Contents

The Cassell
Anagrams
Dictionary

The Cassell Anagrams Dictionary

Samuel C. Hunter

CASSELL

Cassell
Villiers House, 41/47 Strand
London WC2N 5JE

387 Park Avenue South
New York, NY 10016-8810

First published 1982 as *The Dictionary*
of Anagrams by Routledge & Kegan Paul Ltd
Second revised edition 1986
Cassell edition first published 1992

British Library Cataloguing-in-Publication Data
A catalogue entry for this book is available
from the British Library.

ISBN 0-304-34258-0

Printed in Great Britain by Cox & Wyman Ltd, Reading.

Contents

Introduction

An anagram is a word, phrase or sentence formed by transposing the letters of a different word, phrase or sentence. Anagrams, principally in respect of phrases and sentences, have a long history: they were known to the Greeks and Romans and were popular throughout Europe during the Middle Ages. Some scientists of the seventeenth century embodied their discoveries in anagrams, and pseudonyms are often anagrams of the original name.

Today, anagrams are frequently used by compilers of crosswords, especially cryptic crosswords, in both clues and solutions although, in the absence until now of any comprehensive anagram dictionary, single-word solutions have often been hidden in the letters of two or more words appearing in the clue construction.

The author of this dictionary, himself a crossword compiler, has, over the last twenty-odd years, collected together the material now incorporated in this work. The collection is confined to single-word anagrams, arranged in strictly alphabetical order, tabulated according to the number of letters (five to fifteen). Words are only given in the plural when, by the addition of the letter 's', further words are possible, for example:

NECTARINES–TRANSIENCE
BALANCE-SHEETS–TEACHABLENESS
CREDENTIALS–CENTRALISED
HELICOPTERS–ELECTORSHIP

Acceptable hyphenated words have been included, but the author has resisted the temptation of including such interesting items as SALVAGES, CEREBELLAR and TEA-GARDEN since their anagrams LAS VEGAS, BEER CELLAR and GREAT DANE involve the use of two separate (un-hyphenated) words, and such a practice would depart from the self-imposed rule outlined above. A number of proper names have been incorporated into this dictionary and these are indicated by an asterisk against the word where it appears in the first column on the pages, e.g.

*HILDEBRAND–BRIDLE-HAND
*PTERELAUS–PULSE-RATE
*CORNELIUS–INCLOSURE

*MINNESOTA–NOMINATES
*LANCASTER–ANCESTRAL

Each of the above pairs, and of course all the other groups included, also appear in their alternative settings. Thus HILDEBRAND, above, will also be found under its anagram BRIDLE-HAND. This cross-referencing equally applies to cases where more than one anagram is applicable. For instance ELIMINATORS, MISRELATION, ORIEN-TALISM and RELATIONISM appear separately in the eleven-letter section, each giving the three alternative anagrammatic words. Thus whatever the known word, its anagram will immediately be available when reference is made to that section of the Dictionary dealing with the appropriate number of letters.

This anagram dictionary is the only one of its kind ever published and will be invaluable not just to crossword compilers and to many of those millions who regularly attempt to solve crossword puzzles the world over, but also to an ever-increasing number of people for whom anagrams have a special appeal and fascination. This is evident from the popularity of numerous radio and television panel programmes that serve anagrams in their fare – fair enough?

HAPPY ANAGRAMMING!

Five letters

ABACA Caaba
ABASH Sabah
ABASK Kasba
ABEAM Ameba
ABELE Albee
ABETS Baste, Bates, Beast, Beats, Besat, Esbat, Sebat, Tabes
ABLED Baled, Blade
ABLER Baler, Blare, Blear
ABLES Bales, Basel, Basle, Blaes, Blase, Bleas, Sable
ABLET Blate, Bleat, Table
ABODE Adobe
ABORD Board, Broad, Dobra, Dorab
ABORT Boart, Rabot, Tabor
ABOUT U-boat
ABRIM Imbar
ABRIN Bairn, Brain, Brian
* **ABRUS** Brusa, Bursa
ABSEY Abyes
ABSIT Baits
ABUTS Tabus, Tsuba, Tubas
ABYES Absey
ABYSS Bassy
ACERA Areca, Ceara
ACERB Brace, Caber, Cabre
ACERS Acres, Cares, Carse, Races, Sacre, Scare, Scrae, Serac
ACHES Chase
ACHOR Orach, Roach
ACIDS Asdic, Cadis
ACLIS Laics, Salic, Scail
ACORN Racon
ACRED Arced, Cadre, Cared, Cedar, Dacre, Raced

ACRES Acers, Cares, Carse, Races, Sacre, Scare, Scrae, Serac
ACRID Caird, Cardi, Daric, Dirac
ACTED Cadet, Ectad
ACTIN Antic
ACTON Canto, Cotan, Octan
ACTOR Crato, Croat, Rocta, Taroc
ACUTE Ceuta
ADDER Aredd, Dared, Dread, Dreda, Readd
ADDLE Daled, Dedal, Laded
ADEEM Edema, Medea
* **ADENI** Andie, Denia, Diane, Edina
ADEPS Sepad, Spade, Spaed
ADEPT Pated, Taped
ADIOS Aidos
ADITS Ditas, Staid
* **ADLER** Alder, Daler
ADMAN Daman
ADMEN Amend, Mande, Maned, Medan, Menad, Named
ADOBE Abode
ADORE Oared, Oread
ADORN Andro, Donar, Radon, Nardo
ADOWN Downa
ADRET Dater, Rated, Tared, Trade, Tread
ADSUM Dumas, Mauds
ADULT Tauld, Dault
ADUST Dauts
AEGER Agree, Eager, Eagre, Ragee
AESIR Aries, Arise, Raise, Resai, Riesa, Serai, Seria
AFIRE Feria

*AFRIC Farci
AFRIT Frati
AFTER Trefa
AGAIT Taiga
AGAPE Apage
AGATE Gaeta
AGGER Eggar, Gager
AGGRY Raggy
AGIST Gaits, Staig
AGLEE Eagle
AGNEL Angel, Angle, Galen, Genal, Glean
*AGNES Geans, Genas, Senga
AGONE Genoa, Onega
AGREE Aeger, Eager, Eagre, Ragee
AGRIN Garni, Grain
AHEMS Hames, Heams, Shame, Shema
AHINT Hiant
AHOLD Halo'd
*AIDAN Diana, Naiad
AIDED Idia'd
AIDER Aired, Irade, Redia
AIDES Aside, Ideas, Sadie
*AIDIN India
AIDOS Adios
AIERY Ayrie
AILED Delia, Eliad, Ideal
AIMED Amide, Media
AIMER Maire, Marie, Ramie, Rimae
AIRED Aider, Irade, Redia
AIRTS Astir, Raits, Sitar, Sitra, Stair, Stria, Tarsi, Trias
AISLE Elias, Slaie
*AISNE Anise, Siena
AITCH Atchi
AJWAN Jawan
*AKRON Koran, Krona
ALANG Lagan
ALARM Malar, Ramal
*ALBAN Banal, Laban
ALBEE Abele

ALBIN Blain
ALCES Claes, Laces, Scale
ALDER Adler, Daler
*ALDIS Dalis, Dials, Slaid
*ALDUS Lauds, Udals
ALEFT Fetal
ALERT Alter, Artel, Later, Ratel, Taler, Telar
ALGAE Galea
*ALGER Elgar, Glare, Lager, Large, Regal, Relga
ALGIN Align, Gilan, Laing, Liang, Ligan, Linga
ALGOR Argol, Goral, Largo, Orgal
ALGUM Almug, Glaum, Mulga
*ALICE Celia, Ileac
ALIEN Aline, Anile, Elain, Elian, Laine, Liane
ALIGN Algin, Gilan, Laing, Liang, Ligan, Linga
ALINE Alien, Anile, Elain, Elian, Laine, Liane
ALISH Hails
ALIVE Avile, Velia
*ALLAN Nalla
ALL-BE Be-all, Bella, Label
ALL-IN Lalin
ALLOD Do-all
ALLOT All-to, Atoll
ALLOY Loyal
ALL-TO Allot, Atoll
ALMAH Halma, Hamal
*ALMAS Lamas
ALMEH Hemal
ALMES Amsel, Lames, Leams, Males, Meals, Melas, Mesal, Salem, Samel, Selma
ALMRY Marly
ALMUG Algum, Glaum, Mulga
ALOFT Float, Flota
ALONE Olean
ALONG Anglo, Logan, Golan, Longa

ALOOF Loofa
ALPEN Nepal, Panel, Pelan, Penal, Plane, Plena
ALTAR Artal, Ratal, Talar
ALTER Alert, Artel, Later, Ratel, Taler, Telar
*****ALTON** Notal, Talon, Tolan, Tonal
ALTOS Salto, Sloat, Stola, Talos, Tolas
ALURE Ureal
*****ALVES** Elvas, Laves, Salve, Slave, Vales, Valse, Veals
*****ALVIN** Anvil, Nival, Vilna, Vinal
*****ALVIS** Salvi, Silva, Vails, Valis, Vials
AMAIN Amnia, Anima, Mania
AMASS Assam, Massa
AMBER Brame, Bream, Embar
AMBLE Blame, Embla, Mabel, Melba
AMBOS Bomas, Moabs, Sambo
AMBRY Barmy
AMEBA Abeam
AMEER Ramee, Reame
AMEND Admen, Mande, Maned, Medan, Menad, Named
AMENE Enema, Meane
AMENS Manes, Manse, Means, Mensa, Names, Samen
AMENT Manet, Meant
AMIDE Aimed, Media
AMIGO Imago
AMINE Anime, Maine, Menia, Minae
AMISS Missa
AMITY Atimy
AMNIA Amain, Anima, Mania
AMONG Mango
AMORT Morat
AMOUR Moura
AMPLE Maple, Pelma
AMPLY Palmy

AMSEL Almes, Lames, Leams, Males, Meals, Melas, Mesal, Salem, Samel, Selma
ANCLE Calne, Clean, Lance, Lenca
ANCON Canon, Conan
*****ANDES** Danes, Deans, Desna, Sedan, Snead
*****ANDIE** Adeni, Denia, Diane, Edina
ANDRO Adorn, Donar, Radon, Nardo
ANEAR Arena
*****ANETO** Atone, Oaten, Onate
ANGEL Agnel, Angle, Glean, Galen, Genal
ANGER Areng, Range, Regan, Renga
ANGLE Agnel, Angel, Galen, Genal, Glean
*****ANGLO** Along, Golan, Logan, Longa
ANGOR Argon, Groan, Nagor, Ongar, Orang, Organ
ANGRY Rangy
ANGST Gants, Gnats, Stang, Tangs
ANILE Alien, Aline, Elain, Elian, Laine, Liane
ANILS Nails, Salin, Slain, Snail
ANIMA Amain, Amnia, Mania
ANIME Amine, Maine, Menai, Minae
ANISE Aisne, Siena
ANKER Karen, Naker, Nerka, Ranke
ANKHS Hanks, Khans, Shank
*****ANNAM** Manna, Naman
ANNAT Tanna
*****ANNES** Senna
*****ANNIE** Inane
ANTAR Antra, Ratan
ANTED Dante

ANTES Etnas, Nates, Nesta, Senta, Stane, Stean, Teans

ANTIC Actin

ANTIS Saint, Satin, Stain, Tains, Tanis

ANTRA Antar, Ratan

ANTRE Retan

ANVIL Alvin, Nival, Vilna, Vinal

APAGE Agape

APART Trapa

APERS Asper, Pares, Parse, Pears, Prase, Presa, Rapes, Reaps, Spaer, Spare, Spear

APERT Pater, Peart, Petar, Petra, Prate, Taper, Trape

APERY Payer, Peary, Repay

APEST Paste, Pates, Peats, Septa, Spate, Speat, Tapes

APHIS Apish, Spahi

APISH Aphis, Spahi

APISM Sampi

APNEA Paean

APORT Porta, Prato

APPAL Papal

APPEL Apple, Pepla

APPLE Appel, Pepla

APRIL Pilar, Prial

APRON No-par

APSES Passe, Spaes

APSOS Psoas, Soaps

APTLY Patly, Platy, Typal

*ARABS Arbas, Basra, Sabra

ARBAS Arabs, Basra, Sabra

*ARCAS Sacra

ARCED Acred, Cadre, Cared, Cedar, Dacre, Raced

*ARCHY Chary

ARCUS Carus, Scaur

*ARDEA Aread

ARDEB Bader, Barde, Bared, Beard, Bread, Breda, Debar

*ARDEN Dearn, Derna, Redan

ARDES Dares, Dears, Rased, Reads

ARD-RI Raird

AREAD Ardea

ARECA Acera, Ceara

AREDD Adder, Dared, Dread, Dreda, Readd

AREDE Areed, Deare, Eared, Reade, Reeda

AREED Arede, Deare, Eared, Reade, Reeda

AREFY Faery, Freya

ARENA Anear

ARENG Anger, Range, Regan, Renga

ARETE Eater, Reate, Taree

ARETS Aster, Astre, Earst, Rates, Reast, Resat, Stare, Strae, Tares, Tarse, Tears, Teras

ARETT Tater, Tetra, Treat

ARGIL Glair, Grail, Lairg

ARGOL Algor, Goral, Largo, Orgal

ARGON Angor, Groan, Nagor, Ongar, Orang, Organ

*ARGOS Sargo

ARGOT Groat

ARGUE Auger

*ARGUS Gaurs, Sugar

*ARIAN Naira

*ARIES Aesir, Arise, Raise, Resai, Riesa, Serai, Seria

ARIOT Ratio

ARISE Aesir, Aries, Raise, Resai, Riesa, Serai, Seria

ARISH Hairs, Shari

ARKED Daker, Drake, Raked

ARLES Earls, Lares, Laser, Lears, Rales, Reals, Seral

*ARLON Loran, Lorna

ARMED Derma, Dream, Madre, Ramed

ARMER Rearm

ARMET Mater, Metra, Tamer, Terma, Trema

ARMOR Maror, Morra

ARNEE Ranee
ARNOT Orant, Toran, Trona
AROID Radio
AROSE Soare
ARRET Rater, Retar, Tarre, Terra
ARSES Asser, Rases, Rasse, Sarse,
  Sears
ARSIS Rissa, Saris
ARSON Roans, Sonar
ARTAL Altar, Ratal, Talar
ARTEL Alert, Alter, Later, Ratel,
  Taler, Telar
ARTSY Satyr, Stray, Trays
ARUMS Ramus, Rusma, Sarum
ARVAL Larva, Lavra
***ARYAN** Nayar
***ASBEN** Banes, Beans
 ASCII Isiac
 ASCOT Coast, Coats, Costa,
  Scoat, Tosca
 ASCUS Casus
 ASDIC Acids, Cadis
 ASHEN Hanse, Shane
 ASHES He-ass, Seahs, Sesha,
  Sheas
 ASHET Haets, Haste, Hates,
  Heast, Heats
***ASIAN** Naias
 ASIDE Aides, Ideas, Sadie
 ASKED Kades
 ASKER Eskar, Kesar, Rakes,
  Reaks, Saker, Skear
 ASKEW Wakes, Wekas
 ASPEN Napes, Neaps, Panes,
  Peans, Snape, Sneap, Spane,
  Spean
 ASPER Apers, Pares, Parse, Pears,
  Prase, Presa, Rapes, Reaps,
  Spaer, Spare, Spear
 ASPIC Capis, Picas, Scapi, Spica
***ASSAM** Amass, Massa
 ASSER Arses, Rases, Rasse, Sarse,
  Sears
 ASSES Sasse, Sessa

ASSET Easts, Sates, Seats, Tasse,
  Tessa
ASSOT Oasts, Stoas, Tasso
ASTEL Least, Leats, Salet, Slate,
  Stael, Stale, Steal, Stela, Taels,
  Tales, Teals, Tesla
ASTER Arets, Astre, Earst, Rates,
  Reast, Resat, Stare, Strae, Tares,
  Tarse, Tears, Teras
ASTIR Airts, Raits, Sitar, Sitra,
  Stair, Stria, Tarsi, Trias
***ASTOR** Roast, Rotas, Sarto, Taros,
  Toras, Troas
ASTRE Arets, Aster, Earst, Rates,
  Reast, Resat, Stare, Strae, Tares,
  Tarse, Tears, Teras
ASWAY Aways
ASWIM Swami
ATCHI Aitch
***ATHOL** Loath, Lotah
***ATHOS** Hoast, Hosta, Oaths,
  Shoat
ATIMY Amity
ATLAS Salta
ATMAN Manta
ATOLL Allot, All-to
ATOMS Moats, Stoma
ATONE Aneto, Oaten, Onate
ATONY Ayont
ATRIA Riata, Taira, Tiara
ATRIP Parti, Tapir
ATTAR Tatar
ATTIC Tacit
AUBIN Bunia, Nubia
AUGER Argue
AUGHT Ghaut
AUMIL Miaul
AUNTS Saunt
AURAL Laura
AURIC Curia
AVENS Evans, Naves, Sevan,
  Vanes
AVERS Raves, Saver, Vares
AVERT Tarve, Taver, Trave

AVILE Alive, Velia
AVINE Naive, Naevi, Neiva
AWAYS Asway
AWING Wigan
AWNED Dewan, Waned
AWNER Narew
AXILS Salix
AXONS Naxos, Saxon
AYGRE Gayer, Yager
AYONT Atony
AYRIE Aiery
AZOTE Toaze

BABUL Bubal
BACCO Bocca, Caboc
BACON Banco, Coban
***BADER** Ardeb, Barde, Bared,
  Beard, Bread, Breda, Debar
BADGE Begad, Debag
BADLY Baldy
BAGEL Belga, Gabel, Gable
BAGRE Barge, Begar, Berga,
  Garbe
BAILS Basil, Labis
***BAILY** Bialy
***BAIRD** Braid, Rabid
BAIRN Abrin, Brain, Brian
BAITS Absit
BAKER Brake, Break, Kebar
BALAS Balsa, Basal, Sabal
BALDY Badly
BALED Abled, Blade
BALER Abler, Blare, Blear
BALES Ables, Basel, Basle, Blaes,
  Blase, Bleas, Sable
BALSA Balas, Basal, Sabal
***BALTS** Blast, Blats
BANAL Alban, Laban
BANCO Bacon, Coban
BANDS S-band
BANES Asben, Beans
BANTU Tabun
BARDE Ardeb, Bader, Bared,
  Beard, Bread, Breda, Debar

BARDY Darby
BARED Ardeb, Bader, Barde,
  Beard, Bread, Breda, Debar
BARES Baser, Bears, Braes, Saber,
  Sabre
BARET Bater, Berta, Taber
BARGE Bagre, Begar, Berga,
  Garbe
BARIC Carib, Rabic
BARKY Braky
BARMY Ambry
***BARTS** Brast, Brats
BARYE Bayer, Beray, Yerba
BASAL Balas, Balsa, Sabal
BASED Beads
***BASEL** Ables, Bales, Basle, Blaes,
  Bleas, Blase, Sable
BASER Bares, Bears, Braes, Saber,
  Sabre
BASES Basse
BASIL Bails, Labis
BASIN Sabin
BASIS Bassi
***BASLE** Ables, Bales, Basel, Blaes,
  Bleas, Blase, Sable
***BASRA** Arabs, Arbas, Sabra
BASSE Bases
BASSI Basis
BASSY Abyss
BASTE Abets, Bates, Beast, Beats,
  Besat, Esbat, Sebat, Tabes
BASTO Boast, Boats, Sabot, Sobat
  Tobas
BATER Baret, Berta, Taber
BATES Abets, Baste, Beast, Beats,
  Besat, Esbat, Sebat, Tabes
BATHE Beath
BAULK Kabul
BAYED Beady
***BAYER** Barye, Beray, Yerba
BAYLE Belay
BAYOU Boyau
BAZAR Braza, Zabra
BEADS Based

BEADY Bayed
BE-ALL All-be, Bella, Label
BEAMY Embay, Maybe
BEANS Asben, Banes
BEARD Ardeb, Bader, Barde,
　Bared, Bread, Breda, Debar
BEARS Bares, Baser, Braes, Saber,
　Sabre
BEAST Abets, Baste, Bates, Beats,
　Besat, Esbat, Sebat, Tabes
BEATH Bathe
BEATS Abets, Bates, Beast, Beast,
　Besat, Esbat, Sebat, Tabes
BEAUT Butea, Taube, Tubae
BECHE Beech
BEDEL Beeld, Bleed, Debel
BEDIM Imbed
BEDYE Debye
BEECH Beche
BEELD Bedel, Bleed, Debel
BEELE Belee
BEETS Beset, Betes
BEGAD! Badge, Debag
BEGAR Bagre, Barge, Berga,
　Garbe
BEGIN Being, Binge
BEING Begin, Binge
*****BEIRA** Beria, Eibar
BELAH Hable
BELAY Bayle
BELEE Beele
BELGA Bagel, Gabel, Gable
BELIT Blite
*****BELLA** All-be, Be-all, Label
BELOW Bowel, Elbow
BELTS Blest, Blets
BENDS S.bend
BENDY By-end
BENTY Tenby
BERAY Barye, Bayer, Yerba
*****BERGA** Bagre, Barge, Begar,
　Garbe
*****BERIA** Beira, Eibar
BEROE Boree

*****BERTA** Baret, Bater, Taber
BESAT Abets, Baste, Bates, Beast,
　Beats, Esbat, Sebat, Tabes
BESET Beets, Betes
BESIT Bites
BESOM Mebos
BESOT Betso, Botes
BETES Beets, Beset
BETID Bidet, Debit
BETON T-bone
BETSO Besot, Botes
*****BETSY** Bytes
*****BETTE** Tebet
*****BETTI** Tibet
BEVER Breve
*****BEVIS** Vibes
BIALY Baily
BIDER Bride, Debir, Diber, Rebid
BIDET Betid, Debit
BIERS Birse, Bries, Ribes
BIGLY Bilgy
BILES Eblis
BILGE Gibel
BILGY Bigly
*****BINCA** Cabin
BINGE Begin, Being
BIRLE Liber
BIROS Boris
BIRSE Biers, Bries, Ribes
BITER Brite, Tiber, Tribe
BITES Besit
BLADE Abled, Baled
BLAES Bales, Basel, Basle, Bleas,
　Blase, Sable
BLAIN Albin
*****BLAKE** Bleak
BLAME Amble, Embla, Mabel,
　Melba
BLAND L-band
BLARE Abler, Baler, Blear
BLASE Ables, Bales, Basel, Basle,
　Blaes, Bleas, Sable
BLAST Balts, Blats
BLATE Ablet, Bleat, Table

BLATS Balts, Blast
BLEAK Blake
BLEAR Abler, Baler, Blare
BLEAS Ables, Bales, Basel, Basle,
   Blaes, Blase, Sable
BLEAT Ablet, Blate, Table
BLEED Bedel, Beeld, Debel
BLEST Belts, Blets
BLETS Belts, Blest
BLIST Stilb
BLITE Belit
*BLOIS Boils
BLORE Borel, Roble
BLUDE Blued
BLUED Blude
BLUER Brule, Ruble
BLUES Bulse
BLUID Build
BLURS Burls, Slurb
BLUSH Buhls
BOARD Abord, Broad, Dobra,
   Dorab
BOART Abort, Rabot, Tabor
BOAST Basto, Boats, Sabot, Sobat,
   Tobas
BOATS Basto, Boast, Sabot, Sobat,
   Tobas
BOBAC Cabob
BOBAK Kabob
BOCCA Bacco, Caboc
*BODEN Boned
BODHI Dhobi
BODLE Lobed
*BOERS Bores, Brose, Robes, Sober
BOGLE Globe
BOHEA Obeah
BOILS Blois
BOLAR Labor, Lobar
BOLOS Lobos, Obols, Sobol
BOLUS Lobus
BOMAS Ambos, Moabs, Sambo
BONED Boden
BONER Borne
BONEY Boyne, Ebony

BONGO Boong
BONUS Bosun, Bouns
BOOBY Yobbo
BOOMS Bosom
BOONG Bongo
BOONS Boson
BOORD Brood, Dobro
BOORS Sorbo
BOOSE Oboes
BOOST Boots
BOOTS Boost
BORDE Bored, Brode, Orbed,
   Robed
BORED Borde, Brode, Orbed,
   Robed
BOREE Beroe
BOREL Blore, Roble
BORES Boers, Brose, Robes, Sober
*BORIS Biros
BORNE Boner
BORNU Bourn, Bruno
BORTS Strob
BOSOM Booms
BOSON Boons
BOSUN Bonus, Bouns
BOTES Besot, Betso
BOULT U-Bolt
BOUNS Bonus, Bosun
BOURN Bornu, Bruno
BOUSY Buoys, Byous
BOUTS Tsubo
BOWEL Below, Elbow
BOYAU Bayou
*BOYNE Boney, Ebony
BRACE Acerb, Caber, Cabre
BRAES Bares, Baser, Bears, Saber,
   Sabre
BRAID Baird, Rabid
BRAIL Libra
BRAIN Abrin, Bairn, Brian
BRAKE Baker, Break, Kebar
BRAKY Barky
BRAME Amber, Bream, Embar
BRASH Shrab

BRAST Barts, Brats
BRATS Barts, Brast
BRAUL Lubra
BRAZA Bazar, Zabra
BRAZE Zebra
BREAD Ardeb, Bader, Barde,
Bared, Beard, Breda, Debar
BREAK Baker, Brake, Kebar
BREAM Amber, Brame, Embar
*BREDA** Ardeb, Bader, Barde,
Bared, Beard, Bread, Debar
BREDE Breed
BREED Brede
BREEM Breme, Ember
BREER Brere
BREME Breem, Ember
BRERE Breer
BREVE Bever
*BRIAN** Abrin, Bairn, Brain
BRIDE Bider, Debir, Diber, Rebid
BRIEF Fiber, Fibre
BRIES Biers, Birse, Ribes
BRITE Biter, Tiber, Tribe
BROAD Abord, Board, Dobra,
Dorab
BRODE Borde, Bored, Orbed,
Robed
BROME Omber, Ombre
BROMO Broom, Ombro
BROOD Boord, Dobro
BROOM Bromo, Ombro
BROSE Boers, Bores, Robes, Sober
BROTH Throb
*BRUIN** Burin, Rubin
BRUIT Tibur
BRULE Bluer, Ruble
BRUME Umber, Umbre
*BRUNO** Bornu, Bourn
BRUNT Burnt
*BRUSA** Abrus, Bursa
BRUSH Buhrs, Burhs, Bursh,
Shrub
BRUST Burst, Strub
BRUTE Buret, Rebut, Tuber

BUBAL Babul
BUDGE Debug
BUGLE Bulge
BUHLS Blush
BUHRS Brush, Burhs, Bursh,
Shrub
BUILD Bluid
BULGE Bugle
BULSE Blues
BUNIA Aubin, Nubia
BUNKS Knubs
BUOYS Bousy, Byous
BURAN Unbar, Urban
BURET Brute, Rebut, Tuber
BURHS Brush, Buhrs, Bursh,
Shrub
BURIN Bruin, Rubin
BURLS Blurs, Slurb
*BURMA** Rumba, Umbra
BURNT Brunt
BURSA Abrus, Brusa
BURSE Rebus, Suber
BURST Brust, Strub
BUSED Debus
*BUTEA** Beaut, Taube, Tubae
BUYER Ebury
BWANA Nawab
BY-END Bendy
BYOUS Bousy, Buoys
BYTES Betsy

*CAABA** Abaca
CABER Acerb, Brace, Cabre
CABIN Binca
CABLE Caleb
CABOB Bobac
CABOC Bacco, Bocca
CABRE Acerb, Brace, Caber
CACHE Chace
CACTI Ticca
CADES Cased, Daces
CADET Acted, Ectad
CADGE Caged
CADIS Acids, Asdic

CADRE Acred, Arced, Cared,
 Cedar, Dacre, Raced
CAESE Cease
CAGED Cadge
CAGER Grace
*CAHER Chare, Rache, Reach
CAINS Canis, Incas, Sican
CAIRD Acrid, Cardi, Daric, Dirac
CAIRN In-car
*CALEB Cable
CALIN Linac
CALKS Lacks, Slack
CALLS Scall
*CALNE Ancle, Clean, Lance,
 Lenca
*CALOR Carol, Claro, Coral, Lorca
CALPS Claps, Clasp, Scalp
CALVE Cavel, Clave
CAMEL Macle
CAMPS Scamp
CAMUS Caums, Musca, Sumac
CANED Dance
CANEH Hance, Nache
CANER Carne, Crane, Crena,
 Nacre, Rance
CANES Scena
CANID Cnida
*CANIS Cains, Incas, Sican
CANNY Nancy
CANOE Ocean
CANON Ancon, Conan
CANST Cants, Scant
CANTO Acton, Cotan, Octan
CANTS Canst, Scant
CAPED Paced
CAPEL Caple, Place
CAPER Crape, Pacer, Perca, Recap
CAPES Caspe, Paces, Scape,
 Space
*CAPIS Aspic, Picas, Scapi, Spica
CAPLE Capel, Place
CAPON Copan
CAPOT Coapt
*CAPRI Carpi, Picra

CARAT Carta
CARDI Acrid, Caird, Daric, Dirac
CARDS Scard
CARED Acred, Arced, Cadre,
 Cedar, Dacre, Raced
CARER Crare, Racer
CARES Acers, Acres, Carse,
 Races, Sacre, Scare, Scrae, Serac
CARET Carte, Cater, Crate, React,
 Recta, Trace
*CARIB Baric, Rabic
CARLE Clare, Clear
*CARNE Caner, Crane, Crena,
 Nacre, Rance
CAROB Coarb, Cobar, Cobra
CAROL Calor, Claro, Coral, Lorca
CAROM Marco
*CARPI Capri, Picra
CARPS Craps, Scarp, Scrap
CARSE Acers, Acres, Cares,
 Races, Sacre, Scare, Scrae, Serac
CARTA Carat
CARTE Caret, Cater, Crate, React,
 Recta, Trace
CARTS Scart, Scrat
CARUS Arcus, Scaur
CARVE Caver, Crave, Varec
CASAL Scala
CASCO Cocas
CASED Cades, Daces
CASES Casse
*CASPE Capes, Paces, Scape,
 Space
CASSE Cases
CASTE Cates, Scate, Sceat, Taces
CASUS Ascus
CATER Caret, Carte, Crate, React,
 Recta, Trace
CATES Caste, Scate, Sceat, Taces
*CATHY Yacht
CAULD Claud, Ducal
CAULS Lucas
CAUMS Camus, Musca, Sumac
CAUSE Sauce

CAVEL Calve, Clave
CAVER Carve, Crave, Varec
CAVIN Vinca
CEARA Acera, Areca
CEASE Caese
CEBUS Cubes
CEDAR Acred, Arced, Cadre,
  Cared, Dacre, Raced
CEDER Cered, Creed
CEILS Ciels, Leics, Sicel, Slice
*CELIA Alice, Ileac
*CENIS Since
CENSE Scene
CENTO Conte, Notec
CENTS Scent
*CERAM Crame, Cream, Crema,
  Macer, Merca
CERED Ceder, Creed
*CERES Crees, Scree
CERGE Grece
CERIA Erica
CERIN Crine, Nicer
CEROS Cores, Corse, Score
CERTS Crest
*CEUTA Acute
CHACE Cache
CHACO Coach
CHAIN Chian, China
CHAMS Chasm
CHANT Natch
CHAOS Oshac
CHAPE Cheap, Peach
CHAPS Pasch
CHAPT Patch
CHARD Darch
CHARE Caher, Rache, Reach
CHARM March
CHARS Crash
CHART Ratch
CHARY Archy
CHASE Aches
CHASM Chams
CHATS Scath
CHAWS Schwa

CHEAP Chape, Peach
CHEAT Tache, Teach, Theca
CHEEK Keech
CHEER Reech
CHELA Leach
CHERT Retch
CHEST Stech, Techs
*CHIAN Chain, China
CHIEF Fiche
CHIEL Chile, Elchi
*CHIEM Chime, Miche
CHIEN Chine, Niche
CHILE Chiel, Elchi
CHILI Lichi
CHIME Chiem, Hemic, Miche
CHINA Chain, Chian
CHINE Chien, Niche
CHIRT Crith, Richt
CHITS Stich
CHIVY Vichy
CHOIR Ichor
CHORE Ocher, Ochre, Roche
CHOSE Soche
CHOUT Couth, Ought, Touch
CHUET Chute, Teuch
CHURL Lurch
CHURN Runch
CHUTE Chuet, Teuch
CIDER Cried, Dicer, Riced
CIELS Ceils, Leics, Sicel, Slice
CIGAR Craig
CILIA Iliac
*CILLA Lilac
*CINNA Incan
*CINTO Tonic
CITAL Ictal, Tical
CITED Edict, Ticed
CIVES Vices
CIVET Evict
CLADE Decal, Laced
CLAES Alces, Laces, Scale
CLAIM Malic
CLANS Lancs
CLAPS Calps, Clasp, Scalp

*CLARE Carle, Clear
CLARO Calor, Carol, Coral, Lorca
CLASP Calps, Claps, Scalp
*CLAUD Cauld, Ducal
CLAVE Calve, Cavel
CLAYS Scaly
CLEAN Ancle, Calne, Lance,
Lenca
CLEAR Carle, Clare
CLEAT Eclat, Ectal, Lacet
CLEEP Clepe
*CLEON Clone, Colne
CLEPE Cleep
CLIME Melic
CLOAM Comal
CLODS Colds, Scold
CLOKE Locke
CLONE Cleon, Colne
CLOSE Coles, Socle
CLOUD Could
CLOUS Locus
CLOWS Cowls, Scowl
CLUED Dulce
CLUES Cluse, Luces
CLUSE Clues, Luces
CNIDA Canid
COACH Chaco
COAPT Capot
COARB Carob, Cobra, Cobar
COAST Ascot, Coats, Costa,
Scoat, Tosca
COATS Ascot, Coast, Costa,
Scoat, Tosca
*COBAN Bacon, Banco
*COBAR Corob, Coarb, Cobra
COBRA Carob, Coarb, Cobar
COCAS Casco
CODER Cored, Credo, Decor
CODES Coeds, Cosed
CODEX Coxed
CODLE Dolce
COEDS Codes, Cosed
COFFS Scoff
COGON Congo

COIGN Incog
COINS Icons, Scion, Sonic
COLDS Clods, Scold
COLES Close, Socle
*COLIN Nicol
*COLNE Cleon, Clone
COLOR Crool
COMAL Cloam
COMBO Coomb
COMER Crome
COMET Comte
COMTE Comet
*CONAN Ancon, Canon
CONES Cosen, Cosne, Scone,
Sonce
*CONGO Cogon
CONNE Nonce
CONTE Cento, Notec
COOMB Combo
COOMS Cosmo
COONS Scoon
COOPS Copos, Scoop
COOST Coots, Scoot
COOTS Coost, Scoot
*COPAN Capon
COPER Crope
COPES Copse, Pecos, Scope
COPOS Coops, Scoop
COPSE Copes, Pecos, Scope
CORAL Calor, Carol, Claro, Lorca
CORDS Scrod
COREA Ocrea
CORED Coder, Credo, Decor
CORER Crore
CORES Ceros, Corse, Score
CORGI Orgic
CORKY Rocky
CORNO Croon
CORNS Scorn
CORNY Crony
CORPS Crops
CORSE Ceros, Cores, Score
COSEC Secco
COSED Codes, Coeds

COSEN Cones, Cosne, Scone, Sonce
COSMO Cooms
*****COSNE** Cones, Cosen, Scone, Sonce
COSTA Ascot, Coats, Coast, Scoat, Tosca
COSTE Cotes, Escot, Estoc, Scote
COTAN Acton, Canto, Octan
COTES Coste, Escot, Estoc, Scote
COUDE Douce
COULD Cloud
COUPS Scoup
COURT Crout, Turco
COUTH Chout, Oucht, Touch
COVES Scove, Voces
COWLS Clows, Scowl
COXED Codex
CRABS Scrab
CRAFT Fract
CRAGS Scrag
CRAIG Cigar
CRAKE Creak
CRAME Ceram, Cream, Crema, Macer, Merca
CRAMS Scram
CRANE Caner, Carne, Crena, Nacre, Rance
CRANS Scran
CRAPE Caper, Pacer, Perca, Recap
CRAPS Carps, Scarp, Scrap
CRARE Carer, Racer
CRASH Chars
CRASS Scars
CRATE Caret, Carte, Cater, React, Recta, Trace
*****CRATO** Actor, Croat, Rocta, Taroc
CRAVE Carve, Caver, Varec
CRAWS Scraw
CREAK Crake
CREAM Ceram, Crame, Crema, Macer, Merca
CREDO Coder, Cored, Decor
CREED Cered, Ceder

CREEP Crepe, Perce
*****CREES** Ceres, Scree
*****CREIL** Relic
*****CREMA** Ceram, Crame, Cream, Macer, Merca
CRENA Caner, Carne, Crane, Nacre, Rance
*****CREON** Crone, Oncer, Recon
CREPE Creep, Perce
CREST Certs
*****CRETE** Erect, Terce
CREWS Screw
CRIED Cider, Dicer, Riced
CRIER Ricer
CRIES Crise, Erics, Icers, Seric
CRINE Cerin, Nicer
CRISE Cries, Erics, Icers, Seric
CRISP Scrip
CRITH Chirt, Richt
*****CROAT** Actor, Crato, Rocta, Taroc
CROME Comer
CRONE Creon, Oncer, Recon
CRONY Corny
CROOL Color
CROON Corno
CROPE Coper
CROPS Corps
CRORE Corer
CROUT Court, Turco
CROWS Scrow
CRUDE Cured
CRUDY Curdy
CRUEL Lucre, Ulcer
CRUET Cuter, Eruct, Recut, Truce
CRUSE Cures, Curse, Sucre
CRUST Cruts, Curst
CRUTS Crust, Curst
CRUVE Curve
CUBES Cebus
CUFFS Scuff
CULLS Scull
CUMIN Mucin
*****CUNEO** Ounce
CUPID Pudic

CURBS Scrub
CURDY Crudy
CURED Crude
CURER Curre, Recur
CURES Cruse, Curse, Sucre
CURIA Auric
CURRE Curer, Recur
CURSE Cruse, Cures, Sucre
CURST Crust, Cruts
CURVE Cruve
CUTER Cruet, Eruct, Recut, Truce
CUT-IN Incut, Tunic
CUTIS Ictus
CYARS Scary, Scray
CYDER Decry
CYLIX Xylic
*****CYRIL** Lyric

DACES Cades, Cased
*****DACRE** Acred, Arced, Cadre,
   Cared, Cedar, Raced
*****DAGON** Donga, Gonad, Gonda
DAGOS Gadso, Goads
DAILY Lydia
*****DAIRI** Radii
DAIRY Diary
DAISY Sayid
*****DAKAR** Kadar
DAKER Arked, Drake, Raked
DALED Addle, Dedal, Laded
DALER Adler, Alder
DALES Deals, Lades, Leads, Slade
DALIS Aldis, Dials, Slaid
DALLE Della, Ladle
DALLY Laldy
DALTS Stal'd
DAMAN Adman
DAMAR Drama
DAMES Demas, Desma, Meads
*****DAMON** Monad, Nomad
DANCE Caned
*****DANES** Andes, Deans, Desna,
   Sedan, Snead
*****DANTE** Anted

DARAF Fa'ard, Farad
DARBY Bardy
*****DARCH** Chard
DARED Adder, Aredd, Dread,
   Dreda, Readd
DARER Drear
DARES Ardes, Dears, Rased,
   Reads
DARGA Garda
DARIC Acrid, Caird, Cardi, Dirac
DARTS Drats, Strad
DARZI Izard
DASHY Hyads, Shady
*****DATEL** Dealt, Delta, Lated
DATER Adret, Rated, Tared,
   Trade, Tread
DATES Sated, Stade, Stead,
   Teads, Tsade
DAUKS Sudak
DAULT Adult, Tauld
DAUTS Adust
DEALS Dales, Lades, Leads, Slade
DEALT Datel, Delta, Lated
DEANS Andes, Danes, Desna,
   Sedan, Snead
DEARE Arede, Areed, Eared,
   Reade, Reeda
DEARN Arden, Derna, Redan
DEARS Ardes, Dares, Rased,
   Reads
DEARY Deray, Rayed, Ready,
   Yeard
DEATH Hated
DEAVE Evade
DEBAG Badge, Begad
DEBAR Ardeb, Bader, Bared,
   Barde, Beard, Bread, Breda
DEBEL Bedel, Beeld, Bleed
*****DEBIR** Bider, Bride, Diber, Rebid
DEBIT Betid, Bidet
DEBUG Budge
DEBUS Bused
DEBUT Tubed
DEBYE Bedye

DECAL Clade, Laced
DECOR Coder, Cored, Credo
DECRY Cyder
DEDAL Addle, Daled, Laded
DEENS Denes, Dense, Edens, Needs
DEEPS Speed
DEFER Freed, Refed
*DEGAS Gades
DEIFY Edify
DEIGN Dinge, Nidge, Nigde
DEILS Idles, Sidle, Sield, Slide
DE-INK Inked
DEISM Dimes, Disme
DEIST Diets, Dites, Edits, Sited, Stied, Tides
DELAY Delya, Leady
DELES Edsel, Leeds, Seled
*DELIA Ailed, Eliad, Ideal
*DELLA Dalle, Ladle
*DELOS Doles, Dosel, Lodes, Solde, Soled
DELTA Datel, Dealt, Lated
DELVE Devel
*DELYA Delay, Leady
*DEMAS Dames, Desma, Meads
DEMIC Medic
DEMIT Timed
DEMON Monde
DEMOS Domes, Modes
DEMUR Mured
DENAY Nayed
DENES Deens, Dense, Edens, Needs
DENGU Nudge
*DENIA Adeni, Andie, Diane, Edina
DENIM Mined
*DENIS Dines, Enids, Nides, Sdein, Snide
DENSE Deens, Denes, Edens, Needs
DENTS Stend, Tends
DE-OIL Oiled

DEPOD Doped
DEPOT Opted, Poted, Toped
DERAY Deary, Rayed, Ready, Yeard
DERED Dreed
DERES Drees, Redes, Reeds, Seder
DERMA Armed, Dream, Madre, Ramed
*DERNA Arden, Dearn, Redan
DERRY Dryer, Redry, Ryder
*DESMA Dames, Demas, Meads
*DESNA Andes, Danes, Deans, Sedan, Snead
DETER Treed
DEUCE Educe
DEVAS Saved, Vades, Vedas
DEVEL Delve
DEVIL Lived, Vilde
DEWAN Awned, Waned
*DEWAR Wader, Wared
*DEWEY Weedy
DHOBI Bodhi
DHOLE Holed
DIACT Dicta
DIALS Aldis, Dalis, Slaid
*DIANA Aidan, Naiad
*DIANE Adeni, Andie, Denia, Edina
DIARY Dairy
*DIBER Bider, Bride, Debir, Rebid
DICED Eddic
DICER Cider, Cried, Riced
DICHT Ditch
DICTA Diact
DIETS Deist, Dites, Edits, Sited, Stied, Tides
DIKER Irked
DIKES Skied
DILLY Idyll
DIMER Mired, Rimed
DIMES Deism, Disme
DINAR Drain, Drina, Indra, Nadir
DINER Indre, Rined

DINES Denis, Enids, Nides, Sdein, Snide
DINGE Deign, Nidge, Nigde
DINGO Doing, Gondi
DINGY Dying
DINIC Indic
DIODE Dodie
*****DIRAC** Acrid, Caird, Cardi, Daric
DIRER Drier, Reird, Rider
DIRGE Gride, Ridge
DIRTS Strid
DISCO Sodic
DISME Deism, Dimes
DITAL Tidal
DITAS Adits, Staid
DITCH Dicht
DITED Tided
DITES Deist, Diets, Edits, Sited, Stied, Tides
DIVAN Dvina, Viand
DIVER Drive, Rived, Verdi
DIVES Vised
DO-ALL Allod
DOBRA Abord, Board, Broad, Dorab
*****DOBRO** Boord, Brood
*****DODIE** Diode
DOERS Dorse, Doser, Rodes, Rosed
DOEST Dotes, Tosed
DOGIE Geoid
DOING Dingo, Gondi
DOITS Odist
DOLCE Codle
DOLER Drole, Older
DOLES Delos, Dosel, Lodes, Solde, Soled
DOLIA Idola, Iodal
DOLLY Lloyd
DOLOR Drool, Loord
DOMAL Modal
DOMES Demos, Modes
*****DONAR** Adorn, Andro, Radon, Nardo

DONEE Enode
*****DONET** Noted, Toned
DONGA Dagon, Gonad, Gonda
*****DONNE** End-on, On-end
DONOR Doorn, Rondo
DOOLE Looed
DOOLS Soldo
DOOMS Dsomo, Moods, Sodom
DOOMY Moody
*****DOONE** Odeon
DOORN Donor, Rondo
DOORS Roods, Ordos, Sordo
DOPED De-pod
DOPER Pedro, Pored, Roped
DOPES Posed, Spode
DORAB Abord, Board, Broad, Dobra
*****DORAS** Dorsa, Roads, Rodas, Sorda
DOREE Erode
DORPS Drops, Prods, Sprod
DORSA Doras, Roads, Rodas, Sorda
DORSE Doers, Doser, Rodes, Rosed
DOSEH Hosed, Shoed
DOSEL Delos, Doles, Lodes, Solde, Soled
DOSER Doers, Dorse, Rodes, Rosed
DOTED Todde
DOTES Doest, Tosed
DOUAR Doura
DOUCE Coude
DOURA Douar
DOVER Drove, Roved, Vedro
DOVIE Video
DOWEL Dowle, Lowed, Owled
DOWER Rowed
DOWLE Dowel, Lowed, Owled
DOWNA Adown
DOWNS Sownd
DOWRY Rowdy, Wordy
DOWSE Sowed

*DOYLE Odyle, Yodel, Yodle
DOZEN Zoned
DRAIL Laird, Liard
DRAIN Dinar, Drina, Indra, Nadir
DRAKE Arked, Daker, Raked
DRAMA Damar
DRAPE Padre, Pared, Raped,
  Repad
DRATS Darts, Strad
DRAVE Raved, Revda, Varde
DRAWS Sward, Wards
DREAD Adder, Aredd, Dared,
  Dreda, Readd
DREAM Armed, Derma, Madre,
  Ramed
DREAR Darer
*DREDA Adder, Aredd, Dared,
  Dread, Readd
DREED Dered
DREES Deres, Redes, Reeds,
  Seder
DRENT Trend
DREUL Lured, Ruled
DRIED Redid
DRIER Direr, Reird, Rider
DRIES Rides, Sider, Sired
DRILY Lyrid
*DRINA Dinar, Drain, Indrà, Nadir
D-RING Grind
DRIVE Diver, Rived, Verdi
DROLE Doler, Older
DROME Moder
DRONE Endor, Roden, Ronde
DROOL Dolor, Loord
DROPS Dorps, Prods, Sprod
DROSS Sords
DROVE Dover, Roved, Vedro
DROWS Sword, Words
DRUPE Duper, Dupre, Perdu,
  Prude, Pured
DRUSE Dures
DRYAD Ydrad
DRYER Derry, Redry, Ryder
DSOMO Dooms, Moods, Sodom

DUCAL Cauld, Claud
DUELS Dules, Dulse, Leuds,
  Slued
DULCE Clued
DULES Duels, Dulse, Leuds,
  Slued
DULSE Duels, Dules, Leuds,
  Slued
*DUMAS Adsum, Mauds
DUNGY Gundy
DUPER Drupe, Dupre, Prude,
  Pured
DUPES Pseud, Spued
DUPLE Puled, Upled
*DUPRE Drupe, Duper, Perdu,
  Prude, Pured
DURAS Rudas, Sudra
DURED Udder
*DUREN Runed, Under, Unred,
  Urned
*DURER Ruder
DURES Druse
DURGA Guard
DURST Turds
DUSTY Study
*DVINA Divan, Viand
DWALE Lawed, Waled, Weald
DWINE Edwin, Widen, Wined
DYING Dingy
DYNAM Mandy
*DYSON Synod

EAGER Aeger, Agree, Eagre,
  Ragee
EAGLE Aglee
EAGRE Aeger, Agree, Eager,
  Ragee
EARED Arede, Areed, Deare,
  Reade, Reeda
EARLS Arles, Lares, Laser, Lears,
  Rales, Reals, Seral
EARLY Layer, Leary, Rayle, Relay
EARNS Nares, Nears, Saner,
  Snare

EARST Arets, Aster, Astre, Rates, Reast, Resat, Stare, Strae, Tares, Tarse, Tears, Teras

EARTH Harte, Hater, Heart, Herat, Rathe, Thera, Thrae

EASEL Easle, Lease

EASES Sease

EASLE Easel, Lease

EASTS Asset, Sates, Seats, Tasse, Tessa

EATEN Enate

EATER Arete, Reate, Taree

EAT-IN Teian, Tenia, Tinea

EAVES Seave

* **EBLIS** Biles

EBONY Boney, Boyne

* **EBURY** Buyer

ECLAT Cleat, Ectal, Lacet

ECTAD Acted, Cadet

ECTAL Cleat, Eclat, Lacet

EDEMA Adeem, Medea

* **EDDIC** Diced

* **EDENS** Deens, Denes, Dense, Needs

* **EDGAR** Gerda, Grade, Radge, Raged

EDGER Greed

EDGES Sedge

EDICT Cited, Ticed

EDIFY Deify

EDILE Elide

* **EDINA** Adeni, Andie, Denia, Diane

EDITS Deist, Diets, Dites, Sited, Stied, Tides

* **EDSEL** Deles, Leeds, Seled

EDUCE Deuce

* **EDWIN** Dwine, Widen, Wined

EGERS Grees, Grese, Segre, Serge

EGEST Geest, Geste

EGGAR Agger, Gager

EGGER Grege

EGRET Greet, Reget

* **EIBAR** Beira, Beria

EIGNE Genie

EIKON Koine

EISEL Elsie, Esile

ELAIN Alien, Aline, Anile, Elian, Laine, Liane

E-LA-MI Maile, Melia

ELAND Laden, Lande, Laned

* **ELAPS** Lapse, Leaps, Pales, Peals, Pleas, Salep, Sepal, Slape, Spale, Speal

ELATE Telae

* **ELATH** Ethal, Lathe

ELBOW Below, Bowel

* **ELCHE** Leech

ELCHI Chiel

ELDIN Lined

ELERS Leers, Leres, Reels, Sleer

ELEVE Levee

* **ELGAR** Alger, Glare, Lager, Large, Regal, Relga

* **ELGIN** Ingle, Ligne, Nigel

ELIAD Ailed, Delia, Ideal

* **ELIAN** Alien, Aline, Anile, Elain, Laine, Liane

* **ELIAS** Aisle, Slaie

ELIDE Edile

* **ELIOT** Toile

* **ELLIS** Lisle

* **ELMAN** Leman, Lemna

* **ELMER** Merel, Merle

ELOIN Olein

ELOPS Lopes, Olpes, Poles, Slope, Spole

* **ELSIE** Eisel, Esile

ELSIN Lenis, Liens, Lines, Nelis, Niles, Silen

ELVAN Levan, Navel, Venal

* **ELVAS** Laves, Salve, Selva, Slave, Vales, Valse, Veals

ELVER Lever, Revel

ELVES Veles

* **ELVIS** Evils, Levis, Lives, Slive, Veils, Vleis

EMBAR Amber, Brame, Bream

EMBAY Beamy, Maybe
EMBER Breem, Breme
*****EMBLA** Amble, Blame, Mabel, Melba
EMBUS Sebum
EMEND Mende
EMIRS Meris, Mires, Miser,
Reims, Riems, Rimes
EMITS Items, Meist, Metis, Mites,
Smite, Stime, Times
EMONG Genom, Gnome
EMONY Money
ENARM Marne, Namer, Reman
ENATE Eaten
END-ON Donne, On-end
*****ENDOR** Drone, Roden, Ronde
ENDOW Nowed, Owned,
Woden, Woned
ENDUE Undee
ENEMA Amene, Meane
ENEMY Yemen
ENEWS Ensew, Sewen, Weens
ENGLE Glene
*****ENIDS** Denis, Dines, Nides,
Sdein, Snide
*****ENNIS** Innes, Nines
ENODE Donee
ENORM Moner, Morne
ENROL Loner, Loren, Lorne,
Nerol
ENSEW Enews, Sewen, Weens
ENSUE Neuse
ENTAL Laten, Leant
ENTER Etern, Rente, Terne, Treen
ENTIA Eat-in, Taine, Teian, Tenia,
Tinea
ENTRY Yrent
ENVOI Ovine
*****EOLIC** Oleic
EORLS Leros, Lores, Loser, Orles,
Osler, Roles, Soler, Sorel
EOSIN Noise
EPHAS Heaps, Pesah, Phase,
Shape
EPHOD Hoped

EPHOR Hoper
EPICS Sepic, Spice
EPRIS Peris, Piers, Pries, Prise,
Ripes, Speir, Spier, Spire
EPSOM Mopes, Poems, Pomes
EPURE Puree, Rupee
EQUIP Pique
ERASE Saree
*****ERATO** Orate, Roate
ERECT Crete, Terce
ERGON Genro, Goner, Grone,
Negro
ERGOS Goers, Gores, Gorse,
Ogres, Sergo, Soger
ERGOT Roget
*****ERICA** Ceria
ERICK Icker
ERICS Cries, Crise, Icers, Seric
*****ERITH** Their
ERNES Renes, Sneer
*****ERNIE** Irene
*****ERNST** Rents, Stern, Terns
ERODE Doree
EROSE Soree
ERUCT Cruet, Cuter, Recut, Truce
ERVEN Nerve, Never, Vener
Verne
ERVIL Liver, Livre, Rivel, Viler
ESBAT Abets, Baste, Bates, Beast,
Beats, Besat, Sebat, Tabes
ESCOT Coste, Cotes, Estoc, Scote
ESHER Heres, Herse, Sheer,
Shere
ESILE Eisel, Elsie
ESKAR Asker, Kesar, Rakes,
Reaks, Saker, Skear
ESKER Reeks, Reesk, Skeer
ESNEH Sheen
ESNES Essen, Sense
*****ESSEN** Esnes, Sense
*****ESSEX** Sexes
ESTER Reest, Reset, Retes, Steer,
Stere, Teers, Teres, Terse, Trees
ESTOC Coste, Cotes, Escot, Scote

*ESTON Etons, Notes, Onset, Seton, Steno, Stone, Tenos, Tones

ESTOP Poets, Potes, Stoep, Stope, Topes

ESTRO Roset, Rotes, Store, Tores, Torse

ETENS Steen, Teens, Tense

ETERN Enter, Rente, Terne, Treen

ETHAL Elath, Lathe

ETHEL Lethe

ETHER There, Three

ETHIC Theic

ETHOS Shote, Those

ETHYL Lythe

ETNAS Antes, Nates, Nesta, Senta, Stane, Stean, Teans

*ETONS Eston, Notes, Onset, Seton, Steno, Stone, Tenos, Tones

ETUIS Suite

ETYMA Matey, Meaty

EUROS Roues, Rouse

*EURUS Usure

EUSOL Louse, Ousel, Seoul

EVADE Deave

*EVANS Avens, Naves, Sevan, Vanes

EVENS Neves, Seven

EVERT Revet

EVERY Veery

EVETS Steve

EVICT Civet

EVILS Elvis, Levis, Lives, Slive, Veils, Vleis

EWERS Resew, Sewer, Sweer, Weser

EWEST Sweet

*EWING Winge

EXALT Latex, Taxel

EXEEM Exeme

EXEME Exeem

EXERT Retex

EXILE Lexie

EXIST Exits, Sixte

EXITS Exist, Sixte

EXORS Oxers, Sorex

EXTRA Retax, Taxer

*EYETI Eytie

EYRAS Rasey, Sayer, Years

*EYTIE Eyeti

FA'ARD Daraf, Farad

FACER Farce

FADER Fared, Freda

FAERY Arefy, Freya

FAINT Fanti

FAIRS Farsi, Fiars

FAKER Freak

FAKIR Kafir

FALSE Feals, Fleas, Leafs

*FANTI Faint

FARAD Fa'ard, Daraf

FARCE Facer

FARED Fader, Freda

FARES Farse, Fears, Safer

FARLE Feral, Flare

FARSE Fares, Fears, Safer

FARSI Fairs, Fiars

FASTI Fiats

*FATES Feast, Feats, Festa

FATSO Softa

FAUNS Fusan, Snafu

FAURD Fraud

*FAUST Stufa, Tufas

FEALS False, Fleas, Leafs

FEARS Fares, Farse, Safer

FEAST Fates, Feats, Festa

FEATS Fates, Feast, Festa

FECHT Fetch

FELID Field, Filed, Flied

*FELIS Files, Flies, 'Slife

FELTY Flyte, Lefty

FEMAL Flame, Fleam

FEMUR Fumer

FERAL Farle, Flare

FERIA Afire

FERLY Flyer

*FERMO Forme, Frome
FERRY Fryer, Refry
FESTA Fates, Feast, Feats
FETAL Aleft
FETCH Fecht
FETOR Foret, Forte
FEUDS Fused
FIARS Fairs, Farsi
FIATS Fasti
FIBER Brief, Fibre
FIBRE Brief, Fiber
FICHE Chief
*FIDEL Felid, Field, Filed, Flied
FIELD Felid, Fidel, Filed, Flied
FIEND Fined
FIERY Reify
FILAR Flair, Frail
FILED Felid, Fidel, Field, Flied
FILER Flier, Lifer, Rifle
FILES Felis, Flies, 'Slife
FILET Flite
FINED Fiend
FINER Infer
*FINKE Knife
FIRED Fried
FIRER Frier
FIRES Fries, Serif
FIRST Frist, Frits, Rifts
FIRTH Frith
FIXER Refix
FLAIR Filar, Frail
FLAKE Fleak
FLAME Femal, Fleam
FLARE Farle, Feral
FLEAK Flake
FLEAM Femal, Flame
FLEAS False, Feals, Leafs
FLEER Refel
FLESH Shelf
FLIED Felid, Fidel, Field, Filed
FLIER Filer, Lifer, Rifle
FLIES Felis, Files, 'Slife
FLITE Filet
FLOAT Aloft, Flota

FLOOK Kloof
FLOTA Aloft, Float
FLOUR Flour, Furol
FLUES Fuels, Fusel
FLUOR Flour, Furol
FLYER Ferly
FLYTE Felty, Lefty
FOALS Loafs, Solfa
FONDU Found
FOOTS 'Sfoot
FORDO Frodo
FORET Fetor, Forte
FORGE Gofer
FORGO Groof
FORME Fermo, Frome
*FORST Forts, Frost
FORTE Fetor, Foret
FORTH Froth
FORTH Forth
FORTS Forst, Frost
FOSSA Sofas
FOUND Fondu
FOUNT Futon
FRACT Craft
FRAIL Filar, Flair
FRATI Afrit
FRAUD Faurd
FREAK Faker
*FREDA Fader, Fared
FREED Defer, Refed
FREER Frere, Refer
FREIT Refit
FRERE Freer, Refer
*FREYA Arefy, Faery
FRIED Fired
FRIER Firer
FRIES Fires, Serif
FRIST First, Frits, Rifts
FRITH Firth
FRITS First, Frist, Rifts
*FRODO Fordo
*FROME Fermo, Forme
FROST Forst, Forts
FROTH Forth

FRYER Ferry, Refry
FUELS Flues, Fusel
FUGLE Guelf
FUMER Femur
FURAN Unfar
FUROL Flour, Fluor
*FUSAN Fauns, Snafu
FUSED Feuds
FUSEL Flues, Fuels
FUSTY Yufts
FUTON Fount

GABEL Bagel, Belga, Gable
GABLE Bagel, Belga, Gabel
*GABON Obang
GADES Degas
GADGE Gaged
GADSO Dagos, Goads
GADUS Gauds
*GAETA Agate
GAGED Gadge
GAGER Agger, Eggar
GAITS Agist, Staig
GALEA Algae
GALED Glade, Glead
*GALEN Agnel, Angel, Angle,
   Genal, Glean
*GALLE Legal
GALLY Gyall
GALUT Gault
GAMED Madge
GAMER Grame, Marge, Regma
GAMIC Magic
GAMIN Ngami
GAMMA Magma
GANTS Angst, Gnats, Stang,
   Tangs
GAPED Padge, Paged
GAPER Grape, Pager, Pagre
GAPES Gaspe,Pages
GARBE Bagre, Barge, Begar,
   Berga
*GARDA Darga
GARNI Agrin, Grain

GASES Sages
*GASPE Gapes, Pages
GATER Grate, Great, Greta,
   Targe, Terga
GATES Geats, Stage
*GATUN Gaunt
GAUDS Gadus
*GAULS Gusla
GAULT Galut
GAUMS Magus, Sagum
GAUNT Gatun
GAUPS Pagus
GAURS Argus, Sugar
GAVEL Gavle, Glave
*GAVLE Gavel, Glave
GAYER Aygre, Yager
GAZEL Glaze
GAZER Graze
GEANS Agnes, Genas, Senga
GEARS Rages, Sager, Sarge, Segar
GEATS Gates, Stage
GEEST Egest, Geste
GEIST Geits, Gites, Tiges
GEITS Geist, Gites, Tiges
GELID Glide
GENAL Agnel, Angel, Angle,
   Galen, Glean
GENAS Agnes, Geans, Senga
GENIE Eigne
*GENOA Agone, Onega
GENOM Emong, Gnome
GENRE Gerne, Green, Negre
*GENRO Ergon, Goner, Grone,
   Negro
GENUS Negus
GEODE Ogeed
GEOID Dogie
GERBE Grebe
*GERDA Edgar, Grade, Radge,
   Raged
GERNE Genre, Green, Negre
GESSO Segos
GESTE Egest, Geest
GEYAN Gynae

GHAST Ghats
GHATS Ghast
GHAUT Aught
GHOST Goths
GHOUL Lough
GIANT Tangi
GIBEL Bilge
*GILAN Algin, Align, Laing, Liang, Linga
GILET Legit
GIRON Groin, Ringo
GIRTH Grith, Right
GIRTS Grist, Grits, Strig, Trigs
GISMO Misgo
GITES Geist, Geits, Tiges
GIVER Virge
GLADE Galed, Glead
GLAIR Argil, Grail, Lairg
GLANS Langs, Slang
GLARE Alger, Elgar, Lager, Large, Regal, Relga
GLARY Gyral
GLASS Slags
GLAUM Algum, Almug, Mulga
GLAUR Gular
GLAVE Gavel, Gavle
GLAZE Gazel
GLAZY Zygal
GLEAD Galed, Glade
GLEAN Agnel, Angel, Angle, Galen, Genal
GLEDE Gleed, Ledge
GLEED Glede, Ledge
GLEES Leges
GLENE Engle
GLIDE Gelid
GLOBE Bogle
GLODE Lodge, Loged, Ogled
GLOSS Slogs
GLUED Luged
GLUER Gruel, Luger
GLUES Gules, Gusle, Luges
GLUEY Guyle
GNASH Hangs

GNATS Angst, Gants, Stang, Tangs
GNAWS Swang, Wangs
GNOME Emong, Genom
GOADS Dagos, Gadso
GOALS Gaols, Lagos
GODET Toged
GODLY Goldy
GODSO Goods
GOERS Ergos, Gores, Gorse, Ogres, Orges, Sergo, Soger
GOFER Forge
*GOLAN Along, Anglo, Lagon, Longa
GOLDY Godly
GONAD Dagon, Donga, Gonda
*GONDA Dagon, Donga, Gonad
*GONDI Dingo, Doing
GONER Ergon, Genro, Grone, Negro
GONIA Ngaio
GOODS Godso
GORAL Algor, Argol, Largo, Orgal
GORED Rodge
GORER Roger
GORES Ergos, Goers, Gorse, Ogres, Sergo, Soger
GORGE Grego
GORSE Ergos, Goers, Gores, Ogres, Sergo, Soger
*GOTHS Ghost
GOUTS Gusto
GOUTY Guyot
GOWAN Wagon, Wonga
GRACE Cager
GRADE Edgar, Gerda, Radge, Raged
GRAIL Argil, Glair, Lairg
GRAIN Agrin, Garni
GRAIP Pagri
GRAMA Magar
GRAME Gamer, Marge, Regma
GRAPE Gaper, Pager, Parge

GRASP Sprag
GRATE Gater, Great, Greta,
  Targe, Terga
GRAZE Gazer
GREAT Gater, Grate, Greta,
  Targe, Terga
GREBE Gerbe
GRECE Cerge
GREED Edger
GREEN Genre, Gerne, Negre,
GREES Egers, Grees, Segre, Serge
GREET Egret, Reget
GREGE Egger
GREGO Gorge
GREIN Niger, Reign, Renig, Ringe
GREIT Tiger, Tigre
GRESE Egers, Grees, Segre, Serge
*****GRETA** Gater, Grate, Great,
  Targe, Terga
GREVE Verge
GRIDE Dirge, Ridge
GRIND D-ring
GRIPS Prigs, Sprig
GRIST Girts, Grits, Strig, Trigs
GRITH Girth, Right
GRITS Girts, Grist, Strig, Trigs
GROAN Angor, Argon, Nagor,
  Ongar, Orang, Organ
GROAT Argot
GROIN Giron, Ringo
GROMA Margo
GRONE Ergon, Genro, Goner,
  Negro
GROOF Forgo
GROWN Wrong
GRUEL Gluer, Luger
GUARD Durga
*****GUELF** Fugle
GULAR Glaur
GULES Glues, Gusle, Luges
GUNDY Dungy
GUSLA Gauls
GUSLE Glues, Gules, Luges
GUSTO Gouts

GUSTY Gutsy
GUTSY Gusty
GUYLE Gluey
GUYOT Gouty
GYALL Gally
GYELD Ledgy
GYNAE Geyan
GYRAL Glary
GYRUS Surgy

HABLE Belah
HACKS Shack
*****HADES** Heads, Sadhe, Shade
HADJI Jihad
HAETS Ashet, Haste, Hates,
  Heast, Heats
HAFTS Shaft
HAILS Alish
HAIRS Arish, Shari
HAITS Saith, Taish, Thais
HAKES Shake
HALED Heald
HALES Halse, Heals, Leash,
  Selah, Shale, Sheal
HALLO Holla
HALLS Shall
HALMA Almah, Hamal
HALMS Shalm
HALO'D Ahold
HALOS Shoal, Shola, Solah
HALSE Hales, Heals, Leash,
  Selah, Shale, Sheal
HALTS Laths, Shalt, Stahl
HALVE Havel
HAMAL Almah, Halma
HAMES Ahems, Heams, Shame,
  Shema
HANCE Caneh, Nache
HANDS Shand
HANDY Haydn
HANGS Gnash
HANKS Ankhs, Khans, Shank
*****HANSE** Ashen, Shane
*****HANTS** Shan't, Snath

HAPLY Phyla
HARAM Marah
HARDS Shard
HARDY Hydra
HARED Heard
HAREM Herma
HARES Hears, Rheas, Share,
 Shear
HARIM Ihram, Hiram
HARKS Shark
HARMS Marsh, Shram
HARNS Sharn
HARPS Sharp
HARST Harts, Raths, Tahrs,
 Thars, Trash
*HARTE Earth, Hater, Heart,
 Herat, Rathe, Thera, Thrae
HARTS Harst, Raths, Tahrs,
 Thars, Trash
HASPS Shaps
HASTE Ashet, Haets, Hates,
 Heast, Heats
HASTY Yasht
HATED Death
HATER Earth, Harte, Heart,
 Herat, Rathe, Thera, Thrae
HATES Ashet, Haets, Haste,
 Heast, Heats
HAUNT Unhat
*HAVEL Halve
HAVES Shave, Sheva
HAWMS Shawm, Whams
*HAYDN Handy
HAYED Heady
HAZEL Zahle
HEADS Hades, Sadhe, Shade
HEADY Hayed
HEALD Haled
HEALS Hales, Halse, Leash,
 Selah, Shale, Sheal
HEAMS Ahems, Hames, Shame,
 Shema
HEAPS Ephas, Pesah, Phase,
 Shape

HEARD Hared
HEARS Hares, Rheas, Share,
 Shear
HEART Earth, Harte, Hater,
 Herat, Rathe, Thera, Thrae
HE-ASS Ashes, Seahs, Sesha,
 Sheas
HEAST Ashet, Haets, Haste,
 Hates, Heats
HEATS Ashet, Haets, Haste,
 Hates, Heast
HEAVE Hevea
HEAVY Yahve
HEDON Honed
HEELS Heles, Sheel
HEIRS Hires, Shier, Shire
HEIST Shite, Sithe, Thies
HELES Heels, Sheel
HELLS Shell, She'll
HELOT Hotel, Thole
HELPS Plesh
HEMAL Almeh
HE-MAN Maneh
HEMIC Chiem, Chime, Miche
HENDS Shend
*HENRI Rhein, Rhine
HENRY Rhyne
HEPAR Phare, Raphe
*HERAT Earth, Harte, Hater,
 Heart, Rathe, Thrae, Thera
HERDS Sherd, Shred
HERES Esher, Herse, Sheer, Shere
HERMA Harem
*HEROD Horde
HERON Honer, Horne, Rhone
HEROS Hoers, Horse, Shoer,
 Shore
HERSE Esher, Heres, Sheer, Shere
*HERTS Resht, Tehrs
HEVEA Heave
HEWER Where
HIANT Ahint
HIDER Hired, Rehid
HIDES Shide, Shied

HIGHT Thigh
HIKES Sheik
HILLS Shill
*__HINDU__ Unhid
HINGE Neigh
*__HIRAM__ Harim, Ihram
HIRED Hider, Rehid
HIRES Heirs, Shier, Shire
HIVES Shive
HOARD Rhoda
HOARS Saroh
HOAST Athos, Hosta, Oaths, Shoat
HOCKS Shock
HOERS Heros, Horse, Shoer, Shore
HOIKS Shiko
HOLED Dhole
HOLES Sheol, Shole
HOLLA Hallo
*__HOLST__ Holts, Sloth
HOLTS Holst, Sloth
HOMER Horme
HONED Hedon
HONER Heron, Horne, Rhone
HONES Hosen, Shone
HOOKS Shook
HOOTS Shoot, Sooth, Sotho
HOPED Ephod
HOPER Ephor
HORDE Herod
HORME Homer
*__HORNE__ Heron, Rhone, Horer
HORNS Shorn
*__HORSA__ Orsha
HORSE Heros, Hoers, Shoer, Shore
HORST Short
*__HORTA__ Thora, Torah
*__HORUS__ Hours
HOSED Doseh, Shoed
HOSEN Hones, Shone
HOSTA Athos, Hoast, Oaths, Shoat

HOSTS Shots, Stosh
HOTEL Helot, Thole
HOURS Horus
HOVES Shove
HOWES Whose
HOWRE Whore
HOWSO Whoso, Woosh
HSIEN Shine
HUCKS Shuck
HUERS Shure, Usher
HUMOR Mohur
HUMPS Sumph
HUNTS Shunt
HURST Hurts
HURTS Hurst
HYADS Dashy, Shady
HYADY Hayed
*__HYDRA__ Hardy
*__HYLAS__ Shaly

IAIDO Oidia
ICERS Cries, Crise, Erics, Seric
ICHOR Choir
ICKER Erick
ICONS Coins, Scion, Sonic
ICTAL Cital, Tical
ICTUS Cutis
IDEA'D Aided
IDEAL Ailed, Delia, Eliad
IDEAS Aides, Aside, Sadie
IDIOM Imido, Modii
IDLER Riled
IDLES Deils, Sidle, Sield, Slide
*__IDOLA__ Dolia, Iodal
*__IDOLS__ Isold, Lidos, Silo'd, Sloid, Soldi, Solid
IDYLL Dilly
IHRAM Harim, Hiram
ILEAC Alice, Celia
ILEUS Lieus
ILIAC Cilia
ILIAN Inial
ILLTH Thill
*__ILMEN__ Limen, Milne

IMAGO Amigo
IMAMS Maims, Miasm
IMBAR Abrim
IMBED Bedim
IMIDO Idiom, Modii
IMINE Minie
INANE Annie
INAPT Paint, Patin, Pinta
INARM Marin, Minar
*****INCAN** Cinna
IN-CAP Panic
IN-CAR Cairn
*****INCAS** Cains, Canis, Sican
INCOG Coign
INCUR Runic
INCUT Cut-in, Tunic
*****INDIA** Aidin
*****INDIC** Dinic
*****INDRA** Dinar, Drain, Drina,
  Nadir
*****INDRE** Diner, Rined
INDUE Nudie
*****INDUS** Nidus
INEPT Nepit
INERM Miner
INERT Inter, Niter, Nitre, Retin,
  Terni, Trine
INFER Finer
INGLE Elgin, Ligne, Nigel
INGOT Tigon, Toing
INIAL Ilian
INKED De-ink
INKER Re-ink
INKLE Klein, Liken
INNER Renin
*****INNES** Ennis, Nines
INORB Robin
INPUT Put-in
INROS Irons, Ornis, Roins, Rosin
INSET Neist, Nesti, Senti, Set-in,
  Sient, Stein, Tines
INTER Inert, Niter, Nitre, Retin,
  Terni, Trine

INTRA Nitra, Riant, Tarin, Train,
  Trani
INURE Urine
INURN Run-in
INUST Suint, Tunis, Units
*****INVAR** Ravin
IODAL Dolia, Idola
IOTAS Ostia, Stoai
IRADE Aider, Aired, Redia
IRATE Terai
*****IRENE** Ernie
*****IRISH** Rishi, Sirih
IRKED Diker
IRONS Inros, Ornis, Roins, Rosin
*****ISIAC** Ascii
*****ISLAM** Limas, Mails, Malis, Milas,
  Salmi, Simla
ISLES Lisse, Siles
ISLET Istle, Steil, Stile, Teils, Tiles
*****ISOLD** Idols, Lidos, Silod, Sloid,
  Soldi, Solid
*****ISOLT** Solti, Toils
*****ISPRA** Pairs, Paris, Parsi
ISSUE Susie
ISTLE Islet, Steil, Stile, Teils, Tiles
*****ITALY** Laity
ITCHY Tichy
ITEMS Emits, Meist, Metis, Mites,
  Smite, Stime, Times
ITHER Rithe
IVIES Visie
IZARD Darzi

JADED Jedda
JANES Jeans
JANTU Jaunt, Junta, Tunja
JAPES Jaspe
JARUL Jural
*****JASON** Joans, Jonas
JASPE Japes
JAUNT Jantu, Junta, Tunja
JAWAN Ajwan
JEANS Janes
*****JEDDA** Jaded

JIHAD Hadji
*JOANS Jason, Jonas
*JOHAN Jonah
*JONAH Johan
*JONAS Jason, Joans
JORAM Major
JOTUN Junto
JUNTA Jantu, Jaunt, Tunja
JUNTO Jotun
JURAL Jarul

KABOB Bobak
*KABUL Baulk
*KADAR Dakar
KADES Asked
*KAFIR Fakir
KAILS Kalis, Laiks, Laski, Skail
KAIMS Kamis, Maiks, Smaik
KAINS Kinas, Kisan, Nasik, Skain
KALES Lakes, Leaks, Slake
KALIS Kails, Laiks, Laski, Skail
KAMIS Kaims, Maiks, Smaik
KANES Skane, Skean, Snake,
    Sneak
KANTS Stank, Tanks
KARAT Katar
*KAREN Anker, Naker, Nerka,
    Ranke
KARMA Makar
KARST Karts, Skart, Strak, Stark
KARTS Karst, Skart, Stark, Strak
KASBA Abask
*KATAR Karat
*KATES Keats, Skate, Skeat, Stake,
    Steak, Takes, Teaks
KAYAK Yakka
KAYLE Leaky
*KEATS Kates, Skate, Skeat, Stake,
    Steak, Takes, Teaks
KEBAR Baker, Brake, Break
*KEDAH Kheda
KEECH Cheek
KEELS Leeks, Skeel, Sleek
KEENS Knees, Skene, Sneek

KEEPS Peeks, Pekes, Speke
KEIRS Kiers, Siker, Skier
KELPS Skelp, Spelk
KENOS Nokes, Snoek, Snoke,
    Soken
KEPIS Kipes, Pikes, Pisek, Spike
KESAR Asker, Eskar, Rakes,
    Reaks, Saker, Skear
KHANS Ankhs, Hanks, Shank
KHEDA Kedah
KIERS Keirs, Siker, Skier
KILEY Kylie, Ylike
KILLS Skill
KILNS Links, Slink
KINAS Nasik, Kains, Kisan, Skain
KINKS Skink
KIPES Kepis, Pikes, Pisek, Spike
KISAN Kains, Kinas, Nasik, Skain
KITES Skite, Tikes
*KLEIN Inkle, Liken
KLOOF Flook
KNAPS Spank
KNARS Krans, Narks, Ranks,
    Skran, Snark
KNEAD Naked
KNEES Keens, Skene, Sneek
KNIFE Finke
KNIPS Pinks, Pinsk, Spink
KNITS Skint, Stink, Tinks
KNOPS Knosp
KNOSP Knops
KNOTE Token
KNOTS Stonk
KNOWE Woken
KNOWS Snowk
KNUBS Bunks
KOFFS Skoff
*KOINE Eikon
KOLAS Skoal
KOLOS Looks, Sokol
KOPER Poker, Proke
*KORAN Akron, Krona
KOROS Rooks
KOTOS Stook, Tokos

KRAIT Traik
KRANS Knars, Narks, Ranks,
 Skran, Snark
KRAUT Kurta
KRONA Akron, Koran
KURTA Kraut
KYLIE Kiley, Ylike
KYLOE Yokel
*KYOTO Tokyo
KYTES Skyte, Tykes

*LABAN Alban, Banal
LABEL All-be, Be-all, Bella
LABIS Bails, Basil
LABOR Bolar, Lobar
LACED Clade, Decal
LACES Alces, Claes, Scale
LACET Cleat, Eclat, Ectal
LACEY Yecla
LACKS Calks, Slack
LADAS Salad, Salda
LADED Addle, Daled, Dedal
LADEN Eland, Lande, Laned
LADES Dales, Deals, Leads, Slade
*LADIN Linda
LADLE Dalle, Della
LAGAN Alang
LAGER Alger, Elgar, Glare, Large,
 Regal, Relga
*LAGOS Gaols, Goals
LAICS Aclis, Salic, Scail
LAIKS Kails, Kalis, Laski, Skail
LAINE Alien, Aline, Anile, Elain,
 Liane
*LAING Algin, Align, Gilan, Liang,
 Ligan, Linga
LAIRD Drail, Liard
*LAIRG Argil, Glair, Grail
LAIRY Riyal
LAITH Lathi
LAITY Italy
LAKES Kales, Leaks, Slake
LALDY Dally
*LALIN All-in

LAMAS Almas
LAMED Medal
LAMER Marle, Ramle, Realm
LAMES Almes, Amsel, Leams,
 Males, Meals, Melas, Mesal,
 Salem, Samel, Selma
LAMPS Palms, Plasm, Psalm
*LANAI Liana
*LANAS Nalas, Nasal
LANCE Ancle, Calne, Clean,
 Lenca
*LANCS Clans
LANDE Eland, Laden, Laned
LANED Eland, Laden, Lande
LANES Leans, Neals, Senal, Slane
LANGS Glans, Slang
LAPEL Pella
LAPIN Plain
LAPIS Pails, Spail, Spial
LAPSE Elaps, Leaps, Pales, Peals,
 Pleas, Salep, Sepal, Slape, Spale,
 Speal
LARDY Lyard, Rydal
LARES Arles, Earls, Laser, Lears,
 Rales, Reals, Seral
LARGE Alger, Elgar, Glare, Lager,
 Regal, Relga
LARGO Algor, Argol, Goral,
 Orgal
*LARNE Learn, Lerna, Renal
LARUM Mural, Rumal
*LARUS Sural, Urals
LARVA Arval, Lavra
LASER Arles, Earls, Lares, Lears,
 Rales, Reals, Seral
*LASKI Kails, Kalis, Laiks, Skail
LASSO Solas
LATED Datel, Dealt, Delta
LATEN Ental, Leant
LATER Alert, Alter, Artel, Ratel,
 Taler, Telar
LATEX Exalt, Taxel
LATHE Elath, Ethal
LATHI Laith

LATHS Halts, Shalt, Stahl
LAUDS Aldus, Udals
LAUND Ulnad
LAURA Aural
LAVAS Vasal
LAVED Valed
LAVER Ravel, Reval, Velar
LAVES Elvas, Salve, Selva, Slave,
  Vales, Valse, Veals
LAVRA Arval, Larva
LAWED Dwale, Waled, Weald
*****LAWES** Swale, Sweal, Wales,
  Weals
LAWNY Wanly
LAXER Relax
LAYER Early, Leary, Rayle, Relay
LAY-UP Uplay
LAZED Zelda
L-BAND Bland
L-DOPA Podal
LEACH Chela
LEADS Dales, Deals, Lades, Slade
LEADY Delay, Delya
LEAFS False, Feals, Fleas
LEAKS Kales, Lakes, Slake
LEAKY Kayle
LEAMS Almes, Amsel, Lames,
  Males, Meals, Melas, Mesal,
  Salem, Samel, Selma
LEANS Lanes, Neals, Senal, Slane
LEANT Ental, Laten
LEAPS Elaps, Lapse, Pales, Peals,
  Pleas, Salep, Sepal, Slape, Spale,
  Speal
LEAPT Lepta, Palet, Pelta, Petal,
  Plate, Pleat, Tepal
LEARE Leear
LEARN Larne, Lerna, Renal
LEARS Arles, Earls, Lares, Laser,
  Rales, Reals, Seral
LEARY Early, Layer, Rayle, Relay
LEASE Easel, Easle
LEASH Hales, Halse, Heals,
  Selah, Shale, Sheal

LEAST Astel, Leats, Salet, Slate,
  Stael, Stale, Steal, Stela, Taels,
  Tales, Teals, Tesla
LEATS Astel, Least, Salet, Slate,
  Stael, Stale, Steal, Stela, Taels,
  Tales, Teals, Tesla
LEAVE Veale
LEAVY Vealy
LEDGE Glede, Gleed
LEDGY Gyeld
LEEAR Leare
LEECH Elche
*****LEEDS** Deles, Edsel, Seled
LEEKS Keels, Skeel, Sleek
LEERS Leres, Reels, Sleer
LEERY Leyre
LEETS Sleet, Steel, Stele, Teels
LEFTY Felty, Flyte
LEGAL Galle
LEGER Regel, Regle
LEGES Glees
LEGIT Gilet
*****LEICS** Ceils, Ciels, Sicel, Slice
LEIRS Liers, Riels, Riles, Risel,
  Siler, Slier
*****LEITH** Lieth, Lithe
LEMAN Elman, Lemna
*****LEMNA** Elman, Leman
LEMON Melon, Monel
LENCA Ancle, Calne, Clean,
  Lance
*****LENIN** Linen
LENIS Elsin, Liens, Lines, Nelis,
  Niles, Silen
LENOS Solen
LENTO Olent, Olten
LEPER Repel
LEPID Piel'd, Piled, Plied
LEPIS Piles, Plies, Slipe, Spiel,
  Spile
LEPRA Paler, Parle, Pearl, Repla
LEPTA Leapt, Palet, Pelta, Petal,
  Plate, Pleat, Tepal
LERES Leers, Reels, Sleer

LERNA Larne, Learn, Renal
*****LEROS** Eorls, Lores, Loser, Orles,
	Osler, Roles, Soler, Sorel
*****LETHE** Ethel
LEUDS Duels, Dules, Dulse,
	Slued
LEVAN Elvan, Navel, Venal
LEVEE Eleve
LEVER Elver, Revel
LEVIN Liven
*****LEVIS** Elvis, Evils, Lives, Slive,
	Veils, Vleis
*****LEWES** Sewel, Sweel, Weels,
	Wesel
LEWIS Weils, Wiels, Wiles
*****LEXIE** Exile
LEXIS Silex
*****LEYRE** Leery
LIANA Lanai
LIANE Alien, Aline, Anile, Elain,
	Laine
LIANG Algin, Align, Gilan, Laing,
	Ligan, Linga
*****LIARD** Drail, Laird
LIART Trail, T-rail, Trial
LIBER Birle
*****LIBRA** Brail
LICHI Chili
LICKS Slick
LIDOS Idols, Isold, Silod, Sloid,
	Soldi, Solid
LIENS Elsin, Lines, Nelis, Lenis,
	Niles, Silen
LIERS Leirs, Riels, Riles, Risel,
	Siler, Slier
LIETH Leith, Lithe
LIEUS Ileus
LIFER Filer, Flier, Rifle
LIGAN Algin, Align, Gilan, Laing,
	Liang, Linga
LIGER Rigel
LIGNE Elgin, Ingle, Nigel
LIKEN Inkle, Klein
LIKER Rilke

LIKES Sikel
LILAC Cilla
LILTS Still, Tills
LIMAS Islam, Mails, Malis, Milas,
	Salmi, Simla
LIMEN Ilmen, Milne
LIMES Miles, Misle, Slime, Smile
LIMSY Misly, Slimy
LINAC Calin
*****LINDA** Ladin
LINED Eldin
LINEN Lenin
LINES Elsin, Lenis, Liens, Nelis,
	Niles, Silen
LINGA Algin, Align, Gilan, Laing,
	Liang, Ligan
LINGS Sling
LINGY Lying
LINKS Kilns, Slink
LISLE Ellis
LISPS Slips
*****LISSA** Sails, Silas, Sisal
LISSE Isles, Siles
LITAS Tails
LITER Litre, Relit, Tiler
LITHE Leith, Lieth
LITHO Thiol, Tholi
LITRE Liter, Relit, Tiler
LIVED Devil, Vilde
LIVEN Levin
LIVER Ervil, Livre, Rivel, Viler
LIVES Elvis, Evils, Levis, Slive,
	Veils, Vleis
LIVRE Ervil, Liver, Rivel, Viler
*****LLEYN** Nelly
*****LLOYD** Dolly
LOAFS Foals, Sol-fa
LOAMS Lomas, Salmo, Sloam
LOANS Salon, Sloan, Solan, Solna
LOATH Athol, Lotah
LOAVE Volae
LOBAR Bolar, Labor
LOBED Bodle
LOBOS Bolos, Obols, Sobol

LOBUS Bolus
*****LOCKE** Cloke
LOCUS Clous
LODEN Olden
LODES Delos, Doles, Dosel, Solde, Soled
LODGE Glode, Loged, Ogled
LOESS Loses, Sloes, Soles
*****LOGAN** Along, Anglo, Golan, Longa
LOGED Glode, Lodge, Ogled
LOGES Ogles, Segol
*****LOIRE** Oiler, Oriel, Reoil
LOMAS Loams, Salmo, Sloam
LONER Enrol, Loren, Lorne, Nerol
LONGA Along, Anglo, Golan, Logan
LOOED Doole
LOOES Loose, Oleos, Soole
LOOFA Aloof
LOOKS Kolos, Sokol
LOOMS Mools, Sloom
LOONS Snool, Solon
LOOPS Pools, Sloop, Spool
LOORD Dolor, Drool
LOOSE Looes, Oleos, Soole
LOOTS Lotos, Sloot, Sotol, Stool, Tools
LOPED Poled
LOPES Elops, Olpes, Poles, Slope, Spole
LOPPY Polyp
LORAN Arlon, Lorna
*****LORCA** Calor, Carol, Claro, Coral
*****LOREN** Enrol, Loner, Lorne, Nerol
LORES Eorls, Leros, Loser, Orles, Osler, Roles, Soler, Sorel
LORIS Roils
*****LORME** Morel
*****LORNA** Arlon, Loran
*****LORNE** Enrol, Loner, Loren, Nerol

LOSER Eorls, Leros, Lores, Orles, Osler, Roles, Soler, Sorel
LOSES Loess, Sloes, Soles
LOTAH Athol, Loath
LOTES Stole, Telos, Toles
LOTOS Loots, Sloot, Sotol, Stool, Tools
LOTUS Louts, Soult
LOUGH Ghoul
LOUND Nould
LOUPE Poule
LOUSE Eusol, Ousel, Seoul
LOUSY Louys
LOUTS Lotus, Soult
*****LOUYS** Lousy
LOVAT Volta
LOVED Voled
LOVES Slove, Solve, Voles
LOWED Dowel, Dowle, Owled
LOWER Owler, Rowel
LOWNE Nowel
LOWNS Swoln
LOWSE Sowle
LOYAL Alloy
LUBRA Braul
*****LUCAS** Cauls
LUCES Clues, Cluse
LUCRE Cruel, Ulcer
LUGED Glued
*****LUGER** Gluer, Gruel
LUGES Glues, Gules, Gusle
LUMEN Melun
LUMPS Plums, Slump
LUMPY Plumy
LUNAR Ulnar, Urnal
LUNGS Slung
LUPPA Pupal
LUPUS Pulus
LURCH Churl
LURED Dreul, Ruled
LURER Ruler
LYARD Lardy, Rydal
*****LYDIA** Daily
LYING Lingy

LYRES Slyer
LYRIC Cyril
LYRID Drily
LYSES Sleys, Yssel
LYSOL Solly
*****LYTHE** Ethyl

*****MABEL** Amble, Blame, Embla,
　Melba
MACER Ceram, Crame, Cream,
　Crema, Merca
MACKS Smack
MACLE Camel
MADGE Gamed
MADRE Armed, Derma, Dream,
　Ramed
MAGAR Grama
MAGIC Gamic
MAGMA Gamma
MAGUS Gaums, Sagum
MAIDS Midas
MAIKS Kaims, Kamis, Smaik
MAILE E-la-mi, Melia
MAILS Islam, Limas, Malis, Milas,
　Salmi, Simla
MAIMS Imams, Miasm
*****MAINE** Amine, Anime, Menai,
　Minae
MAINS Manis, Minas
MAIRE Aimer, Marie, Ramie,
　Rimae
MAIST Tamis
MAJOR Joram
MAKAR Karma
MALAR Alarm, Ramal
*****MALAY** Yamal
MALES Almes, Amsel, Lames,
　Leams, Meals, Melas, Mesal,
　Salem, Samel, Selma
MALIC Claim
MALIS Islam, Limas, Mails, Milas,
　Salmi, Simla
MALLS Small
*****MALTA** Talma, Tamal

MALTS Smalt
MANDE Admen, Amend, Maned,
　Medan, Menad, Named
*****MANDY** Dynam
MANED Admen, Amend, Medan,
　Menad, Named
MANEH He-man
MANES Amens, Manse, Means,
　Mensa, Names, Samen
*****MANET** Ament, Meant
MANGE Megan
MANGO Among
MANIA Amain, Amnia, Anima
*****MANIS** Mains, Minas
MANNA Annam, Naman
MANOR Morna, Norma, Ramon,
　Roman
MANSE Amens, Manes, Means,
　Mensa, Names, Samen
MANTA Atman
MANTO Toman
MANUS Mauns
*****MAORI** Mario, Moira, Moria
MAPLE Ample, Pelma
*****MARAH** Haram
*****MARAS** Samar
*****MARAT** Tamar
MARCH Charm
*****MARCO** Carom
MARES Maser, Mears, Reams,
　Smear
MARGE Gamer, Grame, Regma
*****MARGO** Groma
*****MARIE** Aimer, Ramie, Rimae,
　Maire
*****MARIN** Inarm, Minar
*****MARIO** Maori, Moira, Moria
MARLE Lamer, Ramle, Realm
MARLY Almay
*****MARNE** Enarm, Namer, Reman
MAROR Armor, Morra
*****MAROS** Moras, Osram, Roams
MARSH Harms, Shram
MARTS Smart, Trams

MARYS Symar
MASER Mares, Mears, Reams,
　Smear
MASON Moans, Monas, Osman
MASSA Amass, Assam
MASSE Mesas, Seams
MASTY Mayst
MATED Tamed
MATER Armet, Metra, Tamer,
　Terma, Trema
MATES Meats, Mesta, Satem,
　Steam, Tames, Teams
MATEY Etyma, Meaty
MATIN Tamin
MATZO Motza
MAUDS Adsum, Dumas
MAUND Munda, Undam, Unmad
MAUNS Manus
MAWRS Swarm, Warms
MAYBE Beamy, Embay
*****MAYEN** Meany, Yamen
MAYOR Moray
MAYST Masty
MEADS Dames, Demas, Desma
MEALS Almes, Amsel, Lames,
　Leams, Males, Melas, Mesal,
　Salem, Samel, Selma
MEANE Amene, Enema
MEANS Amens, Manes, Manse,
　Mensa, Names, Samen
MEANT Ament, Manet
MEANY Mayen, Yamen
MEARS Mares, Maser, Reams,
　Smear
MEASE Seame
*****MEATH** Thame, Thema
MEATS Mates, Mesta, Satem,
　Steam, Tames, Teams
MEATY Etyma, Matey
MEBOS Besom
MEDAL Lamed
*****MEDAN** Admen, Amend, Mande,
　Maned, Menad, Named
*****MEDEA** Adeem, Edema

MEDIA Aimed, Amide
MEDIC Demic
MEERS Meres, Merse
MEETS Metes, Steem, Steme,
　Teems, Temes, Temse
*****MEGAN** Mange
MEISM Mimes
MEIST Emits, Items, Metis, Mites,
　Smite, Stime, Times
MELAS Almes, Amsel, Lames,
　Leams, Males, Meals, Mesal,
　Salem, Samel, Selma
*****MELBA** Blame, Amble, Embla,
　Mabel
*****MELIA** E-la-mi, Maile
MELIC Clime
MELLS Smell
MELON Lemon, Monel
*****MELOS** Moles
MELTS Smelt
*****MELUN** Lumen
MEMOS Momes, Somme
MENAD Admen, Amend, Mande,
　Maned, Medan, Named
*****MENAI** Amine, Anime, Maine,
　Minae
*****MENDE** Emend
MENES Mense, Mesne, Neems,
　Semen
*****MENSA** Amens, Manse, Manes,
　Means, Names, Samen
MENSE Menes, Mesne, Neems,
　Semen
*****MERCA** Ceram, Crame, Cream,
　Cerma, Macer
MEREL Elmer, Merle
MERES Meers, Merse
MERIL Miler
*****MERIS** Emirs, Mires, Miser,
　Reims, Riems, Rimes
MERIT Miter, Mitre, Remit, Timer
MERLE Elmer, Merel
*****MERSE** Meers, Meres

MESAL Almes, Amsel, Lames,
  Leams, Males, Meals, Melas,
  Salem, Samel, Selma
MESAS Masse, Seams
MESNE Menes, Mense, Neems,
  Semen
MESON Nomes, Omens
*MESTA Mates, Meats, Satem,
  Steam, Tames, Teams
MESTO Motes, Smote, Tomes
METED Temed
METER Metre, Retem
METES Meets, Steem, Steme,
  Teems, Temes, Temse
METIS Emits, Items, Meist, Mites,
  Smite, Stime, Times
*METOL Motel
METRA Armet, Mater, Tamer,
  Terma, Trema
METRE Meter, Retem
*METSU Muset, Mutes
MIASM Imams, Maims
MIAUL Aumil
MICHE Chiem, Chime, Hemic
MICRO Romic
*MIDAS Maids
*MILAS Islam, Limas, Mails, Malis,
  Salmi, Simla
MILER Meril
MILES Limes, Misle, Slime, Smile
MILKS Sklim
*MILNE Ilmen, Limen
*MILOS Moils
MIMES Meism
MINAE Amine, Anime, Maine
MINAR Inarm, Marin
MINAS Manis, Mains
MINED Denim
MINER Inerm
MINES Nimes
*MINIE Imine
MINKS Minsk
*MINOS Simon
*MINOT Timon, Tomin

*MINSK Minks
MIRED Dimer, Rimed
MIRES Emirs, Meris, Miser,
  Reims, Riems Rimes,
MISDO Odism
MISER Emirs, Meris, Mires,
  Reims, Riems, Rimes
MISES Seism, Semis
MISGO Gismo
MISLE Limes, Miles, Slime, Smile
MISLY Limsy, Slimy
MISSA Amiss
MISSY Mysis
MISTY Stimy
MITER Merit, Mitre, Remit, Timer
MITES Emits, Items, Meist, Metis,
  Smite, Stime, Times
MITRE Merit, Miter, Remit, Timer
MITTS Smitt
MIXER Re-mix
*MOABS Ambos, Bomas, Sambo
MOANS Mason, Monas, Osman
MOATS Atoms, Stoma
*MOCHA Mohac
MOCKS Smock
MODAL Domal
MODEL Moled
MODER Drome
MODES Demos, Domes
MODII Idiom, Imido
MOERS Mores, Morse, Omers,
  Smore
*MOHAC Mocha
MOHUR Humor
MOILS Milos
*MOIRA Maori, Mario, Moria
MOIST Omits
MOKES Smoke
MOLAL Molla, Ollam
MOLAR Moral, Romal
MOLED Model
MOLES Melos
MOLLA Molal, Ollam
MOMES Memos, Somme

MONAD Damon, Nomad
*MONAS Mason, Moans, Osman
MONDE Demon
MONEL Lemon, Melon
MONER Enorm, Morne
*MONET Monte, Moten
MONEY Emony
MONTE Monet, Moten
MOODS Dooms, Dsomo, Sodom
MOODY Doomy
MOOLS Looms, Sloom
MOONS Nomos
*MOORE Romeo
MOORS Moros, Ormos, Rooms,
    Smoor
MOORY Roomy
MOOTS Smoot, Stoom, Tooms
MOPER Proem, Prome
MOPES Epsom, Poems, Pomes
MOPSY Myops
MORAL Molar, Romal
MORAS Maros, Osram, Roams
MORAT Amort
MORAY Mayor
MOREL L'Orme
MORES Moers, Morse, Omers,
    Smore
MORIA Maori, Mario, Moira
*MORNA Manor, Norma, Ramon,
    Roman
MORNE Enorm, Moner
*MOROS Moors, Ormos, Rooms,
    Smoor
MORRA Armor, Maror
MORSE Moers, Mores, Omers,
    Smore
MORTS Storm, Troms
MOTEL Metol
MOTEN Monet, Monte
MOTES Mesto, Smote, Tomes
MOTET Motte, Totem
MOTHY Y-moth
MOTTE Motet, Totem
MOTZA Matzo

MOUES Mouse
MOULS Solum
MOUNT Muton, Notum
*MOURA Amour
MOURN Munro, Muron
MOUSE Moues
MOUST Smout
MOVER Vomer
MOWER Remow, Rowme
MUCIN Cumin
MUCKS Smuck
*MUCOR Mucro
MUCRO Mucor
MUIST Musit, Tuism
MULES Mulse
MULGA Algum, Almug, Glaum
MULSE Mules
*MUNDA Maund, Undam, Unmad
*MUNRO Mourn, Muron
MURAL Larum, Rumal
MURED Demur
MURES Muser, Remus, Serum,
    Sumer
*MUREX Rumex
MURLY Rumly
*MURON Mourn, Munro
*MUSCA Camus, Caums, Sumac
*MUSCI Music
MUSED Sedum
MUSER Mures, Remus, Serum,
    Sumer
MUSES Musse
MUSET Metsu, Mutes
MUSIC Musci
MUSIT Muist, Tuism
MUSSE Muses
MUTES Metsu, Muset
MUTON Mount, Notum
MVULE Velum
MYOPS Mopsy
MYSIS Missy

NACHE Caneh, Hance

NACRE Caner, Carne, Crane, Crena, Rance
NADIR Dinar, Drain, Drina, Indra
NAEVE Veena, Venae
NAEVI Avine, Naive, Neiva
NAGOR Angor, Argon, Groan, Ongar, Orang, Organ
NAIAD Aidan, Diana
*****NAIAS** Asian
NAILS Anils, Salin, Slain, Snail
NAIRA Arian
*****NAIRN** Narni
NAIVE Avine, Naevi, Neiva
NAKED Knead
NAKER Anker, Karen, Nerka, Ranke
NALAS Nasal, Lanas
NALLA Allan
NAMAN Annam, Manna
NAMED Admen, Amend, Mande, Maned, Medan, Menad
NAMER Enarm, Marne, Reman
NAMES Amens, Manes, Manse, Means, Mensa, Samen
*****NAMUR** Ruman, Unarm, Urman
*****NANCY** Canny
NAPES Aspen, Neaps, Panes, Peans, Snape, Sneap, Spane, Spean
NAPOO Poona
*****NARDO** Adorn, Andro, Donar, Radon
NARES Earns, Nears, Saner, Snare
*****NAREW** Awner
NARIS Rains, Ranis
NARKS Knars, Krans, Ranks, Skran, Snark
*****NARNI** Nairn
NASAL Lanas, Nalas
*****NASIK** Kains, Kinas, Kisan, Skain
NASTY Tansy
NATCH Chant

NATES Antes, Etnas, Nesta, Senta, Stean, Stane, Teans
NATTY Tanty
NAVEL Elvan, Levan, Venal
NAVES Avens, Evans, Sevan, Vanes
NAWAB Bwana
*****NAXOS** Axons, Saxon
*****NAYAR** Aryan
NAYED Denay
NAZES Senza
*****NDOLA** Nodal, Oland
*****NEALS** Lanes, Leans, Senal, Slane
NEAPS Aspen, Napes, Panes, Peans, Snape, Sneap, Spane, Spean
NEARS Earns, Nares, Saner, Snare
NEATH Thane
NECKS Sneck
NEEDS Deens, Denes, Dense, Edens
NEEMS Menes, Mense, Mesne, Semen
*****NEGEV** Venge
NEGRE Genre, Gerne, Green
*****NEGRO** Ergon, Genro, Goner, Grone
NEGUS Genus
NEIGH Hinge
NEIST Inset, Nesti, Senti, Set-in, Sient, Stein, Tines
*****NEIVA** Avine Naevi, Naive
NEIVE Nieve
NELIS Elsin, Lenis, Liens, Lines, Niles, Silen
*****NELLY** Lleyn
*****NEPAL** Alpen, Panel, Pelan, Penal, Plane, Plena
NEPER Preen, Repen
NEPIT Inept
NERKA Anker, Karen, Naker, Ranke

NEROL Enrol, Loner, Loren, Lorne
NERVE Erven, Never, Vener, Verne
*NESKI Skein, Skien
*NESTA Antes, Etnas, Nates, Senta, Stane, Stean, Teans
NESTI Inset, Neist, Senti, Set-in, Sient, Stein, Tines
NETTY Tenty
*NEUSE Ensue
NEVER Erven, Nerve, Vener, Verne
*NEVES Evens, Seven
*NEVIS Sevin, Venis, Veins, Vines, Visne
NEVUS Venus
NEWER Renew
NEXUS Unsex
*NGAIO Gonia
NGAMI Gamin
NICER Cerin, Crine
NICHE Chien, Chine
NICKS Snick
NICOL Colin
NIDES Denis, Dines, Enids, Sdein, Snide
NIDGE Deign, Dinge, Nigde
NIDOR Rodin
NIDUS Indus
NIEVE Neive
NIFFS Sniff
*NIGDE Deign, Dinge, Nidge
*NIGEL Elgin, Ingle, Ligne
*NIGER Grein, Reign, Renig, Ringe
*NIGHT Thing
*NILES Elsin, Lenis, Liens, Lines, Nelis, Selin
*NIMES Mines
NINES Ennis, Innes
NISSE Sines
NISUS Sinus
NITER Inert, Inter, Nitre, Retin, Terni, Trine

NITON Noint
*NITRA Intra, Riant, Tarin, Train, Trani
NITRE Inert, Inter, Niter, Retin, Teri, Trine
NITTY Tinty
NIVAL Alvin, Anvil, Vilna, Vinal
*NOBEL Noble
NOBLE Nobel
NODAL Ndola, Oland
NODES Nosed, Sonde
NODUS Sound, Unsod
NOINT Niton
NOISE Eosin
NOKES Soken
NOMAD Damon, Monad
NOMES Meson, Omens
*NOMOS Moons
NONCE Conne
*NONES Sonne
NONET Tenon, Tonne
NOOKS Snook
NOOPS Poons, Snoop, Spoon
NO-PAR Apron
*NORAH Rhona, Rohan
NORMA Manor, Morna, Ramon, Roman
NORSE Noser, Oners, Rones, Senor, Seron, Snore, Ronse,
NORTH Thorn
NOSED Nodes, Sonde
NOSER Norse, Oners, Rones, Ronse, Senor, Seron, Snore
NOSES Sones, Sonse
NOTAL Alton, Talon, Tolan, Tonal
*NOTEC Cento, Conte
NOTED Donet, Toned
NOTER Ronte, Tenor, Toner, Trone
NOTES Eston, Etons, Onset, Seton, Steno, Stone, Tenos, Tones
NOTUM Mount, Muton

*NOTUS Snout, Stoun, Tonus
NOULD Lound
NOUNS Unson
NOVEL Venlo, Vlone
NOWED Endow, Owned, Woden, Woned
*NOWEL Lowne
*NOWRA Rowan
NUBIA Aubin, Bunia
NUDGE Dengu
NUDIE Indue
NURSE Runes
NYULA Unlay, Yulan

OARED Adore, Oread
OASIS Ossia
OASTS Assot, Stoas, Tasso
OATEN Aneto, Atone, Onate
OATHS Athos, Hoast, Hosta, Shoat
OBANG Gabon
OBEAH Bohea
OBEYS Syboe
OBOES Boose
OBOLS Bolos, Lobos, Sobol
OCEAN Canoe
OCHER Chore, Ochre, Roche
OCHRE Chore, Ocher, Roche
OCREA Corea
OCTAN Acton, Canto, Cotan
ODDER Roded
*ODEON Doone
ODISM Misdo
ODIST Doits
ODYLE Doyle, Yodel, Yodle
ODYLS Sloyd
O'ERBY Ybore
OFFER Reffo
OGEE'D Geode
OGIVE Vogie
OGLED Glode, Lodge, Loged
OGLES Loges, Segol
OGRES Ergos, Goers, Gores, Gorse, Sergo, Soger

OIDIA Iaido
OILED De-oil
OILER Loire, Oriel, Re-oil
*OLAND Ndola, Nodal
OLDEN Loden
OLDER Doler, Drole
*OLEAN Alone
OLEIC Eolic
OLEIN Eloin
OLENT Lento, Olten
OLEOS Looes, Loose, Soole
*OLIVA Viola, Voila
OLIVE Viole, Voile
OLLAM Molal, Molla
OLPES Elops, Lopes, Poles, Slope, Spole
OLTEN Lento, Olent
OMBER Brome, Ombre
OMBRE Brome, Omber
OMBRO Bromo, Broom
OMENS Meson, Nomes
OMERS Moers, Mores, Morse, Smore
OMITS Moist
ONATE Aneto, Atone, Oaten
ONCER Creon, Crone, Recon
*ONEGA Agone, Genoa
ON-END Donne, End-on
ONERS Norse, Noser, Rones, Ronse, Senor, Seron, Snore
*ONGAR Angor, Argon, Goran, Nagor, Orang, Organ
ONSET Eston, Etons, Notes, Seton, Steno, Stone, Tenos, Tones
OPALS Palos, Salop
OPENS Peons, Pones, Posen, Snoep
*OPOLE Poole
OPTED Depot, Poted, Toped
OPTIC Picot, Topic
ORACH Achor, Roach
ORALS Solar, Soral

ORANG Angor, Argon, Groan, Nagor, Ongar, Organ

ORANT Arnot, Toran, Trona

ORATE Erato, Roate

ORBED Borde, Bored, Brode, Robed

*__ORCUS__ Scour

ORDOS Doors, Roods, Sordo

OREAD Adore, Oared

ORGAL Algor, Argol, Goral, Largo

ORGAN Angor, Argon, Groan, Nagor, Ongar, Orang

ORGIC Corgi

ORGUE Rogue, Rouge

ORIEL Loire, Oiler, Re-oil

ORLES Eorls, Leros, Lores, Loser, Osler, Roles, Soler, Sorel,

*__ORMOS__ Moors, Moros, Rooms, Smoor

ORNIS Inros, Irons, Roins, Rosin

ORPIN Proin

*__ORSHA__ Horsa

*__ORTON__ Troon

ORVAL Volar

OSHAC Chaos

OSIER Rosie, Siero

*__OSLER__ Eorls, Leros, Lores, Loser, Orles, Roles, Soler, Sorel

*__OSMAN__ Mason, Moans, Monas

OSRAM Maros, Moras, Roams

OSSIA Oasis

OSTIA Iotas, Stoai

OTARY Yarto

OTHER Throe

OTTAR Tarot, Troat

OTTER Torte, Toter

OUCHT Chout, Couth, Touch

OUGHT Tough

OUNCE Cuneo

OUSEL Eusol, Louse, Seoul

*__OUSES__ Souse

OUTER Outre, Route, Toure

OUTRE Outer, Route, Toure

OVALS Salvo, Volas

OVERS Roves, Serov, Servo, Verso

OVERT Trove, Voter

OVINE Envoi

OVIST Visto

OWERS Owser, Resow, Serow, Sower, Swore, Worse

OWLED Dowel, Dowle, Lowed

OWLER Lower, Rowel

OWLET Towel

OWNED Endow, Nowed, Woden, Woned

OWNER Rewon, Rowen

OWSER Owers, Resow, Serow, Sower, Swore, Worse

OXERS Exors, Sorex

PACED Caped

PACER Caper, Crape, Perca, Recap

PACES Capes, Caspe, Scape, Space

PADAR Padra

PADGE Gaped, Paged

PADLE Paled, Pedal, Plead

PADRA Padar

RADRE Drape, Pared, Raped, Repad

PAEAN Apnea

PAGAN Panga

PAGED Gaped, Padge

PAGER Gaper, Grape, Parge

PAGES Gapes, Gaspe

PAGLE Plage

PAGRI Graip

PAGUS Gaups

PAILS Lapis, Spail, Spial

PAINS Pinas, Spain, Spina

PAINT Inapt, Patin, Pinta

PAIRS Ispra, Paris, Parsi

PALAS Salpa

PALAY Playa

PALED Padle, Pedal, Plead

PALER Lepra, Parle, Pearl, Repla
PALES Elaps, Lapse, Leaps, Peals, Pleas, Salep, Sepal, Slape, Spale, Speal
PALET Leapt, Lepta, Pelta, Petal, Plate, Pleat, Tepal
PALLS Spall
PALMS Lamps, Plasm, Psalm
PALMY Amply
*****PALOS** Opals, Salop
PALPI Pipal
PALSY Plays, Splay, Spyal
PANCE Pecan
PANDY Pydna
PANEL Alpen, Nepal, Pelan, Penal, Plane, Plena
PANES Aspen, Napes, Neaps, Peans, Snape, Sneap, Spane, Spean
PANGA Pagan
PANGS Spang
PANIC In-cap
PANNE Penna
PANTO Paton
PAPAL Appal
PARDI Rapid
PARDS Prads, Sprad
PARED Drape, Padre, Raped, Repad
PARER Raper
PARES Apers, Asper, Parse, Pears, Prase, Presa, Rapes, Reaps, Spaer, Spare, Spear
PARGE Gaper, Grape, Pager
*****PARIS** Ispra, Pairs, Parsi
PARKS Spark
PARLE Lepra, Paler, Pearl, Repla
PARLY Pyral
PAROL Polar, Poral
*****PAROS** Proas, Psora, Sapor, Sopra, Spora
PARSE Apers, Asper, Pares, Pears, Prase, Presa, Rapes, Reaps, Spaer, Spare, Spear

*****PARSI** Ispra, Pairs, Paris
PARTI Atrip, Tapir
PARTS Prats, Spart, Sprat, Strap, Traps
PARTY Praty, Yrapt
*****PASCH** Chaps
PASPY Sappy
PASSE Apses, Spaes
PASTE Apest, Pates, Peats, Septa, Spate, Speat, Tapes
PASTY Patsy, Pyats
PATCH Chapt
PATED Adept, Taped
PATEN Tapen
PATER Apert, Peart, Petar, Petra, Prate, Taper, Trape
PATES Apest, Paste, Peats, Septa, Spate, Speat, Tapes
PATIN Inapt, Paint, Pinta
PATIO Topia
PATLY Aptly, Platy, Typal
*****PATON** Panto
PATSY Pasty, Pyats
PATTE Tapet
*****PATTI** Pitta
*****PAULS** Pulas, Spaul
PAVES Spave, Vespa
PAVID Vapid
PAWLS Spawl
PAWNS Spawn
PAYER Apery, Peary, Repay
PAYSD Spayd
PEACH Chape, Cheap
PEAKS Spake, Speak
PEALS Elaps, Lapse, Leaps, Pales, Pleas, Salep, Sepal, Slape, Spale, Speal
PEANS Aspen, Napes, Neaps, Panes, Snape, Sneap, Spane, Spean
PEARL Lepra, Paler, Parle, Repla
PEARS Apers, Asper, Pares, Parse, Prase, Presa, Rapes, Reaps, Spaer, Spare, Spear

PEART Apert, Pater, Petar, Petra, Prate, Taper, Trape

PEARY Apery, Payer, Repay

PEATS Apest, Paste, Pates, Septa, Spate, Speat, Tapes

PECAN Pance

PECKS Speck

*PECOS Copes, Copse, Scope

PEDAL Padle, Paled, Plead

*PEDRO Doper, Pored, Roped

PEEKS Keeps, Pekes, Speke

PEELS Sleep, Speel

PEERS Perse, Prees, Prese, Speer, Spree

PEKES Keeps, Peeks, Speke

*PEKIN Penki

*PELAN Alpen, Nepal, Panel, Penal, Plane, Plena

*PELLA Lapel

PELLS Spell

PELMA Ample, Maple

PELTA Leapt, Lepta, Palet, Petal, Plate, Pleat, Tepal

PELTS Slept, Spelt

PENAL Alpen, Nepal, Panel, Pelan, Plane, Plena

PENDS Spend

PENIS Pines, Snipe, Spine

*PENKI Pekin

PENNA Panne

PENTS Spent

PEONS Opens, Pones, Posen, Snoep

PEONY Poney

PEPLA Appel, Apple

*PERCA Caper, Crape, Pacer, Recap

PERCE Creep, Crepe

PERDU Drupe, Dupre, Duper, Prude, Pured

PERDY Predy

PERIL Piler, Plier

*PERIM Prime

PERIS Epris, Piers, Pries, Prise, Ripes, Speir, Spier, Spire

PERMS Sperm

*PERON Prone

PERRY Pryer, Ryper

PERSE Peers, Prees, Prese, Speer, Spree

PERTS Prest, Strep

*PESAH Ephas, Heaps, Phase, Shape

PESOS Poses, Posse, Speos

PETAL Leapt, Lepta, Palet, Pelta, Plate, Pleat, Tepal

PETAR Apert, Pater, Peart, Petra, Prate, Taper, Trape

PETER Petre, Ptere, Repet

*PETRA Apert, Pater, Peart, Petar, Prate, Taper, Trape

PETRE Peter, Ptere, Repet

PETRI Piert, Tripe

PETTO Topet

PEYSE Seepy

PHARE Hepar, Raphe

PHASE Ephas, Heaps, Pesah, Shape

PHEON Phone

PHESE Sheep

*PHOCA Poach

PHONE Pheon

PHYLA Haply

PICAS Aspic, Capis, Scapi, Spica

PICKS Spick

PICOT Optic, Topic

PICRA Capri, Carpi

PIEL'D Lepid, Piled, Plied

PIEND Pined

PIERS Epris, Peris, Pries, Prise, Ripes, Speir, Spier, Spire

PIERT Petri, Tripe

PIETS Piste, Spite, Stipe

PIKES Kepis, Kipes, Pisek, Spike

*PILAR April, Prial

PILED Lepid, Piel'd, Plied

PILER Peril, Plier

PILES Lepis, Plies, Slipe, Spiel, Spile
PILLS Spill
PINAS Pains, Spain, Spina
PINED Piend
PINER Repin, Ripen
PINES Penis, Snipe, Spine
PINKS Knips, Pinsk, Spink
*PINSK Knips, Pinks, Spink
PINTA Inapt, Paint, Patin
PINTO Piton, Point, Ponti, Potin
PIPAL Palpi
PIPER Priep
PIPUL Pupil
PIQUE Equip
*PIRAN Pirna
*PIRNA Piran
*PISEK Kepis, Kipes, Pikes, Spike
PISKY Spiky
PISTE Piets, Spite, Stipe
PITAS Spait, Stipa, Tapis
PITON Pinto, Point, Ponti, Potin
*PITTA Patti
PLACE Capel, Caple
PLAGE Pagle
PLAIN Lapin
PLANE Alpen, Nepal, Panel, Pelan, Penal, Plena
PLASM Lamps, Palms, Psalm
PLATE Leapt, Lepta, Palet, Pelta, Petal, Pleat, Tepal
PLATS Spalt, Splat
PLATY Aptly, Patly, Typal
PLAYA Palay
PLAYS Palsy, Splay, Spyal
PLEAD Padle, Paled, Pedal
PLEAS Elaps, Lapse, Leaps, Plaes, Peals, Salep, Sepal, Slape, Spale, Speal
PLEAT Leapt, Lepta, Palet, Pelta, Petal, Plate, Tepal
PLENA Alpen, Nepal, Panel, Pelan, Penal, Plane
PLESH Helps

PLIED Lepid, Piel'd, Piled
PLIER Peril, Piler
PLIES Lepis, Piles, Slipe, Spiel, Spile
PLOTS Polts, Stolp
PLOYS Slopy, Pylos
PLUMS Lumps, Slump
PLUMY Lumpy
*PLUTO Poult
PLYER Reply
POACH Phoca
POCKS Spock
PODAL L-dopa
PODEX Poxed
POEMS Epsom, Mopes, Pomes,
POESY Poyse, Sepoy
POETS Estop, Potes, Stoep, Stope, Topes
POINT Pinto, Piton, Ponti, Potin
POKAL Polka
POKER Koper, Proke
POKES Spoke
POLAR Parol, Poral
POLED Loped
POLER Prole
POLES Elops, Lopes, Olpes, Slope, Spole
POLIS Spoil
POLKA Pokal
POLTS Plots, Stolp
POLYP Loppy
POMES Epsom, Mopes, Poems
PONES Opens, Peons, Posen, Snoep
PONEY Peony
*PONTI Pinto, Piton, Point, Potin
POOFS Spoof
*POOLE Opole
POOLS Loops, Sloop, Spool
*POONA Napoo
POONS Noops, Snoop, Spoon
POORT Porto, Troop
POPSY Psyop, Soppy
PORAL Parol, Polar

PORED Doper, Pedro, Roped

PORER Prore, Repro, Roper

PORES Poser, Prose, Ropes, Soper, Spore

PORTA Aport, Prato

***PORTE** Repot, Retop, Tepor, Toper, Trope

***PORTO** Poort, Troop

PORTS Sport, Strop

POSED Dopes, Spode

***POSEN** Opens, Peons, Pones, Snoep

POSER Pores, Prose, Ropes, Soper, Spore

POSES Pesos, Posse, Speos

POSIT Topis

POSSE Pesos, Poses, Speos

POTED Depot, Opted, Toped

POTES Estop, Poets, Stoep, Stope, Topes

POTIN Pinto, Piton, Point, Ponti

POTTY Typto

POULE Loupe

POULT Pluto

POUPT Top-up

POUTS Spout, Stoup, Toups

POXED Podex

POYSE Poesy, Sepoy

PRADS Pards, Sprad

PRASE Apers, Asper, Pares, Parse, Pears, Presa, Rapes, Reaps, Spaer, Spare, Spear

PRATE Apert, Pater, Peart, Petar, Petra, Taper, Trape

***PRATO** Aport, Porta

PRATS Parts, Spart, Sprat, Strap, Traps

PRATY Party, Yrapt

PRAYS Raspy, Spray

PREDY Perdy

PREEN Neper, Repen

PREES Peers, Perse, Prese, Speer, Spree

PRESA Apers, Asper, Pares, Parse, Pears, Prase, Rapes, Reaps, Spaer, Spare, Spear

PRESE Peers, Perse, Prees, Speer, Spree

PRESS Spers

PREST Perts, Strep

PREXY Pyrex

PREYS Pryse, Pyres, Rypes, Spyre, Ypres

PRIAL April, Pilar

***PRIAM** Prima

PRIDE Pried, Redip, Riped

PRIED Pride, Redip, Riped

PRIEP Piper

PRIER Riper

PRIES Epris, Peris, Piers, Prise, Ripes, Speir, Spier, Spire

PRIGS Grips, Sprig

PRIMA Priam

PRIME Perim

PRIMS Prism

PRISE Epris, Peris, Piers, Pries, Ripes, Speir, Spier, Spire

PRISM Prims

PROAS Paros, Psora, Sapor, Sopra, Spora

PROBE Rebop

PRODS Dorps, Drops, Sprod

PROEM Moper, Prome

PROIN Orpin

PROKE Koper, Poker

PROLE Poler

***PROME** Mopes, Proem

PRONE Peron

PRORE Porer, Repro, Roper

PROSE Pores, Poser, Ropes, Soper, Spore

PROUD Pudor

PRUDE Drupe, Duper, Dupre, Perdu, Pured

PRYER Perry, Ryper

PRYSE Preys, Pyres, Rypes, Spyre, Ypres

PSALM Lamps, Palms, Plasm
PSEUD Dupes, Spued
PSOAS Apsos, Soaps
PSORA Paros, Proas, Sapor,
Sopra, Spora
PSYOP Popsy, Soppy
PTERE Peter, Petre, Repet
PUDIC Cupid
PUDOR Proud
PUERS Pures, Purse, Sprue, Super
*PULAS Pauls, Spaul
PULED Duple, Upled
PULES Pulse, Spule
PULSE Pules, Spule
PULUS Lupus
PUNKS Spunk
PUNTO Put-on, Ton-up, Unpot,
Untop
PUPAL Luppa
PUPIL Pipul
PURED Drupe, Duper, Dupre,
Perdu, Prude
PUREE Epure, Rupee
PURER Purre
PURES Puers, Purse, Sprue, Super
PURIN Unrip
PURLS Slurp
PURRE Purer
PURSE Puers, Pures, Sprue, Super
PURSY Pyrus, Syrup
PUT-IN Input
PUT-ON Punto, Ton-up, Unpot,
Untop
PUTTI Titup
PYATS Pasty, Patsy
*PYDNA Pandy
*PYLOS Ploys, Slopy
PYRAL Parly
PYRES Preys, Pryse, Rypes, Spyre
PYREX Prexy
*PYRUS Pursy, Syrup

QUABS Squab
QUADS Squad

QUATS Squat
QUIBS Squib
QUIDS Squid
QUIET Quite
QUIST Quits, Squit
QUITE Quiet
QUITS Quist, Squit
QUOTE Toque

RABIC Baric, Carib
RABID Baird, Braid
RABOT Abort, Boart, Tabor
RACED Acred, Arced, Cadre,
Cared, Cedar, Dacre
RACER Carer, Crare
RACES Acers, Acres, Cares,
Carse, Sacre, Scare, Scrae, Serac
RACHE Caher, Chare, Reach
RACON Acorn
RADGE Edgar, Gerda, Grade,
Raged
RADII Dairi
RADIO Aroid
RADON Adorn, Andro, Donar,
Nardo
RAGAS Sagar
RAGED Edgar, Gerda, Grade,
Radge
RAGEE Aeger, Agree, Eager,
Eagre
RAGER Regar
RAGES Gears, Sager, Sarge, Segar
RAGGY Aggry
RAIDS Sidra
RAINS Naris, Ranis
RAIRD Ard-ri
RAISE Aesir, Aries, Arise, Resai,
Riesa, Serai, Seria
RAITS Airts, Astir, Sitar, Sitra,
Stair, Stria, Tarsi, Trias
RAKED Arked, Daker, Drake
RAKES Asker, Eskar, Kesar,
Reaks, Saker, Skear

RALES Arles, Earls, Lares, Laser,
  Lears, Reals, Seral
RAMAL Alarm, Malar
RAMED Armed, Derma, Dream,
  Madre
RAMEE Ameer, Reame
RAMIE Aimer, Maire, Marie,
  Rimae
RAMIS Simar
*RAMLE Lamer, Marle, Realm
RAMON Manor, Morna, Norma,
  Roman
RAMUS Arums, Rusma, Sarum
RANCE Caner, Carne, Crane,
  Crena, Nacre
RANEE Arnee
RANGE Anger, Areng, Regan,
  Renga
RANGY Angry
RANIS Naris, Rains
RANKE Anker, Karen, Naker,
  Nerka
RANKS Knars, Krans, Narks,
  Skran, Snark
RANTS Starn, Tarns
RANTY Tyran
RAPED Drape, Padre, Pared,
  Repad
RAPER Parer
RAPES Apers, Asper, Pares,
  Parse, Pears, Prase, Presa,
  Reaps, Spaer, Spare, Spear
RAPHE Hepar, Phare
RAPID Pardi
RASED Ardes, Dares, Dears,
  Reads
RASES Arses, Asser, Rasse, Sarse,
  Sears
RASPY Prays, Spray
RASSE Arses, Asser, Rases, Sarse,
  Sears
*RASTA Ratas, Tasar
RATAL Altar, Artal, Talar
RATAN Antra, Antar

RATAS Rasta, Tasar
RATCH Chart
RATED Adret, Dater, Tared,
  Trade, Tread
RATEL Alert, Alter, Artel, Later,
  Taler, Telar
RATER Arret, Retar, Tarre, Terra
RATES Arets, Aster, Astre, Earst,
  Reast, Resat, Stare, Strae, Tares,
  Tarse, Tears, Teras
RATHE Earth, Harte, Hater,
  Heart, Herat, Thera, Thrae
RATHS Harst, Harts, Tahrs,
  Thars, Trash
RATIO Ariot
RATTY Tarty
RAVED Drave, Revda, Varde
RAVEL Laver, Reval, Velar
RAVES Avers, Saver, Vares
RAVIN Invar
RAYED Deary, Deray, Ready,
  Yeard
RAYLE Early, Layer, Leary, Relay
*RAYNE Renay, Yearn
RAZED Zerda
REACH Caher, Chare, Rache
REACT Caret, Carte, Cater, Crate,
  Recta, Trace
READD Adder, Aredd, Dared,
  Dread
*READE Arede, Areed, Deare,
  Eared, Reeda
READS Ardes, Dares, Dears,
  Rased
READY Deary, Deray, Rayed,
  Yeard
REAKS Asker, Eskar, Kesar,
  Rakes, Saker, Skear
REALM Lamer, Marle, Ramle
REALS Arles, Earls, Lares, Laser,
  Lears, Rales, Seral
REAME Ameer, Ramee
REAMS Mares, Maser, Mears,
  Smear

REAPS Apers, Asper, Pares, Parse, Pears, Prase, Presa, Rapes, Spaer, Spare, Spear
RE-ARM Armer
REARS Sarre, Serra
REAST Arets, Aster, Astre, Earst, Rates, Resat, Stare, Strae, Tares, Tarse, Tears, Teras
REATE Arete, Eater, Taree
REBID Bider, Bride, Debir, Diber
REBOP Probe
REBUS Burse, Suber
REBUT Buret, Brute, Tuber
RECAP Caper, Crape, Pacer, Perca
RECON Creon, Crone, Oncer
RECTA Caret, Carte, Cater, Crate, React, Trace
RECTI Trice
RECUR Curer, Curre
RECUT Cruet, Cuter, Eruct, Truce
REDAN Arden, Dearn, Derna
REDDY Ydred
REDES Deres, Drees, Reeds, Seder
REDIA Aider, Aired, Irade
REDID Dried
REDIP Pride, Pried, Riped
REDRY Derry, Dryer, Ryder
REDYE Reedy
REECH Cheer
*__REEDA__ Arede, Areed, Deare, Eared, Reade
REEDS Deres, Drees, Redes, Seder
REEDY Redye
REEKS Esker, Reesk, Skeer
REELS Leers, Leres, Sleer
REESK Esker, Reeks, Skeer
REEST Ester, Reset, Retes, Steer, Stere, Teers, Teres, Terse, Trees
REFED Defer, Freed
REFEL Fleer
REFER Freer, Frere
REFFO Offer

REFIT Freit
REFIX Fixer
REFRY Ferry, Fryer
REGAL Alger, Elgar, Glare, Lager, Large, Relga
REGAN Anger, Areng, Range, Renga
REGAR Rager
REGEL Leger, Regle
REGET Egret, Greet
REGLE Leger, Regel
REGMA Gamer, Marge
REGUR Urger
REHID Hider, Hired
*__REICH__ Rheic
REIFY Fiery
REIGN Grein, Niger, Renig, Ringe
*__REIMS__ Emirs, Meris, Mires, Miser, Riems, Rimes
REINK Inker
REINS Resin, Rinse, Risen, Serin, Siren
REIRD Direr, Drier, Rider
REIST Resit, Rites, Siret, Stire, Tiers, Tires, Tries
REIVE Revie, Rieve
RELAX Laxer
RELAY Early, Layer, Leary, Rayle
*__RELGA__ Alger, Elgar, Glare, Lager, Large, Regal
RELIC Creil
RELIT Liter, Litre, Tiler
REMAN Namer
REMIT Merit, Miter, Mitre, Timer
REMIX Mixer
REMOW Mower, Rowme
*__REMUS__ Mures, Muser, Serum, Sumer
RENAL Larne, Learn, Lerna
RENAY Yearn, Rayne
RENES Ernes, Sneer
RENEW Newer
RENGA Anger, Areng, Range, Regan

RENIG Grein, Niger, Reign, Ringe
RENIN Inner
RENTE Enter, Etern, Terne, Treen
RENTS Ernst, Stern, Terns
REOIL Loire, Oiler, Oriel
REPAD Drape, Padre, Pared,
  Raped
REPAY Apery, Payer, Peary
REPEL Leper
REPEN Neper, Preen
REPET Peter, Petre, Ptere
REPIN Piner, Ripen
REPLA Lepra, Paler, Parle, Pearl
REPLY Plyer
REPOT Porte, Retop, Tepor,
  Toper, Trope
REPRO Porer, Prore, Roper
RESAI Aesir, Aries, Arise, Raise,
  Riesa, Serai, Seria
RESAT Arets, Aster, Astre, Earst,
  Rates, Reast, Stare, Strae, Tares,
  Tarse, Tears, Teras
RESAW Sawer, Sware, Swear,
  Wares, Wears
RESAY Eyras, Sayer, Years
RESET Ester, Reest, Retes, Steer,
  Stere, Teers, Teres, Terse, Trees
RESEW Ewers, Sewer, Sweer,
  Weser
RESHT Herts, Tehrs
RESIN Reins, Rinse, Risen, Serin,
  Siren
RESIT Reist, Rites, Siret, Stire,
  Tiers, Tires, Tries
RESOW Owers, Owser, Serow,
  Sower, Swore, Worse
RESTS Tress
RESTY Steyr, Styre, Treys, Tyres
RETAN Antre
RETAR Arret, Rater, Tarre, Terra
RETAX Extra, Taxer
RETCH Chert
RETEM Meter, Metre

RETES Ester, Reest, Reset, Steer,
  Stere, Teers, Teres, Terse, Trees
RETEX Exert
RETIN Inert, Inter, Niter, Nitre,
  Terni, Trine
RETOP Porte, Repot, Tepor,
  Toper, Trope
RETRY Terry, Tryer
*****REUSS** Ruses, Users
*****REVAL** Laver, Ravel, Velar
*****REVDA** Drave, Raved, Varde
REVEL Elver, Lever
REVET Evert
REVIE Reive, Rieve
REWAX Waxer
REWET Tweer, 'Twere
REWON Owner, Rowen
RHEAS Hares, Hears, Share,
  Shear
RHEIC Reich
*****RHEIN** Henri, Rhine
RHINE Henri, Rhein
RHODA Hoard
*****RHONA** Norah, Rohan
*****RHONE** Heron, Honer, Horne
RHYNE Henry
RIANT Intra, Nitra, Tarin, Train,
  Trani
RIATA Atria, Taira, Tiara
*****RIBES** Biers, Birse, Bries
RICED Cider, Cried, Dicer
RICER Crier, Erics, Icers
RICHT Chirt, Crith
RIDER Direr, Drier, Reird
RIDES Dries, Sider, Sired
RIDGE Dirge, Gride
RIELS Leirs, Liers, Riles, Risel,
  Siler, Slier
RIEMS Emirs, Meris, Mires,
  Miser, Reims, Rimes
*****RIESA** Aesir, Aries, Arise, Raise,
  Resai, Serai, Seria
RIEVE Reive, Revie
RIFLE Filer, Flier, Lifer

RIFTS First, Frist, Frits
RIGEL Liger
RIGHT Girth, Grith
RILED Idler
RILES Leirs, Liers, Riels, Risel,
Siler, Slier
*****RILKE** Liker
RIMAE Aimer, Marie, Maire,
Ramie
RIMED Dimer, Mired
RIMES Emirs, Meris, Mires,
Miser, Reims, Riems
RINED Diner, Indre
RINGE Grein, Niger, Reign, Renig
RINGO Giron, Groin
RINSE Reins, Resin, Risen, Serin,
Siren
RIOTS Roist, Rosit, Tiros, Torsi,
Trios
RIPED Pride, Pried, Redip
RIPEN Piner, Repin
RIPER Prier
RIPES Epris, Peris, Piers, Pries,
Prise, Speir, Spier, Spire
RISEL Leirs, Liers, Riels, Riles,
Siler, Slier
RISEN Reins, Resin, Rinse, Serin,
Siren
RISHI Irish, Sirih
RISSA Arsis, Saris
RITES Reist, Resit, Siret, Stire,
Tiers, Tires, Tries
RITHE Ither
RIVAL Viral
RIVED Diver, Drive, Verdi
RIVEL Ervil, Liver, Livre, Viler
RIVEN Viner
RIVES Siver
RIVET Tiver
RIYAL Lairy
ROACH Achor, Orach
ROADS Doras, Dorsa, Rodas,
Sorda
ROAMS Maros, Moras, Osram

ROANS Arson, Sonar
ROAST Astor, Rotas, Sarto, Taros,
Toras, Troas
ROATE Erato, Orate
ROBED Borde, Bored, Brode,
Orbed
ROBES Boers, Bores, Brose, Sober
ROBIN Inorb
ROBLE Blore, Borel
ROCHE Chore, Ocher, Ochre
ROCKY Corky
ROCTA Actor, Crato, Croat, Taroc
*****RODAS** Doras, Dorsa, Roads,
Sorda
RODED Odder
*****RODEN** Drone, Endor, Ronde
RODES Doers, Dorse, Doser,
Rosed
RODGE Gored
*****RODIN** Nidor
ROGER Gorer
*****ROGET** Ergot
ROGUE Orgue, Rouge
ROHAN Norah, Rhona
ROILS Loris
ROINS Inros, Irons, Ornis, Rosin
ROIST Riots, Rosit, Tiros, Torsi,
Trios
ROLES Erols, Leros, Lores, Loser,
Orles, Osler, Soler, Sorel
ROMAL Molar, Moral
ROMAN Manor, Morna, Norma,
Ramon
*****ROMEO** Moore
*****ROMIC** Micro
RONDE Drone, Endor, Roden
RONDO Donor, Doorn
RONES Norse, Noser, Oners,
Ronse, Senor, Seron, Snore
*****RONSE** Norse, Noser, Oners,
Rones, Senor, Seron, Snore
RONTE Noter, Tenor, Toner,
Trone
RONTS Snort, Trons

ROODS Doors, Ordos, Sordo
ROOKS Koros
ROOMS Moors, Moros, Ormos, Smoor
ROOMY Moory
ROOST Roots, Stoor, Torso
ROOTS Roost, Stoor, Torso
ROPED Doper, Pedro, Pored
ROPER Porer, Prore, Repro
ROPES Pores, Poser, Prose, Soper, Spore
ROSED Doers, Dorse, Doser, Rodes
ROSET Estro, Rotes, Store, Tores, Torse
*****ROSIE** Osier, Siero
ROSIN Inros, Irons, Ornis, Roins
ROSIT Riots, Roist, Tiros, Torsi, Trios
ROTAS Astor, Roast, Sarto, Taros, Toras, Troas
ROTCH Torch
ROTES Estro, Roset, Store, Tores, Torse
ROUES Euros, Rouse
ROUGE Orgue, Rogue
ROUSE Euros, Roues
ROUST Routs, Stour, Sutor, Torus, Tours
ROUTE Outer, Outre, Toure
ROUTS Roust, Stour, Sutor, Torus, Tours
ROVED Dover, Drove, Vedro
ROVES Overs, Serov, Servo, Verso
ROWAN Nowra
ROWDY Dowry, Wordy
ROWED Dower
ROWEL Lower, Owler
ROWEN Owner, Rewon
ROWME Mower, Remow
ROWTE Tower, Twoer, Wrote
ROWTH Throw, Whort, Worth, Wroth

ROYST Ryots, Story, Stroy, Tyros
RUBIN Bruin, Burin
RUBLE Bluer, Brule
RUDAS Duras, Sudra
RUDER Durer
RUING Unrig
RULED Dreul, Lured
RULER Lurer
RUMAL Larum, Mural
*****RUMAN** Namur, Unarm, Urman
RUMBA Burma, Umbra
*****RUMEX** Murex
RUMLY Murly
RUNCH Churn
RUNED Durem, Under, Unred, Urned
RUNES Nurse
RUNIC Incur
RUN-IN Inurn
RUN-UP Uprun
RUPEE Epure, Puree
RUSES Reuss, Users
RUSMA Arums, Ramus, Sarum
RUSTS Truss
RUTIN Turin
*****RYDAL** Lardy, Lyard
*****RYDER** Derry, Dryer, Redry
RYOTS Royst, Story, Stroy, Tyros
RYPER Perry, Pryer
RYPES Preys, Pryse, Pyres, Spyre, Ypres
*****RYTON** Try-on

*****SAADI** Saida
*****SABAH** Abash
*****SABAL** Balas, Balsa, Basal
*****SABER** Bares, Baser, Bears, Braes, Sabre
SABIN Basin
SABLE Ables, Bales, Basel, Basle, Blaes, Bleas, Blase
SABOT Basto, Boats, Boast, Sobat, Tobas
SABRA Arabs, Arbas, Basra

SABRE Bares, Baser, Bears, Braes,
  Saber
SACRA Arcas
SACRE Acers, Acres, Cares,
  Carse, Races, Scare, Scrae, Serac
SADHE Hades, Heads, Shade
*SADIE Aides, Aside, Ideas
SAFER Fares, Farse, Fears
*SAGAR Ragas
SAGER Gears, Rages, Sarge,
  Segar
SAGES Gases
SAGUM Gaums, Magus
*SAIDA Saadi
SAILS Lissa, Silas, Sisal
SAINS Sasin
SAINT Antis, Satin, Stain, Tains,
  Tanis
SAITH Haits, Taish, Thais
*SAKAI Sakia
SAKER Asker, Eskar, Kesar,
  Rakes
SAKIA Sakai
SALAD Ladas, Salda
SALDA Ladas, Salad
*SALEM Almes, Amsel, Lames,
  Leams, Males, Meals, Melas,
  Mesal, Samel, Selma
SALEP Elaps, Lapse, Leaps, Pales,
  Peals, Pleas, Sepal, Slape, Spale,
  Speal
SALES Salse, Seals, Slaes
SALET Astel, Least, Leats, Slate,
  Stael, Stale, Steal, Stela, Taels,
  Tales, Teals, Tesla
SALIC Aclis, Laics, Scail
SALIN Anils, Nails, Slain, Snail
SALIX Axils
SALMI Islam, Limas, Mails, Malis,
  Milas, Simla
SALMO Loams, Lomas, Sloam
SALON Loans, Sloan, Solan,
  Solna
SALOP Opals, Palos

SALPA Palas
SALSE Sales, Seals, Slaes
*SALTA Atlas
*SALTO Altos, Sloat, Stola, Talos,
  Tolas
SALTY Slaty
SALVE Elvas, Laves, Selva, Slave,
  Vales, Valse, Veals
SALVI Alvis, Silva, Vails, Valis,
  Vials
SALVO Ovals, Volas
*SAMAR Maras
*SAMBO Ambos, Bomas, Moabs
SAMEL Almes, Amsel, Lames,
  Leams, Males, Meals, Melas,
  Mesal, Salem, Selma
SAMEN Amens, Manes, Manse,
  Means, Mensa, Names
SAMEY Seamy, Ysame
*SAMOS Samso
SAMPI Apism
SAMPS Spasm
*SAMSO Samos
SANDY Sdayn
SANER Earns, Nares, Nears,
  Snare
*SANTA Satan, Tsana
SAPOR Poras, Proas, Psora,
  Sopra, Spora
SAPPY Paspy
SAREE Erase
SARGE Gears, Rages, Sager,
  Segar
SARGO Argos
SARIS Arsis, Rissa
SAROH Hoars
SAROS Soars
*SARRE Rears, Serra
SARSE Arses, Asser, Rases,
  Rasse, Sears
*SARTO Astor, Roast, Rotas,
  Taros, Toras, Troas
*SARUM Arums, Ramus, Rusma
SARUS Suras

SASIN Sains
SASSE Asses, Sessa
*****SATAN** Santa, Tsana
SATED Dates, Stade, Stead,
Teads, Tsade
SATEM Mates, Meats, Mesta,
Steam, Tames, Teams
SATES Easts, Asset, Seats, Tasse,
Tessa
SATIN Antis, Saint, Stain, Tains,
Tanis
SATYR Artsy, Stray, Trays
SAUCE Cause
SAULT Talus, Tulsa
SAUNT Aunts
SAURY Surya
SAVED Devas, Vades, Vedas
SAVER Avers, Raves, Vares
SAVIN Sivan, Vains, Vinas
SAWED Wades
SAWER Resaw, Sware, Swear,
Wares, Wears
SAWNY Yawns
SAXON Axons, Naxos
SAYER Eyras, Resay, Years
SAYID Daisy
SAYNE Yeans
SAYST Stays
S-BAND Bands
S-BEND Bends
SCAIL Aclis, Laics, Salic
SCALA Casal
SCALE Alces, Claes, Laces
SCALL Calls
SCALP Calps, Claps, Clasp
SCALY Clays
SCAMP Camps
SCANT Canst, Cants
SCAPE Capes, Caspe, Paces,
Space
SCAPI Aspic, Capis, Picas, Spica
SCARD Cards
SCARE Acers, Acres, Cares,
Carse, Races, Sacre, Scrae, Serac

SCARP Carps, Craps, Scrap
SCARS Crass
SCART Carts, Scrat
SCARY Cyars, Scray
SCATE Caste, Cates, Sceat, Taces
SCATH Chats
SCAUR Arcus, Carus
SCEAT Caste, Cates, Scate, Taces
SCENA Canes
SCENE Cense
SCENT Cents
SCHWA Chaws
SCION Coins, Icons, Sonic
SCOAT Ascot, Coast, Coats,
Costa, Tosca
SCOFF Coffs
SCOLD Clods, Colds
SCONE Cones, Cosen, Cosne,
Sonce
SCOON Coons
SCOOP Coops, Copos
SCOOT Coost, Coots
SCOPE Copes, Copse, Pecos
SCORE Ceros, Cores, Corse
SCORN Corns
SCOTE Coste, Cotes, Escot, Estoc
SCOUP Coups
SCOUR Orcus
SCOVE Coves, Voces
SCOWL Clows, Cowls
SCRAE Acers, Acres, Cares,
Carse, Races, Sacre, Scare, Serac
SCRAB Crabs
SCRAG Crags
SCRAM Crams
SCRAN Crans
SCRAP Carps, Craps, Scarp
SCRAT Carts, Scart
SCRAW Craws
SCRAY Cyars, Scary
SCREE Ceres, Crees
SCREW Crews
SCRIP Crisp
SCROD Cords

SCROW Crows
SCRUB Curbs
SCUFF Cuffs
SCULL Culls
SDAYN Sandy
SDEIN Denis, Dines, Enids, Nides, Snide
SEAHS Ashes, He-ass, Sesha, Sheas
SEALS Sales, Salse, Slaes
SEAME Mease
SEAMS Masse, Mesas
SEAMY Samey, Ysame
SEARS Arses, Asser, Rases, Rasse, Sarse
SEASE Eases
SEATS Asset, Easts, Sates, Tasse, Tessa
SEAVE Eaves
*****SEBAT** Abets, Baste, Bates, Beast, Beats, Besat, Esbat, Tabes
SEBUS Embus
SECCO Cosec
SEDAN Andes, Danes, Deans, Desna, Snead
*****SEDER** Deres, Drees, Redes, Reeds
SEDES Seeds
SEDGE Edges
SEDUM Mused
SEEDS Sedes
SEEPY Peyse
SEGAR Gears, Rages, Sager, Sarge
SEGNI Singe
SEGNO Sogne
SEGOL Loges, Ogles
SEGOS Gesso
*****SEGRE** Egers, Grees, Grese, Serge
SEISM Mises, Semis
SEKOS Skeos, Sokes
SELAH Hales, Halse, Heals, Leash, Shale, Sheal
SELED Deles, Edsel, Leeds

SELIN Elsin, Lenis, Liens, Lines, Nelis, Niles
*****SELMA** Almes, Amsel, Lames, Leams, Males, Meals, Melas, Mesal, Salem, Samel
SELVA Elvas, Laves, Salve, Slave, Vales, Valse, Veals
SEMEN Menes, Mense, Mesne, Neems
SEMIS Mises, Seism
SENAL Lanes, Leans, Neals, Slane
*****SENGA** Agnes, Geans, Genas
SENNA Annes
SENOR Norse, Noser, Oners, Rones, Ronse, Seron, Snore
SENSE Esnes, Essen
*****SENTA** Antes, Etnas, Nates, Nesta, Stane, Stean, Teans
SENTI Inset, Neist, Nesti, Set-in, Sient, Stein, Tines
SENZA Nazes
*****SEOUL** Eusol, Louse, Ousel
SEPAD Adeps, Spade, Spaed
SEPAL Elaps, Lapse, Leaps, Pales, Peals, Pleas, Salep, Slape, Spale, Speal
SEPIC Epics, Spice
SEPOY Poesy, Poyse
SEPTA Apest, Paste, Pates, Peats, Spate, Speat, Tapes
SERAC Acers, Acres, Cares, Carse, Races, Sacre, Scare, Screa
SERAI Aesir, Aries, Arise, Raise, Resai, Riesa, Seria
SERAL Arles, Earls, Lares, Laser, Lears, Rales, Reals
SERGE Egers, Grees, Grese, Segre
*****SERGO** Ergos, Goers, Gores, Gorse, Ogres, Soger
*****SERIA** Aesir, Aries, Arise, Raise, Resai, Riesa, Serai
SERIC Cries, Crise, Erics, Icers
SERIF Fires, Fries

SERIN Reins, Resin, Rinse, Risen, Siren
SERON Norse, Noser, Oners, Rones, Ronse, Senor, Snore
*****SEROV** Overs, Roves, Servo, Verso
SEROW Owers, Owser, Resow, Sower, Swore, Worse
SERRA Rears, Sarre
SERUM Mures, Muser, Remus, Sumer
SERVE Sever, Veers, Verse
SERVO Overs, Roves, Serov, Verso
SESHA Ashes, He-ass, Seahs, Sheas
SESSA Asses, Sasse
SETAE Tease
SET-IN Inset, Neist, Nesti, Senti, Sient, Stein, Tines
SETON Eston, Etons, Notes, Onset, Steno, Stone, Tenos, Tones
SET-TO Totes
SET-UP Stupe, Upset
*****SEVAN** Avens, Evans, Naves, Vanes
SEVEN Evens, Neves
SEVER Serve, Veers, Verse
SEVIN Nevis, Veins, Venis, Vines, Visne
SEWAN Wanes, Weans
SEWED Swede, Sweed, Weeds
SEWEL Lewes, Sweel, Weels, Wesel
SEWEN Enews, Ensew, Weens
SEWER Ewers, Resew, Sweer, Weser
SEWIN Sinew, Swine, Wines
SEXES Essex
'SFOOT Foots
SHACK Hacks
SHADE Hades, Heads, Sadhe
SHADY Dashy, Hyads

SHAFTS Hafts
SHAHI Shiah
SHAKE Hakes
SHALE Hales, Halse, Heals, Leash, Selah, Sheal
SHALL Halls
SHALM Halms
SHALT Halts, Laths, Stahl
SHALY Hylas
SHAME Ahems, Hames, Heams, Shema
SHAMS Smash
SHAND Hands
*****SHANE** Ashen, Hanse
SHANK Ankhs, Hanks, Khans
*****SHANS** Snash
SHAN'T Hants, Snath
SHAPE Ephas, Heaps, Pesah, Phase
SHAPS Hasps
SHARD Hards
SHARE Hares, Hears, Rheas, Shear
*****SHARI** Arish, Hairs
SHARK Harks
SHARN Harns
SHARP Harps
SHAVE Haves, Sheva
SHAWM Hawms, Whams
SHAWS Swash
SHEAL Hales, Halse, Heals, Leash, Selah, Shale
SHEAR Hares, Hears, Rheas, Share
SHEAS Ashes, He-ass, Seahs, Sesha
SHEEL Heels, Heles
SHEEN Esneh
SHEEP Phese
SHEER Esher, Heres, Herse, Shere
SHEET Thees, These
SHEIK Hikes
SHELF Flesh

SHELL Hells, She'll
SHE'LL Hells, Shell
*****SHEMA** Ahems, Hames, Heams, Shame
SHEND Hends
SHEOL Holes, Shole
SHERD Herds, Shred
SHERE Esher, Heres, Herse, Sheer
SHEVA Haves, Shave
SHIAH Shahi
SHIDE Hides, Shied
SHIED Hides, Shide
SHIER Heirs, Hires, Shire
SHIKO Hoiks
SHILL Hills
SHINE Hsien
SHIRE Heirs, Hires, Shier
SHINE Heist, Sithe, Thies
SHITE Heist, Sithe, Thies
SHIVE Hives
SHOAL Halos, Shola, Solah
SHOAT Athos, Hoast, Hosta, Oaths
SHOCK Hocks
SHOED Doseh, Hosed
SHOER Heros, Hoers, Horse, Shore
SHOLA Halos, Shoal, Solah
SHOLE Holes, Sheol
SHONE Hones, Hosen
SHOOK Hooks
SHOOT Hoots, Sooth, Sotho
SHOPS Sophs, Sposh
SHORE Heros, Hoers, Horse, Shoer
SHORN Horns
SHORT Horst
SHOTE Ethos, Those
SHOTS Hosts, Stosh
SHOUT South, Thous
SHOVE Hoves
SHRAB Brash
SHRAM Harms, Marsh

SHRED Herds, Sherd
SHREW Wersh
SHRUB Brush, Buhrs, Burhs, Bursh
SHUCK Hucks
SHUNS Snush
SHUNT Hunts
SHURE Huers, Usher
*****SIBYL** Sybil
*****SICAN** Cains, Canis, Incas
*****SICEL** Ceils, Ciels, Leics, Slice
SIDER Dries, Rides, Sired
SIDLE Deils, Idles, Sield, Slide
*****SIDRA** Raids
SIELD Deils, Idles, Sidle, Slide
*****SIENA** Aisne, Anise
SIENT Inset, Nesti, Neist, Senti, Set-in, Stein, Tines
*****SIERO** Osier, Rosie
SIGHT Thigs
*****SIKEL** Likes
SIKER Keirs, Kiers, Skier
SIKES Skies
*****SILAS** Lissa, Sails, Sisal
SILER Leirs, Liers, Riels, Riles, Risel, Siler
SILES Isles, Lisse
SILEX Lexis
SILLY Slily, Yills
SILO'D Idols, Isold, Lidos, Sloid, Soldi, Solid
SILVA Alvis, Salvi, Vails, Valis, Vials
SIMAR Ramis
*****SIMLA** Islam, Limas, Mails, Malis, Milas, Salmi
*****SIMON** Minos
SINCE Cenis
SINES Nisse
SINEW Sewin, Swine, Wines
SINGE Segni
SINUS Nisus
SIPED Spied
SIPES Spies

SIRED Dries, Rides, Sider
SIREN Reins, Resin, Rinse, Risen, Serin
*SIRET Reist, Resit, Rites, Tiers, Tires, Tries
SIRIH Irish, Rishi
SISAL Lissa, Sails, Silas
SITAR Airts, Astir, Raits, Sitra, Stair, Stria, Tarsi, Trias
SITED Deist, Diets, Dites, Edits, Stied, Tides
SITHE Heist, Shite, Thies
*SITRA Airts, Astir, Raits, Sitar, Stair, Stria, Tarsi, Trias
SITTA Taits
SITUS Suist, Suits
*SIVAN Savin, Vains, Vinas
*SIVAS Visas
SIVER Rives
SIXTE Exist, Exits
SIXTY Xysti
SKAIL Kails, Kalis, Laiks, Laski
SKAIN Kains, Kinas, Kisan, Nasik
*SKANE Kanes, Skean, Snake, Sneak
SKART Karst, Karts, Stark, Strak
SKATE Kates, Keats, Skeat, Stake, Steak, Takes, Teaks
SKEAN Kanes, Skane, Snake, Sneak
SKEAR Asker, Eskar, Kesar, Rakes, Reaks, Saker
*SKEAT Kates, Keats, Skate, Stake, Steak, Takes, Teaks
SKEEL Keels, Leeks, Sleek
SKEER Esker, Reeks, Reesk
SKEET Skete, Steek
SKEIN Neski, Skien
SKELP Kelps, Spelk
SKENE Keens, Knees, Sneek
SKEOS Sekos, Sokes
SKETE Skeet, Steek
SKIED Dikes
SKIEN Neski, Skein

SKIER Keirs, Kiers, Siker
SKIES Sikes
SKILL Kills
SKINK Kinks
SKINT Knits, Stink, Tinks
SKIRT Stirk
SKITE Kites, Tikes
SKLIM Milks
SKOAL Kolas
SKOFF Koffs
SKRAN Knars, Krans, Narks, Ranks, Snark
SKYER Skyre, Syker, Yerks
SKYRE Skyer, Syker, Yerks
SKYTE Kytes, Tykes
SLACK Calks, Lacks
SLADE Dales, Deals, Lades, Leads
SLAES Sales, Salse, Seals
SLAGS Glass
SLAID Aldis, Dalis, Dials
SLAIE Aisle, Elias
SLAIN Anils, Nails, Salin, Snail
SLAKE Kales, Lakes, Leaks
SLANE Lanes, Leans, Neals, Senal
SLANG Glans, Langs
SLAPE Elaps, Lapse, Leaps, Pales, Peals, Pleas, Salep, Sepal, Spale, Speal
SLATE Astel, Least, Leats, Salet, Stael, Stale, Steal, Stela, Taels, Tales, Teals, Tesla
SLATY Salty
SLAVE Elvas, Laves, Salve, Selva, Vales, Valse, Veals
SLEEK Keels, Leeks, Skeel
SLEEP Peels, Speel
SLEER Leers, Leres, Reels
SLEET Leets, Steel, Stele, Teels
SLEPT Pelts, Spelt
SLEYS Lyses, Yssel
SLICE Ceils, Ciels, Leics, Sicel
SLICK Licks
SLIDE Deils, Idles, Sield, Sidle

SLIER Leirs, Liers, Riels, Riles, Risel, Siler
'SLIFE Felis, Files, Flies
SLILY Silly, Yills
SLIME Limes, Miles, Misle, Smile
SLIMY Limsy, Misly
SLING Lings
SLINK Kilns, Links
SLIPE Lepis, Piles, Plies, Spiel, Spile
SLIPS Lisps
SLIPT Spilt, Split, Stilp
SLIVE Elvis, Evils, Levis, Lives, Veils, Vleis
SLOAM Loams, Lomas, Salmo
SLOAN Loans, Salon, Solan, Solna
SLOAT Altos, Salto, Stola, Talos, Tolas
SLOES Loess, Loses, Soles
SLOGS Gloss
SLOID Idols, Isold, Lidos, Silo'd, Soldi, Solid
SLOOM Looms, Mools
SLOOP Loops, Pools, Spool
SLOOT Loots, Lotos, Stool, Tools
SLOPE Elops, Lopes, Olpes, Poles, Spole
SLOPY Ploys, Pylos
SLOTH Holst, Holts
SLOVE Loves, Solve, Voles
SLOYD Odyls
SLUED Duels, Dules, Dulse, Leuds
SLUMP Lumps, Plums
SLUNG Lungs
SLURB Blurs, Burls
SLURP Purls
SLYER Lyres
SLYPE Yelps
SMACK Macks
SMAIK Kaims, Kamis, Maiks
SMALL Malls
SMALT Malts

SMART Marts, Trams
SMASH Shams
SMEAR Mares, Maser, Mears, Reams
SMELL Mells
SMELT Melts
SMILE Limes, Miles, Misle, Slime
SMITE Emits, Items, Meist, Metis, Mites, Stime, Times
SMITT Mitts
SMOCK Mocks
SMOKE Mokes
SMOOR Moors, Moros, Ormos, Rooms
SMOOT Moots, Stoom, Tooms
SMORE Moers, Mores, Morse, Omers
SMOTE Mesto, Motes, Tomes
SMOUT Moust
SMUCK Mucks
SNAFU Fauns, Fusan
SNAIL Anils, Nails, Salin, Slain
SNAKE Kanes, Skane, Skean, Sneak
SNAKY Yanks
SNAPE Aspen, Napes, Neaps, Panes, Peans, Sneap, Spane, Spean
SNARE Earns, Nares, Nears, Saner
SNARK Knars, Krans, Narks, Ranks, Skran
SNARY Yarns
SNASH Shans
SNATH Hants, Shan't
SNEAD Andes, Danes, Deans, Desna, Sedan
SNEAK Kanes, Skane, Skean, Snake
SNEAP Aspen, Napes, Neaps, Panes, Peans, Snape, Spane, Spean
SNECK Necks
*****SNEEK** Keens, Knees, Skene

SNEER Ernes, Renes
SNICK Nicks
SNIDE Denis, Dines, Enids, Nides, Sdein
SNIFF Niffs
SNIPE Penis, Pines, Spine
SNIPY Spiny
SNOEK Kenos, Nokes, Snoke, Soken
SNOEP Opens, Peons, Pones, Posen
SNOKE Kenos, Nokes, Snoek, Soken
SNOOK Nooks
SNOOL Loons, Solon
SNOOP Noops, Poons, Spoon
SNORE Norse, Noser, Oners, Rones, Ronse, Senor, Seron
SNORT Ronts, Trons
SNOUT Notus, Stoun, Tonus
SNOWK Knows
SNUSH Shuns
SOAPS Apsos, Psoas
SOARE Arose
SOARS Saros
*__SOBAT__ Basto, Boast, Boats, Sabot, Tobas
SOBER Boers, Bores, Brose, Robes
SOBOL Bolos, Lobos, Obols
*__SOCHE__ Chose
SOCLE Close, Coles
SODIC Disco
*__SODOM__ Dooms, Dsomo, Moods
SOFAS Fossa
SOFTA Fatso
SOGER Ergos, Goers, Gores, Gorse, Ogres, Sergo
*__SOGNE__ Segno
SOKEN Kenos, Nokes, Snoek, Snoke
SOKES Sekos, Skeos
*__SOKOL__ Kolos, Looks
SOLAH Halos, Shoal, Shola

SOLAN Loans, Salon, Sloan, Solna
SOLAR Orals, Soral
SOLAS Lasso
SOLDE Delos, Doles, Dosel, Lodes, Soled
SOLDI Idols, Isold, Lidos, Silo'd, Sloid, Solid
SOLDO Dools
SOLED Delos, Doles, Dosel, Lodes, Solde
SOLEN Lenos
SOLER Eorls, Leros, Lores, Loser, Orles, Osler, Roles, Sorel
SOLES Loess, Loses, Sloes
SOL-FA Foals, Loafs
SOLID Idols, Isold, Lidos, Silo'd, Sloid, Soldi
*__SOLLY__ Lysol
*__SOLNA__ Loans, Salon, Sloan, Solan
*__SOLON__ Loons, Snool
*__SOLTI__ Isolt, Toils
SOLUM Mouls
SOLUS Souls
SOLVE Loves, Slove, Voles
SOMME Memos, Momes
SONAR Arson, Roans
SONCE Cones, Cosen, Cosne, Scone
SONDE Nodes, Nosed
SONES Noses, Sonse
SONIC Coins, Icons, Scion
SONNE Nones
SONSE Noses, Sones
SONTY Stony
SOOLE Looes, Loose, Oleos
SOOTH Hoots, Shoot, Sotho
*__SOPER__ Pores, Poser, Prose, Ropes, Spore
SOPHS Shops, Sposh
SOPOR Spoor
*__SOPOT__ Stoop, Topos
SOPPY Popsy, Psyop

SOPRA Paros, Proas, Psora,
Sapor, Spora
SORAL Orals, Solar
SORBO Boors
SORDA Doras, Dorsa, Roads,
Rodas
SORDO Doors, Ordos, Roods
SORDS Dross
SOREE Erose
***SOREL** Eorls, Leros, Lores, Loser,
Orles, Osler, Roles, Soler
SOREX Exors, Oxers
SORUS Sours
***SOTHO** Hoots, Shoot, Sooth
SOTOL Loots, Lotos, Sloot, Stool,
Tools
SOULS Solus
***SOULT** Lotus, Louts
SOUND Nodus, Unsod
SOURS Sorus
SOUSE Ouses
SOUTH Shout, Thous
SOWED Dowse
SOWER Owers, Owser, Resow,
Serow, Swore, Worse
SOWLE Lowse
SOWND Downs
SPACE Capes, Caspe, Paces,
Scape
SPADE Adeps, Sepad, Spaed
SPAED Adeps, Sepad, Spade
SPAER Apers, Asper, Pares,
Parse, Pears, Prase, Presa,
Rapes, Reaps, Spare, Spear
SPAES Apses, Passe
SPAHI Aphis, Apish
SPAIL Lapis, Pails, Spial
***SPAIN** Pains, Pinas, Spina
SPAIT Pitas, Stipa, Tapis
SPAKE Peaks, Speak
SPALE Elaps, Lapse, Leaps, Pales,
Peals, Pleas, Salep, Sepal, Slape,
Speal
SPALL Palls

SPALT Plats, Splat
SPALT Plats, Splat
SPANE Aspen, Napes, Neaps,
Panes, Peans, Snape, Sneap,
Spean
SPANG Pangs
SPANK Knaps
SPARE Apers, Asper, Pares,
Parse, Pears, Prase, Presa,
Rapes, Reaps, Spaer, Spear
SPARK Parks
SPART Parts, Prats, Sprat, Strap,
Traps
SPASM Samps
SPATE Apest, Paste, Pates, Peats,
Septa, Speat, Tapes
SPAUL Pauls, Pulas
SPAVE Paves, Vespa
SPAWL Pawls
SPAWN Pawns
SPAYD Paysd
SPEAK Peaks, Spake
SPEAL Elaps, Lapse, Leaps, Pales,
Peals, Pleas, Salep, Sepal, Slape,
Spale
SPEAN Aspen, Napes, Neaps,
Panes, Peans, Snape, Sneap,
Spane
SPEAR Apers, Asper, Pares,
Parse, Pears, Prase, Presa,
Rapes, Reaps, Spaer, Spare
SPEAT Apest, Paste, Pates, Peats,
Septa, Spate, Tapes
SPECK Pecks
SPEED Deeps
SPEEL Peels, Sleep
SPEER Peers, Perse, Prees, Prese,
Spree
SPEIR Epris, Peris, Piers, Pries,
Prise, Ripes, Spier, Spire
***SPEKE** Keeps, Peeks, Pekes
SPELK Kelps, Skelp
SPELL Pells
SPELT Pelts, Slept

SPEND Pends
SPENT Pents
SPEOS Pesos, Poses, Posse
SPERM Perms
SPERS Press
SPIAL Lapis, Pails, Spail
SPICA Aspic, Capis, Picas, Scapi
SPICE Epics, Sepic
SPICK Picks
SPIED Siped
SPIEL Lepis, Piles, Plies, Slipe,
  Spile
SPIER Epris, Peris, Piers, Pries,
  Prise, Ripes, Speir, Spire
SPIES Sipes
SPIKE Kepis, Kipes, Pikes, Pisek
SPIKY Pisky
SPILE Lepis, Piles, Plies, Slipe,
  Spiel
SPILL Pills
SPLIT Slipt, Spilt, Stilp
SPINA Pains, Pinas, Spain
SPINE Penis, Pines, Snipe
SPINK Knips, Pinks, Pinsk
SPINY Snipy
SPIRE Epris, Peris, Piers, Pries,
  Prise, Ripes, Speir, Spier
SPIRT Sprit, Stirp, Strip, Trips
SPITE Piets, Piste, Stipe
SPLAT Plats, Spalt
SPLAY Palsy, Plays, Spyal
SPLIT Slipt, Spilt, Stilp
*SPOCK Pocks
SPODE Dopes, Posed
SPOIL Polis
SPOKE Pokes
SPOLE Elops, Lopes, Olpes,
  Poles, Slope
SPOOF Poofs
SPOOL Loops, Pools, Sloop
SPOON Noops, Poons, Snoop
SPOOR Sopor
SPORA Poras, Proas, Psora,
  Sapor, Sopra

SPORE Pores, Poser, Prose,
  Ropes, Soper
SPORT Ports, Strop
SPOSH Shops, Sophs
SPOUT Pouts, Stoup, Toups
SPRAD Pards, Prads
SPRAG Grasp
SPRAT Parts, Prats, Spart, Strap,
  Traps
SPRAY Prays, Raspy
SPREE Peers, Perse, Prees, Prese,
  Speer
SPRIG Grips, Prigs
SPRIT Spirt, Stirp, Strip, Trips
SPROD Dorps, Drops, Prods
SPRUE Puers, Pures, Purse, Super
SPUED Dupes, Pseud
SPULE Pules, Pulse
SPUNK Punks
SPURT Turps
SPUTA Stupa, Tapus
SPYAL Palsy, Plays, Splay
SPYRE Preys, Pryse, Pyres,
  Rypes, Ypres
SQUAB Quabs
SQUAD Quads
SQUAT Quats
SQUIB Quibs
SQUID Quids
SQUIT Quist, Quits
STACK Tacks
STADE Dates, Sated, Stead,
  Teads, Tsade
*STAEL Astel, Least, Leats, Salet,
  Slate, Stale, Steal, Stela, Taels,
  Tales, Teals, Tesla
STAGE Gates, Geats
*STAHL Halts, Laths, Shalt
STAID Adits, Ditas
STAIG Agist, Gaits
STAIN Antis, Saint, Satin, Tains,
  Tanis
STAIR Airts, Astir, Rites, Sitar,
  Sitra, Stria, Tarsi, Trias

STAKE Kates, Keats, Skate, Skeat, Steak, Takes, Teaks
STAL'D Dalts
STALE Astel, Least, Leats, Salet, Slate, Stael, Steal, Stela, Taels, Tales, Teals, Tesla
STALK Talks
STAMP Tamps
STANE Antes, Etnas, Nates, Nesta, Senta, Stean, Teans
STANG Angst, Gants, Gnats, Tangs
STANK Kants, Tanks
STARE Arets, Aster, Astre, Earst, Rates, Reast, Resat, Strae, Tares, Tarse, Tears, Teras
STARK Karst, Karts, Skart, Strak
STARN Rants, Tarns
STARS Trass, Tsars
START Tarts
STATE Taste, Tates, Teats, Testa
STAVE Vesta
STAYS Sayst
STEAD Dates, Sated, Stade, Teads, Tsade
STEAK Kates, Keats, Skate, Skeat, Stake, Takes
STEAL Astel, Least, Leats, Salet, Slate, Stael, Stale, Stela, Taels, Tales, Teals, Tesla
STEAM Mates, Meats, Mesta, Satem, Tames, Teams
STEAN Antes, Etnas, Nates, Nesta, Senta, Stane, Teans
STECH Chest, Techs
STEED Tedes
STEEK Skeet, Skete
STEEL Leets, Sleet, Stele, Teels
STEEM Meets, Metes, Steme, Teems, Temes, Temse
*__STEEN__ Etens, Teens, Tense
STEER Ester, Reest, Reset, Retes, Stere, Teers, Teres, Terse, Trees
STEIL Islet, Istle, Stile, Teils, Tiles

STEIN Inset, Nesti, Neist, Senti, Set-in, Sient, Tines
STELA Astel, Least, Leats, Salet, Slate, Stael, Stale, Steal, Taels, Tales, Teals, Tesla
STELE Leets, Sleet, Steel, Teels
STELL Tells
STEME Meets, Metes, Steem, Teems, Temes, Temse
STEND Dents, Tends
STENO Eston, Etons, Notes, Onset, Seton, Stone, Tenos, Tones
STENT Tents
STERE Ester, Reest, Reset, Retes, Steer, Teers, Teres, Terse, Trees
STERN Ernst, Rents, Terns
*__STEVE__ Evets
*__STEYR__ Resty, Styre, Treys, Tyres
STICH Chits
STICK Ticks
STIED Deist, Diets, Dites, Edits, Sited, Tides
STIFF Tiffs
STILB Blist
STILE Islet, Istle, Steil, Teils, Tiles
STILL Lilts, Tills
STILP Slipt, Spilt, Split
STILT Tilts
STIME Emits, Items, Meist, Metis, Mites, Smite, Times
STIMY Misty
STING Tings
STINK Knits, Skint, Tinks
STINT Tints, 'Tisn't
STIPA Pitas, Spait, Tapis
STIPE Piets, Piste, Spite
STIRE Reist, Resit, Rites, Siret, Tiers, Tires, Tries
STIRP Spirt, Sprit, Strip, Trips
STOAI Iotas, Ostia
STOAS Assot, Oasts, Tasso
STOAT Toast

STOEP Estop, Poets, Potes, Stope, Topes
STOIT Toits
STOLA Altos, Salto, Sloat, Talos, Tolas
STOLE Lotes, Telos, Toles
***STOLP** Plots, Polts
STOMA Atoms, Moats
STONE Eston, Etons, Notes, Onset, Seton, Steno, Tenos, Tones
STONG Tongs
STONK Knots
STONY Sonty
STOOD To-dos
STOOK Kotos, Tokos
STOOL Loots, Lotos, Sloot, Sotol, Tools
STOOM Moots, Smoot, Tooms
STOOP Sopot, Topos
STOOR Roost, Roots, Torso
STOPE Estop, Poets, Potes, Stoep, Topes
STORE Estro, Roset, Rotes, Tores, Torse
STORK Torsk
STORM Morts, Troms
STORY Royst, Ryots, Stroy, Tyros
STOSH Hosts, Shots
STOUN Notus, Snout, Tonus
STOUP Pouts, Spout, Toups
STOUR Roust, Routs, Sutor, Torus, Tours
STOUT Touts
STOVE Votes
STOWN Towns, Wonts
***STRAD** Darts, Drats
STRAE Arets, Aster, Astre, Earst, Rates, Reast, Resat, Stare, Tares, Tarse, Tears, Teras
STRAK Karst, Karts, Skart, Stark
STRAP Parts, Prats, Spart, Sprat, Traps

STRAW Swart, Warst, Warts, Wrast
STRAY Artsy, Satyr, Trays
STREP Perts, Prest
STREW Trews, Werts, Wrest
STRIA Airts, Astir, Raits, Sitar, Sitra, Stair, Tarsi, Trias
STRID Dirts
STRIG Girts, Grist, Grits, Trigs
STRIP Spirt, Sprit, Stirp, Trips
STROB Borts
STROP Ports, Sport
STROW Trows, Worst, Worts
STROY Royst, Ryots, Story, Tyros
STRUB Brust, Burst
STRUM Turms
STRUT Sturt, Trust
STUCK Tucks
STUDY Dusty
STUFA Faust, Tufas
STUFF Tuffs
STUMP Tumps
STUPA Sputa, Tapus
STUPE Set-up, Upset
STURE Trues
STURT Strut, Trust
STYLE Yelts
STYRE Resty, Steyr, Treys, Tyres
SUAGE Usage
SUAVE Uveas
SUBER Burse, Rebus
SUCRE Cruse, Cures, Curse
SUDAK Dauks
***SUDRA** Duras, Rudas
SUENT Tunes, Unset, Usen't
SUGAR Argus, Gaurs
SUING Using
SUINT Inust, Tunis, Units
SUIST Situs, Suits
SUITE Etuis
SUITS Situs, Suist
SUMAC Camus, Caums, Musca
***SUMER** Mures, Muser, Remus, Serum

SUMPH Humps
*SUNAY Unsay
SUPER Puers, Pures, Purse, Sprue
SURAL Larus, Urals
SURAS Sarus
SURAT Sutra
SURGE Urges
SURGY Gyrus
*SURYA Saury
*SUSIE Issue
SUTOR Roust, Routs, Stour,
     Torus, Tours
SUTRA Surat
SWAGE Wages
SWAIN Wains
SWALE Lawes, Sweal, Wales,
     Weals
SWALY Swayl, Yawls
SWAMI Aswim
SWANG Gnaws, Wangs
SWANK Wanks
SWARD Draws, Wards
SWARE Resaw, Sawer, Swear,
     Wares, Wears
SWARM Mawrs, Warms
SWART Straw, Warst, Warts,
     Wrast
SWASH Shaws
SWATH Thaws
SWAYL Swaly, Yawls
SWEAL Lawes, Swale, Wales,
     Weals
SWEAR Resaw, Sawer, Sware,
     Wares, Wears
SWEAT Tawse, Waste
SWEDE Sewed, Sweed, Weeds
SWEED Sewed, Swede, Weeds
SWEEL Lewes, Sewel, Weels,
     Wesel
SWEEP Weeps
SWEER Ewers, Sewer, Weser
SWEET Ewest
SWEIR Swire, Weirs, Wires, Wiser
SWELL Wells

SWELT Welts
SWILL Wills
SWINE Sewin, Sinew, Wines
SWING Wings
SWINK Winks
SWIPE Wipes
SWIRE Sweir, Weirs, Wires, Wiser
SWISH Whiss
SWITH Whist, Whits, Withs
SWIVE Views, Wives
SWOLN Lowns
SWOON Woons
SWORD Drows, Words
SWORE Owers, Owser, Resow,
     Serow, Sower, Worse
*SYBIL Sibyl
SYBOE Obeys
SYKER Skyer, Skyre, Yerks
SYMAR Marys
SYNOD Dyson
SYRUP Pursy, Pyrus
SYTHE Theys

TABER Baret, Bater, Berta
TABES Abets, Baste, Bates, Beast,
     Beats, Besat, Esbat, Sebat
TABLE Ablet, Blate, Bleat
TABOR Abort, Boart, Rabot
TABUN Bantu
TABUS Abuts, Tsuba, Tubas
TACES Caste, Cates, Scate, Sceat
TACHE Cheat, Teach, Theca
TACIT Attic
TACKS Stack
TAELS Astel, Least, Leats, Salet,
     Slate, Stael, Stale, Steal, Stela,
     Tales, Teals, Tesla
*TAGUS Tsuga
TAHRS Harst, Harts, Raths,
     Thars, Trash
TAIGA Agait
TAILS Litas
*TAINE Eat-in, Entia, Teian, Tenia,
     Tinea

TAINS Antis, Saint, Satin, Stain, Tanis
TAINT Tanti, Titan
TAIRA Atria, Riata, Tiara
TAISH Haits, Saith, Thais
TAITS Sitta
TAKER Terka
TAKES Kates, Keats, Skate, Skeat, Steak, Stake, Teaks
TALAR Altar, Artal, Ratal
TALER Alter, Alert, Artel, Later, Ratel, Telar
TALES Astel, Least, Leats, Salet, Slate, Stael, Stale, Steal, Stela, Taels, Teals, Tesla
TALKS Stalk
TALMA Malta, Tamal
TALON Alton, Notal, Tolan, Tonal
*TALOS** Altos, Salto, Sloat, Stola, Tolas
TALUS Sault, Tulsa
TAMAL Malta, Talma
*TAMAR** Marat
TAMED Mated
TAMER Armet, Mater, Metra, Terma, Trema
TAMES Mates, Meats, Mesta, Satem, Steam, Teams
TAMIN Matin
TAMIS Maist
TAMPS Stamp
TANGI Giant
TANGO Tonga
TANGS Angst, Gants, Gnats, Stang
*TANIS** Antis, Saint, Satin, Stain, Tains
TANKS Kants, Stank
TANNA Annat
TANSY Nasty
TANTI Taint, Titan
TANTY Taint, Titan
TANTY Natty

TAPED Adept, Pated
TAPEN Paten
TAPER Apert, Pater, Peart, Petar, Petra, Prate, Trape
TAPES Apest, Paste, Pates, Peats, Septa, Spate, Speat
TAPET Patte
TAPIR Atrip, Parti
TAPIS Pitas, Spait, Stipa
TAPUS Sputa, Stupa
TARDO Troad
TARED Adret, Dater, Rated, Trade, Tread
*TAREE** Arete, Eater, Reate
TARES Arets, Aster, Astre, Earst, Rates, Reast, Resat, Stare, Strae, Tarse, Tears, Teras
TARGE Gater, Grate, Great, Greta, Terga
TARIN Intra, Nitra, Riant, Train, Trani
TARNS Rants, Starn
TAROC Actor, Crato, Croat, Rocta
TAROS Astor, Roast, Rotas, Sarto, Toras, Troas
TAROT Ottar, Troat
TARRE Arret, Rater, Retar, Terra
TARSE Arets, Aster, Astre, Earst, Rates, Reast, Resat, Stare, Strae, Tares, Tears, Teras
TARSI Airts, Astir, Raits, Sitar, Sitra, Stair, Stria, Trias
TARTS Start
TARTY Ratty
TARVE Avert, Taver, Trave
TASAR Rasta, Ratas
TASSE Asset, Easts, Sates, Seats, Tessa
TASSO Assot, Oasts, Stoas
TASTE State, Tates, Teats, Testa
*TATAR** Attar
TATER Arett, Tetra, Treat
TATES State, Taste, Teats, Testa
TATUS Tauts

TAUBE Beaut, Butea, Tubae
TAULD Adult, Dault
TAUTS Tatus
TAVER Avert, Tarve, Trave
TAWER Water, Wrate
TAWNY Wanty
TAWSE Sweat, Waste
TAXEL Exalt, Latex
TAXER Extra, Retax
TAXES Texas
TAYRA Yarta
T-BONE Beton
T-CART Tract
TEACH Cheat, Tache, Theca
TEADS Dates, Sated, Stade,
   Stead, Tsade
TEAKS Kates, Keats, Skate, Steak,
   Stake, Takes
TEALS Astel, Least, Leats, Salet,
   Slate, Stael, Stale, Steal, Stela,
   Taels, Tales, Tesla
TEAMS Mates, Meats, Mesta,
   Satem, Steam
*TEANS Antes, Etnas, Nates,
   Nesta, Senta, Stane, Stean
TEARS Arets, Aster, Astre, Earst,
   Rates, Reast, Resat, Stare, Strae,
   Tares, Tarse, Teras
TEASE Setae
TEATS State, Taste, Tates, Testa
*TEBET Bette
TECHS Chest, Stech
TECHY Tyche
TEDES Steed
TEELS Leets, Sleet, Steel, Stele
TEEMS Meets, Metes, Steem,
   Steme, Temes, Temse
TEENS Etens, Steen, Tense
TEERS Ester, Reest, Retes, Reset,
   Steer, Stere, Teres, Terse, Trees
TEETH Thete
TEHRS Herts, Resht
*TEIAN Eat-in, Entia, Taine, Tenia,
   Tinea

TEILS Islet, Istle, Steil, Stile, Tiles
TEIND Tined
TELAE Elate
TELAR Alert, Alter, Artel, Later,
   Ratel, Taler
TELEX Texel
TELLS Stell
TELOS Lotes, Stole, Toles
TEMED Meted
*TEMES Meets, Metes, Steem,
   Steme, Teems, Temse
TEMSE Meets, Metes, Steem,
   Steme, Teems, Temes
*TENBY Benty
TENDS Dents, Stend
TENIA Eat-in, Entia, Taine, Teian,
   Tinea
TENON Nonet, Tonne
TENOR Noter, Ronte, Toner,
   Trone
*TENOS Eston, Etons, Notes,
   Onset, Seton, Steno, Stone,
   Tones
TENSE Etens, Steen, Teens
TENTS Stent
TENTY Netty
TEPAL Leapt, Lepta, Palet, Pelta,
   Petal, Plate, Pleat
TEPOR Porte, Repot, Retop,
   Toper, Trope
*TERAI Irate
TERAS Arets, Aster, Astre, Earst,
   Rates, Reast, Resat, Stare, Strae,
   Tares, Tarse, Tears
TERCE Crete, Erect
TERES Ester, Reest, Reset, Retes,
   Steer, Stere, Teers, Terse, Trees
TERGA Gater, Grate, Great,
   Greta, Targe
*TERKA Taker
TERMA Armet, Mater, Metra,
   Tamer, Trema
TERNE Enter, Etern, Rente, Treen

*TERNI Inert, Inter, Niter, Nitre,
  Retin, Trine
TERNS Ernst, Rents, Stern
TERRA Arret, Rater, Retar, Tarre
TERRY Retry, Tryer
TERSE Ester, Reest, Reset, Retes,
  Steer, Stere, Teers, Teres, Trees
TESLA Astel, Least, Leats, Salet,
  Slate, Stael, Stale, Steal, Stela,
  Taels, Tales, Teals
*TESSA Asset, Easts, Sates, Seats,
  Tasse
TESTA State, Taste, Tates, Teats
TETRA Arett, Tater, Treat
TEUCH Chuet, Chute
TEWED Tweed
TEWEL Tweel
TEWIT Twite
*TEXAS Taxes
*TEXEL Telex
*THAIS Haits, Saith, Taish
*THAME Meath, Thema
THANE Neath
THARS Harst, Harts, Raths,
  Tahrs, Trash
THAWS Swath
THECA Cheat, Tache, Teach
THEES Sheet, These
THEIC Ethic
THEIN Thine
THEIR Erith
THEMA Meath, Thame
*THERA Earth, Harte, Hater,
  Heart, Herat, Rathe, Thrae
THERE Ether, Three
THESE Sheet, Thees
THETE Teeth
THEYS Sythe
*THIES Heist, Shite, Sithe
THIGH Hight
THIGS Sight
THILL Illth
THINE Thein
THING Night

THIOL Litho, Tholi
THIRD Thrid
THOLE Helot, Hotel
THOLI Litho, Thiol
*THORA Horta, Torah
THORN North
THOSE Ethos, Shote
THOUS Shout, South
THRAE Earth, Harte, Hater,
  Heart, Herat, Rathe, Thera
THRAW Warth, Wrath
THREE Ether, There
THRID Third
THROB Broth
THROE Other
THROW Rowth, Whort, Worth,
  Wroth
THRUM Thurm
THURM Thrum
TIARA Atria, Riata, Taira
*TIBER Biter, Brite, Tribe
*TIBET Betti
*TIBUR Bruit
TICAL Cital, Ictal
TICCA Cacti
TICED Cited, Edict
TICHY Itchy
TICKS Stick
TIDAL Dital
TIDED Dited
TIDES Deist, Diets, Dites, Edits,
  Sited, Stied
TIERS Reist, Resit, Rites, Siret,
  Stire, Tires, Tries
TIE-UP Uptie
TIFFS Stiff
TIGER Greit, Tigre
TIGES Geist, Geits, Gites
TIGON Ingot, Toing
*TIGRE Greit, Tiger
TIKES Kites, Skite
TILDE Tiled
TILED Tilde
TILER Liter, Litre, Relit

TILES Islet, Istle, Steil, Stile, Teils
TILLS Lilts, Still
TILTS Stilt
TIMED Demit
TIMER Merit, Miter, Mitre, Remit
TIMES Emits, Items, Meist, Metis, Mites, Smite, Stime
*****TIMON** Minot, Tomin
TINEA Eat-in, Entia, Taine, Teian, Tenia
TINED Teind
TINES Inset, Neist, Nesti, Senti, Set-in, Sient, Stein
TINGS Sting
TINKS Knits, Skint, Stink
TINTS Stint, 'Tisn't
TINTY Nitty
TIRED Tride, Tried
TIRES Reist, Resit, Rites, Siret, Stire, Tiers, Tries
TIROS Riots, Roist, Rosit, Torsi, Trios
'TISN'T Stint, Tints
TITAN Taint, Tanti
TITER Titre, Trite
TITRE Titer, Trite
TITUP Putti
TIVER Rivet
TOADY Today
TOAST Stoat
TOAZE Azote
TOBAS Basto, Boats, Boast, Sabot, Sobat
TODAY Toady
TODDE Doted
TO-DOS Stood
TOGED Godet
TOILE Eliot
TOILS Isolt, Solti
TOING Ingot, Tigon
TOITS Stoit
TOKEN Knote
TOKOS Kotos, Stook
*****TOKYO** Kyoto

TOLAN Alton, Notal, Talon, Tonal
TOLAS Altos, Salto, Sloat, Stola, Talos
TOLES Lotes, Stole, Telos
TOLLY Tolyl
TOLYL Tolly
TOMAN Manto
TOMES Mesto, Motes, Smote
TOMIN Minot, Timon
TONAL Alton, Notal, Talon, Tolan
TONED Donet, Noted
TONER Noter, Ronte, Tenor, Trone
TONES Eston, Etons, Notes, Onset, Seton, Steno, Stone, Tenos
TONGA Tango
TONGS Stong
TONIC Cinto
TONNE Nonet, Tenon
TON-UP Punto, Put-on, Unpot, Untop
TONUS Notus, Snout, Stoun
TOOLS Loots, Lotos, Sloot, Sotol, Stool
TOOMS Moots, Smoot, Stoom
TOPED Depot, Opted, Poted
TOPER Porte, Repot, Retop, Tepor, Trope
TOPES Estop, Poets, Potes, Stoep, Stope
TOPET Petto
TOPIA Patio
TOPIC Optic, Picot
TOPIS Posit
TOPOS Stoop, Sopot
TOP-UP Poupt
TOQUE Quote
*****TORAH** Horta, Thora
TORAN Arnot, Orant, Trona
TORAS Astor, Roost, Rotas, Sarto, Taros, Troas

TORCH Rotch
TORES Estro, Roset, Rotes, Store, Torse
TORIC Troic
TORSE Estro, Roset, Rotes, Store, Tores
TORSI Riots, Roist, Rosit, Tiros, Trios
TORSK Stork
TORSO Roots, Roost, Stoor
TORTE Otter, Toter
TORUS Roust, Routs, Stour, Sutor, Tours
*****TOSCA** Ascot, Coast, Coats, Costa, Scoat
TOSED Doest, Dotes
TOTEM Motet, Motte
TOTER Otter, Torte
TOTES Set-to
TOUCH Chout, Couth, Ouch
TOUGH Ought
TOUPS Pouts, Spout, Stoup
*****TOURE** Outer, Outre, Route
TOURS Roust, Routs, Stour, Sutor, Torus
TOUTS Stout
TOWEL Owlet
TOWER Rowte, Twoer, Wrote
TOWNS Stown, Wonts
TOWNY Towyn
*****TOWYN** Towny
TRACE Caret, Carte, Cater, Crate, React, Recta
TRACT T-cart
TRADE Adret, Dater, Rated, Tared, Tread
TRAIK Krait
TRAIL Liart, T-rail, Trial
T-RAIL Liart, Trail, Trial
TRAIN Intra, Riant, Tarin, Nitra, Trani
TRAMS Marts, Smart
*****TRANI** Intra, Nitra, Riant, Tarin, Train

TRANS Rants, Starn
TRAPA Apart
TRAPE Apert, Pater, Peart, Petar, Petra, Prate, Taper
TRAPS Parts, Prats, Spart, Sprat, Strap
TRASH Harst, Harts, Raths, Tahrs, Thars
TRASS Stars, Tsars
TRAVE Avert, Tarve, Taver
TRAYS Artsy, Satyr, Stray
TREAD Dater, Rated, Tared, Trade
TREAT Arett, Tater, Tetra
TREED Deter
TREEN Enter, Etern, Rente, Terne
TREES Ester, Reest, Reset, Retes, Steer, Stere, Teers, Teres, Terse
TREFA After
TREND Drent
TRESS Rests
TREWS Strew, Werts, Wrest
TREYS Resty, Steyr, Styre, Tyres
TRIAL Liart, Trail, T-rail
*****TRIAS** Airts, Astir, Raits, Sitar, Sitra, Stair, Stria, Tarsi
TRIBE Biter, Brite, Tiber
TRICE Recti
TRIDE Tired, Tried
TRIED Tired, Tride
TRIES Reist, Resit, Rites, Siret, Stire, Tiers, Tires
TRIGS Girts, Grist, Grits, Strig
TRINE Inert, Inter, Niter, Nitre, Retin, Terni
TRIOS Riots, Roist, Rosit, Tiros, Torsi
TRIPE Petri, Piert
TRIPS Spirt, Sprit, Stirp, Strip
TRITE Titer, Titre
TROAD Tardo
*****TROAS** Astor, Roast, Rotas, Sarto, Taros, Toras
TROAT Ottar, Tarot

TROIC Toric
***TROMS** Morts, Storm
TRONA Arnot, Orant, Toran
TRONE Noter, Ronte, Tenor, Toner
TRONS Ronts, Snort
***TROON** Orton
TROOP Poort, Porto
TROPE Porte, Repot, Retop, Tepor, Toper
TROUT Tutor
TROVE Overt, Voter
TROWS Strow, Worst, Worts
TRUCE Cruet, Cuter, Eruct, Recut
TRUES Sture
TRUSS Rusts
TRUST Strut, Sturt
TRYER Retry, Terry
TRY-ON Ryton
TSADE Dates, Sated, Stade, Stead, Teads
TSANA Santa, Satan
TSARS Stars, Trass
TSUBA Abuts, Tabus, Tubas
TSUBO Bouts
***TSUGA** Tagus
TUBAE Beaut, Butea, Taube
TUBAS Abuts, Tabus, Tsuba
TUBED Debut
TUBER Brute, Buret, Rebut
TUCKS Stuck
TUFAS Faust, Stufa
TUFFS Stuff
TUISM Muist, Musit
***TULSA** Sault, Talus
TUMPS Stump
TUMPY Umpty
TUNER Urent
TUNES Suent, Unset, Usen't
TUNIC Cut-in, Incut
***TUNIS** Inust, Suint, Units
***TUNJA** Jantu, Jaunt, Junta
***TURCO** Court, Crout
TURDS Durst

***TURIN** Rutin
TURMS Strum
TURPS Spurt
TUTOR Trout
TWAIN Witan
TWEED Tewed
TWEEL Tewel
TWEER Rewet, 'Twere
'TWERE Rewet, Tweer
TWIER Twire, Write
TWILL 'Twill
TWIRE Twier, Write
TWIST Twits
TWITE Tewit
TWITS Twist
TWOER Rowte, Tower, Wrote
***TYCHE** Techy
TYKES Kytes, Skyte
TYNDE Tyned
TYNED Tynde
TYPAL Aptly, Patly, Platy
TYPTO Potty
TYRAN Ranty
TYRES Resty, Steyr, Styre, Treys
TYROS Royst, Ryots, Story, Stroy

U-BOAT About
U-BOLT Boult
UDALS Aldus, Lauds
UDDER Dured
ULCER Cruel, Lucre
ULNAD Laund
ULNAR Lunar, Urnal
UMBER Brume, Umbre
UMBRA Burma, Rumba
UMBRE Brume, Umber
UMPTY Tumpy
UNARM Namur, Ruman, Urman
UNBAR Buran, Urban
UNDAM Maund, Munda, Unmad
UNDEE Endue
UNDER Duren, Runed, Unred, Urned
UNFAR Furan

UNHAT Haunt
UNHID Hindu
UNITE Untie
UNITS Inust, Suint, Tunis
UNLAY Nyula, Yulan
UNLIT Until
UNMAD Maund, Munda, Undam
UNPOT Punto, Put-on, Ton-up, Untop
UNRED Duren, Runed, Under, Urned
UNRIG Ruing
UNRIP Purin
UNSAY Sunay
UNSET Suent, Tunes, Usen't
UNSEX Nexus
UNSOD Nodus, Sound
UNSON Nouns
UNTIE Unite
UNTIL Unlit
UNTOP Punto, Put-on, Ton-up, Unpot
UPLAY Lay-up
UPLED Duple, Puled
UPRUN Run-up
UPSET Set-up, Stupe
UPTIE Tie-up
URALI Urial
*****URALS** Larus, Sural
URBAN Buran, Unbar
UREAL Alure
URENT Tuner
URGER Regur
URGES Surge
URIAL Urali
URINE Inure
URITE Uteri
URMAN Namur, Ruman, Unarm
URNAL Lunar, Ulnar
URNED Duren, Runed, Under, Unred
USAGE Suage
USEN'T Suent, Tunes, Unset
USERS Reuss, Ruses

USHER Huers, Shure
USING Suing
USURE Eurus
UTERI Urite
UVEAL Value
UVEAS Suave

VADED Vedda
VADES Devas, Saved, Vedas
VAILS Alvis, Salvi, Silva, Valis, Vials
VAINS Savin, Sivan, Vinas
VALED Laved
VALES Elvas, Laves, Salve, Selva, Slave, Valse, Veals
VALSE Elvas, Laves, Salve, Selva, Slave, Vales, Veals
VALUE Uveal
VANES Avens, Evans, Naves, Sevan
VAPID Pavid
VARAN Varna
*****VARDE** Drave, Raved, Revda
VAREC Carve, Caver, Crave
VARES Avers, Raves, Saver
VARNA Varan
VASAL Lavas
VEALE Leave
VEALS Elvas, Laves, Salve, Selva, Slave, Vales, Valse
VEALY Leavy
VEDAS Devas, Saved, Vades
*****VEDDA** Vaded
*****VEDIC** Viced
VEDRO Dover, Drove, Roved
VEENA Naeve, Venae
VEERS Serve, Sever, Verse
VEERY Every
VEILS Elvis, Evils, Levis, Lives, Slive, Vleis
VEINS Nevis, Sevin, Venis, Vines, Visne
VELAR Laver, Ravel, Reval
VELES Elves

VELIA Alive, Avile
VELUM Mvule
VENAE Naeve, Veena
VENAL Elvan, Levan, Navel
*VENER Erven, Nerve, Never,
  Verne
VENEY Yeven
VENGE Negev
*VENIS Nevis, Sevin, Veins, Vines,
  Visne
*VENLO Novel, Vlone
*VENUS Nevus
*VERDI Diver, Driver, Rived
VERGE Greve
*VERNE Erven, Nerve, Never,
  Vener
VERSE Serve, Sever, Veers
VERSO Overs, Rovers, Serov,
  Servo
VERST Verts
VERTS Verst
VESPA Paves, Spave
VESTA Stave
VIALS Alvis, Salvi, Silva, Vails,
  Valis
VIAND Divan, Dvina
VIBES Bevis
VICAR Vraic
VICED Vedic
VICES Cives
*VICHY Chivy
VIDEO Dovie
VIEWS Swive, Wives
VIGOR Virgo
VILDE Devil, Lived
VILER Ervil, Liver, Livre, Rivel
*VILES Lives
*VILNA Alvin, Anvil, Nival, Vinal
VINAL Alvin, Anvil, Nival, Vilna
VINAS Savin, Sivan, Vains
VINCA Cavin
VINER Riven
VINES Nevis, Sevin, Veins, Venis,
  Visne

VIOLA Oliva, Voila
VIOLE Olive, Voile
VIRAL Rival
VIRGE Giver
*VIRGO Vigor
VISAS Sivas
VISED Dives
VISIE Ivies
VISIT Vitis
VISNE Nevis, Sevin, Veins, Venis,
  Vines
VISTO Ovist
*VITIS Visit
VLEIS Elvis, Evils, Levis, Lives,
  Slive, Veils
*VLONE Novel, Venlo
VOCES Coves, Scove
VOGIE Ogive
VOGUE Vouge
VOILA Oliva, Viola
VOILE Olive, Viole
VOLAE Loave
VOLAR Orval
VOLAS Ovals, Salvo
VOLED Loved
VOLES Loves, Slove, Solve
VOLET Volte
VOLTA Lovat
VOLTE Volet
VOMER Mover
VOTER Overt, Trove
VOTES Stove
VOUGE Vogue
VOWEL Wolve
VRAIC Vicar

WADER Dewar, Wared
WADES Sawed
WAGES Swage
WAGON Gowan, Wonga
WAINS Swain
WAIST Waits
WAITS Waist
WAKER Wreak

WAKES Askew, Wekas
WALED Dwale, Lawed, Weald
WALES Lawes, Swale, Sweal, Weals
WANED Awned, Dewan
WANES Sewan, Weans
WANGS Gnaws, Swang
WANKS Swank
WANLY Lawny
WANTY Tawny
WARDS Draws, Sward
WARED Dewar, Wader
WARES Resaw, Sawer, Sware, Swear, Wears
WARMS Mawrs, Swarm
WARST Straw, Swart, Warts, Wrast
WARTH Thraw, Wrath
WARTS Straw, Swart, Warst, Wrast
WASPY Yawps
WASTE Sweat, Tawse
WATER Tawer, Wrate
WAXER Rewax
WEALD Dwale, Lawed, Waled
WEALS Lawes, Swale, Sweal, Wales
WEANS Sewan, Wanes
WEARS Resaw, Sawer, Sware, Swear, Wares
WEEDS Sewed, Swede, Sweed
WEEDY Dewey
WEELS Lewes, Sewel, Sweel, Wesel
WEENS Enews, Ensew, Sewen
WEENY Yewen
WEEPS Sweep
WEILS Lewis, Wiels, Wiles
WEIRD Wider, Wired
WEIRS Sweir, Swire, Wires, Wiser
*WEISS** Wises
WEKAS Askew, Wakes
WELLS Swell
WELTS Swelt

WERSH Shrew
WERTS Strew, Trews, Wrest
*WESEL** Lewes, Sewel, Sweel, Weels
*WESER** Ewers, Sewer, Sweer
WHALE Wheal
WHAMS Hawms, Shawm
WHEAL Whale
WHERE Hewer
WHISS Swish
WHIST Swith, Whits, Withs
WHITE Withe
WHITS Swith, Whist, Withs
WHITY Withy
WHORE Howre
WHORT Rowth, Throw, Worth, Wroth
WHOSE Howes
WHOSO Howso, Woosh
WIDEN Dwine, Edwin, Wined
WIDER Weird, Wired
WIELD Wilde, Wiled
WIELS Lewis, Weils, Wiles
WIGAN Awing
*WILDE** Wield, Wiled
WILED Wield, Wilde
WILES Lewis, Weils, Wiels
WILLS Swill
WINED Dwine, Edwin, Widen
WINES Sewin, Sinew, Swine
WINGE Ewing
WINGS Swing
WINKS Swink
WINZE Wizen
WIPES Swipe
WIRED Weird, Wider
WIRER Wrier
WIRES Sweir, Swire, Weirs, Wiser
WISER Sweir, Swire, Weirs, Wires
WISES Weiss
WITAN Twain
WITHE White
WITHS Swith, Whist, Whits
WITHY Whity

WIVES Swive, Views
WIZEN Winze
*****WODEN** Endow, Owned,
   Nowed, Woned
WOKEN Knowe
WOLVE Vowel
WONED Endow, Owned,
   Nowed, Woden
WONGA Gowan, Wagon
WONTS Stown, Towns
WOONS Swoon
WOOSH Howso, Whoso
WORDS Drows, Sword
WORDY Dowry, Rowdy
WORSE Owers, Owser, Resow,
   Serow, Sower, Swore
WORST Strow, Trows, Worts
WORTH Rowth, Throw, Whort,
   Wroth
WORTS Strow, Trows, Worst
WRAST Straw, Swart, Warst,
   Warts
WRATE Tawer, Water
WRATH Thraw, Warth
WREAK Waker
WREST Strew, Trews, Werts
WRIER Wirer
WRIST Writs
WRITE Twier, Twire
WRITS Wrist
WRONG Grown
WROTE Rowte, Tower, Twoer
WROTH Rowth, Throw, Whort,
   Worth

XYLIC Cylix
XYSTI Sixty

YACHT Cathy
YAGER Aygre, Gayer
*****YAHVE** Heavy
YAKKA Kayak
*****YAMAL** Malay
YAMEN Mayen, Meany

YANKS Snaky
YARNS Snary
YARTA Tayra
YARTO Otary
YASHT Hasty
YAWLS Swaly, Swayl
YAWNS Sawny
YAWPS Waspy
YBORE O'erby
YDRAD Dryad
YDRED Reddy
YEANS Sayne
YEARD Deary, Deray, Rayed,
   Ready
YEARN Rayne, Renay
YEARS Eyras, Resay, Sayer
YEAST Yeats
*****YEATS** Yeast
*****YECLA** Lacey
YELPS Slype
YELTS Style
*****YEMEN** Enemy
YERBA Barye, Bayer, Beray
YERKS Syker
YEVEN Veney
YEWEN Weeny
YILLS Silly, Slily
YLIKE Kiley, Kylie
Y-MOTH Mothy
YOBBO Booby
YODEL Doyle, Odyle, Yodle
YODLE Doyle, Odyle, Yodel
YOKEL Kyloe
YPRES Preys, Pryse, Pyres,
   Rypes, Spyre
YRAPT Party, Praty
YRENT Entry
YSAME Samey, Seamy
*****YSSEL** Lyses, Sleys
YUFTS Fusty
YULAN Nyula, Unlay

ZABRA Bazar, Braza
*****ZAHLE** Hazel

ZEBRA Braze　　　　　　**ZONED** Dozen
*** ZELDA** Lazed　　　　　　**ZYGAL** Glazy
ZERDA Razed

Six letters

ABACAS Casaba
ABATER Rabate, Trabea
ABATES Sea-bat
ABATOR Rabato
***ABDERA** Abrade, Abread
ABDEST Basted
***ABDIEL** Bailed, Bidale, Deblai
ABIDED Baddie
ABIDER Air-bed, Braide
ABIDES Biased
ABIENT Binate
ABLAUT Tabula
ABLEST Ablets, Bleats, Stable,
Tables
ABLETS Ablest, Bleats, Stable,
Tables
ABLING Baling
ABLINS Blains
ABOARD Aborad, Abroad,
Baroda
ABORAD Aboard, Abroad,
Baroda
ABORDS Adsorb, Boards, Broads,
Dobras
ABORTS Boarts, Strabo, Tabors
ABRADE Abdera, Abread
ABREAD Abdera, Abrade
ABRINS Bairns, Brains, Brians,
Risban
ABROAD Aboard, Aborad,
Baroda
ABSENT Basnet, Besant
ABUSER Bursae
ACATES Sea-cat
ACCITE Acetic
ACCOIL Calico
ACETIC Accite

ACINAR Arnica, Carina, Crania
ACMITE Micate
ACNODE Canoed, Deacon
ACROSS Oscars
ACTION Atonic, Cation
ACTIVE Cavite
ACTONS Cantos, Cotans, Octans,
Snacot
ACTORS Castor, Castro, Co-star,
Croats, Roctas, Scrota, Tarocs
ACTURE Cauter, Curate
ACUTES Cuesta
ADAMIC Cadmia
ADDERS Dreads, Readds, Sadder
ADDLED Daddle
ADDLES Saddle
ADEEMS Seamed
***ADENIS** Sendai
ADEPTS Pasted
ADHERE Header, Hedera,
Rehead
ADIEUS Suidae
ADMIRE Merida
ADMITS Amidst
***ADONAI** Adonia
***ADONIA** Adonai
***ADONIC** Anodic
ADONIS Sodain
ADORED Deodar, Roaded
ADORER Roared
ADORES Oreads, Soared, Sea-rod
ADRETS Daters, Desart, Stared,
Trades, Treads
***ADRIAN** Andria, Radian
***ADRIEL** Derial, Laired, Lerida,
Railed, Relaid

6

ADSORB Abords, Boards, Broads, Dobras
ADVERB Braved
ADVIEW Waived
ADVISE Avised, Davies, Visaed
AERGE Raggee, Reggae
AERIAL Realia
AERIES Easier
AETHER Heater, Hereat, Reheat
AFFAIR Raffia
AFFEER Raffee
AFIELD Failed
AFREET Terefa
AFROED Fedora
AFTERS Faster, Strafe
AGE-OLD Gaoled
AGEISM Images
AGGERS Eggars, Gagers, Sagger, Seggar
AGNAIL Anglia, Ilagan
AGNAME Manage
AGNISE Easing
AGONIC Angico
AGREED Dragee, Geared
AGREES Eagres, Grease
AGREGE Raggee, Reggae
AHORSE Ashore, Hoarse, Shorea
AIDERS Irades, Raised
AIGLET Ligate, Taigle
AIGRET Gaiter, Triage
AILING Nilgai
AIR-BED Abider, Braide
AIRCAV Caviar
AIRERS Raiser, Serrai, Sierra
AIR-GUN Ugrian
AIRMAN Marian, Marina
AIRMEN Marine, Marnie, Remain
AIR-SEA Araise, Sea-air
AIRTED Raited, Tirade
AISLED Deasil, Ideals, Ladies, Sailed
AISLES Eassil, Laisse, Lassie
ALARIC Racial
ALBATA Atabal, Balata

ALBEDO Doable
ALBEIT Albite, Betail, Libate
* **ALBERT** Labret, Tabler
ALBINO Albion, Alboin
* **ALBION** Albino, Alboin
ALBITE Albeit, Betail, Libate
* **ALBOIN** Albino, Albion
* **ALCAIC** Cicala
ALCEDO Coaled
ALCOVE Coeval, Levoca
* **ALCUIN** Lucian, Lucina, Uncial
ALDERN Darnel, Enlard, Lander, Randle, Reland
ALDERS Dalers, Sardel
* **ALDINE** Alined, Daniel, Delian, Denial, Lead-in, Nailed
* **ALDRED** Ladder, Larded, Raddle
* **ALECTO** Locate
ALEGAR Laager
ALEGER Regale
ALERCE Cereal, Relace
ALERTS Alters, Artels, Laster, Ratels, Resalt, Salter, Slater, Staler, Stelar, Tarsel
ALEVIN Alvine, Valine, Venial
ALEXIN Xenial
* **ALFRED** Fardel, Flared
ALGOID Dialog
ALIBLE Belial, Biella, Labile, Liable
ALIDAD La-di-da
ALIENS Alines, Lianes, Lesina, Saline, Selina, Silane
ALIGNS Ganils, Liangs, Ligans, Lingas, Signal
ALINED Aldine, Daniel, Delian, Denial, Lead-in, Nailed
ALINES Aliens, Lesina, Lianes, Saline, Selina, Silane
ALIPED Elapid, Paidle, Pailed, Pleiad
ALISMA Lamias, Salami
ALLEES Sallee
ALLIED Laldie

ALLIES Sallie
ALLOWS Sallow
ALLUDE Aludel
ALLURE Laurel
ALMAIN Animal, Lamina, Manila
*ALMANY Layman
ALMOIN Molina, Monial, Oilman
ALMOND Dolman
ALMOST Maltos, Smalto
ALMUCE Macule
ALNAGE Angela, Anlage,
  Galena, Lagena
ALPINE Epinal, Nepali, Penial,
  Pineal
ALPIST Pastil, Plaits, Spital
ALSOON Saloon, Solano
*ALTAIR Atrial, Lariat, Latria
ALTARS Astral, Ratals, Talars,
  Tarsal
ALTERN Antler, Learnt, Rental,
  Ternal
ALTERS Alerts, Artels, Laster,
  Ratels, Resalt, Salter, Slater,
  Staler, Stelar, Tarsel
ALUDEL Allude
ALUMNA Manual
ALUMNI Lumina
ALVINE Alevin, Valine, Venial
AMBERS Breams, Embars,
  Sambre
AMBLED Balmed, Bedlam,
  Beldam, Blamed, Lambed
AMBLER Blamer, Lamber,
  Marble, Ramble
AMEERS Ameres, Mersea,
  Ramees, Seamer
AMENDE Amened, Demean
AMENDS Desman, Menads
AMENED Amende, Demean
AMENTA Teaman
AMENTS Manets, Mantes,
  Stamen
AMERCE Careme, Raceme

AMERES Ameers, Mersea,
  Ramees, Seamer
AMICES Camise, Macies
AMIDES Mid-sea
AMIDST Admits
*AMIENS Amines, Inseam, Mesian
AMINES Amiens, Inseam, Mesian
AMMINE Immane
AMNION Minoan
AMORET Teramo
AMOUNT Moutan, Outman
AMOVES Vamose
AMPLER Marple, Palmer
AMPERE Empare
AMREET Remate
AMRITA Tamari
AMUSED Medusa, Sea-mud
AMUSER Maseru, Mauser
AMUSES Assume, Seamus
ANADEM Maenad
ANALOG Angola
ANCHOR Archon, Charon,
  Rancho
ANCILE Celina, Inlace
ANCLES Cleans, Lances, Lencas,
  Senlac
*ANDREW Darwen, Dawner,
  Rawden, Wander, Warden,
  Warned
*ANDRIA Adrian, Radian
ANEATH Athena
ANELED Leaden, Leaned, Nealed
ANEMIC Cinema, Iceman
ANERLY Nearly
*ANGELA Alnage, Anlage,
  Galena, Lagena
ANGERS Ranges, Sanger, Serang
ANGICO Agonic
ANGINA Nagina
ANGLED Dangle, Glenda,
  Lagend
ANGLER Largen, Rangle, Regnal
ANGLET Langet, Tangle
*ANGLIA Agnail, Ilagan

* **ANGLIC** Lacing
* **ANGOLA** Analog
  ANGORA Aragon, Arango, Onagra, Organa
  ANGORS Argons, Groans, Nagors, Orangs, Organs, Sargon, Sarong
* **ANGUIS** Saguin
  ANICUT Nautic
  ANIGHT A'thing, Hating
  ANIMAL Almain, Lamina, Manila
  ANIMAS Maasin, Manias, Manisa, Samian
  ANIONS Nasion
  ANISES Sanies, Sasine
  ANKLED Kendal
  ANLAGE Alnage, Angela, Galena, Lagena
* **ANNIES** Insane, Sienna
  ANNULI Unnail
  ANODIC Adonic
  ANOINT Nation
  ANOMIC Camion, Conima, Manioc
* **ANSELM** Lemans, Mensal
  ANSWER Awners, Resawn
  ANTHEM Hetman
  ANTHER Tehran, Thenar
  ANTICS Incast, Nastic
  ANTLER Altern, Learnt, Rental, Ternal
  ANTLIA Latian, Talian
* **ANTRES** Astern, Retans, Sterna, Transe
* **ANTRIM** Martin
  ANTRUM Truman
* **ANUBIS** Nubias, Unbias
  ANURIA Urania
  ANVILS Silvan
  AORIST Aristo, Artois, Ratios, Satori
  APEDOM Pomade
  APERCU Race-up
  A-PER-SE Parsee, Prease, Serape

APIARY Piraya
APICES Spicae
APLITE Pilate
* **APODES** Saped
  APOLLO Palolo
  APPEND Napped
  APRONS Parson, Prosna
  APTERA Patera, Petara
  APTOTE Tea-pot
  ARABLE Arbela
* **ARAGON** Angora, Arango, Onagra, Organa
  ARAISE Air-sea, Sea-air
  ARANGO Angora, Aragon, Onagra, Organa
* **ARBELA** Arable
  ARBUTE Tauber
  ARCHED Chared
  ARCHES Chares, Chaser, Eschar, Raches, Search
* **ARCHIE** Cahier, Eriach
  ARCHON Anchor, Charon, Rancho
  ARCING Caring, Racing
  ARCKED Carked, Craked, Dacker, Racked
  ARDEBS Beards, Breads, Debars, Sabred, Serdab
  ARDENT Endart, Ranted
  AREDES Deares, Erased, Reseda, Seared
  ARETES Asteer, Easter, Eaters, Reates, Reseat, Saeter, Seater, Staree, Steare, Teaser, Teresa
  ARETTS Astert, Stater, Taster, Taters, Tetras, Treats
  ARGALI Garial
  ARGENT Garnet, Gerant, Gretna
  ARGHAN Hangar
* **ARGIVE** Garvie, Rivage
  ARGONS Angors, Groans, Nagors, Orangs, Organs, Sargon, Sarong

ARGUES Augers, Sauger, Segura,
  Usager
ARGUTE Rugate, Tuareg
ARIELS Asriel, Israel, Relais,
  Resail, Sailer, Serail, Serial
ARIGHT Graith
ARISEN Arsine, Resina, Sarnie
ARISES Raises, Sisera
ARISTA Riatas, Tarsia, Tiaras
ARISTO Aorist, Artois, Ratios,
  Satori
ARKING Raking
ARKITE Karite
ARKOSE Soaker, Oakers, Resoak
* **ARMAGH** Graham
ARMEST Armets, Master, Maters,
  Remast, Stream, Tamers, Tremas
ARMETS Armest, Master, Maters,
  Remast, Stream, Tamers, Tremas
ARMFUL Fulmar
ARMIES Maires
ARMING Ingmar, Ingram,
  Margin
ARMLET Martel
ARMPIT Impart, Partim
* **ARNHEM** Herman
ARNICA Acinar, Carina, Crania
* **ARNOLD** Landor, Lardon,
  Roland, Ronald
AROINT Ration
AROMAS Masora
AROUND Arundo
AROURA Aurora
AROYNT Notary, Troyan
ARPENT Enrapt, Entrap, Panter,
  Parent, Pterna, Trepan
ARRECT Carter, Crater, Tracer
ARREST Arrets, Rarest, Raster,
  Raters, Retars, Sartre, Starer,
  Tarres, Terras
ARRETS Arrest, Rarest, Raster,
  Raters, Retars, Sartre, Starer,
  Tarres, Terras
ARRIDE Raider

ARRISH Harris, Shirra, Sirrah
ARRIVE Rivera, Varier
ARROWY Yarrow
ARSENO Reason, Senora
ARSHIN Shairn
ARSINE Arisen, Resina, Sarnie
ARTELS Alerts, Alters, Laster,
  Ratels, Resalt, Salter, Slater,
  Staler, Stelar, Tarsel
ARTIST Sittar, Strait, Strati, Traits
* **ARTOIS** Aorist, Aristo, Ratios,
  Satori
ARUNDO Around
ASCEND Dances
ASCENT Enacts, Secant, Stance
ASH-BIN Banish
ASHETS Hastes, Tashes
ASH-FLY Flashy
ASHLER Halser, Lasher
ASHMAN Shaman
ASHORE Ahorse, Hoarse, Shorea
* **ASIANS** Niassa
ASIDES Dassie, Sadies
ASKING Gaskin, Kiangs
ASLANT Santal
ASLEEP Elapse, Please, Sapele
ASPECT Epacts
ASPERS Parses, Passer, Prases,
  Repass, Spaers, Spares, Sparse,
  Spears
ASPIRE Paries, Persia, Praise,
  Spirae, Spirea
ASPORT Pastor, Portas, Sap-rot
* **ASRIEL** Ariels, Israel, Relais,
  Resail, Sailer, Serail, Serial
ASSENT Sanest, Snaste, Stanes,
  Steans
ASSERT Asters, Astres, Reasts,
  Stresa, Stares
ASSIGN Signas
ASSIST Stasis
ASSORT Roasts
ASSUME Amuses, Seamus
ASTARE Sea-rat

ASTART Attars, Strata, Tatars
ASTEER Aretes, Easter, Eaters,
  Reates, Reseat, Saeter, Seater,
  Staree, Steare, Teaser, Teresa
ASTERN Antres, Retans, Sterna,
  Transe
ASTERS Assert, Astres, Reasts,
  Stares
ASTERT Aretts, Stater, Taster,
  Taters, Tetras, Treats
ASTRAL Altars, Ratals, Talars,
  Tarsal
ASTRAY Satyra, Tayras
ASTRES Assert, Asters, Reasts,
  Stares, Stresa
ASTREX Extras, Taxers
*ASTRID Triads
ASTUTE Statue
ASWING Sawing
*ATABAL Albata, Balata
ATABEG Tea-bag
*ATHENA Aneath
ATHENE Ethane
*ATHENS Hasten, Snathe, Sneath
  Thanes
ATHING Anight, Hating
ATOCIA Coaita
ATOMIC Matico
ATONAL Latona
ATONED Donate, Nodate
ATONER Ornate, Tenora
ATONES Easton, Seaton
ATONIC Action, Cation
ATOPIC Copita
*ATREUS Auster, Seurat, Urates
ATRIAL Altair, Lariat, Latria
ATRIUM Timaru
ATTACH Chatta
ATTARS Astart, Strata, Tatars
ATTICS Static
ATTIRE Ratite, Tertia, Tiaret
ATTORN Ratton, Rottan
ATTUNE Nutate, Tauten, Tetuan
AUGEND Unaged

AUGERS Argues, Sauger, Segura,
  Usager
AULICS Caulis, Clusia
AUNTER Nature, Neutra, Tea-urn
AUNTIE Uniate
AURATE Aureat
AUREAT Aurate
AUREUS Uraeus
AURORA Aroura
*AUSTEN Nasute, Unseat
AUSTER Atreus, Seurat, Urates
AVAILS Saliva, Salvia, Valais
*AVALON Avlona, Valona
AVENGE Geneva, Vangee
*AVERNO Verona
AVERSE Reaves, Varese
AVERTS Ravest, Starve, Staver,
  Tarves, Tavers, Traves, Vaster
*AVESTA Savate
*AVILES Leavis, Valise
AVISED Advise, Davies, Visaed
AVITAL Latvia
*AVLONA Avalon, Valona
AVOCET Octave
AVOSET Ovates
AVOWER Reavow
AVULSE Values
AWLESS Swales, Sweals
AWNERS Answer, Resawn
AWNING Waning

BACKER Reback
BADDIE Abided
BADGER Barged, Garbed
BAGGIT Gag-bit
BAGNIO Gabion
BAILED Abdiel, Belaid, Bidale,
  Deblai
BAILER Librae
BAIRNS Abrins, Brains, Brians,
  Risban
BAITER Barite, Rebait, Terbia
BAKERS Basker, Brakes, Breaks
BAKING Ink-bag

BALATA Albata, Atabal
BALDED Bladed
***BALDER** Bedral, Blared
BALEEN Enable
BALING Abling
BALMED Ambled, Bedlam, Beldam, Blamed, Lambed
BANDER Brenda
BANGER Graben
BANGLE Bengal
***BANGOR** Barong, Brogan
BANISH Ash-bin
BANKER Barken, Rebank
BANTAM Batman
BANTED Tan-bed
BANTER Barnet
BANZAI Zabian
BARBED Dabber, Debarb
BARBEL Barble, Rabble
BARBET Rabbet
BARBLE Barbel, Rabble
BAREGE Bargee
BARELY Barley, Bleary, Brayle
BAREST Baster, Bestar, Breast, Tarbes
BARETH Bather, Bertha, Breath
BARGED Badger, Garbed
BARGEE Barege
BARITE Baiter, Rebait, Terbia
BARIUM Umbria
BARKED Braked, Debark
BARKEN Banker, Rebank
BARKER Braker
BARKIS Biskra
BARLEY Barely, Bleary, Brayle
***BARNET** Banter
BARNEY Bayern, Bernay, Near-by
***BARODA** Aboard, Aborad, Abroad
BARONG Bangor, Brogan
BARONY Baryon
BARQUE Braque
BARRET Barter
***BARRIE** Ribera

BARSAC Scarab, Scarba
BARTER Barret
BARYON Barony
BASELY Basyle, Belays
BASEST Basset, Bastes, Beasts
BASHED Bedash
BASKER Bakers, Brakes, Breaks
BASNET Absent, Besant
BASSET Basset, Bastes, Beasts
BASTED Abdest
BASTER Barest, Bestar, Breast, Tarbes
BASTES Basest, Basset, Beasts
BASTON Batons
***BASUTO** U-boats
BASYLE Basely, Belays
BATHER Bareth, Bertha, Breath
BATHES Shebat
BATHOS Boshta
BATLET Battel, Battle, Tablet
BATMAN Bantam
BATONS Baston
BATTEL Batlet, Battle, Tablet
BATTER Tabret
BATTLE Batlet, Battel, Tablet
BATTUE Tubate
BAWBLE Wabble
BAWLER Warble
BAWLEY Bye-law
***BAYERN** Barney, Bernay, Near-by
BEAKED Debeak
BEAKER Rebake
BEARDS Ardebs, Breads, Debars, Sabred, Serdab
BEARER Breare
BEASTS Basest, Basset, Bastes
BEATER Berate, Rebate
BEAT-UP Upbeat
BECALM Clambe
BECAME Embace
***BECHAR** Breach, Rechab
BECKED Bedeck
BEDASH Bashed
BEDAUB Daubed

BEDECK Becked
BEDELL Belled
BEDLAM Ambled, Balmed,
　Beldam, Blamed, Lambed
BEDRAL Balder, Blared
BEDRID Bidder, Birded, Brided
BEDROP Probed
BEDSIT Bidets, Debits
BEDUCK Bucked
BEDUNG Bunged
BEDUST Bestud, Busted, Debuts
BEDYDE Bedyed
BEDYED Bedyde
BEE-FLY Feebly
BEFLUM Fumble
BEGILD Bilged
BEGINS Beings, Besing, Binges
BEGIRD Bridge
BEGONE Engobe
BEHEST Thebes
BEINGS Begins, Besing, Binges
BELATE Let-a-be
BELAYS Basely, Basyle
BELDAM Ambled, Balmed,
　Bedlam, Blamed, Lambed
*BELIAL Alible, Biella, Labile,
　Liable
BELIED Debile, Edible
BELIES Iblees
BELIVE Bevile
BELLED Bedell
BELUGA Blague
BEMEAN Bename
BEMETE Beteem
BEMIRE Bireme
BEMOIL Emboil, Emboli, Mobile
BENAME Bemean
BENDER Rebend
*BENGAL Bangle
BENIGN Bingen
*BENONI Bonnie
BEN-NUT Unbent
BEPATS Bespat
BERATE Beater, Rebate

BERETS Bester
*BERNAY Barney, Bayern, Near-by
BERTHA Bareth, Bather, Breath
*BERTIE Rebite
BESANT Absent, Basnet
BESING Begins, Beings, Binges
BESOMS Emboss
BESORT Osbert, Sorbet, Strobe
BESOTS Betoss
BESPAT Bepats
BESTAR Barest, Baster, Breast,
　Tarbes
BESTER Berets
BESTIR Bister, Bistre, Biters,
　Brites, Tribes
BESTUD Bedust, Busted, Debuts
BETAIL Albeit, Albite, Libate
BETEEM Bemete
BETORN Breton
BETOSS Besots
BETRIM Timber, Timbre
BETROD Debtor
BEVILE Belive
BIASED Abides
BICORN Bicron
BICRON Bicorn
BIDALE Abdiel, Bailed, Deblai
BIDDER Bedrid, Birded, Brided
BIDERS Brides, Debris, Rebids
BIDETS Bedsit, Debits
*BIELLA Alible, Belial, Labile,
　Liable
BIGGIN Gibing
BILGED Begild
BILLER Rebill
BINARY Brainy
BINATE Abient
BINDER Brined, Inbred, Rebind
*BINGEN Benign
BINGES Begins, Beings, Besing
BIONIC Niobic
BIRDED Bedrid, Bidder, Brided
BIRDIE Bridie
BIREME Bemire

BIRLED Bridle
BIRLES Birsle
BIRSLE Birles
*BISKRA Barkis
BISTER Bestir, Bistre, Biters, Brites, Tribes
BISTRE Bestir, Bister, Biters, Brites, Tribes
BISTRO Orbits
BITERS Bestir, Bister, Bistre, Brites, Tribes
BITTER Tibert
BLADED Balded
BLADES Sabled
BLAGUE Beluga
BLAINS Ablins
BLAISE Isabel
BLAMED Ambled, Balmed, Bedlam, Beldam, Lambed
BLAMER Ambler, Lamber, Marble, Ramble
BLARED Balder, Bedral
BLEARY Barely, Barley, Brayle
BLEATS Ablest, Ablets, Stable, Tables
BLITHE Thible
BLOATS Oblast
BLONDE Bolden, Dobeln
BLOODS 'Sblood
BLOUSE Boules, Obelus
BLOWED Bowled
BLOWER Bowler
BLOWSE Bowels, Elbows
BLOW-UP Upblow
BLUDGE Bugled, Bulged
BLUEST Bustle, Sublet, Subtle
BLUING Unglib
BLUNGE Bungle
BOARDS Abords, Adsorb, Broads, Dobras
BOARTS Aborts, Strabo, Tabors
BOATEL Lobate, Oblate
BOATER Borate, Orbate, Rebato
BOCHES Bosche

BOGLET Goblet
BOG-ORE Goober
*BOGOTA Tobago
BOILED Bolide
BOILER Reboil
*BOLBEC Cobble
BOLDEN Blonde, Dobeln
BOLDER Bordel
BOLIDE Boiled
BOLTER Rebolt
BOMBED Mobbed
BONING Ningbo
BONNET Bonten
BONNIE Benoni
BONSAI Bosnia
BONTEN Bonnet
BONZER Bronze
BOOERS Booser, Broose, Reboso
BORATE Boater, Orbate, Rebato
BORDEL Bolder
BORDER Roberd
BOREEN Enrobe
BORERS Resorb
BORING Orbing, Robing
*BORNEO Oberon
BOSCHE Boches
BOSHTA Bathos
*BOSNIA Bonsai
BOSSES Obsess
BO-TREE Rebote
BOULES Blouse, Obelus
BOULLE Lobule
BOURGS Burgos
BOURNE Unrobe
BOURNS Suborn
*BOURSE Bouser
BOUSER Bourse
BOUTON Unboot
BOWELS Blowse, Elbows
BOWERS Bowser, Browse
BOWERY Bowyer, Owerby
BOWLED Blowed
BOWLER Blower
BOWSER Bowers, Browse

BOWYER Bowery, Owerby
BRACED Decarb
BRACER Craber
*BRAHMI Mihrab
BRAIDE Abider, Air-bed
BRAIDS Disbar
BRAILS Brasil
BRAINS Abrins, Bairns, Brians,
Risban
BRAINY Binary
BRAIRD Briard
BRAISE Rabies, Serbia
BRAIZE Zeriba
BRAKED Barked, Debark
BRAKER Barker
BRAKES Bakers, Basker, Breaks
*BRAQUE Barque
BRASIL Brails
BRASSE Sabers, Sabres
BRAVED Adverb
BRAWLY Byrlaw
BRAYLE Barely, Barley, Bleary
BREACH Bechar, Rechab
BREADS Ardebs, Beards, Debars,
Sabred, Serdab
BREAKS Bakers, Basker, Brakes
BREAMS Ambers, Embars,
Sambre
BREARE Bearer
BREAST Barest, Baster, Bestar,
Tarbes
BREATH Bareth, Bather, Bertha
BREHON Hebron
*BRENDA Bander
*BRETON Betorn
BREWER Rebrew
*BRIANS Abrins, Bairns, Brains,
Risban
*BRIARD Braird
BRIBED Dibber, Ribbed
BRIBER Ribber
BRIDAL Labrid, Ribald
BRIDED Bedrid, Bidder, Birded
BRIDES Biders, Debris, Rebids

BRIDGE Begird
*BRIDIE Birdie
BRIDLE Birled
BRINED Binder, Inbred, Rebind
BRINES Nebris
BRITES Bestir, Bister, Bistre,
Biters, Tribes
BROADS Abords, Adsorb,
Boards, Dobras
BROGAN Bangor, Barong
BROMES Ombers, Ombres,
Somber, Sombre
BRONZE Bonzer
BROOMS Ombros, Sombor
BROOMY Byroom
BROOSE Booers, Reboso
BROWSE Bowers, Bowser
*BRUGGE Bugger
BRUISE Buries, Busier, Rubies
BRUMAL Labrum, Lumbar,
Umbral
*BRUNEI Rubine
BRUNET Bunter, Burnet
BRUTES Buster, Rebuts, Subter,
Surbet, Tubers
BUCKED Beduck
BUCKLE Lubeck
BUDDER Redbud
BUFFER Rebuff
BUGGER Brugge
BUGLED Bludge, Bulged
BUGLER Bulger, Burgle
BUILDS Sub-lid
BULGED Bugled, Bludge
BULGER Bugler, Burgle
BUMMLE Mumble
BUNDER Burden, Burned,
Unbred
BUNDLE Unbled
BUNGED Bedung
BUNGLE Blunge
BUNKED Debunk
BUNTED But-end
BUNTER Brunet, Burnet

BURBLE Lubber, Rubble
BURDEN Bunder, Burned, Unbred
BURDIE Buried, Rubied
BURGEE Gueber, Guebre
BURGLE Bugler, Bulger
*****BURGOS** Bourgs
BURIED Burdie, Rubied
BURIES Bruise, Busier, Rubies
BURKES Busker
BURLED Deblur
BURLER Burrel
BURNED Bunder, Burden, Unbred
BURNER Reburn
BURNET Brunet, Bunter
BURRED Deburr
BURREL Burler
BURSAE Abuser
BURSAL Labrus
BUSIER Bruise, Buries, Rubies
BUSKER Burkes
BUSMAN Subman
BUSMEN Submen
BUSTED Bedust, Bestud, Debuts
BUSTER Brutes, Rebuts, Subter, Surbet, Tubers
BUSTIC Cubist, Cubits
BUSTLE Bluest, Sublet, Subtle
BUT-END Bunted
BUTTON Nobbut
BY-BLOW Wobbly
BYE-LAW Bawley
BY-FORM Formby
BYRLAW Brawly
BYROOM Broomy

CABRIE Caribe
CADDIE Eddaic
CADENT Canted, Decant
CADETS Casted, Ectads
CADGER Graced
CADMIA Adamic
CADRES Cedars, Sacred, Scared

CAFILA Facial
CAHIER Archie, Eriach
*****CAHORS** Orachs
CAIMAN Maniac
CAISON Casino
*****CALDER** Cradle, Credal
CALICO Accoil
CALIFS Fiscal
CALKED Lacked
CALKER Lacker, Rackle, Recalk
CALLER Cellar, Recall
CALLUS Sulcal
CALMED Macled
CALMER Carmel, Marcel
CALQUE Claque
CALVER Carvel, Claver
CALVES Cavels, Claves, Sclave
CAMARA Maraca
CAMBER Cembra, Crambe
CAMELS Macles, Mascle, Mescal, Scamel
CAMEOS Cosmea
CAMION Anomic, Conima, Manioc
CAMISE Amices, Macies
CAMPED Decamp
*****CANDIA** Dacian
CANDIE Cnidea, Decani
CANDLE Lanced
CANEHS Encash
CANERS Casern, Cranes, Crenas, Rances, Sarcen
CANGUE Uncage
CANINE Encina, Neanic
CANKER Neckar, Reckan
CANNOT Canton
CANOED Acnode, Deacon
CANTED Cadent, Decant
CANTER Carnet, Centra, Creant, Cretan, Nectar, Recant, Tanrec, Trance
CANTLE Cental, Lancet
CANTON Cannot

CANTOR Carton, Contra, Carnot, Craton

CANTOS Actons, Cotans, Octans, Snacot

CANTUS Tucans, Tuscan, Uncast

*CANUTE Uncate

CAPERS Casper, Crapes, Escarp, Pacers, Parsec, Recaps, Secpar, Scrape, Spacer

CAPING Pacing

*CAPOTE Toecap

CAPTAN Catnap

CARBON Corban

CARDER Redcar

CAREEN Enrace, Recane

CAREME Amerce, Raceme

CARESS Carses, Crases, Escars, Scares, Scraes, Seracs

CARETS Cartes, Caster, Caters, Crates, Cresta, Reacts, Recast, Traces

CARIBE Cabrie

CARIES Cerias, Serica

CARINA Acinar, Arnica, Crania

CARING Arcing, Racing

CARKED Arcked, Craked, Dacker, Racked

CARLES Clares, Clears, Sarcel, Scaler, Sclera

*CARLOS Carols, Claros, Corals

*CARMEL Calmer, Marcel

CARNET Canter, Centra, Creant, Cretan, Nectar, Recant, Tanrec, Trance

*CARNOT Cantor, Carton, Contra, Craton

*CAROLE Coaler, Oracle, Recoal

CAROLI Lorica

CAROLS Carlos, Claros, Corals

CAROMS Marcos

CARPED Craped, Redcap

CARPEL Parcel, Placer

CARPET Pre-act

CARROT Trocar

CARSES Caress, Crases, Escars, Scares, Scraes, Seracs

CARTED Cedrat, Crated, Dectra, Redact, Traced

CARTEL Claret, Rectal, Tarcel

CARTER Arrect, Crater, Tracer

CARTES Carets, Caster, Caters, Crates, Cresta, Reacts, Recast, Traces

CARTOL Crotal

CARTON Carnot, Cantor, Contra, Craton

CARVED Craved

CARVEL Calver, Claver

CARVEN Cavern, Craven

CARVER Craver

CASABA Abacas

CASEIN Incase

CASERN Caners, Cranes, Crenas, Rances, Sarcen

CASHED Chased

*CASHEL Chelas, Laches, Sachel

CASHES Chases, Chasse

CASING Signac

CASINO Caison

CASKED Sacked

*CASPER Capers, Crapes, Escarp, Pacers, Parsec, Recaps, Secpar, Scrape, Spacer

CASQUE Sacque

*CASSEL Scales

CASSIA Isaacs

CASTED Cadets, Ectads

CASTER Carets, Cartes, Caters, Crates, Cresta, Reacts, Recast, Traces

CASTLE Cleats, Eclats, Sclate

CASTOR Actors, Castro, Co-star, Croats, Roctas, Scrota, Tarocs

*CASTRO Actors, Castor, Co-star, Croats, Roctas, Scrota, Tarocs

CASUAL Casula, Causal

CASULA Casual, Causal

CATERS Carets, Cartes, Caster, Crates, Cresta, Reacts, Recast, Traces
CATION Action, Atonic
CATNAP Captan
CATRIG Tragic
CATSUP Upcast
CAUDLE Cedula, Claude
CAULIS Aulics, Clusia
CAUSAL Casual, Casula
CAUSED Sauced
CAUSEN Uncase, Usance
CAUSER Cesura, Creusa, Erucas, Saucer
CAUSEY Cayuse
CAUTER Acture, Curate
CAVEAT Vacate
CAVE-IN Incave
CAVELS Calves, Claves, Sclave
CAVERN Carven, Craven
CAVIAR Aircav
CAVIES Vesica
CAVILS Clavis, Slavic
CAVITE Active
CAYUSE Causey
CEASER Crease, Recase, Searce
CEDARN Craned, Dancer, Ranced
CEDARS Cadres, Sacred, Scared
CEDERS Creeds, Screed
CEDRAT Carted, Crated, Dectra, Redact, Traced
*****CEDROS** Coders, Credos, Scored
CEDULA Caudle, Claude
CEILED Cieled, Decile
*****CELINA** Ancile, Inlace
CELLAR Caller, Recall
CEMBRA Camber, Crambe
CENSED Scened
CENSER Screen, Secern
CENSOR Crones, Oncers, Recons
CENTAL Cantle, Lancet
CENTER Centre, Recent, Tenrec

CENTRA Canter, Carnet, Creant, Cretan, Nectar, Recant, Tanrec, Trance
CENTRE Center, Recent, Tenrec
CEORLS Closer, Cresol, Escrol
CERATE Create, Ecarte
CERCUS Cruces
CEREAL Alerce, Relace
*****CEREUS** Ceruse, Cesure, Creuse, Recuse, Rescue, Secure
CERIAS Caries, Serica
CERING Cringe
CERIPH Cipher
CERISE Re-ices
CERITE Certie, Recite, Tierce
CERIUM Uremic
CEROUS Course, Crouse, Crusoe, Source
CERRIS Criers, Ricers
CERTES Erects, Resect, Secret
CERTIE Cerite, Recite, Tierce
CERUSE Cereus, Cesure, Creuse, Recuse, Rescue, Secure
*****CESENA** Encase, Seance, Seneca
CESIUM Miscue
CESSER Recess, Screes
CESTUI Cueist, Cuties
CESTUS Scutes
CESURA Causer, Creusa, Erucas, Saucer
CESURE Cereus, Ceruse, Creuse, Recuse, Rescue, Secure
CETANE Tenace
CETINE Entice
CHAIRS Charis, Rachis
CHALET Thecal, Thecla
CHALKY Hackly
CHANTS Snatch, Stanch
CHAPEL Lepcha, Pleach
CHAPKA Pachak
CHARED Arched
CHARES Arches, Chaser, Eschar, Raches, Search
CHARGE Creagh

*CHARIS Chairs, Rachis
*CHARON Anchor, Archon, Rancho
CHARTS Scarth, Starch
CHASED Cashed
CHASER Arches, Chares, Eschar, Raches, Search
CHASES Cashes, Chasse
CHASSE Cashes, Chases
CHASTE Cheats, Sachet, Scathe, Taches
CHATTA Attach
CHAUNT Nautch
CHEATS Chaste, Sachet, Scathe, Taches
CHEEPS Peches, Speech
CHEERO Choree, Cohere, Echoer, Reecho
CHEERS Creesh
CHEERY Reechy
CHEIRO Coheir, Heroic
CHELAS Cashel, Laches, Sachel
CHENAR Enarch
CHENET Thence
*CHEOPS Epochs
CHESIL Chiels, Chiles, Chisel, Elchis, Schlei
CHESTY Scythe
CHICLE Cliche
CHICON Cochin
CHIDER Dreich, Herdic
CHIELD Childe
CHIELS Chesil, Chiles, Chisel, Elchis, Schlei
CHILDE Chield
CHILES Chesil, Chiels, Chisel, Elchis, Schlei
CHIMED Miched
CHIMER Micher
CHINAR Inarch
CHINED Inched, Niched
CHINES Chinse, Inches, Niches
CHINSE Chines, Inches, Niches
CHIN-UP Punchi

CHIRKS Kirsch, Schrik
CHIRMS Chrism, Smirch
CHIRRE Richer
CHIRTS Christ, Criths
CHISEL Chesil, Chiels, Chiles, Elchis, Schlei
CHOICE Echoic
CHOIRS Ichors, Orchis
CHOKED Hocked
CHOKER Hocker
CHOKEY Hockey
CHOLER Orchel
*CHOLET Clothe
CHOOSE Cohoes
CHOPIN Phonic
CHORAL Lorcha, Orchal
CHOREA Horace, Ochrea, Orache, Rochea
CHOREE Cheero, Cohere, Echoer, Re-echo
CHORES Cosher, Ochres
CHOUSE Ouches
CHOUTS Schout, Scouth
CHRISM Chirms, Smirch
*CHRIST Chirts, Criths
CHYPRE Cypher
CICALA Alcaic
CIDERS Dicers, Scried
CIELED Ceiled, Decile
CIERGE Griece
CIGALE Gaelic
CILICE Icicle
CINDER Crined
CINEMA Anemic, Iceman
CINEOL Nicole
CINQUE Quince
CINTRE Cretin
CIPHER Ceriph
CIRCAR Ric-rac
CIRCLE Cleric
CISTED Edicts
CITHER Ericht, Thrice
CITIES Iciest
CITING Ticing

CITRAL Rictal
CITRIC Critic
CITRIN Nitric
CITRUS Rictus, Rustic
CIVETS Evicts, Vectis
*****CLAIRE** Eclair, Lacier
CLAMBE Becalm
CLAQUE Calque
*****CLARES** Carles, Clears, Sarcel,
    Scaler, Sclera
CLARET Cartel, Rectal, Tarcel
CLAROS Carlos, Carols, Corals
*****CLAUDE** Caudle, Cedula
CLAVER Calver, Carvel
CLAVES Calves, Cavels, Sclave
CLAVIS Cavils, Slavic
CLAYED Lac-dye
CLEANS Ancles, Lances, Lencas,
    Senlac
CLEARS Carles, Clares, Sarcel,
    Scaler, Sclera
CLEATS Castle, Eclats, Sclate
CLEEKS Seckel
CLERIC Circle
CLICHE Chicle
CLIENT Lentic
CLINGY Glycin
CLIPES Splice
CLODLY Coldly
CLOGGY Coggly
CLOKED Locked
CLONUS Consul
CLOSED Dolces
CLOSER Dolces
CLOSER Ceorls, Cresol, Escrol
CLOSET Clotes
CLOTES Closet
CLOTHE Cholet
*****CLOTHO** Coolth
CLOUTS Locust
CLOVER Velcro
CLOVES Scovel
*****CLOVIS** Volsci
*****CLUNES** Uncles

CLUSIA Aulics, Caulis
CLUTCH Cultch
CNIDAE Candie, Decani
COAITA Atocia
COALED Alcedo
COALER Carole, Oracle, Recoal
COARSE Rosace
COATIS Scotia
COBBLE Bolbec
COBRES Scrobe
*****COCHIN** Chicon
COCKER Recock
CODDER Corded
CODEIN Coined
CODERS Cedros, Credos, Scored
COEVAL Alcove, Leroca
COGGLY Cloggy
COHEIR Cheiro, Heroic
COHERE Cheero, Choree, Echoer,
    Re-echo
COHOES Choose
COILED Docile
COINED Codein
COINER Enrico, Orcein, Orcine,
    Recoin
COLDLY Clodly
COLEUS Oscule
COLLIE Ocelli
COLONS Consol
COLTER Lector
COMARB Crambo
COMBAT Tombac
COMBER Recomb
COME-ON Oncome
COMICS Cosmic
COMING Gnomic
COMITY Myotic
COMSAT Mascot, Satcom
CONDER Corned
CONDOR Cordon
CONGAS Gascon, Scogan
CONIES Cosine, Oscine, Soncie
CONIMA Anomic, Camion,
    Manioc

CONINE Connie
CONKED Nocked
CONKER Reckon
*****CONNIE** Conine
*****CONRAD** Dacron
CONSOL Colons
CONSUL Clonus
CONTOS Nostoc, Oncost
CONTRA Carnot, Cantor, Carton, Craton
CONVEY Covyne
COOKER Recook
COOLED Locoed
COOLER Recool
COOLTH Clotho
COONTY Tycoon
COPERS Corpse, Cropes, Proces
COPIED Epodic
COPITA Atopic
COPPIN Pin-cop
COPULA Cupola
CORALS Carlos, Carols, Claros
CORBAN Carbon
CORDED Codder
CORDON Condor
CORERS Crores, Scorer
CORKED Docker, Redock, Rocked
CORKER Recork, Rocker
CORNEA Nocera
CORNED Conder
CORNET Cronet
CORNUS Cronus
CORONA Racoon
CORPSE Copers, Cropes, Proces
CORPUS Croups
CORRIE Orrice
CORSES Crosse, Scores, Scorse
CORSET Cortes, Coster, Escort, Recost, Rectos, Scoter, Sector, Tresco
*****CORTES** Corset, Coster, Escort, Recost, Rectos, Scoter, Sector, Tresco

CORVES Covers
CORVET Covert, Vector
COSHER Chores, Ochres
COSINE Conies, Oscine, Soncie
COSMEA Cameos
COSMIC Comics
COSSET Estocs
CO-STAR Actors, Castor, Castro, Croats, Roctas, Scrota, Tarcos
COSTER Corset, Cortes, Escort, Recost, Rectos, Scoter, Sector, Tresco
COSTUS Custos, Scouts
COTANS Actons, Cantos, Octans, Snacot
COTISE Oecist
COUNTS Tucson
COUPER Croupe, Cuerpo, Recoup
COUPON Uncoop
COURSE Cerous, Crouse, Crusoe, Source
COURTS Crouts, Scruto, Turcos
COUTER Croute
COUTHY Touchy
COUTIL Toluic
COVERS Corves
COVERT Corvet, Vector
COVYNE Convey
COWERS Escrow
COYOTE Oocyte
CRABER Bracer
CRADLE Calder, Credal
CRAKED Arcked, Carked, Dacker, Racked
CRAKES Creaks, Sacker, Screak
CRAMBE Camber, Cembra
CRAMBO Comarb
CRAMES Creams, Macers, Scream
CRAMPS Scramp
CRANED Cedarn, Dancer, Ranced

CRANES Caners, Casern, Crenas, Rances, Sarcen
CRANIA Acinar, Arnica, Carina
CRAPED Carped, Redcap
CRAPES Casper, Capers, Escrap, Pacers, Parsec, Recaps, Secpar, Scrape, Spacer
CRASES Caress, Carses, Escars, Scares, Scraes, Seracs
CRATED Carted, Cedrat, Dectra, Redact, Traced
CRATER Arrect, Carter, Tracer
CRATES Carets, Cartes, Caster, Caters, Cresta, Reacts, Recast, Traces
CRATON Cantor, Carnot, Carton, Contra
CRAVAT Vratca
CRAVED Carved
CRAVEN Carven, Cavern
CRAVER Carver
CRAWLS Scrawl
CREAGH Charge
CREAKS Crakes, Sacker, Screak
CREAKY Yacker
CREAMS Crames, Macers, Scream
CREANT Canter, Carnet, Centra, Cretan, Nectar, Recant, Tanrec, Trance
CREASE Ceaser, Recase, Searce
CREASY Scarey, Scraye
CREATE Cerate, Ecarte
CREDAL Calder, Cradle
CREDIT Direct, Triced
CREDOS Cedros, Coders, Scored
CREEDS Ceders, Screed
CREEPS Crepes, Preces
CREESH Cheers
CREMOR Cromer
CRENAS Caners, Casern, Cranes, Rances, Sarcen
CREPES Creeps, Preces

*****CREPIS** Cripes, Persic, Precis, Prices, Spicer
CRESOL Ceorls, Closer, Escrol
*****CRESTA** Carets, Cartes, Caster, Caters, Crates, Reacts, Recast, Traces
*****CRETAN** Canter, Carnet, Centra, Creant, Nectar, Recant, Tanrec, Trance
CRETIN Cintre
*****CREUSA** Causer, Cesura, Erucas
*****CREUSE** Cereus, Ceruse, Cesure, Recuse, Rescue, Secure
CREWED Decrew
CRIERS Cerris, Ricers
CRIKEY Rickey
*****CRIMEA** Mercia
CRIMED Dermic
CRIMES Scrime
CRIMPS Scrimp
CRINED Cinder
CRINES Scrine
CRINGE Cering
CRIPES Crepis, Persic, Precis, Prices, Spicer
CRISES Scries
CRISPY Cypris
CRISTA Racist
CRITHS Chirts, Christ
CRITIC Critic
*****CROATS** Actors, Castor, Castro, Co-star, Roctas, Scrota, Tarocs
CROCUS Occurs, Roccus, Succor
*****CROMER** Cremor
CRONES Censor, Oncers, Recons
CRONET Cornet
*****CRONOS** Croons
*****CRONUS** Cornus
CROONS Cronos
CROPES Copers, Corpse, Proces
CRORES Corers, Scorer
CROSSE Corses, Scores, Scorse
CROTAL Carlot

CROUPE Couper, Cuerpo,
  Recoup
CROUPS Corpus
CROUSE Cerous, Course, Crusoe,
  Source
CROUTE Couter
CROUTS Courts, Scruto, Turcos
CRUCES Cercus
CRUDER Curred
CRUETS Cruset, Custer, Eructs,
  Rectus, Recuts, Truces
CRUISE Crusie, Curies
CRUNTS Scrunt
CRUSES Curses, Cusser
CRUSET Cruets, Custer, Eructs,
  Rectus, Recuts, Truces
CRUSIE Cruise, Curies
*****CRUSOE** Cerous, Course, Crouse,
  Source
CRUSTY Curtsy
CUBIST Bustic, Cubits
CUBITS Bustic, Cubist
CUEIST Cestui, Cuties
CUERPO Couper, Croupe,
  Recoup
CUESTA Acutes
CUITER Curiet, Uretic
*****CULION** Ulicon, Uncoil
CULTCH Clutch
CULTER Cutler, Reluct
CUMBER Recumb
CUNEAL Launce, Lucena, Unlace
CUPIDS Cuspid, Sidcup
CUPOLA Copula
CURATE Acture, Cauter
CURDLE Curled
CURERS Curser, Recurs
CURIAL Uracil, Uralic, Lauric
CURIES Curise, Crusie
CURIET Cuiter, Uretic
CURLED Curdle
CURRED Cruder
CURSER Curers, Recurs
CURSES Cruses, Cusser

CURSUS Ruscus
CURTSY Crusty
CUSCUS Succus
CUSPID Cupids, Sidcup
CUSSER Cruses, Curses
*****CUSTER** Cruets, Cruset, Eructs,
  Rectus, Recuts, Truces
CUSTOS Costus, Scouts
CUTIES Cestui, Cueist
CUTLER Culter, Reluct
CUTLET Cuttle
CUT-OFF Off-cut
CUT-OUT Outcut
CUTTLE Cutlet
CYDERS Descry
CYPHER Chypre
CYPRIS Crispy

DABBER Barbed, Debarb
*****DACIAN** Candia
DACKER Arcted, Carked,
  Craked, Racked
*****DACRON** Conrad
DADDLE Addled
DAEMON Menado, Moaned,
  Modane, Modena, Nomade
DAFTER Farted, Rafted
DAGGER Ragged
DAGGLE Lagged
DAGOES Dosage, Sea-dog, Sea-
  god
DAIDLE Laddie, Dialed
DAIKER Darkie, Raiked
DAIMEN Damien, Demain,
  Maiden, Mained, Median,
  Medina
DAIMON Domain
*****DAIREN** Darien, Derain, Rained,
  Randie
DALERS Alders, Sardel
*****DALLAS** Sallad
*****DAMIEN** Daimen, Demain,
  Maiden, Mained, Median,
  Medina

DAMMER Rammed
DAMNED Demand, Madden
DAMPER Ramped
DAMSEL Medals
DAMSON Monads, Nomads
DANCER Cedarn, Craned,
  Ranced
DANCES Ascend
DANDER Darned, Narded
DANDLE Landed
DANGER Gander, Garden,
  Grande, Ranged
DANGLE Angled, Glenda,
  Lagend
*****DANIEL** Aldine, Alined, Delian,
  Denial, Lead-in, Nailed
*****DANISH** Dinahs, Sandhi
*****DANITE** Detain, Taiden
DANKER Darken, Narked,
  Ranked
DANTON Donnat
DAPPER Rapped
DAPPLE Lapped, Palped
DARETH Dearth, Hatred, Red-
  hat, Thread
DARGER Garred, Gerard, Grader,
  Regard
*****DARIEN** Dairen, Derain, Rained,
  Randie
DARING Gradin
*****DARIUS** Radius
DARKEN Danker, Narked,
  Ranked
DARKIE Daiker, Raiked
DARKLE Larked
DARNED Dander, Narded
DARNEL Aldern, Enlard, Lander,
  Randle, Reland
DARNER Errand, Redarn, Renard
DARTED Traded
DARTER Dartre, Retard, Retrad,
  Tarred, Trader
DARTRE Darter, Retard, Retrad,
  Tarred, Trader

*****DARWEN** Andrew, Dawner,
  Rawden, Wander, Warden,
  Warned
*****DARWIN** Inward
DASHED Shaded
DASHER Rashed, Shader, Shared
DASHES Sashed, Shades
DASSIE Asides, Sadies
DATERS Adrets, Desart, Stared,
  Trades, Treads
*****DATSUN** Daunts
DAUBED Bedaud
DAUNER Undear, Unread
DAUNTS Datsun
*****DAVIES** Advise, Avised, Visaed
DAWDED Wadded
DAWDLE Waddle
DAWLEY Yawled
DAWNER Andrew, Darwen,
  Rawden, Wander, Warden,
  Warned
DAWTIE Waited
DAY-FLY Ladyfy
DEACON Acnode, Canoed
DEAFER Feared
DEAFLY Flayed
DEALED Delead, Leaded
DEALER Leader, Redeal, Releard
DEANER Dearne, Earned,
  Endear, Neared
DEARER Reader, Reared, Redare,
  Reread
DEARES Aredes, Erased, Reseda,
  Seared
DEARIE Rediae
DEARNE Deaner, Earned,
  Endear, Neared
DEARTH Dareth, Hatred, Red-
  hat, Thread
DEASIL Aisled, Ideals, Ladies,
  Sailed
DEATHS Hasted, 'Sdeath, Tashed
DEAVED Evaded
DEBARB Barbed, Dabber

DEBARK Barked, Braked
DEBARS Ardebs, Beards, Breads,
　Sabred, Serdab
DEBASE Sea-bed
DEBEAK Beaked
DEBILE Belied, Edible
DEBITS Bedsit, Bidets
DEBLAI Abdiel, Bailed, Bidale
DEBLUR Burled
DEBRIS Biders, Brides, Rebids
DEBTOR Betrod
DEBUNK Bunked
DEBURR Burred
DEBUTS Bedust, Bestud, Busted
DECALS Scaled
DECAMP Camped
DECANI Candie, Cnidae
DECANT Cadent, Canted
DECARB Braced
DECIDE De-iced
DECILE Ceiled, Cieled
DECKER Recked
DECREE Recede
DECREW Crewed
*****DECTRA** Carted, Cedrat, Crated,
　Redact, Traced
DEDANS Sadden, Sanded
DEDUCE Deuced, Educed
DEEPEN Peened
DEEPER Peered
DEFANG Fag-end, Fanged
DEFEAT Feated
DEFEND Fended
DEFINE Feed-in
DEFLEX Flexed
DEFLUX Fluxed
DEFORM Formed
DEFOUL Fouled
DEFRAY Frayed
DEGUMS Smudge
DEGUST Gusted
DEHORN Horned

DEHORS Herods, Hordes,
　Horsed, Reshod, Rhodes,
　Shoder, Shored
DEHORT Red-hot
DE-ICED Decide
DEIGNS Design, Dinges, Nidges,
　Sdeign, Signed, Singed
DEISTS Desist, Sisted
DELATE Elated, Tele-ad
DELEAD Dealed, Leaded
*****DELIAN** Aldine, Alined, Daniel,
　Denial, Lead-in, Nailed
DELIST Idlest, Listed, Silted,
　Tildes
DELTAS Desalt, Lasted, Salted,
　Slated, Stadle, Staled
DELUDE Eluded
DEMAIN Daimen, Damien,
　Maiden, Mained, Median,
　Medina
DEMAND Damned, Madden
DEMARK Marked
DEMEAN Amende, Amened
DEMISE Medise
DEMISS Missed
DEMIST Demits, Misted, Stimed
DEMITS Demist, Misted, Stimed
DEMONS Esmond
DEMOTE Emoted
DEMOTH Method, Mothed
DEMURE Emured
DENARY Yarned
DENGUE Unedge
DENIAL Aldine, Alined, Daniel,
　Delian, Lead-in, Nailed,
DENIED Indeed
DENIER Edirne, Nereid, Reined,
　Renied
DENIES Denise, Desine, Seined
*****DENISE** Denies, Desine, Seined
*****DENNIS** Sinned
DENSER Enders, Resend, Sender
DENTED Tended
DENTEX Extend

DENTIN Indent, Intend, Tinned
*DENTON Tendon
DENUDE Dudeen, Duende, Dundee, Endued
*DENVER Nerved, Revend, Vender, Verden
DEODAR Adored, Roaded
DEPART Drapet, Parted, Petard, Prated, Traped
DEPEND Pended
DEPERM Permed, Premed
DEPLOY Podley, Ployed
DEPONE Opened
DEPORT Ported, Red-top
DEPOSE Epodes, Speedo
DEPOTS Despot, Posted, Stoped
DERAIL Adriel, Laired, Lerida, Railed, Relaid
DERAIN Rained, Randie
DERATE Redate, Teared
DERHAM Harmed
DERIDE Diedre
DERING Dinger, Engird, Girned, Ringed
DERIVE Reived, Revied, Rieved
DERMAL Marled, Medlar
DERMIC Crimed
DERNED Redden
DERRIS Driers, Reirds, Riders, Sirred
DERVIS Divers, Drives
DESALT Deltas, Lasted, Salted, Slated, Stadle, Staled
DESART Adrets, Daters, Stared, Trades, Treads
DESCRY Cyders
DESERT Deters, Rested
DESIGN Deigns, Dinges, Nidges, Sdeign, Signed, Singed
DESINE Denies, Denise, Seined
DESIRE Eiders, Reside
DESIST Deists, Sisted
DESMAN Amends, Menads
DESPIN Piends, Sniped, Spined

DESPOT Depots, Posted, Stoped
DETAIL Dietal, Dilate, Tailed
DETAIN Danite, Taiden
DETENT Netted, Tented
DETERS Desert, Rested
DETEST Tested
DETORT Dotter, Rotted
DETOUR Douter, Outred, Redout, Routed, Toured
DEUCED Deduce, Educed
DEUCES Educes, Seduce
*DEURNE Endure, Enured
DEVEST Vested
DEVILS Slived
DEVISE Sieved, Viseed
DEVOID Voided
DEVOIR Voider
DEVOTE Vetoed
*DEWALI Wailed
DEWANI Edwina, Wained
DEWILY Widely, Wieldy
DEWING Winged
DEWITT Witted
DEWLAP Pawled
DIADEM Maided
DIALED Daidle, Laddie
DIALOG Algoid
DIAMYL Milady
DIAPER Paired, Pardie, Repaid
DIAXON Dioxan
DIBBER Bribed, Ribbed
DICERS Ciders, Scried
DICKER Ricked
DIDDER Ridded
DIDDLE Lidded
DIDOES Diodes
DIEDRE Deride
DIESEL Ediles, Elides, Sedile, Seidel, Seiled
DIESES Seised
DIETAL Detail, Dilate, Tailed
DIETED Edited
DIETER Re-edit, Retied, Tiered
DIFFER Riffed

DIGEST Gisted
DIGGER Rigged
DIKERS Risked
DILATE Detail, Dietal, Tailed
DILDOE Doiled
DIMBLE Limbed
DIMMER Rimmed
DIMPLE Limped
DINAHS Danish, Sandhi
DINERS Rinsed
DINGER Dering, Engird, Ginred,
　Ringed
DINGES Deigns, Design, Nidges,
　Sdeign, Signed, Singed
DINGEY Dyeing
DINGLE Elding, Engild, Gliden,
　Ingled
DINING Indign, Niding
DINKEY Kidney
DINNLE Linden, Linned
DINTED Tinded
DIODES Didoes
*****DIONES** Donsie, Edison, Nidose,
　Noised, No-side, Onside, Side-
　on
DIOXAN Diaxon
DIPLOE Dipole, Peloid
DIPOLE Diploe, Peloid
DIPPER Ripped
DIRECT Credit, Triced
DIREST Driest, Ridest, Stride
DIRGES Grides, Grised, Ridges
DIRKED Kidder
DIRLED Riddel, Riddle
DISARM Marids
DISBAR Braids
DISHED Eddish
DISHES Hissed
*****DISNEY** Sidney
DISPEL Disple, Lisped, Sliped,
　Spiled
DISPLE Dispel, Lisped, Sliped,
　Spiled
DISTAL Ditals

DISUSE Issued
DITALS Distal
DITHER Rideth
DITONE Intoed
DIURNA Durian
DIVERS Dervis, Drives
DIVERT Verdit
DIVEST Stived, Vedist
DOABLE Albedo
DOBBER Robbed
*****DOBELN** Blonde, Bolden
DOBRAS Abords, Adsorb,
　Boards, Broads
DOCILE Coiled
DOCKER Corked, Redock,
　Rocked
DODDER Rodded
DODGER Red-dog
DODMAN Odd-man
DOESN'T Donets, Ostend,
　Stoned
DOGATE Dotage, Togaed
DOG-END God-den
DOGGER Gorged
DOGLEG Logged
DOILED Dildoe
DOINGS Dosing
DOLCES Closed
DOLINE Indole, Leonid
DOLIUM Idolum, Moduli
DOLMAN Almond
DOLOSE Loosed, Oodles, Sooled
DOMAIN Daimon
DOMIFY Modify
DOMINE Monied
DONATE Atoned, Nodate
*****DONETS** Doesn't, Ostend,
　Stoned
DONNAT Danton
DONSIE Diones, Edison, Nidose,
　Noised, No-side, Onside, Side-
　on
DONUTS Stound
DOOVER Overdo

DOPERS Pedros, Prosed
DOPIER Period
DOPING Pongid
DOPPER Proped
*__DORCAS__ Dracos
*__DORIAN__ Inroad, Ordain
DORING Roding
DORMIE Moider
DORSEL Droles, Resold, Solder
DORSER Orders
DORSES Dosers, Dosser, Sordes
*__DORSET__ Doters, Sordet, Sorted,
Stored, Strode, Trodes
DOSAGE Dagoes, Sea-dog, Sea-
god
DOSERS Dorses, Dosser, Sordes
DOSING Doings
DOSSER Dorses, Dosers, Sordes
DOSSIL Sloids, Solids
DOTAGE Dogate, Togaed
DOTERS Dorset, Sordet, Sorted,
Stored, Strode, Trodes
DOTTER Detort, Rotted
DOTTLE Lotted
DOUCHE Ouched
DOURER Ordure
DOUSER Roused, Soured
DOUSES Soused
DOUTER Detour, Outred,
Redout, Routed, Toured
DOWELS Slowed, Sowled
DOWERS Dowser, Drowse,
Worsed
DOWLAS Woalds
DOWNER Wonder
DOWSER Drowse, Dowers,
Worsed
DOWSES Sowsed
DRACOS Dorcas
DRAGEE Agreed, Geared
DRAGON Gardon, Gondar
DRAMAS Madras
DRAPED Padder, Parded, Praded

DRAPES Padres, Parsed, Rasped,
Repads, Spader, Spared, Spread
DRAPET Depart, Parted, Petard,
Prated, Traped
DRAUNT Durant, Tundra
DRAWED Edward, Warded
DRAWER Redraw, Reward,
Warder, Warred
DRAYED Yarded
DREADS Adders, Readds, Sadder
DREARY Yarred
DREICH Chider, Herdic
DRIERS Derris, Reirds, Riders,
Sirred
DRIEST Direst, Ridest, Stride
DRIVEN Verdin
DRIVES Dervis, Divers
DROGUE Drouge, Gourde,
Rogued, Rouged
DROICH Orchid, Rhodic
DROLES Dorsel, Resold, Solder
DROLLY Lordly
DROMES Smored
DRONED Nodder
DRONES Rondes, Snored, Sorned
DRONGO Gordon, Grodno
DROOME Moored, Roomed
DROUGE Drogue, Gourde,
Rogued, Rouged
DROWSE Dowser
DRUIDS Siddur
DRUPEL Purled
DRUPES Dupers, Perdus, Prudes,
Pursed
*__DRUSES__ Duress
DUALIN Lindau, Unlaid
DUBBER Rubbed
DUCKER Rucked
DUDEEN Denude, Duende,
Dundee, Endued
DUENDE Denude, Dudeen,
Dundee, Endued
DUETTO Touted
DUFFEL Duffle, Luffed

DUFFER Ruffed
DUFFLE Duffel, Luffed
DUKERY Duyker
DULIAS Lusiad
DUMOSE Moused, Soumed, Usedom
DUMPLE Lumped, Plumed
__DUNBAR__ Durban
DUNCES Secund
__DUNDEE__ Denude, Dudeen, Duende, Endued
DUNDER Durden
DUNGED Nudged
DUNITE United, Untied
DUNNER Undern
DUPERS Drupes, Perdus, Prudes, Pursed
DUPION Unipod
DURANT Draunt, Tundra
__DUNBAR__ Durban
__DURBAN__ Dunbar
DURDEN Dunder
DURESS Druses
DURIAN Diurna
DURING Ungird
DUSTER Redust, Rudest, Rusted
DUYKER Dukery
DWALES Swaled, Wealds
DWINED Winded
DWINES Widens, Widnes
DYEING Dingey
DYNAMO Monday

EAGLET Galtee, Gelate, Legate, Teagle, Telega
EAGRES Agrees, Grease
__EALING__ Genial, Linage
EAR-CAP Parcae
EARFUL Ferula
EARING Gainer, Graine, Regain, Regian, Regina
EARNED Dearne, Deaner, Endear, Neared
EARNER Nearer, Re-earn

EARTHS Haters, Hearts, Rathes, Sarthe, 'Sheart
EARTHY Hearty
EASELS Easles, Eassel, Leases
EASIER Aeries
EASING Agnise
EASLES Easels, Eassel, Leases
EASSEL Easels, Easles, Leases
EASSIL Aisles, Laisse, Lassie
EASTED Seated, Sedate, Teased
EASTER Aretes, Asteer, Eaters, Reates, Reseat, Saeter, Seater, Steare, Staree, Teaser, Teresa
__EASTON__ Atones, Seaton
EATCHE Hecate, Thecae
EATERS Aretes, Asteer, Easter, Reates, Reseat, Saeter, Seater, Steare, Staree, Teaser, Teresa
EATEST Estate, Teaset, Testae
EATHLY Hyetal
EATING Ingate, Tangie, Teaing
ECARTE Cerate, Create
ECHOER Cheero, Choree, Cohere, Re-echo
ECHOIC Choice
ECLAIR Claire, Lacier
ECLATS Castle, Cleats, Sclate
ECTADS Cadets, Casted
__EDDAIC__ Caddie
EDDISH Dished
__EDENIC__ Incede
EDIBLE Belied, Debile
EDICTS Cisted
EDILES Diesel, Elides, Sedile, Seidel, Seiled
__EDIRNE__ Denier, Nereid, Reined, Renied
__EDISON__ Diones, Donsie, Nidose, Noised, No-side, Onside, Side-on
EDITED Dieted
EDITOR Rioted, Tie-rod, Triode
EDUCED Deduce, Deuced
EDUCES Deuces, Seduce
__EDWARD__ Drawed, Warded

*EDWINA Dewani, Wained
EEL-SET Steele
EGALLY Galley
EGERAN Enrage, Genera
EGGARS Aggers, Gagers, Sagger, Seggar
EGGLER Legger
EGOIST Stogie
EGRESS Greses, Serges
EGRETS Greets, Regest, Regets
EIDENT Endite
EIDERS Desire, Reside
EIGHTH Height
EIGNES Genies, Seeing, Siegen
*ELAEIS Laesie
ELANCE Enlace
ELANDS Ladens, Landes, Sendal
ELANET Lateen
ELAPID Aliped, Paidle, Pailed, Pleiad
ELAPSE Asleep, Please, Sapele
ELATED Delate, Tele-ad
ELATER Relate, Tralee
ELATES Steale, Stelae, Teasel
ELBOWS Blowse, Bowels
*ELBRUS Rubles
ELCHIS Chesil, Chiels, Chiles, Chisel, Schlei
ELDEST Steeld
ELDING Dingle, Engild, Gilden, Ingled
*ELDRED Reddle
ELECTS Select
ELEVEN Enleve
ELIDES Diesel, Ediles, Sedile, Seidel, Seiled
ELISOR Lories, Oilers, Oriels, Reoils, Serlio, Soiler
*ELMINA Maline, Menial
*ELMIRA Mailer, Remail
ELOIGN Legion
ELOINS Esloin, Insole, Lesion, Oleins, Sileno, Solein
*ELSTOW Lowest, Owlets, Towels

*ELTHAM Hamlet, Thelma
ELUANT Lunate
*ELUARD Lauder
ELUDED Delude
ELURES Saurel
ELUTOR Outler
ELWAND Wandle
ELYTRA Lyrate, Raylet, Realty, Telary
EMBACE Became
EMBAIL Lambie
EMBARS Ambers, Breams, Sambre
EMBOIL Bemoil, Emboli, Mobile
EMBOLI Bemoil, Emboil, Mobile
EMBOSS Besoms
EMEERS Seemer
EMERGE Mergee
EMESIS Missee
E-METER Meeter
EMIGRE Regime
*EMMAUS Summae
EMOTED Demote
EMPARE Ampere
EMPIRE Epimer, E-prime
EMULGE Legume
EMURED Demure
EMURES Resume
ENABLE Baleen
ENACTS Ascent, Secant, Stance
ENAMOR Merano, Moaner, Monera
ENARCH Chenar
ENCASE Cesena, Seance, Seneca
ENCASH Canehs
ENCINA Canine, Neanic
ENDART Ardent, Ranted
ENDEAR Deaner, Dearne, Earned, Neared
ENDERS Denser, Resend, Sender
ENDEST Nested, Sedent, Tensed
ENDEWS Sweden
ENDING Ginned
ENDITE Eident

ENDIVE Envied, Veined
ENDOWS Snowed
ENDUED Denude, Dudeen,
Duende, Dundee
ENDUES Ensued
ENDURE Deurne, Enured
ENDURO Undoer
ENEMAS Enseam, Seamen
ENERGY Greeny, Ygerne
ENERVE Evener, Veneer
ENEWED Weened
ENFIRE Ferine, Fernie, Fineer,
Infere, Refine
ENFOLD Fondle
ENGILD Dingle, Elding, Gilden,
Ingled
ENGIRD Dering, Dinger, Girned,
Ringed
ENGLUT Gluten
ENGOBE Begone
ENGRAM German, Manger,
Ragmen
ENIGMA Gamine
ENISLE Ensile, Nelies, Nelsie,
Senile, Silene
ENLACE Elance
ENLARD Aldern, Darnel, Lander,
Randle, Reland
ENLEVE Eleven
ENLIST Inlets, Listen, Silent,
Tinsel
ENODAL Loaden, Loaned
ENOSIS Eosins, Essoin, Noesis,
Noises, Ossein, Seison, Sonsie
ENRACE Careen, Recane
ENRAGE Egeran, Genera
ENRAIL Larine, Linear, Nailer,
Renail
ENRAPT Arpent, Entrap, Panter,
Parent, Pterna, Trepan
ENRICH Nicher, Richen
*****ENRICO** Coiner, Orcein, Orcine,
Recoin
ENRING Ginner

ENROBE Boreen
ENSATE Sateen, Senate, Steane
ENSEAM Enemas, Seamen
ENSEAR Serena
ENSILE Enisle, Nelies, Nelsie,
Senile, Silene
ENSOUL Nousle, Olenus, Unsole
ENSUED Endues
ENSURE Enures, Unsere
ENTAIL Tenail
ENTERA Neater, Rateen, Renate
ENTERS Ernest, Nester, Rentes,
Resent, Sterne, Strene, Tenser,
Ternes
ENTICE Cetina
ENTIRE Nerite
ENTOIL Lionet, Nilote
ENTRAP Arpent, Enrapt, Panter,
Parent, Pterna, Trepan
ENTREE Eterne, Retene
ENURED Deurne, Endure,
ENURES Ensure, Unsere
ENVIED Endive, Veined
ENVIER Nievre, Venire, Verein
ENVIES Neives, Nieves
ENWRAP Pawner, Repawn
EONISM Miseno, Monies,
Simeon, Simone
EOSINS Enosis, Essoin, Noesis,
Noises, Ossein, Seison, Sonsie
EOSTRE Retose, Stereo
EPACTS Aspect
EPARCH Preach
EPEIRA Percia
EPHORS Hopers, Posher
EPICAL Plaice, Plicae
EPIGON Pigeon
EPIMER Empire, E-Prime
*****EPINAL** Alpine, Nepali, Penial,
Pineal
*****EPIRUS** Uprise
EPOCHA Phocae
EPOCHS Cheops
EPODES Depose, Speedo

EPODIC Copied
*__EPPING__ Pig-pen
E-PRIME Empire, Epimer
EPULIS Pileus
EQUALS Lasque, Quesal, Squeal
ERASED Aredes, Deares, Reseda, Seared
ERASER Serrae
ERBIUM Imbrue
ERECTS Certes, Resect, Secret
*__ERFURT__ Returf, Turfer
ERG-TEN Gerent, Regent
*__ERHARD__ Harder
ERIACH Archie
*__ERICHT__ Cither, Thrice
ERINGO Ignore, Origen, Region
*__ERIVAN__ Rave-in, Ravine, Vainer, Vanier
*__ERNEST__ Enters, Nester, Rentes, Resent, Sterne, Strene, Tenser, Ternes
EROTIC Tercio
ERRAND Darner, Redarn, Renard
ERRANT Ranter, Terran
ERRING Ringer
*__ERROLL__ Orrell, Reroll, Roller
ERUCAS Causer, Cerusa, Creusa, Saucer
ERUCTS Cruets, Cruset, Custer, Rectus, Recuts, Truces
ERUPTS Purest
ERYNGO Groyne
ESCAPE Peaces
ESCARP Capers, Casper, Crapes, Pacers, Parsec, Recaps, Scrape, Secpar, Spacer
ESCARS Caress, Carses, Crases, Scares, Scraes, Seracs
ESCHAR Arches, Chares, Chaser, Raches, Search
ESCORT Corset, Cortes, Coster, Recost, Rectos, Scoter, Sector, Tresco
ESCROC Soccer

ESCROL Ceorls, Closer, Cresol
ESCROW Cowers
ESLOIN Eloins, Insole, Lesion, Oleins, Sileno, Solein
*__ESMOND__ Demons
ESPIAL Lipase, Plaise
ESPRIT Priest, Pteris, Ripest, Sitrep, Sprite, Stripe, Tripes
ESSIVE Sieves
ESSOIN Enosis, Noesis, Noises, Ossein, Seison, Sonsie
ESTATE Eatest, Teaset, Testae
ESTEEM Mestee
*__ESTHER__ Ethers, Hester, Threes
ESTOCS Cosset
ESTOPS Posset, Stoeps, Stopes
ESTRAY Reasty, Stayer, Stayre, Yarest
ESTRUM Muster, Stumer
ESTRUS Russet, Surest, Tusser
ETALON Lean-to, Tolane
ETAPES Peseta
ETERNE Entree, Retene
ETHANE Athene
ETHERS Esther, Hester, Threes
ETHICS Itches, Theics
*__ETHIOP__ Ophite
ETHYLS Shelty
*__ETNEAN__ Neaten
ETRIER Reiter, Retire
ETTLES Settle
ETYMON Toymen
EUNOMY Euonym
EUONYM Eunomy
EVADED Deaved
EVADER Reaved, Veader
EVANID Invade
*__EVELYN__ Evenly
EVENER Enerve, Veneer
EVENLY Evelyn
EVENTS Steven
EVERTS Revest, Revets, Sterve, Treves, Verset, Vester
EVICTS Civets, Vectis

EVILLY Lively, Vilely
EVINCE Venice
EVITES Stieve
EXCEPT Expect
EXERTS Exsert
EXILES Ilexes
EXISTS Sexist
EXPECT Except
EXSERT Exerts
EXTEND Dentex
EXTRAS Astrex, Taxers

FACIAL Cafila
FACIAS Fascia
FACILE Fecial
FACTOR Forcat
FACULA Faucal
FADETH Hafted
FAERIE Feriae
FAG-END Defang, Fanged
FAILED Afield
FAKERY Freaky
FAKIRS Friska, Kafirs
FALCON Flacon
FALL-IN Infall
FALSER Farles, Flares, Flaser
FAMINE Infame
FANGED Defang, Fag-end
FANGLE Flange
FARDEL Alfred, Flared
FARFEL Raffle
FARLES Falser, Flares, Flaser
FARING Grafin
FAR-OUT Fautor, Foutra
FARMED Framed
FARMER Framer
FARTED Dafter, Rafted
FARTER Frater, Rafter
FASCIA Facias
FASCIO Fiasco
FASTEN Nefast, Stefan
FASTER Afters, Strafe
FATHER Freath
FAUCAL Facula

FAULTS Flatus
FAUTOR Far-out, Foutra
FEALTY Featly
FEALED Leafed
FEARED Deafer
FEASTS Safest
FEATED Defeat
FEATLY Fealty
FECIAL Facile
FEDORA Afroed
FEEBLY Bee-fly
FEEDER Feered, Reefed, Refeed
FEED-IN Define
FEELER Refeel
FEERED Feeder, Reefed, Refeed
FEINTS Finest, Infest
FELTER Feltre, Refelt, Reflet,
    Trefle
FELTRE Felter, Refelt, Reflet,
    Trefle
FENDED Defend
*FENRIS Infers
FEODAL Foaled, Loafed
FERIAE Faerie
FERIAS Fraise, Sea-fir
FERINE Enfire, Fernie, Fineer,
    Infere, Refine
*FERNIE Enfire, Ferine, Fineer,
    Infere, Refine
FERITY Freity
FERULA Earful
FERULE Fueler, Refuel
FESTER Freest, Freets
FETORS Fortes, Forest, Foster,
    Softer
FETTER Frette
FEUTRE Refute
FIASCO Fascio
FIDGET Gifted
FIERCE Recife
FILETS Flites, Itself, Stifle
FILLER Refill
FILTER Lifter, Trifle
FINDER Friend, Redfin, Re-find

FINEER Enfire, Ferine, Fernie, Infere, Refine
FINELY Lenify
FINEST Feints, Infest
FINGER Fringe
FINISH Fish-in
FINLET Infelt
FIREST Freits, Refits, Resift, Rifest, Sifter, Strife
FIRTHS Friths, Shrift
FISCAL Califs
FISHER Sherif
FISH-IN Finish
FISTED Sifted
FIT-OUT Outfit
FITTER Titfer
FLACON Falcon
FLANGE Fangle
FLARED Alfred, Fardel
FLARES Falser, Farles, Flaser
FLASER Falser, Farles, Flares
FLASHY Ash-fly
FLATUS Faults
FLAUNT Unflat
FLAYED Deafly
FLECHE Fleech
FLEECH Fleche
FLESHY Shelfy
FLEXED Deflex
FLITES Filets, Itself, Stifle
FLORAE Loafer
FLORET Lofter
FLORID Ilford
FLOUTS Loftus
FLOWED Fowled, Wolfed
FLOWER Fowler, Reflow, Wolfer
FLUENT Netful, Unfelt, Unleft
FLUXED Deflux
FOALED Feodal, Loafed
FODDER Forded
FOETAL Folate
FOETOR Footer, Refoot, Tofore
FOILER Folier
FOLATE Foetal

FOLDER Refold
FOLIER Foiler
FONDER Fronde
FONDLE Enfold
FOOLED Loofed
FOOTER Foetor, Refoot, Tofore
FORAYS Forsay
FORBYE Fore-by
FORCAT Factor
FORCES Fresco
FORDED Fodder
FORE-BY Forbye
FOREDO Roofed
FOREST Fetors, Fortes, Foster, Softer
*FORMBY By-form
FORMED Deform
FORMER Reform
FORPIT Profit
FORSAY Forays
FORTES Fetors, Forest, Foster, Softer
FORTHY Frothy
FOSTER Fetors, Forest, Fortes, Softer
FOULED Defoul
FOUNTS Unsoft
FOUTER Foutre
FOUTRA Far-out, Fautor
FOUTRE Fouter
FOWLED Flowed, Wolfed
FOWLER Flower, Reflow, Wolfer
FRAISE Ferias, Sea-fir
FRAMED Farmed
FRAMER Farmer
FRATER Farter, Rafter
FRAYED Defray
FREAKY Fakery
FREATH Father
FREEST Fester, Freets
FREETS Fester, Freest
FREITS Firest, Refits, Resift, Rifest, Sifter, Strife
FREITY Ferity

FRESCO Forces
FRETTE Fetter
FRIEND Finder, Redfin, Refind
FRINGE Finger
FRINGY Frying
FRISKA Fakirs, Kafirs
FRITHS Firths, Shrift
*FRONDE Fonder
FROREN Frorne
FRORNE Froren
FROTHY Forthy
FRYING Fringy
FUELER Ferule, Refuel
FULMAR Armful
FUMBLE Beflum
FURDER Furred
FURRED Furder
FUTTER Tufter

GABION Bagnio
GADDER Graded
GADGES Sagged
GADGET Tagged
GADINE Gained
GAELIC Cigale
GAG-BIT Baggit
GAGERS Sagger, Seggar
GAINED Gadine
GAINER Earing, Graine, Regain,
    Regian, Regina
GAINLY Laying
GAINST Giants, Sating,
GAITER Aigret, Triage
GALENA Alnage, Angela,
    Anlage, Lagena
GALING Gingal, Laggin
GALLEY Egally
GALLON Gollan
GALOON Lagoon, Loango
GALORE Gaoler, Regalo
*GALTEE Eaglet, Gelate, Legate,
    Teagle, Telega
GAMELY Gleamy, Mygale
GAMETE Metage

GAMIER Imager, Maigre, Mirage
GAMINE Enigma
GAMING Gigman
GAMMER Gramme
GANDER Danger, Garden,
    Grande, Ranged
GANGED Nagged
GANGER Grange, Gregan,
    Nagger
GANGLE Laggen
GANTED Tag-end, Tanged
GANTRY Gyrant
GAOLED Age-old
GAOLER Galore, Regalo
GAPERS Gasper, Grapes, Parges,
    Sparge
GAPING Paging
GARBED Badger, Barged
GARDEN Danger, Gander,
    Grande, Ranged
GARDON Dragon, Gondar
GARGET Tagger
GARGLE Gregal, Lagger, Raggle
GARIAL Argali
GARNER Ranger
GARNET Argent, Gerant, Gretna
GAROUS Rugosa
GARRED Darger, Gerard, Grader,
    Regard
GARRET Garter, Grater
GARTER Garret, Grater
GARVIE Argive, Rivage
GAS-BAG Sag-bag
*GASCON Gongas, Scogan
GASKIN Asking, Kiangs
GASMEN Manges, Megans
GASPER Gapers, Grapes, Parges,
    Sparge
*GASTON Sontag, Tangos,
    Tongas, Tsonga
GATHER Rageth
GAUCHO Guacho
GAUFER Gaufre
GAUFRE Gaufer

GAYEST Stagey
GEARED Agreed, Dragee
*****GEIGER** Greige, Reggie
GELATE Eaglet, Galtee, Legate, Teagle, Telega
GELDER Ledger, Red-leg
GENERA Egeran, Enrage
GENEVA Avenge, Vangee
GENIAL Ealing, Linage
GENIES Eignes, Seeing, Siegen
GENIUS Sueing
GENUAL Lagune, Langue
GERALD Glared
GERANT Argent, Garnet, Gretna
*****GERARD** Darger, Garred, Grader, Regard
GERENT Erg-ten, Regent
GERMAN Engram, Manger, Ragmen
GERMED Merged
GERMON Monger, Morgen
*****GERONA** Onager, Orange
GERUND Nudger
*****GERVAS** Graves
*****GHEBER** Ghebre
*****GHEBRE** Gheber
GHOULS Loughs, Slough
GIANTS Gainst, Sating
GIBING Biggin
GIFTED Fidget
GIGMAN Gaming
GILDED Glided
GILDEN Dingle, Elding, Engild, Ingled
GILDER Girdle, Glider, Lidger, Regild, Ridgel
GILPIN Piling
GIMMER Megrim
GINETE Teeing
GINGAL Galing, Laggin
GINGER Nigger
GINGKO Ginkgo
GINGLE Liggen, Niggle
GINKGO Gingko

GINNED Ending
GINNEL Lingen
GINNER Enring
GIRDED Grided, Ridged
GIRDER Regird
GIRDLE Gilder, Glider, Lidger, Regild, Ridgel
GIRNED Dering, Dinger, Engird, Ringed
GIRNEL Linger
GIRONS Grison, Groins, Rosing, Signor
*****GIRTON** Roting, Trigon
*****GIRVAN** Raving
GISTED Digest
GLAIVE Vagile
GLARED Gerald
GLAURY Raguly
GLEAMY Gamely, Mygale
GLEDES Gleeds, Ledges, Sledge
GLEDGE Legged
GLEEDS Gledes, Ledges, Sledge
*****GLENDA** Angled, Dangle, Lagend
GLIDED Gilded
GLIDER Gilder, Girdle, Lidger, Regild, Ridgel
*****GLIRES** Grilse
GLOBIN Goblin, Lobing
GLOVER Grovel
GLOWER Reglow
GLUING Luging
GLUTEN Englut
GLUTIN Luting, Ungilt
GLYCIN Clingy
*****GLYNIS** Lyings, Lysing, Singly
GNAWED Gwenda
GNEISS Singes
*****GNETUM** Nutmeg
GNOMIC Coming
GOBLET Boglet
GOBLIN Globin, Lobing
GOD-DEN Dog-end
GODETS Stodge

GOGLET Logget, Toggle
GOIDEL Goldie
GOITER Goitre
GOITRE Goiter
GOLDEN Longed
*GOLDIE Goidel
GOLIAS Oil-gas
GOLLAN Gallon
GONDAR Dragon, Gardon
*GONVIL Loving, Voling
GOOBER Bog-ore
GOONEY Oogeny
GORAMY Morgay
*GORDON Drongo, Grodno
GORGED Dogger
GORING Gringo
GORSES Ogress, Sogers
GO-STOP Stop-go
GOURDE Drogue, Drouge,
  Rogued, Rouged
GRABEN Banger
GRACED Cadger
GRADED Gadder
GRADER Darger, Garred, Gerard,
  Regard
GRADIN Daring
GRADUS Guards
*GRAEME Meager, Meagre
GRAFIN Faring
*GRAHAM Armagh
GRAINE Earing, Gainer, Regain,
  Regian, Regina
GRAINS Rasing, Sangir
GRAINY Raying
GRAITH Aright
GRAMME Gammer
*GRANDE Danger, Gander,
  Garden, Gnared, Ranged
GRANGE Ganger, Gregan,
  Naggar
*GRANTH Thrang
GRAPES Gapers, Gasper, Parges,
  Sparge
GRATED Targed

GRATER Garret, Garter
GRATES Greats, Ragest, Stager,
  Targes
GRATIN Rating, Taring, Tringa
GRATIS Striga
GRAVES Gervas
GREASE Agrees, Eagres
GREASY Yagers
*GREATS Grates, Ragest, Stager,
  Targes
GREAVE Regave
GREENE Renege
GREENY Energy, Ygerne
GREETS Egrets, Regest, Regets
GREEVE Verges
GREGAL Gargle, Lagger, Raggle
*GREGAN Ganger, Grange,
  Nagger
GREIGE Geiger, Reggie
*GRENAA Reagan
GRESES Egress, Serges
*GRETNA Argent, Garnet, Gerant
GREVES Verges
GRIDED Girded, Ridged
GRIDES Dirges, Grised, Ridges
GRIECE Cierge
GRIESY Grysie
GRIEVE Regive
GRILSE Glires
GRINGO Goring
GRIPER Regrip
GRISED Dirges, Grides, Ridges
GRISON Girons, Groins, Rosing,
  Signor
GROANS Angors, Argons,
  Nagors, Orangs, Organs,
  Sargon, Sarong
*GRODNO Drongo, Gordon
GROINS Girons, Grison, Rosing,
  Signor
GROOVE Overgo
GROPER Porger
GROSER Rogers
GROSET Storge

GROUTY Yogurt
GROUSE Orgues, Rogues, Rouges, Rugose
GROVEL Glover
GROWER Regrow
GROYNE Eryngo
GRUDGE Rugged
GRUNTS Strung
GRYSIE Griesy
GUANIN Ungain
GUARDS Gradus
GUEBER Burgee, Guebre
GUEBRE Burgee, Gueber
GUELPH Pleugh
GUESTS Gusset
GUIANA Iguana
GUILER Ligure, Reguli, Uglier
GUISER Regius
GULDEN Lunged
GUNSEL Lunges
GUNTER Gurnet, Urgent
GURGLE Lugger
GURNET Gunter, Urgent
GUSSET Guests
GUSTED Degust
GWENDA Gnawed
GYRANT Gantry

HACKLY Chalky
HADJIS Jagdish, Jihads
HAERES Hearse
HAFTED Fadeth
HAGDEN Hanged
HAILED Halide
HALDEN Handel, Handle
HALIDE Hailed
HALING Hlaing
HALLAN Nallah
HALLOO Holloa
HALSED Lashed
HALSER Ashler, Lasher
HALSES Hassle, Lashes, Selahs, Shales, Sheals
HALTED Lathed

HALTER Lather, Thaler
HAMLET Eltham, Thelma
HAMMAL Mahmal
HANDEL Halden, Handle
HANDER Harden
HANDLE Halden, Handel
HANGAR Arghan
HANGED Hagden
HANGER Rehang
HANG-UP Uphang
HANKER Harken
HANTLE Lathen, Thenal
HAPTIC Pathic, Phatic
HARASS Hassar
HARDEN Hander
HARDER Erhard
HARD-UP Purdah
HAREEM Hermae
HARELD Harled, Herald
HAREMS Masher, Shamer
HARKEN Hanker
HARLED Hareld, Herald
HARLEM Mahler, Ramleh
HARLOT Lothar, Thoral
HARMED Derham
HARRIS Arrish, Shirra, Sirrah
HASHER Rehash
HASLET Lathes, Shelta, Thales
HASPED Pashed, Phased, Shaped
HASSAR Harass
HASSLE Halses, Lashes, Selahs, Shales, Sheals
HASTED Deaths, 'Sdeath, Tashed
HASTEN Athens, Snathe, Sneath, Thanes
HASTES Ashets, Tashes
HATERS Earths, Hearts, Rathes, Sarthe, 'Sheart
HATING A'thing, Anight
HATRED Dareth, Dearth, Redhat, Thread
HATTER Threat
HAULER Rehaul
HAUNTS Sunhat, Unhats, Ushant

HAVENS Hesvan, Shaven
HAVERS Shaver
HAWSER Rewash, Washer,
  Whares
HEADER Adhere, Hedera,
  Rehead
HEALER Reheal
HEARER Rehear
HEARSE Haeres
HEARTS Earths, Haters, Rathes,
  Sarthe, 'Sheart
HEARTY Earthy
HEATER Aether, Hereat, Reheat
HEATHS Sheath
HEAVES Sheave
*****HEBRON** Brehon
HECATE Eatche, Thecae
HECTOR Rochet, Rotche, Tocher,
  Troche
*****HEDERA** Adhere, Header,
  Rehead
HEELER Reheel
HEIGHT Eighth
HEISTS Shiest, Shites, Sithes,
  Theiss, Thesis
HELIUM Humlie
HELOTS Hostel, Hotels, Tholes
HELVES Shelve
HEMINS Inmesh
HEPARS Phares, Phrase, Raphes,
  Seraph, Shaper, Sherpa, Sphaer
HERALD Hareld, Harled
HERDIC Chider, Dreich
HEREAT Aether, Heater, Reheat
HEREIN Inhere, Rheine
HEREON Rehone
HERMAE Hareem
*****HERMAN** Arnhem
HERMIT Mither
*****HERODS** Dehors, Hordes,
  Horsed, Reshod, Rhodes,
  Shoder, Shored
HEROIC Cheiro, Coheir
HEROIN Hornie

HERONS Honers, Nosher,
  Rhones, Senhor
HERPES Hesper, Pheers, Sphere
*****HESPER** Herpes, Pheers, Sphere
*****HESSEN** Sheens, Sneesh
*****HESTER** Esther, Ethers, Threes
*****HESVAN** Havens, Shaven
HETMAN Anthem
HEUCHS Sheuch
HEUGHS Hughes, Sheugh
HEWERS Reshew, Wheres
HEWING Whinge
HIELAN Inhale
HIKERS Shriek, Shrike
HILUMS Mulish
HINDIS Sindhi
HINGES Neighs, Senghi
HIPPOS Popish, Shippo
HIRSEL Hirsle, Relish
HIRSLE Hirsel, Relish
*****HISPAR** Parish, Raphis, Shairp
HISSED Dishes
HISSER Shiers, Shires
HISTIE Shi-ite
*****HITLER** Lither
HITMAN Mithan
HITTER Tither
HIVERS Shiver, Shrive
*****HLAING** Haling
HOARSE Ahorse, Ashore, Shorea
HOASTS Hostas, Shoats, Thasos
HOAXED Ox-head
HOCKED Choked
HOCKER Choker
HOCKEY Chokey
HOGNUT Nought
HOIDEN Honied
HOLD-UP Uphold
HOLLOA Halloo
HOLPEN Phenol
HOMAGE Ohmage
HONERS Herons, Nosher,
  Rhones, Senhor
HONEST Sethon, Stheno

HONIED Hoiden
HOPERS Ephors, Posher
*****HORACE** Chorea, Ochrae,
   Orache, Rochea
HORDES Dehors, Herods,
   Horsed, Reshod, Rhodes,
   Shoder, Shored
HORNED Dehorn
HORNET Horten, Thorne, Throne
*****HORNIE** Heroin
HORSED Dehors, Herods,
   Hordes, Reshod, Rhodes,
   Shoder, Shored
HORTEN Hornet, Thorne, Throne
HOSTAS Hoasts, Shoats, Thasos
HOSTED Toshed
HOSTEL Helots, Hotels, Tholes
HOSTRY Rosyth, Shorty
HOTELS Helots, Hostel, Tholes
HOTTER T'other
HOUGHS Shough
HOUNDS Hudson, Unshod
HOUSES Shouse
HOVELS Shovel
HOVERS Shover, Shrove
HOWLET Thowel
HOWRES Reshow, Shower,
   Whores
HSSTAS Hoasts, Sloats, Thasos
*****HUDSON** Hounds, Unshod
*****HUGHES** Heughs, Sheugh
HUMANE Humean
*****HUMEAN** Humane
HUMINE Inhume
HUMLIE Helium
HUMPTY Tumphy
HUNGER Rehung
HURDLE Hurled
HURLED Hurdle
*****HURONS** Onrush
HURTLE Luther
HUSTLE Sleuth
HYETAL Eathly
HYPERS Sphery, Sypher

*****HYPNOS** Syphon
HYSSOP Sposhy

IATRIC Iricia
*****IBADAN** Indaba
*****IBLEES** Belies
ICECAP Ipecac
ICEMAN Anemic, Cinema
ICHORS Choirs, Orchis
ICICLE Cilice
ICIEST Cities
ICKERS Scrike, Sicker
IDEALS Aisled, Deasil, Ladies,
   Sailed
IDIOMS Iodism
IDIOTS Idoist
IDLERS Sidler, Slider
IDLEST Delist, Listed, Silted,
   Tildes
IDOIST Idiots
*****IDOLUM** Dolium, Moduli
IGNARO Oaring, Onagri, Origan
IGNITE Tieing
IGNORE Eringo, Origen, Region
IGUANA Guiana
*****ILAGAN** Agnail, Anglia
*****ILESHA** Sheila
ILEXES Exiles
*****ILFORD** Florid
*****LIKLEY** Likely
IMAGER Gamier, Maigre, Mirage
IMAGES Ageism
IMBRUE Erbium
*****IMELDA** Mailed, Medial
IMMANE Ammine
IMPARL Primal
IMPART Armpit, Partim
IMPELS Milspe, Simple
IMPOST Impots
IMPOTS Impost
IMPURE Umpire
INARCH Chinar
INBRED Binder, Brined, Rebind
INCASE Casein

INCAST Antics, Nastic
INCAVE Cave-in
INCEDE Edenic
INCEPT Pectin, Peinct
INCEST Insect, Nicest, Scient
INCHED Chined, Niched
INCHES Chines, Chinse, Niches
INDABA Ibadan
INDEED Denied
INDENT Dentin, Intend, Tinned
*INDIES** Inside
INDIGN Dining, Niding
INDITE Tineid
INDOLE Doline, Leonid
*INDORE** Ironed
INDUCE Uniced
INDUES Undies
INFALL Fall-in
INFAME Famine
INFELT Finlet
INFERE Enfire, Ferine, Fernie, Fineer, Refine
INFERS Fenris
INFEST Feints, Finest
INGATE Eating, Tangie, Teaing
INGEST Signet, Stinge, Tinges
INGLED Dingle, Elding, Engild, Gilden
INGLES Lignes, Seling, Single
*INGMAR** Arming, Ingram, Margin
INGOES Soigne
INGOTS Stingo, Tigons, Tosing
INGRAM Arming, Ingmar, Margin
*INGRES** Reigns, Renigs, Resign, Ringes, Signer, Singer
*INGRID** Riding
*INGRUM** Muring
INHALE Hielan
INHERE Herein, Rheine
INHUME Humine
INK-BAG Baking
INK-CAP Panick

INKERS Kirsen, Reinks, Sinker
INKLED Kilned, Kindle, Linked
INKLES Likens, Silken
IN-LAWS Salwin
INLACE Ancile, Celina
INLETS Enlist, Listen, Silent, Tinsel
INLIER Nirlie
INLOCK Lock-in
INMATE Tamine
INMESH Hemins
INMOST Monist
INNATE Tinean
INNERS Sinner
INORBS Robins, Sorbin
INROAD Dorian, Ordain
INSANE Annies, Sienna
INSEAM Amiens, Amines, Mesian
INSECT Incest, Nicest, Scient
INSERT Inters, Nitres, Retins, Sinter, Strine, Trines
INSETS Steins, Tessin
INSIDE Indies
INSIST Sit-ins
INSOLE Eloins, Esloin, Lesion, Oleins, Sileno, Solsin
INSPAN Pinnas
INSTAL Latins, Stalin
INSTAR Santir, Sintra, Strain, Trains
INSTEP Spinet, Step-in
INSTOP Piston, Pitons, Points, Potins, Spin-to
INSULT Sunlit
INSURE Inures, Rusine, Urines, Ursine,
INTAKE Kinate, Take-in
INTEND Dentin, Indent, Tinned
INTERN Tinner
INTERS Insert, Nitres, Retins, Sinter, Strine, Trines
INTINE Tinnie
INTIRE Tinier

INTOED Ditone
INTORT Triton
IN-TRAY Tyrian
INTUSE Tenuis, Unites, Unties
INURED Ruined
INURES Insure, Rusine, Urines,
  Ursine
INVADE Evanid
INVERT Virent
INWARD Darwin
INWITH Within
INWORK Work-in
IODISM Idioms
IODOUS Odious
IPECAC Icecap
IRADES Aiders, Raised
IRIDES Irised
IRISED Irides
IRONED Indore
IRONER Renoir
IRONIC Oniric
*****IRTYSH** Shirty, Thyrsi
*****IRVING** Riving, Virgin
*****IRWELL** Willer
ISAACS Cassia
ISABEL Blaise
ISLETS Istles, Sliest, Stiles
ISOLDE Siloed, Soiled
ISOMER Moires, Rimose
*****ISRAEL** Ariels, Asriel, Relais,
  Resail, Sailer, Serail, Serial
ISSUED Disuse
ISSUER Uresis
ISSUES Suisse
ISTLES Islets, Sliest, Stiles
ITCHES Ethics, Theics
ITSELF Filets, Flites, Stifle

JADISH Hadjis, Jihads
JAILER Rejail
JAMBUL Jumbal
*****JANSEN** Nsanje
JAPERS Jasper
JASPER Japers

JEERED Jereed
JERBIL Jirble
JEREED Jeered
JERKIN Jinker
JETONS Jetson
JETSON Jetons
JIHADS Hadjis, Jadish
JINKER Jerkin
JIRBLE Jerbil
JOINER Rejoin
JOLTER Rejolt
JUDAIC Judica
JUDICA Judaic
JUMBAL Jambul

KAFIRS Fakirs, Friska
*****KAISER** Raikes
KALMIA Kamila
KAMILA Kalmia
KARITE Arkite
*****KARROO** Korora
KASHER Shaker
*****KASPAR** Parkas
*****KASSEL** Slakes
KAVASS Vakass
KAYOED Okayed
*****KEARNY** Yanker
KELPIE Pelike
KELSON Sloken
*****KELTIC** Tickle
*****KENDAL** Ankled
*****KERMAN** Marken
KEUPER Peruke
KIANGS Asking, Gaskin
KIDDER Dirked
KIDNEY Dinkey
KILNED Inkled, Kindle, Linked
KILTER Kirtle
KINATE Intake, Take-in
KINDLE Inkled, Kilned, Linked
KIRSCH Chirks, Schrik
KIRSEN Inkers, Reinks, Sinker
KIRTLE Kilter
KISSER Krises, Skiers

KITSCH Schtik, Shtick, Thicks
KNAWEL Wankle
KNOWER Wroken
KORORA Karroo
KRAITS Straik, Traiks
KREESE Reseek, Seeker
KRISES Kisser, Skiers

LAAGER Alegar
LABILE Alible, Belial, Biella, Liable
LABRET Albert, Tabler
LABRID Bridal, Ribald
LABRUM Brumal, Lumbar, Umbral
*****LABRUS** Bursal
LAC-DYE Clayed
LACHES Cashel, Chelas, Sachel
LACIER Claire, Eclair
LACING Anglic
LACKED Calked
LACKER Calker, Rackle, Recalk
*****LACLOS** Locals
LADDER Aldred, Larded, Raddle
LADDIE Daidle, Dialed
LADENS Elands, Landes, Sendal
LA-DI-DA Alidad
LADIES Aisled, Deasil, Ideals, Sailed
LADING Ligand
*****LADINO** Olinda
LADYFY Day-Fly
LAESIE Elaeis
LAGENA Alnage, Angela, Anlage, Galena
LAGEND Angled, Dangle, Glenda
LAGGED Daggle
LAGGEN Gangle
LAGGER Gargle, Gregal, Raggle
LAGGIN Galing, Gingal
LAGOON Galoon, Loango
LAGUNE Genual, Langue
LAIRED Adriel, Derail, Lerida, Railed, Relaid

LAISSE Aisles, Eassil, Lassie
LALDIE Allied
LAMBED Ambled, Balmed, Bedlam, Beldam, Blamed
LAMBER Ambler, Blamer, Marble, Ramble
LAMBIE Embail
LAMELY Mellay
LAMENT Mantel, Mantle, Mental
LAMEST Metals, Samlet
LAMIAS Alisma, Salami
LAMINA Almain, Animal, Manila
LAMING Lingam, Malign
LAMMER Rammel
LAMPAS Palmas, Plasma
LAMPED Palmed
LANCED Candle
LANCER Rancel
LANCES Ancles, Cleans, Lencas, Senlac
LANCET Cantle, Cental
LANDED Dandle
LANDER Aldern, Darnel, Enlard, Randle, Reland
*****LANDES** Elands, Ladens, Sendal
*****LANDOR** Arnold, Lardon, Roland, Ronald
*****LANETT** Latent, Latten, Talent
LANGET Anglet, Tangle
LANGUE Genual, Lagune
LANGUR Lurgan
LANKER Rankle
LANUGO Lugano
*****LAO-TSE** Osteal
*****LAPEER** Leaper, Pealer, Repeal
LAPINS Plains, Spinal
LAPPED Dapple, Palped
LAPPER Rappel
LAPSED Padles, Pedals, Pleads
LARDED Aldred, Ladder, Raddle
LARDON Arnold, Landor, Roland, Ronald
*****LAREDO** Loader, Ordeal, Reload
LARGEN Angler, Rangle, Regnal

LARIAT Altair, Atrial, Latria
LARINE Enrail, Linear, Nailer, Renail
LARKED Darkle
LARVAL Vallar
LASCAR Rascal, Sacral, Sarlac, Scalar
LASHED Halsed
LASHER Ashler, Halser
LASHES Halses, Hassle, Selahs, Shales, Sheals
LASH-UP Sulpha
LASKET Sklate
LASQUE Equals, Quesal, Squeal
LASSES Salses
LASSIE Aisles, Eassil, Laisse
LASTED Deltas, Desalt, Salted, Slated, Stadle, Staled
LASTER Alerts, Alters, Artels, Ratels, Resalt, Salter, Slater, Staler, Stelar, Tarsel
LASTLY Saltly
LATEEN Elanet
LATELY Lealty
LATENT Lanett, Latten, Talent
LATEST Stealt, Taslet
LATHED Halted
LATHEN Hantle, Thenal
LATHER Halter, Thaler
LATHES Haslet, Shelta, Thales
*****LATIAN** Antlia, Talian
LATINS Instal, Stalin
LATISH Tahsil
*****LATONA** Atonal
LATRIA Altair, Atrial, Lariat
LATTEN Lanett, Latent, Talent
LATTER Rattle, Tatler
*****LATVIA** Avital
LAUDER Eluard
LAUNCE Cuneal, Lucena, Unlace
LAUNCH Nuchal, Unchal
LAUREL Allure
LAURIC Uracil
LAVEER Leaver, Reveal, Vealer

LAVERS Ravels, Salver, Serval, Slaver, Valser, Velors, Versal
LAVING Valing
LAWING Waling
LAWNED Walden
LAWYER Warely
LAXISM Smilax
LAYERS Rayles, Relays, Slayer
LAYING Gainly
LAYMAN Almany
LAYMEN Meanly, Namely
LAY-OUT Outlay
LEADED Dealed, Delead
LEADEN Aneled, Leaned, Nealed
LEADER Dealer, Redeal, Releaad
LEAD-IN Aldine, Alined, Daniel, Delian, Denial, Nailed
LEAFED Fealed
LEALTY Lately
LEANED Aneled, Leaden, Nealed
LEAN-TO Etalon, Tolane
LEAPED Pealed, Pedale
LEAPER Lapeer, Pealer, Repeal
LEARES Leaser, Resale, Reseal, Sealer, Searle
LEARNS Ransel
LEARNT Altern, Antler, Rental, Ternal
LEASED Sealed
LEASER Leares, Resale, Reseal, Sealer
LEASES Easels, Easles, Eassel
LEASOW Sea-owl
LEAVER Laveer, Reveal, Vealer
LEAVES Sleave
*****LEAVIS** Aviles, Valise
LECTOR Colter
LEDGER Gelder, Red-leg
LEDGES Gledes, Gleeds, Sledge
LEERED Reeled
LEESES Lessee
LEGATE Eaglet, Galtee, Gelate, Teagle, Telega
LEGGED Gledge

LEGGER Eggler
LEGION Eloign
LEGLIN Lingel, Lingle
LEG-MAN Mangel, Mangle
LEGUME Emulge
LEIGER Lieger
LEMANS Anselm, Mensal
*LEMNOS Lemons, Melons, Solemn
LEMONS Lemnos, Melons, Solemn
LEMONY Myelon
LENCAS Ancles, Cleans, Lances, Senlac
LENDER Relend
LENIFY Finely
LENSES Lessen
LENTIC Client
LENTIL Lintel
*LEONID Doline, Indole
*LEPCHA Chapel, Pleach
LEPTUS Let-ups
*LERIDA Adriel, Derail, Laired, Railed, Relaid
*LESINA Aliens, Alines, Lianes, Saline, Selina, Silane
*LERINS Liners, Nirles
LESION Eloins, Esloin, Insole, Oleins, Sileno, Solein
LESSEE Leeses
LESSEN Lenses
LESSOR Losers, Solers, Sorels
*LESTER Relets, Streel
*LESVOS Solves
LET-A-BE Belate
LET-OUT Outlet
LET-UPS Leptus
LEUCIN Nuclei
LEVEES Sleeve
LEVIED Veiled
LEVIER Liever, Relive, Revile
LEVINS Livens, Sliven, Snivel
LEVITE Velite
*LEVOCA Alcove, Coeval

LEWDER Reweld, Welder
*LEYDEN Needly
LIABLE Alible, Belial, Biella, Labile
LIANAS Salian, Salina
LIANES Aliens, Alines, Lesina, Saline, Selina, Silane
LIANGS Aligns, Ligans, Lingas, Signal
LIBATE Albeit, Albite, Betail
LIBRAE Bailer
LICKER Rickle
*LICOSA Social
LIDDED Diddle
LIDGER Gilder, Girdle, Glider, Regild, Ridgel
LIEDER Relide, Relied
LIEFER Refile, Relief
LIEGER Leiger
LIENAL Lineal
LIERNE Reline
LIEVER Levier, Relive, Revile
LIFTER Filter, Trifle
LIGAND Lading
LIGANS Aligns, Ganils, Liangs, Lingas, Signal
LIGATE Aiglet, Taigle
LIGGEN Gingle, Niggle
LIGGER Riggle
LIGHTS Slight
LIGNES Ingles, Seling, Single
LIGNIN Lining
LIGURE Guiler, Reguli, Uglier
LIKELY Ilkley
LIKENS Inkles, Silken
LILACS Scilla
LILTED Tilled
LIMBED Dimble
LIMENS Meslin, Semlin, Simnel
LIMNED Milden, Mindel
LIMNER Merlin, Milner
LIMPED Dimple
LIMPER Prelim, Rempli, Rimple
LIMPSY Simply

LINAGE Ealing, Genial
LINDAU Dualin, Unlaid
LINDEN Dinnle, Linned
LINEAL Lienal
LINEAR Enrail, Larine, Nailer, Renail
LINERS Lerins, Nirles
LINE-UP Lupine, Unpile, Up-line
LINGAM Laming, Malign
LINGAS Aligns, Liangs, Ligans, Signal
LINGER Girnel
LINGEL Leglin, Lingle
***LINGEN** Ginnel
LINGLE Leglin, Lingel
LINGOT Tiglon, Toling
LINGUA Nilgau
LINING Lignin
LINKED Inkled, Kilned, Kindle
LINNED Dinnle, Linden
LINSEY Lysine
LINTEL Lentil
LIONEL Niello, O'neill
LIONET Entoil, Nilote
LIPASE Espial, Plaise
LIPOMA Pimola
LIPPEN Nipple
LIPPER Prilep, Ripple
LISPED Dispel, Disple, Sliped, Spiled
LISPER Perils, Perlis, Pilers, Pliers
LISTED Delist, Idlest, Silted, Tildes
LISTEN Enlist, Inlets, Silent, Tinsel
LISTER Litres, Relist, Tilers
LITCHI Lithic
LITHER Hitler
LITHIC Litchi
LITMUS Tilmus
LITRES Lister, Relist, Tilers
LITTER Tilter, Titler
LIVELY Evilly, Vilely
LIVENS Levins, Sliven, Snivel

LIVERS Livres, Rivels, Silver, Sliver
LIVERY Verily
LIVEST Vilest
LIVRES Livers, Rivels, Silver, Sliver
LOADEN Enodal, Loaned
LOADER Laredo, Ordeal, Reload
LOAFED Feodal, Foaled
LOAFER Florae
LOANED Enodal, Loaden
LOANER Lorena, Reloan
***LOANGO** Galoon, Lagoon
LOBATE Boatel, Oblate
LOBING Globin, Goblin
LOBOSE Sobole
LOBULE Boulle
LOCALS Laclos
LOCATE Alecto
LOCKED Cloked
LOCKER Relock, Rockel
LOCK-IN Inlock
LOCOED Cooled
LOCK-UP Uplock
LOCUST Clouts
LOFTER Floret
***LOFTUS** Flouts
LOGANS Slogan
LOGGED Dogleg
LOGGER Roggle
LOGGET Goglet, Toggle
***LOIRET** Loiter, Toiler, Triole
LOITER Loiret, Toiler, Triole
LOMENT Melton, Molten
LONGED Golden
LOOFED Fooled
LOOING Olingo
LOOKER Rookle
LOOPED Poodle, Pooled
LOOPER Pooler
LOOSED Dolose, Oodles, Sooled
LOOTED Toledo, Tooled
LOOTER Loreto, Retool, Rootle, Tooler

LOPING Poling
LOPPER Propel
LORCHA Choral, Orchal
LORDLY Drolly
*LORENA Loaner, Reloan
*LORETO Looter, Retool, Rootle,
　Tooler
LORICA Caroli
LORIES Elisor, Oilers, Oriels,
　Reoils, Serlio, Soiler
LOSERS Lessor, Solers, Sorels
LOSING Soling
LOSSES Sossle
LOTHAR Harlot, Thoral
LOTTED Dottle
*LOTTIE Toilet
LOUDEN Nodule, Oundle
LOUDER Loured
LOUGHS Ghouls, Slough
LOURED Louder
LOUSED Souled
LOUSES Ousels, Soleus
LOUVAR Ovular, Valour
LOUVER Louvre, Velour
LOUVRE Louver, Velour
LOVAGE Volage
LOVELY Volley
LOVERS Solver
LOVING Gonvil, Voling
LOWERS Owlers, Rowels, Slower
LOWERY Owlery
LOWEST Elstow, Owlets, Towels
LOWING Owling
LOWISH Owlish
*LOXIAS Oxalis
LUBBER Burble, Rubble
*LUBECK Buckle
*LUCENA Cuneal, Launce, Unlace
*LUCIAN Alcuin, Lucina, Uncial
*LUCINA Alcuin, Lucian, Uncial
LUFFED Duffel, Duffle
LUFFER Ruffle
*LUGANO Lanugo

LUGGER Gurgle
LUGING Gluing
LUITEA Luteia, Lutine, Untile
LUMBAR Brumal, Labrum,
　Umbral
LUMBER Rumble, Umbrel
LUMINA Alumni
LUMINE Unlime
LUMPED Dumple, Plumed
LUMPEN Plenum
LUMPER Replum, Rumple
LUNARY Uranyl
LUNATE Eluant
LUNGED Gulden
LUNGES Gunsel
LUPINE Line-up, Unpile, Up-line
LURDEN Nurled, Rundle
LUSTRE Lurest, Luster, Luters,
　Result, Rulest, Rustle, Sutler,
　Ulster
*LURGAN Langur
LURING Ruling
LUSIAD Dulias
LUSTER Lurest, Lustre, Luters,
　Result, Rulest, Rustle, Sutler,
　Ulster
LUSTRE Lurest, Luster, Luters,
　Result, Result, Rulest, Rustle,
　Sutler, Ulster
LUTEIN Luiten, Lutine, Untile
LUSTRE Lurest, Luster, Luters,
　Result, Rulest, Rustle, Sutler,
　Ulster
*LUTHER Hurtle
LUTINE Luiten, Lutein, Untile
LUTING Glutin, Ungilt
LUTTEN Nutlet
LYINGS Glynis, Lysing, Singly
LYRATE Elytra, Raylet, Realty,
　Telary
LYSINE Lynsey
LYSING Glynis, Lyings, Singly

*MAASIN Animas, Manias,
　　Manisa, Samian
MACERS Crames, Creams,
　　Scream
*MACHEN Manche
MACIES Amices, Camise
MACLED Calmed
MACLES Camels, Mascle,
　　Mescal, Scamel
MACULE Almuce
MADDEN Damned, Demand
MADRAS Dramas
MAENAD Anadem
*MAGYAR Margay
MAHLER Harlem, Ramleh
MAHMAL Hammal
MAHSIR Marish
MAIDED Diadem
MAIDEN Daimen, Damien,
　　Demain, Mained, Median,
　　Medina
MAIGRE Gamier, Imager,
　　Mirage
MAILED Imelda, Medial
MAILER Elmira, Remail
MAIMER Remaim
MAINED Daimen, Damien,
　　Demain, Maiden, Median,
　　Medina
MAINOR Marino, Marion,
　　Mirano
MAIRES Armies
MAKERS Masker
MAKE-UP Upmake
MALATE Meatal, Tamale
MALEIC Malice
MALICE Maleic
MALIGN Laming, Lingam
MALINE Elmina, Menial
*MALONE Melano
MALTOS Almost, Smalto
MANAGE Agname
*MANCHE Machen
MANEGE Menage

MANETS Aments, Mantes,
　　Stamen
MANGEL Leg-man, Mangle
MANGER Engram, German,
　　Ragmen
MANGES Gasmen, Megans
MANGLE Leg-man, Mangel
MANIAC Caiman
MANIAS Animas, Maasin,
　　Manisa, Samian
MANILA Almain, Animal,
　　Lamina
MANIOC Anomic, Camion,
　　Conima
*MANISA Animas, Maasin,
　　Manias, Samian
MANNED Mennad
MANORS Normas, Ramson,
　　Ransom, Romans
MANRED Randem, Redman,
　　Remand
MANSES Messan
MANTAS Tasman
MANTEL Lament, Mantle, Mental
MANTES Aments, Manets,
　　Stamen
MANTIS Matins, Stamin, Tamins
MANTLE Lament, Mantel, Mental
MANTUA Tamanu
MANUAL Alumna
MANURE Menura, Murena
*MAOISM Mimosa
*MAOIST Samiot, Taoism
MAPLES Pelmas, Sample
MAPPER Pamper
MARACA Camara
MARBLE Ambler, Blamer,
　　Lamber, Ramble
MARCEL Calmer, Carmel
*MARCOS Caroms
MARGAY Magyar
MARGIN Arming, Ingmar,
　　Ingram
*MARIAN Airman, Marina

MARIDS Disarm
MARINA Airman, Marian
MARINE Airmen, Marnie, Remain
*MARINO Mainor, Marion, Mirano
*MARION Mainor, Marino, Mirano
MARISH Mahsir
*MARIST Ramist
MARKED Demark
*MARKEN Kerman
MARKER Remark
MARLED Dermal, Medlar
*MARLON Normal
*MARNIE Airmen, Marine, Remain
*MARPLE Ampler, Palmer
MAROON Monaro, Ramoon
*MARREE Reamer
MARRUM Murram
MARTEL Armlet
MARTEN Rament
*MARTHA Matrah
MARTIN Antrim
*MARTOS Morats, Mostar, Stroam, Stroma
MASCLE Camels, Macles, Mescal, Scamel
MASCON Socman
MASCOT Comsat, Satcom
MASERS Ramses, Smears
*MASERU Amuser, Mauser
MASHED Shamed
MASHER Harems, Shamer
MASHES Shames
MASKER Makers
MASONS Namsos, Samson
MASORA Aromas
MASQUE Squame
MASTER Armest, Armets, Maters, Remast, Stream, Tamers, Tremas

MATERS Armest, Armets, Master, Remast, Stream, Tamers, Tremas
MATICO Atomic
MATIES Samite, Semita, Tamise
MATING Taming
MATINS Mantis, Stamin, Tamins
*MATRAH Martha
*MATSUE Meatus
MAUGER Maugre, Murage
MAUGRE Mauger, Murage
MAULER Ramule
*MAUSER Amuser, Maseru
MAWPUS Wampus
MAYEST Steamy
MEAGER Graeme, Meagre
MEAGRE Graeme, Meager
MEANER Rename
MEANLY Laymen, Namely
MEASES Seames, Sesame
MEASLY Samely
MEATAL Malate, Tamale
MEATUS Matsue
MEDALS Damsel
MEDDLE Melded
MEDIAL Imelda, Mailed
MEDIAN Daimen, Damien, Demain, Maiden, Mained, Medina
*MEDINA Daimen, Damien, Demain, Maiden, Mained, Median
*MEDISE Demise
MEDLAR Dermal, Marled
*MEDUSA Amused, Sea-mud
MEERED Redeem, Remede
MEETER E-meter
*MEGANS Gasmen, Manges
MEGERG Megger
MEGGER Megerg
MEGRIM Gimmer
MEITHS Theism, Themis
MELANO Malone
MELDED Meddle

MELEES Samele
MELLAY Lamely
MELOID Moiled
MELONS Lemnos, Lemons,
  Solemn
MELTER Remelt
MELTON Loment, Molten
*MENADO Daemon, Moaned,
  Modane, Modena, Nomade
MENADS Amends, Desman
MENAGE Manege
MENDER Red-men, Remend
MENIAL Elmina, Maline
MENNAD Manned
MENSAL Anselm, Lemans
MENTAL Lament, Mantel, Mantle
MENTOR Merton, Montre
MENURA Manure, Murena
*MERANO Enamor, Moaner,
  Monera
*MERCIA Crimea
MEREST Mestre, Meters, Metres,
  Restem, Termes
MERGED Germed
MERGEE Emerge
*MERIDA Admire
*MERILL Miller, Remill
MERILS Milers, Smiler
MERISM Mimers, Simmer
MERITS Mister, Miters, Mitres,
  Remits, Smiter, Timers
MERLIN Limner, Milner
*MEROPS Mopers, Proems
*MERSEA Ameers, Ameres,
  Ramees, Seamer
*MERSIN Miners
*MERTON Mentor, Montre
MESAIL Mesial, Salemi, Samiel,
  Sliema
MESCAL Camels, Macles, Mascle,
  Scamel
MESIAL Mesail, Salemi, Samiel,
  Sliema

MESIAN Amiens, Amines,
  Inseam
MESLIN Limens, Semlin, Simnel
MESSAN Manses
MESTEE Esteem
*MESTRE Merest, Meters, Metres,
  Restem, Termes
METAGE Gamete
METALS Lamest, Samlet
METEOR Remote
METERS Merest, Mestre, Metres,
  Restem, Termes
METHOD Demoth, Mothed
METIER Re-emit, Retime, Tremie
METRES Merest, Mestre, Meters,
  Restem, Termes
MICATE Acmite
MICHED Chimed
MICHER Chimer
MIDDEN Minded
MID-SEA Amides
*MIERES Misere, Remise
MIHRAB Brahmi
MIKRON Morkin
MILADY Diamyl
MILDEN Limned, Mindel
MILERS Merils, Smiler
MILLER Merill, Remill
*MILNER Limner, Merlin
*MILSPE Impels, Simple
MILTER Rimlet
MIMERS Merism, Simmer
MIMOSA Maoism
MINDED Midden
*MINDEL Limned, Milden
MINDER Remind
MINERS Mersin
MINES Seisms
*MINOAN Amnion
MINTER Remint
MINUET Minute, Munite, Mutine
MINUTE Minuet, Munite, Mutine
MINXES Mixens,
MIRAGE Gamier, Imager, Maigre

*MIRANO Mainor, Marino,
　Marion
MIRIER Rimier
MIRING Riming
MISCUE Cesium
*MISENO Eonism, Monies,
　Simcon, Simone
MISERE Mieres, Remise
MISERS Remiss
MISHAP Pashim
MISLED Slimed, Smiled
MISSAL Salmis
MISSED Demiss
MISSEE Emesis
MISSEL Slimes, Smiles
MISSES Seisms
MIS-SET Smites, Stimes, Tmesis
MISTED Demist, Demits, Stimed
MISTER Merits, Miters, Mitres,
　Remits, Smiter, Timers
MISTLE Smilet
MITERS Merits, Mister, Mitres,
　Remits, Smiter, Timers
MITHAN Hitman
MITHER Hermit
*MITHRA Thairm
MITRAL Ramtil
MITRES Merits, Mister, Miters,
　Remits, Smiter, Timers
MIXENS Minxes
MOANED Daemon, Menado,
　Modane, Modena, Nomade
MOANER Enamor, Merano,
　Monera
MOBBED Bombed
MOBILE Bemoil, Emboil, Emboli
*MODANE Daemon, Moaned,
　Menado, Modena, Nomade
*MODDER Modred
MODELS Seldom
*MODENA Daemon, Menado,
　Modane, Moaned, Nomade
MODERN Morned, Nemrod,
　Normed, Rodmen

MODIFY Domify
MODIUS Odiums, Sodium
*MODRED Modder
MODULI Dolium, Idolum
MOIDER Dormie
*MOIGNO Mooing
MOILED Meloid
MOIRES Isomer, Rimose
MOLARS Morals, Morsal
MOLDER Remold
MOLEST Motels
*MOLINA Almoin, Monial,
　Oilman
MOLINE Oilmen
MOLLAH Ollamh
MOLTEN Loment, Melton
MOMENT Montem
MONADS Damson, Nomads
MONARO Maroon, Ramoon
MONDAY Dynamo
MONERA Enamor, Merano,
　Moaner
MONGER Germon, Morgen
MONIAL Almoin, Molina,
　Oilman
MONIED Domine
MONIES Eonism, Miseno,
　Simeon, Simone
MONISM Nomism, 'Simmon
MONIST Inmost
*MONROE Mooner, Morone
MONTEM Moment
*MONTES Ostmen
MONTRE Mentor, Merton
MOOING Moigno
MOONER Monroe, Morone
MOORED Droome, Roomed
MOOTED Toomed
MOPERS Merops, Proems
MOPISH Ophism
MORALS Molars, Morsal
MORATS Martos, Mostar,
　Stroam, Stroma
MORELS Morsel

MORGAY Goramy
MORGEN Germon, Monger
MORISH Orhesm
MORISH Romish
MORKIN Mikron
MORNAY Romany
MORNED Modern, Nemrod,
  Normed, Rodmen
MORNES Sermon
MORONE Monroe, Mooner
MOROSE Romeos
MORSAL Molars, Morals
MORSEL Morels
*MOSTAR Martos, Morats,
  Stroam, Stroma
MOTELS Molest
MOTHED Demoth, Method
MOT-MOT Tomtom
MOTORS Tromso
MOUNDS Osmund
MOUSED Dumose, Soumed,
  Usedom
MOUSES Mousse, Smouse
MOUSSE Mouses, Smouse
MOUTAN Amount, Outman
MONALS Salmon
MULISH Hilums
MUMBLE Bummle
MUNITE Minuet, Minute, Mutine
MURAGE Mauger, Maugre
MURENA Manure, Menura
MURINE Nerium
MURING Ingrum
MURRAM Marrum
MUSCAT Mustac
MUSHER Rheums
MUSLIN Unslim
MUSMON Summon
MUSTAC Muscat
MUSTER Estrum, Stumer
MUTANT Tutman
MUTINE Minuet, Minute, Munite
MUTISM Summit
MUTUAL Umlaut

MYELON Lemony
MYGALE Gamely, Gleamy
MYOGEN Gemony
MYOSIN Simony
MYOTIC Comity
MYRTLE Termly
MYTHIC Thymic
MYTHUS Thymus

*NABEUL Nebula, Unable, Unbale
NAGGED Ganged
NAGGER Ganger, Grange,
  Gregan
*NAGINA Angina
NAGORS Angors, Argons,
  Groans, Orangs, Organs,
  Sargon, Sarong
NAILED Aldine, Alined, Daniel,
  Delian, Denial, Lead-in
NAILER Enrail, Larine, Linear,
  Renail
NALLAH Hallan
NAMELY Laymen, Meanly
*NAMSOS Masons, Samson
*NAPIER Rapine
*NAPLES Panels, Planes
NAPPED Append
NAPPER Parpen, Rappen
NARDED Dander, Darned
NARINE Ranine
NARKED Darkes, Darken,
  Ranked
NASARD Sandra
NASION Anions
*NASSER Sarsen, Snares
NASTIC Antics, Incast
NASUTE Austen, Unseat
NATION Anoint
NATTER Ratten
NATURE Aunter, Neutra, Tea-urn
NAUTCH Chaunt
NAUTIC Anicut
NEALED Aneled, Leaden, Leaned
NEANIC Canine, Encina

NEAPED Peaned
NEARBY Barney, Bayern, Bernay
NEARED Deaner, Dearne,
　Earned, Endear
NEARER Earner, Re-earn
NEARLY Anerly
NEATEN Etnean
NEATER Entera, Rateen, Renate
NEBRIS Brines
NEBULA Nabeul, Unable, Unbale
*NECKAR Canker, Reckan
NECTAR Canter, Carnet, Centra,
　Creant, Cretan, Recant, Tanrec,
　Trance
NEEDER Reeden
NEEDLY Leyden
NEFAST Fasten, Stefan
NEIGHS Hinges, Senghi
*NEISSE Seines
NEIVES Envies, Nieves
NELIES Ensile, Enisle, Nelsie,
　Senile, Silene
*NELSIE Ensile, Enisle, Nelies,
　Senile, Silene
*NEMROD Modern, Morned,
　Normed, Rodmen
*NEPALI Alpine, Epinal, Penial,
　Pineal
NEPMAN Penman
NEPMEN Penmen
NEREID Denier, Edirne, Reined,
　Renied
NEREIS Seiner, Serein, Serine,
　Sirene
*NERITA Ratine, Retain, Retina,
　Tirane
NERITE Entire
*NERIUM Murine
NERVAL Vernal
NERVED Denver, Revend,
　Vender, Verden
NERVES Nevers, Severn
NESTED Endest, Sedent, Tensed

NESTER Enters, Ernest, Rentes,
　Resent, Sterne, Strene, Tenser,
　Ternes
*NESTON Nonets, Sonnet, Stonen,
　Tenons, Tenson, Tonnes
*NESTOR Noters, Reston, Stoner,
　Strone, Tenors, Tensor, Terson,
　Toners, Trones
*NESTOS Onsets, Setons, Stones
NETFUL Fluent, Unfelt, Unleft
NETHER Threne
NETTED Detent, Tented
NETTER Retent, Tenter
NEURAL Ulnare, Unreal
NEUTER Retune, Tenure, Tureen
*NEUTRA Aunter, Nature, Tea-urn
*NEVERS Nerves, Severn
*NEWARK Wanker
NEWISH Whines
*NIASSA Asians
NICEST Incest, Insect, Scient
NICHED Chined, Inched
NICHER Enrich, Richen
NICHES Chines, Chinse, Inches
*NICOLE Cineol
NIDDER Ridden, Rinded
NIDGES Deigns, Design, Dinges,
　Sdeign, Signed, Singed
NIDGET Tinged
NIDING Dining, Indign
NIDOSE Diones, Donsie, Edison,
　Noised, No-side, Onside, Side-
　on
NIELLO Lionel, O'Neill
NIEVES Envies, Neives
*NIEVRE Envier, Venire, Verein
NIGGER Ginger
NIGGLE Gingle, Liggen
NIGHTY Thingy
NILGAI Ailing
NILGAU Lingua
NILOTE Entoil, Lionet
*NINGBO Boning
NIOBIC Bionic

NIPPLE Lippen
NIPTER Pinter, Pterin
NIRLES Lerins, Liners
NIRLIE Inlier
NITRES Insert, Inters, Retins,
    Sinter, Strine, Trines
NITRIC Citrin
NITTER Retint, Tinter
NIVOSE Vinose
NOBBUT Button
*NOCERA Cornea
NOCKED Conked
NOCTUA Toucan, Uncoat
NODATE Atoned, Donate
NODDER Droned
NODOSE Noosed
NODULE Louden, Oundle
NOESIS Enosis, Eosins, Essoin,
    Noises, Ossein, Seison, Sonsie
NOETIC Notice
NOISED Diones, Donsie, Edison,
    Nidose, No-side, Onside, Side-
    on
NOISES Enosis, Eosins, Essoin,
    Noesis, Ossein, Seison, Sonsie
NOMADE Daemon, Menado,
    Moaned, Modane, Modena
NOMADS Damson, Monads
NOMISM Monism, 'Simmon
NONETS Neston, Sonnet, Stonen,
    Tenons, Tenson, Tonnes
NONIUS Unions, Unison
NOOSED Nodose
NORITE Orient
NORMAL Marlon
*NORMAS Manors, Ramson,
    Ransom, Romans
NORMED Modern, Morned,
    Nemrod, Rodmen
NOSERS Senors, Sensor, Serons,
    Snores
NOSHER Herons, Honers,
    Rhones, Senhor

NO-SIDE Diones, Donsie, Edison,
    Nidose, Noised, Onside, Side-on
NOSIER Senior, Soneri
NOSTOC Contos, Oncost
NOTARY Aroynt, Troyan
NOTERS Nestor, Reston, Stoner,
    Strone, Tenors, Tensor, Terson,
    Toners, Trones
NOTICE Noetic
NOTING Toning
NOTOUR Unroot
NOUGHT Hognut
NOUSLE Ensoul, Olenus, Unsole
NOVELS Sloven
*NSANJE Jansen
NUBIAS Anubis, Unbias
NUBILE Unible
NUCHAL Launch, Unchal
NUCLEI Leucin
NUDGED Dunged
NUDGER Gerund
NUDGES Snudge
NUDITY Untidy
NUNCIO Uncoin
NURLED Lurden, Rundle
NURSED Sunder, Unders, Unreds
NURSER Runers
NUTATE Attune, Tauten, Tetuan
NUTLET Lutten
NUTMEG Gnetum
NUT-OIL Oil-nut, Ultion
NUTRIA Taurin

OAKERS Arkose, Resoak, Soaker,
OARING Ignaro, Onagri, Origan
OBELUS Blouse, Boules
*OBERON Borneo
OBLAST Bloats
OBLATE Boatel, Lobate
OBSESS Bosses
OCCURS Crocus, Roccus, Succor
OCELLI Collie
OCHERY Ochrey

OCHREA Chorea, Horace, Orache, Rochea
OCHRES Chores, Cosher
OCHREY Ochery
*OCTANS Actons, Cantos, Cotans, Snacot
OCTAVE Avocet
ODD-MAN Dodman
ODIUMS Modius, Sodium
ODIOUS Iodous
OECIST Cotise
OFF-CUT Cut-off
OFFPUT Put-Off
OFFSET Set-off
OGRESS Gorses, Sogers
OHMAGE Homage
OILERS Elisor, Lories Oriels, Reoils, Serlio, Soiler
OIL-GAS Golias
OILMAN Almoin, Molina, Monial
OILMEN Moline
OIL-NUT Nut-oil, Ultion
OKAYED Kayoed
OLDEST Stoled
OLEINS Eloins, Esloin, Insole, Lesion, Sileno, Solein
*OLENUS Ensoul, Nousle, Unsole
*OLINDA Ladino
OLINGO Looing
OLIVER Violer
OLIVES Solive, Voiles
*OLIVET Violet
OLIVIN Violin
OLLAMH Mollah
OMBERS Bromes, Ombres, Somber, Sombre
OMBRES Bromes, Ombers, Somber, Sombre
OMBROS Brooms, Sombor
OMENTA To-name
ONAGER Gerona, Orange
ONAGRA Angora, Aragon, Arango, Organa
ONAGRI Ignaro, Oaring, Origan

ONCERS Censor, Crones, Recons
ONCOME Come-on
ONCOST Contos, Nostoc
*O'NEILL Lionel, Niello
ONEYER Oneyre
ONEYRE Oneyer
ONIRIC Ironic
ONRUSH Hurons
ONSETS Nestos, Setons, Stones
ON-SIDE Dinoes, Donsie, Edison, Nidose, Noised, No-side, Side-on
OOCYTE Coyote
OODLES Dolose, Loosed, Sooled
OOGENY Gooney
OPALED Pedalo
OPENED Depone
OPENER Perone, Repone, Reopen
OPENLY Poleyn
OPERAS Pesaro
*OPHISM Mopish
OPHITE Ethiop
OPINED Pioned
OPINES Ponies
OPPUGN Popgun
OPSTER Poster, Presto, Repost, Repots, Retops, Stoper, Topers, Tropes
OPTANT Patton
OPTICS Picots, Topics
OPTING Poting, Toping
OPTION Potion
ORACHE Chores, Horace, Ochrea, Rochea
ORACHS Cahors
ORACLE Carole, Coaler, Recoal
ORANGE Gerona, Onager
ORANGS Angors, Argons, Groans, Nagors Organs, Sargon, Sarong
ORBATE Boater, Borate, Rebato
ORBING Boring, Robing
ORBITS Bistro

ORCEIN Coiner, Enrico, Orcine, Recoin
ORCHAL Choral, Lorcha
ORCHEL Choler
ORCHID Droich, Rhodic
ORCHIS Choirs, Ichors
ORCINE Coiner, Enrico, Orcein, Recoin
ORDAIN Dorian, Inroad
ORDEAL Laredo, Loader, Reload
ORDERS Dorsen
ORDURE Dourer
OREADS Adores, Sea-rod, Soared
*OREGON Orgone
ORGANA Angora, Aragon, Arango, Onagra
ORGANS Angors, Argons, Groans, Nagors, Orangs, Sarong, Sargon
ORGEAT Toe-rag
ORGONE Oregon
ORGUES Grouse, Rogues, Rouges, Rugose
ORIELS Elisor, Lories, Oilers, Reoils, Soiler, Serlio
ORIENT Norite
ORIGAN Ignaro, Oaring, Onagri
*ORIGEN Ernigo, Ignore, Region
*ORIONS Orison
ORISON Orions
ORNATE Atoner, Tenora
ORPINE Pioner
ORPINS Prison, Proins, Ripons
*ORRELL Erroll, Reroll, Roller
ORRICE Corrie
*OSBERT Besort, Sorbet, Strobe
*OSCARS Across
OSCINE Conies, Cosine, Soncie
OSCULE Coleus
OSMUND Mounds
OSSEIN Enosis, Eosins, Essoin, Noesis, Noises, Seison, Sonsie
OSTEAL Lao-tse
*OSTEND Doesn't, Donets, Stoned

OSTENT Teston, Totnes
OSTIUM Timous
OSTLER Relost, Rostel, Sterol, Torsel
OSTMEN Montes
OTHERS Rothes, Throes, Tosher
OTTERS Troste
OUGHED Douche
OUCHES Chouse
OUCHTS Sought, Toughs
OUNDLE Louden, Nodule
OUSELS Louses, Soleus
OUSTED Toused
OUSTER Outers, Routes, Souter, Touser, Trouse
OUTBAR Rubato, Tabour
OUTCUT Cut-out
OUTERS Ouster, Routes, Souter, Touser, Trouse
OUTFIT Fit-out
OUTLAY Lay-out
OUTLER Elutor
OUTLET Let-out
OUTMAN Amount, Moutan
OUTPOP Popout
OUTPUT Put-out
OUTRED Detour, Douter, Redout, Routed, Toured
OUTRIG Rig-out
OUTRUN Run-out
OUTSET Set-out
OUTTOP Puttoo
OVATES Avoset
OVERDO Doover
OVERGO Groove
OVERLY Volery
OVULAR Louvar, Valour
OWERBY Bowery, Bowyer
OWLERS Lowers, Rowels, Slower
OWLERY Lowery
OWLETS Elstow, Lowest, Towels
OWLING Lowing
OWLISH Lowish

OWNERS Resown, Rowens,
Worsen
OWNING Woning
OXALIS Loxias
OX-HEAD Hoaxed
OYSTER Rosety, Storey, Troyes,
Toyers, Tyroes
OZONES Snooze

PACERS Capers, Casper, Crapes,
Escarp, Parsec, Recaps, Scrape,
Secpar, Spacer
PACHAK Chapka
PACING Caping
PACKER Repack
PADANG Padnag
PADDER Draped, Parded, Praded
PADLES Lapsed, Pedals, Pleads
PADNAG Padang
PADRES Drapes, Parsed, Rasped,
Repads, Spader, Spared, Spread
PAELLA Pallae
PAEONS Peason
PAGING Gaping
PAIDLE Aliped, Elapid, Pailed,
Pleiad
PAILED Aliped, Elapid, Paidle,
Pleiad
PAINTS Patins, Pintas, Ptisan
PAIRED Diaper, Pardie, Repaid,
PALEST Palets, Pastel, Peltas,
Petals, Plates, Pleats, Septal,
Staple, Tepals
PALETS Palest, Pastel, Peltas,
Petals, Plates, Pleats, Septal,
Staple, Tepals
PALISH Phials, Silpha
PALLAE Paella
*PALMAS Lampas, Plasma
PALMED Lamped
PALMER Ampler, Marple
PALOLO Apollo
PALPED Dapple, Lapped
PALPUS Slap-up

PALTER Plater
PALTRY Partly
PAMPER Mapper
PANDER Repand
PANELS Naples, Planes
PANICK Ink-cap
PANICS Panisc
PANISC Panics
PANNEL Pennal
PANNUS Sannup, Unsnap,
Unspan
PANTED Pedant, Pentad
PANTER Arpent, Enrapt,
Entrap, Parent, Pterna, Trepan
PAPERS Sapper
PAPERY Prepay, Yapper
PAPULE Upleap
*PARCAE Ear-cap
PARCEL Carpel, Placer
PARDED Draped, Padder,
Praded
PARDIE Diaper, Paried, Repaid
PARENT Arpent, Enrapt,
Entrap, Panter, Pterna, Trepan
PARERS Parser, Rasper, Sparer,
Sparre
PARGES Gapers, Gasper,
Grapes, Sparge
PARIAH Raphia
*PARIAN Pirana
PARIES Aspire, Persia, Praise,
Spirae, Spirea
PARING Raping
PARISH Hispar, Shairp, Raphis
PARKAS Kaspar
PARKER Repark
PARLED Pedlar, Predal
PARLEY Pearly, Player, Replay
PARPEN Napper, Rappen
PARROT Pro-art, Raptor
PARSEC Capers, Casper,
Crapes, Escarp, Pacers, Recaps,
Scrape, Secpar, Spacer
PARSED Drapes, Padres,
Rasped, Repads, Spader,
Spared, Spread

*PARSEE A-per-se, Prease, Serape
PARSER Parers, Rasper, Sparer,
  Sparre
PARSES Aspers, Passer, Prases,
  Repass, Spaers, Spares, Sparse,
  Spears
PARSON Aprons, Prosna
PARTAN Tarpan, Trapan
PARTED Depart, Drapet, Petard,
  Prated, Traped
PARTER Prater, Repart
PARTIM Armpit, Impart
PARTLY Paltry
PARTON Patron, Tarpon
PARURE Uprear
PARVIS Privas
PASHIM Mishap
PASHED Hasped, Phased,
  Shaped
PASHES Phases, Shapes
PASHTO Pathos, Potash
PASSED Sepads, Spades
PASSER Aspers, Parses, Prases,
  Repass, Spaers, Spares, Sparse,
  Spears
PASSIM Sampis
PASTED Adepts
PASTEL Palest, Palets, Peltas,
  Petals, Plates, Pleats, Septal,
  Staple, Tepals
PASTER Paters, Petars, Praest,
  Prates, Repast, Tapers, Trapes
PASTES Spates, Speats, Stapes
PASTIL Alpist, Plaits, Spital
PASTOR Asport, Portas, Sap-rot
PATENS Septan
PATENT Patten
PATERA Aptera, Petara
PATERS Paster, Petars, Praest,
  Prates, Repast, Tapers, Trapes
PATHIC Haptic, Phatic
PATHOS Pashto, Potash
PATINA Taipan
PATINS Paints, Pintas, Ptisan
PATIOS Patois

PATOIS Patios
PATRAS Satrap, Sparta
PATROL Portal
PATRON Parton, Tarpon
PATTEN Patent
PATTLE T-plate
*PATTON Optant
PAVERS Sparve
PAVINS Spavin
PAVISE Spavie
PAWLED Dewlap
PAWNER Enwrap, Repawn
PAYERS Repays, Speary
PEACES Escape
PEALED Leaped, Pedale
PEALER Lapeer, Leaper, Repeal
PEANED Neaped
PEARLY Parley, Player, Replay
PEASON Paeons
PEBBLY Plebby
PECHES Cheeps, Speech
PECTIN Incept, Peinct
PEDALE Leaped, Pealed
PEDALO Opaled
PEDALS Lapsed, Padles, Pleads
PEDANT Panted, Pentad
PEDLAR Parled, Predal
PEDROS Dopers, Prosed
PEENED Deepen
PEERED Deeper
PEEVER Preeve
PEINCT Incept, Pectin
PELIKE Kelpie
*PELION Pinole
PELMAS Maples, Sample
PELMET Temple
PELOID Diploe, Dipole
*PELOPS Peplos
PELOTA Pot-ale
PELTAS Palest, Palets, Pastel,
  Petals, Plates, Pleats, Septal,
  Staple, Tepals
PELTER Petrel
PELTRY Pertly
PENDED Depend

PENGOS Sponge
PENIAL Alpine, Epinal, Nepali, Pineal
PENMAN Nepman
PENMEN Nepmen
PENNAL Pannel
PENSEL Spleen
PENSIL Pilsen, Spelin, Spinel, Spline
PENTAD Panted, Pedant
PEPLOS Pelops
PEPLUS Supple
PERDUS Drupes, Dupers, Prudes, Pursed
PEREIA Epeira
PERILS Lisper, Perlis, Pilers, Pliers
PERIOD Dopier
PERISH Reship, Seriph
PERKIN Pinker
***PERLIS** Lisper, Perils, Pilers, Pliers
PERMED Deperm, Premed
PERMIT Primet
PERNIS Repins, Ripens, Sniper
***PERNOD** Ponder
PERONE Opener, Reopen, Repone
PERSES Preses, Speers, Sperse, Sprees
***PERSIA** Aspire, Paries, Praise, Spirae, Spirea
***PERSIC** Cripes, Crepis, Precis, Prices, Spicer
PERSON Prones
PERSUE Peruse, Purees, Rupees
PERTLY Peltry
PERUKE Keuper
PERUSE Persue, Purees, Rupees
***PESARO** Operas
PESETA Etapes
PESTER Peters, Petres, Pre-set, Pteres, Serpet
***PETAIN** Pineta

PETALS Palest, Palets, Pastel, Peltas, Plates, Pleats, Septal, Staple, Tepals
PETARA Aptera, Patera
PETARD Depart, Drapet, Parted, Prated, Traped
***PETARS** Paster, Paters, Praest, Prates, Repast, Tapers, Trapes
PETERS Pester, Petres, Preset, Pteres, Serpet
PETHER Threep
PETREA Repeat, Retape
PETREL Pelter
PETRES Pester, Peters, Preset, Pteres, Serpet
PETROL Replot
PHARES Hepars, Phrase, Raphes, Seraph, Shaper, Sherpa, Sphaer
PHASED Hasped, Pashed, Shaped
PHASES Pashes, Shapes
PHASIS Spahis
PHATIC Haptic, Pathic
PHEERS Herpes, Hesper, Sphere
PHENOL Holpen
PHIALS Palish, Silpha
PHOCAE Epocha
PHONIC Chopin
PHRASE Hepars, Phares, Raphes, Seraph, Shaper, Sherpa, Sphaer
PHYSIC Scyphi
PHYTON Python, Typhon
PICENE Piecen
PICKER Repick, Ripeck
PICOTE Poetic
PICOTS Optics, Topics
***PICTON** Pontic
PIECEN Picene
PIECER Pierce, Recipe
PIECES Specie
PIENDS Despin, Sniped, Spined
PIERCE Piecer, Recipe
PIGEON Epigon
PIGHTS Spight

PIG-PEN Epping
PIGSNY Spying
*PILATE Aplite
PILERS Lisper, Perils, Perlis, Pliers
PILE-UP Up-pile
PILEUS Epulis
PILING Gilpin
PILOTS Pistol, Postil, Spoilt
PILOUS Poilus
*PILSEN Pensil, Spelin, Spinel, Spline
PIMENT Pitmen
PIMOLA Lipoma
PINCER Prince
PINCOP Coppin
PINEAL Alpine, Epinal, Penial
PINERO Orpine
PINETA Petain
PINGLE Pin-leg
PINITE Tie-pin
PINKER Perkin
*PIN-LEG Pingle
PINNAS Inspan
PINOLE Pelion
PINTAS Paints, Patins, Ptisan
*PINTER Nipter, Pterin
PIOLET Polite
PIONED Opined
PIOTED Podite
PIPERS Sipper
PIPULS Pupils, Slip-up
PIRANA Parian
PIRATE Pratie, Pteria
PIRAYA Apiary
*PIRENE Repine
PISCES Spices
PISSES Sepsis, Speiss
PISTOL Pilots, Postil, Spoilt
PISTON Instop, Pitons, Points, Potins, Spin-to
PITCHY Pythic
PITMEN Piment

PITONS Instop, Piston, Points, Potins, Spin-to
PIT-PAT Tappit
PITSAW Sawpit
PLACER Carpel, Parcel
PLAICE Epical, Plicae
PLAINS Lapins, Spinal
PLAINT Pliant
PLAISE Espial, Lipase
PLAITS Alpist, Pastil, Spital
PLANER Replan
PLANES Naples, Panels
PLANET Platen
PLANTA Platan
PLASMA Lampas, Palmas
PLATAN Planta
PLATEN Planet
PLATER Palter
PLATES Palest, Palets, Pastel, Peltas, Petals, Pleats, Septal, Staple, Tepals
PLAYER Parley, Pearly, Replay
PLEACH Chapel, Lepcha
PLEADS Lapsed, Padles, Pedals
PLEASE Asleep, Elapse, Sapele
PLEATS Palest, Palets, Pastel, Peltas, Petals, Plates, Septal, Staple, Tepals
PLEBBY Pebbly
PLEIAD Aliped, Elapid, Paidle, Pailed
PLEUGH Guelph
PLENUM Lumpen
PLIANT Plaint
PLICAE Epical, Plaice
PLIERS Lisper, Perils, Perlis, Pilers
PLISSE Slipes, Spiels, Spiles
PLOWER Replow
PLOYED Deploy, Podley
PLUG-IN Puling
PLUMED Dumple, Lumped
PLUTON Pulton
POACHY Pochay

POCHAY Poachy
PODITE Pioted
PODLEY Deploy, Ployed
POETIC Picote
POILUS Pilous
POINTE Pontie
POINTS Instop, Piston, Pitons,
　Potins, Spin-to
POISES Posies
POLERS Proles, Splore
POLEYN Openly
POLING Loping
POLITE Piolet
POLYPS Sloppy
POMADE Apedom
PONDER Pernod
PONGID Doping
PONIES Opines
PONTEE Poteen
PONTES Posnet
*PONTIC Picton
PONTIE Pointe
POODLE Looped, Pooled
POOLED Looped, Poodle
POOLER Looper
POPERY Pyrope
POPGUN Oppugn
POPISH Hippos, Shippo
POPOUT Out-pop
PORERS Prores, Proser, Ropers
PORGER Groper
PORING Proign, Roping
PORKER Proker
PORRET Porter, Pretor, Report
PORTAL Patrol
PORTAS Asport, Pastor, Sap-rot
PORTED Deport, Red-top
PORTER Porret, Pretor, Report
PORTLY Protyl
POSEUR Souper, Uprose
POSHER Ephors, Hopers
POSIES Poises
POSITS Ptosis
POSNET Pontes

POSSET Estops, Stoeps, Stopes
POSTED Depots, Despot, Stoped
POSTER Opster, Presto, Repost,
　Repots, Retops, Stoper, Topers,
　Tropes
POSTIE Sopite
POSTIL Pilots, Pistol, Spoilt
POT-ALE Pelota
POTASH Pashto, Pathos
POTEEN Pontee
POTFUL Topful
POT-HAT Top-hat
POTHER Thorpe
POTING Opting, Toping
POTINS Instop, Piston, Pitons,
　Points, Spin-to
POTION Option
POTMAN Tampon, Topman
POTMEN Topmen
POULES Souple
POUNCE Uncope
POURED Rouped
POURER Repour
POUSSE Spouse
POUTER Roupet, Troupe
*PRADED Daperd, Padder, Parded
*PRAEST Paster, Paters, Petars,
　Prates, Repast, Tapers, Trápes
PRAISE Aspire, Paries, Persia,
　Spirae, Spirea
PRANGS Sprang
PRASES Aspers, Parses, Passer,
　Repass, Spaers, Spares, Sparse,
　Spears
PRATED Depart, Drapet, Parted,
　Petard, Traped
PRATER Parter, Repart
PRATES Paster, Paters, Petars,
　Praest, Repast, Tapers, Trapes
PRATIE Pirate, Pteria
PREACH Eparch
PRE-ACT Carpet
PRE-ARM Ramper
PREASE A-per-se, Parsee, Serape

PRECES Creeps, Crepes
PRECIS Cripes, Crepis, Persic, Prices, Spicer
PREDAL Parled, Pedlar
PREEVE Peever
PRELIM Limper, Rempli, Rimple
PREMED Deperm, Permed
PREPAY Papery, Yapper
*****PREROV** Prover
PRESES Perses, Speers, Sperse, Sprees
PRESET Pester, Peters, Petres, Pteres, Serpet
PRESTO Opster, Poster, Repost, Repots, Retops, Stopes, Topers, Tropes
PRETOR Porret, Porter, Report
PRE-WAR Rewrap, Warper
PRIALS Spiral
PRICES Cripes, Crepis, Persic, Precis, Spicer
PRIDES Prised, Redips, Risped, Spider, Spired
PRIERS Sprier
PRIEST Sprier
PRIEST Esprit, Pteris, Ripest, Sitrep, Sprite, Stripe, Tripes
*****PRILEP** Lipper, Ripple
PRIMAL Imparl
PRIMES Simper
PRIMET Permit
PRIMUS Purims, Purism
PRINCE Pincer
PRINTS Sprint
*****PRIPET** Tipper
PRISED Prides, Redips, Risped, Spider, Spired
PRISES Speirs, Spires
PRISON Orpins, Proins, Ripons
*****PRIVAS** Parvis
PRO-ART Parrot, Raptor
PROBED Bedrop
PROCES Copers, Corpse, Cropes
PROEMS Merops, Mopers

PROFIT Forpit
PROIGN Poring, Roping
PROINS Orpins, Prison, Ripons
PROKER Porker
PROLES Polers, Splore
PRONES Person
PRONGS Sprong
PRONTO Proton
PROPED Dopper
PROPEL Lopper
PRORES Porers, Proser, Ropers
PROSED Dopers, Pedros
PROSER Porers, Prores, Ropers
PROSIT Tripos
*****PROSNA** Aprons, Parson
PROTON Pronto
PROTYL Portly
*****PROUST** Sprout, Stroup, Stupor
PROVER Prerov
PRUDES Drupes, Dupers, Perdus, Pursed
PRUNES Spurne
PTERES Pester, Peters, Petres, Preset, Serpet
PTERIA Pirate, Pratie
PTERIN Nipter, Pinter
*****PTERIS** Esprit, Priest, Ripest, Sitrep, Sprite, Stripe, Tripes
PTERNA Arpent, Enrapt, Entrap, Panter, Parent, Trepan
PTISAN Paints, Patins, Pintas
PTOSIS Posits
PUDENT Punted
PUISNE Supine
PULING Plug-in
PULPER Purple, Repulp
PULTON Pluton
PUMPER Repump
PUNCHI Chin-up
PUNIER Purine, Unripe
PUNISH Unship
PUNNET Unpent
PUNTED Pudent

PUNTOS Put-ons, Ton-ups, Unstop
PUPILS Pipuls, Slip-up
PURDAH Hard-up
PUREES Persue, Peruse, Rupees
PURELY Purley
PUREST Erupts
PURGES Spurge
***PURIMS** Primus, Purism
PURINE Punier, Unripe
PURISM Primus, Purims
PURIST Spruit, Stir-up, Uprist, Upstir
PURLED Drupel
***PURLEY** Purely
PURPLE Pulper, Repulp
PURSED Drupes, Dupers, Perdus, Prudes
***PUSHTO** Tophus, Upshot
PUSHTU Shut-up
PUT-OFF Offput
PUT-ONS Puntos, Ton-ups, Unstop
PUT-OUT Output
PUTTOO Outtop
PUZZEL Puzzle
PUZZLE Puzzel
PYROPE Popery
PYTHIC Pitchy
PYTHON Phyton, Typhon

QUAILS Squail
QUAINT Quinta
QUAKES Squeak
QUARTE Quatre
QUATRE Quarte
QUEEST Queest
QUESAL Equals, Lasque, Squeal
QUILLS Squill
QUINCE Cinque
QUINSY Squiny
QUINTA Quaint
QUINTS Squint

QUIRES Quseir, Risque, Squier, Squire
QUIRTS Squirt
QUOTER Roquet, Torque
***QUSEIR** Quires, Risque, Squier, Squire

RABATE Abater, Trabea
RABATO Abator
RABBET Barbet
RABBLE Barbel, Barble
RABIES Braise, Serbia
RACEME Amerce, Careme
RACE-UP Apercu
RACHES Arches, Chares, Chaser, Eschar, Search
RACHIS Chairs, Charis
RACIAL Alaric
RACING Arcing, Caring
RACIST Crista
RACKED Arcked, Carked, Craked, Dacker
RACKET Retack, Tacker
RACKLE Calker, Lacker, Recalk
RACOON Corona
RADDLE Aldred, Ladder, Larded
RADIAN Adrian, Andria
RADOME Roamed
RADIUS Darius
RAFFEE Affeer
RAFFIA Affair
RAFFLE Farfel
RAFTED Dafter, Farted
RAFTER Farter, Frater
RAGEST Grates, Greats, Stager, Targes
RAGETH Gather
RAGGED Dagger
RAGGEE Agrege, Reggae
RAGGLE Gargle, Gregal, Lagger
RAGMEN Engram, German, Manger
RAG-TAG Tag-rag
RAGULY Glaury

RAIDER Arride
RAIKED Daiker, Darkie
*****RAIKES** Kaiser
RAILED Adriel, Derail, Laired, Lerida, Relaid
RAILER Rerail
RAINED Dairen, Darien, Derain, Randie
*****RAINER** Renira
RAISED Aiders, Irades
RAISER Airers, Serrai, Sierra
RAISES Arises, Sisera
RAISIN Sirian
RAITED Airted, Tirade
RAKING Arking
RAKISH Shikar
RAMATE Retama
RAMBLE Ambler, Blamer, Lamber, Marble
RAMCAT Tarmac
RAMEES Ameers, Ameres, Seamer, Mersea
RAMENT Marten
*****RAMIST** Marist
RAMLEH Harlem, Mahler
RAMMED Dammer
RAMMEL Lammer
RAMOON Maroon, Monaro
RAMPED Damper
RAMPER Pre-arm
RAMSON Manors, Normas, Ransom, Romans
RAMSES Masers, Smears
RAMTIL Mitral
RAMULE Mauler
RANCED Cedarn, Craned, Danced
RANCEL Lancer
RANCES Caners, Casern, Cranes, Crenas, Sarcen
RANCHO Anchor, Archon, Charon
RANDEM Manred, Redman, Remend

RANDIE Dairen, Darien, Darain, Rained
RANDLE Aldern, Darnel, Enlard, Lander, Reland
RANDOM Rodman
RANGED Danger, Gander, Garden, Gnared, Grande
RANGER Garner
RANGES Angers, Sanger, Serang
RANINE Narine
RANGLE Angler, Largen, Regnal
RANKED Danker, Darken, Narked
RANKER Rerank
RANKLE Lanker
RANSEL Learns
RANSOM Manors, Normas, Ramson, Romans
RANTED Ardent, Endart
RANTER Errant, Terran
RAPHES Hepars, Phares, Phrase, Seraph, Shaper, Sherpa, Sphear
*****RAPHIA** Pariah
RAPHIS Hispar, Parish, Shairp
RAPIDS Sparid, Spraid
RAPIER Repair
RAPINE Napier
RAPING Paring
RAPIST Tapirs
RAPPED Dapper
RAPPEL Lapper
RAPPEN Napper, Parpen
RAPTOR Parrot, Pro-art
RARELY Rearly
RAREST Arrest, Arrets, Raster, Raters, Retars, Sartre, Starer, Tarres, Terras
RASANT Ratans
RASCAL Lascar, Sacral, Sarlac, Scalar
RASHED Dasher, Shader, Shared
RASHER Sharer
RASHES Shares, Shears
RASING Grains, Sangir

RASPED Drapes, Padres, Parsed, Repads, Spader, Spared, Spread

RASPER Parers, Parser, Sparer, Sparre

RASTER Arrest, Arrets, Rarest, Raters, Retars, Sartre, Starer, Tarres, Terras

***RASTUS** Straus, Sutras, Tarsus, Tussar

RATALS Altars, Astral, Talars, Tarsal

RATANS Rasant

RATEEN Entera, Neater, Renate,

RATELS Alerts, Alters, Artels, Laster, Resalt, Salter, Slater, Slater, Stelar, Tarsel

RATERS Arrest, Arrets, Rarest, Raster, Retars, Sartre, Starer, Tarres, Terras

RATHES Earths, Haters, Hearts, Sarthe, Sheart

RATINE Nerita, Retain, Retina, Tirane

RATING Gratin, Taring, Tringa

RATION Aroint

RATIOS Aorist, Aristo Artois, Satori

RATITE Attire, Tertia, Tiaret

RATLIN Trinal

RATTAN Tantra, Tartan

RATTED Tarted, Tetrad

RATTEN Natter

RATTLE Latter, Tatler

RATTLY Tartly

RATTON Attorn, Rottan

RAVE-IN Erivan, Ravine, Vainer, Vanier

RAVELS Lavers, Salver, Serval, Slaver, Valser, Velars, Versal

RAVEST Averts, Starve, Staver, Tarves, Tavers, Traves, Vaster

REVETH Thrave

RAVINE Erivan, Rave-in, Vainer, Vanier

RAVING Girvan

***RAWDEN** Andrew, Darwen, Dawner, Wander, Warden, Warned

RAWING Waring

RAYING Grainy

RAYLES Layers, Relays, Slayer

RAYLET Elytra, Lyrate, Realty, Telary

***RAYNER** Yarner

RAYNES Renays, Sarney, Senary, Yearns

REACTS Carets, Cartes, Caster, Caters, Crates, Cresta, Recast, Traces

READDS Adders, Dreads, Sadder

READER Dearer, Reared, Redare, Reread

REAGAN Grenaa

REALIA Aerial

REALLY Re-ally

RE-ALLY Really

REALTY Elytra, Lyrate, Raylet, Telary

REAMED Remade, Remead

REAMER Marree

REARED Dearer, Reader, Redare, Reread

REARLY Rarely

REASON Arseno, Senora

REASTS Assert, Asters, Astres Stares, Stresa

REATES Aretes, Asteer, Easter, Eaters, Reseat, Saeter, Seater, Staree, Steare, Teaser, Teresa

REAVED Evader, Veader

REAVES Averse, Varese

REAVOW Avower

REBACK Backer

REBAIT Baiter, Berite, Terbia

REBAKE Beaker

REBANK Banker, Barken

REBATE Beater, Berate

REBATO Boater, Borate, Orbate

REBEND Bender
REBIDS Biders, Brides, Debris
REBILL Biller
REBIND Binder, Brined, Inbred
REBITE Bertie
REBOIL Boiler
REBOLT Bolter
REBOSO Booers, Broose
REBOTE Bo-tree
REBREW Brewer
REBUFF Buffer
REBURN Burner
REBUTS Brutes, Buster, Subter, Surbet, Tubers
RECALK Calker, Lacker, Rackle
RECALL Caller, Cellar
RECANE Careen, Enrace
RECANT Canter, Carnet, Centra, Creant, Cretan, Nectar, Tanrec, Trance
RECAPS Capers, Casper, Crapes, Escarp, Pacers, Parsec, Secpar, Scrape, Spacer
RECASE Ceaser, Crease, Searce
RECAST Carets, Cartes, Caster, Caters, Crates, Cresta, Reacts, Traces
RECEDE Decree
RECENT Center, Centre, Tenrec
RECESS Cesser, Screes
*****RECHAB** Bechar, Breach
*****RECIFE** Fierce
RECIPE Piecer, Pierce
RECITE Cerite, Certie, Tierce
RECKAN Canker, Neckar
RECKED Decker
RECKON Conker
RECOAL Carole, Coaler, Oracle,
RECOCK Cocker
RECOIN Coiner, Enrico, Orcien, Orcine
RECOMB Comber
RECONS Censor, Crones, Oncers
RECOOK Cooker

RECOOL Cooler
RECORK Corker, Rocker
RECOST Corset, Cortes, Coster, Escort, Rectos, Scoter, Sector, Tresco
RECOUP Couper, Croupe, Cuerpo
RECTAL Cartel, Claret, Tarcel
RECTOS Corset, Cortes, Coster, Escort, Recost, Scoter, Sector, Tresco
RECTUS Cruets, Cruset, Custer, Eructs, Recuts, Truces
RECUMB Cumber
RECURS Curers, Curser
RECUSE Cereus, Ceruse, Cesure, Creuse, Rescue, Secure
RECUTS Cruets, Cruset, Custer, Eructs, Rectus, Truces
REDACT Carted, Cedrat, Crated, Dectra, Traced
REDANS Sander, Snared
REDARE Dearer, Reader, Reared, Reread
REDARN Darner, Errand, Renard
REDATE Derate, Teared
REDBUD Budder
REDCAP Carped, Craped
*****REDCAR** Carder
REDDEN Derned
REDDLE Eldred
RED-DOG Dodger
REDFIN Finder, Friend, Re-find
REDEAL Dealer, Leader, Relead
REDEEM Meered, Remede
RED-HAT Dareth, Dearth, Hatred, Thread
RED-HOT Dehort
REDIAE Dearie
REDIPS Prides, Prised, Risped, Spider, Spired
*****REDLEG** Gelder, Ledger
REDMAN Manred, Random, Remand

RED-MEN Mender, Remend
REDOCK Corked, Docker, Rocked
REDOUT Detour, Douter, Outred, Routed, Toured
REDRAW Drawer, Reward, Warder, Warred
RED-TOP Deport, Ported
REDUST Duster, Rudest, Rusted
RE-EARN Earner, Nearer
RE-ECHO Cheero, Chores, Cohere, Echoer
REECHY Cheery
REEDEN Needer
RE-EDIT Dieter, Retied, Tiered
REEFED Feeder, Feered, Refeed
REELED Leered
REELER Re-reel
RE-EMIT Metier, Retime, Tremie
REESTY Steery, Yester
REEVED Veered
REEVES Severe
REFEED Feeder, Feered, Reefed
REFEEL Feeler
REFELT Felter, Feltre, Reflet, Trefle
REFILE Liefer, Relief
REFILL Filler
RE-FIND Finder, Friend, Redfin
REFINE Enfire, Ferine, Fernie, Fineer, Infere
REFITS Firest, Freits, Resift, Rifest, Sifter, Strife
REFLET Felter, Feltre, Refelt, Trefle
REFLOW Flower, Fowler, Wolfer
REFOLD Folder
REFOOT Foetor, Footer, Tofore
REFORM Former
REFUEL Ferule, Fueler
REFUTE Feutre
REGAIN Earing, Gainer, Graine, Regian, Regina
REGALE Aleger

REGALO Galore, Gaoler
REGARD Darger, Garred, Gerard, Grader
REGAVE Greave
REGENT Erg-ten, Gerent
REGEST Egrets, Greets, Regets
REGETS Egrets, Greets, Regest
REGGAE Agrege, Raggee
*****REGGIE** Geiger, Greige
REGIAN Earing, Gainer, Graine, Regain, Regina
REGILD Gilder, Girdle, Glider, Lidger, Ridgel
REGILT Riglet
REGIME Emigre
REGINA Earing, Gainer, Graine, Regain, Regian
REGION Eringo, Ignore, Origen
REGIRD Girder
REGIUS Guiser
REGIVE Grieve
REGLOW Glower
REGNAL Angler, Largen, Rangle
REGRIP Griper
REGROW Grower
REGULI Guiler, Ligure, Uglier
REHANG Hanger
REHASH Hasher
REHAUL Hauler
REHEAD Adhere, Header, Hedera
RE-HEAL Healer
REHEAR Hearer
REHEAT Aether, Heater, Hereat
REHEEL Heeler
REHONE Hereon
REHUNG Hunger
RE-ICES Cerise
REIGNS Ingres, Renigs, Resign, Ringes, Signer, Singer
REINED Denier, Edirne, Nereid, Renied
REINKS Inkers, Kirsen, Sinker

REIRDS Derris, Driers, Riders, Sirred
REISTS Resist, Resits, sister
REITER Etrier, Retire
REIVED Derive, Revied, Rieved
REIVER Riever, Verier
REIVES Revies, Revise, Rieves
REJAIL Jailer
REJOIN Joiner
REJOLT Jolter
REKNIT Tinker
RELACE Alerce, Cereal
RELAID Adriel, Derail, Laired, Lerida, Railed
RELAIS Ariels, Asriel, Israel, Resail, Sailer, Serail, Serial
RELAND Aldern, Darnel, Enlard, Lander, Randle
RELATE Elater, Tralee
RELAYS Layers, Rayles, Slayer
RELEAD Dealer, Leader, Redeal
RELEND Lender, Rendle
RELETS Lester, Streel
RELICS Slicer
RELICT Tricel
RELIDE Lieder, Relied
RELIED Lieder, Relide
RELIEF Liefer, Refile
RELIES Resile
RELINE Lierne
RELISH Hirsel, Hirsle
RELIST Lister, Litres, Tilers
RELIVE Levier, Liever, Revile
RELOAD Laredo, Loader, Ordeal
RELOAN Loaner, Lorena
RELOCK Locker, Rockel
RELOSE Resole
RELOST Ostler, Rostel, Sterol, Torsel
RELUCT Culter, Cutler
REMADE Reamed, Remead
REMAIL Elmira, Mailer
REMAIM Maimer
REMAIN Airmen, Marine, Marnie

REMAND Manred, Randem, Redman
REMARK Marker
REMAST Armest, Armets, Master, Maters, Stream, Tamers, Tremas
REMATE Amreet
REMEAD Reamed, Remade
REMEDE Meered, Redeem
REMELT Melter
REMEND Mender, Red-men
REMILL Merill, Miller
REMIND Minder
REMINT Minter
REMISE Mieres, Misere
REMISS Misers
REMITS Merits, Mister, Miters, Mitres, Smiter, Timers
REMOLD Molder
REMORA Roamer
REMOTE Meteor
REMPLI Limper, Prelim, Rimple
RENAIL Enrail, Larine, Linear, Nailer
RENAME Meaner
***RENARD** Darner, Errand, Redarn
RENATE Entera, Neater, Rateen
RENAYS Raynes, Sarney, Senary, Yearns
RENEGE Greene
RENIED Denier, Edirne, Nereid Reined
RENIGS Ingres, Reigns, Resign, Ringes, Signer, Singer
***RENIRA** Rainer
RENNET Tenner
***RENOIR** Ironer
RENOWN Wonner
RENTAL Altern, Antler, Learnt, Ternal
RENTED Tender, Terned
RENTER Rerent

RENTES Enters, Ernest, Nester, Resent, Sterne, Strene, Ternes, Tenser

RENULE Unreel

RE-OILS Elisor, Lories, Oilers, Serlio, Soiler

RE-OPEN Opener, Perone, Repone

REPACK Packer

REPADS Drapes, Padres, Parsed, Rasped, Spader, Spared, Spread

REPAID Diaper, Paired, Pardie

REPAIR Rapier

REPAND Pander

REPARK Parker

REPART Parter, Prater

REPASS Aspers, Parses, Passer, Prases, Spaers, Spares, Sparse, Spears

REPAST Paster, Paters, Petars, Praest, Prates, Tapers, Trapes

REPAWN Enwrap, Pawner

REPAYS Payers, Speary

REPEAL Lapeer, Leaper, Pealer

REPEAT Petrea, Retape

REPICK Picker, Ripeck

REPINE Pirene

REPINS Pernis, Ripens, Sniper

REPLAN Planer

REPLAY Parley, Pearly, Player

REPLOT Petrol

REPLOW Plower

REPLUM Lumper, Rumple

REPONE Opener, Perone, Reopen

REPORT Porret, Porter, Pretor

REPOST Opster, Poster, Presto, Repots, Retops, Stoper, Topers, Tropes

REPOTS Opster, Poster, Presto, Repost, Retops, Stoper, Topers, Tropes

REPOUR Pourer

REPULP Pulper, Purple

REPUMP Pumper

RE-RAIL Railer

RERANK Ranker

RE-RATE Retear, Tearer, Terrae

RE-READ Dearer, Reader, Reared, Redare

REREEL Reeler

RERENT Renter

REROLL Erroll, Orrell, Roller

REROOT Rooter, Torero

RESAIL Ariels, Asriel, Israel, Relais, Sailer, Serail, Serial

RESALE Leares, Leaser, Reseal, Sealer, Searle

RESALT Alerts, Alters, Artels, Laster, Ratels, Salter, Slater, Staler, Stelar, Tarsel

RESAWN Answer, Awners

RESAWS Sawers, Swears, Wrasse

RESCUE Cereus, Ceruse, Cesure, Creuse, Recuse, Secure

RESEAL Leares, Leaser, Resale, Sealer, Searle

RESEAT Aretes, Asteer, Easter, Eaters, Reates, Saeter, Seater, Staree, Steare, Teaser, Teresa

RESEAU Urease

RESECT Certes, Erects, Secret

*RESEDA Aredes, Deares, Erased, Seared

RESEED Seeder

RESEEK Kreese, Seeker

RESELL Seller

RESEND Denser, Enders, Sender

RESENT Enters, Ernest, Nester, Rentes, Sterne, Strene, Ternes, Tenser

RESETS Steers, Steres

RESHEW Hewers, Wheres

RESHIP Perish, Seriph

RESHOD Dehors, Herods, Hordes, Horsed, Rhodes, Shoder, Shored

RESHOW Howres, Shower, Whores

RESIDE Desire, Eiders
RESIFT Firest, Freist, Refits, Rifest, Sifter, Strife
RESIGN Ingres, Reigns, Renigs, Ringes, Signer, Singer
RESILE Relies
RESINA Arisen, Arsine, Sarnie
RESIST Reists, Resits, Sister
*****RESITA** Satire, Striae
RESITE Reties
RESITS Reists, Resist, Sister
RESOAK Arkose, Oakers, Soaker
RESOLD Dorsel, Droles, Solder
RESOLE Relose
RESORB Borers
RESORT Roster, Sorter, Storer
RESOWN Owners, Rowens, Worsen
RESOWS Sowser
RESTED Desert, Deters
RESTEM Merest, Mestre, Meters, Metres, Termes
RESTIR Triers
*****RESTON** Nestor, Noters, Stoner, Strone, Tenors, Tensor, Terson, Toners, Trones
RESULT Lurest, Luster, Lustre, Luters, Rulest, Rustle, Sutler, Ulster
RESUME Emures
RETACK Racket, Tacker
RETAIL Retial, Tailer
RETAIN Nerita, Ratine, Retina, Tirane
RETAMA Ramate
RETANS Antres, Astern, Sterna, Transe
RETAPE Petrea, Repeat
RETARD Darter, Dartre, Retrad, Tarred, Trader
RETARS Arrest, Arrets, Rarest, Raster, Raters, Sartre, Starer, Tarres, Terras
RETEAR Re-rate, Tearer, Terrae

RETENE Entree, Eterne
RETELL Teller
RETENT Netter, Tenter
RETEST Setter, Street, Tester
RETHAW Thawer, Wreath
RETIAL Retail, Tailer
RETIED Dieter, Re-edit, Tiered
RETIES Re-site
RETILL Rillet, Tiller
RETIME Metier, Re-emit, Tremie
RETINA Nerita, Ratine, Retain, Tirane
RETINS Insert, Inters, Nitres, Sinter, Strine, Trines
RETINT Nitter, Tinter
RETIRE Etrier, Reiter
RETOOL Looter, Loreto, Rootle, Tooler
RETOPS Opster, Poster, Presto, Repost, Repots, Stoper, Topers, Tropes
RETORT Rotter, Torret
RETOSE Eostre, Stereo
RETOSS Rosets, Sorest, Sortes, Stores, Torses, Tosser
RETOUR Roture, Router, Tourer
RETRAD Darter, Dartre, Retard, Tarred, Trader
RETRIM Trimer
RETUND Runted, Turned
RETUNE Neuter, Tenure, Tureen
RETURF Erfurt, Turfer
RETURN Turner
RETUSE Sûréte, Tereus
*****REUTER** Ureter
REVAMP Vamper
REVEAL Laveer, Leaver, Vealer
REVEND Denver, Nerved, Vender, Verden
REVERS Server, Verser
REVERY Verrey
REVEST Everts, Revets, Sterve, Treves, Verset, Vester
REVETO Revote, Vetoer

REVETS Everts, Revest, Sterve,
Treves, Verset, Vester
REVIED Derive, Reived, Rieved
REVIES Reives, Revise, Rieves
REVIEW Viewer
REVILE Levier, Liever, Relive
REVISE Reives, Revies, Rieves
REVOTE Reveto, Vetoer
REWARD Drawer, Redraw,
Warder, Warred
*****REWARI** Warier
REWARM Warmer
REWARN Warner, Warren
REWASH Hawser, Washer,
Whares
REWEAR Wearer
REWELD Lewder, Welder
REWIND Winder
REWORK Worker
REWRAP Pre-war, Warper
*****RHEINE** Herein, Inhere
RHESUS Rushes, Ushers
RHETOR Rother
RHEUMS Musher
RHINES Shiner, Shrine
*****RHODES** Dehors, Herods,
Hordes, Horsed, Reshod,
Shoder, Shored
RHODIC Droich, Orchid
RHONES Herons, Honers,
Nosher, Senhor
RHYTON Thorny
*****RIALTO** Tailor
RIATAS Arista, Tarsia, Tiaras
RIBALD Bridal, Labrid
RIBBED Bribed, Dibber
RIBBER Briber
RIBBON Robbin
*****RIBERA** Barrie
RICERS Cerris, Criers
RICHEN Enrich, Nicher
RICHER Chirre
RICKED Dicker
RICKEY Crikey

RICKLE Licker
RIC-RAC Circar
RICTAL Citral
RICTUS Citrus, Rustic
RIDDED Didder
RIDDEL Dirled, Riddle
RIDDEN Nidder, Rinded
RIDDLE Dirled, Riddel,
RIDENT Tinder, Trined
RIDERS Derris, Driers, Reirds,
Sirred
RIDEST Direst, Driest, Stride
RIDETH Dither
RIDGED Girded, Grided
RIDGEL Gilder, Girdle, Glided,
Lidger, Regild
RIDGES Dirges, Grides, Grised
RIDING Ingrid
RIEVED Derive, Reived, Revied
RIEVER Reiver, Verier
RIEVES Reives, Revies, Revise
RIFEST Firest, Freits, Refits,
Resift, Sifter, Strife
RIFFED Differ
RIGGED Digger
RIGGLE Ligger
RIGLET Regilt
RIG-OUT Outrig
RILLES Siller
RILLET Retill, Tiller
RIMIER Mirier
RIMING Miring
RIMLET Milter
RIMMED Dimmer
RIMOSE Isomer, Moires
RIMPLE Limper, Prelim, Rempli
RINDED Nidder, Ridden
RINGED Dering, Dinger, Engird,
Girned
RINGER Erring
RINGES Ingres, Reigns, Renigs,
Resign, Signer, Singer
RINSED Diners
RIOTED Editor, Tie-rod, Triode

RIPECK Picker, Repick
RIPENS Pernis, Repins, Sniper
RIPEST Esprit, Priest, Pteris, Sitrep, Sprite, Stripe, Tripes
*RIPONS Orpins, Prison, Proins
RIPPED Dipper
RIPPLE Lipper, Prilep
RISBAN Abrins, Bairns, Brains, Brians
RISETH Rithes, Shrite, Theirs, Thiers
RISING Siring
RISKED Dikers
RISPED Prides, Prised, Redips, Spider, Spired
RISQUE Quires, Quseir, Squire, Squier
RITHES Riseth, Shrite, Theirs, Thiers
RITTER Territ, Tirret, Triter
RIVAGE Argive, Garvie
RIVELS Livers, Livres, Silver, Sliver
*RIVERA Arrive, Varier
RIVETH Thrive
RIVETS Stiver, Strive, Tivers, Trevis, Verist
RIVING Irving, Virgin
RIVOSE Vireos, Virose
ROADED Adored, Deodar
ROAMED Radome
ROAMER Remora
ROARED Adorer
ROASTS Assort
ROBBED Dobber
ROBBIN Ribbon
ROBERD Border
ROBING Boring, Orbing
ROBINS Inorbs, Sorbin
ROBUST Turbos
ROCCUS Crocus, Occurs, Succor
ROCHEA Chorea, Horace, Ochrea, Orache

ROCHET Hector, Rotche, Tocher, Troche
ROCKED Corked, Docker, Redock
ROCKEL Locker, Relock
ROCKER Corker, Recork
ROCTAS Actors, Castor, Castro, Co-star, Croats, Scrota, Tarocs
RODDED Dodder
RODENT To-rend
RODING Doring
RODMAN Random
RODMEN Modern, Morned, Nemrod, Normed
RODNEY Yonder
ROGERS Groser
ROGGLE Logger
ROGUED Drogue, Drouge, Gourde, Rouged
ROGUES Grouse, Orgues, Rouges, Rugose
*ROLAND Arnold, Landor, Lardon, Ronald
ROLLER Erroll, Orrell, Reroll,
ROLL-UP Uproll
ROMANS Manors, Normas, Ramson, Ransom
*ROMANY Mornay
*ROMEOS Morose
ROMERO Roomer
*ROMISH Morish
*RONALD Arnold, Landor, Lardon, Roland
RONDEL Rondle
RONDES Drones, Snored, Sorned
RONDLE Rondel
RONEOS Seroon, Sooner
ROOFED Foredo
ROOKLE Looker
ROOMED Droome, Moored
ROOMER Romero
ROOSES Sorose
ROOTER Torero

ROOTLE Looter, Loreto, Retool, Tooler

ROPERS Porers, Prores, Proser

ROPING Poring, Proign

ROQUET Quoter, Torque

RORTER Terror

ROSACE Coarse

ROSETS Retoss, Sorest, Sortes, Stores, Torses, Tosser

ROSETY Oyster, Storey, Toyers, Troyes, Tyroes

ROSING Girons, Grison, Groins, Signor

ROSTEL Ostler, Relost, Sterol, Torsel

ROSTER Resort, Sorter, Storer

ROSTRA Sartor

ROSYTH Hostry, Shorty

ROTATE To-tear

ROTCHE Hector, Rochet, Tocher, Troche

ROTHER Rhetor

***ROTHES** Others, Throes, Tosher

ROTING Girton, Trigon

ROTTAN Attorn, Ratton

ROTTED Detort, Dotter

ROTTEN To-rent

ROTTER Retort, Torret

ROTULA Torula

ROTUND Untrod

ROTURE Retour, Router, Tourer

ROUGED Drogue, Drouge, Gourde, Rogued

ROUGES Grouse, Orgues, Rogues, Rugose

ROUNCE Uncore

ROUPED Poured

ROUPET Pouter, Troupe

ROUSED Douser, Soured

ROUSES Serous

ROUSTS Stours, Sutors, Tussor

ROUTED Detour, Douter, Outred, Redout, Toured

ROUTER Retour, Roture, Tourer

ROUTES Ouster, Outers, Souter, Touser, Trouse

ROVEST Stover, Strove, Voters

ROVETH Throve

ROWELS Lowers, Owlers, Slower

ROWENS Owners, Resown, Worsen

ROWERS Worser

ROWEST Rowtes, Sowter, Stower, Stowre, Towers, Towser, Twoers

ROWTED Trowed

ROWTES Rowest, Sowter, Stower, Stowre, Towers, Towser, Twoers

RUBATO Outbar, Tabour

RUBBED Dubber

RUBBET Tubber

RUBBLE Burble, Lubber

RUBIED Burdie, Buried

RUBIES Bruise, Buries, Busier

RUBINE Brunei

RUBLES Elbrus

RUCKED Ducker

RUDEST Duster, Redust, Rusted

RUEING Rugine

RUFFED Duffer

RUFFES Suffer

RUFFLE Luffer

RUGATE Argute, Tuareg

RUGGED Grudge

RUGINE Rueing

RUGOSA Garous

RUGOSE Grouse, Orgues, Rogues, Rouges

RUINED Inured

RULEST Lurest, Luster, Lustre, Luters, Result, Rustle, Sutler, Ulster

RULING Luring

RUMBAS Sambur, Umbras

RUMBLE Lumber, Umbrel

RUMPLE Lumper, Replum

RUNDLE Lurden, Nurled

RUNERS Nurser
RUNNET Tunner, Unrent
RUN-OUT Outrun
RUNTED Retund, Turned
RUNWAY Unwary
RUPEES Persue, Peruse, Purees
RUSCUS Cursus
RUSHES Rhesus, Shures, Ushers
RUSINE Insure, Inures, Urines,
  Ursine
RUSSET Estrus, Surest, Tusser
RUSTED Duster, Redust, Rudest
RUSTIC Citrus, Rictus
RUSTLE Lurest, Luster, Lustre,
  Result, Rulest, Sutler, Ulster
RUTTER Turret
RUTTLE Turtle

SABERS Brasse, Sabres
SABLED Blades
SABRED Ardebs, Beards, Breads,
  Debars, Serdab
SABRES Brasse, Sabers
SACHEL Cashel, Chelas, Laches
SACHEM Schema
SACHET Chaste, Cheats, Scathe,
  Taches
SACKED Casked
SACKER Crakes, Creaks, Screak
SACQUE Casque
SACRAL Lascar, Rascal, Sarlac,
  Scalar
SACRED Cadres, Cedars, Scared
SADDEN Dedans, Sanded
SADDER Adders, Dreads, Readds
SADDLE Addles
*SADIES Asides, Dassie
SADIST Saidst, Staids
SAETER Aretes, Asteer, Easter,
  Eaters, Reates, Reseat, Seater,
  Staree, Steare, Teaser, Teresa
SAFEST Feasts
SAG-BAG Gas-bag
SAGENE Senega

SAGEST Stages
SAGGED Gadges
SAGGER Aggers, Eggars, Gagers,
  Seggar
SAGUIN Anguis
SAIDST Sadist, Staids
SAILED Aisled, Deasil, Ideals,
  Ladies
SAILER Ariels, Asreil, Israel,
  Relais, Resail, Serail, Serial
SAINTS Santis, Satins, Sistan,
  Stains
SALAMI Alisma, Lamias
*SALEMI Mesail, Mesial, Samiel,
  Sliema
*SALIAN Lianas, Salina
SALINA Lianas, Salian
SALINE Aliens, Alines, Aniles,
  Lesina, Lianes, Selina, Silane
SALITE Saltie
SALIVA Avails, Salvia, Valais
SALLAD Dallas
SALLEE Allees
SALLET Stella
*SALLIE Allies
SALLOW Allows
SALMIS Missal
SALMON Monals
SALOON Alsoon, Solano
SALSES Lasses
SALTED Deltas, Desalt, Lasted,
  Slated, Stadle, Staled
SALTER Alerts, Alters, Artels,
  Laster, Ratels, Resalt, Slater,
  Staler, Stelar, Tarsel
SALTIE Salite
SALTLY Lastly
SALTUS Saults, Tussal
SALVED Slaved, Valsed
SALVER Lavers, Ravels, Serval,
  Slaver, Valser, Velars, Versal
SALVIA Avails, Saliva,
  Valais
*SALWIN In-laws

*SAMBRE Ambers, Breams,
  Embars
 SAMBUR Rumbas, Umbras
 SAMELY Measly
*SAMIAN Animas, Maasin,
  Manias, Manisa
 SAMIEL Mesail, Mesial, Salemi,
  Sliema
*SAMIOT Maoist, Taoism
 SAMITE Maties, Semita, Tamise
 SAMLET Lamest, Metals
 SAMPIS Passim
 SAMPLE Maples, Pelmas
 SAMSHU Shamus
*SAMSON Masons, Namsos
 SANDED Dedans, Sadden
 SANDER Redans, Snared
 SANDHI Danish, Dinahs
*SANDRA Nasard
 SANEST Assent, Snaste, Stanes,
  Steans
*SANGER Angers, Ranges,
  Serang
*SANGIR Grains, Rasing
 SANIES Anises, Sasine
 SANITY Satiny, Stay-in
 SANNUP Pannus, Unsnap,
  Unspan
 SANTAL Aslant
 SANTIR Instar, Sintra, Strain,
  Trains
*SANTIS Saints, Satins, Sistan,
  Stains
 SANTON Sonant
 SANTUR Saturn
 SAPELE Asleep, Elapse, Please
 SAPPER Papers
 SAP-ROT Asport, Pastor, Portas
 SARCEL Carles, Clares, Clears,
  Scaler, Sclera
 SARCEN Caners, Casern, Cranes,
  Crenas, Rances
 SARDEL Alders, Dalers

*SARGON Angors, Argons,
  Groans, Nagors, Orangs,
  Organs, Sarong
*SARGUS Sugars
 SARLAC Lascar, Rascal, Sacral,
  Scalar
 SARNEY Senary, Raynes, Renays,
  Yearns
 SARNIE Arisen, Arsine, Resina
 SARONG Angors, Argons,
  Groans, Nagors, Orangs,
  Organs, Sargon
 SARSEN Nasser, Snares
*SARTHE Earths, Haters, Hearts,
  Rathes, Sheart
 SARTOR Rostra
*SARTRE Arrest, Arrets, Rarest,
  Raster, Raters, Retars, Starer,
  Tarres, Terras
 SASHED Dashes, Shades
 SASHES She-ass
 SASINE Anises, Sanies
 SATCOM Comsat, Mascot
 SATEEN Ensate, Senate, Steane
 SATING Gainst, Giants
 SATINS Saints, Santis, Sistan,
  Stains
 SATINY Sanity, Stay-in
 SATIRE Resita, Striae
 SATORI Aorist, Aristo, Artois,
  Ratios
*SATURN Santur
 SATYRA Astray, Tayras
 SAUCED Caused
 SAUCER Causer, Cesura, Creusa,
  Erucas
 SAUGER Argues, Augers, Segura,
  Usager
 SAULTS Saltus, Tussal
 SAUREL Elures
 SAVATE Avesta
 SAWDER Seward, Sweard,
  Waders
 SAWERS Resaws, Swears, Wrasse

SAWING Aswing
SAWN-UP Supawn
SAW-PIT Pitsaw
SAW-SET Sweats, Tawses, Wastes
SAWYER Swayer
SAYEST Yeasts
'SBLOOD Bloods
SCAITH Taisch
SCALAR Lascar, Rascal, Sacral, Sarlac
SCALED Decals
SCALER Carles, Clares, Clears, Sarcel, Sclera
SCALES Cassel
SCAMEL Camels, Macles, Mascle, Mescal
SCAPED Spaced
SCARAB Barsac, Scarba
*****SCARBA** Barsac, Scarab
SCARED Cadres, Cedars, Sacred
SCARER Scarre
SCARES Caress, Carses, Crases, Escars, Scraes, Seracs
SCAREY Creasy, Scraye
SCARRE Scarer
SCARTH Charts, Starch
*****SCARUS** Scaurs
SCAURS Scarus
SCATHE Chaste, Cheats, Sachet, Taches
SCEATT Stacte, Tacets
SCENED Censed
SCHEMA Sachem
SCHEME Smeech
SCHLEI Chesil, Chiels, Chiles, Chisel, Elchis
SCHOUT Chouts, Scouth
SCHRIK Chirks, Kirsch
SCHTIK Kitsch, Shtick, Thicks
SCIENT Incest, Insect, Nicest
*****SCILLA** Lilacs
SCLATE Castle, Cleats, Eclats
SCLAVE Calves, Cavels, Claves

SCLERA Carles, Clares, Clears, Sarcel, Scaler
*****SCOGAN** Congas, Gascon
SCORED Cedros, Coders, Credos
SCORER Corers, Crores
SCORES Corses, Crosse, Scorse
SCORSE Corses, Crosse, Scores
SCOTER Corset, Cortes, Coster, Escort, Recost, Rectos, Sector, Tresco
SCOTIA Coatis
SCOUTH Chouts, Schout
SCOUTS Costus, Custos
SCOVEL Cloves
SCRAMP Cramps
SCRAPE Capers, Casper, Crapes, Escarp, Pacers, Parsec, Recaps, Secpar, Spacer
SCRAWL Crawls
SCRAYE Creasy, Scarey
SCREAK Crakes, Creaks, Sacker
SCREAM Crames, Creams, Macers
SCREED Ceders, Creeds
SCREEN Censer, Secern
SCREES Cesser, Recess
SCRIED Ciders, Dicers
SCRIES Crises
SCRIKE Ickers, Sicker
SCRIME Crimes
SCRIMP Crimps
SCRINE Crines
SCROBE Cobres
SCROTA Actors, Castor, Castro, Co-star, Croats, Roctas, Tarocs
SCRUNT Crunts
SCRUTO Courts, Crouts, Turcos
SCUTES Cestus
SCYPHI Physic
SCYTHE Chesty
'SDEATH Deaths, Hasted, Tashed
SDEIGN Deigns, Design, Dinges, Nidges, Signed, Singed
SEA-BAT Abates

SEA-BED Debase
SEA-CAT Acates
SEA-DOG Dagoes, Dosage, Sea-god
SEA-FIR Ferias, Fraise
SEA-GOD Dagoes, Dosage, Sea-dog
SEALED Leased
SEALER Leares, Leaser, Resale, Reseal, Searle
SEAMED Adeems
SEAMEN Enemas, Enseam
SEAMER Ameers, Ameres, Mersea, Ramees
SEAMES Meases, Sesame
SEA-MUD Amused, Medusa
*****SEAMUS** Amuses, Assume
SEA-OWL Leasow
SEANCE Cesena, Encase, Seneca
SEA-RAT Astare
SEARCE Ceaser, Crease, Recase
SEARCH Arches, Chares, Chaser, Eschar, Raches
SEARED Aredes, Deares, Erased, Reseda
*****SEARLE** Leares, Leaser, Resale, Reseal, Sealer
SEA-ROD Adores, Oreads, Soared
SEATED Easted, Sedate, Teades, Teased
SEATER Aretes, Asteer, Easter, Eaters, Reates, Reseat, Saeter, Staree, Steare, Teaser, Teresa
*****SEATON** Atones, Easton
SECANT Ascent, Enacts, Stance
SECERN Censer, Screen
SECKEL Cleeks
SECPAR Capers, Casper, Crapes, Escarp, Pacers, Parsec, Recaps, Scrape, Spacer
SECRET Certes, Erects, Resect

SECTOR Corset, Cortes, Coster, Escort, Recost, Rectos, Scoter, Tresco
SECUND Dunces
SECURE Cereus, Ceruse, Cesure, Creuse, Recuse, Rescue
SEDATE Easted, Seated, Teades, Teased
SEDENT Endest, Nested, Tensed
SEDILE Diesel, Ediles, Elides, Seidel, Seiled
SEDUCE Deuces, Educes
SEEDER Reseed
SEEING Eignes, Genies, Siegen
SEEKER Kreese, Reseek
SEEMER Emeers
SEETHE Te-hees
*****SEFTON** Soften
SEGGAR Aggers, Eggars, Gagers, Sagger
*****SEGURA** Argues, Augers, Sauger, Usager
SEIDEL Diesel, Ediles, Elides, Sedile, Seiled
SEILED Diesel, Ediles, Elides, Sedile, Seidel
SEINED Denies, Denise, Desine
SEINER Nereis, Serein, Serine, Sirene
SEINES Neisse
SEISED Dieses
SEISMS Misses
SEISON Enosis, Eosins, Essoin, Noesis, Noises, Ossein, Sonsie
SELAHS Halses, Hassle, Lashes, Shales, Sheals
SELDOM Models
SELECT Elects
*****SELINA** Aliens, Alines, Lesina, Lianes, Saline, Silane
SELING Ingles, Lignes, Single
SELLER Resell
SELVES Vessel
*****SEMELE** Melees

SEMITA Maties, Samite, Tamise
SEMLIN Limens, Meslin, Simnel
SEMPER Sempre
SEMPRE Semper
SENARY Raynes, Renays, Sarney, Yearns
SENATE Ensate, Sateen, Steane
*SENDAI Adenis
SENDAL Elands, Ladens, Landes
SENDER Denser, Enders, Resend
SEND-UP Unsped, Upends, Upsend
*SENECA Cesena, Encase, Seance
SENEGA Sagene
SENGHI Hinges, Neighs
*SENHOR Herons, Honers, Nosher, Rhones
SENILE Enisle, Ensile, Nelies, Nelsie, Silene
SENIOR Nosier, Soneri
*SENLAC Ancles, Cleans, Lances, Lencas
SENNIT Sinnet, Tennis
SENORA Arseno, Reason
SENORS Nosers, Sensor, Serons, Snores
SENSOR Nosers, Senors, Snores
SEPADS Passed, Spades
SEPHEN Sphene
SEPSIN Snipes, Spines
SEPSIS Pisses, Speiss
SEPTAL Palest, Palets, Pastel, Peltas, Petals, Plates, Pleats, Staple, Tepals
SEPTAN Patens
SERACS Caress, Carses, Crases, Escars, Scares, Scraes
SERAIL Ariels, Asriel, Israel, Relais, Resail, Sailer, Serial
SERANG Angers, Ranges, Sanger
SERAPE A-per-se, Parsee, Prease
SERAPH Hepars, Phares, Phrase, Raphes, Shaper, Sherpa, Sphaer
*SERBIA Braise, Rabies

SERDAB Ardebs, Beards, Breads, Debars, Sabred
SEREIN Nereis, Seiner, Serine, Sirene
SERENA Ensear
*SERETH Threes
SERGES Egress, Greses
SERIAL Ariels, Asriel, Israel, Relais, Resail, Sailer, Serail
SERICA Caries, Cerias
SERINE Nereis, Seiner, Serein, Sirene
SERIPH Perish, Reship
*SERLIO Elisor, Lories, Oilers, Oriels, Reoils, Soiler
SERMON Mornes
SERONS Nosers, Senors, Sensor, Snores
SEROON Roneos, Sooner
SEROUS Rouses
SERPET Pester, Peters, Petres, Preset, Pteres
SERRAE Eraser
*SERRAI Airers, Raiser, Sierra
SERRAN Snarer
SERVAL Lavers, Ravels, Salver, Slaver, Valser, Velars, Versal
SERVED Versed
SERVER Revers, Verser
SERVES Severs, Sevres, Verses
*SERVIA Varies
SESAME Meases, Seames
SESTET Testes, Tsetse
SESTON Tossen
*SESTOS Tosses
*SETHON Honest, Stheno
SET-OFF Offset
SETONS Nestos, Onsets, Stones
SET-OUT Outset
SETTEE Testee
SETTER Retest, Street, Tester
SETTLE Ettles
*SEURAT Atreus, Auster, Urates
SEVERE Reeves

*SEVERN Nerves, Nevers
SEVERS Serves, Sevres, Verses
*SEVRES Serves, Severs, Verses
SEWARD Sawder, Sweard,
  Waders
SEWING Swinge, Winges
SEXIST Exists
SEXTAN Texans
SHADED Dashed
SHADER Dasher, Rashed, Shared
SHADES Dashes, Sashed
SHAIRN Arshin
*SHAIRP Hispar, Parish, Raphis
SHAKER Kasher
*SHAKTI Skaith
SHALES Halses, Hassle, Lashes,
  Selahs, Sheals
SHAMAN Ashman
SHAMED Mashed
SHAMER Harems, Masher
SHAMES Mashes
SHAMUS Samshu
SHAPED Hasped, Phased
SHAPER Hepars, Phares, Phrase,
  Raphes, Seraph, Sherpa, Sphaer
SHAPES Pashes, Phases
SHARED Dasher, Rashed, Shader
SHARER Rasher
SHARES Rashes, Shears
SHAVEN Havens, Hesvan
SHAVER Havers
SHEALS Halses, Hassle, Lashes,
  Selahs, Shales
SHEARS Rashes, Shares
SHEART Earths, Haters, Hearts,
  Rathes, Sarthe
SHE-ASS Sashes
SHEATH Heaths
SHEAVE Heaves
*SHEBAT Bathes
SHEENS Hessen, Sneesh
SHEETS Theses
SHEILA Ilesha
SHELFY Fleshy

*SHELTA Haslet, Lathes, Thales
SHELTY Ethyls
SHELVE Helves
*SHENSI Shines
SHERIF Fisher
*SHERPA Hepars, Phares, Phrase,
  Raphes, Seraph, Shaper, Sphaer
SHEUCH Heuchs
SHEUGH Heughs, Hughes
SHEWEL Wheels
SHIERS Hisser, Shires
SHIEST Heists, Shites, Sithes,
  Theiss, Thesis
*SHIITE Histie
SHIKAR Rakish
SHINER Rhines, Shrine
*SHINES Shensi
SHINTO Tonish
SHIPPO Hippos, Popish
SHIRES Hisser, Shiers
SHIRRA Arrihs, Harris, Sirrah
SHIRTY Irtysh, Thyrsi
SHITES Heists, Shiest, Sithes,
  Theiss
SHIVER Hivers, Shrive
SHOATS Hoasts, Hostas, Thasos
SHODER Dehors, Herods,
  Hordes, Horsed, Reshod,
  Rhodes, Shored
SHOOTS Sothos
SHOREA Ahorse, Ashore, Hoarse
SHORED Dehors, Herods,
  Hordes, Horsed, Reshod,
  Rhodes, Shoder
SHORTY Hostry, Rosyth
SHOUGH Houghs
SHOUSE Houses
SHOVEL Hovels
SHOVER Hovers, Shrove
SHOWER Howres, Reshow,
  Whores
SHRIEK Hikers, Shrike
SHRIFT Firths, Friths
SHRIKE Hikers, Shriek

SHRINE Rhines, Shiner
SHRITE Riseth, Rithes, Theirs, Thiers
SHRIVE Hivers, Shiver
SHROVE Hovers, Shover
SHTICK Kitsch, Schtik, Thicks
SHUT-UP Pushtu
SIALIC Silica
SICKER Ickers, Scrike
*****SIDCUP** Cupids, Cuspid
SIDDUR Druids
SIDE-ON Diones, Donsie, Edison, Nidose, Noised, No-side, Onside
SIDLER Idlers, Slider
*****SIDNEY** Disney
*****SIEGEN** Eignes, Genies, Seeing
SIENNA Annies, Insane
SIERRA Airers, Raiser, Serrai
SIESTA Tassie
SIEVED Devise, Viseed
SIEVES Essive
SIFTED Fisted
SIFTER Firest, Freits, Refits, Resift, Rifest, Strife
*****SIGNAC** Casing
SIGNAL Aligns, Liangs, Ligans, Lingas
SIGNAS Assign
SIGNED Deigns, Design, Dinges, Nidges, Sdeign, Singed
SIGNER Ingres, Reigns, Renigs, Resign, Ringes, Singer,
SIGNET Ingest, Stinge, Tinges
SIGN-IN Sing-in
SIGNOR Girons, Grison, Groins, Rosing
SILANE Aliens, Alines, Lesina, Lianes, Saline, Selina
*****SILENE** Enisle, Ensile, Nelies, Nelsie, Senile
*****SILENO** Eloins, Esloin, Insole, Lesion, Oleins, Solein
SILENT Enlist, Inlets, Listen, Tinsel

SILICA Sialic
SILKEN Inkles, Likens
SILLER Rilles
SILOED Isolde, Soiled
SILPHA Palish, Phials
SILTED Delist, Idlest, Listed, Tildes
SILVAE Aviles, Leavis, Valise
SILVAN Anvils
SILVER Livers, Livres, Rivels, Sliver
*****SIMEON** Eonism, Miseno, Monies
SIMMER Mimers, Merism
'SIMMON Monism, Nomism
SIMNEL Limens, Meslin, Semlin
SIMONE Eonism, Miseno, Monies, Simeon
SIMONY Myosin
SIMPER Primes
SIMPLE Impels, Milspe
SIMPLY Limpsy
*****SINDHI** Hindis
SINEWY Winsey
SINGED Deigns, Design, Dinges, Nidges, Sdeign, Signed
SINGER Ingres, Reigns, Renigs, Resign, Ringes, Singer
SINGES Gneiss
SING-IN Sign-in
SINGLE Ingles, Lignes, Seling
SINGLY Glynis, Lyings, Lysing
SINKER Inkers, Kirsen, Reinks
SINNED Dennis
SINNER Inners
SINNET Sennit, Tennis
SINTER Insert, Inters, Nitres, Retins, Strine, Trines
SINTOC Tocsin, Tonics
SINTRA Instar, Sentir, Strain, Trains
SIPPER Pipers
SIRENE Nereis, Seiner, Serein, Serine
*****SIRIAN** Raisin

SIRING Rising
SIRRAH Arrish, Harris, Shirra
SIRRED Derris, Driers, Reirds, Riders
*****SISERA** Arises, Raises
*****SISTAN** Saints, Santis, Satins, Stains
SISTED Deists, Desist
SISTER Reists, Resist, Resits
SISTRA Sitars, Stairs
SITARS Sistra, Stairs
*****SITHES** Heists, Shiest, Shites, Theiss, Thesis
SITING Tingis
SIT-INS Insist
SITREP Esprit, Priest, Pteris, Ripest, Sprite, Stripe, Tripes
SITTAR Artist, Strait, Strati, Traits
SITTER Titers, Titres, Triste
SKAITH Shakti
SKATED Staked, Tasked
SKATER Strake, Streak, Takers, Tasker
SKEELY Sleeky
SKERRY Skryer
SKEWER Wesker
SKIERS Kisser, Krises
SKLATE Lasket
SKRYER Skerry
SLAKES Kassel
SLAP-UP Palpus
SLATED Deltas, Desalt, Lasted, Salted, Stadle, Staled
SLATER Alerts, Alters, Artels, Laster, Ratels, Resalt, Salter, Staler, Stelar, Tarsel
SLATES Stales, Steals, Tassel, Teslas
SLAVED Salved, Valsed
SLAVER Lavers, Ravels, Salver, Serval, Valser, Velars, Versal
*****SLAVIC** Cavils, Clavis
SLAYER Layers, Rayles, Relays
SLEAVE Leaves

SLEDGE Gledes, Gleeds, Ledges
SLEEKY Skeely
SLEETY Steely
SLEEVE Levees
SLEUTH Hustle
SLICER Relics
SLIDER Idlers, Sidler
*****SLIEMA** Mesail, Mesial, Salemi, Samiel
SLIEST Islets, Istles, Stiles
SLIGHT Lights
SLIMED Misled, Smiled
SLIMES Missel, Smiles
SLIPED Dispel, Disple, Lisped, Spiled
SLIPES Plisse, Spiels, Spiles
SLIP-UP Pipuls, Pupils
SLIVEN Snivel
SLIVED Devils
*****SLIVEN** Levins, Livens, Snivel
SLIVER Livers, Livres, Rivels, Silver
SLOGAN Logans
SLOIDS Dossil, Solids
SLOKEN Kelson
SLOPPY Polyps
SLOUGH Ghouls, Loughs
SLOVEN Novels
SLOWED Dowels, Sowled
SLOWER Lowers, Owlers, Rowels
SLYEST Styles
SMALTO Almost, Maltos
SMEARS Masers, Ramses
SMEATH Thames
SMEECH Scheme
SMEETH Themes
SMILAX Laxism
SMILED Misled, Slimed
SMILER Merils, Milers
SMILES Missel, Slimes
SMILET Mistle
SMIRCH Chirms, Chrism
SMITER Merits, Mister, Miters, Mitres, Remits, Timers

SMITES Misset, Stimes, Tmesis
SMORED Dromes
SMOUSE Mouses, Mousse
SMUDGE Degums
SNACOT Actons, Cantos, Cotans, Octans
SNARED Redans, Sander
SNARER Serran
SNARES Nasser, Sarsen
SNASTE Assent, Sanest, Stanes, Steans
SNATCH Chants, Stanch
SNATHE Athens, Hasten, Sneath, Thanes
SNEATH Athens, Hasten, Snathe, Thanes
SNEESH Hessen, Sheens
SNIPED Despin, Piends, Spined
SNIPER Pernis, Repins, Ripens
SNIPES Sepsin, Spines
SNIVEL Levins, Livens, Sliven
SNOOPY Spoony
SNOOZE Ozones
SNORED Drones, Rondes, Sorned
SNORER Sorner
SNORES Nosers, Senors, Serons, Sensor
SNOWED Endows
SNUDGE Nudges
SOAKER Arkose, Oakers, Resoak
SOAPED Apodes
SOARED Adores, Oreads, Searod
SOBEIT Tobies
SOBOLE Lobose
SOCCER Escroc
SOCIAL Licosa
SOCMAN Mascon
SODAIN Adonis
SODIUM Odiums, Modius
SOFTEN Sefton
SOFTER Fetors, Forest, Fortes, Foster
SOGERS Gorses, Ogress

SOIGNE Ingoes
SOILED Isolde, Siloed
SOILER Elisor, Lories, Oilers, Oriels, Reoils, Serlio
SOLANO Alsoon, Saloon
SOLDER Dorsel, Droles, Resold
SOLEIN Eloins, Esloin, Insole, Lesion, Oleins, Sileno
SOLEMN Lemnos, Lemons, Melons
SOLENT Stolen, Telson
SOLERS Lessor, Losers, Sorels
SOLEUS Louses, Ousels
SOLIDS Dossil, Sloids
SOLING Losing
SOLIVE Olives, Voiles
SOLLER Sorell
SOLUTE Tousle
SOLVER Lovers
SOLVES Lesvos
SOMBER Bromes, Ombers, Ombres, Sombre
*SOMBOR** Brooms, Ombros
SOMBRE Bromes, Ombers, Ombres, Somber
SONANT Santon
SONCIE Conies, Cosine, Oscine
SONERI Nosier, Senior
SONNET Neston, Nonets, Stonen, Tenons, Tenson, Tonnes
SONSIE Enosis, Eosins, Essoin, Noesis, Noises, Ossein, Seison
*SONTAG** Gaston, Tangos, Tongas, Tsonga
SOOLED Dolose, Loosed, Oodles
SOONER Roneos, Seroon
SOPITE Postie
SORBET Besort, Osbert, Strobe
SORBIN Inorbs, Robins
SORDES Dorses, Dosers, Dosser
SORDET Dorset, Doters, Sorted, Stored, Strode, Trodes
SORELL Soller
SORELS Lessor, Losers, Solers

SOREST Retoss, Rosets, Sortes, Stores, Torses, Tosser
SORNED Drones, Rondes, Snored
SORNER Snorer
SOROSE Rooses
SORTED Dorset, Doters, Sordet, Stored, Strode, Trodes
SORTER Resort, Roster, Storer
SORTES Retoss, Rosets, Sorest, Stores, Torses, Tosser
SORTIE Tiroes, Tories
SOSSLE Losses
*****SOTHOS** Shoots
SOUGHT Oughts, Toughs
SOULED Loused
SOUMED Moused, Dumose, Usedom
SOUPER Poseur, Uprose
SOUPLE Poules
SOURCE Cerous, Course, Crouse, Crusoe
SOURED Douser, Roused
SOUSED Douses
SOUTER Ouster, Outers, Routes, Touser, Trouse
SOWLED Dowels, Slowed
SOWSED Dowses
SOWSER Resows
SOWTER Rowest, Rowtes, Stower, Stowre, Towers, Towser, Twoers
SPACED Scaped
SPACER Capers, Casper, Crapes, Escarp, Pacers, Parsec, Recaps, Scrape, Secpar
SPADER Drapes, Padres, Parsed, Rasped, Repads, Spared, Spread
SPADES Passed, Sepads
SPAERS Aspers, Parses, Passer, Prases, Repass, Spares, Sparse, Spears
SPAHIS Phasis
SPARED Drapes, Padres, Parsed, Rasped, Repads, Spader, Spread

SPARER Parers, Parser, Rasper, Sparre
SPARES Aspers, Parses, Passer, Prases, Repass, Spaers, Sparse, Spears
SPARGE Gapers, Gasper, Grapes, Parges
SPARID Rapids, Spraid
SPARRE Parers, Parser, Rasper, Sparer
SPARSE Aspers, Parses, Passer, Prases, Repass, Spaers, Spares, Spears
*****SPARTA** Patras, Satrap
SPARTH Thraps
SPARVE Pavers
SPATES Pastes, Speats, Stapes
SPAVIE Pavise
SPAVIN Pavins
SPEARS Aspers, Parses, Passer, Prases, Repass, Spaers, Spares, Sparse
SPEARY Payers, Repays
SPEATS Pastes, Spates, Stapes
SPECIE Pieces
SPEECH Cheeps, Peches
SPEEDO Depose, Epodes
SPEERS Perses, Preses, Sperse, Sprees
SPEIRS Prises, Spires
SPEISS Pisses, Sepsis
SPELIN Pensil, Pilsen, Spinel, Spline
SPERSE Perses, Preses, Speers, Sprees
SPHAER Hepars, Phares, Phrase, Rephes, Seraph, Shaper, Sherpa
SPHENE Sephen
SPHERE Herpes, Hesper, Pheers
SPHERY Hypers, Sypher
SPICAE Apices
SPICER Cripes, Crepis, Persic, Precis, Prices
SPICES Pisces

SPIDER Prides, Prised, Redips, Risped, Spired

SPIELS Plisse, Slipes, Spiles

SPIGHT Pights

SPILED Dispel, Disple, Lisped, Sliped

SPILES Plisse, Slipes, Spiels

SPINAL Lapins, Plains

SPINAR Sprain

SPINED Despin, Piends, Sniped

SPINEL Pensil, Pilsen, Spelin, Spline

SPINES Sepsin, Snipes

SPINET Instep, Step-in

SPIN-TO Instop, Piston, Pitons, Points, Potins

SPIRAE Aspire, Paries, Persia, Praise, Spirea

SPIRAL Prials

SPIREA Aspire, Paries, Persia, Praise, Spirae

SPIRED Prides, Prised, Redips, Risped, Spider

SPIRES Prises, Speirs

SPIRTS Sprits, Stirps, Strips

SPITAL Alpist, Pastil, Plaits

SPITES Stipes

SPLICE Clipes

SPLEEN Pensel

SPLINE Pensil, Pilsen, Spelin, Spinel

SPLORE Polers, Proles

SPOILT Pilots, Pistol, Postil

SPONGE Pengos

SPOONY Snoopy

SPOSHY Hyssop

SPOUSE Pousse

SPOUTS Stoups, Toss-up, Uptoss

SPRAID Rapids, Sparid

SPRAIN Spinar

SPRANG Prangs

SPREAD Drapes, Padres, Parsed, Rasped, Repads, Spader, Spared

SPREES Perses, Preses, Speers, Sperse

SPRIER Priers

SPRINT Prints

SPRITE Esprit, Priest, Pteris, Ripest, Sitrep, Stripe, Tripes

SPRITS Spirts, Stirps, Strips

SPRONG Prongs

SPROUT Proust, Stroup, Stupor

SPRUIT Purist, Stir-up, Uprist, Upstir

SPUNGE Unpegs

SPURGE Purges

SPURNE Prunes

SPYING Pigsny

SQUAIL Quails

SQUAME Masque

SQUEAK Quakes

SQUEAL Equals, Lasque, Quesal

SQUIER Quires, Quseir, Risque, Squire

SQUILL Quills

SQUINT Quints

SQUINY Quinsy

SQUIRE Quires, Quseir, Risque, Squier

SQUIRT Quirts

STABLE Ablest, Ablets, Bleats, Tables

STACTE Tacets, Sceatt

STADLE Deltas, Desalt, Lasted, Salted, Slated, Staled

STAGER Grates, Greats, Ragest, Targes

STAGES Sagest

STAGEY Gayest

STAIDS Sadist, Saidst

STAIRS Sistra, Sitars

STAINS Saints, Santis, Satins, Sistan

STAKED Skated, Tasked

STALED Deltas, Desalt, Lasted, Salted, Slated, Stadle

STALER Alerts, Alters, Artels, Laster, Ratels, Resalt, Salter, Slater, Stelar, Tarsel

STALES Slates, Steals, Tassel, Teslas

*****STALIN** Instal, Latins

STAMEN Aments, Manets

STAMIN Mantis, Matins, Tamins

STANCE Ascent, Enacts, Secant

STANCH Chants, Snatch

STANES Assent, Sanest, Snaste, Steans

STAPES Pastes, Spates, Speats,

STAPLE Palest, Palets, Pastel, Peltas, Petals, Plates, Pleats, Septal, Tepals

STARCH Charts, Scarth

STARED Adrets, Daters, Desart, Trades, Treads

STAREE Aretes, Asteer, Easter, Eaters, Reates, Reseat, Saeter, Seater, Steare, Teaser, Teresa

STARER Arrest, Arrets, Rarest, Raster, Raters, Retars, Sartre, Tarres, Terras

STARES Assert, Asters, Astres, Reasts, Stresa

STARVE Averts, Ravest, Staver, Tarves, Tavers, Traves, Vaster

STASIS Assist

STATED Tasted

STATER Aretts, Astert, Taster, Taters, Tetras, Treats

STATES Tasset, Tastes

STATIC Attics

STATOR Tarots, Troats

STATUE Astute

STAVER Averts, Ravest, Starve, Tarves, Tavers, Traves, Vaster

STAVES Vestas

STAWED Wadset, Wasted

STAYED Steady

STAYER Estray, Reasty, Stayre, Yarest

STAY-IN Sanity, Satiny

STAYRE Estray, Reasty, Stayer, Yarest

STEADY Stayed

STEALE Elates, Stelae, Teasel

STEALS Slates, Stales, Tassel, Teslas

STEALT Latest, Taslet

STEAMY Mayest

STEANE Ensate, Sateen, Senate

STEANS Assent, Sanest, Snaste, Stanes

STEARE Aretes, Asteer, Easter, Eaters, Reates, Reseat, Saeter, Seater, Staree, Teaser, Teresa

STEELD Eldest

*****STEELE** Eel-set

STEELY Sleety

STEERS Resets, Steres

STEERY Reesty, Yester

STEEVE Vestee

*****STEFAN** Fasten, Nefast

STEINS Insets, Tessin

STELAE Elates, Steale, Teasel

STELAR Alerts, Alters, Artels, Laster, Ratels, Salter, Slater, Staler, Tarsel

*****STELLA** Sallet

STEP-IN Instep, Spinet

STEREO Eostre, Retose

STERES Resets, Steers

STERIC Trices

STERNA Astern, Antres, Retans, Transe

*****STERNE** Enters, Ernest, Nester, Rentes, Resent, Strene, Tenser, Ternes

STEROL Ostler, Relost, Rostel, Torsel

STERVE Everts, Revest, Revets, Treves, Verset, Vester

STEVEN Events

STEWED Tweeds, Wested

STEWER Sweert, Wester

STIEVE Evites
*** STHENO** Honest, Sethon
STIFLE Filets, Flites, Itself
STILAR Trails, Trials
STILES Islets, Istles, Sliest
STILET Titles
STIMED Demist, Demits, Misted
STIMES Misset, Smites, Tmesis
STINGE Ingest, Signet, Tinges
STINGO Ingots, Tigons, Tosing
STINGY Styling, Tyings
STIPES Spites
STIRPS Spirts, Sprits, Strips
STIR-UP Purist, Spruit, Uprist, Upstir
STIVED Divest, Vedist
STIVER Rivets, Strive, Tivers, Trevis, Verist
STODGE Godets
STOEPS Estops, Posset, Stopes
STOGIE Egoist
STOKER Stroke, Trokes
STOLED Oldest
STOLEN Solent, Telson,
STONED Donets, Doesn't, Ostend
STONEN Neston, Nonets, Sonnet, Tenons, Tenson, Tonnes
STONER Nestor, Noters, Reston, Strone, Tenors, Tensor, Terson, Toners, Trones
STONES Nestos, Onsets, Setons
STOPED Depots, Despot, Posted
STOPER Opster, Poster, Presto, Repost, Repots, Retops, Topers, Tropes
STOPES Estops, Posset, Stoeps
STOP-GO Go-Stop
STORAX Taxors
STORED Dorset, Doters, Sordet, Sorted, Strode, Trodes
STORER Resort, Roster, Sorter
STORES Retoss, Rosets, Sorest, Sortes, Torses, Tosser

STOREY Oyster, Rosety, Toyers, Troyes, Tyroes
STORGE Groset
STOUND Donuts
STOUPS Spouts, Toss-up, Uptoss
STOURS Rousts, Sutors, Tussor
STOVER Rovest, Strove, Voters
STOWED Towsed
STOWER Rowest, Rowtes, Sowter, Stowre, Towers, Towser, Twoers
STOWRE Rowest, Rowtes, Sowter, Stower, Towers, Towser, Twoers
*** STRABO** Aborts, Boarts, Tabors
STRACK Tracks
STRAFE Afters, Faster,
STRAIK Kraits, Traiks
STRAIN Instar, Santir, Sintra, Trains
STRAIT Artist, Sittar, Strati, Traits
STRAKE Skater, Streak, Takers, Tasker
STRAMP Tramps
STRATA Astart, Attars, Tatars
STRATI Artist, Sittar, Strait, Traits
*** STRAUS** Rastus, Sutras, Tarsus Tussar
STRAWY Swarty, Wastry
STREAK Skater, Strake, Takers, Tasker
STREAM Armest, Armets, Master, Maters, Remast, Tamers, Tremas
STREEK Tereks
STREEL Lester, Relets
STREET Retest, Setter, Tester
STRENE Enters, Ernest, Nester, Rentes, Resent, Sterne, Tenser, Ternes
*** STRESA** Assert, Asters, Astres, Reasts, Stares
STRIAE Resita, Satire
STRICK Tricks

STRIDE Direst, Driest, Ridest
STRIFE Firest, Freits, Refits, Resift, Rifest, Sifter
STRIGA Gratis
STRIKE Trikes
*__STRINE__ Insert, Inters, Nitres, Retins, Sinter, Trines
STRIPE Esprit, Priest, Pteris, Ripest, Sitrep, Sprite, Tripes
STRIPS Spirts, Sprits, Stirps
STRIVE Rivets, Stiver, Tivers, Trevis, Verist
STROAM Martos, Morats, Mostar, Stroma
STROBE Besort, Osbert, Sorbet
STRODE Dorset, Doters, Sordet, Sorted, Stored, Trodes
STROKE Stoker, Trokes
STROLL Trolls
STROMA Martos, Morats, Mostar, Stroam
STRONE Nestor, Noters, Reston, Stoner, Tenors, Tensor, Terson, Toners, Trones
STROUD Tudors
STROUP Proust, Sprout, Stupor
STROUT Trouts, Tutors
STROVE Rovest, Stover, Voters
STRUCK Trucks
STRUNG Grunts
STUMER Estrum, Muster
STUPOR Proust, Stroup, Sprout
STYING Stingy, Tyings
STYTHE Tethys
STYLES Slyest
SUABLE Usable
SUABLY Usably
SUBLET Bluest, Bustle, Subtle
SUBLID Builds
SUBMAN Busman
SUBMEN Busmen
SUBORN Bourns
SUBTER Brutes, Buster, Rebuts, Surbet, Tubers

SUBTLE Bluest, Bustle, Sublet
SUCCOR Crocus, Occurs, Roccus
SUCCUS Cuscus
SUDDER Udders
SUEING Genius
SUFFER Ruffes
SUGARS Sargus
*__SUIDAE__ Adieus
*__SUISSE__ Issues
SUITES Tissue
SULCAL Callus
SULPHA Lash-up
SUMMAE Emmaus
SUMMIT Mutism
SUMMON Musmon
SUNDER Nursed, Unders, Unreds
SUN-DOG Sun-god, Ungods
SUN-GOD Sun-dog, Ungods
SUN-HAT Haunts, Unhats, Ushant
SUNLIT Insult
SUNSET Unsets
SUPAWN Sawn-up
SUPINE Puisne
SUPPER Uppers
SUPPLE Peplus
SURBET Brutes, Buster, Rebuts, Subter, Tubers
SUREST Estrus, Russet, Tusser
SURETE Retuse, Tereus
SUTLER Lurest, Luster, Lustre, Luters, Result, Rulest, Rustle, Ulster
SUTORS Rousts, Stours, Tussor
SUTRAS Rastus, Straus, Tarsus, Tussor
SUTURE Uterus
SWALED Dwales, Wealds
SWALES Awless, Sweals
SWARTH Thraws, Warths, Wraths
SWARTY Strawy, Wastry
SWARVE Wavers

SWATHE Wheats
SWAYER Sawyer
SWEALS Awless, Swales
SWEARD Sawder, Seward,
  Waders
SWEARS Resaws, Sawers, Wrasse
SWEATS Sawset, Tawses, Wastes
*****SWEDEN** Endews
SWEERT Stewer, Wester
SWEIRT Twiers, Twires, Wriest,
  Writes
SWINGE Sewing, Winges
SWIPED Wisped
SWIPER Wipers
SWITHE Whites, Withes
SWOUND Wounds
SYPHER Hypers, Sphery
SYPHON Hypnos
SYRTES Tressy

TABBED Tebbad
TABLER Albert, Labret
TABLES Ablest, Ablets, Bleats,
  Stable
TABLET Batlet, Battel, Battle
TABORS Aborts, Boarts, Strabo
TABOUR Outbar, Rubato
TABRET Batter
TABULA Ablaut
TACETS Sceatt, Stacte
TACHES Chaste, Cheats, Sachet,
  Scathe
TACKER Racket, Retack
TACTIC Tic-tac
TAG-END Ganted, Tanged
TAGGED Gadget
TAGGER Garget
*****TAGORE** Orgeat
TAG-RAG Rag-tag
TAHSIL Latish
*****TAIDEN** Danite, Detain
TAIGLE Aiglet, Ligate
TAILED Detail, Dietal, Dilate

TAILER Retail, Retial
TAILOR Rialto
TAIL-UP Tipula, Tulipa
TAINTS Tanist, Titans
TAIPAN Patina
TAISCH Scaith
TAKE-IN Intake, Kinate
TAKERS Skater, Strake, Streak,
  Tasker
TAKE-UP Uptake
TALARS Altars, Astral, Ratals,
  Tarsel
TALENT Lanett, Latent, Latten
TALIAN Antlia, Latian
TALLER Tellar
TAMALE Malate, Meatal
TAMARI Amrita
TAMANU Mantua
TAMERS Armest, Armets,
  Master, Maters, Remast, Stream,
  Tremas
TAMINE Inmate
TAMING Mating
TAMINS Mantis, Matins, Stamin
TAMISE Maties, Samite, Semita
TAMPON Potman, Topman
TAN-BED Banted
TANGED Ganted, Tag-end
TANGIE Eating, Ingate, Teaing
TANGLE Anglet, Langet
TANGOS Gaston, Sontag,
  Tongas, Tsonga
TANIST Taints, Titans
TANNAH Thanna
TANNIC Tin-can
TANREC Canter, Carnet, Centra,
  Creant, Cretan, Nectar, Recant,
  Trance
*****TANTRA** Rattan, Tartan
*****TAOISM** Maoist, Samiot
TAPERS Paster, Paters, Petars,
  Praest, Prates, Repast, Trapes
TAPIRS Rapist
TAPPIT Pit-pat

*TARBES Barest, Baster, Bestar, Breast

TARCEL Cartel, Claret, Rectal

TARGED Grated

TARGES Grates, Greats, Ragest, Stager

TARING Gratin, Rating, Tringa

TARMAC Ramcat

TAROCS Actors, Castor, Castro, Co-star, Croats, Roctas, Scrota

TAROTS Stator, Troats

TARPAN Partan, Trapan

TARPON Parton, Patron

TARRED Darter, Dartre, Retard, Retrad, Trader

TARRES Arrest, Arrets, Rarest, Raster, Raters, Retars Sartre, Starer, Terras

TARSAL Altars, Astral, Ratals, Talars

TARSEL Alerts, Alters, Artels, Laster, Ratels, Resalt, Salter, Slater, Staler, Stelar

TARSIA Arista, Riatas, Tiaras

*TARSUS Rastus, Straus, Sutars, Tussar

TARTAN Rattan, Tantra

TARTED Ratted, Tetrad

TARTLY Rattly

TARVES Averts, Ravest, Starve, Staver, Tavers, Traves, Vaster

TASHED Deaths, Hasted, 'Sdeath

TASHES Ashets, Hastes

TASKED Skated, Staked

TASKER Skater, Strake, Streak, Takers

TASLET Latest, Stealt

*TASMAN Mantas

TASSEL Slates, Stales, Steals, Teslas

TASSET States, Tastes

TASSIE Siesta

TASTED Stated

TASTER Aretts, Astert, Stater, Taters, Tetras, Treats

TASTES States, Tasset

*TATARS Astart, Attars, Strata

TATERS Aretts, Astert, Stater, Taster, Tetras, Treats

TATLER Latter, Rattle

*TAUBER Arbute

TAUNTS Tutsan

TAUPES Tuapse

TAURIC Urtica

TAURIN Nutria

TAUTEN Attune, Nutate, Tetuan

TAVERS Averts, Ravest, Starve, Staver, Tarves, Traves, Vaster

TAWERS Waster, Waters

TAWERY Watery

TAWSES Sawset, Sweats, Wastes

TAWTIE Twaite

TAXERS Astrex, Extras

TAXING Xangti

TAXORS Storax

TAYRAS Astray, Satyra

TEABAG Atabeg

TEADES Easted, Seated, Sedate, Teased

TEAGLE Eaglet, Gelate, Galtee, Legate, Telega

TEAING Eating, Ingate, Tangie

TEAMAN Amenta

TEA-POT Aptote

TEARED Derate, Redate

TEARER Rerate, Retear, Terrae

TEASED Easted, Seated, Sedate, Teades

TEASEL Elates, Steale, Stelae

TEASER Aretes, Asteer, Easter, Eaters, Reates, Reseat, Saeter, Seater, Staree, Steare, Teresa

TEA-SET Eatest, Estate, Testae

TEA-URN Aunter, Nature, Neutra

TEAZEL Teazle

TEAZLE Teazel

TEBBAD Tabbed

TEEING Ginete
TEETER Terete
TE-HEES Seethe
*TEHRAN Anther, Thenar
TELARY Eyltra, Lyrate, Raylet,
  Realty
TELE-AD Delate, Elated
TELEGA Eaglet, Galtee, Gelate,
  Legate, Teagle
TELLAR Taller
TELLER Retell
TELSON Solent, Stolen
TEMPLE Pelmet
TENACE Cetane
TENAIL Entail
TENDED Dented
TENDER Rented, Terned
TENDON Denton
TENNER Rennet
TENNIS Sennit, Sinnet
TENONS Neston, Nonets,
  Sonnet, Stonen, Tenson, Tonnes
TENORA Atoner, Ornate
TENORS Nestor, Noters, Reston,
  Strone, Stoner, Tensor, Terson,
  Toners, Trones
TENREC Center, Centre, Recent
TENSED Endest, Nested, Sedent
TENSER Enters, Ernest, Nester,
  Rentes, Resent, Sterne, Strene,
  Ternes
TENSON Neston, Nonets,
  Sonnet, Stonen, Tenons, Tonnes
TENSOR Nestor, Noters, Reston,
  Stoner, Strone, Tenors, Terson,
  Toners, Trones
TENTED Detent, Netted
TENTER Netter, Retent
TENUIS Intuse, Unites, Unties
TENURE Neuter, Retune, Tureen
TENUTO Teuton
TEPALS Palest, Palets, Pastel,
  Peltas, Petals, Plates, Pleats,
  Septal, Staple

*TERAMO Amoret
TERAPH Threap
TERBIA Baiter, Barite,
  Rebait
TERCIO Erotic
TEREFA Afreet
TEREKS Streek
*TERESA Aretes, Asteer, Easter,
  Eaters, Reates, Reseat, Saeter,
  Seater, Staree, Steare, Teaser
TERETE Teeter
*TEREUS Retuse, Surete
*TERMES Merest, Mestre, Meters,
  Metres, Restem
TERMLY Myrtle
TERMOR Tremor
TERNAL Altern, Antler, Learnt,
  Rental
TERNED Rented, Tender
TERNES Enters, Ernest, Nester,
  Rentes, Resent, Tenser, Sterne,
  Strene
TERRAE Rerate, Retear, Tearer
*TERRAN Errant, Ranter
TERRAS Arrest, Arrets, Rarest,
  Raster, Raters, Retars, Sartre,
  Starer, Tarres
TERRIT Ritter, Tirret, Triter
TERROR Rorter
*TERSON Nestor, Noters, Reston,
  Storen, Strone, Tensor, Terson,
  Toners, Trones
TERTIA Attire, Ratite, Tiaret
TESLAS Slates, Stales, Steals,
  Tassel
*TESSIN Insets, Steins
TESTAE Eatest, Estate, Teaset
TESTED Detest
TESTEE Settee
TESTER Retest, Setter, Street
TESTES Sestet, Tsetse
TESTON Ostent, Totnes
*TETHYS Stythe
TETRAD Ratted, Tarted

TETRAS Aretts, Astert, Stater, Taster, Taters, Treats
*** TETUAN** Attune, Nutate, Tauten
*** TEUTON** Tenuto
TEWING Twinge
TEXANS Sextan
THAIRM Mithra
THALER Halter, Lather
*** THALES** Haslet, Lathes, Shelta
*** THAMES** Smeath
THANES Athens, Hasten, Snathe, Sneath
THANNA Tannah
*** THASOS** Hoasts, Hostas, Shoats
THAWED Wadeth
THAWER Rethaw, Wreath
*** THEBES** Behest
THECAE Eatche, Hecate
THECAL Chalet, Thecla
*** THECLA** Chalet, Thecal
THEICS Ethics, Itches
THEIRS Riseth, Rithes, Shrite, Thiers
THEISM Meiths, Themis
*** THEISS** Heists, Shiest, Shites, Sithes, Thesis
THEIST Thetis, Tithes
*** THELMA** Eltham, Hamlet
THEMES Smeeth
*** THEMIS** Meiths, Theism
THENAL Hantle, Lathen
THENAR Anther, Tehran
THENCE Chenet
THESES Sheets
THESIS Heists, Shiest Shites, Sithes, Theiss
*** THETIS** Theist, Tithes
THIBLE Blithe
THICKS Kitsch, Schtik, Shtick
*** THIERS** Riseth, Rithes, Shrite, Theirs
THINGY Nighty
THIRST Thrist, T-Shirt
THOLES Helots, Hostel, Hotels

THORAL Harlot, Lothar
*** THORNE** Hornet, Horten, Throne
THORNY Rhyton
THORPE Pother
THOWEL Howlet
THRANG Granth
THRAPS Sparth
THRAVE Raveth
THRAWS Swarth, Warths, Wraths
THREAD Dareth, Dearth, Hatred, Red-hat
THREAP Teraph
THREAT Hatter
THREEP Pether
THREES Esther, Ethers, Hester
THRENE Nether
THRICE Cither, Ericht
THRIST Thirst, T-Shirt
THRIVE Riveth
THROES Others, Rothes, Tosher
THRONE Hornet, Horten, Thorne
THROVE Roveth
THRUST Truths
THYMIC Mythic
THYMUS Mythus
THYRSI Irtysh, Shirty
TIARAS Arista, Riatas, Tarsia
*** TIARET** Attire, Ratite, Tertia
*** TIBERT** Bitter
TIC-TAC Tactic
TICING Citing
TICKLE Keltic
TIEING Ignite
TIE-PIN Pinite
TIERCE Cerite, Certie, Recite
TIERED Dieter, Re-edit, Retied
TIE-ROD Editor, Rioted, Triode
TIGLON Lingot, Toling
TIGONS Ingots, Stingo, Tosing
TILDES Delist, Idlest, Listed, Silted
TILERS Lister, Litres, Relist
TILLED Lilted

TILLER Retill, Rillet
TILMUS Litmus
TILTED Titled
TILTER Litter, Titler
*TIMARU Atrium
TIMBER Betrim, Timbre
TIMBRE Betrim, Timber
TIMERS Merits, Mister, Miters,
   Mitres, Remits, Smiter
TIMOUS Ostium
TIN-CAN Tannic
TINDED Dinted
TINDER Rident, Trined
TINEAN Innate
TINEAS Tisane
TINEID Indite
TINGED Nidget
TINGES Ingest, Signet, Stinge
TINGIS Siting
TINIER Intire
TINKER Reknit
TINNED Dentin, Indent, Intend
TINNER Intern
TINNIE Intine
TINSEL Enlist, Inlets, Listen,
   Silent
TINTER Nitter, Retint
TIPPER Pripet
TIPULA Tail-up, Tulipa
TIRADE Airted, Raited
*TIRANE Nerita, Ratine, Retain,
   Retina
TIROES Sortie, Tories
TIRRET Ritter, Territ, Triter
TISANE Tineas
TISSUE Suites
TITANS Taints, Tanist
TITERS Sitter, Titres, Triste
TITFER Fitter
TITHER Hitter
TITHES Theist, Thetis
TITLED Tilted
TITLER Litter, Tilter
TITLES Stilet

TITRES Sitter, Titers, Triste
TIVERS Rivets, Stiver, Strive,
   Trevis, Verist
TMESIS Misset, Smites, Stimes
*TOBAGO Bogota
TOBIES Sobeit
TOCHER Hector, Rochet, Rotche,
   Troche
TOCSIN Sintoc, Tonics
TOE-CAP Capote
TOE-RAG Orgeat
TOFORE Foetor, Footer, Refoot
TOGAED Dogate, Dotage
TOGGLE Goglet, Logget
TOILER Loiret, Loiter, Triole
TOILET Lottie
TOLING Lingot, Tiglon
TOLANE Etalon, Lean-to
TOLEDO Looted, Tooled
TOLUIC Coutil
TOMBAC Combat
TOMTOM Mot-mot
TO-NAME Omenta
TONERS Nestor, Noters, Reston,
   Stoner, Strone, Tenors, Tensor,
   Terson, Trones
TONGAS Gaston, Sontag,
   Tangos, Tsonga
TONICS Sintoc, Tocsin
TONING Noting
TONISH Shinto
TONNES Neston, Nonets,
   Sonnet, Stonen, Tenons, Tenson
TON-UPS Puntos, Put-ons,
   Unstop
TOOLED Looted, Toledo
TOOLER Looter, Loreto, Retool,
   Rootle
TOOMED Mooted
TOPERS Opster, Poster, Presto,
   Repost, Repots, Retops, Stoper,
   Tropes
TOPFUL Potful
TOP-HAT Pot-hat

TOPHUS Pushto, Upshot
TOPICS Optics, Picots
TOPING Opting, Poting
TOPMAN Potman, Tampon
TOPMEN Potmen
TO-REND Rodent
TO-RENT Rotten
TORERO Rooter
TORIES Sortie, Tiroes
TORPID Tripod
TORQUE Quoter, Roquet
TORRET Retort, Rotter
TORSEL Ostler, Relost, Rostel,
  Sterol
TORSES Retoss, Rosets, Sorest,
  Sortes, Stores, Tosser
***TORULA** Rotula
TOSHED Hosted
TOSHER Others, Rothes, Throes
TOSING Ingots, Stingo, Tigons
TOSSEN Seston
TOSSER Retoss, Rosets, Sorest,
  Sortes, Stores, Torses
TOSSES Sestos
TOSS-UP Spouts, Stoups, Uptoss
TO-TEAR Rotate
***TOTNES** Ostent, Teston
T'OTHER Hotter
TOUCAN Noctua, Uncoat
TOUCHY Couthy
TOUGHS Oughts, Sought
TOURED Detour, Douter,
  Outred, Redout, Routed
TOURER Retour, Roture, Router
TOUSED Ousted
TOUSER Ouster, Outers, Routes,
  Souter, Trouse
TOUSLE Solute
TOUTED Duetto
TOWELS Elstow, Lowest, Owlets
TOWERS Rowest, Rowtes,
  Sowter, Stower, Stowre, Towser,
  Twoers
TOWING Wigton

TOWSED Stowed
TOWSER Rowest, Rowtes,
  Sowter, Stower, Stowre, Towers,
  Twoers
TOYERS Oyster, Rosety, Storey,
  Troyes, Tyroes
TOYMEN Etymon
T-PLATE Pattle
TRABEA Abater, Rabate
TRACED Carted, Cedrat, Crated,
  Dectra, Redact
TRACER Arrect, Carter, Crater
TRACES Carets, Cartes, Caster,
  Caters, Crates, Cresta, Reacts,
  Recast
TRACKS Strack
TRADED Darted
TRADER Darter, Dartre, Retard,
  Retrad, Tarred
TRADES Adrets, Daters, Desart,
  Stared, Treads
TRAGIC Catrig
TRAIKS Straik, Kraits
TRAINS Instar, Santir, Sintra,
  Strain
TRAITS Artist, Strait, Sittar,
  Strati
***TRALEE** Elater, Relate
0**TRAMPS** Stramp
TRANCE Canter, Carnet, Centra,
  Creant, Cretan, Nectar, Recant,
  Tanrec
TRANSE Antres, Astern, Retans,
  Sterna
TRAPAN Partan, Tarpan
TRAPED Depart, Drapet, Parted,
  Petard, Prated

TRAPES Paster, Paters, Petars,
  Praest, Prates, Repast, Tapers
TRAVEL Averts, Ravest, Strarve,
  Staver, Tarves, Tavers, Vaster
TREADS Adrets, Daters, Desart,
  Stared, Trades

TREATS Aretts, Astert, Stater, Taster, Taters, Tetras
***TRENTO** Rotten
TREFLE Felter, Feltre, Refelt, Reflet
TREMAS Armest, Armets, Master, Maters, Remast, Stream, Tamers
TREMIE Metier, Re-emit, Retime
TREMOR Termor
TREATY Yatter
TREPAN Arpent, Enrapt, Entrap, Panter, Parent, Pterna
***TRESCO** Corset, Cortes, Coster, Escort, Recost, Rectos, Scoter, Sector
TRESSY Syrtes
***TREVES** Everts, Revest, Revets, Sterve, Verset, Vester
TREVET Vetter
TREVIS Rivets, Stiver, Strive, Tivers, Verist
TRIADS Astrid
TRIAGE Aigret, Gaiter
TRIALS Stilar, Trails
TRIBES Bestir, Bister, Bistre, Biters, Brites
TRICED Credit, Direct
***TRICEL** Relict
TRICES Steric
***TRICIA** Iatric
TRICKS Strick
TRIERS Restir
TRIFLE Filter, Lifter
TRIGON Girton, Roting
TRIKES Strike
TRIMER Retrim
TRINAL Ratlin
TRINED Rident, Tinder
TRINES Insert, Inters, Nitres, Retins, Sinter, Strine
TRINGA Gratin, Rating, Taring
TRIODE Editor, Rioted, Tie-rod
TRIOLE Loiret, Loiter, Toiler

TRIPES Esprit, Priest, Pteris, Ripest, Sitrep, Sprite, Stripe
TRIPOD Torpid
TRIPOS Prosit
TRISTE Sitter, Titers, Titres
TRITER Ritter, Territ, Tirret
TRITON Intort
TRIUNE Uniter, Untire
TROATS Stator, Tarots
TROCAR Carrot
TROCHE Hector, Rochet, Rotche, Tocher
TRODES Dorset, Doters, Sordet, Sorted, Stored, Strode
TROKES Stoker, Stroke
TROLLS Stroll
***TROMSO** Motors
TRONES Nestor, Noters, Reston, Stoner, Strone, Tenors, Tensor, Terson, Toners
TROPES Opster, Poster, Presto, Repost, Repots, Retops, Stoper, Topers
***TROSTE** Otters
TROUPE Pouter, Roupet
TROUSE Ouster, Outers, Routes, Souter, Touser
TROUTS Strout, Tutors
TROUTY Try-out
TROWED Rowted
TROWEL Wortle
***TROYAN** Aroynt, Notary
***TROYES** Oyster, Rosety, Storey, Toyers, Tyroes
TRUCES Cruets, Cruset, Custer, Eructs, Rectus, Recuts
TRUCKS Struck
TRUEST Utters
***TRUMAN** Antrum
TRUTHS Thrust
TRYING Tyring
TRY-OUT Trouty
TSETSE Sestet, Testes
T-SHIRT Thirst, Thrist

TSONGA Gaston, Sontag, Tangos, Tongas
*****TUAPSE** Taupes
*****TUAREG** Argute, Rugate
TUBATE Battue
TUBBER Rubbet
TUBERS Brutes, Buster, Rebuts, Subter, Surbet
TUCANS Cantus, Tuscan, Uncast
*****TUCSON** Counts
*****TUDORS** Stroud
TUFTER Futter
*****TULIPA** Tail-up, Tipula
TUMPHY Humpty
TUNDRA Draunt, Durant
TUNERS Unrest
TUNNEL Unlent
TUNNER Runnet, Unrent
TURBOS Robust
*****TURCOS** Courts, Crouts, Scruto
TUREEN Neuter, Retune, Tenure
TURFER Erfurt, Returf
TURNED Retund, Runted
TURNER Return
TURNIP Turpin
TURN-UP Upturn
*****TURPIN** Turnip
TURRET Rutter
TURTLE Ruttle
*****TUSCAN** Cantus, Tucans, Uncast
TUSSAL Saltus, Saults
TUSSAR Rastus, Sutras, Straus, Tarsus
TUSSER Estrus, Russet, Surest
TUSSOR Rousts, Stours, Sutors
TUTMAN Mutant
TUTORS Strout, Trouts
TUTSAN Taunts
TWAITE Tawtie
TWEEDS Stewed, Wested
TWIERS Sweirt, Twires, Wriest, Writes
TWINER Winter
TWINES Wisent

TWINGE Tewing
TWIRES Sweirt, Twiers, Wriest, Writes
TWOERS Rowest, Rowtes, Sowter, Stower, Stowre, Towers, Towser
TYCOON Coonty
TYINGS Stingy, Stying
*****TYPHON** Phyton, Python
*****TYRIAN** In-tray
TYRING Trying
TYROES Oyster, Rosety, Storey, Toyers, Troyes

U-BOATS Basuto
UDDERS Sudder
UGLIER Guiler, Ligure, Reguli
*****UGRIAN** Air-gun
*****UHLANS** Unlash
ULICON Culion, Uncoil
ULLING Ungill
ULNARE Neural, Unreal
ULSTER Lurest, Luster, Lustre, Luters, Result, Rulest, Rustle, Sutler
ULTION Oil-nut, Nut-oil
UMBELS Umbles
UMBLES Umbels
UMBRAL Brumal, Labrum, Lumbar
UMBRAS Rumbas, Sambur
UMBREL Lumber, Rumble
*****UMBRIA** Barium
UMLAUT Mutual
UMPIRE Impure
UNABLE Nabeul, Nebula, Unbale
UNAGED Augend
UNBALE Nabeul, Nebula, Unable
UNBARE Unbear, Urbane
UNBEAR Unbare, Urbane
UNBENT Ben-nut
UNBIAS Anubis, Nubias
UNBLED Bundle
UNBOOT Bouton

UNBRED Bunder, Burden, Burned
UNCAGE Cangue
UNCASE Causen, Usance
UNCAST Cantus, Tucans, Tuscan
UNCATE Canute
UNCHAL Launch, Nuchal
UNCIAL Alcuin, Lucian, Lucina
UNCLES Clunes
UNCOAT Noctua, Toucan
UNCOIL Culion, Ulicon
UNCOIN Nuncio
UNCOOP Coupon
UNCOPE Pounce
UNCORE Rounce
UNDEAR Dauner, Unread
UNDERN Dunner
UNDERS Nursed, Sunder, Unreds
UNDIES Indues
UNDOER Enduro
UNDOES Undose
UNEDGE Dengue
UNFELT Fluent, Netful, Unleft
UNFIST Unfits
UNFITS Unfist
UNFLAT Flaunt
UNFURL Urnful
UNGAIN Guanin
UNGILL Ulling
UNGILT Glutin, Luting
UNGIRD During
UNGIRT Untrig
UNGLIB Bluing
UNGODS Sundog, Sungod
UNGUAL Ungula
UNGULA Ungual
UNHATS Haunts, Sunhat, Ushant
UNHURT Unruth
*****UNIATE** Auntie
UNIBLE Nubile
UNICED Induce
UNIONS Nonius, Unison
UNIPOD Dupion

UNISON Nonius, Unions
UNITED Dunite, Untied
UNITER Triune, Untire
UNITES Intuse, Tenuis, Unties
UNLACE Cuneal, Launce, Lucena
UNLADE Unlead
UNLAID Dualin, Lindau
UNLASH Uhlans
UNLEAD Unlade
UNLEFT Fluent, Netful, Unfelt
UNLENT Tunnel
UNLIME Lumine
UNLIVE Unveil
UNNAIL Annuli
UNNEST Unsent
UNPEGS Spunge
UNPENT Punnet
UNPILE Line-up, Lupine, Up-line
UNPINS Unspin
UNREAD Dauner, Undear
UNREAL Neural, Ulnare
UNREDS Nursed, Sunder, Unders
UNREEL Renule
UNRENT Runnet, Tunner
UNREST Tuners
UNRING Urning
UNRIPE Punier, Purine
UNROBE Bourne
UNROOT Notour
UNRUDE Unrued
UNRUED Unrude
UNRUTH Unhurt
UNSEAT Austen, Nasute
UNSENT Unnest
UNSERE Ensure, Enures
UNSETS Sunset
UNSHIP Punish
UNSHOD Hounds, Hudson
UNSLIM Muslin
UNSNAP Pannus, Sannup, Unspan
UNSOFT Founts
UNSOLE Ensoul, Nousle, Olenus

UNSPAN Pannus, Sannup, Unsnap
UNSPED Send-up, Upends, Upsend
UNSPIN Unpins
UNSTOP Puntos, Put-ons, Ton-ups
UNSUED Unused
UNTAME Unteam
UNTEAM Untame
UNTIDY Nudity
UNTIED Dunite, United
UNTIES Intuse, Tenuis, Unites
UNTILE Luiten, Lutein, Lutine,
UNTIRE Triune, Uniter
UNTRIG Ungirt
UNTROD Rotund
UNUSED Unsued
UNVEIL Unlive
UNWARP Unwrap
UNWARY Runway
UNWRAP Unwarp
UPBEAT Beat-up
UPBLOW Blow-up
UPCAST Catsup
UPDRAW Upward
UPENDS Send-up, Unsped, Upsend
UPHANG Hang-up
UPHOLD Hold-up
UPLEAP Papule
UP-LINE Line-up, Lupine, Unpile
UPLOCK Lock-up
UPMAKE Make-up
UPPERS Supper
UP-PILE Pile-up
UPRATE Uptear
UPREAR Parure
UPRISE Epirus
UPRIST Purist, Spruit, Stir-up, Upstir
UPROLL Roll-up
UPROSE Poseur, Souper

UPSEND Send-up, Unsped, Upends
UPSHOT Pushto, Tophus
UPSTIR Purist, Spruit, Stir-up, Uprist
UPSWAY Upways
UPTAKE Take-up
UPTEAR Uprate
UPTOSS Spouts, Stoups, Toss-up
UPTURN Turn-up
UPWARD Updraw
UPWAYS Upsway
UPWIND Wind-up
URACIL Curial, Lauric, Uralic
URAEUS Aureus
*****URALIC** Curial, Lauric, Uracil
URANYL Lunary
*****URANIA** Anuria
URATES Atreus, Auster, Seurat
URBANE Unbare, Unbear
UREASE Reseau
UREMIC Cerium
URESIS Issuer
URETER Reuter
URETIC Cuiter, Curiet
URGENT Gunter, Gurnet
URINES Insure, Inures, Rusine, Ursine
URNEFUL Unfurl
URNING Unring
URSINE Insure, Inures, Rusine, Urines
URTICA Tauric
USABLE Suable
USABLY Suably
USAGER Argues, Augers, Sauger, Segura
USANCE Causen, Uncase
*****USEDOM** Dumose, Moused, Soumed
*****USHANT** Haunts, Sunhat, Unhats
USHERS Rhesus, Rushes
UTERUS Suture
UTTERS Truest

VACATE Caveat
VAGILE Glaive
VAINER Erivan, Rave-in, Ravine, Vanier
VAKASS Kavass
*****VALAIS** Avails, Saliva, Salvia
VALETS Vestal
VALINE Alevin, Alvine, Venial
VALING Laving
VALISE Aviles, Leavis, Silvae
VALLAR Larval
*****VALONA** Avalon, Avlona
VALOUR Louvar, Ovular
VALSED Salved, Slaved
VALSER Lavers, Ravels, Salver, Serval, Slaver, Velars, Versal
VALUES Avulse
VAMOSE Amoves
VAMPER Revamp
VANGEE Avenge, Geneva
*****VANIER** Erivan, Rave-in, Ravine, Vainer
*****VARESE** Averse, Reaves
VARIER Arrive, Rivera
VARIES Servia
VARLET Travel
VASTER Averts, Ravest, Starve, Staver, Tarves, Tavers, Traves
VEADER Evader, Reaved
VEALER Laveer, Leaver, Reveal
*****VECTIS** Civets, Evicts
VECTOR Corvet, Covert
*****VEDIST** Divest, Stived
VEERED Reeved
VEILED Levied
VEINED Endive, Envied
VELARS Lavers, Ravels, Salver, Serval, Slaver, Valser, Versal
VELATE Veleta
*****VELCRO** Clover
VELETA Velate
VELITE Levite
VELOUR Louver, Louvre

VENDER Denver, Nerved, Revend, Verden
VENEER Enerve, Evener
VENIAL Alevin, Alvine, Valine
*****VENICE** Evince
VENIRE Envier, Nievre, Verein
*****VERDEN** Denver, Nerved, Revend, Vender
VERDIN Driven
VERDIT Divert
VEREIN Envier, Nievre, Venire
VERGEE Greeve
VERGES Greves
VERIER Reiver, Riever
VERILY Livery
VERISM Vermis
VERIST Rivets, Stiver, Strive, Tivers, Trevis
VERMIS Verism
VERNAL Nerval
*****VERONA** Averno
VERREY Revery
VERSAL Lavers, Ravels, Salver, Serval, Slaver, Valser, Velars
VERSED Served
VERSER Revers, Server
VERSES Serves, Severs, Sevres
VERSET Everts, Revets, Revest, Sterve, Treves, Vester,
VESICA Cavies
VESSEL Selves
VESTAL Valets
VESTAS Staves
VESTED Devest
VESTEE Steeve
VESTER Everts, Revest, Revets, Sterve, Treves, Verset
VETOED Devote
VETOER Reveto, Revote
VETTER Trevet
VIEWER Review
VIEWLY Wively
VILELY Evilly, Lively
VILEST Livest

VINOSE Nivose
VIOLER Oliver
VIOLET Olivet
VIOLIN Olivin
VIRENT Invert
VIREOS Rivose, Virose
VIRGIN Irving, Riving
VIROSE Rivose, Vireos
VISAED Advise, Avised, Davies
VISEED Devise, Sieved
VISTAL Vitals
VIVERS Vivres
VIVRES Vivers
VITALS Vistal
VOIDED Devoid
VOIDER Devoir
VOILES Olives, Solive
VOLAGE Lovage
VOLERY Overly
VOLING Gonvil, Loving
VOLLEY Lovely
VOLSCI Clovis
VOTERS Rovest, Stover, Strove
VOWELS Wolves
*VRATCA Cravat

WABBLE Bawble
WADDED Dawded
WADDLE Dawdle
WADERS Sawder, Seward, Sweard
WADETH Thawed
WADSET Stawed, Wasted
WAGGEL Waggle
WAGGLE Waggel
WAILED Dewali
WAINED Dewani, Edwina
WAITED Dawtie
WAIVED Adview
*WALDEN Lawned
WALING Lawing
WALRUS Wrauls
WAMPUS Mawpus

WANDER Andrew, Darwen, Dawner, Rawden, Warden, Warned
WANDLE Elwand
WANING Awning
WANKER Newark
WANKLE Knawel
WARBLE Bawler
WARDED Drawed, Edward
WARDEN Andrew, Darwen, Dawner, Rawden, Wander, Warned
WARDER Drawer, Redraw, Reward, Warred
WARDOG War-god
WARELY Lawyer
WAR-GOD Wardog
WARIER Rewari
WARING Rawing
WARMER Rewarm
WARNED Andrew, Darwen, Dawner, Rawden, Wander, Warden
WARNER Rewarn, Warren
WARPER Pre-war, Rewarp
WARRED Drawer, Redraw, Reward, Warder
WARREN Rewarn, Warner
WARTHS Swarth, Thraws, Wraths
WASHER Hawser, Rewash, Whares
WASHEN Whenas
WASTED Stawed, Wadset
WASTER Tawers, Waters
WASTES Sawset, Sweats, Tawses
WASTRY Strawy, Swarty
WATERS Tawers, Waster
WATERY Tawery
WAVERS Swarve
WEALDS Dwales, Swaled
WEARER Rewear
WEENED Enewed
WELDER Lewder, Reweld

WELKIN Winkle
*****WENDIC** Winced
*****WESKER** Skewer
WESTED Stewed, Tweeds
WESTER Stewer, Sweert
WHARES Hawser, Rewash, Washer
WHEATS Swathe
WHEELS Shewel
WHENAS Washen
WHERES Hewers, Reshew
WHINES Newish
WHINGE Hewing
WHITER Wither, Writhe
WHITES Swithe, Withes
WHORES Howres, Reshow, Shower
WIDELY Dewily, Wieldy
WIDENS Dwines, Widnes
*****WIDNES** Dwines, Widens
WIELDY Dewily, Widely
*****WIGNER** Winger
*****WIGTON** Towing
WILLER Irwell
WINCED Wendic
WINDED Dwined
WINDER Rewind
WIND-UP Upwind
WINGED Dewing
WINGER Wigner
WINGES Sewing, Swinge
WINKER Wrekin
WINKLE Welkin
WINSEY Sinewy
WINTER Twiner
WIPERS Swiper
WISENT Twines
WISPED Swiped
WITHER Whiter, Writhe
WITHES Swithe, Whites
WITHIN Inwith
WITTED Dewitt
WIVELY Viewly

WOALDS Dowlas
WOBBLY By-blow
WOLFED Flowed, Fowled
WOLFER Flower, Fowler, Reflow
WOLVES Vowels
WONDER Downer
WONING Owning
WONNER Renown
WORKER Rework
WORK-IN Inwork
WORSED Dowers, Dowser, Drowse
WORSEN Owners, Resown, Rowens
WORSER Rowers
WORTLE Trowel
WOUNDS Swound
WRASSE Resaws, Sawers, Swears
WRATHS Swarth, Thraws, Warths
WRAULS Walrus
WREATH Rethaw, Thawer
*****WREKIN** Winker
WRIEST Sweirt, Twiers, Twires, Writes
WRITES Sweirt, Twiers, Twires, Wriest
WRITHE Whiter, Wither
WROKEN Knower

XANGTI Taxing
XENIAL Alexin

YACKER Creaky
YAGERS Greasy
YAMENS Yes-man
YANKER Kearny
YAPPER Papery, Prepay
YARDED Drayed
YARELY Yearly
YAREST Estray, Reasty, Stayer, Stayre
YARNED Denary
YARNER Rayner

YARRED Dreary
YARROW Arrowy
YATTER Treaty
YAWLED Dawley
YEARLY Yarely
YEARNS Raynes, Renays, Sarney, Senary
YEASTS Sayest
YES-MAN Yamens
YESTER Reesty, Steery

***YGERNE** Energy, Greeny
YOGURT Grouty
YONDER Rodney

***ZABIAN** Banzai
ZAFFER Zaffre
ZAFFRE Zaffer
ZENDIK Zinked
ZERIBA Braize
ZINKED Zendik

Seven letters

AARONIC Conaria, Ocarina
ABACTOR Acrobat, Boat-car
ABATERS Abreast, Tea-bars
ABETTOR Taboret
ABIDDEN Bandied
ABIDERS Airbeds, Braised,
  Darbies Seabird, Sidebar
ABLUENT Tunable
ABORDED Boarded, Road-bed
ABORTED Borated, Tabored
ABORTER Arboret, Taborer
ABREACT Bearcat, Cabaret
ABREAST Abaters, Tea-bars
ABRIDGE Brigade
ABSCISE Scabies, Ecbasis
* **ABSECON** Beacons
ABSTAIN Tsabian
ABUSERS Surbase
ABYSMAL Balsamy
ACARIAN Acarina
ACARIDS Ascarid
* **ACARINA** Acarian
ACATOUR Autocar
ACCOMPT Compact
ACCOYLD Cacodyl
ACCRUAL Caracul
ACCRUED Cardecu
ACCRUES Accurse, Accuser
ACCURSE Accrues, Accuser
ACCUSED Succade
ACCUSER Accrues, Accurse
ACERBIC Breccia
ACEROUS Carouse
ACETOSE Coatees
ACHENES Enchase
ACHINGS Cashing, Chasing
ACIFORM Formica

ACOLYTE Cotylae
ACONITE Anoetic
ACORNED Dracone
ACRASIN Arnicas, Carinas,
  Sarcina
ACRILAN Carinal, Clarain,
  Cranial
ACROBAT Abactor, Boat-car
ACROGEN Cornage
ACROTER Creator, Reactor
ACTINAL Alicant
ACTINGS Casting
ACTINON Cantion, Contain
ACTIONS Cations, Scotian
ACTRESS Casters, Castres,
  Recasts
ADAMITE Amidate
ADAPTER Readapt
* **ADELINE** Aliened, Delaine
ADERMIN Amerind, Inarmed
ADHERED Redhead
ADHERER Reheard
ADHERES Headers, Hearsed,
  Reheads, Sheared
ADMIRAL Amildar
ADMIRER Madrier, Married
ADMIRES Misread, Sidearm
ADONISE Anodise, Diasone,
  Sodaine
ADOPTER Readopt
ADORERS Drosera, Rear-dos
ADORING Gordian, Gradino,
  Roading
ADORNED Road-end
ADORNER Readorn
ADPRESS Spreads
ADVERSE Evaders

7

ADVERTS Starved
AEDILES Deiseal
AEOLIST Isolate
AEROSOL Roseola
AETATIS Satiate
AFREETS Fearest, Feaster, Seafret
AGELESS Sealegs
AGELONG Legnago
AGGRESS Saggers, Seggars
AGISTER Aigrets, Gaiters, Seagirt, Stagier, Strigae, Triages
AGISTOR Orgiaist
AGNAMED Managed
AGNAMES Manages, Mesagna
AGONIES Agonise
AGONISE Agonies
AGROUND Durango
AGUE-FIT Fatigue
AHUNGRY Hungary
AIDANCE Canidae
AIGRETS Agister, Gaiters, Seagirt, Stagier, Strigae, Triages
AILANTO Laotian
AILERON Alerion, Alienor
AILMENT Aliment
AIMLESS Melissa, Mesails, Samlies, Seismal
*****AINTREE** Retinae, Trainee
AIRBALL Barilla
AIR-BASE Arabise
AIR-BATH Bharati
AIRBEDS Abiders, Braised, Darbies, Sea-bird, Sidebar
AIRBELL Braille, Liberal
AIRFLUE Failure
AIRINGS Arising, Raising, Sairing
AIRLESS Resails, Sailers, Serails, Serials
AIR-SACS Ascaris
AIRSTOP Parotis
*****ALAMEIN** Almaine, Laminae, Limnaea

*****ALBERTA** Latebra, Ratable
*****ALBERTI** Librate, Tablier, Triable, Trilabe
ALBERTS Blaster, Labrets, Stabler, Tablers
ALBINOS Asbolin
ALBUMEN Balneum
ALECOST Lactose, Locates, Scatole, Talcose
ALEMBIC Emblica
ALERION Aileron, Alienor
ALERTED Altered, Delater, Redealt, Related, Treadle
ALERTLY Elytral
ALGATES Lastage
ALGEBAR Algebra
ALGEBRA Algebar
*****ALGENIB** Belgian, Bengali
*****ALGERIA** Lairage, Railage, Regalia
*****ALGIERS** Lea-rigs
ALICANT Actinal
ALIENED Adeline, Delaine
ALIENER Realine
ALIENOR Aileron, Alerion
ALIGNED Dealing, Leading
ALIGNER Engrail, Learing, Nargile, Realign, Reginal
ALIMENT Ailment
ALINING Nailing
ALIPEDS Elapids, Lapides, Paidles, Palsied, Pleiads
*****ALISTER** Realist, Retails, Saltier, Saltire, Slatier, Tailers
ALIUNDE Unideal
ALLEDGE Alleged
ALLEGED Alledge
ALLERGY Gallery, Largely, Regally
ALL-HAIL Hallali
ALL-HEAL Heal-all
ALLONGE Galleon
ALL-OVER Overall
ALLURED Udaller

*ALMAINE Alamein, Laminae, Limnaea
*ALMERIC Carmiel, Claimer, Miracle, Reclaim
ALMOIGN Loaming
ALMONDS Dolmans
ALMONER Moneral, Nemoral
ALMS-FEE Females
ALMUCES Macules, Mascule
ALOETIC Coalite
ALPINES Spaniel
*ALSAGER Laagers
ALSIRAT Lariats
ALTERED Alerted, Delater, Redealt, Related, Treadle
ALTERER Realter, Relater
ALTERNE Enteral, Eternal, Teleran
ALTESSE Tealess, Teasels
*ALTHING Halting, Lathing
ALUMING Mauling
ALYSSUM Asylums
AMARANT Maranta
AMASSER Reamass
AMBERED Breamed, Embread
AMBLING Balming, Blaming, Lambing
AMBONES Bemoans
AMBULET Mutable
*AMELIAS Malaise
AMENDED Deadmen
AMENDER Enarmed, Meander, Reamend, Renamed
AMENDES Demeans
AMENING Meaning
AMENITY Anytime
AMENTIA Animate
AMERCED Creamed, Racemed
AMERCER Creamer
*AMERIND Adermin, Inarmed
*AMHARIC Machair
AMHERST Hamster
AMIDATE Adamite
AMILDAR Admiral

AMMETER Metamer
AMMINES Misname
AMNIONS Onanism, Mansion
*AMORETS Maestro
AMOUNTS Saumont
AMUSERS Assumer, Erasmus, Masseur, Mausers
ANAPEST Peasant
ANCONES Sonance
ANCRESS Caserns
ANDANTE Dantean
ANELING Eanling, Leaning, Nealing
ANETHOL Athlone, Ethanol
ANGELIC Anglice, Galenic, Legnica
*ANGELUS Lagunes
ANGERED Derange, Enraged, Grandee, Grenade
ANGINAL Anglian
*ANGLIAN Anginal
ANGLICE Angelic, Galenic, Legnica
ANGLIFY Flaying
ANGLIST Lasting, Salting, Slating, Staling
ANGRIER Earring, Grainer, Rangier, Rearing
ANGRIES Earings, Erasing, Gainers, Regains, Regians, Reginas, Searing, Seraing, Seringa
ANGRILY Nargily
ANGUINE Guanine
ANGULAR Granula
ANIGHTS Hasting, Shangti, Tashing
ANIMATE Amentia
ANIMIST Intimas
ANKLETS Asklent
ANNELID Lindane
ANNEXER Reannex
ANNOYED Anodyne

ANODISE Adonise, Diasone, Sodaine
ANODYNE Annoyed
ANOETIC Aconite
ANOINTS Nations, Onanist
ANOSMIC Camions, Maniocs, Masonic
ANSWERS Rawness
ANTEING Antigen, Gentian
*****ANTEROS** Atoners, Nor'east, Senator, Treason
ANTHERS Hanster, Thenars
ANTIARS Artisan, Sinatra, Tsarina
*****ANTIBES** Basinet, Besaint, Bestain
ANTICOR Carotin, Cortina
ANTIGEN Anteing, Gentian
*****ANTIPAS** Patinas
ANTIQUE Quinate
ANTI-RED Detrain, Tanride, Trade-in, Trained
ANTI-SEX Sextain
ANTLERS Rentals, Saltern, Sternal
ANYTIME Amenity
ANUROUS Uranous
APANAGE Pangaea
APERTLY Peartly, Prelaty, Pteryla
APERTOR Patrero, Praetor, Prorate
APHETIC Hepatic
APLENTY Net-play, Penalty
APLITES Talipes
APOSTIL Topsail
APOSTLE Pelotas, Pot-ales
APPENDS Snapped
APPLIES Lappies
APPRESS Sappers
APPULSE Papules
APRICOT Parotic, Patrico
APRONED Operand, Padrone, Pandore
APTNESS Patness

ARABISE Air-base
ARAMAIC Cariama
ARANEID Ariadne, Ranidae
ARAWAKS Sarawak
ARBITER Rarebit
ARBORED Boarder, Broader, Reboard
ARBORET Aborter, Taborer
ARCADES Sea-card
*****ARCHIES** Cahiers, Cashier
ARCHING Chagrin, Charing
ARCKING Carking, Craking, Racking
ARCTOID Carotid
ARDECHE Reached
*****ARDITES** Asterid, Astride, Diaster, Disrate, Staider, Staired, Tirades
AREDING Dearing, Deraign, Gradine, Grained, Reading
AREFIES Faeries, Freesia, Sea-fire
ARETTED Treated
*****ARGONNE** Garonne
*****ARIADNE** Araneid, Ranidae
ARICIAN Icarian
ARIETTA Ratitae
ARIETTE Iterate
ARISING Airings, Raising, Sairing
ARISTAE Astaire, Asteria, Atresia
ARLBERG Garbler
ARMREST Smarter
ARNICAS Acrasin, Carinas, Sarcina
ARNOTTO Otranto, Rattoon
*****ARNSIDE** Sandier, Sardine
ARPENTS Entraps, Panters, Parents, Pastern, Persant, Trepans
ARSENIC Cerasin, Sarcine
*****ARTEMIS** Imarets, Maestri, Maister, Misrate, Semitar, Smartie
ARTICLE Recital

ARTISAN Antiars, Sinatra, Tsarina

ARTISTE Attires, Ratites, Striate, Tastier

ARTISTS Sittars, Straits, Tsarist

ARTLESS Lasters, Salters, Slaters, Tarsels

ARTSMAN Mansart, Mantras, Star-man

ARTSMEN Martens, Sarment, Smarten

* **ARUNDEL** Launder, Lurdane, Rundale

ASBOLIN Albinos

ASCARID Acarids

ASCARIS Air-sacs

ASCITES Ectasis

ASCITIC Sciatic

ASCRIBE Brescia

ASEPTIC Spicate

ASHLERS Lashers, Slasher

ASININE Insanie

ASKINGS Gaskins

ASKLENT Anklets

ASPERGE Pre-ages, Presage

ASPERSE Parsees, Praeses, Preasse, Serapes

ASPHALT Taplash

ASPIRED Despair, Diapers, Praised

ASPIRER Parries, Praiser, Rapiers, Raspier, Repairs

ASPIRES Paresis, Praises, Serapis, Spireas

ASPREAD Parades, Saperda

ASSUAGE Sausage

ASSUMER Amusers, Erasmus, Masseur, Mausers

ASSURER Rasures

* **ASTAIRE** Aristae, Asteria, Atresia

ASTEISM Matisse, Samites, Tamises

ASTELIC Castile, Elastic, Laciest, Latices, Salicet

ASTERIA Aristae, Atresia, Astaire

ASTERID Ardites, Astride, Diaster, Disrate, Staider, Staired, Tirades

ASTHORE Earshot

ASTILBE Bastile, Bestial, Blastie, Stabile

ASTRAND Tar-sand

ASTRIDE Ardites, Asterid, Disrate, Staider, Tirades

ASTYLAR Satyral

ASUNDER Danseur, Saunder

ASYLUMS Alyssum

ATELIER Realtie

ATHEISM Hamites

ATHEIST Staithe

ATHIRST Rattish, Tartish

* **ATHLONE** Anethol, Ethanol

ATINGLE Elating, Gelatin, Genital, Langite

ATLASES Sea-salt

ATOMICS Somatic

ATOMIES Atomise, Osmiate, Samiote

ATOMISE Atomies, Osmiate, Samiote

ATONERS Anteros, Nor-east, Senator, Treason

ATRAZIN Tzarina

ATRESIA Aristae, Astaire, Asteria

ATTIRES Artiste, Ratites, Striate, Tastier

ATTRITE Tattier, Titrate

ATTUNED Nutated, Taunted

ATTUNES Nutates, Tautens, Tetanus, Unstate

AUCTION Caution

AUDILES Deasiul

AUGMENT Mutagen

AUNTERS Natives, Saunter, Sea-turn, Tea-urns

AUNTIES Sinuate

* **AUSTENS** Senatus, Unseats

AUTOCAR Acatour

AUTOCUE Couteau
AVARICE Caviare
AVENGER Engrave, Genevra
AVERTED Tavered
AVIETTE Evitate
AVODIRE Avoider
AVOIDER Avodire
AWELESS Weasels
AWESOME Waesome
AXLE-PIN Explain

*__BAALITE__ Labiate
BABBLED Blabbed
BABBLER Blabber, Brabble
*__BACKETS__ Backset, Setback
BACK-OUT Out-back
BACKSET Backets, Set-back
BAGARRE Barrage
BALDIES Disable
BALDEST Blasted, Stabled
BALDING Blading
BALLAST Ballats
BALLATS Ballast
BALLMEN Bellman
BALLUTE Bullate
BALMIER Embrail, Mirabel,
　Mirable, Remblai
BALMING Ambling, Blaming,
　Lambing
BALNEUM Albumen
BALSAMY Abysmal
BANDIED Abidden
BANDORE Broaden
BANSHEE Has-been
BANTAMS Batsman
BARBELS Rabbles, Slabber
BARBETS Rabbets, Stabber
BARGING Garbing
BARILLA Air-ball
BARINGS Sabring
*__BARISAL__ Basilar
BARLESS Bra-less
BARKING Braking

BARMIER Embrail, Mirabel,
　Mirable, Remblai
BARONET Reboant
BARRAGE Bagarre
BARYTES Betrays
BASILAR Barisal
BASKING Ink-bags
BASINET Antibes, Besaint,
　Bestain
*__BASSEIN__ Sabines
BASTARD Tabards
BASTERS Bestars, Brasset, Breasts
BASTILE Astilbe, Bestial, Blastie,
　Stabile
BASTION Obtains
BASTING Batings
BATINGS Basting
BATSMAN Bantams
BATTENS Test-ban
BATTIER Biretta, Rabbite, Terabit
BATTLER Blatter, Brattle
BEACONS Absecon
BEADLES Bedales
BEAMERS Besmear
BEAMING Big-name
BEARCAT Abreact, Cabaret
BEARDED Breaded
*__BEATLES__ Belates
BECALMS Scamble
BECHARM Brecham, Chamber,
　Chambre
*__BEDALES__ Beadles
BEDERAL Bleared
BEDLESS Blessed
BEDRAIL Ridable
BED-ROCK Brocked
BEDROOM Boredom, Broomed
BEDSORE Sobered
BEDTIME Betimed
BEECHES Beseech
BEEFIER Freebie
BEEHIVE Hive-bee
BELACED Debacle
BELATED Bleated

BELATES Beatles
BELDAME Bemedal
BELGARD Garbled
*__BELGIAN__ Algenib, Bengali
BELLIED Delible
BELLMAN Ballmen
*__BELTANE__ Tenable
BELLOWS Boswell
BEMEDAL Beldame
BEMOANS Ambones
BENDIER Inbreed
*__BENGALI__ Algenib, Belgian
BENMOST Entombs
BENTEAK Betaken
BERATED Betread, Debater,
Rebated
BERGAMA Megabar
*__BERNARD__ Brander, Rebrand
BERRIED Briered
BESAINT Antibes, Basinet,
Bestain
BESEECH Beeches
BESHREW Hebrews
BESINGS Bigness
BESMEAR Beamers
BESPAKE Bespeak
BESPEAK Bespake
BESTAIN Antibes, Basinet,
Besaint
BESTARS Basters, Brasset, Breasts
BESTEAD Debates
BESTIAL Astilbe, Bastile, Stabile
BESTILL Billets
BESTORM Mobster
BESTREW Webster
BESTRID Bistred
BESTUCK Buckets
BETAKEN Benteak
BETHUMB Bumpeth
BETIDED Debited
BETIMED Bedtime
BETRAYS Barytes
BETREAD Berated, Debater,
Rebated

*__BHARATI__ Air-bath
BHEESTI Bhistee
BHISTEE Bheesti
BIG-NAME Beaming
BIGNESS Besings
BIGOTED Dog-bite
*__BIKANER__ Brankie, Break-in,
Inbreak
BILBOES Lobbies
BILLETS Bestill
BILOBED Lobbied
BILTONG Bloting, Bolting
BIOGENY Obeying
BIPEDAL Piebald
BIPOLAR Parboil
BIRCHEN Brechin
BIRDING Briding
BIRETTA Battier, Ratbite, Terabit
BIRSLED Bridles
BIRSLES Ribless
BISTRED Bestria
BITTERN Britten
BIZARRE Brazier
BLABBED Babbled
BLABBER Babbler, Brabble
BLADING Balding
BLAMING Ambling, Balming,
Lambing
BLARETH Blather, Halbert
BLASTED Baldest, Stabled
BLASTER Alberts, Labrets,
Stabler, Tablers
BLASTIE Astible, Bastile, Bestial,
Stabile
BLATHER Blareth, Halbert
BLATTER Battler, Brattle
BLEARED Bederal
BLEATED Belated
BLEATER Retable
BLENDER Reblend
BLESSED Bedless
BLETHER Herblet
BLINDER Brindle
BLISTER Bristle, Riblets

BLOATED Lobated
BLOATER Latrobe
BLOCKER Reblock
BLOOMER Rebloom
BLOTING Biltong, Bolting
BLOTTED Bottled
BLOTTER Bottler
BLOUSED Doubles
BLOWFLY Fly-blow
BLOWING Bowling
BLOW-OUT Outblow, Outbowl
BLUBBER Bubbler
BLUDGER Burgled
BLUE-ROT Boulter, Trouble
BLUNDER Bundler
BLUNGED Bungled
BLUNGER Bungler
BLUSHES Bushels
BLUSTER Brustle, Bustler,
   Butlers, Subtler
BOARDED Aborded, Raod-bed
BOARDER Arbored, Broader,
   Reboard
BOARING Grobian
BOASTER Boaters, Borates,
   Rebatos, Sorbate
BOAT-CAR Abactor, Acrobat
BOATERS Boaster, Borates,
   Rebatos, Sorbate
BOAT-FLY Flyboat
BOCAGES Boscage
BOLSTER Bolters, Lobster,
   Rebolts
BOLTERS Bolster, Lobster,
   Rebolts
BOLTING Biltong, Bloting
BOMBING Mobbing
BONDAGE Dogbane
BONE-DRY Dry-bone
BONE-OIL Obelion
BOOKIES Booksie
BOOKSIE Bookies
BOOSTED Deboost
BORACIC Braccio

BORATED Aborted, Tabored
BORATES Boaster, Boaters,
   Rebatos, Sorbate
BOREDOM Bedroom, Broomed
BORSCHT Bortsch
BORTSCH Borscht
BOSCAGE Bocages
BOSHTER Bothers
BOSSING Obsigns
*****BOSWELL** Bellows
BOTHERS Boshter
BOTTLED Blotted
BOTTLER Blotter
BOULDER Doubler
BOULTED Doublet
BOULTER Blue-rot, Trouble
BOUNCED Buncoed
BOUNDEN Unboned
BOUNDER Rebound, Unbored,
   Unorbed, Unrobed
*****BOURGES** Brogues, Rose-bug
BOWELED Elbowed
BOW-HAND Handbow
BOWDLER Bowlder, Low-bred
BOWLDER Bowdler, Low-bred
BOWLING Blowing
BOXWOOD Wood-box
BOXWORK Workbox
BRABBLE Babbler, Blabber
BRACCIO Boracic
BRAILLE Air-bell, Liberal
BRAISED Abides, Airbeds,
   Darbies, Sea-bird, Sidebar
BRAISES Brassie
BRAKING Barking
BRA-LESS Barless
BRANDER Bernard, Rebrand
BRANKIE Bikaner, Break-in,
   Inbreak
BRASSET Basters, Bestars, Breasts
BRASSIE Braises
BRATTLE Battler, Blatter
BRAWLED Warbled
BRAWLER Warbler

BRAWLIE Wirable
BRAZIER Bizarre
BREADED Bearded
BREAK-IN Bikaner, Brankie,
  Inbreak
BREAK-UP Upbreak
BREAMED Ambered, Embread
BREASTS Basters, Bestars, Brasset
BREATHE Herb-tea
BRECCIA Acerbic
BRECHAM Chamber, Chambre
*****BRECHIN** Birchen
BREEDER Rebreed
*****BRESCIA** Ascribe
BRIBING Ribbing
BRICOLE Corbeil
BRIDING Birding
BRIDLES Birsled
BRIEFED Debrief
BRIERED Berried
BRIGADE Abridge
BRINDLE Blinder
BRINING Inbring
BRISTLE Blister, Riblets
BRISURE Bruiser, Buriers
*****BRITTEN** Bittern
BRITTLE Triblet
BROADEN Bandore
BROADER Arbored, Boarder,
  Reboard
BROCHAN Charbon
BROCKED Bed-rock
BROGUES Bourges, Rose-bug
BROOKED Red-book
BROOMED Bdroom, Boredom
BRUCKLE Buckler
BRUISED Burdies, Bus-ride
BRUISER Brisure, Buriers
BRUMOUS Umbrous
BRUNETS Bunters, Burnets,
  Bursten
BRUSHER Rebrush
BRUSTLE Bluster, Bustler,
  Butlers, Subtler

BUBBLER Blubber
BUCKETS Bestuck
BUCKLER Bruckle
BUCKSAW Sawbuck
BUGLING Bulging
BUILDER Reblind
BUILD-UP Upbuild
BUILT-IN Inbuilt
BUILT-UP Upbuilt
BULGING Bugling
BULLACE Cue-ball
BULLATE Ballute
BUMMLED Mumbled
BUMPETH Bethump
BUNCOED Bounced
BUNDLER Blunder
BUNGLED Blunged
BUNGLER Blunger
BUNTERS Brunets, Burnets,
  Bursten
BURGLED Bludger
BURBLES Lubbers, Rubbles,
  Slubber
BURDASH Rhabdus
BURDIES Bruised, Busride
BURIERS Brisure, Bruiser
*****BURMESE** Embrues
*****BURNLEY** Leyburn
BURN-OUT Outburn
*****BURSLEM** Lumbers, Rumbles,
  Slumber, Umbrels
BURSTEN Brunets, Bunters,
  Burnets
BURST-UP Upburst
BURTHEN Unberth
BURYING Rubying
BUSHELS Blushes
BUSHIER Bushire
*****BUSHIRE** Bushier
BUSKING Sub-king
BUS-MILE Sublime
BUS-RIDE Bruised, Burdies

BUS-STOP Post-bus
BUSTLER Bluster, Brustle, Butlers, Subtler
BUSSING Subsign
BUTANES Sunbeat
BUTLERS Bluster, Brustle, Bustler, Subtler
BYREMAN Myrbane

CABARET Abreact, Bearcat
CACHETS Catches
CACKLED Clacked
CACKLER Clacker, Crackle
CACODYL Accoyld
CADENUS Uncased
CAESTUS Cuestas
CAHIERS Archies, Cashier
CAIMANS Camansi, Maniacs
CAIN-HEN Enchain
*****CAIRENE** Cinerea
CAISSON Casinos, Cassino
CALCINE Laccine
*****CALEDON** Celadon
CALENDS Candles
CALIBER Calibre
CALIBRE Caliber
CALICHE Chalice
CALIPER Replica
CALIVER Caviler, Clavier, Valeric, Velaric
CALKERS Lackers, Recalks, Slacker
CALKING Lacking
CALLERS Cellars, Recalls, Scleral
CALLUNA Lacunal
CALMANT Clamant
CALMEST Camlets
CALORIE Cariole, Loricae
CALTROP Proctal
*****CALVARY** Cavalry
CAMANSI Caimans, Maniacs
CAMARAS Maracas, Marasca, Mascara
*****CAMBRAI** Cambria

CAMBREL Clamber
*****CAMBRIA** Cambrai
CAMERAL Caramel
*****CAMERON** Cremona, Menorca, Romance
CAMIONS Anosmic, Maniocs, Masonic
*****CAMLETS** Calmest
*****CAMPARI** Picamar
CAMPERS Scamper
CAMPLED Clamped
CANALED Candela, Decanal
CANDELA Canaled, Decanal
*****CANDIDE** Candied
CANDIED Candide
CANDIES Incased
*****CANDLES** Calends
CANDOUR Caudron
*****CANIDAE** Aidance
CANNERS Scanner
CANTHUS Chaunts, Staunch
CANTION Actinon, Contain
CANTLES Centals, Lancets, Scantle
CANTRED Tancred, Tranced
CAPABLE Pacable
CAPALIN Panicle, Pelican
CAPITAL Placita
CAPITAN Captain
*****CAPITOL** Coal-pit, Optical, Pit-coal, Topical
*****CAPRESE** Escaper, Percase, Respace
CAPSULA Pascual, Scapula
CAPSULE Lace-ups, Specula
CAPTAIN Capitan
CAPTION Paction, Pontiac
CARACUL Accrual
*****CARACAS** Cascara
CARAMEL Cameral
CARBIDE Decibar
CARDECU Accrued
CARDERS Scarred
CAREENS Caserne, Enraces

CAREERS Creaser
CARGOES Corsage, Socager
CARIAMA Aramaic
CARINAL Acrilan, Clarain, Cranial
CARINAS Acrasin, Arnicas, Sarcina
CARIOLE Calorie, Loricae
CARIOUS Curiosa
CARKING Arcking, Craking, Racking
CARLINE Linacre
CARLIST Citrals
*****CARLUKE** Caulker
CARMART Tramcar
*****CARMIEL** Almeric, Claimer, Miracle, Reclaim
CARMINE Crimean, Mercian
CARNAGE Cranage
CARNOSE Coarsen, Corneas, Narcose, Sea-corn
CAROCHE Coacher
*****CAROLUS** Oculars, Oscular
CAROTID Arctoid
CAROTIN Anticor, Cortina
CAROUSE Acerous
CARPELS Clasper, Parcels, Placers, Reclasp, Scalper
CARPERS Scarper, Scraper
CARPETS Pre-acts, Precast, Spectra
CARPING Craping
CARRIES Scarier
CARTELS Clarets, Scarlet, Tarcels
*****CARTIER** Cirrate, Erratic
CARTING Crating, Tracing
CARTOON Coranto, Cortona
CARVING Craving
CASABAS Cassaba
CASCADE Saccade
CASCARA Caracas
CASEMEN Menaces
CASERNE Careens, Enraces
CASERNS Ancress

CASHIER Archies, Cahiers
CASHING Achings, Chasing
CASINOS Caisson, Cassino
CASKING Sacking
CASSABA Casabas
CASSINO Caisson, Casinos
CASSOCK Cossack
CASTERS Actress, Castres, Recasts
*****CASTILE** Astelic, Elastic, Laciest, Latices, Salicet
CASTING Actings
CAST-OFF Offcast
*****CASTRES** Actress, Casters, Recasts
CATCHES Cachets
CATCHUP Upcatch
CATERED Cedrate, Cerated, Created, Reacted
CATERER Recrate, Retrace, Terrace
*****CATIONS** Actions, Scotian
CATKINS Catskin
CATRIGS Gastric, Tragics
*****CATRINE** Ceratin, Certain, Creatin, Crinate, Nacrite
CATSKIN Catkins
CATTILY Tacitly
CATTISH Tachist
CATTIER Citrate
CAUDRON Candour
CAULKER Carluke
CAULOME Leucoma
CAUSERS Cesuras, Saucers, Sucrase
CAUSING Saucing
CAUTION Auction
CAVALRY Calvary
CAVIARE Avarice
CAVILER Caliver, Clavier, Valeric, Velaric
CEASING Incages
CEDRATE Catered, Cerated, Created, Reacted

*CEDRELA Cleared, Creedal, Declare, Relaced
CEILING Cieling, Lignice
CELADON Caledon
CELLARS Callers, Recalls, Scleral
*CELSIUS Sluices
CENSING Scening
CENSUAL Launces, Unlaces, Unscale
CENTALS Cantles, Lancets, Scantle
CENTARE Crenate, Re-enact
CENTAUR Untrace
CENTIMO Entomic, Metonic, Tonemic
CENTRED Credent, Red-cent
CERAMET Cremate, Meercat
CERAMIC Racemic
CERASIN Arsenic, Sarcine
CERATED Catered, Cedrate, Created, Reacted
CERATES Creates, Ecartes, Secreta
CERATIN Catrine, Certain, Creatin, Crinate, Nacrite
CEREALS Rescale
CERESIN Cerines, Sincere
CERINES Ceresin, Sincere
CERIPHS Ciphers, Spheric
CERIUMS Murices
CEROTIC Orectic
CERTAIN Catrine, Ceratin, Creatin, Crinate, Nacrite
CERTIFY Cretify, Rectify
CERUSED Recused, Reduces, Rescued, Secured, Seducer
CESSION Cosines, Oscines
CESS-PIT Septics
CESTODA Coasted
CESTODE Tedesco
CESURAL Secular
CESURAS Causers, Saucers, Sucrase
*CHAGRES Charges, Creaghs

CHAGRIN Arching, Charing
CHAINED Echidna
*CHALDEE Cheadle, Leached
CHALETS Latches, Satchel
CHALICE Caliche
CHALKED Hackled
CHALKER Hackler
CHAMBER Becharm, Brecham, Chambre
CHAMBRE Becharm, Brecham, Chamber
CHAMOIS Chamiso
CHANCER Chancre
CHANGED Ganched
CHANGES Ganches
CHANSON Non-cash
CHANTER Tranche
CHANTIE Teach-in
*CHANUTE Unteach
CHAPTER Patcher, Repatch
CHARBON Brochan
CHARGES Chagres, Creaghs
CHARING Arching, Chagrin
CHARIOT Haricot
*CHARLES Larches, Rachels
CHARMED Decharm, Marched
CHARMER Marcher
CHARNEL Larchen
CHARPOY Corypha
CHARTED Ratched
CHARTER Rechart
CHASERS Crashes, Eschars
CHASING Achings, Cashing
CHASTEN Natches
CHATTED Datchet
CHATTEL Latchet
CHATTER Ratchet
CHAUNTS Canthus, Staunch
CHAWING Chinwag
*CHEADLE Chaldee, Leached
CHEAPEN Ha'pence
CHEAPER Peacher
CHEATER Hectare, Rechate, Recheat, Reteach, Teacher

CHECKER Recheck
CHECK-IN Chicken
CHEERLY Lechery
CHEER-UP Upcheer
CHELOID Helcoid
CHELONE Echelon
***CHELSEA** Leaches, Selache
CHENARS Ranches
CHERMES Schemer
***CHESTER** Etchers, Retches
CHETAHS Hatches
CHIASMS Schisma
CHICANO Noachic
CHICKEN Check-in
CHILDER Chirled
***CHILEAN** Lachine
CHIMING Miching
CHINING Inching, Niching
CHINWAG Chawing
CHIRLED Childer
CHIRTED Ditcher
CHISELS S-chisel
CHOKERS Hockers, Shocker
CHOKING Hocking
CHOLERA Chorale
CHOLINE Helicon
CHOOSER Soroche
CHOPINE Phocine
CHORALE Cholera
CHORALS Lorchas, Scholar
CHORDAL Dorlach
CHOREES Coheres, Echoers,
  Rechose
CHORIST Ostrich
CHOROID Ochroid
CHOUSED Douches, Hocused
CHOWDER Cowherd
CHURNED Runched
CIDARIS Sciarid
CIELING Ceiling, Lignice
CIERGES Grecise
CINDERS Discern, Rescind
CINEMAS Emiscan
CINEREA Cairene

CIPHERS Ceriphs, Spheric
CIRRATE Cartier, Erratic
CIRROSE Corries, Crosier,
  Orrices
CISTERN Cretins
CITADEL Deltaic, Dialect, Edictal
CITIZEN Zincite
CITRALS Carlist
CITRATE Cattier
CITRENE Enteric, Enticer, Tercine
CITRINE Crinite, Inciter, Neritic
***CITROEN** Noticer
CLACKED Cackled
CLACKER Cackler, Crackle
CLAIMED Decimal, Declaim,
  Medical
CLAIMER Almeric, Carmiel,
  Miracle, Reclaim
CLAMANT Calmant
CLAMBER Cambrel
CLAMPED Campled
CLANGED Glanced
CLARAIN Acrinal, Carinal,
  Cranial
CLARETS Cartels, Scarlet, Tarcels
CLARINO Clarion, Locrian
CLARION Clarino, Locrian
CLASPED Scalped
CLASPER Carpels, Parcels,
  Placers, Reclasp, Scalper
CLASSED Declass
CLASSER Reclass, Sarcels, Scalers
CLAVIER Caliver, Caviler,
  Valeric, Velaric
CLAYPIT Typical
CLEANED Elanced, Enlaced
CLEANER Reclean, Relance
CLEANSE Elances, Enlaces,
  Scalene
CLEAN-UP Unplace
CLEARED Cedrela, Creedal,
  Declare, Relaced
CLEMENT Tlemcen
CLIENTS Stencil

CLIMBER Reclimb
CLINGER Cringle
CLINKER Crinkle
CLIPPER Cripple
CLOBBER Cobbler
CLOCKED Cockled
CLOCKER Cockler
CLODDED Coddled
CLOGGED Coggled
CLOKING Locking
CLOSE-IN Conseil, Inclose
CLOSEST Closets
CLOSE-UP Couples, Opuscle, Upclose
CLOSURE Colures
CLOTTER Crottle
CLOTURE Coulter
CLUMBER Crumble
CLUMPER Crumple
CLUSTER Culters, Custrel, Cutlers, Relucts
COACHER Caroche
COAGENT Cognate
COALERS Escolar, Oracles, Recoals, Solacer
COAL-GAS Gas-coal
*****COALITE** Aloetic
COAL-PIT Capitol, Optical, Pit-coal, Topical
COARSEN Carnose, Corneas, Narcose, Sea-corn
COASTED Cestoda
COASTER Coaters, Recoast, Recoats
COATERS Coaster, Recoast, Recoats
COATEES Acetose
COATING Cotinga
COBBLER Clobber
COCAINE Oceanic
COCKILY Colicky
COCKLED Clocked
COCKLER Clocker
COCKSHY Shy-cock

CODDLED Clodded
CODDLES Scolded
CODILLE Collide, Collied
CODLING Lingcod
COEXIST Exotics
COFFERS Scoffer
COGGLED Clogged
COGNATE Coagent
COGNISE Coignes
COHERES Chorees, Echoers, Rechose
COIGNES Cognise
COINERS Crinose, Cronies, Recoins, Sericon
*****COLENSO** Console
COLICKY Cockily
COLLIER Corelli
COLITIS Solicit
COLLIDE Codille, Collied
COLLIED Collide, Codille
COLLIER Corelli
COLLOPS Scollop
COLLUMS Mollusc
COLORER Recolor
COLTERS Corslet, Costrel, Croslet, Lectors
COLURES Closure
COMBERS Recombs, Scomber
COME-OFF Off-come
*****COMINES** Incomes, Mesoric
COMMITS Comtism
COMPACT Accompt
COMPARE Compear
COMPEAR Compare
COMPEER Compere
COMPERE Compeer
COMPILE Polemic
*****COMTISM** Commits
CONARIA Aaronic, Ocarina
CONATUS Toucans, Uncoats
CONCENT Connect
CONDERS Corsned, Scorned
CONDIGN Conding
CONDING Condign

CONDITE Ctenoid, Deontic, D-notice, Noticed
CONDUIT Noctuid
CONGERY Cryogen
CONICAL Laconic
CONIFER Fir-cone, Inforce
CONKING Nocking
CONNECT Concent
CONSEIL Close-in, Inclose
*****CONSETT** Contest
CONSIST Tacsins
CONSOLE Colenso
CONSORT Crotons
CONSTER Cornets, Cronets
CONSUME Muscone
CONSUTE Contuse
CONTAIN Actinon, Cantion
CONTEST Consett
CONTOUR Cornuto, Crouton
CONTUSE Consute
COOLANT Octonal
COOLERS Creosol, Recools
COOLEST Ocelots
COOLING Locoing
COOPERS Scooper
COPIERS Persico
COPINGS Copsing
COPSING Copings
COPULAR Cupolar
COPYISM Miscopy
CORANTO Cartoon
CORBEIL Bricole
CORDATE Red-coat
CORELLA Ocellar
*****CORELLI** Collier
CORKIER Rockier
CORKING Rocking
CORK-LEG Grockle
CORNAGE Acrogen
CORNEAS Carnose, Coarsen, Narcose, Sea-corn
CORNERS Scorner
CORNETS Conster, Cronets
CORNUAL Courlan

CORNUTE Counter, Recount, Trounce
CORNUTO Contour, Crouton
CORONAL Locarno
CORONER Crooner
CORONET Cotrone
CORPSES Process
CORRIES Cirrose, Crosier, Orrices
CORSAGE Cargoes, Socager
CORSITE Erotics
CORSLET Colters, Costrel, Croslet, Lectors
CORSNED Conders, Scorned
*****CORTINA** Anticor, Carotin
*****CORTONA** Cartoon, Coranto
*****CORYPHA** Charpoy
COSINES Cession, Oscines
COSMIST Scotism
*****COSSACK** Cassock
COSTEAN Octanes
COSTING Gnostic
COSTREL Colters, Corslet, Croslet, Lectors
COTINGA Coating
*****COTINUS** Suction, Unstoic
*****COTRONE** Coronet
COTTISE Scottie
COTYLAE Acolyte
COULTER Cloture
COUNSEL Unclose
COUNTER Cornute, Recount, Trounce
COUPLES Close-up, Opuscle, Upclose
COUPLET Octuple
COUPONS Soupcon, Uncoops
COURLAN Cornual
COURSED Scoured
COURSER Scourer
COURSES Croesus, Scourse, Scouser, Sources, Sucrose
COURTED Eductor
COUSINS Socinus

COUTEAU Autocue
COVERER Recover
COWHERD Chowder
COWRIES Scowrie
CRACKLE Cackler, Clacker
CRADLES Scalder
CRAKING Arking, Carking,
  Racking
CRAMPIT Ptarmic
CRANAGE Carnage
CRANIAL Acrilan, Carinal,
  Clarain
CRANING Rancing
CRANIUM Cumarin
CRAPING Carping
CRAPPLE Epicarp
CRASHES Chasers, Eschars
CRATING Carting, Tracing
CRAVING Carving
CREAGHS Chagres, Charges
CREAMED Amerced, Racemed
CREAMER Amercer
CREASED Decares, Searced
CREASER Careers
CREATED Catered, Cedrate,
  Cerated, Reacted
CREATES Cerates, Ecartes,
  Secreta
CREATIN Catrine, Ceratin,
  Certain, Crinate, Nacrite
CREATOR Acroter, Reactor
CRECHES Screech
CREDENT Centred, Red-cent
CREEDAL Cedrela, Cleared,
  Declare, Relaced
CREMATE Ceramet, Meercat
CREMONA Cameron, Menorca,
  Romance
CRENATE Centare, Re-enact
CREOSOL Coolers, Recools
* **CRESPIN** Pincers, Princes
CRESSET Re-sects, Secrets
CRETIFY Certify, Rectify
CRETINS Cistern

CRETISM Metrics
* **CRIMEAN** Carmine, Mercian
CRIMSON Microns
CRINATE Catrine, Ceratin,
  Certain, Creatin, Nacrite
CRINGES Scringe
CRINGLE Clinger
CRINITE Citrine, Inciter, Neritic
CRINKLE Clinker
CRINOSE Coiners, Cronies,
  Recoins, Sericon
CRIPPLE Clipper
CRISPED Discerp
CROCKED Red-cock
* **CROESUS** Courses, Scourse,
  Scouser, Sources, Sucrose
CRONETS Conster, Cornets
CRONIES Coiners, Crinose,
  Recoins, Sericon
CROODLE Decolor
CROOKED Rock-doe
CROONER Coroner
CROQUET Rocquet
CROSIER Cirrose, Corries,
  Orrices
CROSLET Colters, Corslet,
  Costrel, Lectors
CROSSED Scorsed
CROSSER Recross, Scorers,
  Scorser
CROSSES Scorses
CROTALS Scrotal
CROTONS Consort
CROTTLE Clotter
CROUPED Produce
CROUPER Procure
CROUTON Contour, Cornuto
CROWDED Decrowd
CROWNED Decrown
CROWNER Recrown
* **CROYDON** Corydon
CRUDDLE Cuddler, Curdled
CRUDEST Crusted

CRUELLS Culles, Sculler
CRUELTY Cutlery
CRUISED Discure
CRUISER Curries, Sucrier
CRUISES Crusies, Cuisser,
CRUIVES Cursive
CRUMBLE Clumber
CRUMPLE Clumper
CRUSIES Cruises, Cuisser
CRUSTAE Curates
CRUSTAL Curtals
CRUSTED Crudest
CRYINGS Scrying
CRYOGEN Congery
CTENOID Condite, D-notice,
  Deontic, Noticed
CUDDLER Cruddle, Curdled
CUDDLES Scuddle
CUE-BALL Bullace
CUESTAS Caestus
CUISSER Cruises, Crusies
CULDEES Seclude
CULEBRA Curable
*****CULLERA** Cure-all
CULLERS Cruells, Sculler
CULTERS Cluster, Custrel,
  Cutlers, Relucts
CUMARIN Cranium
CUMBERS Recumbs, Scumber
CUMMERS Scummer
CUNNERS Scunner
CUPOLAR Copular
CUPPERS Scupper
CUPRITE Picture
CURABLE Culebra
CURACAO Curacoa
CURACOA Curacao
CURATES Crustae
CURDLED Cruddle, Cuddler,
CURDLES Scudler
CURE-ALL Cullera
CURINGS Cursing
CURIOSA Carious
CURRIES Cruiser, Sucrier

CURSING Curings
CURSIVE Cruives
CURTAIL Trucial
CURTAIN Turacin
CURTALS Crustal
CURTESY Curtesy
CURTSEY Curtesy
CUSPATE Teacups
CUSTREL Cluster, Culters,
  Cutlers, Relucts
CUTLERS Cluster, Culters,
  Custrel, Relucts
CUTLERY Cruelty
CUTLETS Cuttles, Scuttle
CUTTERS Scutter
CUTTLES Cutlets, Scuttle
CYTASES Ecstasy

DABBLER Drabble, Rabbled
DABBLES Slabbed
*****DACIANS** Scandia
DADDLES Saddled
DAEMONS Monades, Nomades
DAGGLES Slagged
DAHLINE Inhaled
DAILIES Sedilia
DAIMONS Domains, Madison
DAIRIES Diaries, Diarise
DALLIED Dialled
DALLIER Dialler, Rallied
DALLIES Disleal, Sallied,
DAMAGER Megarad
DAMPISH Phasmid
DANGLED Gladden
DANGLER Gnarled
DANGLES Slanged
*****DANITES** Detains, Instead,
  Sainted, Satined, Stained
DANSEUR Asunder, Saunder
DANSKER Darkens
*****DANTEAN** Andante
*****DANTIST** Distant
DAPPLES Slapped

DARBIES Abiders, Airbeds, Braised, Sea-bird, Sidebar
DARKENS Dansker
DARLING Larding
DARNELS Enlards, Landers, Relands, Slander, Snarled
DARNERS Errands, Randers
DARNING Narding
DARREIN Drainer
DARSHAN Hansard
DARTERS Retards, Starred, Traders
DARTING Trading
DASHING Shading
DASYURE Daysure
DATARIA Radiata
*****DATCHET** Chatted
DAUBERS Subedar
DAUNTED Undated
DAWDLED Waddled
DAWDLER Drawled, Waddler
DAWDLES Swaddle, Waddles
DAWTIES Waisted
DAYSMAN Man-days
DAYSURE Dasyure
DAYWORK Workday
DEADMEN Amended
DEAD-SET Sedated, Steaded
DEAFEST Defeats, Feasted
DEAD-SET Steaded
DEALING Aligned, Leading
DEANERY Ne'erday, Renayed, Yearned
DEAREST Derates, Estrade, Reasted, Redates
DEARIES Readies
DEARING Areding, Deraign, Gradine, Grained
DEARTHS Hardest, Hardset, Hatreds, Red-hats, Threads, Trashed
DEASIUL Audiles
DEAVING Evading
DEBACLE Belaced

DEBATER Berated, Betread, Rebated
DEBATES Bestead
DEBITED Be-tided
DEBITOR Deorbit, Orbited
DEBOOST Boosted
DEBRIFF Briefed
DECAMPS Scamped
DECANAL Canaled, Candela
DECANTS Descant, Scanted
DECARES Creased, Searced
*****DECATUR** Educrat, Traduce
DECAYER Redecay
DECHARM Charmed, Marched
DECIBAR Carbide
DECIDER Decried
DECIMAL Claimed, Declaim, Medical
DECLAIM Claimed, Decimal, Medical
DECLARE Cedrela, Cleared, Creedal, Relaced
DECLASS Classed
DECOLOR Croodle
DECREED Receded
DECREES Recedes, Seceder
DECREET Erected
DECREWS Screwed
DECRIAL Radicel, Radicle
DECRIED Decider
DECRIES De-icers
DECROWD Crowded
DECROWN Crowned
DEDIMUS Muddies
DEDUCES Seduced
DEEDING Deigned
DEEPEST Steeped
DEFACER Refaced
DEFAULT Faulted
DEFEATS Deafest, Feasted
DEFIANT Fainted
DEFILED Fielded
DEFILER Fielder, Refiled
DEFINER Refined, Enfired

DEFLOUR Floured
DEFORMS Serfdom
DEFROCK Frocked
DEFROST Frosted
DEFUSER Refused
DEHORTS Shorted
DE-ICERS Decries
DEIFIED Edified
DEIFIER Edifier
DEIGNED Deeding
*****DEIRDRE** Derider, Redried, Ridered
DEISEAL Aediles
*****DEISTIC** Diciest
DELAINE Adeline, Aliened
DELAPSE Elapsed, Pleased
DELATER Alerted, Altered, Redealt, Related, Treadle
DELATOR Leotard
DELAYER Layered, Relayed
DELETES Sleeted, Steeled
DELIBLE Bellied
DELIGHT Lighted
DELIMIT Limited
DELIRIA Irideal
DELIVER Livered, Relived, Reviled
*****DELORME** Modeler, Remodel
DELTAIC Citadel, Dialect, Edictal
DELUDER Dreuled
DEMAINS Maidens, Mandies, Medians, Sideman
DEMEANS Amendes
DEMERGE Emerged
DEMERIT Dimeter, Edremit, Merited, Mitered, Retimed
DEMERSE Emersed, Redeems
*****DEMETER** Metered
DEMI-GOD Megiddo
DEMIREP Epiderm, Impeder, Remiped
DEMISED Medised, Misdeed
DEMOUNT Mounted
DENIALS Lead-ins, Snailed

*****DENISON** Ondines
DENOTES Tenedos
DENSITY Destiny
DENTALS Slanted, Standel, Stendal
DENTARY Rent-day
DENTELS Nestled
DENTING Tending
DENTIST Distent, Stinted
DENTURE Retuned, Untreed
DEONTIC Condite, Ctenoid, D-notice, Noticed
DEORBIT Debitor, Orbited
DEPAINT Painted, Patined
DEPETER Petered
DEPICTS Discept
DEPONES Spondee
DEPORTS Red-tops, Sported
DEPOSER Reposed
DEPOSIT Dopiest, Posited, Topside
DEPRAVE Pervade, Repaved
DEPRESS Pressed, Spersed
DEPRIVE Prieved
DERAIGN Areding, Dearing, Gradine, Grained, Reading
DERAILS Sideral
DERANGE Angered, Enraged, Grandee, Grenade
DERATES Dearest, Estrade, Reasted, Redates
DERAYED Yearded
DERIDER Deirdre, Redried, Ridered
DERIDES Desired, Resided
DERIVER Redrive
DERIVES Deviser, Diverse, Revised
DERRIES Desirer, Dreiser, Resider, Serried
DERVISH Shrived
DESCANT Decants, Scanted
DESCEND Scended
DESCENT Scented

DESERTS Dessert, Tressed
DESERVE Severed
DESIRED Derides, Resided
DESIRER Derries, Dreiser, Resider, Serried
DESKILL Skilled
DESMANS Madness
DESPAIR Aspired, Diapers, Praised
DESPISE Pedesis
DESPOIL Diploes, Dipoles, Peloids, Soliped, Spoiled
DESSERT Deserts, Tressed
DESTINY Density
DETAINS Danites, Instead, Sainted, Satined, Stained
DETERGE Greeted
DETOURS Dourest, Douters, Outreds, Rousted
DETRACT Tracted
DETRAIN Anti-red, Tanride, Trade-in, Trained
*****DETROIT** Dottier
DEVISER Derives, Diverse, Revised
DEVISOR Devoirs, Visored, Voiders
DEVOIRS Devisor, Visored, Voiders
DEVOLVE Evolved
DEVOTER Revoted
DEWATER Tarweed, Watered,
DHURRIE Hurried
DIALECT Citadel, Deltaic, Edictal
DIALING Glaidin, Gliadin
DIALLED Dallied
DIALLER Dallier, Rallied
DIANDER Drained
DIAPERS Aspired, Despair, Praised
DIARIES Dairies, Diarise
DIARISE Dairies, Diaries
*****DIASONE** Adonise, Anodise, Sodaine

DIASTER Ardites, Asterid, Astride, Disrate, Staider, Staired, Tirades
DIATOMS Distoma, Mastoid
DIBBLER Dribble
DICERAS Sidecar, Radices
DICIEST Deistic
DICKENS Snicked
DIDDLER Riddled
*****DIERAMA** Madeira
DIESELS Idlesse
DIETING Editing, Ignited
DIETIST Ditties, Tidiest
DIGESTS Disgest
DIGNITY Tidying
DIGONAL Dog-nail, Loading
DILATER Red-tail, Trailed
DILUENT Untiled
DILUTED Luddite
DIMETER Demerit, Edremit, Merited, Mitered, Retimed
DIMNESS Missend
DIMPLES Simpled
DINDLES Slidden
DINGING Nidging
DINGLES Engilds, Singled
DINTING Tinding
DIOPTER Dioptre, Peridot, Proteid
DIOPTRE Diopter, Peridot, Proteid
DIPLOES Despoil, Dipoles, Peloids, Soliped, Spoiled
DIPNOAN Non-paid, Pandion
DIPOLES Despoil, Diploes, Peloids, Soliped, Spoiled
*****DIPTERA** Pirated
DIRHAMS Midrash
DIRT-PIE Riptide, Tiderip
DISABLE Baldies
DISCEPT Depicts
DISCERN Cinders, Rescind
DISCERP Crisped
DISCURE Cruised

DISEASE Seaside
DISGEST Digests
DISGOWN Dowsing
DISHING Hidings, Shindig
DISHORN Dronish
DISJUNE Jundies
DISLEAL Dallies, Sallied
DISNEST Dissent
DISPONE Spinode
DISPORT Torpids, Tripods
DISRATE Ardites, Asterid,
Astride, Diaster, Staider, Staired,
Tirades
DISROOT Toroids
DISSEAT Saidest
DISSENT Disnest
DISSERT Strides
DISTANT Dantist
DISTENT Dentist, Stinted
DISTOMA Diatoms, Mastoid
DITCHER Chirted
DITTIES Dietist, Tidiest
DIVERGE Grieved
DIVERSE Derives, Deviser,
Revised
DIVERTS Strived
DIVINER Drive-in
*DNIEPER** Repined, Ripened
D-NOTICE Condite, Ctenoid,
Deontic, Noticed
DOCKETS Stocked
DODGERS Gorsedd
DOESKIN Sekondi
DOGBANE Bondage
DOG-BITE Bigoted
DOGEARS Dog's-ear
DOGEATE Goateed
DOG-ENDS Goddens, God-send
DOG-FISH Fish-god
DOGGREL Roggled
DOGHEAD Godhead
DOGHOOD Godhood
DOG-LEGS Slogged
DOGLESS Godless

DOGLIKE Godlike
DOG-NAIL Digonal, Loading
DOG'S-EAR Dogears
DOGSHIP Godship
DOG'S-RUE Drogues, Gourdes,
Groused
DOGWOOD Wood-god
DOILIES Idolise
DOLINES Leonids, Sondeli
DOLMANS Almonds
DOMAINS Daimons, Madison
DOMINES Misdone
*DOMINGO** Dooming
DONATED Nodated
DONATES Onstead
DONATOR Odorant, Tornado
DONE-FOR Fordone
*DONGOLA** Gondola
DOOMING Domingo
DOORMAN Madrono
DOORMEN Morendo
DOPIEST Deposit, Posited,
Topside
*DORIANS** Inroads, Nidaros,
Ordains, Sadiron
DORKING Kingrod
DORLACH Chordal
DORMANT Mordant
DORMIES Misdoer, Moiders
DORSELS Rodless, Solders
*DORSTEN** Rodents, Snorted
DOTTIER Detroit
DOTTLES Slotted
DOUBLER Boulder
DOUBLES Bloused
DOUBLET Boulted
DOUBTER Obtrude, Outbred,
Redoubt
DOUCETS Scouted
DOUCHES Choused, Hocused
DOUREST Detours, Douters,
Outreds, Rousted
DOUTERS Detours, Dourest,
Outreds, Rousted

DOWAGER Wordage
DOWSING Disgown
DRABBLE Dabbler, Rabbled
DRACONE Acorned
DRAFTER Redraft
DRAGGLE Gargled, Raggled
DRAG-MAN Grandam, Grandma
DRAG-NET Granted
DRAGOON Gadroon
DRAINED Diander
DRAINER Darrein
DRAPERS Sparred
DRAPIER Parried
DRAPPIE Prepaid
DRAWING Warding
DRAWLED Dawdler, Waddler
DRAW-OUT Outdraw, Outward
DRAYAGE Yardage
DRAYING Yarding
DRAYMAN Yardman
DREAMER Rearmed
DREEING Energid, Enridge,
  Reeding, Reigned
*DREISER Derries, Desirer,
  Resider
*DRESDEN Reddens
DRESSER Redress
DREULED Deluder
DRIBBLE Dibbler
DRILLER Redrill
DRIVE-IN Diviner
DROGUES Dog's-rue, Gourdes,
  Groused
DROGUET Grouted
DRONISH Dishorn
DROOPER Redroop
DROPLET Pretold
DROP-NET Portend, Protend
*DROSERA Adorers, Rear-dos
*DROWNED Wondred
DRUGGED Grudged
DRUMBLE Rumbled
DRUSIAN Durians, Sundari
*DRY-BONE Bone-dry

DUCTILE Include
DUETTOS Testudo
DULCINE Include, Nuclide
DULCITE Ductile
DULOSIS Solidus
DUMAIST Stadium
DUMPIER Umpired
DUMPLES Slumped
*DUNMORE Mourned
DUNGING Nudging
DURAMEN Manured, Maunder,
  Unarmed
DURANCE Uncared, Unraced
*DURANGO Aground
*DURANTE Natured, Unrated,
  Untread
DURIANS Drusian, Sundari
DURMAST Mustard
DUSTERS Trussed
DUSTIER Studier
DUST-PAN Stand-up, Upstand
DWINING Winding
DYELINE Needily

EANLING Aneling, Leaning,
  Nealing
EAR-DROP Padrero
EAR-FLAP Parafle
EARFULS Ferulas, Fur-seal,
  Refusal
EARINGS Angries, Erasing,
  Gainers, Regains, Regians,
  Reginas, Searing, Seraing,
  Seringa
EARLESS Leasers, Resales,
  Reseals, Sealers
EARNEST Eastern, Nearest
EARNETH Earthen, Hearten,
  Neareth, Teheran
EARNING Engrain, Grannie,
  Nearing
EARRING Angrier, Grainer,
  Rangier, Rearing
EARSHOT Asthore

EARTHED Hearted, Red-heat
EARTHEN Earneth, Hearten, Neareth, Teheran
EARTHLY Heartly, Lathery
EAST-END Standee
EASTERN Earnest, Nearest
EASTERS Reseats, Saeters, Seaters, Teasers, Tessera
EASTING Gastein, Genista, Ingates, Ingesta, Seating, Signate, Tangies, Tsigane, Teasing
EASTLIN Elastin, Entails, Salient, Slainte, Staniel, Tenails
ECARTES Cerates, Creates, Secreta
ECBASIS Abscise, Scabies
ECHELON Chelone
*****ECHIDNA** Chained
ECHOERS Chorees, Coheres, Rechose
ECHOIST Toisech
ECSTASY Cytases
ECTASIS Ascites
*****EDENTON** Tenoned
*****EDGWARE** Rag-weed, Wagered
EDICTAL Citadel, Deltaic, Dialect
EDIFIED Deified
EDIFIER Deifier
EDITING Dieting, Ignited
EDITION Tenioid
EDITORS Roisted, Rosited, Sortied, Steroid, Storied, Tie-rods, Triodes
*****EDREMIT** Dimeter, Demerit, Merited, Mitered, Retimed
EDUCRAT Decator, Traduce
EDUCTOR Courted
EIGHTHS Heights, Highest, High-set
EILDING Eliding
EITHERS Heister
ELANCED Cleaned, Enlaced

ELANCES Cleanse, Enlaces, Scalene
ELAPIDS Alipeds, Lapides, Paidles, Palsied, Pleiads
ELAPSED Delapse, Pleased
ELASTIC Astelic, Castile, Laciest, Latices, Salicet
ELASTIN Eastlin, Entails, Salient, Slainte, Staniel, Tenails
ELATERS Laertes, Relates, Stealer
ELATING Atingle, Gelatin, Genital, Langite
ELATION Toenail
ELBOWED Boweled
ELECTOR Electro
*****ELECTRA** Telecar, Treacle
ELECTRO Elector
ELEGIES Elegise
ELEGISE Elegies
ELEGIST Elegits
ELEGITS Elegist
ELF-WORT Felwort
ELIDING Eilding
ELISION Isoline, Lionise
ELITISM Limiest, Limites
ELLAGIC Gallice
ELOGIST Logiest
*****ELOHIST** Eoliths, Hostile
ELOIGNS Legions, Lignose, Lingoes, Sloe-gin
ELOPERS Leprose
ELUDING Indulge
ELUTION Line-out, Outline
ELYTRAL Alertly
EMANATE Enemata, Manatee
EMANIST Inmates, Inmeats, Mista'en, Samnite, Tamines
EMBLICA Alembic
EMBRAIL Balmier, Mirabel, Mirable, Remblai
EMBREAD Ambered, Breamed
EMBRUES Burmese
EMERGED Demerge
EMERSED Demerse, Redeems

EMICANT Nematic
EMIGRES Regimes, Remiges
EMIRATE Meatier
EMISCAN Cinemas
EMITTER Termite
EMPALED Emplead
EMPANEL Emplane
EMPIRES Emprise, Epimers,
  Imprese, Premise, Spireme
EMPLANE Empanel
EMPLEAD Empaled
EMPRISE Empires, Epimers,
  Imprese, Premise, Spireme
EMPTIES Septime
EMPTION Pimento
ENAMOUR Euroman, Neuroma
ENARMED Amender, Meander,
  Reamend, Renamed
ENATION Etonian, Noetian
ENCAVED Vendace
ENCHAIN Cain-hen
ENCHARM Marchen
ENCHASE Achenes
ENCLASP Spancel
ENCLAVE Valence
ENCODES Seconde
ENCORES Necrose
ENCRATY Nectary
ENDARCH Ranched
END-GAME Maneged
ENDLANG England
ENDINGS Sending
ENDOWER Re-endow
ENDURES End-user, Ensured
ENDUROS Oresund, Resound,
  Sounder, Undoers, Unrosed
END-USER Endures, Ensured
ENDWISE Sinewed
ENEMATA Emanate, Manatee
ENERGIC Generic
ENERGID Dreeing, Enridge,
  Reeding, Reigned
ENEWING Weening
*****ENFIELD** Enfiled

ENFILED Enfield
ENFIRED Refined, Definer
ENFRAME Freeman
ENGILDS Dingles, Singled
ENGINED Needing
*****ENGLAND** Endlang
ENGLISH Shingle
ENGORES Negroes
ENGRAIL Aligner, Learing,
  Nargile, Realign, Reginal
ENGRAIN Earning, Grannie,
  Nearing
ENGRAVE Avenger, Genevra
ENIGMAS Gamines, Seaming
ENISLED Ensiled, Linseed,
  Nelides
ENISLES Ensiles, Sensile, Silenes
ENJOYER Re-enjoy
ENLACED Cleaned, Elanced
ENLACES Cleanse, Elances,
  Scalene
ENLARDS Darnels, Landers,
  Relands, Slander
ENLARGE General, Gleaner
ENLIGHT Lighten
ENLOCKS Slocken
ENRACES Careens, Caserne
ENRAGED Angered, Derange,
  Grandee, Grenade
ENRIDGE Dreeing, Energid,
  Reeding, Reigned
ENRIVEN Innerve, Nervine
ENROBES Ensober
ENROUGH Roughen
ENSIGNS Sensing
ENSILED Enisled, Linseed,
  Nelides
ENSILES Enisles, Sensile, Silenes
ENSLAVE Leavens
ENSNARL Lanners
ENSOBER Enrobes
ENSTEEP Steepen
ENSTYLE Tensely
ENSURED Endures, End-user

ENTAILS Eastlin, Elastin, Salient, Slainte, Staniel, Tenails
ENTASIS Saintes, Sestina, Staines, Tansies, Tisanes
ENTERAL Alterne, Eternal, Teleran
ENTERER Re-enter, Terreen, Terrene
ENTERIC Citrene, Enticer, Tercine
ENTERON Tenoner
ENTHEAL Lethean
ENTICER Citrene, Enteric, Tercine
ENTIRES Entries, Steiner, Teniers, Trenise
ENTOILS Lionets, Tonsile
ENTOMBS Benmost
ENTOMIC Centimo, Metonic, Tonemic
ENTOPIC Nepotic
ENTOTIC Tonetic
ENTOZOA Tan-ooze
ENTRAIL Latiner, Latrine, Ratline, Reliant, Retinal, Trenail
ENTRAIN Trannie
ENTRANT Tranent
ENTRAPS Arpents, Panters, Parents, Pastern, Persant, Trepans
ENTREAT Ratteen, Ternate
ENTRIES Entires, Steiner, Teniers, Trenise
ENTRISM Minster, Minters, Remints
ENTRIST Nitters, Retints, Stinter, Tinters
ENTRUST Nutters
ENVIERS Inverse, Versine, Viersen
ENVIOUS Niveous, Veinous
ENWRAPS Pawners, Repawns, Spawner
EOLITHS Elohist, Hostile

*EPACRIS Ice-spar, Scrapie, Serapic
EPARCHY Preachy
EPHEBOS Phoebes
*EPHRAIM Rephaim
EPICARP Crappie
EPIDERM Demirep, Impeder, Remiped
EPIDOTE Opetide
EPIGRAM Primage
EPILATE Pileate
EPIMERS Empires, Emprise, Imprese, Premise, Spirema
EPSILON Pinoles
ERASING Angries, Earings, Gainers, Regains, Regians, Reginas, Searing, Seraing, Seringa
*ERASMUS Amusers, Assumer, Masseur, Mausers
ERECTED Decreet
ERECTER Re-erect
EREPSIN Repines
ERETHIC Etheric, Heretic
*EREWHON Nowhere, Whereon
ERGATES Restage
ERINGOS Ignores, Regions, Signore
ERINITE Niterie
ERMINED Meriden
*ERNESTS Nesters, Resents, Streens, Strenes
ERODING Gironde, Groined, Ignored, Negroid, Redoing
EROTICS Corsite
EROTISM Moister, Mortise
ERRANDS Darners, Randers
ERRATIC Cartier, Cirrate
ERRATUM Maturer
ERUPTED Reputed
ESCAPER Caprese, Percase, Respace
ESCHARS Chasers, Crashes
ESCHEAT Teaches

ESCOLAR Coalers, Oracles, Recoals, Solacer
ESLOINS Insoles, Lesions, Lioness
ESPARTO Pro-east, Proteas, Seaport
ESPINEL Pensile, Sleep-in
ESPOUSE Poseuse
ESPYING Pigsney
ESQUIRE Queries
ESSOINS Session
*****ESSONNE** Oneness
*****ESTORIL** Estriol, Loiters, Toilers
ESTOVER Overset, Revotes, Setover, Vetoers
ESTRADE Dearest, Derates, Reasted, Redates
ESTREAT Restate, Retaste, Tearest
ESTREPE Steeper
ESTRIOL Estoril, Loiters, Toilfers
ESTROUS Oestrus, Ousters, Sourest, Souters, Tousers, Trouses, Trousse, Tussore
ETACISM Sematic
ETAMINE Matinee
ETCHERS Chester, Retches
ETERNAL Alterne, Enteral, Teleran
ETHANOL Anethol, Athlone
ETHERIC Erethic, Heretic
ETHIOPS Peshito
ETHNICS Sthenic
ETONIAN Enation, Noetian
ETOURDI Ioduret, Outride
ETRIERS Reiters, Retires, Retries, Terries
EUCLASE Sea-luce
EUROMAN Enamour, Neuroma
EVADERS Adverse
EVADING Deaving
EVITATE Aviette
EVOLUTE Veloute
EVOLVED Devolve

EVOLVER Revolve
EXACTER Excreta
EXAMPLE Exempla
EXCIDES Excised
EXCISED Excides
EXCITOR Xerotic
EXEMPLA Example
EXCRETA Exacter
EXCURSE Excuser
EXCUSER Excurse
EXPIRES Prexies
EXOTICS Coexist
EXPLAIN Axle-pin
EX-TERNS Sextern
EYELIDS Seedily
EYEWALL Walleye

FACTURE Furcate
FAERIES Arefies, Freesia, Sea-fire
*****FAEROES** Faroese
FAIENCE Fiancee
FAILURE Air-flue
FAINTED Defiant
FALL-GUY Fugally
FALLOUT Outfall
FALSEST Fatless
FALSIES Filasse
FALTERS Falster
FALSTER Falters
FANCIER Francie
FANCIES Fascine, Fiances
FANGLED Flanged
FANNELL Flannel
FANNIES Fenians
FARMING Framing
FARMOST Formats
*****FAROESE** Faeroes
FARRIER Ferrari
FARTING Ingraft, Rafting
FASCINE Fancies, Fiances
FASTENS Fatness
*****FASTNET** Fattens
FATHERS Shafter
FATIGUE Ague-fit

FATLESS Falsest
FATNESS Fastens
FATTENS Fastnet
FAULTED Default
FAULTER Refutal, Tearful
FAUNIST Fustian, Infaust
FEALING Finagle, Leafing
FEAREST Afreets, Feaster, Sea-fret
FEARETH Feather, Terefah
FEASTED Deafest, Defeats
FEASTER Afreets, Fearest, Sea-fret
FEATHER Feareth, Terefah
FEBRILE Felibre
FEDORAS Seaford
FEEDING Feigned
FEELING Fleeing
FEERING Feigner, Freeing, Reefing
FEIGNED Feeding
FEIGNER Feering, Freeing, Reefing
*FELIBRE Febrile
FELLATE Leaflet
FELSITE Lefties, Liefest
FELWORT Elf-wort
FEMALES Alms-fee
FEMINAL Inflame
FENGITE Feteing
*FENIANS Fannies
*FERRARI Farrier
FERRITE Fir-tree
FERROUS Furores
FERULAS Earfuls, Fur-seal, Refusal
FETEING Fengite
FETICHE Fitchee
FIANCEE Faience
FIANCES Fancies, Fascine
FICKLED Flicked
FIELDED Defiled
FIELDER Defiler, Refiled
FIGHTER Freight

FILASSE Falsies
FILTERS Lifters, Stifler, Trifles
FINAGLE Fealing, Leafing
FIR-CONE Conifer, Inforce
FIREDOG Firegod
FIREGOD Firedog
FIR-TREE Ferrite
FISHERS Serfish, Sherifs
FISH-GOD Dogfish
FISHNET Net-fish
FISSURE Fussier
FISTING Sifting
FITCHEE Fetiche
FITNESS Infests
FIZZING Gin-fizz
FLANGED Fangled
FLANNEL Fannell
FLANEUR Funeral
FLAYING Anglify
FLECKER Freckle
FLEEING Feeling
*FLEMISH Himself
FLESHER Herself
FLETTON Fontlet
FLICKED Fickled
FLIRTED Trifled
FLIRTER Trifler
FLOATER Floreat, Refloat
*FLODDEN Fondled
FLOOSIE Foliose
FLOREAT Floater, Refloat
FLOURED Deflour
FLOWERY Rye-wolf
FLOWING Fowling, Wolfing
FLUSTER Fluters, Restful
FLUTERS Fluster, Restful
FLUVIAL Vialful
FLY-BLOW Blowfly
FLYBOAT Boatfly
FLY-OVER Overfly
FLY-RAIL Frailly
FOALING Loafing
FOCUSER Refocus
FOG-RING Forging

FOISTER Forties
*****FOLIGNO** Fooling, Looting
FOLIOSE Floosie
FONDLED Flodden
FONDLER Forlend
FONTLET Fletton
FOOLING Foligno, Loofing
FOOTHOT Hot-foot
FOOT-JAW Jaw-foot
FORAMEN Foreman
FORDONE Done-for
FOREMAN Foramen
FOREMEN Formene
FORGERY Frogery
FORGING Fog-ring
FORLEND Fondler
FORMATS Farmost
FORMENE Foremen
*****FORMICA** Aciform
FORTIES Foister
FORWARD Froward
FOUNDER Refound
FOWLING Flowing, Wolfing
FRAILLY Fly-rail
FRAMING Farming
*****FRANCIE** Fancier
FRANTIC Infarct, Infract
FRECKLE Flecker
FREE-ARM Refiame
FREEBIE Beefier
FREEING Feering, Feigner,
  Reefing
FREEMAN Enframe
FREESIA Arefies, Faeries, Sea-fire
FREIGHT Fighter
FRESHER Refresh
FRETFUL Truffle
FRETSAW Wafters
FRISEUR Frisure, Surfier
FRISURE Friseur, Surfier
FROCKED Defrock
FROGERY Forgery
FROSTED Defrost
FROWARD Forward

FUGALLY Fall-guy
FULL-PAY Playful
FUNERAL Flaneur
FUNFAIR Ruffian
FURCATE Facture
FURORES Ferrous
FUR-SEAL Earfuls, Ferulas,
  Refusal
FUSSIER Fissure
FUSTIAN Faunist, Infaust

GABBLER Grabble
GABNASH Nashgab
GADGETS Stagged
GADROON Dragoon
GAGSTER Gargets, Stagger,
  Taggers
GAHNITE Heating
GAINERS Angries, Erasing,
  Earings, Regains, Regians,
  Reginas, Searing, Seraing,
  Seringa
GAITERS Agister, Aigrets, Sea-
  girt, Stagier, Strigae, Triages
*****GALENIC** Angelic, Anglice,
  Legnica
GALLATE Tallage
GALLEON Allonge
GALLERY Allergy, Largely,
  Regally
*****GALLICE** Ellagic
GALLING Gingall
GALL-NUT Nut-gall
GAMBLER Gambrel
GAMBREL Gambler
GAMETES Maesteg, Metages
GAMINES Enigmas, Seaming
GANCHES Changes
GANCHED Changed
GANGERS Granges, Naggers,
  Snagger
GANGING Nagging
GANTING Tanging
GARBLED Belgard

GARBLER Arlberg
GARBING Barging
*****GARDENA** Grenada
*****GARDNER** Grander
GARGETS Gagster, Stagger,
  Taggers
GARGLED Draggle, Raggled
GARMENT Margent, Ragment
GARNERS Rangers
GARNETS Sargent, Stanger,
  Strange
GARNISH Rashing, Sharing
*****GARONNE** Argonne
GAS-COAL Coal-gas
GASKINS Askings
GAS-MAIN Magians, Siamang
GASPING Pagings
GAS-RING Ragins, Sirgang
*****GASTEIN** Easting, Genista,
  Ingates, Ingesta, Seating,
  Signate, Tangies, Teasing,
  Tsigane
GASTRIC Catrigs, Tragics
GASTRIN Gratins, Ratings,
  Staring
GATEMAN Magenta, Magnate
GATEWAY Getaway
GATINGS Staging
GAUDGIE Guidage
GAUFFER Gauffre
GAUFFRE Gauffer
*****GAUMONT** Montagu
GAVILAN Vaginal
GELATIN Atingle, Elating,
  Genital, Langite
GELDERS Ledgers, Red-legs,
  Sledger
GELDING Gingled, Niggled
GENERAL Enlarge, Gleaner
GENERIC Energic
GENESIS Seeings
*****GENEVRA** Avenger, Engrave
GENISTA Easting, Gastein,

Ingates, Ingesta, Seating,
Signate, Tangies, Teasing,
Tsigane
GENITAL Atingle, Elating,
  Gelatin, Langite
GENITOR Negrito, Trigone
GENTIAN Anteing, Antigen
GENUINE Ingenue
*****GERAINT** Granite, Ingrate,
  Tangier, Tearing
*****GERMAIN** Reaming
GERMANE Mangere
*****GESTAPO** Postage, Potages
GESTATE Tageted
GET-AWAY Gateway
GIBBONS Sobbing
GILDERS Girdles, Gliders,
  Grisled, Lidgers, Ridgels, Regilds
GILDING Gliding
*****GINEVRA** Reaving, Vinegar
GIN-FIZZ Fizzing
GINGALL Galling
GINGERS Niggers, Snigger
GINGERY Greying, Niggery
GINGLED Gelding, Niggled
GINGLES Niggles, Sniggle
GINNERY Renying
GINTRAP Parting, Prating,
  Traping
GIRASOL Glorias
GIRDING Griding, Ridging
GIRDLED Glidder, Griddle
GIRDLES Gilders, Gliders,
  Grisled, Lidgers, Regilds, Ridgels
*****GIRESUN** Reusing
GIRKINS Griskin, Risking
GIRLOND Lording
GIRNELS Lingers, Singler, Slinger
GIRNING Ringing
*****GIRONDE** Eroding, Groined,
  Ignored, Negroid, Redoing
GIRTHED Righted
GISARME Imagers, Mirages

GITTERN Retting
GLACIER Gracile
GLADDEN Dangled
GLAIDIN Dialing, Gliadin
GLAIRIN Lairing, Railing
GLANCED Clanged
GLAREAL Grallae
GLEANER Enlarge, General
GLEEING Gleneig, Neglige
GLEEMAN Melange
*GLENEIG Gleeing, Neglige
GLIADIN Dialing, Glaidin
GLIDDER Girdled, Griddle
GLIDERS Gilders, Girdles,
   Grisled, Lidgers, Regilds, Ridgels
GLIDING Gilding
GLIMPSE Megilps
GLINTED Tingled
GLISTEN Lingets, Singlet, Tingles
GLISTER Gristle
GLOATER Legator, Ortegal
*GLORIAS Girasol
GLUTINS Lusting, Lutings,
   Singult, Sutling
GLUTTED Guttled
GMELINA Leaming, Mealing
GNARING Ranging
GNARLED Dangler
GNAT-NET Tangent
GNOSTIC Costing
GOATEED Dogeate
*GOBELIN Ignoble, Inglobe
GODDENS Dog-ends, Godsend
GODHEAD Doghead
GODHOOD Doghood
GODLESS Dogless
GODLIKE Doglike
GODLING Golding, Lodging
GODSEND Dog-ends, Goddens
GODSHIP Dogship
*GOLDING Godling, Lodging
GONDOLA Dongola
*GORDIAN Adoring, Gradino,
   Roading

GORSEDD Dodgers
GOSLING Oglings
GOSNICK Socking
GOURDES Dog's-rue, Drogues,
   Groused
GRABBLE Gabbler
GRACILE Glacier
GRADDAN Grandad
GRADINE Areding, Dearing,
   Deraign, Grained, Reading
GRADING Niggard
GRADINO Adoring, Gordian,
   Roading
GRAFTER Regraft
GRAINED Areding, Dearing,
   Deraign, Gradine, Reading
GRAINER Angrier, Earring,
   Rangier, Rearing
*GRALLAE Glareal
GRANDAM Drag-man, Grandma
GRANDEE Angered, Derange,
   Enraged, Grenade
GRANDER Gardner
GRANDMA Drag-man, Grandam
GRANGES Gangers, Naggers,
   Snagger
GRANITE Geraint, Ingrate,
   Tangier, Tearing
GRANNIE Earning, Engrain,
   Nearing
GRANTED Drag-net
GRANTEE Greaten, Negater,
   Reagent
GRANTER Regrant
GRANULA Angular
GRANULE Unlarge, Unregal
GRAPHER Regraph
GRASPED Sparged
GRASPER Regrasp, Sparger
GRATING Targing
GRATINS Gastrin, Ratings,
   Staring
GRAUPEL Plaguer
GRAVELS Verglas

GRAVURE Verruga
GREATEN Grantee, Negater, Reagent
GREATER Regrate
GREAVES Servage
GRECISE Cierges
GREENED Reneged
GREENER Reneger
GREETED Deterge
GREETER Regreet
GREMIAL Lamiger
GREMLIN Merling, Mingler
GREMMIE Immerge
*****GRENADA** Gardena
GRENADE Angered, Derange, Enraged, Grandee
GREYING Gingery, Niggery
GRIDDLE Girdled, Glidder
GRIDING Girding, Ridging
GRIEVED Diverge
GRIFFIN Riffing
GRINDER Regrind
GRINNED Rending
GRISKIN Girkins, Risking
GRISLED Gilders, Girdles, Gliders, Regilds, Ridgels
GRISTLE Glister
GROBIAN Boaring
GROCKLE Cork-leg
GROINED Eroding, Gironde, Ignored, Negroid, Redoing
GROUPER Regroup
GROUPIE Pirogue
GROUSED Dug's-rue, Drogues, Gourdes
GROUTED Droguet
GROWN-UP Upgrown
GRUDGED Drugged
GRUMOSE Morgues
GRUNTED Trudgen
GRUTTEN Turgent
GUANINE Anguine
GUBBINS Subbing
GUELDER Reglued

GUERDON Undergo, Ungored
GUIDAGE Gaudgie
GULLIES Ligules
GUNSHIP Pushing
GUNSHOT Hognuts, Noughts, Shotgun
GURGLES Luggers, Slugger
GUSTAVE Vaguest
GUTTLED Glutted
GYRATED Tragedy

HABITAT Tabitha
HABITED Thebaid
HACKLED Chalked
HACKLER Chalker
HACKLES Shackle
HAFFIRS Raffish
HAG-RIDE Headrig
HAIRNET Inearth
HALBERT Blareth, Blather
HALLALI All-hail
HALLOWS Shallow
HALSING Lashing
HALTERS Harslet, Hastler, Herstal, Lathers, Slather, Thalers
HALTING Althing, Lathing
HAMBLES Shamble
*****HAMBURG** Murghab
*****HAMITES** Atheism
HAMMERS Shammer
HAMSTER Amherst
HANDBOW Bow-hand
HANDLES Handsel
HAND-OFF Offhand
HANDSEL Handles
HANG-OUT To-Hunga
HANKERS Harkens, Shanker
HANKING Khingan
*****HANSARD** Darshan
HANSTER Anthers, Thenars
HA'PENCE Cheapen
HAPLESS Plashes
HAPTICS Spathic

HARDEST Dearths, Hardset, Hatreds, Red-hats, Threads, Trashed
HARDIER Harried
HARDIES Shadier
HARDSET Dearths, Hardest, Hatreds, Red-hats, Threads, Trashed
HAREING Hearing
HARICOT Chariot
HARKEES Reshake
HARKENS Hankers, Shanker
HARKERS Sharker
HARPERS Phraser, Sharper
HARRIED Hardier
HARSLET Halters, Hastler, Herstal, Lathers, Slather, Thalers
HARVEST Thraves
HAS-BEEN Banshee
HASLETS Hatless, Hasselt
HASPING Pashing, Phasing, Shaping
*HASSELT Haslets, Hatless
HASSLED Slashed
HASSLES Slashes
HASTIER Sheriat
HASTING Anights, Shangti, Tashing
HASTLER Halters, Harslet, Herstal, Lathers, Slather, Thalers
HATCHES Chetahs
HATEFUL Heatful
HATLESS Haslets, Hasselt
HATREDS Dearths, Hardest, Hardset, Red-hats, Threads, Trashed
HATTERS Rathest, Shatter, Stareth, Threats
HAULING Laugh-in
HAUNTER Unearth, Unheart, Urethan
HAVINGS Shaving
HAWKISM Mawkish
HAWSERS Swasher, Washers

HEADERS Adheres, Hearsed, Reheads, Sheared
HEADPAN Pan-head
HEADPIN Pin-head
HEADRIG Hag-ride
HEAL-ALL All-heal
HEARERS Rehears, Reshare, Shearer
HEARING Hareing
HEARSED Adheres, Headers, Reheads, Sheared
HEARTED Earthed, Red-heat
HEARTEN Earneth, Earthen, Neareth, Teheran
HEARTLY Earthly, Lathery
HEATERS Reheats, Theresa
HEATFUL Hateful
HEATING Gahnite
HEAVERS Reshave
*HEBREWS Beshrew
HECTARE Cheater, Rachate, Recheat, Reteach, Teacher
HECTORS Rochets, Rotches, Tochers, Torches, Troches
HEEDERS Heredes
HEEDING Neighed
HE-GOATS Hostage, She-goat
HEIGHTS Eighths, Highest, High-set
HEINOUS In-house
HEIRDOM Homerid
HEIRESS Herisse
HEISTER Eithers
HELCOID Cheloid
HELICES Lichees
HELICON Choline
HELLERS Sheller
HEPATIC Aphetic
HEP-CATS Patches
HEPSTER Sperthe
HEPTADS Spathed, T-shaped
HEPTANE Phenate
HERBLET Blether
HERB-TEA Breathe

HEREDES Heeders
HERETIC Erethic, Etheric
HERISSE Heiress
HERNIAL Inhaler
HEROINS Inshore
HEROISM Himeros, Moreish
HERSELF Flesher
***HERSTAL** Halters, Harslet,
  Hastler, Lathers, Slather, Thalers
HETAIRA Rhaetia
HEWINGS Shewing, Whinges
HICATEE Teachie
HIDINGS Dishing, Shindig
HIGHEST Eighths, Heights,
  High-set
HIGH-SET Eighths, Heights,
  Highest
***HIMEROS** Heroism, Moreish
HIMSELF Flemish
HINDERS Shrined
HINDGUT Updight
HINTING In-thing, Nithing
HIP-BONE Hopbine
HISTORY Toryish
***HITLERS** Slither
HITTING Tithing
HIVE-BEE Beehive
HOARSEN Hornsea, Senhora
***HOBBISM** Mobbish
HOCKERS Chokers, Shocker
HOCKING Choking
HOCUSED Choused, Douches
HOG-MANE Mohegan
HOGNUTS Gunshot, Noughts,
  Shotgun
HOISTER Shortie
HOLIDAY Hyaloid
HOLSTER Hostler
***HOMERIC** Moriche
HOMERID Heirdom
HOODMAN Manhood
HOOKERS Reshook
HOOTERS Reshoot, Shooter,
  Soother

HOPBINE Hip-bone
HOPPERS Shopper
HORMONE Moorhen
HORNETS Shorten, Threnos,
  Thrones
***HORNSEA** Hoarsen, Senhora
HORRENT Norther
HORSING Shoring
HOSTAGE He-goats, She-goat
HOSTILE Elohist, Eoliths
HOSTING Toshing
HOSTLER Holster
HOT-FOOT Foothot
HOTPOTS Hot-spot, Pot-shot
HOT-SPOT Hotpots, Pot-Shot
HOTTING To-night
HOUNDS Hudson, Unshod
HOWEVER Whoever
HUDDLER Hurdled
***HULSEAN** Unheals, Unleash,
  Unshale
HUMIDOR Rhodium, Mid-hour
***HUNGARY** Ahungry
HUNTERS Shunter
HURDLED Huddler
HURRIED Dhurrie
HURRIES Rushier
HURTFUL Ruthful
HURTING Ungirth, Unright
HURTLES Hustler, Thurles
HUSTLER Hurtles, Thurles
HYALOID Holiday
HYDRATE Thready
HYDROUS Shroudy

IATRICS Satiric
***ICARIAN** Arician
***ICELAND** Inlaced
ICEPACK Pack-ice
ICEPANS Inscope, Pincase
ICE-SPAR Epacris, Scrapie,
  Serapic
ICINESS Incises
IDENTIC Incited

IDLESSE Diesels
IDOLISE Doilies
IGNAROS Origans, Signora, Soaring
IGNITED Dieting, Editing
IGNITER Nigrite, Tiering, Tigrine
IGNITOR Rioting
IGNOBLE Gobelin, Inglobe
IGNORED Eroding, Gironde, Groined, Negroid, Redoing
IGNORES Eringos, Regions, Signore
ILLUDES Ill-uses, Sullied
ILL-USED Illudes, Sullied
ILL-USES Sullies
IMAGERS Gisarme, Mirages
IMARETS Artemis, Maestri, Maister, Misrate, Semitar, Smartie
IMBRUES Imburse
IMBRUTE Terbium
IMBURSE Imbrues
IMMERGE Gremmie
IMPAINT Timpani
IMPALED Implead, Pelamid
IMPALER Impearl, Lempira, Palmier
IMPANEL Maniple
IMPASTE Pastime
IMPEARL Impaler, Lempira, Palmier
IMPEDER Epiderm, Impeder, Remiped
IMPEDES Semiped
IMPETUS Imputes
IMPLATE Palmiet
IMPLEAD Implaed, Pelamid
IMPONES Peonism, Pi-meson
IMPORTS Tropism
IMPOSER Promise, Semi-pro
IMPRESA Sampire
IMPRESE Empires, Emprise, Epimers, Premise, Spireme

IMPRESS Persism, Premiss, Simpers
IMPREST Permits
IMPUGNS Spuming
IMPUTES Impetus
INAPTLY Ptyalin
INARMED Adermin, Amerind
INBREAK Bikaner, Brankie, Break-in
INBREED Bendier
INBRING Brining
IN-BUILT Built-in
INCAGES Ceasing
INCASED Candies
INCEPTS Inspect, Pectins
INCHING Chining, Niching
INCISED Indices
INCISES Iciness
INCITED Identic
INCITER Citrine, Crinite, Neritic
INCLOSE Close-in, Conseil
INCLUDE Dulcine, Nuclide
INCOMES Comines, Mesonic
INCUDES Incused, Induces
INCUSED Incudes, Induces
*****INDESIT** Indites
INDEXER Reindex
INDICES Incised
INDITER Nitride
INDITES Indesit
INDOORS Sondrio, Sordino
INDORSE Rosined, Sordine
INDUCER Uncried
INDUCES Incudes, Incused
INDULGE Eluding
INEARTH Hairnet
INFARCT Frantic, Infract
INFAUST Faunist, Fustian
INFEFTS Stiffen
INFESTS Fitness
INFIDEL Infield
INFIELD Infidel
INFLAME Feminal
INFORCE Conifer, Fir-cone

INFRACT Frantic, Infarct
INGATES Easting, Gastein,
  Genista, Ingesta, Seating,
  Signate, Tangies, Teasing,
  Tsigane
INGENUE Genuine
INGESTA Easting, Gastein,
  Genista, Ingates, Seating,
  Signate, Tangies, Teasing,
  Tsigane
INGINES Insigne, Seining
INGLOBE Ignoble, Gobelin
INGRAFT Farting, Rafting
INGRAIN Raining
INGRATE Geraint, Granite,
  Tangier, Tearing
INGRESS Resigns, Signers,
  Singers
INGROUP Pouring, Rouping
INHALED Dahline
INHALER Hernial
INHERES Inherse, Reshine
INHERSE Inheres, Reshine
IN-HOUSE Heinous
INK-BAGS Basking
INKLESS Kinless
INKLING Kilning, Linking
*INKSTER Kirsten, Reinkes,
  Stinker, Tinkers
INLACED Iceland
INLAYER Nailery
INLYING Lying-in
INMATES Emanist, Inmeats,
  Mista'en, Samnite, Tamines
INMEATS Emanist, Inmates,
  Mista'en, Samnite, Tamines
INNERVE Enriven, Nervine
INNINGS Inn-sign, Sinning
INN-SIGN Innings, Sinning
INQUEST Quintes
INROADS Dorians, Inroads,
  Ordains, Sadiron
INSANIE Asinine
INSCAPE Icepans, Pincase

INSCULP Sculpin, Unclips
INSEAMS Samisen
INSHORE Heroins
INSIGHT Shiting
INSIGNE Ingines, Seining
INSOFAR Snofari
INSOLES Esloins, Lesions,
  Lioness
INSPECT Incepts, Pectins
INSPIRE Pirnies, Spinier
INSTATE Satinet
INSTEAD Danites, Detains,
  Sainted, Satined, Stained
INSTEPS Spinets, Step-ins
INSULAR Urinals, Ursinal
INSULIN Inulins
INSULSE Silenus
INSURER Ruiners
INSURES Serinus, Sunrise
INTAKES Take-ins
INTEGER Retinge, Teering,
  Treeing
INTERIM Termini, Mintier
IN-THING Hinting, Nithing
INTIMAE Miniate
INTIMAS Animist
INTONER Ternion
INTONES Sonnite, Tension
INTREAT Iterant, Nattier, Nitrate,
  Tartine, Tertian
INTRUDE Turdine, Untired,
  Untried
INULINS Insulin
INURING Ruining
INVADER Ravined
INVERSE Enviers, Versine,
  Viersen
INVERTS Striven, Ventris
INVITER Vitrine
IODURET Etourdi, Outride
IRATELY Reality
IRENICS Sericin, Sirenic
IRIDEAL Deliria
IRKSOME Smokier

IRONIES Noisier
ISLEMAN Malines, Menials, Seminal
ISMATIC Itacism
ISOLATE Aeolist
ISOLINE Elision, Lionise
ISOTRON Nitroso, Torsion
ISSUANT Sustain
ITACISM Ismatic
ITERANT Intreat, Nattier, Nitrate, Tartine, Tertian
ITERATE Ariette
IVRESSE Revises
IVORIST Visitor

JACKMAN Manjack
JALOUSE Jealous
JAW-FOOT Foot-jaw
JEALOUS Jalouse
JOINTER Rejoint
JOLTERS Jostler, Rejolts
JOSTLER Jolters, Rejolts
JOYANCE Joycean
*****JOYCEAN** Joyance
*****JUANITA** Tijuana
JUNDIES Disjune

KAISERS Sea-risk
*****KARENNI** Rankine
*****KASHING** Shaking
*****KATRINE** Kenitra
KAYOING Okaying
KEELERS Sleeker
KEENING Kneeing
KEEPING Peeking
KELTERS Skelter
*****KENITRA** Katrine
KERATIN Kreatin
KESTREL Skelter
*****KHINGAN** Hanking
KIDNAPS Skid-pan
KILNING Inkling, Linking
KILTING Kitling
KIMMERS Skimmer

KING-PIN Pinking
KING-ROD Dorking
KINLESS Inkless
KINSHIP Pinkish
KIPPERS Skipper
*****KIRSTEN** Inkster, Reknits, Stinker, Tinkers
KISSING Skiings
KITCHEN Thicken
KITLING Kilting
KITTLES Skittle
KNARLED Rankled
KNEADER Reknead
KNEEING Keening
KNITTER Trinket
KNOCKER Reknock
KNOCK-ON No-knock
KREATIN Keratin
KURSAAL Rusalka

LAAGERS Alsager
LABELER Relabel
LABIATE Baalite
LABOURS Sub-oral
LABRETS Alberts, Blaster, Stabler, Tablers
LACCINE Calcine
LACEMAN Maclean, Manacle
LACE-UPS Capsule, Specula
*****LACHINE** Chilean
LACIEST Astelic, Castile, Elastic, Latices, Salicet
LACKERS Calkers, Recalks, Slacker
LACKING Calking
LACONIC Conical
LACTOSE Alecost, Locates, Scatole, Talcose
LACUNAL Calluna
LADDERS Raddles, Saddler
LADYISH Shadily
*****LAERTES** Elaters, Relates, Stealer
LAGUNES Angelus

LAIRAGE Algeria, Railage, Regalia
LAIRING Glairin, Railing
*** LAMAISM** Miasmal
LAMBING Ambling, Balming, Blaming
LAMIGER Gremial
LAMINAE Alamein, Almaine, Limnaea
LAMINAL Manilla
LAMINAR Railman
LAMPATE Palmate
LAMPERS Marples, Palmers, Sampler
LAMPING Palming
LAMPREY Palmery
LANCETS Cantles, Centals, Scantle
LANDERS Darnels, Enlards, Relands, Slander, Snarled
LAND-LAW Lawland
LANGITE Atingle, Elating, Gelatin, Genital
LANGUID Lauding
LANNERS Ensnarl
LANSING Linsang
LANTERN Trannel
*** LAOTIAN** Ailanto
LAPIDES Alipeds, Elipads, Paidles, Palsied, Pleiads
LAPPERS Rappels, Slapper
LAPPIES Applies
LAPPING Palping
LAPPISH Palship, Shiplap
LAPSING Palings, Sapling, Spaling
LAPWING Pawling
LARCHEN Charnel
LARCHES Charles, Rachels
LARDING Darling
LARDOON Orlando
LARGELY Allergy, Gallery, Regally
LARIATS Alsirat

*** LARIDAE** Radiale
LASABLE Sabella, Salable
LASHERS Ashlers, Slasher
LASTAGE Algates
LASHING Halsing
LASSOER Oarless
LASTERS Artless, Salters, Slaters, Tarsels
LASTING Anglist, Salting, Slating, Staling
LATCHES Chalets, Satchel
LATCHET Chattel
LATEBRA Alberta, Ratable
LATHERS Halters, Harslet, Hastler, Herstal, Slather, Thalers
LATHERY Earthly, Heartly
LATHING Althing, Halting
LATICES Astelic, Castile, Elastic, Laciest, Salicet
*** LATINER** Entrail, Latrine, Ratline, Reliant, Retinal, Trenail
LATRINE Entrail, Latiner, Ratline, Reliant, Retinal, Trenail
*** LATROBE** Bloater
LATTICE Tactile, Talcite
*** LATVIAN** Valiant
LAUDING Languid
LAUGH-IN Hauling
LAUNCES Censual, Unlaces, Unscale
LAUNDER Arundel, Lurdane, Rundale
*** LAURENS** Ulnares
LAVAGES Salvage
LAVEERS Leavers, Reveals, Several, Vealers
LAYERED Delayer, Relayed
LAYINGS Slaying
LAYOVER Overlay
LAWLAND Land-law
LEACHED Chaldee, Cheadle
LEACHES Chelsea, Selache
LEADING Aligned, Dealing
LEAD-INS Denials, Snailed

LEAFING Fealing, Finagle
LEAFLET Fellate
LEAGUER Regulae
LEAKING Linkage
LEAMING Gmelina, Mealing
*****LEANDER** Learned
LEANING Aneling, Eanling,
　Nealing
LEAPERS Pealers, Pleaser,
　Preseal, Relapse, Repeals
LEAPING Pealing
LEA-RIGS Algiers
LEARING Aligner, Engrail,
　Nargile, Realign, Reginal
LEARNED Leander
LEARNER Relearn
LEASERS Earless, Resales,
　Reseals, Sealers
LEASING Linages, Sealing
LEATHER Tar-heel
LEAVENS Enslave
LEAVERS Laveers, Reveals,
　Several, Vealers
LECHERY Cheerly
LECTORS Colters, Corslet,
　Costrel, Croslet
LEDGERS Gelders, Red-legs,
　Sledger
LEECHES Scheele
LEEMOST Omelets
LEERING Reeling
LEFTIES Felsite, Liefest
*****LEGASPI** Paigles
LEGATOR Gloater, Ortegal
LEGIONS Eloigns, Lignose,
　Lingoes, Sloe-gin
LEG-SPIN Pingles, Pin-legs,
　Spignel
*****LEGNAGO** Agelong
*****LEGNICA** Angelic, Galenic
LEISTER Retiles, Sterile
*****LEITRIM** Limiter, Relimit
LEMMING Memling
*****LEMNIAN** Lineman, Melanin

LEMPIRA Impaler, Impearl,
　Palmier
LENDERS Relends, Slender
LENTISK Tinkles
LEONIDS Dolines, Sondeli
LEOPARD Paroled
LEOTARD Delator
*****LEPANTO** Polenta
LEPROSE Elopers
LEPROUS Pelorus, Perlous,
　Sporule
LESIONS Esloins, Insoles, Lioness
*****LESSING** Singles
LESSONS Sonless
LETHEAN Entheal
LETTERN Nettler
LETTERS Settler, Sterlet, Trestle
*****LETTISH** Listeth, Lithest, Thistle
LEUCOMA Caulome
LEVELER Relevel
LEVIERS Lievres, Relives,
　Reviles, Servile, Veilers
*****LEVITES** Velites
*****LEYBURN** Burnley
LIASSIC Silicas
LIBERAL Air-bell, Braille
LIBRATE Alberti, Tablier, Triable,
　Trilabe
LICENSE Selenic, Silence
LICHEES Helices
LICKERS Rickles, Sickler, Slicker
LIDGERS Gilders, Girdles,
　Gliders, Grisles, Regilds, Ridgels
LIEFEST Felsite, Lefties
*****LIESTAL** Tailles, Tallies
*****LIEVRES** Leviers, Relives,
　Reviles, Servile, Veilers
LIFTERS Filters, Stifler, Trifles
LIFTMAN Man-lift
LIGATED Taigled
LIGHTED Delight
LIGHTEN Enlight
LIGHTER Relight
*****LIGNICE** Ceiling, Cieling

LIGNITE Tigline
LIGNOSE Eloigns, Legions, Lingoes, Sloe-gin
LIGROIN Roiling
LIGULAS Lugsail
LIGULES Gullies
LILTING Tilling
LIMACEL Micella
LIMBATE Timbale
LIMIEST Elitism, Limites
LIMITED Delimit
LIMITER Leitrim, Relimit
LIMITES Elitism, Limiest
LIMNAE Alamein, Almaine, Laminae
LIMNERS Merlins, Smerlin
LIMPERS Prelims, Rimples, Simpler
LIMPEST Limpets
LIMPETS Limpest
*LINACRE Carline
LINAGES Leasing, Sealing
*LINARES Nailers
LINCHET Tinchel
LINDANE Annelid
LINEMAN Lemnian, Melanin
LINE-OUT Elution, Outline
LINE-UPS Lupines, Spinule, Unpiles, Up-lines
LINGCOD Codling
LINGERS Girnels, Singler, Slinger
LINGETS Glisten, Singlet, Tingles
LINGISM Sliming, Smiling
LINGOES Eloigns, Legions, Lignose, Sloe-gin
LINGUAL Lingula
LINGULA Lingual
LINKAGE Leaking
LINKING Inkling, Kilning
LINSANG Lansing
LINSEED Enisled, Ensiled, Nelides
LINTERS Snirtle
LIONESS Esloins, Insoles, Lesions

LIONETS Entoils, Tonsile
LIONISE Elision, Isoline
LIPPERS Ripples, Slipper
LIP-READ Pedrail, Predial
LIQUATE Tequila
LISMORE Moilers, Semilor
LISPING Pilings, Spiling
LISTETH Lettish, Lithest, Thistle
LISTING Silting
LITERAL Tallier
LITHATE Tile-hat
LITHEST Lettish, Thistle, Listeth
LITOTES Toilets
LITTERS Slitter, Stilter, Testril, Tilters, Titlers
LITTERY Tritely
LIVE-OUT Outlive, Ovulite
LIVERED Deliver, Relived, Reviled
LOADERS Ordeals, Reloads, Sea-lord
LOADING Digonal, Dog-nail
LOAFERS Safrole
LOAFING Foaling
LOAMIER Morelia
LOAMING Almoign
LOANERS Orleans, Reloans, Salerno
LOATHER Rat-hole
LOATHLY Tally-ho
LOBATED Bloated
LOBBERS Slobber
LOBBIED Bilobed
LOBBIES Bilboes
LOBSTER Bolster, Bolters, Rebolts
LOBULES Soluble
*LOCARNO Coronal
LOCATES Alecost, Lactose, Scatole, Talcose
LOCHIAS Scholia
LOCKING Cloking
LOCOING Cooling
LOCOMEN Monocle
*LOCRIAN Clarino, Clarion

LOCULES Ocellus
LOCUSTA Talcous
LODGING Godling, Golding
LOFTIER Trefoil
LOGGERS Roggles, Slogger
LOGIEST Elogist
LOITERS Estoril, Estriol, Toilers
LOMENTA Omental, Telamon
LOOFING Foligno, Fooling
LOOKOUT Outlook
LOOPERS Spooler
LOOPING Pooling
LOOSING Olingos, Sooling
LOOTING Tooling
LORCHARS Chorals, Scholar
LORDING Girlond
*LORETTA Retotal
LORICAE Calorie, Cariole
*LORINDA Ordinal
LOUDENS Nodules, Unsoled
LOUDEST Tousled
LOUNDER Roundel, Roundle
LOUSIER Soilure
LOUTING Tung-oil
LOVABLE Volable
LOVERED Reloved
LOW-BRED Bowdler, Bowlder
LOWINGS Slowing, Sowling
LOXYGEN Xylogen
LUBBERS Burbles, Rubbles,
  Slubber
LUCARNE Nuclear, Unclear
LUDDITE Diluted
LUGGERS Gurgles, Slugger
LUGSAIL Ligulas
LUMBERS Burslem, Rumbles,
  Slumber, Umbrels
LUMPERS Replums, Rumples,
  Slumper
LUMPING Pluming
LUNATED Undealt
LUNIEST Untiles, Utensil
LUPINES Line-ups, Spinule,
  Unpiles, Up-lines

LURDANE Arundel, Launder,
  Rundale
LUSTING Glutins, Lutings,
  Singult, Sutling
LUSTRED Rustled, Strudel
LUTINGS Glutins, Lusting,
  Sutling, Singult
LYDDITE Tiddley
LYING-IN Inlying

MACHAIR Amharic
*MACLEAN Laceman, Manacle
MACULES Almuces, Mascule
MADEIRA Dierama
*MADERNO Roadmen
*MADISON Daimons, Domains
MADNESS Desmans
MADRIER Admirer, Married
MADRONA Mandora, Monarda,
  Roadman
MADRONO Doorman
*MAESTEG Gametes, Metages
MAESTRI Artemis, Imarets,
  Maister, Misrate, Semitar,
  Smartie
MAESTRO Amorets
MAGENTA Gateman, Magnate
*MAGIANS Gas-main, Siamang
*MAGINOT Moating
MAGNATE Gateman, Magenta
MAGNETO Megaton, Montage
MAIDENS Demains, Mandies,
  Medians, Sideman
*MAIGRET Migrate, Ragtime
MAILERS Realism, Remails
MAINTOP Ptomain, Tampion,
  Timpano
MAISTER Artemis, Imarets,
  Maestri, Misrate, Semitar,
  Smartie
MALAISE Amelias
MALATES Maltase, Tamales
*MALINES Isleman, Menials,
  Seminal

MALISON Monials, Osmanli, Soliman, Somnial
MALKINS Slamkin
MALTASE Malates, Tamales
MANACLE Laceman, Maclean
MANAGED Agnamed
MANAGES Agnames, Mesagna
MANATEE Emanate, Enemata
MAN-DAYS Daysman
*****MANDIES** Demains, Maidens, Medians, Sideman
MANDIOC Monacid, Monadic, Nomadic
MANDORA Madrona, Monarda, Roadman
MANEGED End-game
*****MANGERE** Germane
MANHOOD Hoodman
MANIACS Caimans, Camansi
MANIHOC Mohican
MANILLA Laminal
MANIOCS Anosmic, Camions, Masonic
MANIPLE Impanel
MANITOU Tinamou
MANJACK Jackman
MANLIER Marline, Mineral, Railmen, Ramline
MAN-LIFT Liftman
MANNOSE Name-son
MANRENT Remnant, Rent-man
MANSART Artsman, Mantras, Star-man
MANSART Artsman, Mantras, Star-man
MANSION Amnions, Onanism
MAN-TRAP Rampant
MANTRAS Artsman, Mansart, Star-man
MANURED Duramen, Maunder, Unarmed
MANURES Surname
MARACAS Camaras, Marasca, Mascara

*****MARANTA** Amarant
MARASCA Camaras, Maracas, Mascara
MARBLED Rambled
MARBLER Rambler
MARCHED Charmed, Decharm
MARCHEN Encharm
MARCHER Charmer
MARCHES Mesarch, Schmear
*****MARCONI** Minorca, Romanic
*****MARGATE** Regmata
MARGENT Garment, Ragment
MARGOSA Smarago
MARINER Rein-aim
MARINES Remains, Seminar, Sirname
*****MARISTS** Ramists, Tsarism
MARITAL Martial
MARLINE Manlier, Mineral, Railmen, Ramline
MARPLES Lampers, Palmers, Sampler
MARRIED Admirer, Madrier
MARRIES Simarre
*****MARSTON** Matrons, Transom
MARTENS Artsmen, Sarment, Smarten
MARTIAL Marital
MARTIAN Martina, Tamarin
*****MARTINA** Martian, Tamarin
MASCARA Camaras, Maracas, Marasca
MASCULE Almuces, Macules
MASHERS Shamers, Smasher
MASHIES Messiah
MASHING Shaming
MASONIC Anosmic, Camions, Maniocs
MASSEUR Amusers, Assumer, Erasmus, Mausers
*****MASSINE** Messina
MASTERY Mayster, Streamy
MASTICH Tachism
MASTICS Miscast

MASTOID Diatoms, Distoma
MATCHER Rematch
MATINEE Etamine
*MATISSE Asteism, Samites, Tamises
MATRONS Marston, Transom
MATROSS Stroams
MATTERS Smatter
MATURER Erratum
MATURES Strumae
MAULING Aluming
MAUNDER Duramen, Manured,
  Unarmed
MAUSERS Amusers, Assumer,
  Erasmus, Masseur
MAWKISH Hawkism
MAXI-MIN Mini-max
*MAY-MORN Rommany
MAYSTER Mastery, Streamy
MEALIES Sea-mile
MEALING Gmelins, Leaming
MEANDER Amender, Enarmed,
  Reamend, Renamed
MEANETH Methane
MEANING Amening
MEATIER Emirate
MEDIALS Misdeal, Mislead
MEDIANS Demains, Maidens,
  Mandies, Sideman
MEDICAL Claimed, Decimal,
  Declaim
MEDICOS Miscode
MEDISED Demised, Misdeed
MEDUSAN Sudamen
MEERCAT Ceramet, Cremate
MEETING Teeming
MEGABAR Bergama
MEGARAD Damager
MEGASSE Message
MEGATON Magneto, Montage
*MEGIDDO Demi-god
MEGILPS Glimpse
*MEILHAC Michael
*MEISSEN Misseen, Nemesis,
  Siemens

MELANGE Gleeman
MELANIN Lemnian, Lineman
MELDING Mingled
*MELISSA Aimless, Mesails,
  Samiels, Seismal
MELTERS Remelts, Smelter
*MEMLING Lemming
MENACES Casemen
MENIALS Isleman, Malines,
  Seminal
MENIVER Minever
*MENORCA Cameron, Cremona,
  Romance
MENTORS Monster, Montres
MERCERY Remercy
*MERCIAN Carmine, Crimean
*MERIDEN Ermined
MERINOS Mersion
MERITED Demerit, Dimeter,
  Edremit, Mitered, Retimed
MERLING Gremlin, Mingler
MERLINS Limners, Smerlin
MERSION Merinos
*MESAGNA Agnames, Manages
MESAILS Aimless, Melissa,
  Samiels, Seismal
MESARCH Marsche, Schmear
MESONIC Comines, Incomes
MESSAGE Megasse
*MESSIAH Mashies
MESSIER Remises
MESSINA Massine
MESSINS Sensism
MESS-TIN Missent
METAGES Gametes, Maesteg
METAMER Ammeter
METERED Demeter
METHANE Meaneth
METIERS Re-emits, Retimes,
  Triseme
METONIC Centimo, Entomic,
  Tonemic
METRICS Cretism
METTLES Stemlet

MIASMAL Lamaism
MICELLA Limacel
*MICHAEL Meilhac
MICHING Chiming
MICRONS Crimson
MID-EAST Misdate
MID-HOUR Humidor, Rhodium
*MIDRASH Dirhams
MID-TERM Trimmed
MIGRATE Maigret, Ragtime
MILLETS Mistell
MILREIS Slimier
MIMOSAS Mosaism
MINARET Raiment
MINERAL Manlier, Marline,
  Railmen, Ramline
*MINERVA Vermian
MINEVER Meniver
MINGLED Melding
MINGLER Gremlin, Merling
MINIATE Intimae
MINIBUS Minisub
MINI-MAX Maxi-min
MINIMUS Minisum, Miniums
MINISUB Minibus
MINISUM Minmus, Miniums
MINIUMS Minimus, Minisum
MINORCA Marconi, Romanic
MINSTER Entrism, Minters,
  Remints
MINTAGE Teaming, Tegmina
MINTERS Entrism, Minster,
  Remints
MINTIER Interim, Termini
MINTOES Moisten
MINUEND Unmined
MINUETS Minutes, Mistune,
  Mutines
MINUTES Minuets, Mistune,
  Mutines
*MIRABEL Balmier, Embrail,
  Mirabel, Remblai
MIRABLE Balmier, Embrail,
  Mirabel, Remblai

MIRACLE Almeric, Carmiel,
  Claimer, Reclaim
MIRAGES Gisarme, Imagers
MIRIEST Mistier, Rimiest
MISCAST Mastics
MISCITE Semitic
MISCODE Medicos
MISCOPY Copyism
MISDATE Mid-east
MISDEAL Medials, Mislead
MISDEED Demised, Medised
MISDIET Stimied
MISDOER Dormies, Moiders
MISDONE Domines
MISEASE Siamese
MISLEAD Medials, Misdeal
MISMATE Tammies
MISNAME Ammines
MISRATE Artemis, Imarets,
  Maestri, Maister, Semitar,
  Smartie
MISREAD Admires, Sidearm
MISSEEN Meissen, Nemesis,
  Siemens
MISSEND Dimness
MISSENT Mess-tin
MISSILE Similes
MISTA'EN Emanist, Inmates,
  Inmeats, Samnite, Tamines
MISTELL Millets
MISTERY Smytrie
MISTICO Somitic
MISTIER Miriest, Rimiest
MISTING Smiting
MISTRAL Ramtils
MISTUNE Minuets, Minutes,
  Mutines
MISUSER Mussier, Surmise
MITERED Demerit, Edremit,
  Dimeter, Merited, Retimed
MITERER Trireme
MITTENS Smitten
MOANERS Romanes
MOATING Maginot

MOBBING Bombing
MOBBISH Hobbism
MOBSTER Bestorm
MODELER Delorme, Remodel
MODERNS Rodsmen
*** MOHEGAN** Hog-mane
MOHICAN Manihoc
MOIDERS Dormies, Misdoer
MOIDORE Moodier
MOILERS Lismore, Semilor
MOISSAC Mosaics
MOISTEN Mintoes
MOISTER Erotism, Mortise
MOLDERS Smolder
MONACID Mandioc, Monadic,
  Nomadic
MONADES Daemons, Nomades
MONADIC Mandioc, Monacid,
  Nomadic
MONARCH Nomarch
MONARDA Madrona, Mandora,
  Roadman
MONERAL Almoner, Nemoral
MONIALS Malison, Osmanli,
  Soliman, Somnial
MONISTS Stimson
MONOCLE Locomen
MONOSIS Simoons
MONSTER Mentors, Montres
MONTAGE Magneto, Megaton
*** MONTAGU** Gaumont
MONTRES Mentors, Monster
MONTURE Mounter, Remount
MOODIER Moidore
MOONIES Noisome
MOORAGE Roomage
MOOR-HEN Hormone
MOORING Rooming
MOOTING Tooming
MORAINE Romaine
MORDANT Dormant
MOREISH Heroism, Himeros
*** MORELIA** Loamier
MORENDO Doormen

MORGUES Grumose
MORICHE Homeric
*** MORINGA** Roaming
MORONIC Omicron
MORTISE Erotism, Moister
MOSAICS Moissac
MOSAISM Mimosas
MOTHERS Smother, Thermos
MOTIVED Vomited
MOULDER Remould
MOUNTED Demount
MOUNTER Monture, Remount
MOURNED Dunmore
MOUSERS Smouser
MUDDIES Dedimus
MUGGERS Smugger
MUMBLED Bummled
MUNDANE Unmaned, Unnamed
*** MUNSTER** Sternum
MURDERS Smurred
*** MURGHAB** Hamburg
MURICES Ceriums
MUSCONE Consume
MUSLIMS Slumism
MUSSELS Sumless
MUSSIER Misuser, Surmise
MUSTARD Durmast
MUSTILY Mytilus
MUTABLE Ambulet
MUTAGEN Augment
MUTINES Minuets, Minutes,
  Mistune
MYOSOTE Toysome
MYRBANE Byreman
MYTILUS Mustily

NACRITE Catrine, Ceratin,
  Certain, Creatin, Crinate
NAGGERS Gangers, Granges,
  Snagger
NAGGING Ganging
NAILERS Linares
NAILERY Inlayer
NAILING Alining

NAME-SON Mannose
NAPPERS Parpens, Parsnep,
Snapper
NARCOSE Carnose, Coarsen,
Corneas, Sea-corn
NARDING Darning
NARGILE Aligner, Engrail,
Learing, Realign, Reginal
NARGILY Angrily
NARKING Ranking
NASHGAB Gabnash
NASTIER Ratines, Resiant,
Restain, Retains, Retinas,
Retsina, Stainer, Starnie, Stearin
NASTILY Saintly
NATCHES Chasten
NATIONS Anoints, Onanist
NATTIER Intreat, Iterant, Nitrate,
Tartine, Tertian
NATURED Durante, Unrated,
Untread
NATURES Aunters, Saunter, Sea-
turn, Tea-urns
NAVARIN Nirvana
NEALING Aneling, Eanling,
Leaning
NEAPING Peaning
NEAREST Earnest, Eastern
NEARETH Earneth, Earthen,
Hearten, Teheran
NEARING Earning, Engrain,
Grannie
NECROSE Encores
NECTARY Encraty
NEEDERS Serened, Sneered
NEEDILY Dyeline
NEEDING Engined
NE-ERDAY Deanery, Renayed,
Yearned
NEGATER Grantee, Greaten,
Reagent
NEGATUR Ungrate
NEGLIGE Gleeing, Gleneig
NEGRITO Genitor, Trigone

*NEGROES Engores
NEGROID Eroding, Gironde,
Groined, Ignored, Redoing
NEIGHED Heeding
NEITHER Therein
*NELIDES Enisled, Ensiled,
Linseed
NEMATIC Emicant
NEMESIS Meissen, Misseen,
Siemens
NEMORAL Almoner, Moneral
NEPHRIC Phrenic, Pincher
NEPOTIC Entopic
NERITIC Citrine, Crinite, Inciter
NERVATE Veteran
NERVINE Enriven, Innerve
NESTERS Ernests, Resents,
Streens, Strenes
NESTING Tensing
NESTLED Dentels
NESTLER Relents
NET-FISH Fish-net
NET-PLAY Aplenty, Penalty
NETTING Tenting
NETTLER Lettern
NEUROMA Enamour, Euroman
*NEUQUEN Unqueen
NEUTERS Retunes, Tenures,
Tureens, Unterse
NEUTRAL Renault
NICHING Chining, Inching
NICKELS Slicken
NICKERS Snicker
NICTATE Tetanic
*NIDAROS Dorians, Inroads,
Ordains, Sadiron
NIDGING Dinging
NIFFLES Sniffle
NIGGARD Grading
NIGGERS Gingers, Snigger
NIGGERY Gingery, Greying
NIGGLED Gelding, Gingled
NIGGLES Gingles, Sniggle
NIGRINE Reining

NIGRITE Igniter, Tiering, Tigrine,
NILGAIS Sailing
*__**NIPIGON** Opining
NIPPERS Snipper
NIRVANA Navarin
NITERIE Erinite
NITHING Hinting, In-thing
NITRATE Intreat, Iterant, Nattier,
  Tartine, Tertian
NITRIDE Inditer
NITROSO Isotron, Torsion
NITTERS Entrist, Retints, Stinter,
  Tinters
NIVEOUS Envious, Veinous
*__**NOACHIC** Chicano
NOCKING Conking
NOCTUID Conduit
NODATED Donated
NODULES Loudens, Unsoled
*__**NOETIAN** Enation, Etonian
NOETICS Notices, Section
NOISIER Ironies
NOISOME Moonies
NO-KNOCK Knock-on
NOMADES Daemons, Monades
NOMADIC Mandioc, Monacid,
  Monadic
NOMARCH Monarch
NON-CASH Chanson
NON-PAID Dipnoan, Pandion
NONSTOP Pontons
NOOLOGY Onology
NOR'EAST Anteros, Atoners,
  Senator, Treason
NORTHED Thonder, Thorned,
  Throned
NORTHER Horrent
NOSE-RAG Onagers, Oranges
NOTICED Condite, Ctenoid,
  Deontic, D-notice
NOTICER Citroen
NOTICES Noetics, Section
NOTINGS Stoning

NOUGHTS Gunshot, Hognuts,
  Shotgun
NOVALIA Valonia
NOWHERE Erewhon, Whereon
NUCLEAR Lucarne, Unclear
NUCLIDE Dulcine, Include
NUDGING Dunging
NUPTIAL Patulin, Unplait
NUTATED Attuned, Taunted
NUTATES Attunes, Tautens,
  Tetanus, Unstate
NUT-GALL Gall-nut
NUTTERS Entrust
NUT-WOOD Woodnut
NUZZLES Snuzzle

OARLESS Lassoer
OBELION Bone-oil
OBEYING Biogeny
OBLIGER Oilberg
OBSERVE Obverse, Verbose
OBSIGNS Bossing
OBTAINS Bastion
OBTRUDE Doubter, Outbred,
  Redoubt
OBVERSE Observe, Verbose
OCARINA Aaronic, Conaria
OCEANIC Cocaine
OCELLAR Corella
OCELLUS Locules
OCELOTS Coolest
OCHROID Choroid
OCTANES Costean
OCTONAL Coolant
OCTUPLE Couplet
OCULARS Carolus, Oscular
ODDNESS Soddens
ODORANT Donator, Tornado
OERSTED Teredos
OESTRUS Estrous, Ousters,
  Sourest, Souters, Tousers,
  Trouses, Trousse, Tussore
OEUVRES Overuse
OFFCAST Cast-off

OFF-COME Come-off
OFFENDS Send-off
OFFERER Reoffer
OFFHAND Hand-off
OFF-SPIN Spin-off
OFF-STEP Step-off
OFF-TAKE Take-off
OGLINGS Gosling
OILBERG Obliger
OILINGS Siloing, Soiling
OIL-LAMP Oil-palm, Palm-oil
OIL-PALM Palm-oil, Oil-lamp
OIL-SEED Seed-oil
OIL-TREE Troelie
OKAYING Kayoing
OLDSTER Strodle
OLINGOS Loosing, Sooling
*****OLIVIER** Rilievo
OLIVINE Violine
OMELETS Leemost
OMENTAL Lomenta, Telamon
OMICRON Moronic
OMNEITY Omniety
OMNIETY Omniety
OMNIETY Omniety
ONAGERS Nose-rag, Oranges
ONANISM Amnions, Mansion
ONANIST Anoints, Nations
ONDINES Denison
ON-DRIVE Vine-rod
ONENESS Essonne
ONE-STEP Pentose, Pontees, Posteen, Poteens
*****ONESUND** Nesound, Sounden, Undoens, Endonus, Unnosed
ONOLOGY Noology
ONSHORE Sorehon
ONSTEAD Donates
*****ONTARIO** Oration
OOLITES Ostiole, Stoolie
OPEN-AIR Pea-iron
OPERAND Aproned, Padrone, Pandore

OPERANT Paterno, Pronate, Protean
OPETIDE Epidote
OPINING Nipigon
OPPOSER Propose
OPPRESS Porpess
OPTICAL Capitol, Coalpit, Pit-coal, Topical
OPTIONS Positon, Potions
*****OPUNTIA** Utopian
OPUSCLE Close-up, Couples, Upclose
ORACHES Roaches
ORACLES Coalers, Escolar, Recoals, Solacer
ORANGES Nose-rag, Onagers
ORATING Tragion
ORATION Ontario
ORBITED Debitor, Deorbit
ORDAINS Dorians, Inroads, Nidaros, Sadiron
ORDEALS Loaders, Reloads, Sealord
ORDERER Reorder
ORDINAL Lorinda
ORECTIC Cerotic
*****ORESTES** Osseter, Stereos
*****ORESUND** Endorus, Resound, Sounder, Undoers, Unrosed
ORGEATS Storage, Tagsore
ORGIAST Agistor
ORIGANS Ignaros, Signora, Soaring
ORIGINS Signior
*****ORKNEYS** Yonkers
*****ORLANDO** Lardoon
ORLEANS Loaners, Reloans, Salerno
*****ORPHISM** Rompish
ORPINES Sinoper
ORRICES Cirrose, Corries, Crosier
*****ORTEGAL** Gloater, Legator
ORTHITE Thorite

OSCHEAL Sea-loch
*OSCINES Cession, Cosines
OSCULAR Carolus, Oculars
*OSMANLI Malison, Monials,
  Soliman, Somnial
OSMIATE Atomies, Atomise,
  Samiote
OSSETER Orestes, Stereos
OSTENTS Stetson
OSTIOLE Oolites, Stoolie
OSTRICH Chorist
*OTRANTO Arnotto, Rattoon
OUSTERS Estrous, Oestrus,
  Sourest, Souters, Tousers,
  Trouses, Trousse, Tussore
OUSTING Outings, Outsing,
  Tousing
OUTARDE Outdare, Outread,
  Readout
OUT-BACK Back-out
OUTBLOW Blow-out, Outbowl
OUTBOWL Blow-out, Outblow
OUTBRED Doubter, Obtrude,
  Redoubt
OUTBURN Burnout
OUTDARE Outarde, Outread,
  Readout
OUTDRAW Drawout, Outward
OUTFALL Fall-out
OUTGRIN Outring, Routing,
  Touring
OUTHIRE Routhie
OUTINGS Ousting, Outsing,
  Tousing
OUTJEST Outjets
OUTJETS Outjest
OUTLINE Elution, Line-out
OUTLIVE Live-out, Ovulite
OUTLOOK Lookout
OUTPASS Passout
OUTPOST Outtops, Puttoos,
  Stop-out
OUTPULL Pull-out
OUTRATE Out-tear

OUTREAD Outarde, Outdare,
  Readout
OUTREDS Detours, Dourest,
  Douters, Rousted
OUTRIDE Etourdi, Ioduret
OUTRING Outgrin, Routing,
  Touring
OUTSELL Sell-out
OUTSEND Send-out
OUTSERT Stouter, Touters
OUTSIDE Tedious
OUTSING Ousting, Outings
  Tousing
OUTSPIN Sit-upon, Spin-out
OUTSTEP Toupets
OUTTAKE Take-out
OUT-TEAR Outrate
OUTTOPS Outpost, Puttoos,
  Stop-out
OUTTURN Turn-out
OUTWALK Walk-out
OUTWARD Drawout, Outdraw
OUTWASH Wash-out
OUTWITH Without
OUTWORK Work-out
OUTWORN Worn-out
OVERALL All-over
OVERATE Over-eat
OVER-EAT Over-ate
OVERFLY Fly-over
OVERLAY Lay-over
OVERLIE Relievo
OVERPLY Plovery
OVERRUN Run-over
OVERSET Estover, Revotes,
  Setover, Vetoers
OVERUSE Oeuvres
OVULITE Live-out, Outlive
*OWENISM Winsome

PACABLE Capable
PACINGS Scaping, Spacing
PACK-ICE Icepack
PACTION Caption, Pontiac

PADDLES Spaddle

PADRERO Ear-drop

PADRONE Aproned, Operand, Pandore

PADRONI Poniard

PAD-TREE Predate, Readept, Red-tape, Retaped, Tapered

PAGINGS Gasping

PAIDLES Alipeds, Elapids, Lapides, Palsied, Pleiads

PAIGLES Legaspi

PAINTED Depaint, Patined

PAINTER Patenir, Pertain, Pine-tar, Repaint

PALETTE Peltate

PALINGS Lapsing, Sapling, Spaling

PALMARY Palmyra

PALMATE Lampate

PALMERS Lampers, Marples, Sampler

PALMERY Lamprey

PALMIER Impaler, Impearl, Lempira

PALMIET Implate

PALMING Lamping

PALM-OIL Oil-lamp, Oil-palm

PALMYRA Palmary

PALPING Lapping

PALSHIP Lappish, Shiplap

PALSIED Alipeds, Elapids, Lapides, Paidles, Pleiads

PALTERS Persalt, Plaster, Platers, Psalter, Spartel, Stapler

PANDEAN Pannade

*****PANDION** Dipnoan, Non-paid

PANDITS Sandpit

PANDORE Aproned, Operand, Padrone

PANELER Repanel

*****PANGAEA** Apanage

PAN-HEAD Headpan

PANICLE Capelin, Pelican

PANNADE Pandean

PANNERS Spanner

PANTERS Arpents, Entraps, Parents, Pastern, Persant, Trepans

PANTHER Penarth

PANTIES Patines, Sapient, Spinate

PANTINE Pinnate

PANTLER Planter, Replant

PAPERER Prepare, Repaper

PAPULES Appluse

PARADES Aspread, Saperda

PARAFLE Earflap

PARBOIL Bipolar

PARCELS Carpels, Clasper, Placers, Reclasp, Scalper

PARENTS Arpents, Entraps, Panters, Pastern, Persant, Trepans

PARESIS Aspires, Praises, Serapis, Spireas

PARETIC Picrate

PARINGS Parsing, Rasping, Sparing

PARISON Soprani

PARKERS Reparks, Sparker

PARLEYS Parsley, Players, Replays, Sparely

PARODIC Picador

PAROLED Leopard

PAROLES Reposal

PAROTIC Apricot, Patrico

PAROTIS Airstop

PARPENS Nappers, Parsnep, Snapper

PARRIED Drapier

PARRIES Aspirer, Praiser, Rapiers, Raspier, Repairs

*****PARSEES** Asperse, Praeses, Preasse, Serapes

PARSERS Raspers, Sparers, Sparser

PARSING Parings, Rasping, Sparing

PARSLEY Parleys, Players, Replays, Sparely
PARSNEP Nappers, Parpens, Snapper
PARTANS Spartan, Tarpans, Trapans
PARTIAL Patrial
PARTIES Piaster, Piastre, Pirates, Praties, Traipse
PARTING Gin-trap, Prating, Traping
PARTITE Tearpit
PARTLET Platter, Prattle
PARTONS Patrons, Strap-on, Tarpons
PARTURE Rapture
PARULIS Uprisal
PARVISE Paviers, Paviser
PASCUAL Capsula, Scapula
PASHING Hasping, Plasing
PASSIVE Pavises
PASSMAN Sampans
PASSOUT Outpass
PASTERN Arpents, Entraps, Panters, Parents, Persant, Trepans
*****PASTEUR** Pasture, Upstare
PASTIME Impaste
PASTURE Pasteur, Upstare
PATCHES Hep-cats
PATCHER Chapter, Repatch
*****PATENIR** Painter, Pertain, Pine-tar, Repaint
PATINAS Antipas
PATINED Depaint, Painted
PATINES Panties, Sapient, Spinate
PATNESS Aptness
PATRERO Apertor, Praetor, Prorate
PATRIAL Partial
PATRICO Apricot, Parotic
PATRONS Partons, Strap-on, Tarpons

PATTERN Reptant
PATTERS Spatter, Tapster
PATTLES Peltast, Spattle
PATULIN Nuptial, Unplait
PAVIERS Parvise, Paviser
PAVISER Parvise, Paviers
PAVISES Passive
PAWLING Lapwing
PAWNERS Enwraps, Repawns, Spawner
PAY-BILL Pliably
PEACHER Cheaper
PEA-IRON Open-air
PEALERS Leapers, Pleaser, Preseal, Relapse, Repeals
PEALING Leaping
PEANING Neaping
PEANUTS Unpaste
PEARLED Pleader, Replead
PEARLIN Plainer, Praline
PEARTLY Apertly, Prelaty, Pteryla
PEASANT Anapest
*****PECHORA** Poacher
PECTINE Pentice
PECTINS Incepts, Inspect
PEDESIS Despise
PEDICEL Pedicle
PEDICLE Pedicel
PEDRAIL Lip-read, Predial
PEEKING Keeping
PEELERS Sleeper, Speeler
PEERESS Presees
PEERING Preeing
PELAMID Impaled, Implead
PELICAN Capelin, Panicle
PELITIC Tie-clie
PELMETS Stempel, Stemple, Temples
*****PELOIDS** Despoil, Diploes, Dipoles, Soliped, Spoiled
PELORIA Rape-oil
PELORUS Leprous, Perlous, Sporule

PELOTAS Apostle, Pot-ales
PELTAST Pattles, Spattle
PELTATE Palette
PELTERS Petrels, Prestel, Respe
  Spelter
PENALTY Aplenty, Net-play
*PENARTH Panther
PENATES Pesante
PENCILS Splenic
PENNATE Pentane
PENNIES Pinenes
PENSILE Espinal, Sleep-in
PENSIVE Vespine
PENTANE Pennate
PENTICE Pectine
PENTOSE One-step, Pontees,
  Posteen, Poteens
PENULTS Unspelt
PEONISM Impones, Pi-meson
PERACID Preacid
PERBEND Prebend
PERCALE Replace
PERCASE Caprese, Escaper,
  Respace
PER-CENT Precent
PERCEPT Precept
PERCUSS Spruces
PERDUES Perused
PEREION Pioneer
PERFECT Prefect
PERFORM Perform
PERIDOT Diopter, Dioptre,
  Proteid
PERIOST Pterois, Reposit, Riposte
PERIQUE Re-equip, Repique
PERJINK Prejink
PERLITE Reptile
PERLOUS Leprous, Pelorus,
  Sporule
PERMITS Imprest
PERRIES Reprise, Respire
PERSALT Palters, Plaster, Platers,
  Psalter, Spartel, Stapler
PERSANT Arpents, Entraps,

Panters, Parents, Pastern,
  Trepans
*PERSEID Predies, Preside,
  Speired
*PERSEUS Persues, Peruses
*PERSIAN Rapines
PERSICO Copiers
*PERSISM Impress, Premiss,
  Simpers
PERSIST Priests, Spriest, Sprites,
  Stirpes, Stripes
PERSUES Perseus, Peruses
PERTAIN Painter, Pine-tar,
  Patenir, Repaint
PERTUSE Reputes
PERUSAL Serpula
PERUSED Perdues
PERUSES Perseus, Persues
PERVADE Deprave, Repaved
PERVERT Prevert
PESANTE Penates
*PESHITO Ethiops
PETEMAN Tempean
PETERED Depeter
PETRELS Pelters, Prestel, Respelt,
  Spelter
PETROUS Posture, Pouters,
  Proteus, Septuor, Spouter,
  Troupes
*PETULAS Pulsate, Puteals,
  Spatule
PEWTERS Reswept
PHAETON Phonate
PHASING Hasping, Pashing,
  Shaping
PHASMID Dampish
PHENATE Heptane
PHILTER Philtre
PHILTRE Philter
PHOCINE Chopine
PHOEBES Ephebos
PHONATE Phaeton
PHRASED Sharped

PHRASER Harpers, Sharper
PHRENIC Nephric, Pincher
PHYTOID Typhoid
PIASTER Parties, Piastre, Pirates, Praties, Traipse
PIASTRE Parties, Piaster, Pirates, Praties, Traipse
PICADOR Parodic
PICAMAR Campari
PICKETS Skeptic
PICKLER Prickle
PICRATE Paretic
PICTURE Cuprite
PIEBALD Bipedal
PIECERS Pierces, Precise, Recipes, Respice
PIERCER Reprice
PIERCES Piecers, Precise, Recipes, Respice
PIETIST Pitesti
PIGSKIN Spiking
PIGSNEY Espying
PILEATE Epilate
PILINGS Lisping, Spiling
PILULES Pullies
PIMENTO Emption
PI-MESON Impones, Peonism
PINCASE Icepans, Inscape
PINCERS Crespin, Princes
PINCHER Nephric, Phrenic
PINCHES Sphenic
PINENES Pennies
PINE-TAR Painter, Patenir, Pertain, Repaint
PINGERS Springe
PINGLES Leg-spin, Pin-legs, Spignal
PIN-HEAD Head-pin
PININGS Sniping
PINKING King-pin
PINKISH Kinship
PIN-LEGS Leg-spin, Pingles, Spignel
PINNATE Pantine

PINNERS Spinner
PINNETS Spinnet, Ten-pins
PINOLES Epsilon
PINTLES Plenist
PIOLETS Pistole, Ploesti
PIONEER Pereion
***PIRAEUS** Spuriae, Upraise
PIRATED Diptera
PIRATES Parties, Piaster, Piastre, Praties, Traipse
PIRNIES Inspire, Spinier
PIROGUE Groupie
PISMIRE Primsie
PISTOLE Piolets, Ploesti
PITCOAL Capitol, Coal-pit, Optical, Topical
***PITESTI** Pietist
PITTERS Spitter, Tipster
PLACERS Carpels, Clasper, Parcels, Reclasp, Scalper
PLACITA Capital
PLACOID Podalic
PLAGUER Graupel
PLAINER Pearlin, Praline
PLAITED Taliped
PLAITER Replait
PLANTER Pantler, Replant
PLASHER Spheral
PLASHES Hapless
PLASMIC Psalmic
PLASTER Palters, Persalt, Platers, Psalter, Spartel, Stapler
PLATANS Saltpan
PLATERS Palters, Persalt, Plaster, Psalter, Spartel, Stapler
PLATTER Partlet, Prattle
PLAYERS Parleys, Parsley, Replays, Sparely
PLAYFUL Full-pay
PLEADER Pearled, Replead
PLEASED Delapse, Elapsed
PLEASER Leapers, Pealers, Preseal, Relapse, Repeals
PLEATER Prelate, Replate

PLECTRE Prelect
***PLEIADS** Alipeds, Elapids, Lapides, Paidles, Palsied
PLENIST Pintles
PLESSOR Preloss, Splores
PLIABLY Pay-bill
***PLOESTI** Piolets, Pistole
PLOPPED Poppled
PLOTFUL Topfull
PLOUTER Poulter
PLOVERY Overply
PLUMBIC Upclimb
PLUMING Lumping
PLUTEUS Pustule
POACHER Pechora
PODALIC Placoid
POINTEL Pontile, Potline, Top-line
POINTER Protein, Pterion, Repoint, Tropine
POISONS Poisson
POISSON Poisons
POITREL Politer
POLEMIC Compile
POLENTA Lepanto
PONIARD Padroni
POLITER Poitrel
POLOIST Topsoil
PONDERS Respond
PONTEES One-step, Pentose, Posteen, Poteens
***PONTIAC** Caption, Paction
PONTILE Pointel, Potline, Top-line
PONTONS Nonstop
POODLES Spooled
POOLING Looping
POOREST Pooters, Stooper
POOTERS Poorest, Stooper
POPERIN Propine
POPPLED Plopped
POPSTER Stopper, Toppers
PORCHES Porsche
PORGIES Serpigo

PORPESS Oppress
PORRETS Porters, Presort, Pretors, Reports, Sporter
***PORSCHE** Porches
PORTAGE Potager
PORTEND Drop-net, Protend
PORTENT Torpent
PORTERS Porrets, Presort, Pretors, Reports, Sporter
PORTICO Prootic
PORTIRY Torpify
POSEUSE Espouse
POSITED Deposit, Dopiest, Topside
POSITON Options, Potions
POSTAGE Gestapo, Potages
POST-BOY Potboys
POST-BUS Bus-stop
POSTEEN One-step, Pentose, Pontees, Poteens
POSTERN Preston
POSTING Stoping
POSTMAN Tampons, Topsman
POSTURE Petrous, Pouters, Proteus, Septuor, Spouter, Troupes
POTAGER Portage
POTAGES Gestapo, Postage
POT-ALES Apostle, Pelotas
POTAMIC Tampico
POTASSA Sapotas
POTBOYS Post-boy
POTEENS One-step, Pentose, Pontees, Posteen
POTENTS Ten-spot
POTHERS Strophe, Thorpes
POTHOLE Tophole
POTIONS Options, Positon
POTLINE Pointel, Pontile, Topline
POT-LUCK Putlock
POT-SHOT Hotpots, Hotspot
POTTERS Protest, Spotter
POTTIES Tiptoes
POTWORK Topwork

POULTER Plouter
POUNCED Uncoped
POUNDER Unroped
POURING Ingroup, Rouping
POUSSIN Spinous
POUTERS Petrous, Posture,
   Proteus, Septuor, Spouter,
   Troupes
PRAESES Asperse, Parsees,
   Preasse, Serapes
PRAETOR Apertor, Patrero,
   Prorate
PRAISED Aspired, Despair,
   Diapers
PRAISER Aspirer, Parries,
   Rapiers, Raspier, Repairs
PRAISES Aspires, Paresis,
   Serapis, Spireas
PRALINE Pearlin, Plainer
PRATIES Parties, Piaster, Piastre,
   Pirates, Traipse
PRATING Gin-trap, Parting,
   Traping
PRATTLE Partlet, Platter
PRAWNED Pre-dawn
PRAWNER Prewarn
PRAYERS Respray, Sprayer
PREACHY Eparchy
PREACID Peracid
PRE-ACTS Carpets, Precast,
   Spectra
PRE-AGES Asperge, Presage
PREASSE Asperse, Parsees,
   Praeses, Serapes
PREBEND Perbend
PRECAST Carpets, Pre-acts,
   Spectra
PRECENT Per-cent
PRECEPT Percept
PRECISE Piecers, Pierces,
   Recipes, Respice
PRECITE Receipt
PREDATE Pad-tree, Readept,
   Red-tape, Retaped, Tapered

PRE-DAWN Prawned
PREDIAL Lip-read, Pedrail
PREDIES Perseid, Preside,
   Speired
PREDIET Pre-edit
PREDONE Reponed
PRE-EDIT Prediet
PREEING Peering
PREFECT Perfect
PREFORM Perform
PREJINK Perjink
PRELATE Pleater, Replate
PRELATY Apertly, Peartly,
   Pteryla
PRELECT Plectre
PRELIMS Limpers, Rimples,
   Simpler
PRELOSS Plessor, Splores
PREMATE Tampere, Tempera
PREMIER Reprime
PREMISE Empires, Emprise,
   Epimers, Imprese, Spireme
PREMISS Impress, Simpers,
   Persism
PREPAID Drappie
PREPARE Paperer, Repaper
PRESAGE Asperge, Pre-ages
PRESEAL Leapers, Pealers,
   Pleaser, Relapse, Repeals
PRESEES Peeress
PRESELL Respell, Speller
PRESENT Repents, Serpent
PRESHIP Shipper
PRESIDE Perseid, Predies,
   Speired
PRESORT Porrets, Porters,
   Pretors, Reports, Sporter
PRESSED Depress, Spersed
PRESSER Repress
PRESS-UP Suppers
PRESTEA Repaste, Repeats,
   Retapes, Sea-pert
*****PRESTEL** Pelters, Petrels, Spelter,
   Respelt

*PRESTON Postern
PRESUME Supreme
PRE-TEEN Terpene
PRETOLD Droplet
PRETORS Porrets, Porters,
Presort, Reports, Sporter
*PREVERT Pervert
PREVOID Provide
PREWARN Prawner
PREWRAP Wrapper
PREXIES Expires
PRICKLE Pickler
PRIESTS Persist, Spriest, Sprites,
Stirpes, Stripes
PRIEVED Deprive
PRIMAGE Epigram
PRIMSIE Pismire
PRINCES Crespin, Pincers
PRINTER Reprint
PRISAGE Spairge
PRISING Risping, Spiring
PRISTIS Spirits, Tripsis
PROCESS Corpses
PROCTAL Caltrop
PROCURE Crouper
PRODUCE Crouped
PRO-EAST Esparto, Proteas,
Seaport
PRO-ETTE Treetop
PROGENY Pyrogen
PROMISE Imposer
PRONAOS Soprano
PRONATE Operant, Paterno,
Protean
PROOFER Reproof
PROOTIC Portico
PROPERS Prosper
PROPINE Poperin
PROPOSE Opposer
PRORATE Apertor, Patrero,
Praetor
PROSPER Propers
PROTEAN Operant, Paterno,
Pronate

PROTEAS Esparto, Pro-East,
Seaport
PROTEID Diopter, Dioptre,
Peridot
PROTEIN Pointer, Pterion,
Repoint, Tropine
PROTEND Drop-net, Portend
PROTEST Potters, Spotter
*PROTEUS Petrous, Posture,
Pouters, Septuor, Spouter,
Troupes
PROTIST Tropist
PROVIDE Prevoid
PROXIES Siporex
PRUDENT Prunted, Uptrend
PUERIST Requits
PRUNERS Spurner
PRUNTED Prudent, Uptrend
PRUSSIC Scirpus
PRYINGS Springy
PSALMIC Plasmic
PSALTER Palters, Persalt, Plaster,
Platers, Spartel, Stapler
PTARMIC Crampit
PTERION Pointer, Protein,
Repoint, Tropine
PTEROIS Periost, Reposit, Riposte
PTERYLA Apertly, Prelaty,
Peartly
PTOMAIN Maintop, Tampion,
Timpano
PTYALIN Inaptly
PULINGS Pusling
PULLIES Pilules
PULL-OUT Outpull
PULPITS Split-up
PULSATE Petulas, Puteals,
Spatule
PULSING Pulings
PULSION Upsilon
PUNCHER Unperch
PUNIEST Punties
PUNKIES Spunkie
PUNNETS Unspent

PUNSTER Punters
PUNTERS Punster
PUNTIES Puniest
PURITAN Up-train
PURSUED Usurped
PURSUER Usurper
PUSHING Gunship
*PUSHTOO Shoot-up, Upshoot
PUSTULE Pluteus
PUTEALS Petulas, Pulsate,
  Spatule
PUTLOCK Pot-luck
PUTTERS Sputter
PUTTOOS Outpost, Outtops,
  Stop-out
PYRALID Rapidly
PYRITES Stripey
PYROGEN Progeny

QUEERER Requere
QUERIES Esquire
QUERIST Requits
QUESTER Request
QUESTOR Quoters, Roquets,
  Torques
QUIETER Requite
QUINATE Antique
QUINNAT Quintan
QUINTAN Quinnat
QUINTES Inquest
QUOTERS Quester, Roquets,
  Torques

RABATTE Tabaret
RABBETS Barbets, Stabber
RABBLED Dabbler, Drabble
RABBLES Barbels, Slabber
RACEMED Amerced, Creamed
RACEMIC Ceramic
*RACHELS Charles, Larches
RACINGS Sacring, Scaring
RACISTS Sacrist
RACKETS Restack, Retacks,
  Stacker, Tackers

RACKING Arcking, Carking,
  Craking
RADDLES Ladders, Saddler
RADIALE Laridae
RADIANS Sindara
RADIATA Dataria
RADIATE Tiaraed
RADICEL Decrial, Radicle
RADICES Diceras, Sidecar
RADICLE Decrial, Radicel
RAFFISH Haffirs
RAFTING Farting, Ingraft
RAGGLED Draggle, Gargled
RAGINGS Gas-ring, Sirgang
RAGMENT Garment, Margent
RAGTIME Maigret, Migrate
RAG-WEED Edgware, Wagered
RAILAGE Algeria, Lairage,
  Regalia
RAILING Glairin, Lairing
RAILMAN Laminar
RAILMEN Manlier, Marline,
  Mineral, Ramline
RAIMENT Minaret
RAINING Ingrain
RAISING Airings, Arising,
  Sairing
RAKINGS Sarking
RALLIED Dallier, Dialler
RAMBLED Marbled
RAMBLER Marbler
*RAMESES Seamers
*RAMISTS Marists, Tsarism
RAMLINE Manlier, Marline,
  Mineral, Railmen
RAMPANT Mantrap
RAMTILS Mistral
RANCHED Endarch
RANCHES Chenars
RANCING Craning
*RANDERS Darners, Errands
RANGERS Garners
RANGIER Angrier, Earring,
  Grainer, Rearing

RANGING Gnaring
*****RANIDAE** Araneid, Ariadne
RANKEST Tankers
*****RANKINE** Karenni
RANKING Narking
RANKLED Knarled
RAPE-OIL Peloria
RAPIDLY Pyralid
RAPIERS Aspirer, Parries, Praiser, Raspier, Repairs
RAPINES Persian
RAPPELS Lappers, Slapper
RAPTURE Parture
RAREBIT Arbiter
RASHEST Trashes
RASHING Garnish, Sharing
RASORES Soarers
RASPERS Parsers, Sparers, Sparser
RASPIER Aspirer, Parries, Praiser, Rapiers, Repairs
RASPING Parings, Parsing, Sparing
RASURES Assurer
RATABLE Alberta, Latebra
RATBITE Battier, Biretta, Terabit
RATCHED Charted
RATCHEL Trachle, Relatch
RATCHET Chatter
RATHEST Hatters, Shatter, Stareth, Threats
RAT-HOLE Loather
RATINES Nastier, Resiant, Restain, Retains, Retinas, Retsina, Stainer, Starnie, Stearin
RATINGS Gastrin, Gratins, Staring
*****RATITAE** Arietta
RATITES Artiste, Attires, Striate, Tastier
RATLINE Entrail, Latiner, Latrine, Reliant, Retinal, Trenail
RATTEEN Entreat, Ternate
RATTERS Restart, Starter

RATTING Tarting
RATTISH Athirst, Tartish
RATTLES Slatter, Starlet, Startle, Tatlers, Telstar
RATTOON Arnotto, Otranto
RAUNCHY Unchary
RAVINED Invader
RAVINES Servian, Vansire
RAWHEAD Warhead
RAWNESS Answers
RAYLESS Slayers
REACHED Ardeche
REACTED Catered, Cedrate, Cerated, Created
REACTOR Acroter, Creator
READAPT Adapter
READEPT Padtree, Predate, Red-tape, Retaped, Tapered
READERS Redares, Redsear, Rereads
READIES Dearies
READING Areding, Dearing, Deraign, Gradine, Grained,
READOPT Adopter
READORN Adorner
READ-OUT Outarde, Outdare, Outread
REAGENT Grantee, Greaten, Negater
REALIGN Aligner, Engrail, Learing, Nargile, Reginal
REALINE Aliener
REALISE Saliere
REALISM Mailers, Remails
REALIST Alister, Retails, Saltier, Saltire, Slatier, Tailers
REALITY Irately
REALTER Alterer, Relater
REALTIE Atelier
*****REALTOR** Relator
REAMASS Amasser
REAMEND Amender, Enarmed, Meander, Renamed
REAMING Germain

REANNEX Annexer
REAPERS Spearer
REAR-DOS Adorers, Drosera
REARING Angrier, Earring,
Grainer, Rangier
REARMED Dreamer
REASTED Dearest, Derates,
Estrade, Redates
REAVING Ginevra, Vinegar
REBATED Berated, Betread,
Debater
REBATER Terebra
REBATOS Boaster, Boratrs,
Boaters, Sorbate
REBLEND Blender
REBLOCK Blocker
REBLOOM Bloomer
REBOANT Baronet
REBOARD Arbored, Boarder,
Broader
REBOLTS Bolster, Bolters, Lobster
REBOUND Bounder, Unbored,
Unorbed, Unrobed
REBRAND Bernard, Brander
REBREED Breeder
REBRUSH Brusher
REBUILD Builder
RECALKS Calkers, Lackers,
Slacker
RECALLS Callers, Cellars, Scleral
RECASTS Actress, Casters,
Castres
RECEDED Decreed
RECEDES Decrees, Seceder
RECEIPT Precite
RECEPTS Respect, Scepter,
Sceptre, Specter, Spectre
RECHART Charter
RECHATE Cheater, Hectare,
Recheat, Reteach, Teacher
RECHEAT Cheater, Hectare,
Rechate, Reteach, Teacher
RECHECK Checker

RECHOSE Chorees, Coheres,
Echoers
RECIPES Piecers, Pierces, Precise,
Respice
RECITAL Article
RECLAIM Almeric, Carmiel,
Claimer, Miracle
RECLASP Carpels, Clasper,
Parcels, Placers, Scalper
RECLASS Classer, Sarcels, Scalers
RECLEAN Cleaner, Relance
RECLIMB Climber
RECOALS Coalers, Escolar,
Oracles, Solacer
RECOAST Coaster, Coaters,
Recoats
RECOATS Coaster, Coaters,
Recoast
RECOINS Coiners, Crinose,
Cronies, Sericon
RECOLOR Colorer
RECOMBS Combers, Scomber
RECOOLS Coolers, Creosol
RECOUNT Cornute, Counter,
Trounce
RECOVER Coverer
RECRATE Caterer, Retrace,
Terrace
RECROSS Crosser, Scorers,
Scorser
RECROWN Crowner
RECTIFY Certify, Cretify
RECUMBS Cumbers, Scumber
RECURED Reducer
RECURES Rescuer, Securer
RECUSED Cerused, Reducer,
Rescued, Secured, Seducer
REDARES Readers, Red-sear,
Rereads
REDATES Dearest, Derates,
Estrade, Reasted
RED-BOOK Brooked
RED-CAPS Scarped, Scraped
RED-CENT Centred, Credent

RED-COAT Cordate
RED-COCK Crocked
REDDENS Dresden
REDDEST Tedders
BEDDISH Shidder
REDDLES Sledder
REDEALT Alerted, Altered, Delater, Related, Treadle
REDECAY Decayer
REDEEMS Demerse, Emersed
RED-HATS Dearths, Hardest, Hardset, Hatreds, Threads, Trashed
RED-HEAD Adhered
RED-HEAT Earthed, Hearted
RED-LEGS Geldes, Ledgers, Sledger
REDNESS Resends, Senders
REDOING Eroding, Gironde, Groined, Ignored, Negroid
REDORSE Reredos, Rose-red
REDOUBT Doubter, Obtrude, Outbred
REDOUND Rounded, Underdo
REDRAFT Drafter
REDRESS Dresser
REDRIED Deirdre, Derider, Ridered
REDRILL Driller
REDRIVE Deriver
REDROOP Drooper
RED-SEAR Readers, Redares, Rereads
RED-TAIL Dilater, Trailed
RED-TAPE Pad-tree, Predate, Readept, Retaped, Tapered
RED-TOPS Deports, Sported
REDUCER Recured
REDUCES Cerused, Recused, Rescued, Secured, Seducer
REDWING Wringed
REEDILY Yielder
REEDING Dreeing, Energid, Enridge, Reigned

RE-EDITS Reisted, Re-sited
REEFING Feering, Feigner, Freeing
REELING Leering
REEMING Regimen
RE-EMITS Metiers, Retimes, Triseme
RE-ENACT Centare, Crenate
RE-ENDOW Endower
RE-ENJOY Enjoyer
RE-ENTER Enterer, Terreen, Terrene
RE-EQUIP Perique, Repique
RE-ERECT Erecter
REESTED Steered
REEVING Veering
REFACED Defacer
REFILED Defiler, Fielder
REFINED Definer, Enfired
REFINER Reinfer
REFLOAT Floater, Floreat
REFOCUS Focuser
REFOUND Founder
REFRAME Free-arm
REFRESH Fresher
REFUSAL Earfuls, Ferulas, Furseal
REFUSED Defuser
REFUTAL Faulter, Tearful
REGAINS Angries, Erasing, Earings, Gainers, Regians, Reginas, Searing, Seraing, Seringa
REGALIA Algeria, Lairage, Railage
REGALLY Allergy, Gallery, Largely
REGIANS Angries, Erasing, Earings, Gainers, Regains, Reginas, Searing, Seraing, Seringa
REGILDS Gilders, Gliders, Grisled, Lidgers, Ridgels
REGIMEN Reeming

REGIMES Emigres, Remiges
REGINAL Aligner, Engrail,
Learing, Nargile, Realign
REGINAS Angries, Earsing,
Earings, Gainers, Regains,
Regians, Searing, Seraing,
Seringa
REGIONS Eringos, Ignores,
Signore
REGLUED Guelder
REGMATA Margate
REGRAFT Grafter
REGRANT Granter
REGRAPH Grapher
REGRASP Grasper, Sparger
REGRATE Greater
REGREET Greeter
REGRIND Grinder
REGROUP Grouper
REGROWN Wronger
REGULAE Leaguer
REHEADS Adheres, Headers,
Hearsed, Sheared
REHEARD Adherer
REHEARS Hearers, Reshare,
Shearer
REHEATS Heaters, Theresa
REIGNED Dreeing, Energid,
Enridge, Reeding
REIN-ARM Mariner
REINDEX Indexer
REINFER Refiner
REINING Nigrine
REINTER Rentier, Terrine
REISTED Re-edits, Resited
REITERS Etriers, Retires, Retries,
Terries
REIVING Rieving
REJOINT Jointer
REJOLTS Jolters, Jostler
REKNEAD Kneader
REKNITS Inkster, Kirsten,
Stinker, Tinkers
REKNOCK Knocker

RELABEL Labeler
RELACED Cedrela, Cleared,
Creedal, Declare
RELANCE Cleaner, Reclean
RELANDS Darnels, Enlards,
Landers, Slander, Snarled
RELAPSE Leapers, Pealers,
Pleaser, Preseal, Repeals
RELATCH Ratchel, Trachle
RELATED Alerted, Altered,
Delater, Redealt, Treadle
RELATER Alterer, Realter
RELATES Elaters, Laertes, Stealer
RELATOR Realtor
RELAYED Delayer, Layered
RELEARN Learner
RELENDS Lenders, Slender
RELENTS Nestler
RELEVEL Leveler
RELEVER Reveler
RELIANT Entrail, Latiner,
Latrine, Ratline, Retinal, Trenail
RELIEVO Overlie
RELIGHT Lighter
RELIMIT Leitrim, Limiter
RELIVER Reviler
RELIVED Deliver, Livered,
Reviled
RELIVES Leviers, Lievres,
Reviles, Servile, Veilers
RELOADS Loaders, Ordeals, Sea-
lord
RELOANS Loaners, Orleans,
Salerno
RELOVED Lovered
RELOVES Resolve
RELUCTS Cluster, Culters,
Custrel, Cutlers
REMAILS Mailers, Realism
REMAINS Marines, Seminar,
Sirname
REMANET Remeant
REMATCH Matcher

REMBLAI Balmier, Embrail,
Mirabel, Mirable
REMEANT Remanet
REMELTS Melters, Smelter
REMERCY Mercery
REMIGES Emigres, Regimes
REMINTS Entrism, Minster,
Minters
REMIPED Demirep, Epiderm,
Impeder
REMISES Messier
REMNANT Manrent, Rentman
REMODEL Delorme, Modeler
REMOULD Moulder
REMOUNT Monture, Mounter
RENAMED Amender, Enarmed,
Meander, Reamend
****RENAULT** Neutral
RENAYED Deanery, Ne'erday,
Yearned
RENDING Grinned
RENEGED Greened
RENEGER Greener
RENTALS Antlers, Saltern,
Sternal
RENT-DAY Dentary
RENTERS Rerents, Sterner
RENTIER Reinter, Terrine
RENTING Ringent, Ring-net,
Terning
RENT-MAN Manrent, Remnant
RENVOIS Version
RENYING Ginnery
REOFFER Offerer
REORDER Orderer
REPAINT Painter, Patenir,
Pertain, Pine-tar
REPAIRS Aspirer, Parries,
Praiser, Rapiers, Raspier
REPANEL Paneler
REPAPER Paperer, Prepare
REPARKS Parkers, Sparker
REPASTE Prestea, Repeats,
Retapes, Sea-pert

REPATCH Chapter, Patcher
REPAVED Deprave, Pervade
REPAWNS Enwraps, Pawners,
Spawner
REPEALS Leapers, Pealers,
Pleaser, Preseal, Relapse
REPEATS Prestea, Repaste,
Retapes, Sea-pert
REPENTS Present, Serpent
****REPHAIM** Ephraim
REPHASE Reshape, Sphaere
REPINED Dnieper, Ripened
REPINES Erepsin
REPIQUE Perique, Re-equip
REPLACE Percale
REPLAIT Plaiter
REPLANT Pantler, Planter
REPLATE Pleater, Prelate
REPLAYS Parleys, Parsley,
Players, Sparely
REPLEAD Pearled, Pleader
REPLICA Caliper
REPLIES Spieler
REPLUMS Burslem, Lumpers,
Rumples, Slumper
REPOINT Pointer, Protein,
Pterion, Tropine
REPONED Predone
REPORTS Porrets, Porters,
Presort, Pretors, Sporter
REPOSAL Paroles
REPOSED Deposer
REPOSIT Periost, Pterois, Riposte
REPRESS Presser
REPRICE Piercer
REPRIME Premier
REPRINT Printer
REPRISE Perries, Respire
REPROOF Proofer
REPTANT Pattern
REPTILE Perlite
REPUTED Erupted
REPUTES Pertuse
REQUERE Queerer

REQUEST Quester
REQUITE Quieter
REQUITS Querist
RERATED Retrade, Retread, Treader
RERATES Retears, Serrate, Tearers
REREADS Readers, Redares, Redsear
REREDOS Redorse, Rose-read
RERENTS Renters, Sterner
RESAILS Airless, Sailers, Serails, Serials
RESALES Earless, Leasers, Reseals, Sealers
RESCALE Cereals
RESCIND Cinders, Discern
RESCUED Cerused, Recused, Reduces, Rescued, Secured, Seducer
RESCUER Recures, Securer
RESEALS Earless, Leasers, Resales, Sealers
RESEATS Easters, Saeters, Seaters, Teasers, Tessera
RESEAUS Seasure, Ureases
RE-SECTS Cresset, Secrets
RESENDS Redness, Senders
RESENTS Ernests, Nesters, Streens, Strenes
RESERVE Reveres, Reverse, Severer
RESHAKE Harkees
RESHAPE Rephase, Sphaere
RESHARE Hearers, Reshears, Shearer
RESHAVE Heavers
RESHIFT Shifter
RESHINE Inheres, Inherse
RESHOOK Hookers
RESHOOT Hooters, Shooter, Soother
RESIANT Nastier, Ratines, Restain, Retains, Retinas,

Retsina, Stainer, Starnie, Stearin
RESIDED Derides, Desired
RESIDER Derries, Desirer, Dreiser, Serried
RESIDUE Ureides
RESIGHT Sighter
RESIGNS Ingress, Signers, Singers
RESITED Re-edits, Reisted
RESOLVE Reloves
RESOUND Enduros, Oresund, Sounder, Undoers, Unrosed
RESPACE Caprese, Escaper, Percase
RESPEAK Speaker
RESPECT Recepts, Scepter, Sceptre, Specter, Spectre
RE-SPELL Presell, Speller
RE-SPELT Pelters, Petrels, Prestel, Spelter
RESPICE Piecers, Pierces, Precise, Recipes
RESPIRE Perries, Reprise
RESPLIT Spirtle
RESPOND Ponders
RESPRAY Prayers, Sprayer
RESTACK Rackets, Retacks, Stacker, Tackers
RESTAFF Staffer
RESTAGE Ergates
RESTAIN Nastier, Ratines, Resiant, Retains, Retinas, Retsina, Stainer, Starnie, Stearin
RESTAMP Stamper, Tampers
RESTART Ratters, Starter
RESTATE Estreat, Retaste, Tearest
REST-DAY Strayed
RESTFUL Fluster, Fluters
RESTIFF Stiffer
RESTING Stinger
RESTIVE Servite, Veriest
RESTOCK Rockets

RESTUFF Stuffer
RESTYLE Tersely
RESURGE Reurges
RESWEAR Rewears, Swearer,
Wearers
RESWEEP Sweeper, Weepers
RESWELL Sweller
RESWEPT Pewters
RETABLE Bleater
RETACKS Rackets, Restack,
Stacker, Tackers
RETAILS Alister, Realist, Saltier,
Saltire, Slatier, Tailers
RETAINS Nastier, Ratines,
Resiant, Restain, Retinas,
Retsina, Stainer, Starnie, Stearin
RETAKES Sakeret
RETAPED Pad-tree, Predate,
Readept, Red-tape, Tapered
RETAPES Prestea, Repaste,
Repeats, Sea-pert
RETARDS Darters, Starred,
Traders
RETASTE Estreat, Restate, Tearest
RETCHES Chester, Etchers
RETEACH Cheater, Hectare,
Rechate, Recheat, Teacher
RETEARS Rerates, Serrate,
Tearers
RETHANK Thanker
RETHINK Thinker
RETICLE Tiercel
RETILED Tile-red
RETILES Leister, Sterile
RETILLS Rillets, Stiller, Tillers,
Trellis
RETIMED Demerit, Dimeter,
Edremit, Merited, Mitered
RETIMES Metiers, Re-emits,
Triseme
RETINAE Aintree, Trainee
RETINAL Entrail, Latiner,
Latrine, Ratline, Reliant,
Trenail

RETINAS Nastier, Ratines,
Resiant, Restain, Retains,
Retsina, Stainer, Starnie, Stearin
RETINGE Integer, Teering,
Treeing
RETINTS Nitters, Stinter, Tinters
RETINUE Reunite, Uterine
RETIRAL Retrial, Trailer
RETIRED Retried
RETIRER Terrier
RETIRES Etriers, Reiters, Retries,
Terries
RETOAST Rosetta, Rotates,
Toaster, To-tears
RETORTS Rotters, Stertor
RETOTAL Loretta
RETOUCH Toucher
RETOURS Rouster, Routers,
Tourers, Trouser
RETRACE Caterer, Recrate,
Terrace
RETRACK Tracker
RETRADE Rerated, Retread,
Treader
RETRAIN Terrain, Trainer
RETRATE Retreat, Treater
RETREAD Rerated, Retrade,
Treader
RETREAT Retrate, Treater
RETRIAL Retiral, Trailer
RETRIED Retired
RETRIES Etriers, Reiters, Retires,
Terries
RETSINA Nastier, Ratines,
Resiant, Restain, Retains,
Retinas, Stainer, Starnie, Stearin
RETTING Gittern
RETUNED Denture, Untreed
RETUNES Neuters, Tenures,
Tureens, Unterse
RETWIST Twister, Witster,
Witters
REUNITE Retinue, Uterine
REURGES Resurge

REUSING Giresun
REUTTER Utterer
REVEALS Laveers, Leavers,
Several, Vealers
REVELER Relever
REVENUE Unreeve
REVERES Reserve, Reverse,
Severer
REVERSE Reserve, Reveres,
Severer
REVERSI Reviser
REVESTU Versute, Vesture,
REVILED Deliver, Livered,
Relived
REVILER Reliver
REVILES Leviers, Lievres,
Relives, Servile, Veilers
REVISED Derives, Deviser,
Diverse
REVISER Reversi
REVISES Ivresse
REVISIT Visiter
REVOLVE Evolver
REVOTED Devoter
REVOTES Estover, Overset,
Setover, Vetoers
REWAGER Wagerer
REWAKEN Wakener
REWARMS Swarmer, Warmers
REWATER Waterer
REWEARS Reswear, Swearer,
Wearers
REWEIGH Weigher
REWIDEN Widener
REWORDS Sworder
REWOUND Wounder
RHABDUS Burdash
***RHAETIA** Hetaira
***RHAETIC** Theriac
RHODIUM Humidor, Mid-hour
RIBBING Bribing
RIBLESS Birsles
RIBLETS Blister, Bristle
RICHEST Estrich

RICKETS Sickert, Sticker, Tickers
RICKLES Lickers, Sickler, Slicker
RIDABLE Bedrail
RIDDELS Riddles, Slidder
RIDDLED Diddler
RIDDLES Riddels, Slidder
RIDERED Deirdre, Derider,
Redried
RIDGELS Gilders, Girdles,
Gliders, Lidgers, Regilds
RIDGING Girding, Griding
RIEVING Reiving
RIFFING Griffin
RIGHTED Girthed
RIGHT-UP Upright
RILIEVO Oliver
RILLETS Retills, Stiller, Tillers,
Trellis
RIMIEST Miriest, Mistier
RIMLESS Smilers
RIMPLES Limpers, Prelims,
Simpler
RINGENT Renting, Ring-net,
Terning
RINGING Girning
RINGLET Tingler, Tringle
RING-NET Renting, Ringent,
Terning
RIOTERS Roister
RIOTING Ignitor
RIPENED Dnieper, Repined
RIPOSTE Periost, Pterois, Reposit
RIPPLES Lippers, Slipper
RIPPLET Tippler, Tripple
RIPTIDE Dirt-pie, Tiderip
RISKING Girkins, Griskin
RISPING Prising, Spiring
RITUALS Trisula
RIVERET Riveter
RIVETED Tivered
RIVETER Riveret
ROACHES Oraches
ROAD-BED Aborded, Boarded
ROAD-END Adorned

ROADING Adoring, Gordian, Gradino
ROADMAN Mandora, Modrana, Monarda
ROADMEN Maderno
ROAMING Moringa
ROASTED Rosated, Torsade
ROCHETS Hectors, Rotches, Tochers, Torches, Troches
*ROCK-DOE Crooked
ROCKETS Restock
ROCKIER Corkier
ROCKING Corking
ROCK-TAR Tarrock
ROCQUET Croquet
RODENTS Dorsten, Snorted
RODLESS Dorsels, Solders
RODSMEN Moderns
ROGGLED Doggrel
ROGGLES Loggers, Slogger
ROGUING Rouging
ROILING Ligroin
ROISTED Editors, Rosited, Sortied, Steroid, Storied, Tie-rods, Triodes
ROISTER Rioters
*ROLANDS Rosland
ROLL-TOP Trollop
ROMAINE Moraine
ROMANCE Cameron, Cremona, Menorca
*ROMANES Moaners
*ROMANIC Marconi, Minorca
*ROMMANY May-morn
ROMPISH Orphism
RONDEAU Unoared
RONDURE Rounder, Unorder
ROOMAGE Moorage
ROOMING Mooring
ROOSTED Stoored
ROOSTER Rooters, Toreros
ROOTERS Rooster, Toreros
ROOTLET Tootler

ROQUETS Questor, Quoters, Torques
ROSATED Roasted, Torsade
ROSEATE Tea-rose
ROSE-BUG Borgues, Brogues
ROSE-CUT Scouter
ROSEOLA Aerosol
ROSE-RED Redorse, Reredos
ROSETTA Retoast, Rotates, Toaster, To-tears
ROSIEST Sorites, Sorties, Stories
ROSINED Indorse, Sordine
ROSITED Editors, Roisted, Sortied, Steroid, Storied, Tie-rods, Triodes
ROSLAND Rolands
ROTATED Troated
ROTATES Retoast, Rosetta, Toaster, To-tears
ROTCHES Hectors, Rochets, Tochers, Torches, Troches
ROTCHIE Theoric
ROTTERS Retorts, Stertor
ROUGHEN Enrough
ROUGING Roguing
ROULADE Urodela
ROUNDED Redound, Underdo
ROUNDEL Lounder, Roundle
ROUNDER Rondure, Unorder
ROUNDLE Lounder, Roundel
ROUND-UP Unproud
ROUPING Ingroup, Pouring
ROUSANT Santour
ROUSING Souring
ROUSTED Detours, Dourest, Douters, Outreds
ROUSTER Retours, Routers, Tourers, Trouser
ROUTERS Rouster, Retours, Tourers, Trouser
ROUTHIE Out-hire
ROUTING Outgrin, Outring, Touring
ROWDILY Wordily

RUBBLES Burbles, Lubbers, Slubber
RUBELLA Rulable
RUBINES Suberin
RUBYING Burying
RUCKLES Sculker, Suckler
RUFFIAN Funfair
RUINATE Taurine, Uranite, Urinate
RUINERS Insurer
RUINING Inuring
RUINOUS Urinous
RULABLE Rubella
RUMBLED Drumble
RUMBLES Burslem, Lumbers, Slumber, Umbrels
RUMPLES Lumpers, Replums, Slumper
RUNCHED Churned
RUNDALE Arundel, Launder, Lurdane
RUNDLET Trundle
RUN-OVER Overrun
RUSALKA Kursaal
RUSHIER Hurries
RUSSETS Trusses
RUSTLED Lustred, Strudel
RUTHFUL Hurtful
RUTTERS Truster, Turrets
RYE-WOLF Flowery

SABELLA Lasable, Salable
SABINES Bassein
SABRING Barings
SACCADE Cascade
SACKBUT Subtack
SACKING Casking
SACRIFY Scarify
SACRING Racings, Scaring
SACRIST Racists
SADDLED Daddles
SADDLER Ladders, Raddles
SADIRON Dorians, Inroads, Nidaros, Ordains

SAETERS Easters, Reseats, Seaters, Teasers, Tessera
SAFROLE Loafers
SAGE-TEA Sea-gate
SAGGERS Aggress, Seggars
SAIDEST Disseat
SAILERS Airless, Resails, Serails, Serials
SAILING Nilgais
SAINTED Danites, Detains, Instead, Satined, Stained
*****SAINTES** Entasis, Sestina, Staines, Tansies, Tisanes
SAINTLY Nastily
SAIRING Airings, Arising, Raising
*****SAIVITE** Sivaite
SAKERET Retakes
SALABLE Lasable, Sabella
*****SALERNO** Loaners, Orleans, Reloans
SALICET Astelic, Castile, Elastic, Laciest, Latices
SALICIN Sinical
SALIENT Eastlin, Elastin, Entails, Slainte, Staniel, Tenails
SALIERE Realise
SALLIED Dallies, Disleal
SALTERN Antlers, Rentals, Sternal
SALTERN Antlers, Rentals, Sternal
SALTERS Artless, Lasters, Slaters, Tarsels
SALTIER Alister, Realist, Retails, Saltire, Slatier, Tailers
SALTING Anglist, Lasting, Slating, Staling
SALTIRE Alister, Realist, Retails, Saltier, Slatier, Tailers
SALTPAN Platans
SALVAGE Lavages
SALVING Slaving, Valsing

SAMIELS Aimless, Melissa, Mesails, Seismal
SAMIOTE Atomies, Atomise, Osmiate
SAMISEN Inseams
SAMITES Asteism, Matisse, Tamises
*****SAMNITE** Emanist, Inmates, Inmeats, Mista'en, Tamines
SAMOYED Someday
SAMPANS Passman
SAMPIRE Impresa
SAMPLER Lampers, Marples, Palmers
*****SANCTUS** Tuscans
SANDERS Sarsden
SANDIER Arnside, Sardine
SAND-PIT Pandits
SANGRIA Sarangi
SANHITA Shaitan
SANIOUS Suasion
SANTOUR Rousant
SAPERDA Aspread, Parades
SAPIENT Panties, Patines, Spinate
SAPLING Lapsing, Palings, Spaling
SAPOTAS Potassa
SAPPERS Appress
SARANGI Sangria
*****SARAWAK** Arawaks
SARCELS Classer, Reclass, Scalers
SARCINA Acrasin, Arnicas, Carinas
SARCINE Arsenic, Cerasin
SARDINE Arnside, Sandier
*****SARGENT** Garnets, Stanger, Strange
SARKING Rakings
SARMENT Artsmen, Martens, Smarten
SARSDEN Sanders
SATCHEL Chalets, Latches
SATEENS Senates, Sensate

SATIATE Aetatis
SATINED Danites, Detains, Instead, Sainted, Stained
SATINET Instate
SATIRES Tirasse
SATIRIC Iatrics
SATYRAL Astylar
SAUCERS Causers, Cesuras, Sucrase
SAUCIER Uricase
SAUCING Causing
SAUMONT Amounts
*****SAUNDER** Asunder, Danseur
SAUNTER Aunters, Natures, Sea-turn, Tea-urns
SAUSAGE Assuage
SAVINES Vinasse
SAVIOUR Various
SAWBUCK Bucksaw
SAW-GATE Wastage
SAWWHET Wet-wash
SCABIES Abscise,Ecbasis
SCADDLE Scalded
SCALDED Scaddle
SCALDER Cradles
SCALENE Cleanse, Elances, Enlaces
SCALERS Classer, Reclass, Sarcels
SCALPED Clasped
SCALPER Carpels, Clasper, Parcels, Placers, Reclasp
SCAMBLE Becalms
SCAMPED Decamps
SCAMPER Campers
SCANDIA Dacians
SCANNER Canners
SCANTED Decants, Descant
SCANTLE Cantles, Centals, Lancets
SCAPING Pacings, Spacing
SCAPULA Capsula, Pascual
SCARIER Carries
SCARIFY Sacrify
SCARING Racings, Sacring

SCARLET Cartels, Clarets, Tarcels
SCARPED Red-caps, Scraped
SCARPER Carpers, Scraper
SCARRED Carders
SCATOLE Alecost, Lactose, Locates, Talcose
SCENDED Descend
SCENING Censing
SCENTED Descent
SCEPTER Recepts, Respect, Sceptre, Specter, Spectre
SCEPTRE Recepts, Respect, Scepter, Specter,Spectre
*****SCHEELE** Leeches
SCHEMER Chermes
S-CHISEL Chisels
SCHISMA Chiasms
SCHMEAR Marches, Mesarch
SCHOLAR Chorals, Lorchas
SCHOLIA Lochias
SCIARID Cidaris
SCIATIC Ascitic
*****SCIRPUS** Prussic
SCLERAL Callers, Cellars, Recalls
SCOFFER Coffers
SCOLDED Coddles
SCOLLOP Collops
SCOMBER Combers, Recombs
SCOOPER Coopers
SCORERS Crosser, Recross, Scorser
SCORNED Conders, Corsned
SCORNER Corners
SCORSED Crossed
SCORSER Crosser, Recross, Scorers
*****SCOTIAN** Actions, Cations
*****SCOTISM** Cosmist
*****SCOTTIE** Cottise
SCOURED Coursed
SCOURER Courser
SCOURSE Courses, Croesus, Scouser, Sources, Sucrose

SCOUSER Courses, Croesus, Scourse, Sources, Sucrose
SCOUTED Doucets
SCOUTER Rose-cut
SCOWRIE Cowries
SCRAPED Red-caps, Scarped
SCRAPER Carpers, Scarper
SCRAPIE Epacris, Ice-spar, Serapic
SCREECH Creches
SCREICH Scriech
SCREWED Decrews
SCRIECH Screich
SCRIEVE Service
SCRINGE Cringes
SCROTAL Crotals
SCROUGE Scourge
SCRYING Cryings
SCUDDLE Cuddles
SCUDLER Curdles
SCULKER Ruckles, Suckler
SCULLER Cruells, Cullers
SCULPIN Insculp, Unclips
SCUMBER Cumbers, Recumbs
SCUMMER Cummers
SCUNNER Cunners
SCUPPER Cuppers
SCUTTER Cutters
SCUTTLE Cutlets, Cuttles
SDEIGNE Seeding
SEA-BIRD Abiders, Airbeds, Braised, Darbies, Sidebar
SEA-BLUE Sueable
SEA-CARD Arcades
SEA-CORN Carnose, Coarsen, Corneas, Narcose
SEA-FIRE Arefies, Faeries, Freesia
*****SEAFORD** Fedoras
SEA-FOWL Sea-wolf
SEA-FRET Afreets, Fearest, Feaster
SEA-GATE Sage-tea
SEA-GIRT Agister, Aigrets, Gaiters, Stagier, Strigae, Triages

SEAGULL Sullage, Ullages
SEA-KING Sinkage
SEA-LEGS Ageless
SEALERS Earless, Leasers, Resales, Reseals
SEALING Leasing, Linages
SEA-LOCH Oscheal
SEA-LORD Loaders, Ordeals, Reloads
SEA-LUCE Euclase
SEAMERS Rameses
SEA-MILE Mealies
SEAMING Enigmas, Gamines
SEA-MONK Sokeman
SEA-PERT Prestea, Repaste, Repeats, Retapes
SEAPORT Esparto, Pro-east, Proteas
SEARCED Creased, Decares
SEARING Angries, Earings, Erasing, Gainers, Regains, Regians, Reginas, Searing, Seringa
SEA-RISK Kaisers
SEA-SALT Atlases
SEASIDE Disease
SEASURE Reseaus, Ureases
SEA-TERM Steamer
SEATERS Easters, Reseats, Saeters, Teasers, Tessera
SEATING Easting, Gastein, Genista, Ingates, Ingesta, Signate, Tangies, Teasing, Tsigane
SEA-TURN Aunters, Natures, Saunter, Tea-urns
SEA-WOLF Sea-fowl
SECEDER Decrees, Recedes
SECLUDE Culdees
SECONDE Encodes
SECRETA Cerates, Creates, Ecartes
SECRETS Cresset, Re-sects
SECTION Noetics, Notices

SECULAR Cesural
SECURED Cerused, Recused, Reduces, Rescued, Seducer
SECURER Recures, Rescuer
SEDATED Dead-set, Steaded
SEDILIA Dailies
SEDUCED Deduces
SEDUCER Cerused, Recused, Reduces, Rescued, Secured
SEEDILY Eyelids
SEEDING Sdeigne
SEED-OIL Oil-seed
SEEINGS Genesis
SEEKING Skeeing
SEETHED Sheeted
SEETHER Sheeter, Therese
SEGGARS Aggress, Saggers
SEINING Ingines, Insigne
SEISMAL Aimless, Melissa, Mesails, Samiels
*SEKONDI Doeskin
SELACHE Chelsea, Leaches
*SELENGA Senegal
SELENIC License, Silence
SELFIST Stifles
SELL-OUT Outsell
SEMATIC Etacism
SEMILOR Lismore, Moilers,
SEMINAL Isleman, Malines, Menials
SEMINAR Marines, Remains, Sirname
SEMIPED Impedes
SEMI-PRO Imposer, Promise
SEMITAR Artemis, Imarets, Maestri, Maister, Misrate, Smartie
SEMITIC Miscite
SENATES Sensate, Sateens
SENATOR Anteros, Atoners, Nor-east, Treason
SENATUS Austens, Unseats
SENDERS Redness, Resends
SENDING Endings

SEND-OFF Offends
SEND-OUT Outsend, Snouted
SEND-UPS Suspend, Upsends
*SENEGAL Selenga
*SENHORA Hoarsen, Hornsea
SENSATE Sateens, Senates
SENSILE Enisles, Ensiles, Silenes
SENSING Ensigns
SENSISM Messins
SENSUAL Unseals
*SENUSSI Senusis
*SENUSIS Senussi
SEPTATE Spattee
SEPTICS Cess-pit
SEPTIME Empties
SEPTUOR Petrous, Posture,
  Pouters, Proteus, Spouter,
  Troupes
SERAILS Airless, Resails, Sailers,
  Serials
*SERAING Angries, Earings,
  Erasing, Gainers, Regains,
  Regians, Reginas, Searing,
  Seringa
SERAPES Sperse, Parsees,
  Preases, Preasse
*SERAPIC Epacris, Ice-spar,
  Scrapie
*SERAPIS Aspires, Paresis,
  Praises, Spireas
SERENED Needers, Sneered
SERENER Sneerer
SERFDOM Deforms
SERFISH Fishers, Sherifs
*SERVIAN Ravines, Vansire
SERIALS Airless, Resails, Sailers,
  Serails
SERICIN Irenics, Sirenic
SERICON Coiners, Crinose,
  Cronies, Recoins
SERINGA Angries, Earings,
  Erasing, Gainers, Regains,
  Regians, Reginas, Searing,
  Seraing

SERINUS Insures, Sunrise
SERPENT Present, Repents
SERPIGO Porgies
SERPULA Perusal
SERRATE Rerates, Retears,
  Tearers
SERRIED Derries, Desirer,
  Dreiser, Resider
SERVAGE Greaves
SERVICE Scrieve
SERVILE Leviers, Lievres,
  Relives, Reviles, Veilers
SERVING Versing
*SERVITE Restive, Veriest
SESELIS Sessile
SESOTHO Soothes
SESSILE Seselis
SESSION Essoins
SESTINA Entasis, Tisanes
SESTOLE Toeless
SET-BACK Backset, Backets
SET-LINE Tensile
SETOVER Estover, Overset,
  Revotes, Vetoers
SETTERS Streets, Tersest, Testers
SETTING Testing
SETTLER Letters, Sterlet, Trestle
SETTLOR Slottler
SETWALL Swallet, Wallets
SEVERAL Laveers, Leavers,
  Reveals, Vealers
SEVERED Deserve
SEVERER Reserve, Reveres,
  Reverse
SEXTAIN Antisex
SEXTERN Ex-terns
SHACKLE Hackles
SHADIER Hardies
SHADILY Ladyish
SHADING Dashing
SHAFTER Fathers
SHAITAN Sanhita
SHAKING Kashing
SHALLOW Hallows

SHAMBLE Hambles
SHAMERS Mashers, Smasher
SHAMING Mashing
SHAMMER Hammers
SHANGTI Anights, Hasting Tashing
SHANKER Hankers, Harkens
SHAPING Hasping, Pashing, Phasing
SHARING Garnish, Rashing
SHARKER Harkers
SHARPED Phrased
SHARPER Harpers, Phraser
SHATTER Hatters, Rathest, Stareth, Threats
SHAVING Havings
SHEARED Adheres, Headers, Hearsed, Reheads
SHEARER Hearers, Rehears, Reshare
SHEETED Seethed
SHEETER Seether, Therese
SHE-GOAT He-goats, Hostage
SHELLER Hellers
SHERIAT Hastier
SHERIFS Fishers, Serfish
SHEWING Hewings, Whinges
SHICKER Skreich, Skriech
SHIDDER Reddish
SHIFTER Reshift
SHINDIG Dishing, Hidings
SHINGLE English
SHIPLAP Lappish, Palship
SHIPPER Preship
SHITING Insight
SHOCKER Chokers, Hockers
SHOOTER Hooters, Reshoot, Soother
SHOOT-UP Pushtoo, Upshoot
SHOPPER Hoppers
SHORING Horsing
SHORTED Dehorts
SHORTEN Hornets, Threnos, Thrones

SHORTIA Thorias
SHORTIE Hoister
SHOTGUN Gunshot, Hognuts, Noughts
SHOUTED Southed
SHOUTER Souther
SHRINED Hinders
SHRIVED Dervish
SHROUDY Hydrous
SHUNTER Hunters
SHYCOCK Cockshy
SHYSTER Thyrses
SIAMANG Gas-main, Magians
*SIAMESE Misease
*SICKERT Rickets, Sticker, Tickers
SICKLED Slicked
SICKLER Lickers, Rickles, Slicker
SIDEARM Admires, Misread
SIDEBAR Abiders, Air-beds, Braised, Darbies, Sea-bird
SIDECAR Diceras, Radices
SIDEMAN Demains, Maidens, Mandies, Medians
SIDERAL Derails
SIDEWAY Wayside
SIDLING Sliding
SIEMENS Meissen, Misseen, Nemesis
SIFTING Fisting
SIGHTER Resight
SIGNARY Syringa
SIGNATE Easting, Gastein, Genista, Ingates, Ingesta, Seating, Tangies, Teasing, Tsigane
SIGNERS Ingress, Resigns, Singers
SIGNING Singing
SIGNIOR Origins
*SIGNORA Ignaros, Origans, Soaring
*SIGNORE Eringos, Ignores, Regions
SILENCE License, Selenic

SILENES Enisles, Ensiles, Sensile
SILENUS Insulse
SILICAS Liassic
SILOING Oilings, Soiling
SILTING Listing
SIMARRE Marries
SIMILES Missile
SIMOONS Monosis
SIMPERS Impress, Persism,
  Premiss
SIMPLED Dimples
SIMPLER Limpers, Prelims,
  Rimples
*SINATRA Antiars, Artisan,
  Tsarina
SINCERE Ceresin, Cerines
*SINDARA Radians
SINEWED Endwise
SINGERS Ingress, Resigns,
  Signers
SINGING Signing
SINGLED Dingles, Engilds
SINGLER Girnels, Lingers,
  Slinger
SINGLES Lessing
SINGLET Glisten, Lingets,
  Tingles
SINGULT Glutins, Lusting,
  Lutings, Sutling
SINICAL Salicin
SINKAGE Sea-king
SINNING Innings, Inn-sign
SINOPER Orpines
SINUATE Aunties
SIPHONS Sonship
SIPOREX Proxies
SIPPLED Slipped
SIRENIC Irenics, Sericin
SIRGANT Gas-ring, Ragings
SIRNAME Marines, Remains,
  Seminar
SISTRUM Trismus, Truisms
*SITTANG Stating, Tasting
SITTARS Artists, Straits, Tsarist

SITTINE Tiniest, Tinties
SITUATE Usitate
SIT-UPON Outspin, Spin-out
*SIVAITE Saivite
SKATING Staking, Takings,
  Tasking
SKEEING Seeking
SKELTER Kestrel
SKEPTIC Pickets
SKID-PAN Kidnaps
SKIINGS Kissing
SKILLED Deskill
SKIMMER Kimmers
SKIPPER Kippers
SKIRRET Skirter, Striker
SKIRTER Skirret, Striker
SKITTLE Kittles
SKIVING Vikings
SKREICH Shicker, Skriech
SKRIECH Shicker, Skreich
SLABBED Dabbles
SLABBER Barbels, Rabbles
SLACKER Calkers, Lackers,
  Recalks
SLAGGED Daggles
SLAINTE Eastlin, Elastin, Entails,
  Salient, Staniel, Tenails
SLAMKIN Malkins
SLANDER Darnels, Enlards,
  Landers, Relands, Snarled
SLANGED Dangles
SLANTED Dentals, Standel,
  Stendal
SLAPPED Dapples
SLAPPER Lappers, Rappels
SLASHED Hassled
SLASHER Ashlers, Lashers
SLASHES Hassles
SLATERS Artless, Lasters, Salters,
  Tarsels
SLATHER Halters, Harslet,
  Hastler, Herstal, Lathers,
  Thalers

SLATIER Alister, Realist, Retails, Saltier, Saltire, Tailers

SLATING Anglist, Lasting, Salting, Staling

SLATTER Rattles, Starlet, Startle, Tatlers, Telstar

SLAVING Salving, Valsing

SLAYERS Rayless

SLAYING Layings

SLEDDER Reddles

SLEDGER Gelders, Ledgers, Red-legs

SLEEKER Keelers

SLEEPER Peelers, Speeler

SLEEP-IN Espinel, Pensile

SLEETED Deletes, Steeled

SLENDER Lenders, Relends

SLEWING Swingel, Swingle

SLICKED Sickled

SLICKEN Nickels

SLICKER Lickers, Rickles, Sickler

SLIDDEN Dindles

SLIDDER Riddels, Riddles

SLIDING Sidling

SLIMIER Milreis

SLIMING Lingism, Smiling

SLINGER Girnels, Lingers, Singler

SLIPPED Sippled

SLIPPER Lippers, Ripples

SLITHER Hitlers

SLITTER Litters, Stilter, Testril, Tilters, Titlers

SLOBBER Lobbers

SLOCKEN Enlocks

SLOE-GIN Eloigns, Legions, Lignose, Lingoes

SLOGGED Dog-legs

SLOGGER Loggers, Roggles

SLOTTED Dottles

SLOTTER Settlor

SLOWING Lowings, Sowling

SLUBBER Burbles, Lubbers, Rubbles

SLUGGER Gurgles, Luggers

SLUICES Celsius

SLUMBER Burslem, Lumbers, Rumbles, Umbrels

SLUMISM Muslims

SLUMPED Dumples

SLUMPER Lumpers, Replums, Rumples

SMARAGO Margosa

SMARTEN Artsmen, Martens, Sarment

SMARTER Armrest

SMARTIE Artemis, Imarets, Maestri, Maister, Misrate, Semitar

SMASHER Mashers, Shamers

SMATTER Matters

SMELTER Melters, Remelts

SMERLIN Limners, Merlins

SMILERS Rimless

SMILING Lingism, Sliming

SMITING Misting, Stiming, Timings

SMITTEN Mittens

SMOKIER Irksome

SMOLDER Molders

SMOTHER Mothers, Thermos

SMOUSER Mousers

SMURRED Murders

SMUGGER Muggers

SMYTRIE Mistery

SNAGGER Gangers, Granges, Naggers

SNAILED Denials, Lead-ins

SNAPPED Appends

SNAPPER Nappers, Parsnep, Parpens

SNARLED Darnels, Enlards, Landers, Relands, Slander

SNEAK-UP Unspeak

SNEAPED Speaned

SNEERED Needers, Serened

SNEERER Serener

SNICKED Dickens

SNICKER Nickers
SNIFFLE Niffles
SNIGGER Gingers, Niggers
SNIGGLE Gingles, Niggles
SNIPING Pinings
SNIPPER Nippers
SNIRTLE Linters
SNOFARI Insofar
SNOOPED Spooned
SNOOPER Spooner
SNORING Sorning
SNORTED Dorsten, Rodents
SNOTTER Stentor, Torsten
SNOUTED Outsend, Send-out
SNUZZLE Nuzzles
SOARERS Rasores
SOARING Ignaros, Origans,
   Signora
SOBBING Gibbons
SOCAGER Cargoes, Corsage
*****SOCINUS** Cousins
SOCKING Gosnick
SODAINE Adonise, Anodise,
   Diasone
SODDENS Oddnes
SOILING Oilings, Siloing
SOILURE Lousier
SOKEMAN Sea-monk
SOLACER Coalers, Escolar,
   Oracles, Recoals
SOLDERS Dorsels, Rodless
SOLDIER Solider
SOLICIT Colitis
SOLIDER Soldier
SOLIDUS Dulosis
*****SOLIMAN** Malison, Monials,
   Osmanli, Somnial
SOLIPED Despoil, Dipoles,
   Diploes, Peloids, Spoiled
SOLUBLE Lobules
SOMATIC Atomics
SOMEDAY Samoyed
SOMITIC Mistico

SOMNIAL Malison, Monials,
   Osmanli, Soliman
SONANCE Ancones
SONDELI Dolines, Leonids
*****SONDRIO** Indoors, Sordino
SONLESS Lessons
SONNETS Stenson, Tensons
*****SONNITE** Intones, Tension
SONSHIP Siphons
SOOLING Loosing, Olingos
SOOTHES Sesotho
SOOTHER Hooters, Reshoot,
   Shooter
SOPRANI Parison
SOPRANO Pronaos
SORBATE Boaster, Boaters,
   Borates, Rebatos
SORDINE Indorse, Rosined
SORDINO Indoors, Sondrio
SOREHON Onshore
SORITES Rosiest, Sorties, Stories
SORNING Snoring
SOROCHE Chooser
SORTIED Editors, Roisted,
   Rosited, Steroid, Storied,
   Tie-rods, Triodes
SORTIES Rosiest, Sorites, Stories
SORTING Storing, Trigons
SOUCHET Touches
SOUNDER Enduros, Oresund,
   Resound, Undoers, Unrosed
SOUPCON Coupons, Uncoops
SOURCES Courses, Croesus,
   Scourse, Scouser, Sucrose
SOUREST Estrous, Oestrus,
   Ousters, Souters, Tousers,
   Trouses, Trousse, Tussore
SOURING Rousing
SOUTERS Estrous, Oestrus,
   Ousters, Sourest, Tousers,
   Trouses, Trousse, Tussore
SOUTHED Shouted
SOUTHER Shouter
SOVIETS Stovied

SOWLING Lowings, Slowing
SPACING Pacings, Scaping
SPADDLE Paddles
SPAIRGE Prisage
SPALING Lapsing, Palings, Sapling
SPANCEL Enclasp
SPANIEL Alpines
SPANNER Panners
SPARELY Parleys, Parsley, Players, Replays
SPARERS Parsers, Raspers, Sparser
SPARGED Grasped
SPARGER Grasper, Regrasp
SPARING Parings, Parsing, Rasping
SPARKER Parkers, Reparks
SPARRED Drapers
SPARSER Parsers, Raspers, Sparers
SPARTAN Partans, Tarpans, Trapans
*SPARTEL Palters, Persalt, Plaster, Platers, Psalter, Stapler
SPATHED Heptads, T-shaped
SPATHIC Haptics
SPATTEE Septate
SPATTER Patters, Tapster
SPATTLE Pattles, Peltast
SPATULE Petulas, Pulsate, Puteals
SPAWNER Enwraps, Pawners, Repawns
SPEAKER Respeak
SPEANED Sneaped
SPEARER Reapers
SPECTER Recepts, Respect, Scepter, Sceptre, Spectre
SPECTRA Carpets, Pre-acts, Precast
SPECTRE Recepts, Respect, Scepter, Sceptre, Specter
SPECULA Capsule, Lace-ups

SPEEDER Speered
SPEELER Peelers, Sleeper
SPEERED Speeder
SPEIRED Perseid, Predies, Preside
SPELDIN Spindle, Splined
SPELLER Presell, Respell
SPELTER Pelters, Petrels, Prestel, Respelt
SPERSED Depress, Pressed
SPERTHE Hepster
SPHAERE Rephase, Reshape
SPHENIC Pinches
SPHERAL Plasher
SPHERIC Ceriphs, Ciphers
SPICATE Aseptic
SPIELER Replies
SPIGNEL Leg-spin, Pingles, Pin-legs
SPIKING Pigskin
SPILING Lisping, Pilings
SPINATE Panties, Patines, Sapient
SPINDLE Speldin, Splined
SPINETS Insteps, Step-ins
SPINIER Inspire, Pirnies
SPINNER Pinners
SPINNET Tenpins, Pinnets
SPINODE Dispone
SPIN-OFF Off-spin
SPINOUS Poussin
SPIN-OUT Outspin, Sit-upon
SPINULE Line-ups, Lupines, Unpiles, Up-lines
SPIRANT Spraint
SPIREAS Aspires, Paresis, Praises, Serapis
SPIREME Empires, Emprise, Epimers, Imprese, Premise
SPIRING Prising, Risping
SPIRITS Pristis, Tripsis
SPIRTED Striped
SPIRTLE Resplit
SPITTER Pitters, Tipster

SPLENIC Pencils
SPLINED Speldin, Spindle
SPLIT-UP Pulpits
SPLORES Plessor, Pre-loss
SPOILED Despoil, Dipoles,
  Diploes, Peloids, Soliped
SPONDEE Despone
SPOOLED Poodles
SPOOLER Loopers
SPOONED Snooped
*SPOONER Snooper
SPORTED Deports, Red-tops
SPORTER Porrets, Porters,
  Presort, Pretors, Reports
SPORULE Leprous, Pelorus,
  Perlous
SPOTTER Potters, Protest
SPOUTER Petrous, Posture,
  Pouters, Proteus, Septuor,
  Troupes
SPRAINT Spirant
SPRAYER Prayers, Respray
SPREADS Adpress
SPRIEST Persist, Priests, Sprites,
  Stirpes, Stripes
SPRINGE Pingers
SPRINGY Pryings
SPRITES Persist, Priests, Spriest,
  Stirpes, Stripes
SPRUCES Percuss
SPUMING Impugns
SPUNKIE Punkies
SPURIAE Pireaus, Upraise
SPURNER Pruners
SPUTTER Putters
STABBED Tebbads
STABBER Barbets, Rabbets
STABILE Astilbe, Bastile, Bestial,
  Blastie
STABLED Baldest, Blasted
STABLER Alberts, Blaster,
  Labrets, Tablers
STACKER Rackets, Restack,
  Retacks, Tackers

STACKET Tackets
STADIUM Dumaist
STAFFER Restaff
STAGGED Gadgets
STAGGER Gagster, Gargets,
  Taggers
STAGIER Agister, Aigrets,
  Gaiters, Sea-girt, Strigae, Triages
STAGING Gatings
STAIDER Ardites, Asterid,
  Astride, Diaster, Disrate, Staired,
  Tirades
STAINED Danites, Detains,
  Instead, Sainted, Satined
STAINER Nastier, Ratines,
  Resiant, Restain, Retains,
  Retinas, Retsina, Stanrie, Stearin
*STAINES Entasis, Saintes,
  Sestina, Tansies, Tisanes
STAIRED Ardites, Asterid,
  Astride, Diaster, Disrate, Staider,
  Tirades
STAITHE Atheist
STAKING Skating, Takings,
  Tasking
STALING Anglist, Lasting,
  Salting, Slating
*STALINO Talions
STALKER Talkers
STAMPER Restamp, Tampers
STANDEE East-end
STANDEL Dentals, Slanted,
  Stendal
STANDER Endarts
STAND-UP Dust-pan, Upstand,
*STANGER Garnets, Sargent,
  Strange
STANIEL Eastlin, Elastin, Entails,
  Salient, Slainte, Tenails
STANNIC Tin-cans
STAPLER Palters, Persalt, Plaster,
  Platers, Psalter, Spartel
STARDOM Tsardom

STARETH Hatters,
Rathest,Shatter, Threats
STARING Gastrin, Gratins,
Ratings
STARLET Rattles, Slatter, Startle,
Tatlers, Telstar
STAR-MAN Artsman, Mansart,
Mantras
STARNIE Nastier, Ratines,
Resiant, Restain, Retains,
Retinas, Retsina, Stainer, Stearin
STARRED Darters, Retards,
Traders
STARTED Tetrads
STARTER Ratters, Restart
STARTLE Rattles, Slatter, Starlet,
Tatlers, Telstar
STARVED Adverts
STATING Sittang, Tasting
STATURE Steuart
STAUNCH Canthus, Chaunts
STAYING Stygian
STEADED Dead-set, Sedated
STEALER Elaters, Laertes, Relates
STEADED Dead-set, Sedated
STEAMER Sea-term
STEARIN Nastier, Ratines,
Resiant, Restain, Retains,
Retinas, Retsina, Stainer, Starnie
STEELED Deletes, Sleeted
STEEPED Deepest
STEEPEN Ensteep
STEEPER Estrepe
STEERED Reested
*STEINER Entires, Entries,
Teniers, Trenise
*STELVIO Violets
STEMLET Mettles
STEMPEL Pelmets, Stemple,
Temples
STEMPLE Pelmets, Stempel,
Temples
STENCIL Clients
*STENDAL Dentals, Slanted,

Standel
*STENSON Sonnets, Tensons
STENTOR Snotter, Torsten
STEP-INS Insteps, Spinets
STEP-OFF Off-step
STEREOS Orestes, Osseter
STERILE Leister, Retiles
STERLET Letters, Settler, Trestle
STERNAL Antlers, Rentals,
Saltern
STERNED Tenders
STERNER Renters, Rerents
STERNUM Munster
STEROID Editors, Roisted,
Rosited, Sortied, Storied, Tie-
rods, Triodes
STERTOR Retorts, Rotters
STETSON Ostents
*STEUART Stature
STEVING Vesting
STEWARD Strawed
STEWART Swatter, Tewarts
STEWING Twinges, Westing
STEW-POT Two-step
STHENIC Ethnics
STICKER Rickets, Sickert, Tickers
STICKLE Tickles
STIFFEN Infefts
STIFFER Restiff
STIFLER Filters, Lifters, Trifles
STIFLES Selfist
STILLER Retills, Rillets, Tillers,
Trellis
STILTER Litters, Slitter, Testril,
Tilters, Titlers
STIMIED Misdiet
STIMING Misting, Smiting,
Timings
*STIMSON Monists
STINGER Resting
STINKER Inkster, Kirsten,
Reknits, Tinkers
STINTED Dentist, Distent

STINTER Entrist, Nitters, Retints, Tinters
STIPPLE Tipples
STIPULA Tipulas
STIRPES Persist, Priests, Spriest, Sprites, Stripes
STIRRED Strider
STIVERS Strives, Treviss, Verists
STOCKED Dockets
STONILY Tylosin
STONING Notings
STOOLIE Oolites, Ostiole
STOOPER Poorest, Pooters
STOORED Roosted
STOOTER Tooters
STOPING Posting
STOP-OUT Outpost, Outtops, Puttoos
STOPPER Popster, Toppers
STOPPLE Topples
STORAGE Orgeats, Tagsore
STORIED Editors, Steroid, Tie-rods, Triodes
STORIES Rosiest, Sorites, Sorties
STORING Sorting, Trigons
STORMER Termors, Tremors
STOTTER Stretto, Totters
STOUTER Outsert, Touters
STOVIES Soviets
STOVING Votings
STOWAGE Towages
STOWING Towsing, Wigston
STRAITS Artists, Sittars, Tsarist
STRANGE Garnets, Gerants, Sargent, Stanger
STRAP-ON Partons, Patrons, Tarpons
STRAWED Steward
STRAYED Rest-day
STREAMY Mastery, Mayster
STREENS Ernests, Nesters, Resents, Strenes
STREETS Setters, Tersest, Testers

STRENES Ernests, Nesters, Resents, Streens
STRETTA Tatters
STRETTO Stotter, Totters
STREWED Wrested
STREWER Wrester
STRIATE Artiste, Attires, Ratites, Tastier
STRIDER Stirred
STRIDES Dissert
STRIGAE Agister, Aigrets, Gaiters, Sea-girt, Stagier, Triages
*****STRIGES** Tigress
STRIKER Skirret, Skirter
STRIPED Spirted
STRIPES Persist, Priests, Spriest, Sprites, Stirpes
STRIPEY Pyrites
STRIVED Diverts
STRIVEN Inverts, Ventris
STRIVES Stivers, Treviss, Verists
STROAMS Matross
STRODLE Oldster
STROPHE Pothers, Thorpes
STROWED Worsted
STRUDEL Lustred, Rustled
STRUMAE Matures
STUDDIE Studied
STUDENT Stunted
STUDIED Dustier
STUDIER Dustier
STUFFER Restuff
STUMBLE Tumbles
STUMPER Sumpter
STUNNER Unstern
STUNTED Student
*****STURNUS** Untruss
STURTED Trusted
*****STYGIAN** Staying
STYLITE Testily
STYRENE Yestern
SUASION Sanious
SUBBING Gubbins
SUBEDAR Daubers

SUBERIN Rubines
SUB-KING Busking
SUBLIME Bus-mile
SUB-ORAL Labours
SUBSIGN Bussing
SUBTACK Sackbut
SUBTLER Bluster, Brustle, Bustler, Butlers
SUCCADE Accused
SUCKLER Ruckles, Sculker
SUCRASE Causers, Cesuras, Saucers
SUCRIER Cruiser, Curries
SUCROSE Courses, Croesus, Scourse, Scouser, Sources
SUCTION Cotinus, Unstoic
SUDAMEN Medusan
SUEABLE Sea-blue
SULLAGE Seagull, Ullages
SULLIED Illudes, Illused
SULLIES Illuses
SULTANE Unslate
SUMLESS Mussels
SUMMIST Summits
SUMMITS Summist
SUMPTER Stumper
SUNBEAR Unbares, Unbears
SUNBEAT Butanes
SUNDARI Drusian, Durians
SUNDERS Undress
SUNNITE Tunnies
SUNRISE Insures, Serinus
SUNROOF Unroofs
SUNROOM Unmoors
SUNSPOT Unstops
SUNTRAP Unstrap
SUNWARD Undraws
SUPPERS Press-up
SUPPING Uppings
SUPREME Presume
SURBASE Abusers
SURFIER Friseur, Frisure
***SURINAM** Uranism
SURMISE Misuser, Mussier

SURNAME Manures
SUSPEND Send-ups, Upsends
SUSPIRE Uprises
SUSTAIN Issuant
SUTLING Glutins, Lusting, Lutings, Singult
SWADDLE Dawdles, Waddles
SWAGING Wagings
SWALLET Setwall, Wallets
SWALLOW Wallows
SWANKER Wankers
SWARMER Rewarms, Warmers
SWASHER Hawsers, Washers
SWATTER Stewart, Tewarts
SWEARER Reswear, Rewears, Wearers
SWEDISH Swished, Whissed
SWEEPER Resweep, Weepers
SWEERED Weeders
SWELLER Reswell
SWELTER Welters, Wrestle
SWILLER Willers
SWINDLE Windles
SWINGEL Slewing, Swingle
SWINGER Wingers
SWINGLE Slewing, Swingel
SWINKER Winkers
SWISHED Swedish, Whissed
SWISHER Wishers
SWISHES Whisses
SWITHER Withers, Writhes
SWORDER Rewords
SYRINGA Signary
SYSTOLE Tyloses

TABARDS Bastard
TABARET Rabatte
***TABITHA** Habitat
TABLEAU Tabulae
TABLERS Alberts, Blaster, Labrets, Stabler
TABLIER Alberti, Librate, Triable, Trilabe
TABORED Aborted, Borated

TABORER Aborter, Arboret
TABORET Abettor
TABULAE Tableau
TACHISM Mastich
TACHIST Cattish
TACITLY Cattily
TACKERS Rackets, Restack, Retacks, Stacker
TACKETS Stacket
TACKLED Talcked
TACTILE Lattice, Talcite
TAGETES Gestate
TAGGERS Gagster, Gargets, Stagger
TAGSORE Orgeats, Storage
TAIGLED Ligated
TAILERS Alister, Realist, Retails, Saltier, Saltire, Slatier
TAILLES Liestal, Tallies
TAKE-OFF Off-take
TAKE-OUT Out-take
TAKINGS Skating, Staking, Tasking
TALCITE Lattice, Tactile
TALCKED Tackled
TALCOSE Alecost, Lactose, Locates, Scatole
TALCOUS Locusta
TALIONS Stalino
TALIPED Plaited
TALIPES Aplites
TALKERS Stalker
TALLAGE Gallate
TALLIER Literal
TALLIES Liestal, Tailles
TALLY-HO Loathly
TAMALES Malates, Maltase
TAMARIN Martian, Martina
TAMINES Emanist, Inmates, Inmeats, Mista'en, Samnite
TAMISES Asteism, Matisse, Samites
TAMMIES Mismate

TAMPERE Premate, Tempera
TAMPERS Restamp, Stamper
***TAMPICO** Potamic
TAMPION Maintop, Ptomain, Timpano
TAMPONS Postman, Topsman
***TANCRED** Cantred, Tranced
TANGENT Gnat-net
***TANGIER** Geraint, Granite, Ingrate, Tearing
TANGIES Easting, Gastein, Genista, Ingates, Ingesta, Seating, Signate, Teasing, Tsigane
TANGING Ganting
TANGLER Trangle
TANGRAM Trangam
TANKERS Rankest
TANNERY Tyranne
TAN-OOZE Entozoa
TANRIDE Anti-red, Detrain, Trade-in, Trained
TANTARA Tartana
TAPERED Pad-tree, Predate, Readept, Red-tape, Retaped
TAPLASH Asphalt
TAP-SHOE Tea-shop
TAPSTER Patters, Spatter
TARCELS Cartels, Clarets, Scarlet
TARDIER Tarried
TARGING Grating
TAR-HEEL Leather
TARPONS Partons, Patrons, Strap-on
TARRIED Tardier
TARRIES Tarsier
TARROCK Rock-tar
TAR-SAND Astrand
TARSELS Artless, Lasters, Salters, Slaters
TARSIER Tarries
TARTANA Tantara
TARTINE Intreat, Iterant, Nattier, Nitrate, Tertian

TARTING Ratting
TARTISH Athirst, Rattish
TARTLET Tattler
TARWEED Dewater, Watered
TASHING Anights, Hasting, Shangti
TASKING Skating, Staking, Takings
TASTIER Artiste, Attires, Ratites, Striate
TASTING Stating, Sittang
TATLERS Rattles, Slatter, Starlet, Startle, Telstar
TATTERS Stretta
TATTIER Attrite, Titrate
TATTLER Tartlet
TAUNTED Attuned, Nutated
TAURINE Ruinate, Uranite, Urinate
TAUTENS Attunes, Nutates, Tetanus, Unstate
TAVERED Averted
TAVERNS Servant, Versant
TAWNIER Tinware
TEA-BARS Abaters, Abreast
TEACHER Cheater, Hectare, Rechate, Recheat, Reteach
TEACHES Escheat
TEACHIE Hicatec
TEACH-IN Chantie
TEACUPS Cuspate
TEALESS Altesse, Teasels
TEAMING Mintage, Tegmina
TEARERS Rerates, Retears, Serrate
TEAREST Estreat, Restate, Retaste
TEARETH Theater, Theatre, Thereat
TEARFUL Faulter, Refutal
TEARING Geraint, Granite, Ingrate, Tangier
TEA-ROSE Roseate
TEARPIT Partite
TEASELS Altesse, Tealess

TEASERS Easters, Reseats, Saeters, Seaters, Tessera
TEA-SHOP Tap-shoe
TEASING Easting, Gastein, Genista, Ingates, Ingesta, Seating, Signate, Tangies, Tsigane
TEA-URNS Aunters, Natures, Saunter, Sea-turn
TEBBADS Stabbed
TEDDERS Reddest
TEDESCO Cestode
TEDIOUS Outside
TEEMING Meeting
TEERING Integer, Retinge, Treeing
TEGMINA Mintage, Teaming
*****TEHERAN** Earneth, Earthen, Hearten, Neareth
TELAMON Lomenta, Omental
TELECAR Electra, Treacle
*****TELERAN** Alterne, Enteral, Eternal
TELESIS Tieless
*****TELSTAR** Rattles, Slatter, Starlet, Startle, Tatlers
TEMPEAN Peteman
TEMPERA Premate, Tampere
TEMPLAR Trample
TEMPLES Pelmets, Stempel, Stemple
TENABLE Beltane
TENAILS Eastlin, Elastin, Entails, Salient, Slainte, Staniel
TENDERS Sterned
TENDING Denting
TENDRIL Trindle
*****TENEDOS** Denotes
*****TENIERS** Entires, Entries, Steiner, Trenise
TENIOID Edition
TENONED Edenton
TENONER Enteron
TEN-PINS Pinnets, Spinnet

TENSELY Enstyle
TENSILE Set-line, Spinnet
TENSING Nesting
TENSION Intones, Sonnite
TENSONS Sonnets, Stenson
TEN-SPOT Potents
TENTERS Testern
TENTING Netting
TENURES Neuters, Retunes,
 Tureens, Unterse
TEQUILA Liquate
TERBIUM Imbrute
TERCINE Citrene, Enteric, Enticer
TEREBRA Rebater
TEREDOS Oersted
TEREFAH Feareth, Feather
TERMINI Interim, Mintier
TERMITE Emitter
TERMORS Stormer, Tremors
TERNATE Entreat, Ratteen
TERNING Renting, Ringent,
 Ring-net
TERNION Intoner
TERPENE Pre-teen
TERRACE Caterer, Recrate,
 Retrace
TERRAIN Retrain, Trainer
TERREEN Enterer, Re-enter,
 Terrene
TERRENE Enterer, Re-enter,
 Terreen
TERRIER Retirer
TERRIES Etriers, Reiters, Retires,
 Retries
TERRINE Reinter, Rentier
TERSEST Setters, Streets, Testers
TERSION Triones
TESSERA Easters, Reseats,
 Saeters, Seaters, Teasers
TERTIAN Intreat, Iterant, Nattier,
 Nitrate, Tartine
TEST-BAN Battens
TESTERN Tenters
TESTERS Setters, Streets, Tersest

TESTIER Trieste
TESTILY Stylite
TESTING Setting
TESTRIL Litters, Slitter, Stilter,
 Tilters, Titlers
TESTUDO Duettos
TETANIC Nictate
TETANUS Attunes, Nutates,
 Tautens, Unstate
TEWARTS Stewart, Swatter
TETRADS Started
THALERS Halters, Harslet,
 Hastler, Herstal, Lathers, Slather
THANKER Rethank
THEATER Teareth, Theatre,
 Thereat
THEATRE Teareth, Theater,
 Thereat
*****THEBAID** Habited
THENARS Anthers, Hanster
THEORIC Rotchie
THEREAT Teareth, Theater,
 Theatre
*****THEREIN** Neither
THERESA Heaters, Reheats
*****THERESE** Seether, Sheeter
THERIAC Rhaetic
THERMOS Mothers, Smother
THICKEN Kitchen
THINKER Rethink
THISTLE Lettish, Listeth, Lithest
THONDER Northed, Thorned,
 Throned
THORIAS Shortia
THORITE Orthite
THORNED Northed, Thonder,
 Throned
THRAVES Harvest
THREADS Dearths, Hardest,
 Hardset, Hatreds, Red-hats,
 Trashed
THREADY Hydrate
THREATS Hatters, Rathest,
 Shatter, Stareth

THRENOS Hornets, Shorten, Thrones
THRONED Northed, Thonder, Thorned
THRONES Hornets, Shorten, Threnos
*****THURLES** Hurtles, Hustler
THWAITE Waiteth
THYRSES Shyster
TIARAED Radiate
TICKERS Rickets, Sickert, Sticker
TICKLER Trickle
TICKLES Stickle
TIDDLEY Lyddite
TIDERIP Dirt-pie, Riptide
TIDIEST Dietist, Ditties
TIDYING Dignity
TIE-CLIP Pelitic
TIERCEL Reticle
TIERING Igniter, Nigrite, Tigrine
TIE-RODS Editors, Roisted, Rosited, Sortied, Steroid, Storied, Triodes
TIGLINE Lignite
TIGRESS Striges
TIGRINE Igniter, Nigrite, Tiering
*****TIJUANA** Juanita
TILE-HAT Lithate
TILE-RED Retiled
TILLERS Retills, Rillets, Stiller, Trellis
TILLING Lilting
TILTERS Litters, Slitter, Stilter, Testril, Titlers
TILTING Titling
TIMBALE Limbate
TIMINGS Misting, Smiting, Stiming
TIMPANI Impaint
TIMPANO Maintop, Ptomain, Tampion
TINAMOU Manitou
TIN-CANS Stannic
TINCHEL Linchet

TINDING Dinting
TINGLED Glinted
TINGLER Ringlet, Tringle
TINGLES Glisten, Lingets, Singlet
TINIEST Sittine, Tinties
TINKERS Inkster, Kirsten, Reknits, Stinker
TINKLER Trinkle
TINKLES Lentisk
TINTERS Entrist, Nitters, Retints, Stinter
TINTIES Sittine, Tiniest
TINWARE Tawnier
TIPPLER Ripplet, Tripple
TIPPLES Stipple
TIPSTER Pitters, Spitter
TIPTOES Potties
TIPULAS Stipula
TIRADES Ardites, Asterid, Astride, Diaster, Disrate, Staider, Staired
TIRASSE Satires
TISANES Entasis, Saintes, Sestina, Staines, Tansies
TITHING Hitting
TITLERS Litters, Slitter, Stilter, Testril, Tilters
TITLING Tilting
TITRATE Attrite, Tattier
TITTERS Tritest
TIVERED Riveted
*****TLEMCEN** Clement
TOASTER Retoast, Rosetta, Rotates, To-tears
TO-BRAKE To-break
TO-BREAK To-brake
TOCHERS Hectors, Rochets, Rotches, Torches, Troches
TOCSINS Consist
TOELESS Sestole
TOENAIL Elation
TO-HUNGA Hang-out
TOILERS Estoril, Estriol, Loiters
TOILETS Litotes

TOISECH Echoist
TONEMIC Centimo, Entomic, Metonic
TONETIC Entotic
TO-NIGHT Hotting
TONSILE Entoils, Lionets
TOOLING Looting
TOOMING Mooting
TOOTERS Stooter
TOOTLER Rootlet
TOPFULL Plotful
TOPHOLE Pothole
TOPICAL Capitol, Coalpit, Optical, Pit-coal
TOPLINE Pointel, Pontile, Potline
TOPPERS Popster, Stopper
TOPPLES Stopple
TOPSAIL Apostil
TOPSIDE Deposit, Dopiest, Posited
TOPSMAN Postman, Tampons
TOPSOIL Poloist
TOPWORK Potwork
TORCHES Hectors, Rochets, Rotches, Tochers, Troches
TOREROS Rooster, Rooters
TORNADO Donator, Odorant
TOROIDS Disroot
TORPEDO Trooped
TORPENT Portent
TORPIDS Disport, Tripods
TORPIFY Portify
TORQUES Questor, Quoters, Roquets
TORSADE Roasted, Rosated
TORSION Isotron, Nitroso
TORSTEN Snotter, Stentor
TORTILE Triolet
TORTIVE Viretot
TORTURE Trouter
TORYISH History
TOSHING Hosting
TOSSILY Tylosis

TO-TEARS Retoast, Rosetta, Rotates, Toaster
TOTTERS Stotter, Stretto
TOUCANS Conatus, Uncoats
TOUCHER Retouch
TOUCHES Souchet
TOUPETS Outstep
TOURERS Retours, Rouster, Routers, Trouser
TOURING Outgrin, Outring, Routing
TOUSERS Estrous Oestrus, Ousters, Sourest, Souters, Trouses, Tussore
TOUSING Ousting, Outsing, Outings
TOUSLED Loudest
TOUTERS Outsert, Stouter
TOWAGES Stowage
TOWLINE Two-line
TOWSING Stowing, Wigston
TOYSOME Myosote
TRACHLE Ratchel, Relatch
TRACING Carting, Crating
TRACKER Retrack
TRACTED Detract
TRADE-IN Anti-red, Detrain, Tanride, Trained
TRADERS Darters, Retards, Starred
TRADING Darting
TRADUCE Decatur, Educrat
TRAGEDY Gyrated
TRAGICS Catrigs, Gastric
TRAGION Orating
TRAILED Dilater, Red-tail
TRAILER Retiral, Retrial
TRAINED Anti-red, Detrain, Tranride, Trade-in
TRAINEE Aintree, Retinae
TRAINER Retrain, Terrain
TRAIPSE Parties, Piaster, Piastre, Pirates, Praties
TRAMCAR Carmart

TRAMPLE Templar
TRANCED Cantred, Tancred
TRANCHE Chanter
*****TRANENT** Entrant
TRANGAM Tangram
TRANGLE Tangler
TRANKUM Turkman
TRANNEL Lantern
TRANNIE Entrain
TRANSOM Marston, Matrons
TRAPANS Partans, Spartan,
  Tarpans
TRAPING Gintrap, Parting,
  Prating
TRASHED Dearths, Hardest,
  Hardset, Hatreds, Red-hats,
  Threads
TRASHES Rashest
TRAVELS Varlets, Vestral
TREACLE Electra, Telecar
TREADER Rerated, Retrade,
  Retread
TREADLE Alerted, Altered,
  Delater, Redealt, Related
TREASON Anteros, Atoners,
  Nor'east, Senator
TREATED Aretted
TREATER Retrate, Retreat
TREEING Integer, Retinge,
  Tearing
TREETOP Proette
TREFOIL Loftier
TRELLIS Retills, Rillets, Stiller,
  Tillers
TREMORS Termors, Stormer
TRENAIL Entrail, Latiner,
  Latrine, Ratline, Reliant, Retinal
TRENISE Entires, Entries, Steiner,
  Teniers
TREPANS Arpents, Entraps,
  Panters, Parents, Pastern,
  Persant
TRESSED Deserts, Dessert
TRESTLE Letters, Settler, Sterlet

TREVISS Stivers, Strives, Verists
TRIABLE Alberti, Librate, Tablier,
  Trilabe
TRIACID Triadic
TRIADIC Triacid
TRIAGES Agister, Aigrets,
  Gaiters, Sea-girt, Stagier, Strigae
TRIBLET Brittle
TRIBUNE Turbine
TRICKLE Tickler
*****TRIESTE** Testier
TRIFLED Flirted
TRIFLER Flirter
TRIFLES Filters, Lifters, Stifler
TRIGONE Genitor, Negrito
TRIGONS Sorting, Storing
TRILABE Alberti, Librate, Tablier,
  Triable
TRIMMED Mid-term
TRINDLE Tendril
TRINGLE Ringlet, Tingler
TRINKET Knitter
TRINKLE Tinkler
TRIODES Editors, Roisted,
  Rosited, Steroid, Sortied,
  Storied, Tie-rods
TRIOLET Tortile
TRIONES Orients, Stonier,
  Tersion
TRIPODS Disport, Torpids
TRIPPLE Ripplet, Tippler
TRIPSIS Pristis, Spirits
TRIREME Miterer
TRISEME Metiers, Re-emits,
  Retimes
TRISMUS Sistrum, Truisms
TRISULA Rituals
TRITELY Littery
TRITEST Titters
TROATED Rotated
TROCHES Hectors, Rochets,
  Rotches, Tochers, Torches
TROELIE Oil-tree
TROLLOP Roll-top

TROOPED Torpedo
TROPINE Pointer, Protein, Pterion, Repoint
TROPISM Imports
TROPIST Protist
TROUBLE Blue-rot, Boulter
TROUNCE Cornute, Counter, Recount
TROUPES Petrous, Posture, Pouters, Proteus, Septuor, Spouter
TROUSER Retours, Rouster, Routers, Tourers
TROUSES Estrous, Oestrus, Ousters, Sourest, Souters, Trousse, Tussore
TROUSSE Estrous, Oestrus, Ousters, Sourest, Souters, Trouses, Tussore
TROUTER Torture
TRUCIAL Curtail
TRUDGEN Grunted
TRUFFLE Fretful
TRUISMS Sistrum, Trismus
TRUNDLE Rundlet
TRUSSED Dusters
TRUSSES Russets
TRUSTED Sturted
TRUSTER Rutters, Turrets
TSABIAN Abstain
TSARDOM Stardom
TSARINA Antiars, Artisan, Sinatra
TSARISM Ramists, Marists
TSARIST Artists, Straits, Sittars
T-SHAPED Heptads, Spathed
TSIGANE Easting, Gastein, Genista, Ingates, Ingesta, Seating, Signate, Tangies, Teasing
TULCHAN Unlatch
TUMBLER Tumbrel
TUMBLES Stumble
TUMBREL Tumbler

TUNABLE Abluent
TUNG-OIL Louting
TUNICLE Untelic
TUNNIES Sunnite
TURACIN Curtain
TURBINE Tribune
TURDINE Intrude, Untired, Untried
TUREENS Neuters, Retunes, Tenures, Unterse
TURGENT Grutten
*****TURKESS** Tuskers
TURKMAN Trankum
TURNIPS Unstrip
TURN-OUT Outturn
TURN-UPS Upturns
TURRETS Rutters, Truster
*****TUSCANS** Sanctus
TUSKERS Turkess
TUSSORE Estrous, Oestrus, Ousters, Sourest, Souters, Tousers, Trouses, Trousse
TWEEDLE Tweeled
TWEELED Tweedle
TWINGES Stewing, Westing
TWISSEL Witless
TWISTER Retwist, Witster, Witters
TWO-LINE Towline
TWOSTEP Stewpot
TYLOSIN Stonily
TYPHOID Phytoid
TYPICAL Claypit
TYRANNE Tannery
TYLOSES Systole
TYLOSIS Tossily
TZARINA Atrazin

UDALLER Allured
ULLAGES Seagull, Sullage
ULNARES Laurens
ULNARIA Uralian
UMBRELS Burslem, Lumbers, Rumbles, Slumber

UMBROUS Brumous
UMPIRED Dumpier
UNAIDED Unidea'd
UNAIRED Uranide
UNARMED Duramen, Manured, Maunder
UNAWNED Unwaned
UNBARES Sun-bear, Unbears
UNBEARS Sun-bear, Unbares
UNBELTS Unblest
UNBERTH Burthen
UNBLEST Unbelts
UNBONED Bounder, Rebound, Unorbed, Unrobed
UNCAPED Unpaced
UNCARED Durance, Unraced
UNCASED Cadenus
UNCHARY Raunchy
UNCLEAR Lucarne, Nuclear
UNCLIPS Insulp, Sculpin
UNCLOSE Counsel
UNCOATS Conatus, Toucans
UNCOOPS Coupons, Soupcon
UNCOPED Pounced
UNCRIED Inducer
UNDATED Daunted
UNDEALT Lunated
UNDERDO Redound, Rounded
UNDERGO Guerdon, Ungored
UNDIGHT Hindgut
UNDOERS Enduros, Oresund, Resound, Sounder, Unrosed
UNDRAPE Unpared, Unraped
UNDRAWS Sunward
UNDRESS Sunders
UNEARTH Haunter, Unheart, Urethan
UNFIRED Unfried
UNFRIED Unfired
UNGIRTH Hurting, Unright
UNGORED Guerdon, Undergo
UNGRATE Negatur
UNHEALS Unleash, Unshale

UNHEART Haunter, Unearth, Urethan
UNIDEA'D Unaided
UNIDEAL Aliunde
UNLACES Censual, Launces, Unscale
UNLARGE Granule, Unregal
UNLATCH Tulchan
UNLEASH Hulsean, Unheals, Unshale
UNMANED Mundane, Unnamed
UNMATED Untamed
UNMINED Minuend
UNMITER Unmitre
UNMITRE Unmiter
UNMOORS Sunroom
UNNAILS Unslain
UNNAMED Mundane, Unmaned
UNNOTED Untoned
UNOARED Rondeau
UNORBED Bounder, Rebound, Unbored, Unrobed
UNORDER Rondure, Rounder
UNPACED Uncaped
UNPANEL Unpenal
UNPARED Undrape, Unraped
UNPASTE Peanuts
UNPENAL Unpanel
UNPERCH Puncher
UNPILES Line-ups, Lupines, Spinule, Up-lines
UNPLACE Clean-up
UNPLAIT Nuptial, Patulin
UNPROUD Round-up
UNQUEEN Neuquen
UNRACED Durance, Uncared
UNRAPED Undrape, Unpared
UNRATED Durante, Natured, Untread
UNRAYED Unready
UNREADY Unrayed
UNREEVE Revenue
UNREGAL Granule, Unlarge

UNRIGHT Hurting, Ungirth
UNROBED Bounder, Rebound, Unbored, Unorbed
UNROBES Unsober
UNROOFS Sunroof
UNROOST Unroots
UNROOTS Unroost
UNROPED Pounder
UNROSED Enduros, Oresund, Resound, Sounder, Undoers
UNSCALE Censual, Launces, Unlaces
UNSENSE Unseens
UNSEALS Sensual
UNSEATS Austens, Senatus
UNSEENS Unsense
UNSENSE Unseens
UNSHALE Hulsean, Unheals, Unleash
UNSLAIN Unnails
UNSLATE Sultane
UNSOBER Unrobes
UNSOLED Loudens, Nodules
UNSPEAK Sneak-up
UNSPELT Penults
UNSPENT Punnets
UNSPILT Unsplit
UNSPLIT Unspilt
UNSTACK Untacks
UNSTATE Attunes, Nutates, Tautens, Tetanus
UNSTERN Stunner
UNSTOIC Cotinus, Suction
UNSTOPS Sunspot
UNSTRAP Suntrap
UNSTRIP Turnips
UNSTUCK Untucks
UNSWEAR Unwares
UNTACKS Unstack
UNTAMED Unmated
UNTEACH Chanute
UNTELIC Tunicle
UNTERSE Neuters, Retunes, Tenures, Tureens

UNTILED Diluent
UNTILES Luniest, Utensil
UNTIRED Intrude, Turdine, Untried
UNTONED Unnoted
UNTRACE Centaur
UNTREAD Durante, Natured, Unrated
UNTREED Denture, Retuned
UNTRIED Intrude, Turdine, Untired
UNTRUSS Sturnus
UNTUCKS Unstuck
UNWANED Unawned
UNWARES Unswear
UPBREAK Break-up
UPBUILD Build-up
UPBUILT Built-up
UPBURST Burst-up
UPCATCH Catch-up
UPCHEER Cheer-up
UPCLIMB Plumbic
UPCLOSE Close-up, Couples, Opuscle
UPGROWN Grown-up
UP-LINES Line-ups, Lupines, Spinule, Unpiles
UPPINGS Supping
UPRAISE Piraeus, Spuriae
UPRIGHT Right-up
UPRISAL Parulis
UPRISES Suspire
UPSENDS Send-ups, Suspend
UPSHOOT Pushtoo, Shoot-up
UPSILON Pulsion
UPSPAKE Upspeak
UPSPEAK Upspake
UPSTAND Dust-pan, Stand-up
UPSTARE Pasteur, Pasture
UPSWARM Warm-ups
UPSWELL Upwells
UP-TRAIN Puritan
UPTREND Prudent, Prunted
UPTURNS Turn-ups

UPWELLS Upswell
***URALIAN** Ulnaria
URANIDE Unaired
URANISM Surinam
URANITE Ruinate, Taurine, Urinate
URANOUS Anurous
UREASES Reseaus, Seasure
UREIDES Residue
URETHAN Haunter, Unearth, Unheart
URICASE Saucier
URINALS Insular, Ursinal
URINATE Ruinate, Taurine, Uranite
URINOUS Ruinous
***URODELA** Roulade
URSINAL Insular, Urinals
USITATE Situate
USURPED Pursued
USURPER Pursuer
UTENSIL Luniest, Untiles
UTERINE Reunite, Retinue
***UTOPIAN** Opuntia
UTTERER Reutter

VAGINAL Gavilan
VAGUEST Gustave
VALENCE Enclave
VALERIC Caliver, Caviler, Clavier, Velaric
VALIANT Latvian
VALONIA Novalia
VALSING Salving, Slaving
VANSIRE Ravines, Servian
VARICES Viscera
VARIOUS Saviour
VARLETS Travels, Vestral
VEALERS Laveers, Leavers, Reveals
VEERING Reeving
VEILERS Leviers, Lievres, Relives, Reviles, Servile
VEINOUS Envious, Niveous

VELARIC Caliver, Caviler, Clavier, Valeric
VELITES Levites
VELOUTE Evolute
VENDACE Encaved
***VENTRIS** Inverts, Striven
VERBOSE Observe, Obverse
VERGLAS Gravels
VERIEST Restive, Servite
VERISTS Stivers, Strives, Treviss
VERMIAN Minerva
VERRUGA Gravure
VERSANT Servant, Taverns
VERSINE Enviers, Inverse, Viersen
VERSION Renvois
VERSING Serving
VERSUTE Revestu, Vesture
VESPINE Pensive
VESTING Steving
VESTRAL Travels, Vartels
VESTURE Revestu, Versute
VETERAN Nervate
VETOERS Estover, Overset, Revotes, Setover
VIALFUL Fluvial
***VIERSEN** Enviers, Inverse, Versine
VIKINGS Skiving
VINASSE Savines
VINEGAR Ginevra, Reaving
VINE-ROD On-drive
VIOLETS Stelvio
VIOLINE Olivine
VIRETOT Tortive
VIRGATE Vitrage
VIRTUAL Vitular
VISCERA Varices
VISITER Revisit
VISITOR Ivorist
VISORED Devisor, Devoirs, Voiders
VITRAGE Virgate
VITRAIN Vitrina

*   **VITRINA** Vitrain
    VITRINE Inviter
    VITULAR Virtual
    VOIDERS Devisor, Devoirs, Visored
    VOLABLE Lovable
    VOLATIC Voltaic
    VOLTAIC Volatic
    VOMITED Motived
    VOTINGS Stoving

WADDLED Dawdled
WADDLER Dawdler, Drawled
WADDLES Dawdles, Swaddle
WAESOME Awesome
WAFTERS Fretsaw
WAGERED Edgware, Ragweed
WAGERER Rewager
WAGINGS Swaging
WAISTED Dawties
WAISTER Waiters, Wariest, Wastrie
WAITERS Waister, Wariest, Wastrie
WAITETH Thwaite
WAKENER Rewaken
WALK-OUT Outwalk
WALLETS Setwall, Swallet
WALLEYE Eyewall
WALLOWS Swallow
*   **WALTERS** Warstle, Wastrel
WANGLER Wrangel, Wrangle
WARBLED Brawled
WARBLER Brawler
WARDING Drawing
WARHEAD Rawhead
WARIEST Waister, Waiters, Wastrie
WARMERS Rewarms, Swarmer
WARM-UPS Upswarm
WARSTLE Walters, Wastrel
WASHERS Hawsers, Swasher
WASH-OUT Outwash
WASTAGE Saw-gate

WASTREL Walters, Warstle
WASTRIE Waister, Waiters, Wariest
WATERED Dewater, Tarweed
WATERER Rewater
WAYSIDE Sideway
WEARERS Reswear, Rewears, Swearer
WEASELS Aweless
WEATHER Whate'er, Whereat, Wreathe
WEBSTER Bestrew
WEDGING Wind-egg
WEEDERS Sweered
WEENING Enewing
WEEPERS Resweep, Sweeper
WEIGHER Reweigh
WELDING Wing-led
WELTERS Swelter, Wrestle
WELTING Winglet
*   **WERTHER** Wherret
WESTING Stewing, Twinges
WETTISH Whitest
WET-WASH Sawwhet
WHATE'ER Weather, Whereat, Wreathe
WHEEDLE Wheeled
WHEELED Wheedle
WHEREAT Whate'er, Weather, Wreathe
WHEREON Erewhon, Nowhere
WHERRET Werther
WHINGES Hewings, Shewing
WHISSED Swedish, Swished
WHISSES Swishes
WHITEST Wettish
WHOEVER However
WIDENER Rewiden
WIGGLER Wriggle
WIGSTON Stowing, Towsing
WILLERS Swiller
WILTING Witling
WING-EGG Wedging
WINDING Dwining

WINDLES Swindel
WINGERS Swinger
WING-LED Welding
WINGLET Welting
WINKERS Swinker
WINSOME Owenism
WIRABLE Brawlie
WISENTS Witness
WISHERS Swisher
WITHERS Switcher, Writhes
WITHOUT Outwith
WITLESS Twissel
WITLING Wilting
WITNESS Wisents
WITSTER Retwist, Twister,
  Witters
***WITTERS** Retwist, Twister,
  Witster
 WOLFING Flowing, Fowling
 WONDRED Drowned
 WOOD-BOX Boxwood
 WOD-GOD Dogwood
 WOODNUT Nutwood
 WORDAGE Dowager
 WORDIER Worried
 WORDILY Rowdily
 WORKBOX Boxwork
 WORKDAY Day-work
 WORK-OUT Outwork
 WORN-OUT Outworn

WORRIED Wordier
WORSTED Strowed
WOUNDER Rewound
***WRANGEL** Wangler, Wrangle
WRANGLE Wangler, Wrangel
WRAPPER Prewrap
WREATHE Whate'er, Weather,
  Whereat
WRESTED Strewed
WRESTER Strewer
WRESTLE Swelter, Welters
WRIGGLE Wiggler
WRINGED Redwing
WRITHES Swither, Withers
WRONGER Regrown

XEROTIC Excitor
XYLOGEN Loxygen

YARDAGE Drayage
YARDING Draying
YARD-MAN Drayman
YEARDED Derayed
YEARNED Deanery, Renayed,
  Ne'erday
YESTERN Styrene
YIELDER Reedily
YONKERS Orkneys

ZINCITE Citizen

Eight letters

*ABDERITE Ebriated
ABELMOSK Smokable
*ABERCARN Canberra
ABETMENT Batement
ABETTALS Statable, Tastable
ABLUENTS Unstable
ABLUTION Abutilon
ABORDING Boarding
ABORTING Borating, Taboring
ABRIDGED Brigaded
ABSORBER Reabsorb
*ABUTILON Ablution
ACARIDAN Arcadian
ACCEPTER Reaccept
ACCOUTER Accoutre
ACCOUTRE Accouter
ACCRUALS Caraculs, Saccular
ACCURATE Carucate
ACCURSED Cardecus
ACETATES Testacea
ACETONES Notecase
ACHERSET Cheaters, Reachest,
  Recheats, Teachers
ACLUTTER Cultrate
ACONITES Canoeist
ACONITIC Cationic
ACOSMIST Massicot
ACREAGES Gear-case
ACRE-INCH Chicaner
ACROLEIN Caroline, Cornelia,
  Creolian
ACROSTIC Socratic
ACTINIDE Ctenidia, Diactine,
  Indicate
ACTINOID Diatonic
ACTUATOR Autocrat
*ADAMITES Adamsite, Diastema

ADAMSITE Adamites, Diastema
ADDUCERS Crusaded
ADENOIDS Anodised
ADHERENT Neatherd, Threaden
ADHERERS Redshare, Reshared
ADHERING Head-ring
ADHIBITS Dishabit
ADJUSTER Readjust
ADOPTERS Asported, Readopts
ADROITLY Dilatory, Idolatry
ADSORBED Roadbeds
ADULATOR Laudator
AEROLOGY Areology
AESTIVAL Salivate
AFFECTER Reaffect
AFFIRMER Reaffirm
AGENESIS Assignee
AGENTIAL Alginate
AGNOSTIC Coasting, Coatings,
  Cotingas
AGONISED Diagnose
*AGROTERA Arrogate
AILERONS Alerions, Alienors,
  Rosaline
AILMENTS Aliments, Manliest,
  Saltmine, Smaltine
AIR-BENDS Brandeis, Brandies,
  Brandise
AIRCREWS Airscrew
AIRPOSTS Prosaist, Protasis
AIRSCREW Aircrews
ALARMING Marginal
ALARMIST Alastrim
ALASTRIM Alarmist
ALBERTA'S Arbalest
ALBICORE Cabriole
ALBURNUM Laburnum

*ALCESTIS Elastics
ALCHEMIC Chemical
*ALCINOUS Unsocial
ALDERMAN Malander
ALERIONS Ailerons, Alienors,
　Rosaline
ALERTING Altering, Integral,
　Relating, Triangle
*ALGERIAN Regalian
ALGERIA'S Gasalier, Regalias
ALGINATE Agential
*ALGERNON Non-glare
ALIENISM Milesian
ALIENIST Latinise, Litanies
ALIENORS Ailerons, Alerions,
　Rosaline
ALIGHTED Gilt-head
ALIGNERS Engrails, Realigns,
　Resignal, Salinger, Sanglier, Seal-
　ing, Signaler
ALIMENTS Ailments, Manliest,
　Saltmine, Smaltine
*ALISTERS Realists, Saltiers,
　Saltires, Slaister
ALKALIES Alkalise
ALKALISE Alkalies
ALL-GIVER Villager
ALLIANCE Canaille
ALLOTTED Totalled
ALL-ROUND Round-all
ALLURING Lingular
ALMADIES Maladies
ALOETICS Societal
ALPINIST Pintails, Tail-spin
ALTERANT Alternat
ALTERING Alerting, Integral,
　Relating, Triangle
ALTERNAT Alterant
ALTITUDE Latitude
ALTRICES Articles, Recitals,
　Selictar, Sterical
ALTRUISM Muralist, Ultraism
ALTRUIST Titulars, Ultraist
ALUNITES Insulate

AMANITIN Maintain
AMASSING Gas-mains,
　Siamangs
AMBIVERT Verbatim
*AMBRIDGE Game-bird
AMATEURS Satu-Mare
AMELCORN Cornmeal
AMENABLE Nameable
AMERCERS Creamers, Screamer
AMERCING Creaming,
　Germanic, Merignac
*AMERICAN Cinerama
*AMERICAS Mesaraic
AMORTISE Atomiser, Mareotis
ANALCIME Calamine
*ANAPOLIS Pianolas, Salopian
ANARCHIC Characin
ANCESTOR Enactors, Escatron,
　Sortan'ce
*ANCHISES Inchases
ANCHORED Rondache
ANCIENTS Canniest, Instance
*ANDERSEN Ensnared
ANDIRONS Iron-sand, Sand-iron
ANDROGEN Dragonne
ANECDOTE Toe-dance
ANEURISM Sumerian
ANGERING Enraging
ANGLINGS Slanging
ANGRIEST Astringe, Ganister,
　Gantries, Granites, Ingrates,
　Reasting, Tangiers
ANIMATED Diamante
ANIMATOR Montaria, Tamanoir
ANISETTE Tetanise
ANKERITE Kreatine
ANNALIST Santalin
ANNEALER Lernaean
ANOINTED Antinode
ANOINTER Inornate, Reanoint
ANORETIC Creation, Reaction
ANOTHER'S Sheraton
ANSWERER Reanswer
ANT-BEARS Ratsbane, Strabane

8

ANTEDATE Edentata
ANTHEMIA Haematin
ANTHESIS Shanties, Sheitans
ANTICOUS Auctions, Cautions
ANTIDOTE Tetanoid
*ANTIGONE Negation
*ANTILOPE Antipole
ANTIMONY Antinomy
ANTINODE Anointed
ANTINOMY Antimony
ANTIPOLE Antilope
ANTIQUES Quantise
ANTI-REDS Detrains, Strained,
  Tan-rides, Trade-ins
ANTI-RUST Naturist
ANTISERA Artesian, Erastian,
  Resinata
ANTISTES Instates, Nastiest,
  Satinets, Titaness
APHETISE Hepatise
APHORISM Morphias
APPARENT Trappean
APPEALER Reappeal
APPEARER Rapparee, Reappear
APRICOTS Patricos, Piscator
*ARANIDAE Areneida
ARBALEST Alberta's
ARBORIST Rib-roast
ARBUSCLE Curables
ARCADIAN Acaridan
ARCADING Cardigan
ARCHAISM Charisma, Machairs
ARCHLUTE Trauchle
*ARENEIDA Aranidae
AREOLOGY Aerology
ARETTING Treating
ARGENTIC Catering, Citrange,
  Creating, Reacting
ARGYRITE Geriatry
ARIDNESS Sardines
ARIETTAS Aristate
ARIETTES Iterates, Treaties,
  Treatise
ARISTATE Ariettas

*ARMENIAN Marianne
ARRAIGNS Srinagar
ARRESTED Retrades, Retreads,
  Serrated, Treaders
ARRESTER Rearrest
ARROGANT Tarragon
ARROGATE Agrotera
ARSENATE Serenata
ARSENICS Cerasins, Raciness,
  Sarcines
ARSENIDE Nearside
ARSENITE Resinate, Sin-eater,
  Stearine, Teresian, Teresina,
  Trainees
ARSONITE Asterion, Notaries,
  Notarise, Rosinate, Senorita
ARTESIAN Antisera, Erastian,
  Resinata
*ARTEVELD Traveled
ARTICLES Altrices, Recitals,
  Selictrar, Sterical
ASCENDER Reascend
ASCRIBED Carbides
ASPERATE Separate
ASPERGED Presaged
ASPERGER Presager
ASPERGES Presages
ASPERSED Repassed
ASPERSES Passeres, Repasses
ASPHODEL Pholades
ASPIRANT Partisan
ASPIRATE Parasite, Septaria
ASPIRING Praising
ASPORTED Adopters, Readopts
ASSAILER Salaries
ASSAYING Gainsays
ASSEMBLE Beamless
ASSENTED East-ends, Standees
ASSENTER Earnests, Reassent,
  Sarsenet
ASSENTOR Essorant, Senators,
  Star-nose, Treasons
ASSERTER Reassert, Serrates

ASSERTOR Assorter, Oratress, Reassort, Roasters
ASSIGNEE Agenesis
ASSIGNER Reassign, Seringas
ASSIGNOR Signoras
ASSISTER Reassist
ASSORTED Torsades
ASSORTER Assertor, Oratress, Reassort, Roasters
ASTATINE Sanitate, Tanaiste
ASTERIDS Diasters, Disaster, Disrates
*ASTERION Arsonite, Notaries, Notarise, Rosinate, Senorita
ASTERISM Maisters, Misrates, Semitars
*ASTEROPE Operates, Protease, Soap-tree
ASTIGMIC Sigmatic
ASTONIED Sedation
ASTRINGE Angriest, Ganister, Gantries, Granites, Ingrates, Reasting, Tangiers
*ASTURIAN Austrian, Saturnia
ASTURIAS Austrias
ATELIERS Earliest
ATHEISMS Mathesis
*ATHERINA Rhaetian
ATHETISE Hesitate
ATHLETIC Thetical
*ATLANTIC Tantalic
ATOMISER Amortise, Mareotis
ATOMISMS Somatism
ATOMISTS Somatist
ATRAZINE Nazarite
ATROCITY Citatory
ATTACHER Reattach
ATTACKER Reattack
ATTAINER Reattain
ATTENDED Dentated
ATTENDER Nattered, Rattened
ATTESTER Reattest
ATTESTOR Testator
ATTRITED Titrated

ATTUNING Taunting
AUCTIONS Anticous, Cautions
AURICLED Radicule
AURICLES Escurial
AUSTRIAN Asturian, Saturnia
*AUSTRIAS Asturias
AUTOCRAT Actuator
AVERTERS Traverse
AVERTING Tavering, Vintager
AWAKENER Reawaken
AWEATHER Wheatear

BAALITES Labiates, Satiable
BABBLING Blabbing
BABISHLY Shabbily
BACHELOR Lochaber
BACKFALL Fall-back
BACK-FIRE Fireback
BACK-HAUL Haul-back
BACK-REST Brackets
BACKWARD Drawback
BAHADURS Subahdar
BAIRNISH Brainish
*BAJOCIAN Jacobian
BAKEMEAT Makebate
BALANCER Barnacle
BALDNESS Bandless
BALE-FIRE Fireable
BALLADES Sabadell
*BALINESE Base-line, Sabeline
BALK-LINE Linkable
BALLOTER Reballot
BALMIEST Timbales
BALMLIKE Lamblike
BALSAMIC Cabalism
BALUSTER Rustable
BANDEROL Oberland
BANDLESS Baldness
BANISHES Banshies
BANSHIES Banishes
*BAREILLY Reliably
BARITONE Obtainer, Reobtain
BARNACLE Balancer
*BARNSLEY Blarneys

BARRACAN Barranca
BARRANCA Barracan
BASALTIC Cabalist
BASCINET Cabinets
BASE-LINE Balinese, Sabeline
BASINETS Bassinet, Bestains, Besaints
BASSINET Basinets, Bestains, Besaints
BATEMENT Abetment
BAUCHLES Chasuble
*__BAUDRONS** Sound-bar
BEADIEST Diabetes
BEADINGS Debasing
BEADSMAN Bedesman, Beam-ends
BEAM-ENDS Beadsman, Bedesman
BEAMLESS Assemble
BEANPOLE Openable
BEARDING Breading
BEARSKIN Inbreaks
BEAVERED Bereaved
BED-CHAIR Chair-bed
BEDESMAN Beadsmen, Beam-ends
BEDMAKER Embarked
BEE-LINES Eisleben
BEETROOT Boot-tree
BEGRUDGE Buggered, Debugger
BEJESUIT Jebusite
BELATING Bleating, Tangible
*__BELGIANS** Bengalis, Signable, Singable
BELLOWED Bowelled
BELLOWER Rebellow
BELONGED Englobed
BEMOILED Emboiled
*__BENGALIS** Belgians, Signable, Singable
BERATING Rebating
BEREAVED Beavered
BERSEEMS Bessemer
BERTHING Brighten

BESAINTS Basinets, Bassinet, Bestains
BESHADOW Bowheads
BESLAVER Servable, Versable
BESORTED Bestrode
BESOTTED Obtested
BESSEMER Berseems
BESTAINS Basinets, Bassinet, Besaints
BESTIARY Sybarite
BESTOWAL Stowable
BESTRODE Besorted
BETIDING Debiting
BETOKENS Steenbok
BETRAYAL Rateably
BETRAYER Teaberry
BETREADS Breasted, Debaters
BIGAMOUS Subimago
BIG-SWOLN Bowlings
BIOCIDAL Diabolic
BIOCLEAN Coinable
BIRDCAGE Cage-bird
BIRD-CALL Call-bird
BIRD-LIKE Kilbride
BIRD-SEED Seed-bird
BIRDSONG Song-bird
BLABBING Babbling
BLANKEST Blankets
BLANKETS Blankest
BLARNEYS Barnsley
BLASTEMA Lambaste
BLASTING Stabling
BLEACHER Rebleach
BLEATERS Restable, Retables
BLEATING Belating, Tangible
BLESSING Glibness
*__BLETILLA** Tillable
BLOATERS Sortable, Storable
BLOATING Bog-Latin, Obligant
BLOTLESS Boltless
BLOTTING Bottling
BLOWFISH Fishbowl
BLUENOSE Nebulose
BLUNGING Bungling

BOARDING Abording
BOASTERS Botsares
BOASTING Bostangi
BOAT-HOOK Book-oath
BODEMENT Entombed
BOG-LATIN Bloating, Obligant
BOLDNESS Bondless
BOLTLESS Blotless
BONDAGES Dogbanes, Dogsbane
BONDLESS Boldness
BONE-FISH Fishbone
BONELESS Noblesse
BOOKCASE Casebook
BOOK-OATH Boat-hook
BOOKWORK Workbook
BOOTJACK Jackboot
BOOTLACE Lace-boot
BOOT-TREE Beetroot
BORATING Aborting, Taboring
BORDELLO Doorbell
BORDURES Suborder
BOSTANGI Boasting
BOTANIES Botanise, Obeisant
BOTANISE Botanies, Obeisant
BOTSARES Boasters
BOTTLING Blotting
BOUNCING Buncoing
BOUNDERS Rebounds, Suborned
BOUNDING Unboding
BOWELLED Bellowed
BOWHEADS Beshadow
BOWLINGS Big-swoln
BOX-WAGON Wagon-box
BRAKEAGE Breakage
BRAINISH Bairnish
BRAKE-MAN Breakman
*****BRANDEIS** Air-bends, Brandies, Brandise
BRANDIES Air-bends, Brandeis, Brandise,
BRANDISE Air-bends, Brandeis Brandies
BRAWLING Warbling

BRACKETS Back-rest
BREADING Bearding
BREAD-NUT Turbaned
BREAKAGE Brakeage
BREAKMAN Brake-man
BREAKOUT Outbreak
BREASTED Betreads, Debaters
BREATHES Hartbees
BRICK-RED Redbrick
BRIDE-ALE Rideable
BRIGADED Abridged
BRIGHTEN Berthing
BRISANCE Carbines
BRISTLED Driblets
BROADWAY Wayboard
BROIDERS Disrober
BROKAGES Grosbeak
BUCKLERS Sub-clerk
BUDGETER Rebudget
BUFFERED Rebuffed
BUGGERED Begrudge, Debugger
BUMMLING Mumbling
BUNCOING Bouncing
BUNGLING Blunging
BUNKERED Debunker
BURLETTA Rebuttal
*****BURNSITE** Turbines
BURNT-OUT Outburnt
BUSH-BRED Shrubbed
BUS-RIDES Disburse, Subsider
BUTCHERS Schubert
BUTTERED Rebutted
BUTTERIS Tributes
BUTTONER Rebutton
BY-PASSER Passer-by

CABALISM Balsamic
CABALIST Basaltic
CABALLER Race-ball
CABINETS Bascinet
CABRIOLE Albicore
CACKLING Clacking
CADASTER Cadastre
CADASTRE Cadaster

CADUCEUS Caucused
CAGE-BIRD Birdcage
CALAMINE Analcime
CALAMINT Claimant
CALANDER Calendar, Landrace
CALCINES Scenical
CALENDAR Calander, Landrace
CALENDER Encradle
CALENDRY Dry-clean
CALIDITY Dialytic
CALIPEES Especial
CALIPERS Replicas, Spiracle
CALIVERS Claviers, Visceral
CALL-BIRD Bird-call
CALLINGS Call-sign
CALL-NOTE Lancelot
CALL-OVER Cover-all, Overcall
CALL-SIGN Callings
CALORIES Carioles, Escorial
CALOTTES Salt-cote
CALOYERS Coarsely
CALUMETS Muscatel
CAMBERED Embraced
CAMBRELS Clambers, Scambler, Scramble
CAMELINE Melaenic
CAMERATE Macerate, Racemate
CAMPAIGN Pangamic
CAMPLING Clamping
CANAILLE Alliance
*****CANARESE** Cesarean
CANARIES Cesarian
CANASTER Caterans
*****CANBERRA** Abercarn
CANCROID Draconic
CANEPHOR Chaperon
CANISTER Creatins, Scantier
CANNIEST Ancients, Instance
CANNINGS Scanning
CANOEIST Aconites
CANONESS Sonances
CANONIST Contains, Sanction
CANOPIES Caponise
CANTEENS Enascent

CANTERED Crenated, Decanter, Nectared, Recanted
CANTICOY Cyanotic
CANTORIS Cast-iron, Nicastro
CAPERING Preignac
CAPITANO Pacation
CAPONIER Ice-apron, Procaine
CAPONISE Canopies
CAPSTONE Open-cast
CAPSULAR Scapular
CARACULS Accruals, Saccular
CARBIDES Ascribed
CARBINES Brisance
CARDECUS Accursed
CARD-GAME Decagram
CARDIGAN Arcading
CARINATE Craniate
CARIOLES Calories, Escorial
CARMINES Cremains
CARNEOUS Nacreous
*****CAROLEAN** Lecanora
*****CAROLINA** Conarial
*****CAROLINE** Acrolein, Cornelia, Creolian
CAROLLED Collared
CARPINGS Scarping, Scraping
CARROTED Redactor
CARRY-OUT Curatory
CARTOONS Corantos, Ostracon
CARUCATE Accurate
CASEBOOK Bookcase
CASHMERE Marchese
CASSETTE Test-case
CAST-IRON Cantoris, Nicastro
CASTLING Catlings
CASTORES Coarsest, Coasters, Recoasts, Socrates
CASUALLY Causally
CATALYSE Stay-lace
CATCHERS Cratches
CATEGORY Grey-coat
CATERANS Canaster
CATERESS Cerastes

CATERING Argentic, Citrange, Creating, Reacting
CATHETER Charette
CATHOUSE Soutache
CATIONIC Aconitic
CATLINGS Castling
CAT'S-TAIL Cattails, Statical
CATTAILS Cat's-tail, Statical
CAUCUSED Caduceus
CAUDILLO Lodicula
CAUSALLY Casually
CAUTIONS Anticous, Acutions
CAVATION Octavian, Vacation
CAVERNED Cravened
CAVITIED Vaticide
CEDAR-NUT Uncarted, Uncrated, Underact, Untraced
CELLARED Recalled
CEMENTER Cerement, Recement
CENSORED Seconder, Seed-corn
CENTAURS Etruscan, Recusant, Untraces
CENTAURY Cyanuret
CENTERED Decenter, Decentre
CENTIARE Creatine, Increate, Iterance
CENTIMOS Centoism
CENTOISM Centimos
CENTROID Crediton, Doctrine
CERAMIST Matrices
CERASINS Arsenics, Raciness, Sarcines
*CERASTES Cateress
CERATOSE Creasote
CEREBRUM Cumberer
CEREMENT Cementer, Recement
CERVELAS Cleavers
CERVICES Crescive, Crevices
CESAREAN Canarese
*CESARIAN Canaries
CESSIONS Cosiness
CESTODES Cosseted
CHAINLET Ethnical
CHAINMAN Chinaman

CHAINMEN Chinamen
CHAIR-BED Bed-chair
CHAIRMAN Charmian
CHALDRON Chondral
CHALKING Hackling
CHANGING Ganching
CHANTERS Snatcher, Stancher, Tranches
CHAPERON Canephor
CHAPITER Patchier, Phreatic
CHARACIN Anarchic
CHARETTE Catheter
CHARISMA Archaism, Machairs
CHARMIAN Chairman
CHARMING Marching
CHARNECO Encroach
CHARPIES Parchesi, Seraphic
CHARTERS Chartres, Recharts, Starcher
CHARTING Ratching
CHARTIST Straicht
*CHARTRES Charters, Recharts, Starcher
CHASUBLE Bauchles
*CHATWOOD Woodchat
CHEATERS Acherset, Reachest, Recheats, Teachers
CHEATING Teaching
CHELATOR Chlorate, Trochlea
CHEMICAL Alchemic
CHEMISTS Schemist
CHENILLE Hellenic
*CHEREMIS Chimeres
CHICANER Acre-inch
CHICK-PEA Peachick
CHILLERS Schiller
CHILLIES Ice-hills
CHIMERES Cheremis
*CHINAMAN Chainman
*CHINAMEN Chainmen
CHINREST Christen, Citherns, Snitcher
CHITTERS Restitch, Stitcher
CHLORATE Chelator, Trochlea

CHLORITE Clothier
CHOIRMAN Harmonic
CHONDRAL Chaldron
CHOPINES Echinops
CHOUSING Hocusing
CHRISTEN Chinrest, Citherns,
  Snitcher
CHROMITE Trichome
CHURNING Runching
CIDER-AND Riddance
CI-DEVANT Vedantic
CILIATES Silicate
*CINERAMA American
CINEREAL Reliance
CINGULUM Glucinum
CIPHERED Decipher
CIPOLINS Psilocin
CISELEUR Ciselure
CISELURE Ciseleur
CISTVAEN Vesicant
CITATORY Atrocity
CITHERNS Chinrest, Christen,
  Snitcher
CITRANGE Argentic, Catering,
  Creating, Reacting
CITRATES Cristate, Scattier
CITREOUS Outcries
CLABBERS Scrabble
CLACKING Cackling
CLAIMANT Calamint
*CLAIRTON Contrail
CLAMBERS Cambrels, Scambler,
  Scramble
CLAMPING Campling
CLANGING Glancing
CLASPING Placings, Scalping
CLATTERS Scrattle
*CLAUDIAN Dulciana
CLAVIERS Calivers, Visceral
CLAY-MARL Lacrymal
CLAY-PIPE Pipeclay
CLEANERS Cleanser, Recleans,
  Relances
CLEANING Elancing, Enlacing

CLEANSER Cleaners, Recleans,
  Relances
CLEAREST Scelerat, Telecars,
  Treacles
CLEAVERS Cervelas
CLEMATIS Climates
CLERKESS Reckless
CLEVEITE Elective
CLIMATES Clematis
CLEAN-OUT Outlance
CLIMAXES Exclaims
CLIMBOUT Outclimb
CLITORIS Cloister, Coistrel,
  Cortiles, Costlier
CLOCKING Cockling
CLODDING Coddling
CLOGGING Coggling
CLOISTER Clitoris, Coistrel,
  Cortiles, Costlier
CLOSE-UPS Scopelus, Upcloses
CLOSURES Sclerous
CLOTHIER Chlorite
CLOUDING Dulcigno
CLUMSILY Cullyism
CLUTCHED Declutch
CLUTTERS Scuttler
COACHMAN Comanche
COARSELY Caloyers
COARSEST Castores, Coasters,
  Recoasts, Socrates
COASTERS Castores, Coarsest,
  Recoasts, Socrates
COASTING Agnostic, Coatings,
  Cotingas
COATINGS Agnostic, Coasting,
  Cotingas
COAT-TAIL Tailcoat
COAXIALS Saxicola
COCKLING Clocking
CODDLERS Scroddle
CODDLING Clodding
CODLINGS Lingcods, Scolding
COEHORNS Schooner
COGGLING Clogging

COHERERS Cosherer
COIFFEUR Coiffure
COIFFURE Coiffeur
COINABLE Bioclean
COINAGES Cosinage
COISTREL Clitoris, Cloister, Cortiles, Costlier
COITIONS Isotonic
COLATION Location
COLLAPSE Escallop
COLLARED Carolled
COLLIERS Orsellic
COLONIES Colonise, Eclosion
COLONISE Colonies, Eclosion
COLOURED Decolour
COLOURER Recolour
*****COMANCHE** Coachman
COMATOSE Moot-case
COMEDIAN Daemonic, Demoniac, Midocean
COMEDIST Docetism, Domestic
COME-DOWN Downcome
COMING-IN Incoming
COMITIES Semiotic
COMPARES Compears, Mesocarp
COMPEARS Compares, Mesocrap
COMPILED Complied
COMPILER Complier
COMPILES Complies, Polemics
COMPLIES Compiles, Polemics
COMPLIED Compiled
COMPLIER Compiler
CONARIAL Carolina
CONARIUM Coumarin
CONATIVE Invocate
CONCERTI Necrotic
CONCETTI Tectonic
CONDOLES Consoled
CONDUITS Discount, Noctuids
CONDYLES Secondly
CONFLATE Falconet
CONFRERE Enforcer, Renforce
CONGREET Co-regent
*****CONGREVE** Converge

CONIFERS Fir-cones, Forensic, Forinsec, Inforces
*****CONISTON** Scontion
CONSERVE Converse
CONSOLED Condoles
CONSOLES Coolness
CONSPIRE Incorpse
CONSTRUE Cornutes, Counters, Recounts, Trounces
CONSULAR Courlans
CONSUMED Mud-cones
CONSUMER Mucrones
CONTAINS Canonist, Sanction
CONTOURS Cornutos, Croutons, Outscorn
CONTRAIL Clairton
CONTRITE Cornetti
CONTUSES Countess
CONVERGE Congreve
CONVERSE Conserve
CONVEYER Reconvey
COOLNESS Consoles
COPULATE Outplace
CORANTOS Cartoons, Ostracon
CORDAGES God's-acre
CO-REGENT Congreet
CORELESS Recloses, Sclerose
CORKIEST Rockiest, Stockier
CORK-TREE Rocketer
CORKWING King-crow
CORKWOOD Rock-wood, Woodrock
*****CORNELIA** Acrolein, Caroline, Creolian
CORNETTI Contrite
CORNICHE Enchoric
CORNMEAL Amelcorn
CORNUTED Trounced
CORNUTES Construe, Counters, Recounts, Trounces
CORNUTOS Contours, Croutons, Outscorn
CORSELET Electors, Electros, Selector

CORSETED Costered, Escorted, Recosted
CORSLETS Costrels, Croslets, Crosslet
CORTILES Clitoris, Cloister, Coistrel, Costlier
*CORVINAE** Veronica
COSHERER Coherers
COSINAGE Coinages
COSINESS Cessions
COSSETED Cestodes
COSTERED Corseted, Escorted, Recosted
COST-FREE Free-cost, Scot-free
COSTLIER Clitoris, Cloister, Coistrel, Cortiles
COSTRELS Corslets, Croslets, Crosslet
COSTUMED Customed
COSTUMER Customer
CO-SURVEY Courtesy
COTELINE Election
COTERIES Esoteric
COTINGAS Agnostic, Coasting, Coatings
COTLANDS Scotland
COUMARIN Conarium
COUNTERS Construe, Cornutes, Recounts, Trounces
COUNTESS Contuses
COUPURES Cupreous
COURAGES Scourage
COURANTE Outrance
COURLANS Consular
COURSERS Cursores, Scourers
COURSING Scouring
COURTESY Co-survey
COURTIER Outcrier
COVER-ALL Call-over, Overcall
COVETING Viet-cong
COWLINGS Scowling
*CRABTREE** Tree-crab
CRANIATE Carinate
*CRANSTON** Scranton

CRAPPIES Epicarps
CRATCHES Catchers
CRAVENED Caverned
CRAWLERS Scrawler
CRAYONED Deaconry
CREAMERS Amercers, Screamer
CREAMING Amercing, Germanic, Merignac
CREASING Grecians, Searcing
CREASOTE Ceratose
CREATINE Centiare, Increate, Iterance
CREATING Argentic, Catering, · Citrange, Reacting
CREATINS Canister, Scantier
CREATION Anoretic, Reaction
CREATIVE Reactive
CREDITED Directed
*CREDITON** Centroid, Doctrine
CREDITOR Director
CREMAINS Carmines
CREMATOR Mercator
CREMOSIN Incomers, Sermonic
CRENATED Cantered, Decanter, Nectared, Recanted
CREOLIAN Acrolein, Caroline, Cornelia
CREPITUS Cuprites, Pictures, Piecrust
CRESCIVE Cervices, Crevices
*CRESSIDA** Discrase, Sidecars
*CRETHEIS** Heretics
CREVICES Cervices, Crescive
CRIBBLES Scribble
CRIMEFUL Merciful
CRINATED Dicentra
CRISPATE Picrates, Practise
CRISTATE Citrates, Scattier
CRITTERS Restrict, Stricter
*CROATION** Raincoat
CROCHETS Crotches
CROSLETS Corslets, Costrels, Crosslet
CROSSING Scorsing

CROSSLET Corslets, Costrels, Croslets
CROTCHES Crochets
CROUTONS Contours, Cornutos, Outscorn
CRUELEST Lectures
CRUISERS Scurries
CRUMPETS Spectrum
CRUNODES Unscored
CRUSADED Adducers
CRUSTIER Recruits
CRUSTILY Rusticly
CRUTCHES Scutcher
CTENIDIA Actinide, Diactine, Indicate
CULLINGS Sculling
CULLIONS Scullion
CULLYISM Clumsily
CULPRITS Spit-curl
CULTIVAR Curvital
CULTRATE Aclutter
CUMBERED Recumbed
CUMBERER Cerebrum
CUNIFORM Nuciform, Unciform
CUPIDITY Pudicity
CUPREOUS Coupures
CUPRITES Crepitus, Pictures, Piecrust
CURABLES Arbuscle
CURATORY Carry-out
CURELESS Recluses
CURSORES Coursers, Scourers
CURTAILS Rustical
CURTAINS Saturnic
CURTNESS Encrusts
CURVITAL Cultivar
CUSTOMED Costumed
CUSTOMER Costumer
CUTTABLE Table-cut
CUTTINGS Tungstic
CYANOTIC Canticoy
CYANURET Centaury
CYSTINES Encystis
CYTISINE Syenitic

DAEMONIC Comedian, Demoniac, Mid-ocean
DAIRYMAN Mainyard
DALESMAN Leadsman
DALESMEN Emendals, Leadsmen
DANGLERS Glanders
DANSEUSE Sudanese
DARNDEST Stranded
DATE-LINE Entailed, Lineated
DATE-PALM Palmated
DATURINE Indurate, Ruinated, Urinated
DAWDLERS Swaddler, Waddlers
DAWDLING Waddling
DAWNERED Wandered
DAWNLIKE Wandlike
DAYLIGHT Light-day
DEACONRY Crayoned
DEADENER Endeared
DEADLIER Derailed
DEAD-LOCK Deck-load
DEANSHIP Headpins, Pinheads
DEARLING Dragline
DEBASING Beadings
DEBATERS Betreads, Breasted
DEBATING Nebit-Dag
DEBITING Betiding
DEBUGGER Begrudge, Buggered
DEBUNKER Bunkered
DECADENT Decanted
DECAGRAM Card-game
DECANTED Decadent
DECANTER Cantered, Crenated, Nectared, Recanted
DECEIVER Received
DECENTER Centered, Decentre
DECENTRE Centered, Decenter
DECIDERS Descried
DECIGRAM Grimaced
DECIMATE Medicate
DECIPHER Ciphered
DECK-LOAD Dead-lock
DECLARES Rescaled

DECLINER Reclined
DECLINES Licensed, Silenced
DECLUTCH Clutched
DECOLOUR Coloured
DECORATE Recoated
DECREETS Resected, Secreted
DECREPIT Depicter
DEERFOOT Refooted
DEER-HORN Dehorner
DEER-LICK Relicked
DEER-PARK Reparked
DEFEATER Redefeat
DEFERRER Referred
DEFILING Fielding
DEFLOWER Flowered, Reflowed
DEFORCES Frescoed
DEFOREST Forested, Fostered
DEFORMER Reformed
DEFRAYER Federary
DEGENDER Gendered
DEGRADER Regarded, Regraded
DEHORNER Deer-horn
DEIFYING Edifying
*****DELAWARE** Weardale
DELETION Entoiled
DELIGHTS Slighted
DELIVERS Desilver, Silvered,
　Slivered
*****DELSARTE** Treadles
DELUDING Indulged, Ungiled
DELUSION Insouled, Unsoiled
DEMANDED Maddened
DEMANDER Remanded
DEMENTIS Sediment, Tidesmen
DEMERITS Demister, Dimeters
DEMERSAL Emeralds
DEMESNES Seedsmen
DEMIREPS Premised, Simpered
DEMISING Medising
DEMISTER Demerits, Dimeters
DEMONESS Enmossed
DEMONIAC Comedian,
　Daemonic, Mid-ocean
DEMOTION Motioned

DEMOUNTS Mudstone,
　Unmodest
DEMURRED Murdered
DEMURRER Murderer
DENARIUS Eridanus, Unraised
DENOTATE Detonate
DENOUNCE Enounced
DENTATED Attended
DENTINES Desinent
DENTURES Sederunt, Underest,
　Underset, Unrested
DENUDERS Sundered
DEPARTED Predated
DEPARTER Reparted
DEPICTER Decrepit
DEPILATE Epilated, Pileated
DEPLETES Steepled
DEPOSITS Side-post, Topsides
DEPRAVED Pervaded
DEPRIVES Prevised
DEPSIDES Despised
DEPUTIES Deputies
DEPUTISE Deputies
DERAILED Deadlier
DERAILER Re-railed
DERANGED Gardened
DERATING Gradient, Treading
DERATION Ordinate, Rationed,
　Rodentia
DERAYING Readying, Yearding
DERELICT Relicted
DERISION Ironside, Resinoid
DERMATIC Time-card
DESCHOOL Schooled
DESCRIBE Escribed
DESCRIED Deciders
DESELECT Selected
DESERTER Redesert
DESERVER Reserved, Reversed
DESIGNED Sdeigned
DESIGNER Energids, Enridges,
　Reedings, Redesign, Resigned
DESILVER Delivers, Silvered,
　Slivered

DESINENT Dentines
DESIRING Residing, Ringside
DESPAIRS Perissad
DESPISED Depsides
DESPISER Disperse, Perseids, Presides
DESPITES Side-step
DESPOTAT Postdate
DESSERTS Destress, Stressed
D'ESTAING Sedating, Steading
*__**DESTERRO**__ Resorted, Restored, Rostered
DESTRESS Desserts, Stressed
DETAILER Elaterid, Retailed
DETAINER Retained
DETESTER Retested
DETHRONE Threnode
DETONATE Denotate
DETRAINS Anti-reds, Strained, Tan-rides, Trade-ins
DEVIANCE Vice-dean
DEVIATES Sedative
DEVISERS Disserve, Dissever
DEWINESS Wideness
DIABETES Beadiest
DIABOLIC Biocidal
DIACTINE Actinide, Ctenidia, Indicate
DIAGNOSE Agonised
DIALYTIC Calidity
DIAMANTE Animated
DIAMETER Remediat
DIARIANS Sardinia
DIASTEMA Adamites, Adamsite
DIASTERS Asterids, Disaster, Disrates
DIASTOLE Isolated, Sodalite, Solidate
DIASTYLE Steadily
DIATONIC Actinoid
*__**DICENTRA**__ Crinated
DIGESTER Erdgeist, Estridge, Redigest
DIGRAPHS Sphragid

DILATORY Adroitly, Idolatry
DIMEROUS Soredium
DIMETERS Demerits, Demister
DIOPTERS Dioptres, Dipteros, Peridots, Portside, Proteids, Riposted
DIOPTRIC Tripodic
DIOPTRES Diopters, Dipteros, Peridots, Portside, Proteids, Riposted
*__**DIOSCURI**__ Sciuroid
DIPTERAL Tripedal
DIPTEROS Diopters, Dioptres, Peridots, Portside, Proteids, Riposted
DIRECTED Credited
DIRECTOR Creditor
DISASTER Asterids, Diasters, Disrates
DISBURSE Bus-rides, Subsider
DISCOUNT Conduits, Noctuids
DISCOVER Divorces
DISCRASE Cressida, Sidecars
DISCREET Discrete
DISCRETE Discreet
DISENDOW Disowned
DISHABIT Adhibits
DISHEVEL She-devil
DISINTER Inditers, Nitrides
DISORBED Disrobed
DISOWNED Disendow
DISPENSE Piedness
DISPERSE Despiser, Perseids, Presides
DISPLODE Lop-sided
DISPONER Prisoned
DISPROVE Prevoids, Provides
DISRATES Asterids, Diasters, Disaster
DISROBED Disorbed
DISROBER Broiders
DISSERTS Distress
DISSERVE Devisers, Dissever
DISSEVER Devisers, Disserve

DISTRAIT Triadist
DISTREAM Misrated, Readmits
DISTRESS Disserts
DISUNITE Nudities
DIVERTER Redivert, Verditer
DIVORCES Discover
*__DNIESTER__ Inserted, Resident,
Sintered
*__DOCETISM__ Comedist, Domestic
DOCTRINE Centroid, Crediton
DOGBANES Bondages,
Dog'sbane
DOGHOUSE Housedog
DOG'SBANE Bondages,
Dogbanes
DOG'S-NOSE Goodness
DOG-WATCH Watchdog
DOLERITE Loitered
DOMAINAL Domaniel
DOMANIAL Domainal
DOMESTIC Docetism, Comedist
DOMIFIED Modified
DOMINATE Nematoid
DOMINIES Minidose
DONATION Nodation
DONATISM Saintdom
DOORBELL Bordello
DOOR-POST Door-stop
DOOR-STOP Door-post
DORMANCY Mordancy
DOURINES Sourdine
DOURNESS Resounds, Sounders
DOVERING Ringdove
DOVETAIL Violated
DOWELLER Rowelled, Welldoer
DOWNCOME Come-down
DOWN-TAKE Take-down
DOWN-TURN Turndown
DOWNWARD Drawdown
DOWNWASH Washdown
DRACONIC Cancroid
*__DRACONIS__ Sardonic
DRAGLINE Dearling
DRAG-NETS Grandest

DRAGONNE Androgen
DRAINAGE Gardenia
DRAINERS Serranid
DRAWBACK Backward
DRAWBORE Wardrobe
DRAWDOWN Downward
DRAWINGS Swarding, Wardings
DREAMING Margined, Mid-
range
DREARING Gairdner, Gardiner
DRESS-TIE Editress, Resisted,
Sistered
DRIBLETS Bristled
DROLLING Lordling
DROWSING Wordings
DRUGGING Grudging
DRUM-BEAT Umbrated
DRY-CLEAN Calendry
DRY-STEAM Steam-dry
DULCIANA Claudian
*__DULCIGNO__ Clouding
DUNGAREE Underage, Ungeared
DUODENAL Unloaded
DUPLEXES Expulsed
DURAMENS Maunders,
Surnamed
DURANCES Unsacred, Unscared
DWINDLES Swindled

EARLIEST Ateliers
EARLSHIP Hare-lips
EARNESTS Assenter, Reassent,
Sarsenet
EARTH-FED Fathered
EARTHIER Heartier
EARTHILY Heartily
EARTHING Hearting, Ingather
EARTHPEA Heart-pea
EASEMENT Estamene
EAST-ENDS Assented, Standees
EASTINGS Giantees, Seatings,
Teasings
EASTLING Galenist, Gelatins,
Genitals, Stealing

EASTLINS Salients, Staniels
EBRIATED Abderite
*ECHINOPS** Chopines
ECHOISMS Mischose
ECLIPSED Pedicels, Pedicles
ECLIPSER Resplice
ECLOSION Colonies, Colonise
*EDENTATA** Antedate
EDGINESS Seedings
EDIFYING Deifying
EDITIONS Sedition
EDITRESS Dress-tie, Resisted, Sistered
EDUCTORS Seductor
EEL-GRASS Gearless, Largesse
EEL-POUTS Outsleep, Sleep-out
EEL-SPEAR Prelease
EFTSOONS Festoons
EGG-SHELL Shell-egg
EGLATERE Regelate, Relegate
EIDOLONS Solenoid
*EINSTEIN** Nineties
*EISLEBEN** Bee-lines
ELANCING Cleaning, Enlacing
ELAPSING Pleasing
ELAPSION Opalines
ELASTICS Alcestis
ELATERID Detailer, Retailed
ELATERIN Entailer, Treenail
ELATIONS Insolate
ELECTION Coteline
ELECTIVE Cleveite
ELECTORS Corselet, Electros, Selector
ELECTRET Tercelet
ELECTROS Corselet, Electors, Selector
ELEGIACS Legacies
ELISIONS Lionises, Oiliness
*ELSEVIER** Relieves
ELVANITE Ventaile
EMBALMER Emmarble
EMBARKED Bed-maker
EMBOILED Bemoiled

EMBRACED Cambered
EMENDALS Dalesmen, Leadsmen
EMERALDS Demersal
EMIGRATE Remigate
EMIRATES Steamier
EMMARBLE Embalmer
EMONGEST Gemstone
EMPANELS Emplanes, Ensample
EMPATHIC Emphatic
EMPERORS Premorse
EMPHASIS Misshape
EMPHATIC Empathic
EMPLANES Empanels, Ensample
EMPLOYER Re-employ
EMPRISES Impresse, Premises, Spiremes
ENACTORS Ancestor, Escatron, Sortance
ENACTURE Uncreate
ENARMING Renaming
ENASCENT Canteens
ENCASHED Enchased
ENCASHES Enchases
. **ENCASTRE** Reascent, Sarcenet
ENCHASED Encashed
ENCHASES Encashes
ENCHORIC Corniche
ENCLOUDS Unclosed
ENCOMIUM Meconium
ENCRADLE Calender
ENCROACH Charneco
ENCRUSTS Curtness
ENCYSTIS Cystines
ENDITING Indigent
ENDURING Unringed
ENERGIDS Designer, Enridges, Reedings, Redesign, Resigned
ENERGIES Energise
ENERGISE Energies
ENERGIST Integers, Reesting, Retinges, Steering, Streigne
ENERVATE Venerate
ENFIRING Infringe, Refining

ENFORCER Confrere, Renforce

ENFOREST Resoften, Softener

ENFRAMED Freedman

ENGIRDED Enridged

ENGIRDLE Lingered, Reedling

ENGLANTE Entangle

ENGLOBED Belonged

ENGRAILS Aligners, Realigns, Resignal, Salinger, Sanglier, Seal-ring, Signaler

ENGROOVE Overgone

ENISLING Ensiling

ENJOINER Re-enjoin

ENKINDLE Enlinked

ENLACING Cleaning, Elancing

ENLINKED Enkindle

ENLISTED Lintseed, Listened

ENLISTEE Selenite

ENLISTER Leinster, Listener, Re-enlist, Relisten

ENMOSSED Demoness

ENORMOUS Nemorous

ENOUNCED Denounce

ENQUIRES Squireen

ENRAGING Angering

ENRAVISH Vanisher

ENRICHED Richened

ENRIDGED Engirded

ENRIDGES Designer, Energids, Redesign, Reedings, Resigned

ENROBING Ring-bone

ENSAMPLE Empanels, Emplanes

ENSHROUD Unhorsed, Unshored

ENSILAGE Lineages

ENSILING Enisling

ENSLAVES Vaneless

ENSNARED Andersen

ENSNARES Nearness

ENSPIRIT Pristine

ENTAILED Date-line, Lineated

ENTAILER Elaterin, Treenail

ENTANGLE Englante

ENTASTIC Nictates, Tetanics

ENTERERS Re-enters, Resenter, Terreens, Terrenes

ENTICERS Scienter, Secretin, Tercines

ENTIRELY Lientery

ENTIRETY Eternity, Trey-tine

ENTOILED Deletion

ENTOMBED Bodement

ENTOZOIC Enzootic

ENTRAILS Latrines, Ratlines, Trenails

ENTREATS Ratteens, Seat-rent

ENTREPOT Tent-rope

ENZOOTIC Entozoic

EPICARPS Crappies

EPILATED Depilate, Pileated

EPILATOR Petiolar, Tail-rope

EPIPLOIC Epipolic

EPIPOLIC Epiploic

EPISODAL Oplised, Sepaloid

EPISTLER Peltries, Perlites, Repliest, Reptiles, Spirelet

EPITAPHS Happiest

EPULOTIC Poultice

EQUATORS Quaestor

EQUINITY Inequity

ERASIONS Sensoria

*****ERASTIAN** Antisera, Artesian, Resinata

ERASURES Reassure

*****ERDGEIST** Digester, Estridge, Redigest

ERECTION Neoteric, Renotice

ERECTORS Secretor

EREMITAL Lemaitre, Materiel, Real-time

ERETHISM Etherism

EREWHILE While-ere, Wire-heel

*****ERIDANUS** Denarius, Unraised

*****ERITREAN** Rain-tree, Retainer

EROTICAL Loricate

ERUPTING Reputing

ESCALLOP Collapse

*ESCATRON Ancestor, Enactors,
  Sortance
ESCOLARS Lacrosse, Solacers
*ESCORIAL Calories, Carioles
ESCORTED Corseted, Costered,
  Recosted
ESCRIBED Describe
ESCURIAL Auricles
ESOTERIC Coteries
ESPALIER Pearlies
ESPECIAL Calipees
ESPOUSAL Sepalous
ESPOUSER Repousse
ESSORANT Assentor, Senators,
  Star-nose, Treasons
ESTAMENE Easement
ESTAMINE Matinees, Seminate
ESTATING Tangiest
ESTIMATE Etatisme
ESTOVERS Oversets
*ESTRAGON Rag-stone, Stone-rag
ESTRANGE Grantees, Greatens,
  Negaters, Reagents, Segreant,
  Sergeant, Sternage
ESTREPED Pestered
ESTRIDGE Digester, Erdgeist,
  Redigest
ESURIENT Retinues, Reunites
ETAGERES Steerage
ETATISME Estimate
ETATISMS Misstate
ETERNITY Entirely, Trey-tine
ETHERISM Erethism
ETHERIST Tee-shirt
ETHICIST Itchiest, Theistic
ETHNICAL Chainlet
ETHOLOGY Theology
*ETRUSCAN Centaurs, Recusant,
  Untraces
EULOGIES Eulogise
EULOGISE Eulogies
EVERTORS Restrove
EVIDENTS Invested
EVILNESS Liveness, Veinless,
  Vileness
EVOCATOR Overcoat
EXCEPTED Expected
EXCITORS Exorcist
EXCLAIMS Climaxes
EXERTING Genetrix
EXORCIST Excitors
EXPANDER Re-expand
EXPECTED Excepted
EXPLODER Explored
EXPLORED Exploder
EXPORTER Re-export
EXPUGNED Expunged
EXPULSED Duplexes
EXPUNGED Expunged
EYEGLASS Glass-eye

FAIRNESS Sanserif
FALCONET Conflate
FALL-BACK Backfall
FALL-TRAP Pratfall, Trap-fall
FALLIBLE Fillable
FALTBOAT Flatboat
FALTERED Reflated
FAMELESS Selfsame
FARMABLE Framable
FARROWED Foreward
FASCIOLE Focalise
FASTENER Fenestra, Refasten
FATHEADS Headfast
FATHERED Earth-fed
FATTRELS Flatters
FEASTFUL Sufflate
FEDERARY Defrayer
FELINITY Finitely
FENESTRA Fastener, Refasten
FERRITIC Terrific
FESTOONS Eftsoons
FICKLING Flicking
FIDICULA Fiducial
FIDUCIAL Fidicula
FIELDING Defiling
FIENDISH Finished

FIGURATE Fruitage
FILLABLE Fallible
FILTERER Refilter
FINESSER Rifeness
FINISHED Fiendish
FINITELY Felinity
FIR-CONES Conifers, Forensic, Forinsec, Inforces
FIREABLE Bale-fire
FIREBACK Backfire
FIRE-POTS Firestop
FIRESTOP Fire-pots
FISH-BONE Bone-fish
FISHBOWL Blowfish
FISH-WORM Worm-fish
FLATBOAT Faltboat
FLAT-IRON Inflator
FLATTERS Fattrels
FLAUNTED Unflated
FLICHTER Rich-left
FLICKING Fickling
FLIRTING Trifling
FLOATERS Forestal, Refloats
FLOUNDER Unfolder
FLOURING Fourling
FLOUTING Outfling
FLOWERED Deflower, Reflowed
FLOWERER Reflower
FLUSHING Lung-fish
FLUTINAS Inflatus
FOCALISE Fasciole
FOLLOW-UP Upfollow
FORELIES Free-soil
FOREMAST Formates, Mort-safe
FOREMEAN Forename
FORENAME Foreman
FORENSIC Conifers, Fir-cones, Forinsec, Inforces
FOREPART Raft-rope
FORESHEW Whereofs
FORESTAL Floaters, Refloats
FORESTED Deforest, Fostered
FORESTER Fosterer, Reforest
FORETELL Toll-free

FOREWARD Farrowed
FORINSEC Conifers, Fir-cones, Forensic, Inforces
FORMALIN Informal
FORMATES Foremast, Mort-safe
FORMULAE Fumarole
FORWARDS Frowards
FORWASTE Software
FOSTERED Deforest, Forested
FOSTERER Forester, Reforest
FOURLING Flouring
FRAMABLE Farmable
FRAME-SAW Saw-frame
FREE-COST Cost-free, Scot-free
FREEDMAN Enframed
FREEPOST Post-free
FREE-REED Refereed
FREE-SHOT Shot-free
FREE-SOIL Forelies
FRENETIC Infecter, Reinfect
FRESCOED Deforces
FROUNCED Unforced
FROWARDS Forwards
FRUITAGE Figurate
FRUMENTY Furmenty
FUMAROLE Formulae
FUNDABLE Unfabled
FURMENTY Frumenty

GAILLARD Galliard
GAINLESS Glassine, Leasings, Sealings
GAINSAYS Assaying
*****GAIRDNER** Drearing, Gardiner
*****GALENIST** Easting, Gelatins, Genitals, Stealing
GALENITE Gelatine, Legatine
GALILEES Legalise
GALLIARD Gaillard
GAME-BIRD Ambridge
GAMESTER Gas-meter
GANCHING Changing

GANISTER Angriest, Astringe, Gantries, Granites, Ingrates, Reasting, Tangiers
GANTRIES Angriest, Astringe, Ganister, Granites, Ingrates, Reasting, Tangiers
*GANYMEDE Megadyne
GARDENED Deranged
GARDENER Garnered
GARDENIA Drainage
*GARDINER Drearing, Gairdner
GARGLING Raggling
GARNERED Gardener
GAROTTER Garrotte
GARRETED Gartered, Regrated, Tredegar
GARRISON Roarings
GARROTTEE Garotter
GARTERED Garreted, Regrated, Tredegar
GASALIER Algeria's, Regalias
GAS-MAINS Amassing, Siamangs
GAS-METER Gamester
GASOLIER Girasole, Seraglio
GAS-RINGS Grassing
*GASTONIA Santiago
GAS-WATER Water-gas
GATE-VEIN Negative
GATHERER Regather
GEAR-CASE Acreages
GEARINGS Greasing
GEARLESS Eel-grass, Largesse
GELATINE Galenite, Legatine
GELATINS Eastling, Galenist, Genitals, Stealing
GELATION Legation
GELDINGS Sledging, Sniggled
GEMATRIA Maritage
GEMSTONE Emongest
GENDERED Degender
GENERATE Green-tea, Renegate, Teenager

GENETRIX Exerting
GENITALS Eastlings, Galenist, Gelatins, Stealing
GENTILES Sleeting, Steeling
*GENTILIS Lignites
GEORGIAN Georgina
*GEORGINA Georgian
GERANIOL Regional
*GERMANIC Amercing, Creaming, Merignac
GERIATRY Argyrite
GERMINAL Maligner, Malinger
GIANTESS Eastings, Seatings, Teasings
GILT-HEAD Alighted
GINGLING Niggling
GIN-SLING Singling, Slinging
GIRASOLE Gasolier, Seraglio
GIRASOLS Grass-oil
*GIRONDIN Non-rigid
GIRTLINE Tireling
*GISBORNE Sobering
GLAD-RAGS Laggards
GLANCING Clanging
GLANDERS Danglers
GLANDULE Ungalled
GLASS-EYE Eye-glass
GLASSINE Gainless, Leasings, Sealings
GLENOIDS Sidelong
GLIBNESS Blessing
GLINTING Tingling
GLOATING Goatling
GLORY-PEA Play-goer
GLOSSINA Lassoing
GLOSSING Goslings
GLUCINUM Cingulum
GLUTTING Guttling
GNASHING Hangings
GNATLING Tangling
GNOMONIC Oncoming
GOATLING Gloating
GOAT'S-RUE Outrages
GOBELINS Ignobles

GOD'S-ACRE Cordages
GOINGS-ON Ongoings
GOLIARDY Gyroidal
GOODNESS Dog's-nose
GOSLINGS Glossing
GRADIENT Derating, Treading
GRAECISM Grimaces
GRAIN-TIN Training
*GRANADOS Sangrado
GRANDEST Drag-nets
GRANITES Angriest, Astringe,
   Ganister, Gantries, Ingrates,
   Reasting, Tangiers .
GRANTEES Estrange, Greatens,
   Negaters, Reagents, Segreant,
   Sergeant, Sternage
GRANTERS Regrants, Stranger
GRANULES Laser-gun
GRASPING Sparing
GRASSING Gas-rings
GRASS-OIL Girasols
GRAUPELS Plaguers, Spergula
GRAVITAS Stravaig
GRAYLING Ragingly
GREASING Gearings
GREATENS Estrange, Grantees,
   Negaters, Reagents, Segreant,
   Sergeant, Sternage
*GRECIANS Creasing, Searcing
GREENING Reneging
GREENISH Sheering
GREEN-TEA Generate, Renegate,
   Teenager
GREMIALS Regalism
GREY-COAT Category
GRIMACED Decigram
GRIMACES Graecism
GROINING Ignoring
GROPINGS Proggins
GROSBEAK Brokages
GROUNDED Underdog, Under-
   god
GRUDGING Drugging
GRUNTERS Restrung

GUANINES Sanguine
GUTTLING Glutting
GYRATION Organity
GYROIDAL Goliardy

HACKLING Chalking
HADDOCKS Shaddock
HADRONIC Rhodanic
HAEMATIN Anthemia
HALCYONS Synochal
HALF-NOTE Half-tone
HALF-TONE Half-note
HALICORE Heroical
HALL-MOOT Moot-hall
HALLOOED Holloaed
HALTERED Lathered
HALTERES Leathers
HAMMERER Rehammer
HANDLESS Handsels
HANDMILL Millhand
HANDOUTS Thousand
HANDOVER Overhand
HANDSELS Handless
HANGINGS Gnashing
HANG-OVER Overhang
HANKERED Harkened
HAPLOIDS Shipload
HAPPIEST Epitaphs
HARA-KIRI Hari-kari
HARDENER Reharden
HARELIPS Earlship
HARI-KARI Hara-kiri
HARKENED Hankered
HARMONIC Choirman
HARP-SEAL Pearl-ash
HARPINGS Phrasing, Sharping
HARSHEST Thrashes
HARTBEES Breathes
HASSLING Lashings, Slangish,
   Slashing
HASTENER Heartens
*HASTINGS Stashing
HATBANDS Sandbath

HATCHERY Thearchy
HATCHETS Thatches
HATEABLE Heatable
HATERENT Threaten
HAUL-BACK Back-haul
HEADFAST Fatheads
HEADINGS Sheading
HEADLONG Long-head
HEADPINS Deanship, Pinheads
HEADRAIL Railhead
HEAD-RING Adhering
HEADSKIN Skinhead
HEALINGS Leashing, Shealing
HEARINGS Hearsing, Shearing
HEARKENS Reshaken
HEARSING Hearings, Shearing
HEARTENS Hastener
HEARTIER Earthier
HEARTILY Earthily
HEARTING Earthing, Ingather
HEARTPEA Earth-pea
HEATABLE Haleable
HEAVINGS Sheaving
HECTORED Tochered
HECTORER Torchere
HEIRLESS Hireless, Relishes
HELISTOP Isopleth, Hoplites,
*HELLENIC Chenille
HEMATICS Misteach, Tachisme
HEPATICS Pastiche, Scaphite
HEPATISE Aphetise
HEPTAGON Pathogen
*HERACLID Heraldic
HERALDIC Heraclid
HERETICS Cretheis
HEROICAL Halicore
HERONSEW Nowheres,
   Whereons
HESITATE Athetise
HESPERID Perished, Shred-pie
HETAIRAI Hetairia
HETAIRIA Hetairai
HIDROTIC Trichoid
HIGHJACK Jack-high

HILL-BORN Hornbill
HILLSIDE Side-hill
HINDERED Rehidden
HINDLEGS Shingled
HIPPINGS Shipping
HIPSTERS Thripses
HIRELESS Heirless, Relishes
HISTIOID Idiotish
HISTORIC Orchitis
HITTABLE Tithable
HOCUSING Chousing
HOGMANAY Mahogany
HOLLOAED Hallooed
HOOTINGS Soothing, Shooting
HOPLITES Helistop, Insopleth
HOPPINGS Shopping
HORNBILL Hill-born
HORSEMAN Shoreman
HORSEMEN Shormen
*HORTENSE Thereons
HOSELESS Shoeless
HOSPODOR Shop-door
HOUSEDOG Doghouse
HOUSETOP Pot-house
HOVER-CAR Overarch
HOWEVERS Whosever
HUMORIST Thoriums
HUNG-OVER Overhung
HUNTINGS Shunting
HUNTRESS Shunters
HUNTSMAN Manhunts
HURTLESS Hustlers, Ruthless
HUSTINGS Unsights
HUSTLERS Hurtless, Ruthless
HUSTLING Sunlight
HYPNOTIC Pythonic, Typhonic
HYPOBOLE Lyophobe

*IBERIANS Siberian
ICE-APRON Caponier, Procaine
ICE-FRONT Infector
ICE-HILLS Chillies
ICE-PLANT Pectinal, Planetic
ICE-STONE Seicento

ICE-WATER Water-ice
IDEALISM Miladies,
IDEATION Iodinate, Taenioid
IDIOTIST Histioid
IDLENESS Linseeds
IDOLATER Tailored
IDOLATRY Adroitly, Dilatory
IDOLISMS Solidism
IDOLISTS Solidist
IGNITERS Resiting, Strigine
IGNOBLES Gobelins
IGNORING Groining
*****ILLINOIS** Illision
ILLISION Illinois
ILL-TIMED Tide-mill
ILMENITE Melinite
IMAGINER Migraine
IMBRUTES Resubmit, Terbiums
IMITANCY Intimacy, Minacity
IMITANTS Titanism
IMITATOR Timariot
IMMERSED Simmered
IMMINENT Miniment
IMPEDING Impinged
IMPELLED Milleped
IMPINGED Impeding
IMPLATES Palmiest, Palmiets,
    Petalism, Septimal
IMPLEADS Misplead
IMPLORED Impolder
IMPLORES Pelorism, Sperm-oil
IMPOLDER Implored
IMPORTER Reimport
IMPRESES Emprises, Premises,
    Spiremes
IMPRESSE Emprises, Premises,
    Spiremes
IMPRINTS Misprint
INACTION Nicotian
IN-AND-OUT Nudation
INBREAKS Brearskin
INBREAKS Bearskin
INCENSES Niceness
INCEPTOR Pretonic

INCHASES Anchises
INCISURE Sciurine
INCLOSER Licensor
INCLUDES Nuclides, Unsliced
INCOMERS Cremosin, Sermonic
INCOMING Coming-in
INCORPSE Conspire
INCREASE Resiance
INCREATE Centiare, Creatine,
    Iterance
INDENTED Intended
INDENTER Intender, Interned,
    Retinned
INDICATE Actinide, Ctenidia,
    Diactine
INDICTER Indirect, Reindict
INDIGENT Enditing
INDIRECT Indicter, Reindict
INDITERS Disinter, Nitrides
INDULGED Deluding, Ungilded
INDURATE Daturine, Ruinated,
    Urinated
INEQUITY Equinity
INFECTER Frenetic, Reinfect
INFECTOR Icc-front
INFESTER Reinfest
INFLAMER Rifleman
INFLATOR Flatiron
INFLATUS Flutinas
INFORCES Conifers, Fir-cores,
    Forensic
INFORMAL Formalin
INFORMER Reinform, Reniform
INFRINGE Enfiring, Refining,
INGATHER Earthing, Hearting
INGENUES Unseeing
INGRAFTS Strafing
INGRATES Angriest, Astringe,
    Ganister, Gantries, Granites,
    Reasting, Tangiers
INGROWTH Throwing, Worthing
INKLINGS Linkings, Slinking
INKWOODS Woodskin
INNOVATE Venation

INORNATE Anointer, Reanoint
INSECURE Sinecure
INSERTED Dniester, Resident, Sintered
INSERTER Reinsert, Reinters, Rentiers, Terrines
INSISTED Tidiness
INSISTER Reinsist, Sinister
INSOLATE Elations
INSOLENT Neilston
INSOULED Delusion, Unsoiled
INSTANCE Ancients, Canniest
INSTATES Antistes, Nastiest, Satinets, Titaness
INSTREAM Minarets, Raiments
INSULATE Alunites
INSULTED Unlisted
INSULTER Lustrine
INSUREDS Sundries
INTAGLIO Ligation, Taglioni
INTEGERS Energist, Reesting, Retinges, Steering, Streigne
INTEGRAL Alerting, Altering, Relating, Triangle
INTENDED Indented
INTENDER Indenter, Interned, Retinned
INTERCUT Tincture
INTEREST Interset, Sternite, Trestine
INTERIMS Minister
INTERNED Indenter, Intender, Retinned
*****INTERPOL** Top-liner
INTERSET Interest, Sternite, Trestine
INTERTIE Retinite
INTIMACY Imitancy, Minacity
INTIMISM Minimist
INTREATS Nitrates, Straiten, Tartines, Tertians, Train-set
INTROITS Tritonis
INVADERS Sandiver
INVENTER Reinvent

INVENTOR Noverint
INVESTED Evidents
INVOCATE Conative
IODINATE Ideation, Taenioid
IRELAND'S Islander
IRON-SAND Andirons, Sand-iron
*****IRONSIDE** Derision, Resinoid
IRONWARE Wear-iron
*****ISABELLA** Sailable
*****ISENGRIM** Remising, Semi-ring
ISLANDER Ireland's
ISOCHEIM Isochime
ISOCHIME Icocheim
ISOCLINE Silicone
ISOLATED Diastole, Sodalite, Solidate
ISOPLETH Helistop, Hoplites
ISOPRENE Pioneers
ISOTHERE Theories, Theorise
ISOTHERM Moithers, Stroheim
ISOTONIC Coitions
ISOTROPY Porosity
ISSUABLE Suasible
ITCHIEST Ethicist, Theistic
ITERANCE Centiare, Creatine, Increate
ITERATES Ariettes, Treaties, Treatise

JACKBOOT Bootjack
JACK-HIGH Highjack
*****JACOBIAN** Bajocian
*****JEBUSITE** Bejesuit
JINGOIST Joisting
JOISTING Jingoist

KERATOSE Kreasote
KEYNOTES Keystone
KEYSTONE Keynotes
KHALIFAT Khilafat
KHILAFAT Khalifat
*****KILBRIDE** Bird-like
KILLINGS Skilling
KING-CROW Corkwing

KREASOTE Keratose
KREATINE Ankerite

LABIATES Baalites, Satiable
*LABRADOR Larboard
LABURNUM Alburnum
LACE-BOOT Bootlace
LACINESS Sanicles
LACROSSE Escolars, Solacers
LACRYMAL Clay-marl
LACTEOUS Locustae, Osculate
LADRONES Solander
LAGGARDS Glad-rags
LAKELETS Skeletal
LAMBASTE Blastema
LAMBKINS Lambskin
LAMBLIKE Balmlike
LAMBSKIN Lambkins
LAMELLAS Small-ale
LAMENESS Maleness, Maneless,
  Nameless, Salesmen
LAMINOSE Semolina
*LAMPETER Palm-tree
LAMPREYS Samplery
*LANCELOT Call-note
LAND-ARMY Maryland
LANDRACE Calander, Calendar
LAPIDATE Talpidae
LAPSTONE Pleonast, Polentas
LAPWINGS Spawling
LARBOARD Labrador
LARGESSE Eel-grass, Gearless
LASER-GUN Granules
LASHINGS Hassling, Slangish,
  Slashing
LASSOING Glossina
LATERITE Literate
LATHERED Haltered
*LATINISE Alienist, Litanies
LATITUDE Altitude
LATRINES Entrails, Ratlines,
  Trenails
LAUDATOR Adulator
LAUNCHER Relaunch

LAVISHER Shrieval
LAYERING Relaying, Yearling
LEADSMAN Dalesman
LEADSMEN Dalesmen, Emendals
*LEANDERS Sand-reel
LEASABLE Saleable
LEASHING Healings, Shealing
LEASINGS Gainless, Glassine,
  Sealings
LEATHERS Halteres
LEAVINGS Sleaving, Svengali
LECANORA Carolean
LECTURES Cruelest
LEERIEST Steelier
LEGACIES Elegiacs
LEGALISE Galilees
LEGALIST Stillage, Tillages
LEGATINE Galenite, Gelatine
LEGATION Gelation
*LEINSTER Enlister, Listener, Re-
  enlist, Relisten
LEISTERS Riteless, Tireless
LENTICEL Lenticle
LENTICLE Lenticel
*LEMAITRE Eremital, Materiel,
  Real-time
LEMURINE Relumine
LEPIDOTE Petioled
LERNAEAN Annealer
LESSENED Needless, Seldseen
LETTERER Reletter
*LEVANTER Relevant   .
LEVERETS Verselet
LEVIABLE Liveable
LEVIRATE Relative
LIBRETTO Tribolet
LICENSED Declines, Silenced
LICENSER Reclines, Silencer
LICENSOR Incloser
LICKINGS Slicking
LIENTERY Entirely
LIFELONG Long-life
LIGATING Taigling
LIGATION Intaglio, Taglioni

LIGHT-DAY Daylight
LIGHTERS Relights, Slighter
LIGNITES Gentilis
LIKEWISE Wise-like
LIMATION Miltonia
LIME-PITS Slime-pit
LIMERICK Rice-milk
LIMITARY Military
LIMITATE Militate
LINEAGES Ensilage
LINEATED Date-line, Entailed
LINESIDE Side-line
LINESMAN Melanins
LINGCODS Codlings, Scolding
LINGERED Engirdle, Reedling
LINGSTER Ringlets, Sterling,
  Tinglers, Tringles
LINGULAR Alluring
LINKABLE Balk-line
LINKINGS Inklings, Slinking
LINKSTER Strinkle, Tinklers,
  Trinkles
LINSEEDS Idleness
LINTSEED Enlisted, Listened
LIONISES Elisions, Oiliness
LIPARITE Reptilia
LISTENED Enlisted, Lintseed
LISTENER Enlister, Leinster, Re-
  enlist, Relisten
LITANIES Alienist, Latinise
LITERATE Laterite
LITHARGE Thirlage
LITTORAL Tortilla
LIVEABLE Leviable
LIVENESS Evilness, Veinless,
  Vileness
LIVEWARE Reviewal
LOBATELY Oblately
LOBATION Oblation
LOCATION Colation
*LOCHABER Bachelor
LOCUSTAE Lacteous, Osculate
LODESMAN Sand-mole
LODICULA Caudillo

LOGGINGS Slogging
LOG-SLATE Tollages
LOITERED Dolerite
LONG-HEAD Headlong
LONG-LIFE Lifelong
LONG-SLIP Pollings
LOOKER-IN Oerlikon
LOOKER-ON Onlooker
LOONIEST Oilstone, Stone-oil
LOP-SIDED Displode
LORDLING Drolling
LORICATE Erotical
LOVE-SUIT Solutive
LOW-DOWNS Slow-down
LUNARIST Luristan
LUNATICS Sultanic
LUNATION Lutonian, Ultonian
LUNETTES Unsettle
LUNG-FISH Flushing
*LURISTAN Lunarist
LUSHNESS Shunless
LUSTRATE Tutelars
LUSTRINE Insulter
LUSTRING Rustling
*LUTONIAN Lunation, Ultonian
LYOPHOBE Hypobole

MACARISM Marasmic
MACARONI Marocain
*MACASSAR Marascas, Mascaras
MACERATE Camerate, Racemate
MACHAIRS Archaism, Charisma
MADDENED Demanded
MADRIGAL Mail-drag
MAESTOSO Osteomas
MAGISTER Migrates, Ragtimes,
  Sterigma
MAHOGANY Hogmanay
MAIDENLY Medianly
MAIL-DRAG Madrigal
MAINTAIN Amanitin
*MAKARIOS Romaikas
MAKEBATE Bakemeat
MAINYARD Dairyman

MAISTERS Asterism, Misrates, Semitars
MALADIES Almadies
MALANDER Alderman
MALENESS Lameness, Maneless, Nameless, Salesmen
MALETOTE Matelote
MALIGNER Germinal, Malinger
MALINGER Germinal, Maligner
MALTSTER Martlets
MANAGERS Semarang
MANDORAS Roadsman
MANELESS Lameness, Maleness, Nameless, Salesmen
MANHUNTS Huntsman
MANLIEST Ailments, Aliments, Saltmire, Smaltine
MANNERED Menander, Remanned
MANORIAL Morainal
MAN-POWER Powerman
MANROPES Proseman
MANTISSA Satanism, Staminas
MARABOUT Tamboura
MARASCAS Macassar, Mascaras
MARASMIC Macarism
MARBLING Rambling
MARCHESE Cashmere
MARCHING Charming
*****MAREOTIS** Amortise, Atomiser
MARGINAL Alarming
MARGINED Dreaming, Mid-range
*****MARIANNE** Armenian
*****MARINIST** Martinis
MARITAGE Gematria
MARKETER Remarket
MAROCAIN Macaroni
*****MARONIAN** Romanian
MARTINIS Marinist
MARTLETS Maltster
*****MARYLAND** Land-army
MASCARAS Macassar, Marascas
*****MASSENET** Tameness

MASSETER Seamster, Sea-terms, Steamers
MASSICOT Acosmist
MASTERED Remasted, Streamed
MASTERER Remaster, Streamer
MASTICOT Stomatic
MATELESS Meatless, Tameless
MATELOTE Maletote
MATERIEL Eremital, Lemaitre, Real-time
MATESHIP Shipmate
MATHESIS Atheisms
MATINEES Seminate
MATRICES Ceramist
MATTRESS Smartest, Smatters
MAUNDERS Duramens, Surnamed
MEAGERLY Meagrely
MEAGRELY Meagerly
MEASURES Reassume
MEATLESS Mateless, Tameless
MECONIUM Encomium
MEDALIST Misdealt
MEDIANLY Maidenly
MEDICATE Decimate
*****MEDISING** Demising
MEGADYNE Ganymede
MEGASTAR Ramsgate
MELAENIC Cameline
MELANICS Meniscal, Mescalin
MELANINS Linesman
MELIBEAN Mineable
MELINITE Ilmenite
MELODIAS Soda-lime
MELODIES Melodise
MELODISE Melodies
MEMORIES Memorise
MEMORISE Memories
MENANDER Mannered, Remanned
MENISCAL Melanics, Mescalin
MENSTRUA Transume
MENSURAL Numerals
MENTALLY Tallymen

*MERCATOR Cremator
MERCIFUL Crimeful
*MERIGNAC Amercing,
Creaming, Germanic
MERISTIC Trisemic
MERRIEST Miterers, Rimester,
Triremes
MERSIONS Minoress
MESARAIC Americas
MESCALIN Melanics, Meniscal
MESOCARP Compares,
Compears
MESOTRON Monteros, Montrose
MESSIDOR Misdoers
METERING Regiment
*METHADON Thanedom
MICELLAR Millrace
MID-OCEAN Comedian,
Daemonic, Demoniac
MID-RANGE Dreaming,
Margined
MIGRAINE Imaginer
MIGRANTS Smarting
MIGRATES Magister, Ragtimes,
Sterigma
MILADIES Idealism
MILDNESS Mindless
*MILESIAN Alienism
MILITARY Limitary
MILITATE Limitate
MILL-HAND Handmill
MILLAIRE Ramillie
MILLEPED Impelled
MIMESTER Meristem, Mismetre
MILL-RACE Micellar
MILTONIA Limation
MINACITY Imitancy, Intimacy
MINARETS Instream, Raiments
MINDLESS Mildness
MINEABLE Melibean
MINIDOSE Dominies
MINIMENT Imminent
MINIMIST Intimism
MINISTER Interims

MINORESS Mersions
MINSTERS Trimness
MINTAGES Steaming
MINUTELY Untimely
MISCHOSE Echoisms
MISDEALT Medalist
MISDOERS Messidor
MISFIELD Misfiled
MISFILED Misfield
MISMETRE Meristem, Mimester
MISPLEAD Impleads
MISPRINT Imprints
MISPRISE Pismires
MISRATED Distream, Readmits
MISRATES Asterism, Maisters,
Semitars
MISREADS Sidearms
MISSHAPE Emphasis
MISSPELL Psellism
MISSTATE Etatisms
MISTEACH Hematics, Tachisme
MISTICOS Stoicism
MISTIMES Semitism
MISTREAT Teratism
MISTRIAL Trialism
MISUNION Unionism
MITERERS Merriest, Rimester,
Triremes
MOCKINGS Smocking
MODIFIED Domified
MOITHERS Isotherm, Stroheim
MOLARITY Morality
MONADISM Nomadism
MONANDRY Normandy
MONARCHS Nomarchs,
Romansch
MONARCHY Nomarchy
*MONASTIR Romanist
MONETISE Semitone
MONISTIC Nomistic
MONOGENY Nomogeny
MONOGRAM Nomogram
MONOLOGY Nomology
MONOTYPE Moon-type

MONTARIA Animator, Tamanoir
MONTEROS Mesotron, Montrose
*****MONTROSE** Mesotron, Monteros
MONTURES Mounters,
Remounts
MOON-TYPE Monotype
MOORINGS Smooring
MOOT-CASE Comatose
MOOT-HALL Hall-moot
MOOTINGS Stooming
MORAINAL Manorial
MORAINES Romanies, Romanise
MORALITY Molarity
MORDANCY Dormancy
MORINGAS Orangism,
Organism, Roamings, Sinogram
MORPHIAS Aphorism
MORT-SAFE Foremast, Formates
MOTIONED Demotion
MOTIONER Remotion
MOTORAIL Motorial
MOTORIAL Motorail
MOULDERS Remoulds,
Smoulder
MOUNTERS Montures,
Remounts
MOUTERER Outremer
MUCRONES Consumer
MUD-CONES Consumed
MUDSTONE Demounts,
Unmodest
MUMBLING Bummling
MUNERARY Numerary
MURALIST Altruism, Ultraism
MURDERED Demurred
MURDERER Demurrer
MURMURER Remurmur
MUSCADIN Scandium
MUSCATEL Calumets
MUTENESS Tenesmus
MUTILATE Ultimate
MUTINOUS Untimous

NACREOUS Carneous

NAMEABLE Amenable
NAME-DROP Pomander
NAMELESS Lameness, Maleness,
Maneless, Salesmen
NAME-PART Parament
NARGHILE Nargileh
NARGILEH Narghile
NASALISE Sea-snail
NASTIEST Antistes, Instates,
Satinets, Titaness
NATANTES Stannate, Tannates
NATIVELY Venality
NATIVISM Vitamins
NATIVIST Visitant
NATTERED Attender, Rattened
NATURIST Anti-rust
NAVIGATE Vaginate
*****NAZARITE** Atrazine
NEARNESS Ensnares
NEARSIDE Arsenide
NEATHERD Adherent, Threaden
*****NEBIT-DAG** Debating
NEBULOSE Bluenose
NECROTIC Concerti
NECTARED Cantered, Crenated,
Decanter, Recanted
NEEDLESS Lessened, Seldseen
NEGATERS Estrange, Grantees,
Greatens, Reagents, Segreant,
Sergeant, Sternage
NEGATION Antigone
NEGATIVE Gate-vein
*****NEILSTON** Insolent
NEMATOID Dominate
NEMOROUS Enormous
NEOPLASM Pleonasm
NEOTERIC Erection, Renotice
NEPHRITE Prehnite, Trephine
NEPOTISM Pimentos
NEPOTIST Point-set, Stone-pit
NERVIEST Reinvest, Servient,
Sirvente
NEUROSIS Resinous
*****NEUSTADT** Unstated, Untasted

*NEUSTRIA Ruinates, Urinates
*NICASTRO Cantoris, Cast-iron
NICENESS Incenses
NICKINGS Snicking
*NICOSIAN Socinian
NICOTIAN Inaction
NICTATES Entastic, Tetanics
NIGER-OIL Religion, Re-oiling
NIGGLING Gingling
NIGHTCAP Patching
NINETIES Einstein
NIPPINGS Snipping
NITRATES Intreats, Straiten,
  Tartines, Tertians, Train-set
NITRIDES Disinter, Inditers
NOBLESSE Boneless
NOCARDIA Orcadian
NOCTUIDS Conduits, Discount
NODATION Donation
NOMADISM Monadism
NOMARCHS Monarchs,
  Romansch
NOMARCHY Monarchy
NOMISTIC Monistic
NOMOGENY Monogeny
NOMOGRAM Monogram
NOMOLOGY Monology
NONESUCH Unchosen
NON-GLARE Algernon
NON-RIGID Girondin
*NORMANDY Monandry
NORTHING Thorning, Throning
NOSELESS Soleness
NOTARIAL Rational
NOTARIES Arsonite, Asterion,
  Notarise, Rosinate, Senorita
NOTARISE Arsonite, Asterion,
  Notaries, Rosinate, Senorita
NOTECASE Acetones
NOTELESS Toneless
NOVELIST Violents
NOVERINT Inventor
NOWHERES Heronsew,
  Whereons

NUCIFORM Cuniform, Unciform
NUCLINES Includes, Unsliced
NUDATION In-and-out
NUDENESS Unsensed
NUDITIES Disunite
NUMBERER Renumber
NUMERALS Mensural
NUMERARY Munerary
NUPTIALS Unplaits
NURLINGS Nursling
NURSLING Nurlings
NUTARIAN Turanian
NUTHATCH Unthatch
NUTTINGS Stunting

OBDURATE Taboured
OBEISANT Botanies, Botanise
*OBERLAND Banderol
OBLATELY Lobately
OBLATION Lobation
OBLIGANT Bloating, Bog-Latin
OBTAINER Baritone, Reobtain
OBTESTED Besotted
OBTURATE Tabouret
OCHEROUS Ochreous
OCHREOUS Ocherous
*OCTAVIAN Cavation, Vacation
OERLIKON Looker-in
OERSTEDS Retossed
OFFENDER Reoffend
OFF-SHOOT Shoot-off
OILINESS Elisions, Lionises
OIL-PRESS Spoilers
OIL-SHALE Shale-oil
OILSTONE Looniest, Stone-oil
OLD-WORLD World-old
OLEANDER Reloaned
ONCOMING Gnomonic
ONGOINGS Goings-on
ONLOOKER Looker-on
ONSETTER Setter-on
OPALINES Elapsion
OPALISED Episodal, Sepaloid
OPENABLE Bean-pole

OPEN-CAST Capstone
OPERABLE Ropeable
OPERANDS Padrones, Pandores, Sarpedon
OPERANTS Paterson, Pronates
OPERATES Asterope, Protease, Soap-tree
OPERATOR Poor-rate
OPSONINS Sponsion
OPTOLOGY Topology
OPTOTYPE Topotype
*ORANGISM** Moringas, Organism, Roamings, Sinogram
ORATRESS Assertor, Assorter, Reassort, Roasters
ORCADIAN Nocardia
ORCHITIS Historic
ORDAINER Reordain
ORDINALS Rosalind
ORDINATE Deration, Rationed, Rodentia
ORGANISE Origanes
ORGANISM Moringas, Orangism, Roamings, Sinogram
ORGANIST Roasting
ORGANITY Gyration
ORIENTAL Relation, Tirolean
ORIGANES Organise
ORNATELY Tyrolean
ORNITHIC Trichion
ORSELLIC Colliers
OSCITANT Tactions
OSCULATE Lacteous, Locustae
OSTEOMAS Maestoso
OSTRACOD Scordato
OSTRACON Cartoons, Corantos
OUTBREAK Breakout
OUTBURNT Burnt-out
OUTCHARM Outmarch
OUTCLASS Soul-scat
OUTCLIMB Climbout
OUTCRIER Courtier
OUTCRIES Citreous
OUTCURES Outcurse

OUTCURSE Outcures
OUTDEVIL Outlived
OUTFLING Flouting
OUTKILLS Outskill
OUTLANCE Clean-out
OUTLIVED Outdevil
OUTMARCH Outcharm
OUTMATES Outsteam
OUTPLACE Copulate
OUTPORTS Outsport
OUTRAGES Goat's-rue
OUTRANCE Courante
OUTRATES Outstare, Out-tears, Rout-seat, Sea-trout
OUTREIGN Routeing
OUTREMER Mouterer
OUTRIDES Outsider
OUTROPER Uprooter
OUTSCORN Contours, Cornutos, Croutons
OUTSHOOT Shoot-out
OUTSIDER Outrides
OUTSKILL Outkills
OUTSLEEP Eel-pouts, Sleep-out
OUTSLIDE Solitude, Toluides
OUTSPORT Outports
OUTSTAND Stand-out
OUTSTARE Outrates, Out-tears, Rout-seat, Sea-trout
OUTSTEAM Outmates
OUTSWEAR Outwears
OUTSWELL Outwells
OUTSWING Outwings
OUT-TEARS Outrates, Outstare, Route-seat, Sea-trout
OUTTHROW Outworth, Throw-out
OUTWATCH Watch-out
OUTWEARS Outswear
OUTWEIGH Weigh-out
OUTWELLS Outswell
OUTWINGS Outswing
OUTWORTH Outthrow, Throwout

OVERACTS Overcast
OVERARCH Hover-car
OVERBLOW Overbowl
OVERBOWL Overblow
OVERBUSY Overbuys
OVERBUYS Overbusy
OVERCALL Call-over, Cover-all
OVERCAST Overacts
OVERCOAT Evocator
OVERDARE Overdear, Overread
OVERDEAL Overlade
OVERDEAR Overdare, Overread
OVERDOER Overrode
OVERDOES Overdose
OVERDOSE Overdoes
OVEREATS Oversate
OVERGONE Engroove
OVERHAND Hand-over
OVERHANG Hangover
OVERHUNG Hung-over
OVERKEEN Overknee
OVERKING Revoking
OVERKNEE Overkeen
OVERLADE Overdeal
OVERLAND Rondavel
OVERLAPS Pro-slave
OVERLIVE Overveil
OVERMANS Oversman
OVERNEAT Renovate
OVERPASS Passover
OVERPOST Overtops, Stop-over
OVER-READ Overdare, Overdear
OVERODE Overdoer
OVERSAIL Valorise
OVERSATE Overeats
OVERSEEN Veronese
OVERSETS Estovers
OVERSLIP Slipover
OVERSMAN Overmans
OVERSPIN Provines
OVERTAKE Take-over
OVERTOPS Overpost, Stop-over
OVERTURE Trouvere
OVERTURN Turnover

OVERVEIL Overlive
OVERWORK Work-over
OXAZINES Saxonize
OYSTERED Storeyed

PACATION Capitano
PACK-MULE Plum-cake
PADRONES Operands, Pandores, Sarpedon
*PAIGNTON Poignant
PAINLESS Spaniels
PAINTERS Pantries, Parentis, Pertains, Pinaster, Repaints
PALENESS Paneless
PALLETED Petalled
PALMATED Date-palm
PALMATES Plateasm
PALMETTE Template
PALMETTO Pot-metal
PALMIEST Implates, Palmiets, Petalism, Septimal
PALMIETS Implates, Palmiest, Petalism, Septimal
PALMISTS Psalmist
PALM-TREE Lampeter
PALM-WINE Wine-plam
PALSYING Splaying
PANDOORS Spadroon
PANDORES Operands, Padrones, Sarpedon
PANELESS Paleness
PANGAMIC Campaign
PANNICLE Pinnacle
PANTILES Plainest
PANTRIES Painters, Parentis, Pertains, Pinaster, Repaints
PAPISHER Sapphire
PARABLES Sparable
PARADISE Sparidae
PARAMENT Name-part
PARASITE Aspirate, Septaria
PARCHESI Charpies, Seraphic
PARENTAL Paternal, Prenatal

*PARENTIS Painters, Pantries,
　Pertains, Pinaster, Repaints
PARIETAL Pteralia
PARISHEN Seraphin
PARLEYED Replayed
*PARMESAN Spearman
PARODIST Parotids
PAROTIDS Parodist
PARROTED Predator, Prorated,
　Teardron
PARSLEYS Sparsely
PARTIALS Triapsal
PARTICLE Prelatic
PARTISAN Aspirant
PARTLETS Platters, Prattles,
　Splatter, Sprattle
PASSER-BY By-passer
*PASSERES Asperses, Repasses
*PASSOVER Overpass
PASTICHE Hepatics, Scaphite
PASTRIES Piastres, Raspiest,
　Tarsipes, Traipses
PASTURAL Spatular
*PATARINE Tarpeian
PATCHERY Petchary
PATCHIER Chapiter, Phreatic
PATCHING Nightcap
PATENTED Pattened
PATERERO Perorate
PATERNAL Parental, Prenatal
*PATERSON Operants, Pronates
PATHOGEN Heptagon
PATRICOS Apricots, Piscator
PATRIOTS Protista
PATTENED Patented
PATTERNS Transept
PEACHERS Preaches, Sea-perch
PEACHICK Chickpea
PEARL-ASH Harp-seal
PEARLERS Relapser
PEARLIES Espalier
PEARTREE Repartee, Repeater
PECTINAL Iceplant, Planetic
PEDALLER Predella

PEDANTIC Pentadic
PEDERAST Predates, Repasted,
　Trapesed
PEDICELS Eclipsed, Pedicles
PEDICLES Eclipsed, Pedicels
PEELINGS Sleeping, Speeling
PEERLESS Sleeper, Speelers
PELORIAS Polarise
PELORISM Implores, Sperm-oil
PELTINGS Pestling
PELTRIES Epistler, Perlites,
　Repliest, Reptiles, Spirelet
PENALISE Sepaline
PENDULAR Underlap, Uplander
PENTADIC Pedantic
PEOPLING Popeling
PERDENDO Pondered
PERIDOTS Diopters, Dioptres,
　Dipteros, Portside, Proteids,
　Riposted
*PERIGORD Porridge
PERIPLUS Supplier
PERISHED Hesperid, Shred-pie
PERISSAD Despairs
PERLITES Epistler, Repliest,
　Reptiles, Spirelet
PERORATE Paterero
PERRADII Prairied
*PERSEIDS Despiser, Disperse,
　Presides
PERSONAS Responsa
PERTAINS Pantries, Painters,
　Parentis, Pinaster, Repaints
PERTHITE Pith-tree, Tephrite,
　Threepit
PERTNESS Presents, Serpents
PERUSERS Pressure
PERVADED Depraved
PERVERSE Preserve
PERVIOUS Previous, Viperous
PESTERED Estreped
PESTLING Peltings
PETALINE Tape-line

PETALISM Implates, Palmiest, Palmiets, Septimal
PETALLED Palleted
PETCHARY Patchery
PETIOLAR Epilator, Tail-rope
PETIOLED Lepidote
PETROSAL Pole-star, Prolates
PETUNIAS Supinate
PHAETONS Stanhope, Stephano
PHENOLIC Pinochle
PHOLADES Asphodel
PHREATIC Chapiter, Patchier
PHRASING Harpings, Sharping
PIANOLAS Anapolis, Salopian
PIASABAS Piassaba
PIASSABA Piasabas
PIASTRES Pastries, Raspiest, Traipses, Tarsipes
PICADORS Sporadic
PICRATES Crispate, Practise
PICTURES Crepitus, Cuprites, Piecrust
PIECRUST Crepitus, Cuprites, Pictures
PIEDNESS Dispense
PIKELETS Spikelet
PILASTER Plaister, Plaiters, Replaits
PILEATED Depilate, Epilated
PILHORSE Polisher, Repolish
PILLAGES Spillage
PIMENTOS Nepotism
PINASTER Painters, Pantries, Parentis, Pertains, Repaints
PINCHERS Pinscher
PINHEADS Deanship, Headpins
PINNACLE Pannicle
PINNINGS Spinning
PINOCHLE Phenolic
PINSCHER Pinchers
PINTAILS Alpinist, Tail-spin
PIONEERS Isoprene
PIPE-CLAY Clay-pipe
PISCATOR Apricots, Patricos

PISMIRES Misprise
PISTOLED Postiled
PISTOLES Spilotes
PITCHERS Spitcher
PITHEADS Spithead
PITH-TREE Perthite, Tephrite, Threepit
PLACINGS Clasping, Scalping
PLAGUERS Graupels, Spergula
PLAINANT Plantain
PLAINEST Pantiles
PLAISTER Pilaster, Plaiters, Replaits
PLAITERS Pilaster, Plaister, Replaits
PLANETIC Ice-Plant, Pectinal
PLANTAIN Plainant
PLANTPOT Pot-plant
PLASHERS Splasher
PLASTERY Psaltery
PLATANES Pleasant, Sea-plant
PLATEASM Palmates
PLATINGS Stapling
PLATTERS Partlets, Prattles, Splatter, Sprattle
PLAY-GOER Glory-pea
PLEADERS Relapsed, Repleads
PLEASANT Platanes, Sea-plant
PLEASING Elapsing
PLEASURE Serpulae
PLEONASM Neoplasm
PLEONAST Lapstone, Polentas
PLOPPING Poppling
*****PLOTINUS** Unspoilt
PLUM-CAKE Pack-Mule
PODISMUS Spodiums
POIGNANT Paignton
POINT-SET Nepotist, Stone-pit
*****POLANDER** Ponderal
POLARISE Pelorias
POLEMICS Compiles, Complies
POLENTAS Lapstone, Pleonast
POLE-STAR Petrosal, Prolates
POLISHER Pilhorse, Repolish

POLITICS Psilotic
POLLINGS Long-slip
POMANDER Name-drop
POMWATER Tapeworm
PONDERAL Polander
PONDERED Perdendo
PONDERER Reponder
PONTOONS Spontoon
POOR-RATE Operator
POPELING Peopling
POPPLING Plopping
PORINESS Pression, Ropiness
POROSITY Isotropy
PORRIDGE Perigord
PORTFIRE Profiter
PORTHOLE Potholer
PORTINGS Sporting
PORTIONS Positron, Sorption
PORTOLAN Pronotal
PORTRESS Sporters
PORTSIDE Diopters, Dioptres, Dipteros, Peridots, Proteids, Riposted
POSHTEEN Potheens
POSINGLY Spongily
POSITION Sopition
POSITRON Portions, Sorption
POSTABLE Potables
POSTDATE Despotat
POST-FREE Freepost
POSTICHE Potiches
POSTILED Pistoled
POSTINGS Signpost, Stopings
POSTLESS Spotless, Stopless
POSTLIKE Spotlike
POST-NOTE Potstone, Topstone
POSTURAL Pulsator
POSTURED Proudest, Sprouted
POSTURER Sprouter, Troupers
POTABLES Postable
POTASHES Spathose
POTHEENS Poshteen
POTHOLER Porthole
POT-HOUSE Housetop

POTICHES Postiche
POT-METAL Palmetto
POT-PLANT Plantpot
POT-ROAST Taproots
POTSTONE Post-note, Topstone
POTTERED Repotted
POTTINGS Spotting
POULTICE Epulotic
POUNCING Uncoping
POUNDERS Presound
POUND-NET Ten-pound
POWERMAN Manpower
PRACTISE Crispate, Picrates
PRAETORS Prorates, Raptores
PRAIRIAL Riparial
PRAIRIED Perradii
PRAISING Aspiring
PRATFALL Fall-trap, Trap-fall
PRATTLES Partlets, Platters, Splatter, Sprattle
PRAYINGS Spraying
PREACHES Peachers, Sea-perch
PREBOAST Probates
PRECIOUS Rice-soup
PREDATED Departed
PREDATES Pederast, Repasted, Trapesed
PREDATOR Parroted, Prorated, Tear-drop
PREDELLA Pedaller
PREDICTS Scripted
PRE-ENTER Repenter
PREHNITE Nophrite, Trephine
PREIGNAC Capering
PRELATIC Particle
PRELEASE Eel-spear
PRELUDES Repulsed
PREMATES Presteam, Temperas
PREMIERS Reprimes, Simperer
PREMISED Demireps, Simpered
PREMISES Emprises, Impresse, Spiremes
PREMORSE Emperors
PRENATAL Parental, Paternal

PRESAGED Asperged
PRESAGER Asperger
PRESAGES Asperges
PRESENTS Pertness, Serpents
PRESERVE Perverse
PRESIDES Despiser, Disperse,
　Perseids
PRESOUND Pounders
PRESSING Spersing, Springes
PRESSION Poriness, Ropiness
PRESS-UPS Suppress
PRESSURE Perusers
PRESTEAM Premates, Temperas
PRETENSE Terpenes
PRETERIT Prettier
PRETONIC Inceptor
*PRETORIA Priorate
PRETTIER Preterit
PREVIOUS Pervious, Viperous
PREVISED Deprives
PREVOIDS Disprove, Provides
PRIESTED Respited
PRIESTLY Spritely
PRIMROSE Promiser
PRINTERS Reprints, Sprinter
PRIORATE Pretoria
PRISONED Disponer
PRISTINE Enspirit
PROBATES Pre-boast
PROCAINE Caponier, Ice-apron
PROCURED Producer
PRODUCER Procured
PROFITER Portfire
PROGGINS Gropings
PROLAPSE Sapropel
PROLATES Petrosal, Pole-star
PROMETAL Temporal
PROMISEE Reimpose
PROMISER Primrose
PRONATES Operants, Paterson
PRONOTAL Portolan
PRORATED Parroted, Predator,
　Tear-drop
PRORATES Praetors, Raptores

PROSAIST Airposts, Protasis
PROSEMAN Manropes
PROSLAVE Overlaps
PROSTYLE Protyles
PROTASIS Airposts, Prosaist
PROTEASE Asterope, Operates,
　Soap-tree
PROTEIDS Diopters, Dioptres,
　Dipteros, Peridots, Portside,
　Riposted
PROTISTA Patriots
PROTYLES Prostyle
PROUDEST Postured, Sprouted
PROVIDES Disprove, Prevoids
PROVINES Overspin
PRUNINGS Spurning
PSALMIST Palmists
PSALTERY Plastery
PSELLISM Misspell
PSILOCIN Cipolins
PSILOTIC Politics
PTERALIA Parietal
PUDICITY Cupidity
PULPITER Repulpit
PULP-WOOD Wood-pulp
PULSATOR Postural
PUNISHER Repunish
PURITANS Rasputin, Uptrains
PURPOSES Supposer
PURRINGS Spurring
PURSLANE Supernal
PURSUING Usurping
PUSH-CART Sharp-cut
PYTHONIC Hypnotic, Typhonic

QUAESTOR Equators
QUANTISE Antiques
QUARTETS Squatter
QUARTILE Requital
QUICKEST Quickset
QUICKSET Quickest

RACE-BALL Caballer
RACEMATE Camerate, Macerate

RACINESS Arasenics, Cerasins, Sarcines
RADICULE Auricled
RAFT-ROPE Forepart
RAGGLING Gargling
RAGINGLY Grayling
RAG-STONE Estragon, Stone-rag
RAGTIMES Magister, Migrates Sterigma
RAILHEAD Headrail
RAIMENTS Instream, Minarets
RAINCOAT Croatian
RAINTREE Eritrean, Retainer
RAMBLING Marbling
*****RAMILLIE** Milliare
*****RAMSGATE** Megastar
RANCHERO Reanchor
RAPPAREE Appearer, Reappear
RAPTORES Praetors, Prorates
RARERIPE Repairer
RASPIEST Pastries, Piastres, Tarsipes, Traipses
*****RASPUTIN** Puritans, Uptrains
RATCHING Charting
RATEABLE Tearable
RATEABLY Betrayal
RATIONAL Notarial
RATIONED Deration, Ordinate, Rodentia
RATLINES Alternis, Entrails, Latrines, Trenails
RATLINGS Starling, Trasling
RATSBANE Ant-bears, Strabane
RATTEENS Entreats, Seat-rent
RATTENED Attender, Nattered
RATTLERS Startler
RATTLINE Trail-net
REABSORB Absorber
REACCEPT Accepter
REACHERS Research, Searcher
REACHEST Acherset, Cheaters, Recheats, Teachers
REACTING Argentic, Catering, Citrange, Creating

REACTION Anoretic, Creation
REACTIVE Creative
READIEST Steadier
READJUST Adjuster
READMITS Distream, Misrated
READOPTS Adopters, Asported
READYING Deraying, Yearding
REAFFECT Affecter
REAFFIRM Affirmer
REAGENTS Estrange, Grantees, Negaters, Segreant, Sergeant, Sternage
REALIGNS Aligners, Engrails, Resignal, Salinger, Sanglier, Seal-ring, Signaler
REALISED Resailed, Sidereal
REALISTS Alisters, Saltiers, Saltires, Slaister
REAL-TIME Eremital, Lemaitre, Materiel
REANCHOR Ranchero
REANOINT Anointer, Inornate
REANSWER Answerer
REAPPEAL Appealer
REAPPEAR Appearer, Rapparee
REARGUED Redargue
REARMING Remargin
REARREST Arrester
REASCEND Ascender
REASCENT Encastre, Sarcenet
REASSENT Assenter, Earnests, Sarsenet
REASSERT Asserter, Serrates
REASSIGN Assigner, Seringas
REASSIST Assister
REASSORT Assertor, Assorter, Oratress, Roasters
REASSUME Measures
REASSURE Erasures
REASTING Angriest, Astringe, Ganister, Gantries, Granites, Ingrates, Tangiers
REATTACH Attacher
REATTACK Attacker

REATTAIN Attainer
REATTEST Attester
REAWAKEN Awakener
REBALLOT Balloter
REBATING Berating
REBELLOW Bellower
REBLEACH Bleacher
REBOUNDS Bounders, Suborned
REBUDGET Budgeter
REBUFFED Buffered
REBUTTAL Burletta
REBUTTED Buttered
REBUTTON Buttoner
RECALLED Cellared
RECANTED Cantered, Crenated,
  Decanter, Nectared
RECANTER Recreant
RECEIVED Deceiver
RECEMENT Cementer, Cerement
RECESSED Seceders
RECHARTS Charters, Chartres,
  Starcher
RECHEATS Acherset, Cheaters,
  Reachest, Teachers
RECISION Soricine
RECITALS Altrices, Articles,
  Selictar, Sterical
RECKLESS Clerkess
RECLEANS Cleaners, Cleanser,
  Relances
RECLINED Decliner
RECLINES Licenser, Silencer
RECLOSES Coreless, Sclerose
RECLUSES Cureless
RECOASTS Castores, Coarsest,
  Coasters, Socrates
RECOATED Decorate
RECOLOUR Colourer
RECONVEY Conveyer
RECORDER Re-record
RECOSTED Corseted, Costered,
  Escorted
RECOUNTS Cornutes, Construe,
  Counters, Trounces

RECOURSE Resource
RECREANT Recanter
RECRUITS Crustier
RECUMBED Cumbered
RECUSANT Centaurs, Etruscan,
  Untraces
RECUSING Rescuing, Securing
REDACTOR Carroted
REDARGUE Reargued
REDBRICK Brick-red
REDEFEAT Defeater
REDELESS Reedless
REDEMISE Remedies
REDENTED Tendered
REDESERT Deserter
REDESIGN Designer, Energids,
  Enridges, Reedings, Resigned
REDIGEST Digester, Estridge
  Erdgeist
REDIVERT Diverter, Verditer
REDOLENT Rondelet
REDSHARE Adherers, Reshared
REEDINGS Designer, Energids,
  Enridges, Redesign, Resigned
REEDLESS Redeless
REEDLING Engirdle, Lingered
REED-STOP Reposted
RE-EMPLOY Employer
RE-ENJOIN Enjoiner
RE-ENLIST Enlister, Leinster,
  Listener, Re-enlist
RE-ENTERS Enteres, Resenter,
  Terreens, Terrenes
REESTING Energist, Integers,
  Retinges, Steering, Streigne
RE-EXPAND Expander
RE-EXPORT Exporter
REFASTEN Fastener, Fenestra
REFEREED Free-reed
REFERENT Rent-free, Tree-fern
REFERRED Deferrer
REFILTER Filterer
REFINING Enfiring, Infringe
REFLATED Faltered

REFLOATS Floaters, Forestal
REFLOWED Deflower, Flowered
REFLOWER Flowerer
REFOOTED Deerfoot
REFOREST Forester, Fosterer
REFORMED Deformer
REFUNDED Underfed
REGALIAN Algerian
REGALIAS Algeria's, Gasalier
REGALISM Gremials
REGARDED Degrader, Regraded
REGATHER Gatherer
REGELATE Eglatere, Relegate
REGIMENT Metering
REGIONAL Geraniol
REGRADED Degrader, Regarded
REGRATED Gartered, Garreted,
　Tredegar
REGRANTS Granters, Stranger
REHAMMER Hammerer
REHARDEN Hardener
REHIDDEN Hindered
REHOUSED Rose-hued, Shore-
　due
REIMPORT Importer
REIMPOSE Promisee
REINDICT Indicter, Indirect
REINFECT Frenetic, Infecter
REINFEST Infester
REINFORM Informer, Reniform
REINFUND Unfriend
REINSERT Inserter, Reinters,
　Rentiers, Terrines
REINSIST Insister, Sinister
REINTERS Inserter, Reinsert,
　Rentiers, Terrines
REINVENT Inventer
REINVEST Nerviest, Servient,
　Sirvente
REISSUED Residues
RELANCES Cleaners, Cleanser,
　Recleans
RELAPSED Pleaders, Repleads
RELAPSER Pearlers

RELATING Alerting, Altering,
　Integral, Triangle
RELATION Oriental, Tirolean
RELATIVE Levirate
RELAUNCH Launcher
RELAYING Layering, Yearling
RELEASED Resealed
RELEGATE Eglatere, Regelate
RELETTER Letterer
RELEVANT Levanter
RELIABLY Bareilly
RELIANCE Cinereal
RELICKED Deer-lick
RELICTED Derelict
RELIEVES Elsevier
RELIGHTS Lighters, Slighter
RELIGION Niger-oil, Re-oiling
RELISHES Heirless, Hireless
RELISTEN Enlister, Leinster,
　Listener, Re-enlist
RELIVING Reviling
RELOANED Oleander
RELUMINE Lemurine
REMANDED Demander
REMANNED Mannered,
　Menander
REMARGIN Rearming
REMARKET Marketer
REMASTED Mastered, Streamed
REMASTER Masterer, Streamer
REMEDIAT Diameter
REMEDIES Redemise
REMIGATE Emigrate
REMISING Isengrim, Semi-ring
REMITTER Trimeter
REMOTION Motioner
REMOULDS Moulders, Smoulder
REMOUNTS Montures, Mounters
REMURMUR Murmurer
RENAMING Enarming
RENAYING Yearning
RENEGATE Generate, Green-tea,
　Teenager
RENEGING Greening

RENFORCE Confrere, Enforcer
RENIFORM Informer, Reinform
RENITENT Tin-terne
RENOTICE Erection, Neoteric
RENOVATE Overneat
RENT-FREE Referrent, Tree-fern
RENTIERS Inserter, Reinsert, Reinters, Terrines
RENUMBER Numberer
REOBTAIN Baritone, Obtainer
REOFFEND Offender
RE-OILING Niger-oil, Religion
REORDAIN Ordainer
REPAINTS Painters, Pantries, Parentis, Pertains, Pinaster
REPAIRER Rareripe
REPARKED Deer-park
REPARTED Departer
REPARTEE Pear-tree, Repeater
REPASSED Aspersed
REPASSES Asperses, Passeres
REPASTED Pederast, Predates, Trapesed
REPEATER Pear-tree, Repartee
REPENTED Repetend
REPENTER Pre-enter
REPERTOR Reporter
REPETEND Repented
REPINING Ripening
REPLAITS Pilaster, Plaister, Plaiters
REPLAYED Parleyed
REPLEADS Pleaders, Relapsed
REPLICAS Calipers, Spiracle
REPLIEST Epistler, Peltries, Perlites, Reptiles, Spirelet
REPOLISH Pilhorse, Polisher
REPONDER Ponderer
REPORTER Repertor
REPOSING Spongier
REPOSTED Reed-stop
REPOTTED Pottered
REPOUSSE Espouser
REPRIMES Premiers, Simperer

REPRINTS Printers, Sprinter
REPRISAL Sarplier
REPRISED Respired, Serriped
REPTILES Epistler, Peltries, Perlites, Repliest, Spirelet
*****REPTILIA** Liparite
REPULPIT Pulpiter
REPULSED Preludes
REPUNISH Punisher
REPUTING Erupting
REQUITAL Quartile
RE-RAILED Derailer
RE-RECORD Recorder
REREWARD Rewarder
RESAILED Realised, Sidereal
RESCALED Declares
RESCREEN Screener
RESCUING Recusing, Securing
RESEALED Released
RESEARCH Reachers, Searcher
RESEASON Seasoner
RESECTED Decreets, Secreted
RESENTER Enterers, Re-enters, Terreens, Terrenes
RESERVED Deserver, Reversed
RESERVER Reverser
RESHAKEN Hearkens
RESHARED Adherers, Redshare
RESIANCE Incrcase
RESICKEN Sickener
RESIDENT Dniester, Inserted, Sintered
RESIDING Desiring, Ringside
RESIDUES Reissued
RESIGNAL Aligners, Engrails, Realigns, Salinger, Sanglier, Seal-ring, Signaler
RESIGNED Designer, Energids, Enridges, Redesign, Reedings
RESILING Riesling
RESILVER Revilers, Silverer, Sliverer
RESINATA Antisera, Artesian, Erastian

RESINATE Arsenite, Sin-eater, Stearine, Teresian, Teresina, Trainees
RESINOID Derision, Ironside
RESINOUS Neurosis
RESISTED Dress-tie, Editress, Sistered
RESISTOR Roisters, Sorriest
RESITING Igniters, Strigine
RESKETCH Sketcher
RESMOOTH Smoother
RESOFTEN Enforest, Softener
RESOLDER Solderer
RESORTED Desterro, Restored, Rostered
RESORTER Restorer, Retrorse
RESOUNDS Dourness, Sounders
RESOURCE Recourse
RESPIRED Reprised, Serriped
RESPITED Priested
RESPLICE Eclipser
RESPONSA Personas
RESPREAD Spreader
RESPRING Springer
RESTABLE Bleaters, Retables
RESTATED Retasted
REST-HOME Theorems
RESTITCH Chitters, Stitcher
RESTLESS Tressels
RESTORED Desterro, Resorted, Rostered
RESTORER Resorter, Retrorse
RESTRAIN Strainer, Terrains, Trainers, Transire
RESTRICT Critters, Stricter
RESTRING Ringster, Stringer
RESTRIVE Reverist, Riverets, Riveters
RESTROVE Evertors
RESTRUNG Grunters
RESUBMIT Imbrutes, Terbiums
RESULTED Ulstered
RESUMMON Summoner
RETABLES Bleaters, Restable

RETAILED Detailer, Elaterid
RETAINED Detainer
RETAINER Eritrean, Raintree
RETASTED Restated
RETEMPER Temperer
RETESTED Detester
RETHATCH Thatcher
RETHREAD Threader
RETHRESH Thresher
RETICLES Sclerite, Tiercels
RETIMING Ring-time
RETINGES Energist, Integers, Reesting, Steering, Streigne
RETINITE Intertie
RETINNED Indenter, Intender, Interned
RETINUED Reunited, Untiered
RETINUES Esurient, Reunites
RETINULA Tenurial
RETOSSED Oersteds
RETRACED Terraced
RETRADES Arrested, Retreads, Serrated, Treaders
RETREADS Arrested, Retrades, Serrated, Treaders
RETRENCH Trencher
RETRORSE Resorter, Restorer
RETUNDED Rudented
REUNITED Retinued, Untiered
REUNITES Esurient, Retinues
REVENANT Venerant
REVERIST Restrive, Riverets, Riveters
REVERSAL Slaverer
REVERSED Deserver, Reserved
REVERSER Reserver
REVERSIS Revisers
REVIEWAL Liveware
REVILERS Resilver, Silverer, Sliverer
REVILING Reliving
REVISERS Reversis
REVISION Visioner
REVOKING Overking

REVOLUTE True-love
REWARDER Rereward
REWEAKEN Weakener
*RHAETEAN** Atherina
RHODANIC Hadronic
RIB-ROAST Arborist
RICE-MILK Limerick
RICE-SOUP Precious
RICHENED Enriched
RICH-LEFT Flichter
RIDDANCE Cider-and
RIDEABLE Bride-ale
RIESLING Resiling
RIFENESS Finesser
RIFLEMAN Inflamer

RING-BONE Enrobing
RING-DOVE Dovering
RINGLESS Slingers
RINGLETS Lingster, Sterling,
Tinglers, Tringles
RING-LOCK Rock-ling
RING-SIDE Desiring, Residing
RINGSTER Restring, Stringer
RING-TAIL Trailing
RING-TIME Retiming
RING-TOSS Sortings
RIPARIAL Prairial
RIPENING Repining
RIPOSTED Diopters, Dioptres,
Dipteros, Peridots, Proteids,
Portside
RIPPLETS Stippler, Tipplers,
Tripples
RIPTIDES Spirited, Tide-rips
RITELESS Leisters, Tireless
RIVALING Virginal
RIVERETS Restrive, Reverist,
Riveters
RIVETERS Restrive, Reverist,
Riverets
RIVETING Tivering
ROADBEDS Adsorbed

ROADSIDE Side-road
ROADSMAN Mandoras
ROAMINGS Moringas,
Orangism, Organism, Sinogram
ROARINGS Garrison
ROASTERS Assertor, Assorter,
Oratress, Reassort
ROASTING Organist
ROCKETER Cork-tree
ROCKIEST Corkiest, Stockier
ROCK-LING Ring-lock
ROCK-WOOD Corkwood,
Woodrock
*RODENTIA** Deration, Ordinate,
Rationed
ROISTERS Resistor, Sorriest
ROISTING Rositing
ROMAIKAS Makarios
*ROMANIAN** Maronian
*ROMANIES** Moraines, Romanise
ROMANISE Moraines, Romanies
*ROMANIST** Monastir
ROMANSCH Monarchs,
Nomarchs
RONDACHE Anchored
RONDAVEL Overland
RONDELET Redolent
RONDURES Rounders, Unorders
ROOSTING Stooring
ROOTIEST Tortoise
ROPEABLE Operable
ROPINESS Poriness, Pression
*ROSALIND** Ordinals
*ROSALINE** Ailerons, Alerions,
Alienors
ROSE-HIPS Seriphos
ROSE-HUED Rehoused,
Shore-due
ROSINATE Arsonite, Asterion,
Notaries, Notarise, Senorita
ROSITING Roisting
ROSTERED Desterro, Resorted
Restored
ROTATING Troating

ROUND-ALL All-round
ROUNDERS Rondures, Unorders
ROUNDEST Tonsored, Unsorted,
  Unstored
ROUSTERS Trousers
ROUTEING Outreign
ROUT-SEAT Outrates, Outstare,
  Out-tears, Sea-trout
ROWELLED Doweller, Welldoer
ROYALIST Solitary
ROYSTING Storying
RUDENTED Retunded
RUDDIEST Sturdied
RUINATED Daturine, Indurate,
  Urinated
RUINATES Neustria, Urinates
RUNCHING Churning
RUSTABLE Baluster
RUSTICAL Curtails
RUSTICLY Crustily
RUSTLING Lustring
RUTHLESS Hurtless, Hustlers

***SABADELL** Ballades
SABELINE Balinese, Base-line
SACCULAR Accruals, Caraculs
SAILABLE Isabella
SAINFOIN Sinfonia
SAINTDOM Donatism
SAINTING Staining
SAINTISM Samnitis
SALARIES Assailer
SALEABLE Leasable
SALESMEN Lameness, Maleless,
  Maneless, Nameless
SALICINE Sicelain, Silicane
SALIENTS Eastlins, Staniels
***SALINGER** Aligners, Engrails,
  Realigns, Resignal, Sanglier,
  Seal-ring, Signaler
SALIVANT Valiants
SALIVATE Aestival
SALLYING Signally, Slangily
***SALOPIAN** Anapolis, Pianolas

SALT-COTE Calottes
SALTIERS Alisters, Realists,
  Saltires, Slaister
SALTIEST Slatiest
SALTIRES Alisters, Realists,
  Saltiers, Slaister
SALTMINE Ailments, Aliments,
  Manliest, Smaltine
SAMNITIS Saintism
SAMPHIRE Seraphim
SAMPLERY Lampreys
SANCTION Canonist, Contains
SANCTITY Scantity
SAND-BATH Hatbands
SAND-DART Standard
SAND-IRON Andirons, Ironsand
SANDIVER Invaders
SAND-MOLE Lodesman
SAND-REEL Leanders
SAND-WORM Swordsman
SANGLIER Aligners, Engrails,
  Realigns, Resignal, Seal-ring,
  Signaler
***SANGRADO** Granados
SANGUINE Guanines
SANICLES Laciness
SANITATE Astatine, Tanaiste
SANITISE Teniasis
SANSERIF Fairness
SANTALIN Annalist
***SANTIAGO** Gastonia
SAPPHIRE Papisher
SAPROPEL Prolapse
SARCENET Encastre, Reascent
SARCINES Arsenics, Cerasins,
  Raciness
SARCITIS Triassic
SARDINES Aridness
***SARDINIA** Diarians
SARDONIC Draconis
SARMENTA Semantra
***SARPEDON** Operands, Padrones,
  Pandores
SARPLIER Reprisal

SARSENET Assenter, Earnests, Reassent
SARPLIER Reprisal
SATANISM Mantissa, Staminas
SATELESS Seatless
SATELLES Tessella
SATIABLE Baalites, Labiates
SATINETS Antistes, Instates, Nastiest, Titaness
SATU-MARE Amateurs
SATURNIA Asturian, Austrian
SATURNIC Curtains
SAUCIEST Suitcase
SAW-FRAME Frame-saw
SAXICOLA Coaxials
SAXONIZE Oxazines
SCALENUS Unscales
SCALPING Clasping, Placings
SCAMBLER Cambrels, Clambers, Scramble
SCANDIUM Muscadin
SCANNING Cannings
SCANTIER Canister, Creatins
SCANTITY Sanctity
SCAPHITE Hepatics, Pastiche
SCAPULAR Capsular
SCARIOUS Urocissa
SCARPING Carpings, Scraping
SCATTIER Citrates, Cristate
SCELERAT Clearest, Telecars, Treacles
SCENICAL Calcines
SCEPTRAL Spectral
SCHEMIST Chemists
SCHILLER Chillers
SCHOOLED Deschool
SCHOONER Coehorns
*** SCHUBERT** Butchers
SCHWERIN Winchers
SCIENTER Enticers, Secretin, Tercines
SCIOLIST Solicits
SCIURINE Incisure
SCIUROID Dioscuri

SCLERITE Reticles, Tiercles
SCLEROSE Coreless, Recloses
SCLEROUS Closures
SCOLDING Codlings, Lingcods
SCONTION Coniston
*** SCOPELUS** Close-ups, Upcloses
SCORDATO Ostracod
SCORSING Crossing
SCOT-FREE Cost-free, Free-cost
SCOTLAND Cotlands
SCOURAGE Courages
SCOURERS Coursers, Cursores
SCOURGED Scrouged
SCOURING Coursing
SCOUTHER Touchers
SCOWLING Cowlings
SCRABBLE Clabbers
SCRAMBLE Cambrels, Clambers, Scambler
*** SCRANTON** Cranston
SCRAPING Carpings, Scarping
SCRATTLE Clatters
SCRAWLER Crawlers
SCREAMER Amercers, Creamers
SCREENED Secerned
SCREENER Rescreen
SCRIBBLE Cribbles
SCRIEVED Serviced
SCRIPTED Predicts
SCRODDLE Coddlers
SCROUGED Scourged
SCROUGER Scourger
SCULLING Cullings
SCULLION Cullions
SCURRIES Cruisers
SCUTCHER Crutches
SCUTTLER Clutters
SDEIGNED Designed
SEA-HORSE Sea-shore
SEA-LEMON Sea-melon
SEALINGS Gainless, Glassine, Leasings

SEAL-RING Aligners, Engrails, Realigns, Resignal, Salinger, Sanglier, Signaler
SEA-MELON Sea-lemon
SEAMSTER Masseter, Sea-terms, Steamers
SEA-PERCH Peachers, Preaches
SEA-PLANE Spelaean
SEA-PLANT Platanes, Pleasant
SEARCHER Reachers, Research
SEARCING Creasing, Grecians
SEARWOOD Wood-sear
SEA-SHORE Sea-horse
SEA-SNALL Nasalise
SEASONER Reseason
SEATBELT Testable
SEA-TERMS Masseter, Seamster, Steamers
SEATINGS Eastings, Giantess, Teasings
SEATLESS Sateless
SEAT-RENT Entreats, Ratteens
SEA-TROUT Outrates, Outstare, Out-tears, Rout-seat
SECEDERS Recessed
SECERNED Screened
SECONDER Censored, Seed-corn
SECONDLY Condyles
SECRETED Decreets, Resected
SECRETES Sesterce
SECRETIN Enticers, Scienter, Tercines
SECRETOR Erectors
SECURING Recusing, Rescuing
SEDATING d'Estaing, Steading
SEDATION Astonied
SEDATIVE Deviates
SEDERUNT Dentures, Underset, Undesert, Unrested
SEDIMENT Dementis, Tidesmen
SEDITION Editions, Tenioids
SEDUCTOR Eductors
SEED-BIRD Bird-seed
SEED-CORN Censored, Seconder

SEEDINGS Edginess
SEEDSMEN Demesnes
SEETHING Sheeting
SEGREANT Estrange, Grantees, Greatens, Negaters, Reagents, Sergeant, Sternage
SEICENTO Ice-stone
SEIZABLE Sizeable
SELDSEEN Lessened, Needless
SELECTED Deselect
SELECTOR Corselet, Electors, Electros
SELENITE Enlistee
SELENIUM Semilune
SELF-LOST Soft-sell
SELFSAME Fameless
SELICTAR Altrices, Articles, Recitals, Sterical
SEMANTRA Sarmenta
*SEMARANG Managers
SEMILUNG Selenium
SEMINATE Matinees
SEMIOTIC Comities
SEMI-RING Isengrim, Remising
SEMITARS Asterism, Maisters, Misrates
SEMITISM Mistimes
SEMITONE Monetise
SEMOLINA Laminose
SENATORS Assentor, Essorant, Star-nose, Treasons
SENORITA Arsonite, Asterion, Notaries, Notarise, Rosinate
SENSORIA Erasions
SENTRIES Trenises
SEPALINE Penalise
SEPALOID Episodal, Opalised
SEPALOUS Espousal
SEPARATE Asperate
SEPTARIA Aspirate, Parasite
SEPTIMAL Implates, Palmiest, Palmiets, Petalism
SERAGLIO Gasolier, Girasole
SERAPHIC Charpies, Parchesi

SERAPHIM Samphire
SERAPHIN Parishen
SERAPIAS Spiraeas
SERENATA Arsenate
SERENING Sneering
SERGEANT Estrange, Grantees,
　Greatens, Negaters, Reagents,
　Segreant, Sternage
SERINGAS Assinger, Reassign
*SERIPHOS Rose-hips
SERMONIC Cremosin, Incomers
SERPENTS Pertness, Presents
SERPULAE Pleasure
SERRANID Drainers
SERRATED Arrested, Retrades,
　Retreads, Treaders
SERRATES Asserter, Reassert
SERRIPED Reprised, Respired
SERVABLE Beslaver, Versable
SERVICED Scrieved
SERVIENT Nerviest, Reinvest,
　Sirvente
SESTERCE Secretes
SESTOLET Teleosts
SETTER-ON Onsetter
SETTER-UP Upsetter
SEVERING Veerings
SEWER-RAT Waterers
SHABBILY Babishly
SHADDOCK Haddocks
*SHAIVISM Shivaism
SHALE-OIL Oil-shale
SHANTIES Anthesis, Sheitans
SHAREMAN Shearman
SHARP-CUT Push-cart
SHARPEST Sharp-set
SHARP-SET Sharpest
SHAWLING Whalings
SHEADING Headings
SHEALING Healings, Leashing
SHEARING Hearings, Hearsing
SHEARMAN Shareman
SHEAVING Heavings
SHE-DEVIL Dishevel

SHEEP-RUN Unsphere
SHEERING Greenish
SHEETING Seething
SHEILING Shieling
SHEITANS Anthesis, Shanties
SHELL-EGG Eggshell
*SHERATON Another's
*SHETLAND Stendhal
SHIELING Sheiling
SHINGLED Hindlegs
SHIPLOAD Haploids
SHIPMATE Mateship
SHIPPING Hippings
*SHIVAISM Shaivism
SHIVERED Shrieved
SHOELESS Hoseless
SHOOTING Hootings, Soothing
SHOOT-OFF Offshoot
SHOOT-OUT Outshoot
SHOP-DOOR Hospodor
SHOPPING Hoppings
SHOPWORK Workshop
SHORE-DUE Rehoused, Rose-
　hued
SHOREMAN Horseman
SHOREMEN Horsemen
SHOT-FREE Free-shot
SHOTTING Tonights
SHOUTING Southing
SHRED-PIE Hesperid, Perished
SHRIEVAL Lavisher
SHRIEVED Shivered
SHRUBBED Bush-bred
SHUNLESS Lushness
SHUNTERS Huntress
SHUNTING Huntings
SIAMANGS Amassing, Gas-
　mains
*SIBERIAN Iberians
*SICELAIN Salicine, Silicane
SICKENER Resicken
SIDEARMS Misreads
SIDECARS Cressida, Discrase
SIDE-HILL Hillside

SIDE-LINE Lineside
SIDELONG Glenoids
SIDE-NOTE Side-tone
SIDE-POST Deposits, Topsides
SIDEREAL Realised, Resailed
SIDE-ROAD Roadside
SIDE-STEP Despites
SIDE-TONE Side-note
SIDEWAYS Waysides
SIDE-WIND Wind-side
SIGMATIC Astigmic
SIGNABLE Belgians, Bengalis,
　Singable
SIGNALER Aligners, Engrails,
　Realigns, Resignal, Sanglier
SIGNALLY Sallying, Slangily
SIGNORAS Assignor
SIGNPOST Postings, Stopings
SILENCED Declines, Licensed
SILENCER Licenser, Reclines
SILENTLY Tinselly
SILICANE Salicine, Sicelain
SILICATE Ciliates
SILICONE Isocline
SILVERED Delivers, Desilver,
　Slivered
SILVERER Resilver, Revilers,
　Sliverer
SIMMERED Immersed
SIMPERED Demireps, Premised
SIMPERER Premiers, Reprimes
SIMULARS Surmisal
SIN-EATER Arsenite, Resinate,
　Stearine, Teresian, Teresina,
　Trainees
SINECURE Insecure
SINFONIA Sainfoin
SINGABLE Belgians, Bengalis,
　Signable
SINGLING Gin-sling, Slinging
SINISTER Insister, Reinsist
SINOGRAM Moringas,
　Orangism, Organism, Roamings

SINTERED Dniester, Inserted,
　Resident
SIPPLING Slipping
SIRVENTE Nerviest, Reinvest,
　Servient
SISTERED Dress-tie, Editress,
　Resisted
SIZEABLE Seizable
SKEAN-DHU Unshaked
SKELETAL Lakelets
SKETCHER Resketch
SKILLING Killings
SKINHEAD Headskin
SKIRTING Striking
SLAISTER Alisters, Realists,
　Saltiers, Saltires
SLANGILY Sallying, Signally
SLANGING Anglings
SLANGISH Hassling, Lashings,
　Slashing
SLASHING Hassling, Lashings,
　Slangish
SLATIEST Saltiest
SLATTERN Trentals
SLAVERER Reversal
*****SLAVONIC** Volscian
SLEAVING Leavings, Svengali
SLEDGING Geldings, Sniggled
SLEEPERS Peerless, Speelers
SLEEPING Peelings, Speeling
SLEEP-OUT Eel-pouts, Outsleep
SLEETING Gentiles, Steeling
SLEWINGS Swingles, Wingless
SLICKETS Stickles
SLICKING Lickings
SLIGHTED Delights
SLIGHTER Lighters, Relights
SLIME-PIT Lime-pits
SLINGERS Ringless
SLINGING Gin-sling, Singling
SLINKING Inklings, Linkings
SLIPOVER Overslip
SLIPPING Sippling
SLIPRAIL Spirilla

SLITTING Stilting, Tiltings, Titlings, Tlingits
SLIVERED Delivers, Desilver, Silvered
SLIVERER Resilver, Revilers, Silverer
SLOGGING Loggings
SLOW-DOWN Low-downs
SLOWNESS Snowless
SMALL-ALE Lamellas
SMALTINE Ailments, Aliments, Saltmine
SMARTEST Mattress, Smatters
SMARTING Migrants
SMATTERS Mattress, Smartest
SMELTERS Termless
SMOCKING Mockings
SMOKABLE Abelmosk
SMOORING Moorings
SMOOTHER Resmooth
SMOULDER Moulders, Remoulds
SNATCHED Stanched
SNATCHES Stanches
SNATCHER Chanters, Stancher, Tranches
SNEAPING Speaning
SNEERING Serening
SNICKING Nickings
SNIGGLED Geldings, Sledging
SNIPPING Nippings
SNITCHER Chinrest, Christen, Citherns
SNOOPIER Spoonier
SNOOPING Spooning
SNOWLESS Slowness
SOAP-TREE Asterope, Operates, Protease
SOBERING Gisborne
SOCIETAL Aloetics
*****SOCINIAN** Nicosian
*****SOCRATES** Castores, Coarsest, Coasters, Recoasts
*****SOCRATIC** Acrostic
SODA-LIME Melodias

SODALITE Diastole, Isolated, Solidate
SOFTENER Enforest, Resoften
SOFT-SELL Self-lost
SOFTWARE Forwaste
SOLACERS Escolers, Lacrosse
SOLANDER Ladrones
SOLDERER Resolder
SOLECIST Solstice
SOLENESS Noseless
SOLENOID Eidolons
SOLICITS Sciolist
SOLIDARE Soredial
SOLIDATE Diastole, Isolated, Sodalite
SOLIDISM Idolisms
SOLIDIST Idolists
SOLITARY Royalist
SOLITUDE Outslide, Toluides
SOLSTICE Solecist
SOLUTIVE Love-suit
SOMATISM Atomisms
SOMATIST Atomists
SOMBERLY Sombrely
SOMBRELY Somberly
SOMERSET Tree-moss
SONANCES Canoness
SONG-BIRD Bird-song
SOOTHING Hootings, Shooting
SOOTIEST Tootsies
SOPITION Position
SOREDIAL Solidare
SOREDIUM Dimerous
SORICINE Recision
SORPTION Portions, Positron
SORRIEST Resistor, Roisters
SORTABLE Bloaters, Storable
SORTANCE Ancestor, Enactors, Escatron
SORTINGS Ring-toss
SORTMENT Torments
SOUL-SCAT Outclass
SOUND-BAR Baudrons
SOUNDERS Dourness, Resounds

SOUNDING Undoings
SOURDINE Dourines
SOUTACHE Cathouse
SOUTERLY Urostyle
SOUTHING Shouting
SPADROON Pandoors
SPANGLER Sprangle
SPANIELS Painless
SPARABLE Parables
SPARGING Grasping
*SPARIDAE Paradise
SPARLING Springal
SPARSELY Parsleys
SPATHOSE Potashes
SPATULAR Pastural
SPAWLING Lapwings
SPAWNING Wingspan
SPEANING Sneaping
SPEARMAN Parmesan
SPECTRAL Sceptral
SPECTRUM Crumpets
SPEELERS Peerless, Sleepers
SPEELING Peelings, Sleeping
SPELAEAN Sea-plane
SPERGULA Graupels, Plaguers
SPERM-OIL Implores, Pelorism
SPERSING Pressing, Springes
SPHRAGID Digraphs
SPIKELET Pikelets
SPILLAGE Pillages
SPILOTES Pistoles
SPINDLED Splendid
SPINNING Pinnings
SPINSTRY Trypsins
SPINULES Splenius
SPIRACLE Calipers, Replicas
SPIRAEAS Serapias
SPIRANTS Spraints
SPIRELET Epistler, Peltries,
    Perlites, Repliest, Reptiles
SPIREMES Emprises, Impresse,
    Premises
SPIRILLA Sliprail
SPIRITED Riptides, Tide-rips

SPIRTING Striping
SPITCHER Pitchers
SPIT-CURL Culprits
*SPITHEAD Pitheads
SPLASHER Plashers
SPLATTER Partlets, Platters,
    Prattles, Sprattle
SPLAYING Palsying
SPLENDID Spindled
SPLENIUS Spinules
SPLITTER Triplets
SPODIUMS Podismus
SPOILERS Oil-press
SPONGIER Reposing
SPONGILY Posingly
SPONSION Opsonins
SPONTOON Pontoons
SPOONIER Snoopier
SPOONING Snooping
SPORADIC Picadors
SPORTERS Portress
SPORTING Portings
SPOTLESS Postless, Stopless
SPOTLIKE Postlike
SPOTTING Pottings
SPRAINTS Spirants
SPRANGLE Spangler
SPRATTLE Partlets, Platters,
    Prattles, Splatter
SPRAYING Prayings
SPREADER Respread
SPRINGAL Sparling
SPRINGER Respring
SPRINGES Pressing, Spersing
SPRINGLE Sperling
SPRINTER Printers, Reprints
SPRITELY Priestly
SPROUTED Postured, Proudest
SPROUTER Posturer, Troupers
SPURNING Prunings
SPURRING Purrings
SQUATTER Quartets
SQUIREEN Enquires
*SRINAGAR Arraigns

STABLING Blasting
STACCATO Stoccata, Toccatas
STAINING Sainting
STAKE-OUT Take-outs
STALLAGE Tallages
STAMINAL Talisman
STAMINAS Mantissa, Satanism
STAMPEDE Step-dame
STAMPING Tampings
STANCHED Snatched
STANCHER Chanters, Snatcher,
　Tranches
STANCHES Snatches
STANDARD Sand-dart
STANDEES Assented, East-ends
STANDOUT Outstand
*****STANHOPE** Phaetons, Stephano
STANIELS Fastlins, Salients
*****STANMORE** Storeman
STANNATE Natantes, Tannates
STAPLING Platings
STARCHER Charters, Chartres,
　Recharts
STARLING Ratlings, Trasling
STAR-NOSE Assentor, Essorant,
　Senators, Treasons
STARTLER Rattlers
STASHING Hastings
STATABLE Abettals, Tastable
STATICAL Cat's-tail, Cattails
STAY-LACE Catalyse
STEADIER Readiest
STEADING d'Estaing, Sedating
STEADILY Diastyle
STEALERS Tearless, Tesseral
STEALING Eastling, Galenist,
　Gelatins, Genitals
STEAM-DRY Dry-steam
STEAMERS Masseter, Seamster,
　Sea-terms
STEAMING Mintages
STEAMIER Emirates

STEARINE Arsenite, Resinate,
　Sin-eater, Teresian, Teresina,
　Trainees
STEELIER Leeriest
STEELING Gentiles, Sleeting
STEENBOK Betokens
STEEPLED Depletes
STEERAGE Etageres
STEERING Energist, Integers,
　Reesting, Retinges, Streigne
*****STENDHAL** Shetland
STEP-DAME Stampede
STEP-DOWN Stewpond
*****STEPHANO** Phaetons, Stanhope
STERICAL Altrices, Articles,
　Recitals, Selictor
STERIGMA Magister, Migrates,
　Ragtimes
STERLING Lingster, Ringlets,
　Tinglers, Tringles
STERNAGE Estrange, Grantees,
　Greatens, Negaters, Reagents,
　Segreant, Sergeant
STERNITE Interest, Interset,
　Trestine
*****STEWART** Swatter, Tewarts
STEWPOND Step-down
STIBBLER Tribbles
STICKETH Thickest, Thickets,
　Thickset
STICKING Tickings
STICKLER Strickle, Ticklers,
　Trickles
STICKLES Slickest
STILBENE Tensible
STILLAGE Legalist, Tillages
STILLING Tillings
STILTING Slitting, Tiltings,
　Titlings, Tlingits
STING-RAY Straying
STINTING Tintings
STIPPLER Ripplets, Tipplers,
　Tripples
STITCHER Chitters, Restitch

STOATING Tangoist, Toasting, Tsingtao
STOCCATA Toccatas, Staccato
STOCKIER Corkiest, Rockiest
STOICISM Misticos
STOMATIC Masticot
STONE-OIL Looniest, Oilstone
STONE-PIT Nepotist, Point-set
STONE-RAG Estragon, Rag-stone
STOOLING Toolings
STOOMING Mootings
STOORING Roosting
STOPINGS Postings, Signpost
STOPLESS Postless, Spotless
STOP-OVER Overpost, Overtops
STOPPING Toppings
STORABLE Bloaters, Sortable
STOREMAN Stanmore
STOREYED Oystered
STORYING Roysting
STOWABLE Bestowal
*****STRABANE** Ratsbane, Ant-bears
STRAFING Ingrafts
STRAICHT Chartist
STRAINED Anti-reds, Detrains, Tan-rides, Trade-ins
STRAINER Restrain, Terrains, Trainers, Transire
STRAITEN Intreats, Nitrates, Tartines, Tertians, Train-set
STRAMMEL Trammels
STRANDED Darndest
STRANGER Granters, Regrants
STRANGLE Tanglers, Trangles
STRAPPER Trappers
STRAVAIG Gravitas
STRAYING Sting-ray
STREAMED Mastered, Remasted
STREAMER Masterer, Remaster
STREIGNE Energist, Integers, Reesting, Retinges, Sterring
STRELITZ Streltzi
STRELTZI Strelitz
STRESSED Desserts, Destress

STREWING Wresting
STRIATED Tardiest
STRICKLE Stickler, Ticklers, Trickles
STRICTER Critters, Restrict
STRIDDLE Tiddlers
STRIDENT Tridents
STRIGINE Igniters, Resiting
STRIKING Skirting
STRINGER Restring, Ringster
STRINKLE Linkster, Tinklers, Trinkles
STRIPING Spirting
STRIPPER Trippers
STRODDLE Strodled, Toddlers
STRODLED Stroddle, Toddlers
*****STROHEIM** Isotherm, Moithers
STROLLER Trollers
STROWING Worsting
STRUMPET Trumpets
STUBBING Tubbings
STUMBLER Tumblers, Tumbrels
STUNTING Nuttings
STURDIED Ruddiest
STURTING Trusting
SUASIBLE Issuable
SUBAHDAR Bahadurs
SUB-ALATE Tableaus
SUB-CLERK Bucklers
SUBIMAGO Bigamous
SUBLIMES Sub-smile
SUB-OPTIC Sub-topic
SUBORDER Bordures
SUBORNED Bounders, Rebounds
SUBSERVE Subverse
SUBSIDER Bus-rides, Disburse
SUB-SMILE Sublimes
SUB-TOPIC Sub-optic
SUBVERSE Subserve
*****SUDANESE** Danseuse
SUFFLATE Feastful
SUITCASE Sauciest
SUITINGS Tissuing
SULTANIC Lunatics

*SUMERIAN Aneurism
SUMMONER Resummon
SUN-BLIND Unblinds
SUN-CURED Uncursed
SUNDERED Denuders
SUNDRIES Insureds
SUNLIGHT Hustling
SUN-SHADE Unsashed,
  Unshades
SUPERATE Upas-tree
SUPERNAL Purslane
SUPINATE Petunias
SUPPLIER Periplus
SUPPOSER Purposes
SUPPRESS Press-ups
SURENESS Suresnes
*SURESNES Sureness
SURFEITS Surfiest
SURFIEST Surfeits
SURMISAL Simulars
SURNAMED Duramens,
  Maunders
*SVENGALI Leavings, Sleaving
SWADDLER Dawdlers, Waddlers
SWAGGING Waggings
SWARDING Drawings, Wardings
SWASHING Washings
SWATTER Stewart, Tewarts
SWEARING Wearings
SWEATIER Weariest
SWEEPING Weepings
SWIGGING Wiggings
SWINDGED Weddings
SWINDLED Dwindles
SWINDLES Wildness, Windless
SWINGLES Slewings, Wingless
SWINKING Winkings
SWISHING Whissing
SWORDMAN Sand-worm
SYBARITE Bestiary
SYENITIC Cytisine
SYNOCHAL Halycons

TABLEAUS Sub-alate

TABLE-CUT Cuttable
TABORING Aborting, Borating
TABOURED Obdurate
TABOURET Obturate
TACHISME Misteach, Hematics
TACITURN Urticant
TACKLING Talcking
TACTIONS Oscitant
TAENIOID Ideation, Iodinate
TAGLIONI Intaglio, Ligation
TAIGLING Ligating
TAIL-COAT Coat-tail
TAILORED Idolater
TAIL-ROPE Epilator, Petiolar
TAIL-SPIN Alpinist, Pintails
TAKE-DOWN Down-take
TAKE-OUTS Stake-out
TAKE-OVER Overtake
TALCKING Tackling
TALISMAN Staminal
TALLAGES Stallage
TALLYMEN Mentally
*TALPIDAE Lapidate
TAMANOIR Animator, Montaria
TAMBOURA Marabout
TAMELESS Mateless, Meatless
TAMENESS Massenet
TAMPINGS Stamping
TANAISTE Astatine, Sanitate
TANGIBLE Belating, Bleating
*TANGIERS Angriest, Astringe,
  Ganister, Gantries, Granites,
  Ingrates, Reasting
TANGIEST Estating
TANGLERS Strangle, Trangles
TANGLING Gnatling
TANGOIST Stoating, Toasting,
  Tsingtao
TANNATES Natantes, Stannate
TAN-RIDES Anti-reds, Detrains,
  Strained, Trade-ins
TANTALIC Atlantic
*TANTRISM Transmit
TAPE-LINE Petaline

TAPEWORM Pomwater
TAPROOTS Pot-roast
TAPWATER Water-tap
TARDIEST Striated
*****TARPEIAN** Patarine
TARRAGON Arrogant
*****TARSIPES** Pastries, Piastres, Raspiest, Traipses
TARTINES Intreats, Nitrates, Straiten, Tertians, Trainset
TAR-WATER Water-rat
TASTABLE Abettals, Statable
TAUNTING Attuning
TAUTNESS Unstates
TAVERING Averting, Vintager
TEABERRY Betrayer
TEACHERS Acherset, Cheaters, Reachest, Recheats
TEACHING Cheating
TEAMWORK Workmate
TEARABLE Rateable
TEAR-DROP Parroted, Predator, Prorated
TEARLESS Stealers, Tesseral
TEASINGS Eastings, Giantess, Seatings
TECTONIC Concetti
TEENAGER Generate, Green-tea, Renegate
TEE-SHIRT Etherist
TELECARS Clearest, Scelerat, Treacles
TELEOSTS Sestolet
TELESTIC Testicle
TEMPERAS Premates, Presteam
TEMPERER Retemper
TEMPLATE Palmette
TEMPORAL Prometal
TENDERED Redented
TENESMUS Muteness
TENIASIS Sanitise
TENORIST Tritones
TEN-POUND Pound-net
TENSIBLE Stilbene

TENT-ROPE Entrepot
TENURIAL Retinula
TEPHRITE Perthite, Pith-tree, Threepit
TERATISM Mistreat
TERBIUMS Imbrutes, Resubmit
TERCELET Electret
TERCINES Enticers, Scienter, Secretin
*****TERESIAN** Arsenite, Resinate, Sin-eater, Stearine, Teresina, Trainees
*****TERESINA** Arsenite, Resinate, Sin-eater, Stearine, Teresian, Trainees
TERMINAL Tram-line
TERMINUS Unmiters, Unmitres
TERMLESS Smelters
TERPENES Pretense
TERRACED Retraced
TERRAINS Restrain, Strainer, Trainers, Transire
TERREENS Enterers, Re-enters, Resenter, Terrenes
TERRENES Enterers, Re-enters, Resenter, Terreens
TERRIFIC Ferritic
TERRINES Inserter, Reinsert, Reinters, Rentiers
TERTIANS Intreats, Nitrates, Straiten, Tartines, Train-set
TESSELLA Satelles
TESSERAL Stealers, Tearless
TESTABLE Seat-belt
TESTACEA Acetates
TESTATOR Attestor
TEST-CASE Cassette
TESTICLE Telestic
TETANICS Entastic, Nictates
TETANISE Anisette
TETANOID Antidote
TETRACID Tetradic
TETRADIC Tetracid
TETRONAL Tolerant

TEWARTS Stewart, Swatter
THANEDOM Methadon
THATCHER Rethatch
THATCHES Hatchets
THEARCHY Hatchery
THEISTIC Ethicist, Itchiest
THEOLOGY Ethology
THEOREMS Rest-home
THEORIES Isothere, Theorise
THEORISE Isothere, Theories
THEORIST Thorites
THEREONS Hortense
THETICAL Athletic
THICKEST Sticketh, Thickets, Thickset
THICKETS Sticketh, Thickest, Thickset
THICKSET Sticketh, Thickest, Thickets
THIRLAGE Litharge
THORACIC Trochaic
THORITES Theorist
THORIUMS Humorist
THORNING Northing, Throning
THOUSAND Handouts
THRASHES Harshest
THREADEN Adherent, Neatherd
THREADER Rethread
THREATEN Haterent
THREEPIT Perthite, Pith-tree, Tephrite
THRENODE Dethrone
THRESHER Rethresh
THRIDACE Tracheid
THRIPSES Hipsters
THRONING Northing, Thorning
THROWING Ingrowth, Worthing
THROW-OUT Outthrow, Outworth
THYROIDS Thyrsoid
THYRSOID Thyroids
TICKINGS Sticking
TICKLERS Stickler, Strickle, Trickles

TIDDLERS Striddle
TIDE-MILL Ill-timed
TIDE-RIPS Riptides, Spirited
TIDESMEN Dementis, Sediment
TIDINESS Insisted
TIERCELS Reticles, Sclerite
TIGER-NUT Uttering
TILLABLE Bletilla
TILLAGES Legalist, Stillage
TILLERED Tredille
TILLINGS Stilling
TILTINGS Stilting, Slitting, Titlings, Tlingits
TIMARIOT Imitator
TIMBALES Balmiest
TIME-CARD Dermatic
TINCTURE Intercut
TINGLERS Lingster, Ringlets, Sterling, Tringles
TINGLING Glinting
TINKLERS Linkster, Strinkle, Trinkles
TINSELLY Silently
TINSTONE Tontines
TIN-TERNE Renitent
TINTINGS Stinting
TIPPLERS Ripplets, Stippler, Tripples
TIRELESS Leisters, Riteless
TIRELING Girtline
TIROLEAN Oriental, Relation
TISSUING Suitings
TITANESS Antistes, Instates, Nastiest, Satinets
TITANISM Imitants
TITHABLE Hittable
TITLINGS Stilting, Tiltings
TITRATED Attrited
TITRATES Tri-state
TITULARS Altruist, Ultraist
TIVERING Riveting
*****TLINGITS** Slitting, Stilting, Tiltings, Titlings

TOASTING Stoating, Tangoist, Tsingtao
TOCCATAS Staccato, Stoccata
TOCHERED Hectored
TODDLERS Stroddle, Strodled
TOE-DANCE Anecdote
TOLERANT Tetronal
TOLLAGES Log-slate
TOLL-FREE Foretell
TOLUIDES Outslide, Solitude
TONELESS Noteless
TONIGHTS Shotting
TONSURED Roundest, Unsorted, Unstored
TONTINES Tinstone
TOOLINGS Stooling
TOOTSIES Sootiest
TOP-LINER Interpol
TOPOLOGY Optology
TOPOTYPE Optotype
TOPPINGS Stopping
TOPSIDES Deposits, Side-post
TOPSTONE Post-note, Potstone
TORCHERE Hectorer
TORMENTS Sortment
TORSADES Assorted
TORTILLA Littoral
TORTOISE Rootiest
TOTALLED Allotted
TOUCHERS Scouther
TOURISTY Yttrious
TOUSLING Tung-oils
TOWNLESS Wontless
TRACHEID Tridance
TRADE-INS Anti-reds, Detrains, Strained, Tan-rides
TRAILING Ringtail
TRAIL-NET Rattline
TRAINEES Arsenite, Resinate, Sin-eater, Stearine, Teresian, Teresina
TRAINERS Restrain, Strainer, Terrains, Transire
TRAINING Grain-tin

TRAIN-SET Intreats, Nitrates, Straiten, Tartines, Tertians
TRAIPSES Pastries, Piastres, Raspiest, Tarsipes
TRAM-LINE Terminal
TRAMMELS Strammel
TRANCHES Chanters, Snatcher, Stancher
TRANGLES Strangle, Tanglers
TRANSEPT Patterns
TRANSIRE Restrain, Strainer, Terrains, Trainers
TRANSMEW Trewsman
TRANSMIT Tantrism
TRANSUME Menstrua
TRAPESED Pederast, Predates, Repasted
TRAP-FALL Fall-trap, Pratfall
TRAPPEAN Apparent
TRAPPERS Strapper
TRASLING Ratlings, Starling
TRAUCHLE Archlute
TRAVELED Arteveld
TRAVERSE Averters
TREACLES Clearest, Scelerat, Telecars
TREADERS Arrested, Retrades, Retreads, Serrated
TREADING Derating, Gradient
TREADLES Delsarte
TREASONS Assentor, Essorant, Senators, Star-nose
TREATIES Ariettes, Iterates, Treatise
TREATING Aretting
TREATISE Ariettes, Iterates, Treaties
***TREDEGAR** Gartered, Garreted, Regrated
TREDILLE Tillered
TREE-CRAB Crabtree
TREE-FERN Referent, Rent-free
TREE-MOSS Somerset
TREENAIL Elaterin, Entailer

TRENAILS Entrails, Latrines, Ratlines
TRENCHER Retrench
TRENISES Sentries
TRENTALS Slattern
TREPHINE Nephrite, Prehnite
TRESSELS Restless
TRESSING Trigness
TRESTINE Interest, Interset, Sternite
TREWSMAN Transmew
TREY-TINE Entirety, Eternity
TRIADIST Distrait
TRIALISM Mistrial
TRIANGLE Alerting, Altering, Integral, Relating
TRIAPSAL Partials
TRIASSIC Sarcitis
TRIBBLES Stibbler
TRIBOLET Libretto
TRIBUNAL Trubinal
TRIBUTES Butteris
TRICHION Ornithic
TRICHOID Hidrotic
TRICHOME Chromite
TRICKLES Stickler, Strickle, Ticklers
TRIDENTS Strident
TRIFLING Flirting
TRIGNESS Tressing
TRIMETER Remitter
TRIMNESS Minsters
TRINGLES Lingster, Ringlets, Sterling, Tinglers
TRINKLES Linkster, Strinkle, Tinklers
TRIPEDAL Dipteral
TRIPLETS Splitter
TRIPODIC Dioptric
TRIPPERS Stripper
TRIPPLES Ripplets, Stippler, Tipplers
TRIREMES Merriest, Miterers, Rimester

TRISEMIC Meristic
TRI-STATE Titrates
TRITONES Tenorist
*** TRITONIS** Introits
TROATING Rotating
TROCHAIC Thoracic
TROCHLEA Chelator, Chlorate
TROLLERS Stroller
TROUNCED Cornuted
TROUNCES Cornutes, Construe, Counters, Recounts
TROUPERS Posturer, Sprouter
TROUSERS Rousters
TROUTING Tutoring
TROUVERE Overture
TRUELOVE Revolute
TRUMPETS Strumpet
TRUSTING Sturting
TRYPSINS Spinstry
*** TSINGTAO** Stoating, Tangoist, Toasting
TUBBINGS Stubbing
TUBE-WORM Worm-tube
TUMBLERS Stumbler, Tumbrels
TUNG-OILS Tousling
TUNGSTIC Cuttings
*** TURANIAN** Nutarian
TURBANED Bread-nut
TURBINAL Tribunal
TURBINES Burnsite
TURNDOWN Down-turn
TURNINGS Unstring
TURNOVER Overturn
TUTELARS Lustrate
TUTORING Trouting
TWISTING Wittings
TYPHONIC Hypnotic, Pythonic
*** TYROLEAN** Ornately

ULCEROUS Urceolus
ULSTERED Resulted
ULTIMATE Mutilate
*** ULTONIAN** Lunation, Lutonian
ULTRAISM Altruism, Muralist

ULTRAIST Altruist, Titulars
UMBELLAR Umbrella
UMBRATED Drumbeat
UMBRELLA Umbellar
UNBELIED Unedible
UNBLINDS Sun-blind
UNBODING Bounding
UNBOILED Unilobed
UNBOMBED Unmobbed
UNBRIBED Unribbed
UNBURDEN Unburned
UNBURNED Unburden
UNCARTED Cedar-nut,
    Uncrated, Underact, Untraced
UNCASKED Unsacked
UNCAUSED Unsauced
UNCHOSEN Nonesuch
UNCIFORM Cuniform, Nuciform
UNCLOSED Enclouds
UNCOPING Pouncing
UNCORKED Unrocked
UNCRATED Cedar-nut,
    Uncarted, Underact, Untraced
UNCREATE Enacture
UNCURSED Sun-cured
UNDASHED Unshaded
UNDENTED Untended
UNDERACT Cedar-nut,
    Uncarted, Uncrated, Untraced
UNDERAGE Dungaree, Ungeared
UNDERAID Unraided
UNDERARM Unmarred
UNDERATE Undereat
UNDER-DOG Grounded,
    Undergod
UNDEREAT Underate
UNDERFED Refunded
UNDERFUR Unfurred
UNDER-GOD Grounded, Underdog
UNDERLAP Pendular, Uplander
UNDERPAY Unprayed
UNDERSEA Unseared
UNDERSET Dentures, Sederunt,
    Undesert, Unrested

UNDESERT Dentures, Sederunt,
    Underset, Unrested
UNDOINGS Sounding
UNDRAPES Unparsed,
    Unrasped, Unspared, Unspread
UNDULOSE Unsouled
UNEDIBLE Unbelied
UNFABLED Fundable
UNFARMED Unframed
UNFISTED Unsifted
UNFLATED Flaunted
UNFOLDER Flounder
UNFORCED Frounced
UNFRAMED Unfarmed
UNFRIEND Reinfund
UNFURRED Underfur
UNGAINLY Unlaying
UNGALLED Glandule
UNGEARED Dungaree, Underage
UNGILDED Deluding, Indulged
UNGIRDED Unridged
UNHALSED Unlashed
UNHASPED Unphased,
    Unshaped
UNHORSED Enshroud,
    Unshored
UNILOBED Unboiled
UNINURED Unruined
UNIONISM Misunion
UNIONIST Inustion
UNKILNED Unlinked
UNLASHED Unhalsed
UNLAYING Ungainly
UNLEASED Unsealed
UNLINKED Unkilned
UNLISTED Insulted
UNLOADED Duodenal
UNLOADER Urodelan
UNLOOPED Unpooled
UNLUMPED Unplumed
UNMARRED Underarm
UNMASHED Unshamed
UNMITERS Terminus, Unmitres
UNMITRES Terminus, Unmiters

UNMOBBED Unbombed
UNMODEST Demounts,
Mudstone
UNNATIVE Venutian
UNNETTED Untented
UNORDERS Rondures, Rounders
UNPAIRED Unrepaid
UNPARSED Undrapes,
Unrasped, Unspared, Unspread
UNPHASED Unhasped,
Unshaped
UNPLAITS Nuptials
UNPLUMED Unlumped
UNPOOLED Unlooped
UNPRAYED Underpay
UNRAIDED Underaid
UNRAISED Denarius
UNRASPED Undrapes,
Unparsed, Unspared, Unspread
UNRENTED Untender
UNREPAID Unpaired
UNRESTED Dentures, Sederunt,
Underset, Undesert
UNRIBBED Unbribed
UNRIDGED Ungirded
UNRIFLED Urnfield
UNRINGED Enduring
UNROCKED Uncorked
UNROUTED Untoured
UNRUINED Uninured
UNSACKED Uncasked
UNSACRED Durances, Unscared
UNSALTED Unslated, Unstaled
UNSASHED Sun-shade,
Unshades
UNSAUCED Uncaused
UNSCALES Scalenus
UNSCARED Durances, Unsacred
UNSCORED Crunodes
UNSEALED Unleased
UNSEARED Undersea
UNSEATED Unsedate, Unteased
UNSEDATE Unseated, Unteased
UNSEEING Ingenues

UNSENSED Nudeness
UNSERVED Unversed
UNSETTLE Lunettes
UNSHADED Undashed
UNSHADES Sun-shade,
Unsashed
UNSHADED Undashed
UNSHAKED Skean-dhu
UNSHAMED Unmashed
UNSHAPED Unhasped,
Unphased
UNSHORED Enshroud,
Unhorsed
UNSIFTED Unfisted
UNSIGHTS Hustings
UNSIGNED Unsinged
UNSINGED Unsigned
UNSLATED Unsalted, Unstaled
UNSLICED Includes, Nuclides
UNSOCIAL Alcinous
UNSOILED Delusion, Insouled
UNSOMBER Unsombre
UNSOMBRE Unsomber
UNSORTED Roundest, Tonsured,
Unstored
UNSOULED Undulose
UNSPARED Undrapes,
Unparsed, Unrasped, Unspread
UNSPHERE Sheep-run
UNSPOILT Plotinus
UNSPREAD Undrapes,
Unparsed, Unrasped, Unspared
UNSTABLE Abluents
UNSTALED Unsalted, Unslated
UNSTATED Neustadt, Untasted
UNSTATES Tautness
UNSTAYED Unsteady
UNSTEADY Unstayed
UNSTORED Roundest, Tonsured,
Unsorted
UNSTRING Turnings
UNTASTED Neustadt, Unstated
UNTEASED Unseated, Unsedate
UNTENDED Undented

UNTENDER Unrented
UNTENTED Unnetted
UNTHATCH Nuthatch
UNTHRUST Untruths
UNTIERED Retinued, Reunited
UNTILTED Untitled
UNTIMELY Minutely
UNTIMOUS Mutinous
UNTITLED Untilted
UNTOURED Unrouted
UNTRACED Cedar-nut,
   Uncrated, Underact
UNTRACES Centaurs, Etruscan,
   Recusant
UNTRUTHS Unthrust
UNVERSED Unserved
UPAS-TREE Superate
UPCLOSES Close-ups, Scopelus
UPFOLLOW Follow-up
UPLANDER Pendular, Underlap
UPROOTER Outroper
UPSETTER Setter-up
UPTRAINS Puritans, Rasputin
URCEOLUS Ulcerous
URINATED Daturine, Indurate,
   Ruinated
URINATES Neustria, Ruinates
URNFIELD Unrifled
UROCISSA Scarious
URODLEAN Unloader
UROSTYLE Souterly
URTICANT Taciturn
USURPING Pursuing
UTTERING Tiger-rut

VACATION Cavation, Octavian
VAGINATE Navigate
VALIANTS Salivant
VALORISE Oversail
VANELESS Enslaves
VANISHER Enravish
VATICIDE Cavitied
VAULTERS Vestural
* **VEDANTIC** Ci-devant

VEERINGS Severing
VEINLESS Evilness, Liveness,
   Vileness
VENALITY Natively
VENATION Innovate
VENERANT Revenant
VENERATE Enervate
VENTAILE Elvanite
* **VENUTIAN** Unnative
VERBATIM Ambivert
VERDITER Diverter, Redivert
* **VERONESE** Overseen
* **VERONICA** Corvinae
VERSABLE Beslaver, Servable
VERSELET Leverets
VESICANT Cistvaen
VESTURAL Vaulters
VICE-DEAN Deviance
VIET-CONG Coveting
VILENESS Evilness, Liveness,
   Veinless
VILLAGER All-giver
VINTAGER Averting, Tavering
VIOLATED Dovetail
VIOLENTS Novelist
VIPEROUS Pervious, Previous
VIRGINAL Rivaling
VIRTUOSE Vitreous
VISCERAL Calivers, Claviers
VISIONER Revision
VISITANT Nativist
VITAMINS Nativism
VITREOUS Virtuose
VOCALIST Voltaics
* **VOLSCIAN** Slavonic
VOLTAICS Vocalist

WADDLERS Dawdlers, Swaddler
WADDLING Dawdling
WAGGINGS Swagging
WAGON-BOX Box-wagon
WAISTERS Waitress
WAITRESS Waisters
WANDERED Dawnered

WANDLIKE Dawnlike
WARBLING Brawling
WARDINGS Drawings, Swarding
WARDROBE Drawbore
WASHDOWN Downwash
WASHINGS Swashing
WATCHDOG Dog-watch
WATCH-OUT Outwatch
WATER-DOG Water-god
WATERERS Sewer-rat
WATER-GAS Gas-water
WATER-GOD Water-dog
WATER-HEN Wreathen
WATER-ICE Ice-water
WATER-RAT Tar-water
WATER-TAP Tap-water
WAYBOARD Broadway
WAYSIDES Sideways
WEAKENER Reweaken
*__WEARDALE__ Delaware
WEARIEST Sweatier
WEARINGS Swearing
WEAR-IRON Ironware
WEDDINGS Swindged
WEEPINGS Sweeping
WEIGH-OUT Outweigh
WELLDOER Doweller, Rowelled
WENCHERS Wrenches
WHALINGS Shawling
WHEATEAR Aweather
WHEREOFS Foreshew
WHEREONS Heronsew,
  Nowheres
WHILE-ERE Erewhile, Wire-heel
WHIRTLES Whistler
WHISSING Swishing
WHISTLER Whirtles
WHIRTLES Whistler
WHOSEVER Howevers
WIDENESS Dewiness
WIGGINGS Swigging
WILDNESS Swindles, Windless
WINCHERS Schwerin
WINDLESS Swindles, Wildness

WIND-SIDE Side-wind
WINE-PALM Palm-wine
WINGLESS Slewings, Swingles
WINGSPAN Spawning
WINKINGS Swinking
WIRE-HEEL Erewhile, While-ere
WISE-LIKE Likewise
WITTINGS Twisting
WONTLESS Townless
WOODCHAT Chatwood
WOOD-LARK Workload
WOOD-PULP Pulp-wood
WOODROCK Corkwood, Rock-
  wood
WOOD-SEAR Searwood
WOOD-SEER Wood-sere
WOOD-SERE Wood-seer
WOODSKIN Inkwoods
WOOD-WORM Wormwood
WORDINGS Drowsing
WORKBOOK Bookwork
WORKLOAD Wood-lark
WORKMATE Teamwork
WORKSHOP Shopwork
WORLD-OLD Old-world
WORM-FISH Fish-worm
WORM-TUBE Tube-worm
WORMWOOD Woodworm
WORSTING Strowing
*__WORTHING__ Ingrowth, Throwing
WREATHEN Water-hen
WRENCHES Wenchers
WRESTING Strewing

XANTHEIN Xanthine
XANTHINE Xanthein

YEARDING Deraying, Readying
YEARLING Layering, Relaying
YEARNING Renaying
YTTRIOUS Touristy

ZOOPATHY Zoophyta
*__ZOOPHYTA__ Zoopathy

Nine letters

ABANDONER Reabandon
ABHORRENT Earth-born
ABORIGINE Baignoire
ABOUT-TURN Turnabout
ABRIDGING Brigading
ACALEPHAN Acephalan
ACCIDENTS Desiccant
ACCLAIMER Reacclaim
ACCOURTED Accoutred
ACCOUTERS Accoutres,
  Coruscate
ACCOUTRED Accourted
ACCOUTRES Accouters,
  Coruscate
ACCRETION Anorectic
ACEPHALAN Acalephan
ACETAMIDE Emaciated
ACIERATED Eradicate
ACROTISMS Castroism,
  Ostracism
ACTIONING Incognita
ADDRESSER Readdress
* **ADLESTROP** Portslade
ADMINICLE Medicinal
ADMISSIVE Misadvise,
  Misavised
ADMONITOR Dominator
ADNASCENT Ascendant
ADSORBATE Tea-boards
ADULATION Laudation
ADULATORY Laudatory
AEROBIONT Reboation
AEROLOGIC Areologic
AEROMETER Areometer
AEROMETRY Areometry
AFFRONTER Reaffront
AGISTMENT Magnetist

AIR-BRIDGE Brigadier
ALCHEMIES Alchemise
ALCHEMISE Alchemies
* **ALGERINES** Releasing
ALGORITHM Logarithm
ALIBILITY Liability
ALIENATOR Rationale
ALIGNMENT Lamenting
ALINEMENT Lineament
ALLERGIES Galleries
ALLOTTING Totalling
ALMANDITE Laminated
ALSATIANS Assailant
ALTERANTS Alternats, Translate
ALTERNATS Alterants, Translate
AMATORIAN Inamorata
* **AMBLESIDE** Demisable
AMNESTIES Meatiness,
  Seminates
AMBERGRIS Gris-amber
AMPLENESS Ensamples
ANACRUSES Assurance
ANALGESIC Angelicas
ANALOGIES Analogise
ANALOGISE Analogies
ANALOGIST Nostalgia
ANAPHORIC Pharaonic
ANARCHIST Cantharis
ANATOMIES Anatomise
ANATOMISE Anatomies
ANCESTRAL Lancaster
ANCHOR-ICE Ice-anchor
ANCHORITE Antechoir
ANCHOVIES Schiavone
ANDESITIC Dianetics, Indicates
* **ANDROCLES** Colanders
ANGELICAL Englacial, Galenical

322

ANGELICAS Analgesic
ANGERLESS Largeness
ANGLESITE Galenites, Gelatines, Teaseling
ANGLE-WORM Lawmonger
* **ANGOSTURA** Argonauts
ANGRINESS Ranginess
ANICONISM Insomniac
ANICONIST Inactions, Nicotians, Onanistic
ANNUITIES Insinuate
ANORECTIC Accretion
ANTECHOIR Anchorite
ANTELOPES Pleonaste
ANTELUCAN Cannulate
ANTENATAL Atlantean, Tantalean
ANTHROPIC Rhapontic
* **ANTICOSTI** Citations
ANTIDOTES Stationed
ANTIGENIC Gentianic
ANTIMERIC Criminate, Metrician
ANTIMONIC Antinomic
ANTINODAL Daltonian
ANTINOMIC Antimonic
ANTIPHONY Typhonian
ANTIPOLES Platonise, Seal-point
ANTI-SERUM Misaunter, Ruminates
ANTI-TRADE Attainder
APARTHEID Hit-parade
APERIENTS Pistareen, Sparteine
APERTNESS Taperness
APERTURES Repasture
APHERSIS Pharisees
APHETIZED Hepatized
APHORISER Pair-horse
APIVOROUS Oviparous
APLUSTRES Pertussal, Supersalt
APOLOGIES Apologise
APOLOGISE Apologies
APPEALING Lagniappe
APPLAUDER Reapplaud
APPLE-JOHN John-apple

APPOINTER Reappoint
APPOINTOR Apportion
APPORTION Appointor
APPRAISED Disappear
APSIDIOLE Episodial
ARC-EN-CIEL Cancelier
ARCHERESS Searchers
AREOLOGIC Aerologic
AREOMETER Aerometer
AREOMETRY Aerometry
* **ARGENTINA** Tanagrine
ARGENTINE Tangerine
ARGENTITE Integrate
* **ARGONAUTS** Angostura
ARILLATED Lardalite
ARMAMENTS Men-at-arms
* **ARMSTRONG** Strongarm
ARRESTING Astringer
ARSENICAL Carnalise
ASCENDANT Adnascent
ASCENSION Canonises
ASCERTAIN Cartesian, Sectarian
ASCITICAL Sciatical
ASCLEPIUS Capsulise
ASHLARING Shangri-la
ASHLERING Narghiles, Nargilehs, Shearling
ASPECTUAL Capsulate, Scapulate
ASPERGILL Pillagers
ASPERGING Presaging
ASPERSING Repassing
ASPIRANTS Partisans, Satin-spar
ASPIRATED Disparate
ASPIRATES Parasites, Satrapies
ASSAILANT Alsatians
ASSAULTER Saleratus
ASSERTION Senoritas
ASSESSING Gassiness
ASSISTANT Santanists
ASSORTING Organists, Roastings
ASSURANCE Anacruses
ASTHENICS Caithness

9

ASTRINGED Gradients
ASTRINGER Arresting
ASTROFELL Forestall
ASTROLABE Roastable
ASTROPHEL Plethoras
ASYNDETIC Cystidean,
Syndicate
ASYNERGIA Gainsayer
*****ATLANTEAN** Antenatal,
Tantalean
ATTAINDER Anti-trade
ATTEMPTER Reattempt
ATTENTION Tentation
ATTENTIVE Tentative
ATTRACTER Reattract
ATTRACTOR Tractator
ATTRITING Titrating
ATTRITION Titration
AUCTIONED Cautioned,
Education, Noctuidae
AUCTORIAL Caliatour
AURISCOPE Parecious
AUTHORESS Share-outs
AUTOCLAVE Vacuolate
AVERTIBLE Veritable

BACK-CHECK Check-back
BACKCLOTH Clothback
BACKGREEN Greenback
BACKSHORE Horseback
BACK-SWEPT Swept-back
BACK-SWING Swing-back
BACKWARDS Drawbacks
BACTERIAL Calibrate
*****BACULITES** Bisulcate
BAIGNOIRE Aborigine
BALE-FIRES Bas-relief
BALKANISE Lake-basin
BANDELIER Breadline
BANDEROLE Bandoleer
BANDOLEER Banderole
BANDOLIER Bird-alone
*****BARBADOES** Baseboard
BARGAINED Gabardine

BARGEPOLE Porbeagle
*****BARNABITE** Rabbinate
BASANITES Sebastian
BASEBOARD Barbadoes
BAS-RELIEF Bale-fires
BASSETING Beastings
BEANPOLES Spealbone
BEARDLESS Breadless
BEASTINGS Basseting
BECHARMED Chambered
BEECH-FERN Free-bench
BELONGING Englobing
BENEDIGHT Benighted
BENIGHTED Benedight
BESAINTED Bestained
BESOTTING Obtesting
BESTAINED Besainted
BESTARRED Redbreast
BIANGULAR Bulgarian
BIGENTIAL Ignitable
BILL-BOARD Broadbill
BIRD-ALANE Drainable
BIRD-ALONE Bandolier
BIRGANDER Debarring
BISULCATE Baculites
BLUENOTES Bluestone
BLUESTONE Bluenotes
BOARD-FOOT Foot-board
BOARDINGS Signboard
BOARDROOM Broadmoor
BOATHOUSE Houseboat
BOB-CHERRY Cherry-bob
BOTHERING Night-robe
BOTTLE-GAS Gas-bottle
BRAINCASE Carabines
BRAKELESS Breakless
BRASSERIE Brassiere
BRASSIERE Brasserie
BREAD-CORN Corn-bread
BREADLESS Beardless
BREADLINE Bandelier
BREAKLESS Brakeless
BREAK-WIND Wind-break
BREAST-PIN Step-bairn

***BRIDGETON** Tonbridge
BRIEFLESS Fiberless, Fibreless
BRIGADIER Air-bridge
BRIGADING Abridging
BROACHERS Shore-crab
BROADBILL Bill-board
BROAD-HEAD Headboard
BROAD-LEAF Loaf-bread
***BROADMOOR** Boardroom
BROADSIDE Sideboard
BROADTAIL Tail-board
BRUSHLESS Shrubless
BRUSHLIKE Shrublike
BUFFERING Rebuffing
***BULGARIAN** Biangular
BULLETRIE Rubellite
BURNED-OUT Out-burned
BURN-SIDES Sideburns
BUTTERING Rebutting
BUTTER-NUT Nut-butter
BYSTANDER Stander-by

CABLE-LAID Cebadilla
CAEN-STONE Cantonese
CAESARIST Staircase
***CAITHNESS** Asthenics
CALAMITES Micaslate
CALENDERS Encradles,
  Esclandre
CALENTURE Crenulate
CALIATOUR Auctorial
CALIBRATE Bacterial
CALIPHATE Hepatical
CALLOSITY Stoically
CALUMNIES Masculine,
  Semunical
CAMBERING Embracing
CAMELINES Mescaline
CAMERATED Demarcate,
  Macerated
CANCELIER Arc-en-ciel
CANCERATE Reactance
CANEPHORE Chaperone
CANE-SUGAR Sugar-cane

CANISTERS Scenarist
CANNULATE Antelucan
CANOEISTS Cessation
CANONISES Ascension
CANOPYING Poignancy
CANTERING Recanting
CANTHARIS Anarchist
CANTILENA Lancinate
CANTINESS Incessant, Instances
***CANTONESE** Caen-stone
CAPOTAINE Copataine
CAPSULARY Scapulary
CAPSULATE Aspectual,
  Scapulate
CAPSULISE Asclepius
CAPTIONED Pactioned
CARABINES Braincase
CARBONISE Escribano
CARCINOMA Macaronic
CARD-PUNCH Punch-card
CARNALISE Arsenical
***CAROLINES** Censorial, Creolians
CAROLLING Collaring
CARTELISE Cerealist
CARTESIAN Ascertain, Sectarian
CART-HORSE Orchestra
CARUCATES Crustacea
CASE-BOUND Subdeacon
CASSOULET Osculates
***CASTALIAN** Satanical
CASTRATED Tadcaster
***CASTROISM** Acrotisms,
  Ostracism
CATALOGUE Coagulate
CATATONIC Toccatina
CATECHISM Schematic
CATILINES Inelastic, Sciential
CAT-SILVER Verticals
CAUTERISM Cerastium
CAUTIONED Auctioned,
  Education, Noctuidae
CAUTIONER Cointreau,
  Recaution
CEBADILLA Cable-laid

CEILINGED Diligence
CELANDINE Decennial
CELEBRATE Erectable
CELLARING Recalling
CELLOIDIN Decillion
CENSORIAL Carolines, Creolians
CENTERING Centreing
CENTIARES Creatines, Iterances,
  Nectarise
CENTIGRAM Cremating
CENTREING Centering
CENTURION Continuer
*CERASTIUM Causterism
*CERATODUS Educators,
  Croustade
CEREALIST Cartelise
CERTIFIED Cretified, Rectified
CERTIFIER Rectifier
CERTITUDE Rectitude
CERTOSINA Creations,
  Narcotise, Reactions
CERULEINS Licensure
CERUSITES Cerussite
CERUSSITE Cerusites
CESSATION Canoeists
CHAMBERED Becharmed
CHANNELER Rechannel
CHANTRESS Snatchers,
  Stanchers
CHAPERONE Canephore
CHAPTERED Repatched
CHARACINS Saccharin
CHARRETTE Chatterer
CHARTERED Three-card
CHARTERER Recharter
CHARTISMS Christmas
CHATTERER Charrette
CHAUNTERS Stauncher
CHEATABLE Teachable
CHECK-BACK Back-check
CHERALITE Etherical, Heretical
CHERRY-BOB Bob-cherry
CHEST-NOTE Chest-tone
CHEST-TONE Chest-note

CHLORITIC Trochilic
CHOLTRIES Clothiers
CHONDRITE Threnodic
CHORISTER Rhetorics
CHRISTIAN Christina, Trichinas
*CHRISTINA Christian, Trichinas
CHRISTMAS Chartisms
CHROMATES Stomacher
CISTERNAL Clarinets, Larcenist
CITATIONS Anticosti
CITHARIST Trachitis
CITRANGES Recasting
CLARINETS Cisternal, Larcenist
CLARIONET Crotaline
CLAUSTRAL Lacustral
CLAYMORES Lacrymose
CLEANSERS Clearness
CLEARNESS Cleansers
CLIENTAGE Genetical
CLIMATURE Tularemic
CLOACALIN Cloacinal, Laconical
CLOACINAL Cloacalin, Laconical
CLODPOLES Scolloped
CLOTHBACK Backcloth
CLOTHIERS Choltries
COAGULATE Catalogue
COASTLINE Sectional
COATDRESS Dresscoat
COAT-FROCK Frock-coat
COAT-STYLE Octastyle
COETERNAL Tolerance
COGNATION Contagion
COGNITION Incognito
COINTREAU Cautioner,
  Recaution
COLANDERS Androcles
COLCOTHAR Ochlocrat
COLLAPSED Scalloped
COLLARING Carolling
COLLINEAR Coralline
COLLUSIVE Colluvies
COLLUVIES Collusive
COLOURMAN Monocular
COMFORTER Recomfort

*COMMELINA Melomanic
COMMENDER Recommend
COMPANIED Compendia
COMPENDIA Companied
COMPLAINT Compliant
COMPLEXED Decomplex
COMPLIANT Complaint
CONCEDERS Crescendo
CONCENTER Concentre,
Connecter, Reconnect
CONCENTRE Concenter,
Connecter, Reconnect
CONCERTED Concreted
CONCRETED Concerted
CONDEMNER Recondemn
CONFIRMER Reconfirm
CONFIRMOR Corniform
CONFORMER Reconform
CONFRERIE Reinforce
CONGERIES Recognise
CONGESTED Decongest
CONGRUITY Outcrying
CONNECTER Concenter,
Concentre, Reconnect
CONNOTATE Notonecta
CONSENTER Cretonnes,
Reconsent
CONSERVED Conversed
CONSERVER Converser
CONSIGNED Seconding
CONSIGNER Necrosing,
Reconsign
CONSOLATE Stone-coal
CONSORTIA Ostracion
CONSPIRES In-process
CONSTRAIN Transonic
CONSULTER Reconsult
CONTADINE Contained
CONTAGION Cognation
CONTAINED Contadine
CONTAINER Crenation,
Narcotine, Rocinante
CONTENDER Recontend
CONTESTER Recontest

CONTINUAL Inoculant
CONTINUED Unnoticed
CONTINUER Centurion
CONVERSED Conserved
CONVERSER Conserver
CONVERTER Reconvert
CO-PARTNER Procreant
COPATAINE Capotaine
COPEMATES Copesmate
COPESMATE Copemates
COPULATED Cupolated
CORALLINE Collinear
CORAL-TREE Correlate
*CORISANDE Dinoceras, Iron-
cased
CORK-BORER Rock-borer
CORKINESS Rockiness
CORN-BREAD Bread-corn
*CORNELIUS Inclosure, Reclusion
CORNIFORM Confirmor
CORNINESS Incensors
CORNUTING Trouncing
CORRELATE Coral-tree
CORSETING Escorting, Recosting
CORUSCATE Accouters,
Accoutres
COTELINES Elections, Selection
COTILLION Octillion
COTTON-GIN Cottoning
COTTONING Cotton-gin
COUNTERED Recounted
COUNTRIES Cretinous,
Neurotics
COURANTES Courtesan,
Nectarous, Outrances
COURBARIL Orbicular
COURTESAN Courantes,
Nectarous, Outrances
COURTIERS Outcriers, Scrutoire
COVERABLE Revocable
CREAMINGS Germanics,
Screaming
CREATABLE Traceable

CREATINES Centiares, Iterances, Nectarise

CREATIONS Certosina, Narcotise, Reactions

CREDITING Directing

CREDITORS Directors, Recordist

CREDITRIX Directrix

CREMATING Centigram

CREMATION Manticore

CRENATION Container, Narcotine, Rocinante

CRENULATE Calenture

*****CREOLIANS** Carolines, Censorial

CREPOLINE Pencil-ore

CRESCENDO Conceders

CRETIFIED Certified, Rectified

CRETINOID Direction

CRETINOUS Countries, Neurotics

CRETONNES Consenter, Reconsent

CRIMELESS Merciless

CRIMINATE Antimeric, Metrician

CRISPATED Practised

CRITERION Tricerion

CRITICISE Sericitic

CROSS-TREE Rectoress

CROTALINE Clarionet

CROUSTADE Educators, Ceratodus

CROWFOOTS Crow's-foot

CROW'S-FOOT Crowfoots

CRUSTACEA Carucates

CTENIDIAL Identical

*****CTESIPHON** Phonetics

CUMBERING Recumbing

CUPOLATED Copulated

CURIALIST Rusticial

CURTATION Ructation

CURTILAGE Graticule

CYSTIDEAN Asyndetic, Syndicate

CYSTOLITH Lithocyst

DAINTIEST Dittanies

*****DALTONIAN** Antinodal

DAMNATORY Mandatory

DATE-LINES Dentalise

DATE-SUGAR Graduates

DATUM-LINE Dentalium

DAUNDERED Undreaded

DAWNERING Wandering

DAY-SCHOOL School-day

DEBARRING Birgander

DECADENTS Descanted

DECALITER Decalitre

DECALITRE Decaliter

DECAMETER Decametre

DECAMETRE Decameter

DECANTERS Descanter

DECASTERE Desecrate

DECELERON Redolence

DECEMVIRI Vermicide

DECENNIAL Celandine

DECILITER Decilitre

DECILITRE Deciliter

DECILLION Celloidin

DECIMALLY Medically

DECIMATED Medicated

DECIMATOR Medicator

DECIMETER Decimetre

DECIMETRE Decimeter

DECLAIMER Reclaimed

DECOLLATE Ocellated

DECOMPLEX Complexed

DECONGEST Congested

DECRETIST Trisected

DECORATED Red-coated

DECRETIST Trisected

DECURIONS Decursion,

DECURSION Decurions

DEER-FENCE Deference

DEER-MOUSE Mouse-deer

DEFERENCE Deer-fence

DEFERMENT Fermented

DEFLATION Defoliant

DEFLORATE Floreated, Refloated

DEFOLIANT Deflation

DEGARNISH Garnished
DEGRADING Niggarded
DEISTICAL Silicated
DELAPSION Palinodes
DELATIONS Insolated
DELIGHTER Relighted
DELIRIANT Drain-tile
DELIVERER Redeliver
DEMANDING Maddening
DEMARCATE Camerated,
  Macerated
DEMEANOUR Enamoured
DEMERSION Domineers,
  Modernise
DEMI-LANCE Endemical
DEMISABLE Ambleside
DEMURRING Murdering
DENATURES Sauntered
DENDRITES Distender
DENOTABLE Detonable
DENOTATED Detonated
DENOUNCER Renounced
DENTALISE Date-lines
DENTALIUM Datum-line
DENTATION Intoned
DEPARTING Predating
DEPASTURE Depurates
DEPLENISH Plenished
DEPLETION Diplotene
DEPLUMING Implunged
DEPOSITOR Droopiest
DEPRAVING Pervading
DEPURATES Depasture
DERANGING Gardening
DEREPRESS Repressed
DESCANTED Decadents
DESCANTER Decanters
DESCENDER Redescend
DESECRATE Decastere
DESERTION Detersion
DESICCANT Accidents
DESIGNING Sdeigning
DESPAIRER Draperies, Repraised
DESTINATE Tetanised

DESULPHER Sulphured
DETERSION Desertion
DETHRONES Shortened
DETONABLE Denotable
DETONATED Denotated
DEVALUATE Evaluated
DEVELOPER Redevelop
DEVITRIFY Fervidity
DIAMETRIC Matricide
DIANETICS Andesitic, Indicates
DIETITIAN Initiated
DIGITISER Dirigiste
DIGNIFIES Signified
DILIGENCE Ceilinged
DILUVIONS Divulsion
DINOCERAS Corisande,
  Iron-cased
DIPLOTENE Depletion
DIRECTING Crediting
DIRECTION Cretinoid
DIRECTORS Creditors, Recordist
DIRECTRIX Creditrix
DIREPTION Perdition
DIRIGISTE Digitiser
DIRTINESS Disinters
DISAPPEAR Appraised
DISCERNED Rescinded
DISCERNER Rescinder
DISCUSSER Rediscuss
DISENDOWS Dowdiness
DISHONEST Hedonists
DISINTERS Dirtiness
DISPARATE Aspirated
DISPLAYER Redisplay
DISSEISOR Siderosis
DISSENTER Residents, Tiredness
DISSOLUTE Outslides, Solitudes
DISSONATE Sedations
DISSUNDER Ruddiness
DISTENDER Dendrites
DISTILLER Redistill
DISTRAINS Sinistrad
DITTANIES Daintiest
DIVULSION Diluvions

DOMINATES Maidstone, Staminode
DOMINATOR Admonitor
DOMINEERS Demersion, Modernise
DOOMWATCH Matchwood
DOVEHOUSE House-dove
DOWDINESS Disendows
DOWELLING Well-doing
DOWNRIGHT Right-down
DOWN-THROW Throw-down
DRAGONISE Grandiose, Organdies, Organised
DRAGOONED Gadrooned
DRAINABLE Bird-alane
DRAIN-TILE Deliriant
DRAPERIES Despairer, Repraised
DRAWBACKS Backwards
DREAMLAND Raddleman
DRESSCOAT Coatdress
DROOPIEST Depositor

EAGERNESS Sea-greens
EAR-RINGED Grenadier, Re-reading
EARTH-BORN Abhorrent
EARTHIEST Heartiest
EARTHLING Haltering, Heartling, Lathering
EARTHWORM Heartworm
EASTER-EGG Segregate
ECONOMIES Economise
ECONOMISE Economies
ECSTASIES Ecstasise
ECSTASISE Ecstasies
EDUCATION Auctioned, Cautioned, Noctuidae
EDUCATORS Ceratodus, Croustade
EDUCTIONS Seduction
EGLANTINE Inelegant
EIDOGRAPH Ideograph
ELECTIONS Cotelines, Selection
ELECTIVES Selective

ELECTRISE Leicester
EMACIATED Acetamide
EMANATIST Staminate
EMANATING Man-eating, Manganite
EMBOILING Bemoiling
EMBRACING Cambering
EMENDATOR Notre-dame
EMERSIONS Sermonise
EMIGRANTS Germanist, Mastering, Remasting, Streaming
EMIGRATED Remigated
EMPAESTIC Space-time
EMPLASTER Palm-trees
ENAMELIST Melanites
ENAMOURED Demeanour
ENCASHING Enchasing
ENCAUSTIC Succinate
ENCHASING Encashing
ENCLASPED Spanceled
ENCRADLES Calenders, Esclandre
*****ENCRATISM** Miscreant
ENCURTAIN Runcinate, Uncertain
ENDARTING Integrand
ENDEARING Engrained, Grenadine
ENDEMICAL Demi-lance
END-PAPERS Snappered
ENERGICAL Generical
ENERGISED Reseeding
ENERGISES Regenesis
ENERVATED Venerated
ENERVATOR Venerator
ENGLACIAL Angelical, Galenical
*****ENGLANDER** Greenland
ENGLOBING Belonging
ENGRAILED Geraldine, Realigned, Redealing, Releading
ENGRAINED Endearing, Grenadine
ENGROSSER Re-engross

ENLARDING Leningrad
ENLIGHTED Lightened
ENLISTING Listening
ENRICHING Richening
ENSAMPLES Ampleness
ENSTATITE Intestate, Satinette
ENSTEEPED Steepened
ENTERTAIN Terentian
ENTITLING Inletting
ENTRANCES Renascent
ENTROPION Pontonier,
  Prenotion
ENTROPIUM Importune
EPARCHIES Parcheesi
EPICENTER Epicentre
EPICENTRE Epicenter
EPIDERMAL Impearled,
  Impleader
EPILATION Polianite
EPISCOPAL Pepsi-cola
EPISODIAL Apsidiole
ERADICATE Acierated
ERASEMENT Mesentera
ERASTIANS Star-anise
ERECTABLE Celebrate
ERECTIONS Necrotise,
  Renotices, Resection, Secretion
ERISTICAL Realistic
*ERITREANS Raintrees, Retainers,
  Ternaries
*ERNESTINE Internees
EROTICISM Isometric, Meroistic
ERUPTIONS Pertusion
ERVALENTA Revalenta
ESCLANDRE Calenders,
  Encradles
ESCORTING Corseting,
  Recosting
ESCRIBANO Carbonise
*ESPERANTO Personate
*ESSLINGEN Lessening
ESTRADIOL Idolaters
ESTRANGES Greatness,
  Sergeants

ESTRAPADE Paederast,
  Separated
ESTREPING Perstinge, Pestering,
  Presteing
ETHERICAL Cheralite, Heretical
ETHOLOGIC Theologic
EVALUTED Devaluate
EVANISHES Heaviness
EVITATION Novitiate
EVITERNAL Intervale
EXAMINATE Exanimate
EXANIMATE Examinate
EXCEPTANT Expectant
EXCEPTING Expecting
EXERTIONS Exsertion
EXHIBITER Re-exhibit
EXPECTANT Exceptant
EXPECTING Excepting
EXPLAINER Re-explain
EXPRESSER Re-express
EXSERTION Exertions

FACTIONAL Falcation
FACTORIES Factorise
FACTORISE Factories
FAITHLESS Flashiest
FALCATION Factional
FALTERING Reflating
FANTASIES Fantasise
FANTASISE Fantasies
FASHIONER Refashion
FERMENTED Deferment
FERVIDITY Devitrify
FIBERFILL Fibrefill
FIBERLESS Briefless, Fibreless
FIBREFILL Fiberfill
FIBRELESS Briefless, Fiberless
FIREIRONS Inferiors
FIRELIGHT Flightier
FIRESTONE Forestine
FIRE-STORM Reformist,
  Restiform
FIRSTLING Flirtings, Triflings
FISH-SPEAR Spearfish

FLASHBACK Half-backs
FLASHIEST Faithless
FLAT-IRONS Frost-nail
FLIGHTIER Firelight
FLIRTINGS Firstling, Triflings
FLOREATED Deflorate, Refloated
FLOWERING Reflowing
FOOT-BOARD Board-foot
FORCE-LAND Land-force
FORE-HORSE Foreshore
FOREMEANS Forenames,
  Freemeson
FORENAMES Foremeans,
  Freemason
FORENIGHT Fothering
FOREPEAKS Forespake,
  Forespeak
FORESHORE Fore-horse
FORESIGHT Gift-horse, Grief-
  shot
FORESPEAK Forepeaks,
  Forespake
FORESPAKE Forepeaks,
  Forespeak
FORESTAGE Fosterage
FORESTALL Astrofell
FORESTINE Firestone
FORESTING Fostering
FORFEITER Reforfeit
FORWARDER Reforward
FORWARDLY Frowardly
FOSTERAGE Forestage
FOSTERING Foresting
FOTHERING Forenight
FOUNDLING Unfolding
FOUR-BY-TWO Two-by-four
FREE-BENCH Beech-fern
FREEMASON Foremeans,
  Forenames
FRESHENER Refreshen
FRIENDING Infringed
FRINGILLA Ill-faring
FROCK-COAT Coat-frock
FROST-NAIL Flat-irons

FROWARDLY Forwardly
FURBISHER Refurbish
FURNISHER Refurnish

GABARDINE Bargained
GADROONED Dragooned
GAINSAYER Asynergia
*GALENICAL Angelical, Englacial
GALENITES Anglesite, Gelatines,
  Teaseling
GALLERIES Allergies
GANDERISM Semigrand
GANGLIONS Singalong
GANTRISIN Straining, Trainings
GARDENING Deranging
GARNISHED Degarnish
GARNISHER Regarnish,
  Resharing
GARRETING Gartering,
  Regrating
GARTERING Garreting,
  Regrating
GAS-BOTTLE Bottle-gas
GASSINESS Assessing
GATHERING Nightgear
GAUNTRIES Signature
GEE-STRING Greetings
GELATINES Anglesite, Galenites,
  Teaseling
GELIDNESS Seedlings
GEMINATES Magnesite,
  Magnetise
GENERATED Renegated
GENERICAL Energical
GENETICAL Clientage
GENITIVAL Vigilante
GENITIVES Ingestive
GENTIANIC Antigenic
GENTILISH Sight-line
GERALDINE Engrailed,
  Realigned, Redealing, Releading
GERMANICS Creamings,
  Scraming

GERMANIST Emigrants, Mastering, Remasting, Streaming
GEYSERITE Tiger's-eye
GIFT-HORSE Foresight, Grief-shot
GIRANDOLE Negroidal, Reloading
GNOMONICS Oncomings
GNOSTICAL Nostalgic
GOING-OVER Overgoing
GOVERNORS Grosvenor
GRADATION Indagator
GRADIENTS Astringed
GRADUATES Date-sugar
GRANDIOSE Dragonise, Organdies, Organised
GRANULITE Traguline
GRATICULE Curtilage
GRAVELESS Verglases
GREATNESS Estranges, Sergeants
GREENBACK Back-green
*GREENLAND Englander
GREETINGS Gee-string
GREGARIAN Gregarina
*GREGARINA Gregarian
GRENADIER Ear-ringed, Rereading
GRENADINE Endearing, Engrained
GRIEF-SHOT Foresight, Gift-horse
GRIS-AMBER Amberaris
GROOMSMAN Monograms, Nomograms
*GROSVENOR Governors
GUSTINESS Gutsiness
GUTSINESS Gustiness
GYMNASTIC Nystagmic
GYRATIONS Signatory

HABERDINE Hebridean
HALF-BACKS Flashback

HALF-GROWN Half-wrong
HALF-WRONG Half-grown
HALLOOING Holloaing
HALTERING Earthling, Heartling, Lathering
HANKERING Harkening
HARKENING Hankering
HARMONICS Man-orchis
HARMONIES Harmonise
HARMONISE Harmonies
HARNESSER Reharness
HARVESTER Reharvest
HAWKNOSED Shake-down
HAUNTINGS Unhasting
HEAD-BOARD Broad-head
HEADLAMPS Lampshade
HEADNOTES Headstone
HEADSTONE Headnotes
HEADWATER Waterhead
HEART-FREE Hereafter
HEARTIEST Earthiest
HEARTLING Earthling, Haltering, Lathering
HEARTSEED Shade-tree
HEARTSOME Horsemeat
HEARTWORM Earthworm
HEAVINESS Evanishes
*HEBRIDEAN Haberdine
HECTORING Tochering
HEDONISTS Dishonest
HELLFIRES Shellfire
HELL-HOLES Shell-hole
HEPATICAL Caliphate
HEPATIZED Aphetized
HEREAFTER Heart-free
HERETICAL Cheralite, Etherical
HERNIATED Inearthed
HESPERIAN Inspheare, Seraphine
HETEROSIS Isotheres, Theorises
HIBERNATE Inbreathe
HISPANIST Saintship
HISTORISM Hit-or-miss
HIT-OR-MISS Historism

HIT-PARADE Apartheid
HOLLOAING Hallooing
HOMELIEST Lithesome
HORSEBACK Backshore
HORSEBANE Horsebean
HORSEBEAN Horsebane
HORSE-BOAT Shoreboat
HORSEFACE Shoreface
HORSE-HOES Horseshoe
HORSELESS Shoreless
HORSEMEAT Heartsome
HORSESHOE Horse-hoes
HORSETAIL Aeroliths,
  Isotheral
HORSEWEED Shoreweed
*HORTENSIA Senhorita
HOUSE-BOAT Boathouse
HOUSE-DOVE Dovehouse
HOUSE-TOPS Posthouse,
  Pothouses
HOUSEWORK Workhouse
HOWSOEVER Whosoever
HOWTOWDIE Whitewood
*HUNTERIAN Ruthenian
HURTFULLY Ruthfully

ICE-ANCHOR Anchor-ice
ICHNOLITE Neolilhic
IDENTICAL Ctenidial
IDEOGRAPH Eidograph
IDOLATERS Estradiol
IGNITABLE Bigential
ILL-FARING Fringilla
ILL-NATURE Tellurian
IMMANTLES Mentalism,
  Simmential
IMMERSING Simmering
IMPARTIAL Primatial
IMPEARLED Epidermal,
  Impleader
IMPETICOS Poeticism
IMPETICSM Poeticism
IMPLANTER Reimplant

IMPLEADER Epidermal,
  Impearled
IMPLUNGED Depluming
IMPORTERS Misreport,
  Reimports
IMPORTUNE Entropium
IMPRESARI Primaries
IMPRESSER Reimpress,
  Simperers
IMPRESSES Premisses
IMPRINTER Reimprint
IMPUGNERS Presuming
INACTIONS Aniconist,
  Nicotians, Onanistic
INAMORATA Amatorian
INBREATHE Hibernate
INCENSORS Corniness
INCEPTORS Inspector, Pre-tonics
INCESSANT Cantiness, Instances
INCLOSURE Cornelius, Reclusion
INCOGNITA Actioning
INCOGNITO Cognition
INCONDITE Nicotined
INCREASES Scenarise
INDAGATOR Gradation
INDENTING Intending
INDICATES Andesitic, Dianetics
INEARTHED Herniated
INELASTIC Catilines, Sciential
INELEGANT Eglantine
INFARCTED Infracted
INFERIORS Fireirons
INFERRING Infringer
INFRACTED Infarcted
INFRINGED Friending
INFRINGER Inferring
INGESTIVE Genitives
INHABITER Reinhabit
INITIATED Dietitian
INLETTING Entitling
INOCULANT Continual
IN-PROCESS Conspires
INSECTILE Selenitic
INSERTING Sintering

INSINUATE Annuities
INSISTENT Tintiness
INSOLATED Delations
INSOMNIAC Aniconism
INSPECTOR Inceptors, Pre-tonics
INSPHEARE Hesperian,
  Seraphine
INSTALLER Reinstall
INSTANCES Cantiness, Incessant
INSTANTER Transient
INSULATOR Solutrian
INSURABLE Sublinear
INSURANCE Nuisancer
INSURGENT Unresting
INTEGRAND Endarting
INTEGRANT Nattering,
  Rattening
INTEGRATE Argentite
INTENDING Indenting
INTER-ARTS Restraint
INTERDASH Tarnished
INTERDEAL Tail-ender
INTERESTS Intersets, Resistent,
  Sternites, Triteness
INTERLACE Lacertine, Reclinate
INTERLOPE Repletion, Terpineol
INTERMITS Terminist
INTERNEES Ernestine
INTERPAGE Pignerate, Repeating
INTERPLAY Painterly, Party-line
INTERPONE Tin-opener
INTERSETS Interests, Resistent,
  Sternites, Triteness
INTERVALE Eviternal
INTESTATE Enstatite, Satinette
INTIMATES Mini-state
INTONATED Dentation
INTRICATE Triactine
INTRIGUED Nigritude
INTRODUCE Reduction
INTROITUS Routinist
INTRUDERS Unstirred
INUNDATES Unsainted,
  Unstained

INVEAGLER Revealing
INVEIGLER Relieving
*INVERNESS Nerviness
INVOLUCRE Volucrine
INWREATHE Near-white
IRON-CASED Corisande,
  Dinocerus
IRONSTONE Serotonin
IRRADIANT Triandria
*ISLAMITIC Italicism
ISMATICAL Lamaistic
*ISOCRATES Ostracise
ISOMETRIC Eroticism, Meroistic
ISOSCELES Solecises
ISOTHERAL Aeroliths, Horsetail
ISOTHERES Heterosis, Theorises
*ISRAELITE Realities
ISSUANCES Sauciness
ITALICISM Islamitic
ITERANCES Centiares, Creatines,
  Nectarise
ITINERANT Nitratine

JACK-PINES Jack-snipe
JACK-SNIPE Jack-pines
JESSERANT Serjeants
*JOHN-APPLE Apple-john

KILOLITER Kilolitre
KILOLITRE Kiloliter
KILOMETER Kilometre
KILOMETRE kilometer
KITCHENED Thickened
KITCHENER Rethicken,
  Thickener
KLENDUSIC Unsickled

LACERTIAN Nectarial
LACERTINE Interlace, Reclinate
LACONICAL Cloacalin, Cloacinal
LACQUERER Relacquer
LACRYMOSE Claymores
LACUSTRAL Claustral
LAGNIAPPE Appealing

LAKE-BASIN Balkanise
LAMAISTIC Ismatical
LAMENTING Alignment
LAMINATED Almandite
LAMPSHADE Headlamps
*LANCASTER Ancestral
LANCEOLAR Olecranal
LANCINATE Cantilena
LAND-FORCE Force-land
LAPIDATES Stapedial
LARCENIST Cisternal, Clarinets
LARDALITE Arillated
LARGENESS Angerless
LARGITION Tailoring
LARVICIDE Veridical
LATESCENT Tentacles
LATHERING Earthling,
  Haltering, Heartling
LATICLAVE Vacillate
LATINISTS Stalinist
LAUDATION Adulation
LAUDATORY Adulatory
LAUGHTERS Slaughter
LAUGHTON'S Onslaught
LAUNDERER Relaunder
LAVATIONS Salvation
LAWMONGER Angle-worm
LEAF-MINER Reinflame
LEASE-LAND Lend-lease
LEICESTER Electrise
LEND-LEASE Lease-lend
*LENINGRAD Enlarding
LESSENING Esslingen
LETTERING Reletting
*LEVANTINE Valentine
LIABILITY Alibility
LICENSING Silencing
LICENSURE Ceruleins
LIGHTENED Enlighted
LIGHTINGS Slighting
LIGHTNESS Nightless
LIMESTONE Milestone
LINEAMENT Alinement
LIONESSES Noiseless

LIQUIDATE Qualitied
LISTENING Enlisting
LISTERISE Sterilise
LITHESOME Homeliest
LITHOCYST Cystolith
LITHOPONE Phonolite
LOAF-BREAD Broad-leaf
LOAF-SUGAR Sugar-loaf
LOGARITHM Algorithm
LOGOTYPES Pestology
LONGSHIPS Sploshing
LONGUETTE Tonguelet
LORICATES Sclerotia, Sectorial
LOWRIE-TOD Tod-lowrie
LUCRATIVE Revictual
LUMBERERS Slumberer
LUMP-SUGAR Sugar-lump,
  Sugar-plum

MACARONIC Carcinoma
MACERATED Camerated,
  Demarcate
MACINTOSH Monachist
MADDENING Demanding
MADRASAHS Madrassah
MADRASSAH Madrasahs
MAGNESITE Geminates,
  Magnetise
MAGNETISE Geminates,
  Magnesite
MAGNETIST Agistment
MAIDSTONE Dominates,
  Staminode
MALENGINE Meningeal
MANDATORY Damnatory
MAN-EATING Emanating,
  Manganite
MANGANITE Emanating, Man-
  eating
*MANICHEES Mechanise
MANICURES Muscarine
MANOEUVER Manoeuvre
MANOEUVRE Manoeuver
MAN-ORCHIS Harmonics

MANTICORE Cremation
MARE'S NEST Steersman
MARE'S TAIL Materials
MARITALLY Martially
*__MARONITES__ Matronise,
Trasimeno
MARSHALER Remarshal
MARTIALLY Maritally
MARTINETS Stream-tin,
Tarentism
MASCULINE Calumnies,
Semuncial
MASONRIED Randomise
MASTERING Emigrants,
Germanist, Remasting,
Streaming
MATCHWOOD Doomwatch
MATERIALS Mare's-tail
MATRICIDE Diametric
MATRONISE Maronites,
Trasimeno
MAUNDERED Undreamed
MEALINESS Messaline
MEANDRIAN Meandrina
MEANDRINA Meandrian
MEANS-TEST Statesmen
MEATINESS Amnesties,
Seminates
MECHANICS Mischance
MECHANISE Manichees
MEDICALLY Decimally
MEDICATED Decimated
MEDICATOR Decimator
MEDICINAL Adminicle
MELANITES Enamelist
MELANOSIS Semolinas
MELOMANIC Commelina
MEN-AT-ARMS Armaments
MENINGEAL Malengine
MENTALISM Immantles,
Simmental
MENTIONER Remention
MERCILESS Crimeless
MEROISTIC Eroticism, Isometric

MESCALINE Camelines
MESENTERA Erasement
MESSALINE Mealiness
METRICIAN Antimeric,
Criminate
METRONOME Monometer,
Monotreme
MICASLATE Calamites
MICROPYLE Polymeric
MILESTONE Limestone
MILLSTONE Stone-mill
MINI-STATE Intimates
*__MINNESOTA__ Nominates
MINORITES Misorient
MISADVISE Admissive,
Misavised
MISAUNTER Anti-serum,
Ruminates
MISAVISED Admissive,
Misadvise
MISCHANCE Mechanics
MISCREANT Encratism
MISCREATE Stream-ice
MISCREDIT Misdirect
MISDEALER Misleader,
Misleared
MISDIRECT Miscredit
MISLEADER Misdealer,
Misleared
MISLEARED Misdealer,
Misleader
MISORIENT Minorites
MISREFORM Reformism
MISRELATE Salimeter
MISREPORT Importers,
Reimports
MISSIONER Remission
MOBILISES Omissible
MODERNISE Demersion,
Domineers
MONACHIST Macintosh
MONERGISM Sommering
*__MONGOLISE__ Neologism
MONOCRACY Nomocracy

MONOCULAR Colourman
MONOGRAMS Groomsman,
  Nomograms
MONOGRAPH Nomograph,
  Phonogram
MONOMETER Metronome,
  Monotreme
MONOTONES Moonstone
MONOTREME Metronome,
  Monometer
MONOTYPIC Toponymic
*****MONTARGIS** Sigmatron,
  Stroaming
MOONSTONE Monotones
MORALISTS Storm-sail
MORPHINES Premonish
MOULDERED Remoulded
MOUSE-DEER Deer-mouse
MOUSETRAP Route-maps
MURDERING Demurring
MURRAINED Unmarried
MUSCARINE Manicures
MUTILATES Stimulate, Ultimates
MUTILATOR Timorlaut

NARCOTINE Container,
  Crenation, Rocinante
NARCOTISE Certosina,
  Creations, Reactions
NARCOTISM Romancist,
  Romantics
NARCOTIST Stratonic, Tractions
NARGHILES Ashlering,
  Nargilehs, Shearling
NARGILEHS Ashlering,
  Narghiles, Shearling
NATIONALS Santolina
NATROLITE Tentorial
NATTERING Integrant, Rattening
NAVIGATED Vaginated
NEAR-WHITE Inwreathe
NECROSING Consigner,
  Reconsign

NECROTISE Erections, Renotices,
  Resection, Secretion
NECTARIAL Lacertian
NECTARISE Centiares, Creatines,
  Iterances
NECTAROUS Courantes,
  Courtesan, Outrances
NEGROIDAL Girandole,
  Reloading
*****NEO-GOTHIC** Theogonic
*****NEOLITHIC** Ichnolite
NEOLOGIES Neologise
NEOLOGISE Neologies
NEOLOGISM Mongolise
NEOTERISM Timoneers
NEPHOLOGY Phenology
NEPHRITIC Phrenitic
NEPHRITIS Phrenitis
NEPHROSIS Phronesis
NERVATION Vernation
NERVINESS Inverness
*****NESTORIAN** Non-satire, Rain-
  stone, Rosinante
NEUROTICS Countries,
  Cretinous
NICCOLOUS Occlusion
NICOTIANS Aniconist, Inactions,
  Onanistic
NICOTINED Incondite
NIGGARDED Degrading
NIGHTGEAR Gathering
NIGHTLESS Lightness
NIGHT-ROBE Bothering
NIGHTWEAR Wreathing
NIGRITUDE Intrigued
NINE-SCORE Recension
NINETY-SIX Sixty-nine
NITRATINE Itinerant
*****NOCTUIDAE** Auctioned,
  Cautioned, Education
NOISELESS Lionesses
NOMINATES Minnesota
NOMOCRACY Monocracy

NOMOGRAMS Groomsman, Monograms
NOMOGRAPH Monograph, Phonogram
NON-SACRED Ordnances
NON-SATIRE Nestorian, Rainstone, Rosinante
NONSUITED Tendinous
NORMALISE Orleanism
NORMALITY Trionymal
NORTHWEST Westnorth
NOSTALGIA Analogist
NOSTALGIC Gnostical
*__NOTONECTA__ Cannotate
*__NOTRE-DAME__ Emendator
NOURISHER Renourish
NOVITIATE Evitation
NUISANCER Insurance
NUMERICAL Melanuric
NUT-BUTTER Butter-nut
NUTRITIVE Vetturini
NUTTINESS Sustinent
NYSTAGMIC Gymnastic

OBALIQUES Obalisque
OBALISQUE Obaliques
OBSCURANT Subcantor
OBTESTING Besotting
OBVERSELY Verbosely
OCCLUSION Niccolous
OCELLATED Decollate
OCHLOCRAT Colcothar
OCTILLION Cotillion
OCULARIST Suctorial
ODOMETERS Osteoderm
OLECRANAL Lanceolar
OMISSIBLE Mobilises
ONANISTIC Aniconist, Inactions, Nicotians
ONCOMINGS Gnomonics
ONSLAUGHT Laughton's
OPERATING Orange-tip, Pignorate
OPERETTAS Poetaster

OPPRESSOR Proposers
OPTICALLY Topically
OPTICIANS Panoistic
OPTOMETER Potometer
OPTOMETRY Potometry
ORANGE-TIP Operating, Pignorate
ORBICULAR Courbaril
ORCADIANS Sarcodina
ORCHESTRA Cart-horse
ORDERLESS Resolders, Solderers
ORDNANCES Non-sacred
ORGANDIES Dragonise, Grandiose, Organised
ORGANISED Dragonise, Grandiose, Organdies
ORGANISTS Assorting, Roastings
ORGAN-PIPE Pipe-organ
ORIENTALS Orleanist, Relations, Tiroleans
ORIGINALS Sailoring, Signorial
ORLEANISM Normalise
ORLEANIST Orientals, Relations, Tiroleans
OSCULATES Cassoulet
OSTEODERM Odometers
*__OSTRACION__ Consortia
OSTRACISE Isocrates
OSTRACISM Acrotisms, Castroism
OSTRINGER Resorting, Restoring, Rostering
OUT-BURNED Burned-out
OUTCRIERS Courtiers, Scrutoire
OUTCRYING Congruity
OUTMASTER Outstream
OUTRANCES Courantes, Courtesan, Nectarous
OUTSLIDES Dissolute, Solitudes
*__OUTSPRING__ Postering, Sprouting
OUTSPRINT Print-outs
OUTSTREAM Outmaster

OUTSTRIKE Strike-out
OUTSTRIPS Posturist
OVERBRAKE Overbreak
OVERBREAK Overbrake
OVERDATES Oversated
OVERGOING Going-over
OVERRATED Overtrade,
Overtread
OVERRATES Overstare
OVERSATED Overdates
OVERSPILL Spill-over
OVERSTARE Overrates
OVERSTREW Overwrest
OVERSWEAR Overwears
OVERTHROW Throw-over
OVERTOWER Overwrote
OVERTRADE Overrated,
Overtread
OVERTREAD Overrated,
Overtrade
OVERWEARS Overswear
OVERWREST Overstrew
OVERWROTE Overtower
OVIPAROUS Apivorous
OWNERSHIP Shipowner

PACTIONAL Placation
PACTIONED Captioned
PAEDERAST Separated,
Estrapade
PAILLASSE Palliasse
PAINTERLY Interplay, Party-line
PAINTRESS Pinasters
PAIR-HORSE Aphoriser
*****PALESTINE** Penalties, Tapelines
PALINODES Delapsion
PALLIASSE Paillasse
PALM-SUGAR Sugar-palm
PALM-TREES Emplaster
PALTERERS Plasterer, Replaster
PALUSTRAL Plaustral
PANOISTIC Opticians
PANTIHOSE Siphonate
PAPILLOTE Popliteal

PARAMEDIC Pre-adamic
PARASITES Aspirates, Satrapies
PARCHEESI Eparchies
PARECIOUS Auriscope
PARENESIS Passerine
PARLEYING Replaying
PAROTITIS Topiarist
PARROTING Prorating
PARTERRES Pre-arrest
PARTISANS Aspirants,
Satin-spar
PARTY-LINE Interplay, Painterly
PASSENGER Sap-greens
PASSERINE Parenesis
PASSIONAL Sponsalia
PATRIARCH Phratriac
PATRICIDE Pediatric
PATRONESS Transpose
PATTERNER Repattern
PECULATES Speculate
PEDIATRIC Patricide
PELAGIANS Pelasgian
PENALTIES Palestine, Tapelines
PENCIL-ORE Crepoline
PENDULATE Unpleated
PENETRANT Repentant
*****PENISTONE** Stone-pine
PENTAMERY Repayment
*****PEPSI-COLA** Episcopal
PEPTONISE Pipestone
PERCALINE Periolean
PERCOLATE Prelocate
PERCUSSOR Procuress
PERDITION Direption
PERFORMED Preformed
PERFORMER Prereform,
Reperform
PERICLASE Sale-price
PERICLEAN Percaline
PERICOPES Periscope
PERISCIAN Precisian
PERISCOPE Pericopes
PERISTOME Temporise
PERMITTER Pretermit

PERSONATE Esperanto
PERSTINGE Estreping, Pestering, Presteign
PERTAINED Repainted
PERTHITIC Tephritic
PERTUSION Eruptions
PERTUSSAL Aplustres, Supersalt
PERVADING Depraving
PESTERING Estreping, Perstinge, Presteign
PESTOLOGY Logotypes
***PETRINISM** Strip-mine
PHARAONIC Anaphoric
PHARISEES Apheresis
PHASELESS Shapeless
PHENOLOGY Nephology
PHONETICS Ctesiphon
PHONOGRAM Monograph, Nomograph
PHONOLITE Lithopone
PHOTOGRAM Tomograph
PHRATRIAC Patriarch
PHRENITIC Nephritic
PHRENITIS Nephritis
PHRONESIS Nephrosis
PICK-TOOTH Tooth-pick
PIECEWORK Work-piece
PIERRETTE Preterite
PIGNERATE Interpage, Repeating
PIGNORATE Operating, Orange-tip
PILLAGERS Aspergill
PINASTERS Paintress
PIPE-ORGAN Organ-pipe
PIPE-STONE Peptonise
PISTAREEN Aperients, Sparteine
PISTOLING Postiling
PISTOLLED Postilled
PLACATION Pactional
PLACATORY Play-actor
PLASTERER Palterers, Replaster
PLATE-RAIL Prelatical
PLATINOUS Pulsation

PLATONISE Antipoles, Seal-point
PLAUSTRAL Palustral
PLEASURER Reperusal
PLAY-ACTOR Placatory
PLENISHED Deplenish
PLENISHES Spleenish
PLEONASTE Antelopes
PLETHORAS Astrophel
PLEURITIS Spirituel
POETASTER Operettas
POETICISM Impeticos
POIGNANCY Canopying
POLIANITE Epilation
POLYESTER Proselyte
POLYMERIC Miropyle
POLYTHENE Telephony
POMOERIUM Prooemium
PONTONIER Prenotion, Entropion
POPLITEAL Papillote
PORBEAGLE Bargepole
***PORTSLADE** Adlestrop
PORTERAGE Reportage
PORTIONER Reportion
PORTRAYED Predatory
POSTERIOR Repositor
POSTHOUSE House-tops, Pothouses
POSTILING Pistoling
POSTILLED Pistolled
POSTURING Outspring, Sprouting
POSTURIST Outstrips
POST-WOMAN Woman-post
POTHOUSES House-tops, Posthouse
POTOMETER Optometer
POTOMETRY Optometry
POTTERING Pottinger, Repotting
POTTINESS Stone-pits
POTTINGER Pottering, Repotting
PRACTISED Crispated
PREACHERS Presearch
PRE-ADAMIC Paramedic

PRE-ARREST Parterres
PRECEDENT Precented
PRECENTED Precedent
PRECISIAN Periscian
PRECREDIT Predirect
PRECURSOR Procurers
PREDATING Departing
PREDATORY Portrayed
PREDESIGN Presigned
PRE-ENTERS Presenter,
  Repenters, Represent
PRE-EXCEPT Pre-expect
PRE-EXPECT Pre-except
PREFORMED Performed
PRELATIAL Plate-rail
PRELATION Rantipole
PRE-LEASED Pre-sealed
PRELOCATE Percolate
PRELUSION Repulsion
PRELUSIVE Pulverise, Repulsive
PRELUSORY Repulsory
PREMISING Simpering
PREMISSES Impresses
PREMONISH Morphines
PRENOTION Entropion,
  Pontonier
PRENTICES Prescient, Reinspect
PREREFORM Performer,
  Reperform
PRE-RESORT Reporters
PRESAGING Asperging
PRESCIENT Prentices, Reinspect
PRE-SEALED Pre-leased
PRESEARCH Preachers
PRESENTED Pretensed,
  Repetends, Serpented
PRESENTER Pre-enters,
  Repenters, Represent
PRESIGNED Predisign
*PRESTEIGN** Estreping, Perstinge,
  Pestering
PRESTRAIN Terrapins, Transpire
PRESUMING Impugners

PRETENSED Presented,
  Repetends, Serpented
PRETERIST Preterits
PRETERITE Pierrette
PRETERITS Preterist
PRETERMIT Permitter
PRE-TONICS Inceptors, Inspector
PRIMARIES Impresari
PRIMATIAL Impartial
PRINTINGS Sprinting
PRINTLESS Splinters
PRINT-OUTS Outsprint
PROCEDURE Reproduce
PROCEEDER Reproceed
PROCREANT Copartner
PROCTITIS Protistic, Tropistic
PROCURERS Precursor
PROCURESS Percussor
PROLETARY Pyrolater
PROOEMIUM Pomoerium
PROPOSERS Oppressor
PRORATING Parroting
PROSELYTE Polyester
PROTESTER Reprotest
PROTHESIS Sophister, Store-ship
PROTISTIC Proctitis, Tropistic
PROUSTIAN Supinator
PSALTRESS Strapless
*PTERELAUS** Pulse-rate
PUBLISHER Republish
PULSATION Platinous
PULSE-RATE Pterelaus
PULVERISE Prelusive, Repulsive
PUMP-WATER Water-pump
PUNCH-CARD Cardpunch
PUNCTILIO Unpolitic
PYROGENIC Recopying
PYROLATER Proletary

QUAKERESS Squeakers
QUALITIED Liquidate
QUICKENER Requicken

RABBINATE Barnabite

RACIALIST Satirical
RADDLEMAN Dreamland
RAIN-CLOUD Uncordial
RAININESS Sirenians
RAIN-STONE Nestorian, Nonsatire, Rosinante
RAINTREES Eritreans, Retainers, Ternaries
RANDOMISE Masonried
RANGINESS Angriness
RANTIPOLE Prelation
RASCALITY Satyrical
RASPINGLY Sparingly
RATHERIPE Three-pair
RATIONALE Alienator
RATTENING Integrant, Nattering
RATTLINGS Startling
REABANDON Abandoner
REACCLAIM Acclaimer
REACTANCE Cancerate
REACTIONS Certosina, Creations, Narcotise
READDRESS Addresser
REAFFRONT Affronter
REALIGNED Engrailed, Geraldine, Redealing, Releading
REALISTIC Eristical
REALITIES Israelite
REAPPLAUD Applauder
REAPPOINT Appointer
REATTEMPT Attempter
REATTRACT Attracter
REBOATION Aerobiont
REBUFFING Buffering
REBUTTING Buttering
RECALLING Cellaring
RECANTING Cantering
RECASTING Cilranges
RECAUTION Cautioner, Cointreau
RECENSION Nine-score
RECHANNEL Channeler
RECHARTER Charterer
RECLAIMED Declaimer

RECLINATE Interlace, Lacertine
RECLUSION Corelius, Inclosure
RECOGNISE Congeries
RECOMFORT Comforter
RECOMMEND Commender
RECONCEAL Concealer
RECONDEMN Condemner
RECONDITE Renoticed
RECONFIRM Confirmer
RECONFORM Conformer
RECONNECT Concenter, Concentre, Connecter
RECONSENT Consenter, Cretonnes
RECONSIGN Consigner, Necrosing
RECONSULT Consulter
RECONTEND Contender
RECONTEST Contester
RECONVERT Converter
RECOPYING Pyrogenic
RECORDIST Creditors, Directors
RECOSTING Corseting, Escorting
RECOUNTED Countered
RECRUITAL Reticular
RECTIFIED Certified, Cretified
RECTIFIER Certifier
RECTITUDE Certitude
RECTORESS Crosstree
RECUMBING Cumbering
RECUSANCE Securance
REDBREAST Bestarred
RED-COATED Decorated
REDEALING Engrailed, Geraldine, Realigned, Releading
REDECRAFT Refracted
REDELIVER Deliverer
REDESCEND Descender
REDEVELOP Developer
REDISCUSS Discusser
REDISPLAY Displayer
REDISTILL Distiller
REDOLENCE Deceleron
REDRAWING Rewarding

RED-TAPIST Spermatid
REDUCTANT Truncated
REDUCTION Introduce
RE-EDITING Reignited
RE-ENGROSS Engrosser
RE-EXHIBIT Exhibiter
RE-EXPLAIN Explainer
RE-EXPRESS Expresser
RE-FASHION Fashioner
REFLATING Faltering
REFLOATED Deflorate, Floreated
REFLOWING Flowering
REFORFEIT Forfeiter
REFORMISM Misreform
REFORMIST Fire-storm,
  Restiform
REFORWARD Forwarder
REFRACTED Redecraft
REFRESHEN Freshener
REFURBISH Furbisher
REFURNISH Furnisher
REGARNISH Garnisher,
  Resharing
REGAUGING Ring-gauge
REGELATED Relegated
REGENESIS Energises
REGRATING Garreting,
  Gartering
REHARNESS Harnesser
REHARVEST Harvester
REIGNITED Re-editing
REIMPLANT Implanter
REIMPORTS Importers,
  Misreport
REIMPRESS Impresser,
  Simperers
REIMPRINT Imprinter
REINFLAME Leaf-miner
REINFORCE Confrerie
REINHABIT Inhabiter
REINSPECT Prentices, Prescient
REINSTALL Installer
REINSURED Surreined
RELACQUER Lacquerer

RELATIONS Orientals, Orleanist,
  Tiroleans
RELATIVES Versatile
RELAUNDER Launderer
RELEADING Engrailed,
  Geraldine, Realigned, Redealing
RELEASING Algerines
RELEGATED Regelated
RELETTING Lettering
RELIANCES Scare-line
RELIEVING Inveigler
RELIGHTED Delighter
RELOADING Girandole,
  Negroidal
REMARSHAL Marshaler
REMASTING Emigrants,
  Germanist, Mastering, Streaming
REMENTION Mentioner
REMIGATED Emigrated
REMISSION Missioner
REMITTERS Trimester, Trimeters
REMOULDED Mouldered
RENASCENT Entrances
RENEGATED Generated
RENOTICED Recondite
RENOTICES Erections, Necrotise,
  Resection, Secretion
RENOUNCED Denouncer
RENOURISH Nourisher
REPAINTED Pertained
REPASSING Aspersing
REPASTURE Apertures
REPATCHED Chaptered
REPATTERN Patterner
REPAYMENT Pentamery
REPEATING Interpage, Pignerate
REPENTANT Penetrant
REPENTERS Pre-enters,
  Presenter, Represent
REPERFORM Performer,
  Prereform
REPERUSAL Pleasurer
REPETENDS Presented,
  Pretensed, Serpented

REPLASTER Palterers, Plasterer
REPLAYING Parleying
REPLETION Interlope, Terpineol
REPORTAGE Porterage
REPORTERS Pre-resort
REPORTION Portioner
REPOSITOR Posterior
REPOTTING Pottering, Pottinger
REPRAISED Despairer, Draperies
REPRESENT Pre-enters,
  Presenter, Repenters
REPRESSED Derepress
REPRISING Respiring, Springier
REPROCEED Proceeder
REPRODUCE Procedure
REPROTEST Protester
REPUBLISH Publisher
REPULSION Prelusion
REPULSIVE Prelusive, Pulverise
REPULSORY Prelusory
REQUICKEN Quickener
REREADING Ear-ringed,
  Grenadier
RESCINDED Discerned
RESCINDER Discerner
RESCUABLE Securable
RESEATING Stingaree
RESECTION Erections, Necrotise,
  Renotices, Secretion
RESECTING Secreting
RESEEDING Energised
RESERVING Reversing
RESHARING Garnisher,
  Regarnish
RESHARPEN Sharpener
RESHORTEN Shortener
RESIDENTS Dissenter, Tiredness
RESISTANT Straitens
RESISTENT Interests, Intersets,
  Sternites, Triteness
RESISTING Sistering
RESLANDER Slanderer
RESOLDERS Orderless, Solderers

RESORTING Ostringer,
  Restoring, Rostering
RESPIRATE Sparterie
RESPIRING Reprising, Springier
RESTATION Stationer
RESTIFORM Fire-storm,
  Reformist
RESTORING Ostringer,
  Resorting, Rostering
RESTRAINT Inter-arts
RESUSPEND Suspender,
  Unpressed
RESWALLOW Swallower,
  Wallowers
RESWEETEN Sweetener
RETAINERS Eritreans, Raintrees,
  Ternaries
RETHICKEN Kitchener,
  Thickener
RETICULAR Recruital
RETIGHTEN Tightener
RETRACING Terracing
REVALENTA Ervalenta
REVARNISH Varnisher
REVEALING Inveagler
REVERENDS Renversed
REVERSING Reserving
REVERSION Versioner
REVICTUAL Lucrative
REVISABLE Verbalise
REVOCABLE Coverable
REWARDING Redrawing
REWARRANT Warranter
RHAPONTIC Anthropic
RHETORICS Chorister
RHETORISE Theoriser
RHODANISE Rhodesian
*RHODESIAN Rhodanise
RICE-WATER Water-rice
RICHENING Enriching
RIFLE-SHOT Short-life
RIGHT-DOWN Downright
RING-GAUGE Regauging
RINGSTAND Stranding

RITUALISE Uralitise
ROASTABLE Astrolabe
ROASTINGS Assorting,
　Organists
*****ROCINANTE** Container,
　Crenation, Narcotine
ROCK-BORER Cork-borer
ROCKINESS Corkiness
ROCK-TRIPE Rope-trick
ROISTERER Terrorise
ROMANCIST Narcotism,
　Romantics
ROMANISER Rosmarine
ROMANTICS Narcotism,
　Romancist
ROPE-TRICK Rock-tripe
*****ROSINANTE** Nestorian, Non-
　satire, Rain-stone
ROSMARINE Romaniser
ROSTERING Ostringer,
　Resorting, Restoring
ROUTE-MAPS Mousetrap
ROUTINIST Introitus
ROWDINESS Windroses,
　Wordiness
ROWEL-SPUR Spur-rowel
RUBELLITE Bulletrie
RUCTATION Curtation
RUDDINESS Dissunder
RUINATION Urination
RUMINATES Anti-serum,
　Misaunter
RUNCINATE Encurtain,
　Uncertain
RUSTICATE Urticates
RUSTICIAL Curialist
RUTHFULLY Hurtfully
*****RUTHENIAN** Hunterian

SACCHARIN Characins
SAIL-BOARD Sail-broad
SAIL-BROAD Sailboard
SAILORING Originals, Signorial
SAINTSHIP Hispanist

SALE-PRICE Periclase
SALERATUS Assaulter
SALEROOMS Salesroom
SALESROOM Salerooms
SALIMETER Misrelate
SALTATION Stational
SALTINESS Slatiness, Stainless
SALTPETER Saltpetre, Steel-trap
SALTPETRE Saltpeter, Steel-trap
SALVATION Lavations
*****SAMARITAN** Sarmatian
*****SANTOLINA** Nationals
SAP-GREENS Passenger
SARCODINA Orcadians
*****SARMATIAN** Samaritan
*****SATANICAL** Castalian
SATANISTS Assistant
SATINETTE Enstatite, Intestate
SATIN-SPAR Aspirants, Partisans
SATIRICAL Racialist
SATRAPIES Aspirates, Parasites
SATURATOR Tartarous
SATURNIAN Turanians
SATYRICAL Rascality
SAUCINESS Issuances
SAUNTERED Denatures
SAVOURILY Variously
SCALLOPED Collapsed
SCAPELESS Spaceless
SCAPULARY Capsulary
SCAPULATE Aspectual,
　Capsulate
SCARE-LINE Reliances
SCARPETTO Spectator
SCATTERER Street-car
SCENARISE Increases
SCENARIST Canisters
SCHEMATIC Catechism
SCHIAVONE Anchovies
SCHOOL-DAY Day-School
SCIATICAL Ascitical
SCIENTIAL Catilines, Inelastic
SCLEROSIS Scoreless
SCLEROTIA Loricates, Sectorial

SCOLLOPED Clodpoles
SCORELESS Sclerosis
SCOURGING Scrouging
SCREAMING Creamings,
  Germanics
SCREENING Secerning
SCREICHED Scrieched
SCREICHES Scrieches
SCRIECHED Screiched
SCRIECHES Screiches
SCRIEVING Servicing
SCROUGING Scourging
SCRUTOIRE Courtiers, Outcriers
SDEIGNING Designing
SEA-BATHER Tabasheer
SEAGREENS Eagerness
SEAL-POINT Antipoles, Platonise
SEA-PARROT Separator
SEARCHERS Archeress
SEA-SPIDER Spear-side
*SEBASTIAN Basanites
SECERNENT Sentencer
SECERNING Screening
SECONDING Consigned
SECRETING Resecting
SECRETION Erections, Necrotise,
  Renotices, Resection
SECTARIAN Ascertain, Cartesian
SECTIONAL Coastline
SECTORIAL Loricates, Sclerotia
SECURABLE Rescuable
SECURANCE Recusance
SEDATIONS Dissonate
SEDERUNTS Undersets,
  Untressed
SEDUCTION Eductions
SEEDLINGS Gelidness
SEGREGATE Easter-egg
SELECTION Cotelines, Elections
SELECTIVE Electives
SELENITIC Insectile
*SELLOTAPE Sole-plate
SEMIGRAND Ganderism

SEMINATES Amnesties,
  Meatiness
SEMOLINAS Melanosis
SEMUNCIAL Calumnies,
  Masculine
SENESCENT Sentences
*SENHORITA Hortensia
SENORITAS Assertion
SENTENCER Secernent
SENTENCES Senescent
SEPARATED Estrapade,
  Paederast
SEPARATOR Sea-parrot
SEPULCHER Sepulchre
SEPULCHRE Sepulcher
SERAPHINE Hesperian,
  Inspheare
SERGEANTS Estranges,
  Greatness
SERICITIC Criticise
SERJEANTS Jesserant
SERMONISE Emersions
SEROTONIN Ironstone
SERPENTED Presented,
  Pretensed, Repetends
SERRATURE Treasurer
SERVICING Scrieving
SESTERTIA Treatises
SETTER-OUT Tetterous
SHADE-TREE Heartseed
SHAKE-DOWN Hawk-nosed
*SHANGRI-LA Ashlaring
SHAPELESS Phaseless
SHARE-OUTS Authoress
SHARPENER Resharpen
SHEARLING Ashlering,
  Narghiles, Nargilehs
SHELLFIRE Hellfires
SHELL-HOLE Hell-holes
SHIPMATES Steamship
SHIPOWNER Ownership
SHIVERING Shrieving
SHOREBOAT Horse-boat
SHORE-CRAB Broachers

SHOREFACE Horseface
SHORELESS Horseless
SHOREWEED Horseweed
SHORTENED Dethrones
SHORTENER Reshorten
SHORT-LIFE Rifle-shot
SHRIEVING Shivering
SHRUBLESS Brushless
SHRUBLIKE Brushlike
SIBILATES Stabilise
SIDEBOARD Broadside
SIDEBURNS Burnsides
SIDEROSIS Disseisor
SIGHT-LINE Gentilish
SIGMATRON Montargis,
  Stroaming
SIGNATORY Gyrations
SIGNATURE Gauntries
SIGNBOARD Boardings
SIGNIFIED Dignifies
SIGNORIAL Sailoring
SILENCING Licensing
SILICATED Deistical
SILVERING Slivering
***SIMMENTAL** Immantles,
  Mentalism
SIMMERING Immersing
SIMPERERS Impresser,
  Reimpress
SIMPERING Premising
SINGALONG Ganglions
SINISTRAD Distrains
SINTERING Inserting
SIPHONATE Pantihose
SIRENIANS Raininess
SISTERING Resisting
SIXTY-NINE Ninety-six
SKREIGHED Skrieghed
SKRIEGHED Skrieghed
SLANDERER Reslander
SLATE-GREY Steel-gray
SLATINESS Saltiness, Stainless
SLAUGHTER Laughters
SLIGHTING Lightings

SLIVERING Silvering
SLUMBERER Lumberers
SMARTENED Tradesmen
SNAPPERED End-papers
SNATCHERS Chantress
SNATCHING Stanching
SNOOPIEST Spconiest
SOI-DISANT Stasidion
SOLDERERS Orderless,
  Resolders
SOLECISES Isosceles
SOLE-PLATE Sellotape
SOLITUDES Dissolute, Outslides
***SOLUTRIAN** Insulator
***SOMMERING** Monergism
SOPHISTER Prothesis, Store-ship
SORTMENTS Sternmost
SPACE-LESS Scapeless
SPACE-TIME Empaestic
SPANCELED Enclasped
SPARINGLY Raspingly
SPARTEINE Aperients, Pistareen
SPARTERIE Respirate
SPEALBONE Beanpoles
SPEAR-SIDE Sea-spider
SPEARWORT Straw-rope
SPEAR-FISH Fish-spear
SPECTATOR Scarpetto
SPECULATE Peculates
SPERMATID Red-tapism
SPILL-OVER Overspill
SPIRITUEL Pleuritis
SPLEENISH Plenishes
SPLINTERS Printless
SPLIT-RING Stripling, Triplings
SPLOSHING Long-ships
SPOLIATOR Troopials
SPONSALIA Passional
SPOONIEST Snoopiest
SPOTTABLE Tabletops
SPRINGIER Reprising, Respiring
SPRINTING Printings
SPROUTING Outspring,
  Posturing

SPUR-ROWEL Rowel-spur
SQUEAKERS Quakeress
STABILISE Sibilates
STAINLESS Saltiness, Slatiness
STAIRCASE Caesarist
STALINIST Latinists
STAMINATE Emanatist
STAMINODE Dominates,
  Maidstone
STANCHERS Chantress,
  Snatchers
STANCHING Snatching
STANDER-BY Bystander
STAPEDIAL Lapidates
STAR-ANISE Erastians
STARINGLY Strayling
STARSHINE Tarnishes
STARTLING Rattlings
STASIDION Sol-disant
STATEABLE Tasteable
STATELESS Tasteless
STATEMENT Testament
STATESIDE Steadiest
STATESMEN Means-test
STATIONAL Saltation
STATIONED Antidotes
STATIONER Restation
STAUNCHER Chaunters
STEADIEST Stateside
STEAMSHIP Shipmates
STEEL-GRAY Slate-grey
STEEL-TRAP Saltpeter, Saltpetre
STEEPENED Ensteeped
STEERSMAN Mare's-nest
STEP-BAIRN Breast-pin
STERILISE Listerise
STERNITES Interests, Intersets,
  Resistent, Triteness
STERNMOST Sortments
STIMULATE Mutilates, Ultimates
STINGAREE Reseating
STOCK-WHIP Whip-stock
STOICALLY Callosity
STOMACHER Chromates

STONE-COAL Consolate
STONE-MILL Millstone
STONE-PINE Penistone
STONE-PITS Pottiness
STORE-SHIP Prothesis, Sophister
STORM-SAIL Moralists
STRAINING Gantrisin, Trainings
STRAITENS Resistant
STRANDING Ringstand
STRAPLESS Psaltress
STRAPPING Trappings
STRATONIC Narcotist, Tractions
STRAW-ROPE Spearwort
STRAYLING Staringly
STREAM-ICE Miscreate
STREAMING Emigrants,
  Germanist, Mastering,
  Remasting
STREAM-TIN Martinets,
  Tarentism
STREET-CAR Scatterer
STRIKE-OUT Outstrike
STRING-PEA Taperings,
  Trapesing
STRIPLING Split-ring, Triplings
STRIP-MINE Petrinism
STROAMING Montargis,
  Sigmatron
STRONGARM Armstrong
STUMBLING Tumblings
SUABILITY Usability
SUBCANTOR Obscurant
SUB-DEACON Case-bound
SUB-DEALER Sub-leader
SUBENTIRE Trubenise
SUB-LEADER Sub-dealer
SUBLINEAR Insurable
SUBSIDIES Subsidise
SUBSIDISE Subsidies
SUBSTRACT Subtracts
SUBTRACTS Substract
SUCCINATE Encaustic
SUCTIONAL Sulcation, Unstoical
SUCTORIAL Ocularist

SUGAR-CANE Cane-sugar
SUGAR-LOAF Loaf-sugar
SUGAR-LUMP Lump-sugar,
  Sugar-plum
SUGAR-PALM Palm-sugar
SUGAR-PLUM Lump-sugar,
  Sugar-lump
SULCATION Suctional, Unstoical
SULPHURED Desulphur
SUMMARIES Summarise
SUMMARISE Summaries
SUNBONNET Unbonnets
SUNBURNED Unburdens
SUNDERING Undersign
SUNFLOWER Unflowers
SUPERSALT Aplustres, Pertussal
SUPINATOR Proustian
SURREINED Reinsured
SUSPENDER Resuspend,
  Unpressed
SUSPIRING Uprisings
SUSTINENT Nuttiness
SWALLOWER Reswallow,
  Wallowers
SWEETENER Resweeten
SWEPT-BACK Back-swept
SWING-BACK Back-swing
SWING-TREE Westering
SWORDPLAY Wordplays
SYNDICATE Asyndetic,
  Cystidean

TABASHEER Sea-bather
TABLETOPS Spottable
TABLE-WORK Work-table
*TADCASTER Castrated
TAILBOARD Broadtail
TAIL-ENDER Interdeal
TAILORING Largition
TANAGRINE Argentina
TANGERINE Argentine
*TANTALEAN Antenatal,
  Atlantean
TAP-CINDER Predicant

TAPELINES Palestine, Penalties
TAPERINGS String-pea,
  Trapesing
TAPERNESS Apertness
TARENTISM Martinets,
  Stream-tin
TARNISHED Interdash
TARNISHES Starshine
TARPAULIN Unpartial
TARTAROUS Saturator
TASTEABLE Stateable
TASTELESS Stateless
TEA-BOARDS Adsorbate
TEACHABLE Cheatable
TEASELING Anglesite, Galenites,
  Gelatines
TELEPHONY Polythene
TELLURIAN Ill-nature
TEMPORISE Peristome
TENDERISE Teredines
TENDINOUS Nonsuited
TENTACLES Latescent
TENTATION Attention
TENTATIVE Attentive
TENTORIAL Natrolite
TEPHRITIC Perthitic
TEREDINES Tenderise
TERENTIAN Entertain
TERMINIST Intermits
TERNARIES Eritreans, Raintrees,
  Retainers
TERPINEOL Interlope, Repletion
TERRACING Retracing
TERRAPINS Prestrain, Transpire
TERRORISE Roisterer
TESTAMENT Statement
TETANISED Destinate
TETTEROUS Setter-out
THEOGONIC Neo-gothic
THEOLOGIC Ethologic
THEORISER Rhetorise
THEORISES Heterosis, Isotheres
THERENESS Threeness
THICKENED Kitchened

THICKENER Kitchener, Rethicken
THREE-CARD Chartered
THREENESS Thereness
THREE-PAIR Ratheripe
THRENODIC Chondrite
THROW-DOWN Down-throw
THROW-OVER Overthrow
TIGER'S-EYE Geyserite
TIGHTENER Retighten
TIMONEERS Neoterism
*TIMORLAUT Mutilator
TIN-OPENER Interpone
TINTINESS Insistent
TIREDNESS Dissenter, Residents
TIROLEANS Orientals, Orleanist, Relations
TITRATING Attriting
TITRATION Attrition
TOCCATINA Catatonic
TOCHERING Hectoring
TOD-LOWRIE Lowrie-tod
TOILET-SET Toilettes
TOILETTES Toilet-set
TOLERANCE Coeternal
TOMOGRAPH Photogram
*TONBRIDGE Bridgeton
TONGUELET Longuette
TONSORIAL Torsional
TOOTH-PICK Pick-tooth
TOP-DRAWER Water-drop
TOPIARIST Parotitis
TOPICALLY Optically
TOPONYMIC Monotypic
TORSIONAL Tonsorial
TORTRICES Trisector
TOTALLING Allotting
TOW-HEADED Two-headed
TRACEABLE Creatable
TRACHITIS Citharist
TRACTATOR Attractor
TRACTIONS Narcotist, Stratonic
TRADESMEN Smartened
TRAGULINE Granulite

TRAININGS Gantrisin, Straining
TRANSHIPS Transship
TRANSIENT Instanter
TRANSLATE Alterants, Alternats
TRANSONIC Constrain
TRANSPIRE Prestrain, Terrapins
TRANSPOSE Patroness
TRANSSHIP Tranships
TRAPESING String-pea, Taperings
TRAPPINGS Strapping
*TRASIMENO Maronites, Matronise
TREADLING Triangled
TREASURER Serrature
TREATISES Sestertia
TRIACTINE Intricate
*TRIANDRIA Irradiant
TRIANGLED Treadling
TRIBUNATE Turbinate
TRICHINAS Christian, Christina
TRIFLINGS Firstling, Flirtings
TRIMESTER Remitters, Trimeters
TRIMETERS Remitters, Trimester
TRIONYMAL Normality
TRIPLINGS Split-ring, Stripling
TRISECTED Decretist
TRISECTOR Tortrices
TRITENESS Interests, Intersets, Resistent, Sternites
TROCHILIC Chloritic
TROOPIALS Spoliator
TROPISTIC Proctitis, Protistic
TROUNCING Cornuting
*TRUBENISE Subentire
TRUNCATED Reductant
TUMBLINGS Stumbling
TUNAREMIC Climature
TURANIANS Saturnian
TURBINATE Tribunate
TURNABOUT About-turn
TWISTABLE Waistbelt
TWO-BY-FOUR Four-by-two
TWO-HEADED Tow-headed

*TYPHONIAN Antiphony

ULTIMATES Mutilates, Stimulate
UNALIGNED Unleading
UNALTERED Unrelated
UNATTUNED Untaunted
UNBEARDED Unbreaded
UNBLASTED Unstabled
UNBLOTTED Unbottled
UNBONNETS Sunbonnet
UNBOTTLED Unblotted
UNBREADED Unbearded
UNBRUSHED Underbush
UNBURDENS Sunburned
UNCATERED Uncreated
UNCERTAIN Encurtain,
  Runcinate
UNCHALKED Unhackled
UNCLAIMED Undecimal,
  Unmedical
UNCLESHIP Siphuncle
UNCORDIAL Rain-cloud
UNCREATED Uncatered
UNDECIMAL Unclaimed,
  Unmedical
UNDEFILED Unfielded
UNDELIGHT Unlighted
UNDERACTS Undercast
UNDERBUSH Unbrushed
UNDERCAST Underacts
UNDERFLOW Wonderful
UNDERNOTE Undertone
UNDERSETS Sederunts,
  Untressed
UNDERSIDE Undesired
UNDERSIGN Sundering
UNDERTIME Unmerited
UNDERTONE Undernote
UNDESERVE Unsevered
UNDESIRED Underside
UNDREADED Daundered
UNDREAMED Maundered
UNELAPSED Unpleased

UNERODING Ungroined,
  Unignored
UNERUPTED Unreputed
UNFEEDING Unfeigned
UNFEELING Unfleeing
UNFEIGNED Unfeeding
UNFIELDED Undefiled
UNFLEEING Unfeeling
UNFLOWERS Sunflower
UNFOLDING Foundling
UNGROINED Uneroding,
  Unignored
UNHACKLED Unchalked
UNHASTING Hauntings
UNHEARSED Unsheared
UNIGNORED Uneroding,
  Ungroined
UNLEADING Unaligned
UNLIGHTED Undelight
UNMARRIED Murrained
UNMEDICAL Unclaimed,
  Undecimal
UNMERITED Undertime
UNNOTICED Continued
UNPARTIAL Tarpaulin
UNPHRASED Unsharped
UNPLEASED Unelapsed
UNPLEATED Pendulate
UNPOLITIC Punctilio
UNPRESSED Resuspend,
  Suspender
UNRASPING Unsparing
UNRELATED Unaltered
UNREPINED Unripened
UNREPUTED Unerupted
UNRESCUED Unsecured
UNRESTING Insurgent
UNRIPENED Unrepined
UNSAINTED Inundates,
  Unstained
UNSECURED Unrescued
UNSEVERED Undeserve
UNSHARPED Unphrased
UNSHEARED Unhearsed

UNSICKLED Klendusic
UNSPARING Unrasping
UNSTABLED Unblasted
UNSTAINED Inundates,
  Unsainted
UNSTIRRED Intruders
UNSTOICAL Suctional, Sulcation
UNSTREWED Unwrested
UNTAUNTED Unattuned
UNTRESSED Sederunts,
  Undersets
UNWRESTED Unstrewed
UPRISINGS Suspiring
URALITISE Ritualise
URINATION Ruination
URTICATES Rusticate
USABILITY Suability

VACILLATE Laticlave
VACUOLATE Autoclave
VAGINATED Navigated
VALENTINE Levantine
VANISHERS Varnishes
VARIOUSLY Savourily
VARNISHER Revarnish
VARNISHES Vanishers
VASTITUDE Vedutista
VEDUTISTA Vastitude
VENERATED Enervated
VENERATOR Enervator
VERBALISE Revisable
VERBALITY Veritably
VERBERATE Vertebrae
VERBOSELY Obversely
VERGLASES Graveless
VERIDICAL Larvicide
VERIFIERS Versifier
VERITABLE Avertible
VERITABLY Verbality
VERMICIDE Decemviri
VERNATION Nervation
VERSATILE Relatives
VERSIFIER Verifiers

VERSIONER Reversion
VERTEBRAE Verberate
VERTICALS Cat-silver
VETTURINI Nutritive
VIGILANTE Genitival
VOLUCRINE Involucre

WAGNERIST Waterings
WAISTBELT Twistable
WALLOWERS Reswallow,
  Swallower
WANDERING Dawnering
WARRANTER Rewarrant
WATERDROP Top-drawer
WATERFLEA Waterleaf
WATERFLOW Waterfowl
WATERFOWL Waterflow
WATERHEAD Head-water
WATERINGS Wagnerist
WATERLEAF Waterflea
WATER-PUMP Pump-water
WATER-RICE Rice-water
WELLDOING Dowelling
WELL-NOTED Well-toned
WELL-TONED Well-noted
WESTERING Swing-tree
WESTNORTH Northwest
WHIP-STOCK Stock-whip
WHITEWOOD Howtowdie
WHOSOEVER Howsoever
WIND-BREAK Break-wind
WINDROSES Rowdiness,
  Wordiness
WOMAN-POST Post-woman
WONDERFUL Underflow
WORDINESS Rowdiness,
  Windroses
WORDPLAYS Swordplay
WORKHOUSE Housework
WORK-PIECE Piecework
WORK-TABLE Table-work
WREATHING Nightwear

Ten letters

ABORTICIDE Bacterioid
ABSORPTION Probations
ACCOURTING Accoutring
ACCOUTRING Accourting
ACCRETIONS Cestracion
*****ACHERONTIC** Anchoretic
ACHROMATIN Machinator
ACIDIMETER Mediatrice
ACTIVATION Cavitation
ADAMANTINE Amantadine,
  Diamantane
ADMINISTER Mistained
ADMONITIVE Dominative
ADMONITION Domination
ADROITNESS Intradoses
ADULTERIES Adulterise
ADULTERISE Adulteries
AEROGRAPHY Areography
AEROLOGIST Areologist
AEROMETRIC Areometric
ALARMINGLY Marginally
ALIENATION Alineation
ALIENATORS Rationales,
  Senatorial
ALIGNMENTS Signalment
ALIENATION Alineation
ALINEATION Alienation
ALLEGORIES Allegorise
ALLEGORISE Allegories
ALLEGORIST Legislator
ALLOSTERIC Corallites
ALMOND-TREE Entodermal
ALPHAMETIC Emphatical
ALTRUISTIC Ultraistic
AMANTADINE Adamantine,
  Diamantane
AMENDATORS Sordamente

AMPHOTERIC Metaphoric
ANAGLYPTIC Play-acting
ANAPAESTIC Sea-captain
ANCHORETIC Acherontic
ANCHORITES Chain-store
ANEMOGRAPH Phanerogam
ANHARMONIC Monarchian
ANTAGONIST Stagnation
ANTIMONIAL Antinomial,
  Lamination
ANTINOMIAL Antimonial,
  Lamination
ANTISEPSIS Inspissate
ANTISEPTIC Psittacine
ANTI-SOVIET Novitiates
ANTITRADES Attainders
APHETIZING Hepatizing
APPERTAINS Satin-paper
APPRENTICE Pine-carpet
APPROACHER Reapproach
ARBALESTER Arrestable
ARBALISTER Breastrail
ARCTOPHILE Cartophile
AREOGRAPHY Aerography
AREOLOGIST Aerologist
AREOMETRIC Aerometric
ARGENTEOUS Entourages
ARRESTABLE Arbalester
ASCERTAINS Cartesians,
  Incrassate, Sectarians
ASCRIPTION Crispation
ASPHALTING Phalangist
ASPIRINGLY Praisingly
ASTRINGENT Integrants
ATTAINDERS Anti-trades
ATTEMPERED Temperated
AUCTIONARY Cautionary

AUCTIONING Cautioning
*__AUSTRALIAN__ Saturnalia

BACTERIOID Aborticide
BANALITIES Insatiable
BANDEROLES Bandoleers,
  Endorsable
BANDOLEERS Banderoles,
  Endorsable
BAND-SPRING String-band
BANTERINGS String-bean
BASKETWORK Workbasket
BAS-RELIEFS Bass-relief
BASS-RELIEF Bas-reliefs
BASSET-HORN Stone-brash
BECHARMING Chambering
BELL-FLOWER Flower-bell
BESAINTING Bestaining
BESTAINING Besainting
BITONALITY Notability
BOLSTERING Lobstering
BOTTLE-HEAD Table-d'hôte
BREAKWATER Waterbreak
BREAST-DEEP Predebates
BREAST-RAIL Arbalister
BRIDLE-HAND Hildebrand
BRIGHTENER Rebrighten
BRIGHTEYES Eyebrights
BRINGING-UP Upbringing
BROADTREAD Treadboard
BURGLARIES Burglarise
BURGLARISE Burglaries

CACOMISTLE Cosmetical
CAMERATING Macerating
CAMERATION Maceration,
  Racemation
CAMPAIGNER Recampaign
CAMPESTRAL Scrap-metal
*__CAMPTONITE__ Pentatomic
CANE-CHAIRS Saccharine
CANTILEVER Trivalence
CAPSULATED Scapulated
CAPTIONING Pactioning

CARD-CASTLE Cat's-cradle
*__CARNOUSTIE__ Cautioners
CAROTENOID Co-ordinate,
  Decoration
CARTESIANS Ascertains,
  Incrassate, Sectarians
CARTOPHILE Arctophile
CATALOGUED Coagulated
CATECHESIS Catechises
CATECHISES Catechesis
CATEGORIES Categorise
CATEGORISE Categories
CAT'S-CRADLE Card-castle
CAUTIONARY Auctionary
CAUTIONERS Carnoustie
CAUTIONING Auctioning
CAVITATION Activation
*__CELTOMANIA__ Neomatical
CENTERINGS Centreings,
  Nigrescent
CENTESIMAL Lemniscate
CENTILITER Centilitre
CENTILITRE Centiliter
CENTIMETER Centimetre
CENTIMETRE Centimeter
CENTRALISE Interlaces,,
  Linecaster
CENTREINGS Centerings,
  Nigrescant
CENTROIDAL Declinator
*__CERINTHIAN__ Interchain
CERTIFYING Cretifying,
  Rectifying
*__CESTRACION__ Accretions
CHAIN-STORE Anchorites
CHALKSTONE Shackleton,
  Shecklaton
CHAMBERING Becharming
CHIMNEYPOT Chimneytop
CHIMNEYTOP Chimneypot
CHRISTENER Rechristen
CHROMOTYPE Cormophyte,
  Ectomorphy
CHRYSOLITE Chrysotile

10

CHRYSOTILE Chrysolite
CISPONTINE Inceptions,
  Inspection
CLOUDINESS Discounsel
COAGULATED Catalogued
COAL-PORTER Percolator
COLLAPSING Scalloping
COLUMNATED Documental
COMMODORES Cosmodrome
COMPOUNDED Decompound
COMPOUNDER Recompound
COMPRESSED Decompress
CONCERTING Concreting
CONCERTINO Concretion
CONCLUSIVE Vice-consul
CONCREATES Consecrate
CONCRETING Concerting
CONCRETION Concertino
CONFRONTER Reconfront
CONSECRATE Concreates
CONSERVANT Conversant
CONSERVING Conversing
CONSTIPATE Costean-pit
CONSTRAINS Transonics, Trans-
  sonic
CONTAINERS Crenations,
  Resanction, Sanctioner
CONTENTING Contingent
CONTINGENT Contenting
CONTRAVENE Covenanter
CONVERSANT Conservant
CONVERSING Conserving
CO-ORDINATE Carotenoid,
  Decoration
CO-RELATION Iconolater,
  Relocation
CORALLITES Allosteric
CORDIERITE Directoire
CORMOPHYTE Chromotype,
  Ectomorphy
CORREPTION Porrection
*****CORTADERIA** Eradicator
COSMETICAL Cacomistle
COSMODROME Commodores

COSTEAN-PIT Constipate
COUNTERING Recounting
COVENANTER Contravene
CREATININE Incinerate
CREATIONAL Laceration,
  Reactional
CREATIVELY Reactively
CREATIVITY Reactivity
CREDENTIAL Interlaced
CREDITABLE Directable
CRENATIONS Containers,
  Resanction, Sanctioner
CRESCENTED Decrescent
CRESCENTIC Eccentrics
CRETIFYING Certifying,
  Rectifying
CRETINISED Indiscreet,
  Indiscrete, Iridescent
CRISPATION Ascription
CRISPBREAD Spider-crab
CROUPINESS Percussion,
  Supersonic
CRUSTINESS Rusticness
CURATESHIP Pasticheur
CYLINDRITE Indirectly

DAME-SCHOOL School-dame
DATUM-PLANE Paludament
DEALERSHIP Leadership
DECIMATING Medicating
DECIMATION Medication
DECLENSION Indolences
DECLINATOR Centroidal
DECOMPOUND Compounded
DECOMPRESS Compressed
DECORATION Carotenoid, Co-
  ordinate
DECRESCENT Crescented
DEER-FOREST Deforester,
  Reforested
DELIGATION Gadolinite,
  Gelatinoid, Intaglioed
DENOMINATE Emendation
DENOTATING Detonating

DENOTATION Detonation
DENOTATIVE Detonatire
DENSIMETER Determines
DENTITIONS Distention
DENUNCIATE Enunciated
DEPOSITION Positioned
DEPRECATOR Tape-record
DEPRESSING Predesigns
DERACINATE Ecardinate
DEROGATION Gerodontia,
  Trogonidae
DESCRIPTOR Predictors
DESPAIRING Diaperings,
  Spinigrade
DETERMINES Densimeter
DETONATING Denotating
DETONATION Denotation
DETONATIVE Denotative
DIAMANTANE Adamantine,
  Amantadine
DIAMANTINE Inanimated,
  Maintained
DIAPERINGS Despairing,
  Spinigrade
DICE-PLAYER Icy-pearled
DICTATIONS Donatistic
DICTIONARY Indicatory
DIGESTIONS Disgestion
DIRECTABLE Creditable
DIRECTIONS Discretion,
  Soricident
DIRECTIVES Discretive
DIRECTOIRE Cordierite
DIRUPTIONS Disruption
DISANIMATE Mediastina
DISCERNING Rescinding
DISCOUNSEL Cloudiness
DISCOUNTER Introduces,
  Reductions
DISCOVERER Rediscover
DISCREETLY Discretely
DISCREPANT Predicants
DISCRETELY Discreetly

DISCRETION Directions,
  Soricident
DISCRETIVE Directives
DISGESTION Digestions
DISPATCHER Redispatch
DISRUPTION Diruptions
DISTENTION Dentitions
DIURNALIST Industrial
DOCUMENTAL Columnated
DOMINATION Admonition
DOMINATIVE Admonitive
*DONATISTIC** Dictations
DRACONITES Narcotised,
  Redactions
DRAGOONING Gadrooning
DYNAMICIST Dynamistic
DYNAMISTIC Dynamicist

EAR-WITNESS Wateriness
EARTHINESS Heartiness
EARTHQUAKE Heartquake
EASTERLING Generalist
EAVESDROPS Overpassed
ECARDINATE Deracinate
ECCENTRICS Crescentic
ECRITOIRES Escritoire
ECTOMORPHY Chromotype,
  Cormophyte
EDITORIALS Idolatries, Idolatrise
EGOCENTRIC Geogentric
ELFISHNESS Fleshiness
EMACULATES Emasculate
EMASCULATE Emaculates
EMBITTERER Timber-tree
EMENDATION Denominate
EMIGRATING Remigating
EMIGRATION Remigation
EMPHATICAL Alphametic
EMPLASTRON Palmerston
ENCLASPING Spanceling
ENCOIGNURE Neurogenic
ENCOPRESIS Precession
ENDEARMENT Man-entered
ENDODERMIS Modernised

ENDORSABLE Banderoles,
  Bandoleers
ENDURINGLY Underlying
ENERVATING Venerating
ENERVATION Veneration
ENERVATIVE Venerative
ENGRAILING Realigning
ENGRASPING Gingersnap
ENIGMATIST Estimating
ENLIGHTING Lightening
ENREGISTER Interreges
ENTHRALDOM Mother-land
ENTHRONISE Rhinestone
ENTODERMAL Almond-tree
ENTOURAGES Argenteous
ENTREATIVE Inveterate
ENTROPIUMS Importunes,
  Resumption
ENUNCIATED Denunciate
EPISTERNAL Presential
EPITHERMAL Hemipteral
ERADICATOR Cortaderia
EROTOGENIC Orogenetic
ESCHAROTIC Octarchies
ESCRITOIRE Ecritoires
ESTIMATING Enigmatist
ETHOLOGIST Theologist
EVISCERATE Tea-service
EXCEPTABLE Expectable
EXCITATION Intoxicate
EXPECTABLE Exceptable
EXPLOITERS Sexploiter
EXTIRPATES Sexpartite
EYEBRIGHTS Brighteyes

FEARLESSLY Self-slayer
FIBERBOARD Fibreboard
FIBERGLASS Fibreglass
FIBREBOARD Fiberboard
FIBREGLASS Fiberglass
FIELDBOOTS Soft-boiled
FILTRATION Flirtation
FIMICOLOUS Music-folio
FINGERLESS Fringeless

*FINNO-UGRIC Ugro-finnic
FIRST-NIGHT First-thing
FIRST-THING First-night
FISHING-ROD Rod-fishing
FITTING-OUT Outfitting
FLESHINESS Elfishness
FLIRTATION Filtration
FLIRTINGLY Triflingly
FLOODWATER Waterflood
FLOWER-BELL Bell-flower
FORECASTER Reforecast
FORTEPIANO Pianoforte
FRINGELESS Fingerless

GADOLINITE Deligation,
  Gelatinoid, Intaglioed
GADROONING Dragooning
GELATINOID Deligation,
  Gadolinite Intaglioed
*GALWEGIANS Glaswegian
GENERALIST Easterling
GENERATING Renegating
GENERATION Renegation
GEOCENTRIC Egocentric
GERMINATES Magnetiser
GERODONTIA Derogation
GINGERSNAP Engrasping
*GLASWEGIAN Galwegians
GLOOMINESS Neologisms
GLYCOSURIA Graciously
GRACIOUSLY Glycosuria
GRADIENTER Intergrade,
  Retreading
GRAMOPHONY Graphonomy,
  Monography
GRANULITES Resaluting
GRAPE-LOUSE Plague-sore
GRAPHOLOGY Logography
GRAPHONOMY Gramophony,
  Monography, Nomography
GRAVEOLENT Lovat-green
GREEDINESS Niger-seeds
GRINDSTONE Stringendo
GROUNDLESS Groundsels

GROUNDSELS Groundless

HARMONICAL Monarchial
HARMONICAS Maraschino
HEADMASTER Headstream
HEADSPRING Springhead
HEADSTREAM Headmaster
HEARTINESS Earthiness
HEARTQUAKE Earthquake
HECTOLITRE Hectoliter
HECTOLITER Hectolitre
HECTOMETRE Hectometer
HECTOMETER Hectometre
HEMIPTERAL Epithermal
HEPATIZING Aphetizing
*****HEPTAMERON** Promethean
HETEROKONT Tenter-hook
HIBERNATED Inbreathed
*****HILDEBRAND** Bridle-hand
HOMILETICS Mesolithic
HOMOLOGIES Homologise
HOMOLOGISE Homologies
HOWSOMEVER Whomsoever
HURTLESSLY Ruthlessly
HYPODORIAN Radiophony

ICONOLATER Co-relation,
  Relocation
ICY-PEARLED Dice-player
IDEALISERS Serialised
IDEALISTIC Italicised
IDEALIZERS Serialized
IDOLATRIES Editorials,
  Idolatrise
IDOLATRISE Editorials,
  Idolatries
IMPENITENT Pentimenti
IMPERFECTS Perfectism
IMPORTANCY Patronymic,
  Pyromantic
IMPORTUNED Minute-drop
IMPORTUNES Entropiums,
  Resumption
IMPRECATED Mercaptide

IMPRECATES Spermaceti
IMPREGNATE Permeating
IMPRESSION Permission
IMPRESSIVE Permissive
IMPRESSURE Presurmise
IMPRISONER Reimprison
INACTIVATE Vaticinate
INANIMATED Diamantine,
  Maintained
INBREATHED Hibernated
INCAUTIONS Insouciant
INCEPTIONS Cispontine,
  Inspection
INCINERATE Creatinine
INCORONATE Nero-antico
INCRASSATE Ascertains,
  Cartesians, Sectarians
INDICATORY Dictionary
INDIRECTLY Cylindrite
INDISCREET Cretinised,
  Indiscrete, Iridescent
INDISCRETE Cretinised,
  Indiscreet, Iridescent
INDOLENCES Declension
INDUSTRIAL Diurnalist
INFARCTION Infraction
INFRACTION Infarction
INOCULATES Inosculate
INOSCULATE Inoculates
INSATIABLE Banalities
INSINUATOR Ruinations,
  Urinations
INSOUCIANT Incautions
INSPECTION Cispontine,
  Inceptions
INSPISSATE Antisepsis
INSTRUMENT Nutriments
INTAGLIOED Deligation,
  Gadolinite, Gelatinoid
INTEGRANTS Astringent
INTERCHAIN Cerinthian
INTERGRADE Retreading,
  Gradienter
INTERLACED Credential

INTERLACES Centralise,
Linecaster
INTERPOSAL Rantipoles
INTERREGES Enregister
INTERVENED Reinvented
INTOXICATE Excitation
INTRADOSES Adroitness
INTREATING Intrigante
INTRENCHER Reintrench
INTRIGANTE Intreating
INTRODUCES Discounter,
Reductions
INVETERATE Entreative
IRIDECTOMY Mediocrity
IRIDESCENT Cretinised,
Indiscreet, Indiscrete
IRIDOSMIUM Osmiridium
IRONSMITHS Mini-shorts
ISENTROPIC Triniscope
ITALICISED Idealistic

JEOPARDIES Jeopardise
JEOPARDISE Jeopardies

KITCHENING Thickening
KNOTTINESS Stinkstone

LACE-PILLOW Pillow-lace
LACERATION Creational,
Reactional
LACUSTRINE Nuclearist
LAMINARISE Seminarial
LAMINATION Antimonial,
Antinomial
LAPIDARIST Triapsidal
LAZINESSES Sleaziness
LEADERSHIP Dealership
LEAD-PENCIL Pencil-lead
***LEBENSRAUM** Mensurable
LEGISLATOR Allegorist
LEMNISCATE Centesimal
LENTAMENTE Tenemental
LETHARGIES Lethargise
LETHARGISE Lethargies

LEVITATION Tonalitive,
Velitation
LIBERTY-MAN Terminably
LIGHTENING Enlighting
LIMITATION Militation
LINECASTER Centralise,
Interlaces
LOBSTERING Bolstering
LOGOGRAPHY Graphology
LOUVER-DOOR Louvre-door
LOUVRE-DOOR Louver-door
LOVAT-GREEN Gravelent
LUSTRELESS Resultless

MACERATING Camerating
MACERATION Cameration,
Racemation
MACHINATOR Achromatin
MAGISTRATE Sterigmata
MAGNETISER Germinates
***MAHOMMEDAN** Mohammedan
MAIN-STREET Martensite,
Misentreat, Terminates
MAINTAINED Adimantine,
Inanimated
MAN-ENTERED Endearment
MANIFESTER Remanifest
MAN-SERVANT Servant-man
MANNERISMS Mismanners
MARASCHINO Harmonicas
MARCESCENT Scarcement
***MARCIONIST** Morticians,
Romanistic
MARGARINES Misarrange
MARGINALLY Alarmingly
MARTENSITE Main-street,
Misentreat, Terminates
MASTERLESS Streamless
MASTERSHIP Shipmaster
MASTER-WORK Work-master
MASTERWORT Storm-water
MATURATION Natatorium
MAUNDERING Undreaming
MEAGERNESS Meagreness

MEAGRENESS Meagerness
MEDIASTINA Disanimate
MEDIATRICE Acidimeter
MEDICASTER Miscreated
MEDICATING Decimating
MEDICATION Decimation
MEDIOCRITY Iridectomy
MENSURABLE Lebensraum
MENTIONERS Minestrone
MERCAPTIDE Imprecated
MERCERIES Mercerise
MERCERISE Merceries
*MESOLITHIC Homiletics
METAPHORIC Amphoteric
METASTABLE Stablemate
METRONOMIC Monometric
MICA-SCHIST Schismatic
MICRO-METER Micro-metre
MICRO-METRE Micro-meter
MILITARIES Militarise
MILITARISE Militaries
MILITATION Limitation
MILLILITER Millilitre
MILLILITRE Milliliter
MILLIMETER Millimetre
MILLIMETRE Millimeter
MINESTRONE Mentioners
MINI-SHORTS Ironsmiths
MINUTE-DROP Importuned
· MISALIGNED Misdealing,
   Misleading
MISARRANGE Margarines
MISCREATED Medicaster
MISDEALING Misaligned,
   Misleading
MISENTREAT Main-street,
   Martensite, Terminates
MISLEADING Misaligned,
   Misdealing
MISMANNERS Mannerisms
MISTRAINED Administer
MODERNISED Endodermis
*MOHAMMEDAN Mahommedan
MONARCHIAL Harmonical

MONARCHIAN Anharmonic
MONARCHIES Monarchise,
   Nomarchies
MONARCHISE Monarchies,
   Nomarchies
MONOGRAPHY Gramophony,
   Graphonomy, Nomography
MONOLOGIST Nomologist,
   Ontologism
MONOMETRIC Metronomic
MONOPOLIES Monopolise
MONOPOLISE Monopolies
MONOTHETIC Nomothetic
MORTICIANS Marcionist,
   Romanistic
MOTHER-AND Enthraldom
MOULDERING Remoulding
MUSIC-FOLIO Fimicolous
*MUSTELINAE Semi-lunate
MUTILATORS Stimulator

NARCOTISED Draconites,
   Redactions
NATATORIUM Maturation
NATURISTIC Unartistic
NECTAREOUS Raconteuse
NECTARINES Transience
NECTARLIKE Trancelike
NEGATIVISM Time-saving
NEOLOGISMS Gloominess
NEOMATICAL Celtomania
NEOPLASTIC Pleonastic
*NEOTIANISM Semination
NEPHROLOGY Phrenology
NERO-ANTICO Incoronate
NEUROGENIC Encoignure
NEUROLYSIS Resinously
NIGER-SEEDS Greediness
NIGHT-WATCH Watch-night
NIGRESCENT Centerings,
   Centreings
NOMARCHIES Monarchies,
   Monarchise

NOMOGRAPHY Gramophony, Graphonomy, Monography
NOMOLOGIST Monologist, Ontologism
NOMOTHETIC Monothetic
NOSTOLOGIC Oncologist
NOSTOPATHY Photonasty
NOTABILITY Bitonality
NOTARIALLY Rationally
NOTELESSLY Tonelessly
NOVITIATES Anti-Soviet
NUCLEARIST Lacustrine
NUTRIMENTS Instrument

OCTARCHIES Escharotic
OLIVACEOUS Violaceous
ONCOLOGIST Nostologic
ONTOLOGISM Monologist, Nomologist
OPEN-STITCH Pitchstone
OPISOMETER Opsiometer
OPSIOMETER Opisometer
OPTOLOGIST Topologist
ORANGE-LILY Regionally
ORCHESTRAL Trochlears
ORNAMENTER Reornament
OROGENETIC Erotogenic
OSMIRIDIUM Iridosmium
OUTBREATHE Thereabout
OUTFITTING Fitting-out
OUTLANDERS Outslander
OUTSLANDER Outlanders
OUTSTRETCH Stretch-out
OVERDRAPES Overspread, Spread-over
OVERDRAWER Overreward
OVERLIGHTS Overslight
OVERMASTER Overstream
OVERPASSED Eavesdrops
OVERREWARD Overdrawer
OVERSLIGHT Overlights
OVERSPREAD Overdrapes, Spread-over
OVERSTRAIN Overtrains

OVERSTRIKE Strikeover
OVERTRAINS Overstrain
OVERSTREAM Overmaster

PACTIONING Captioning
*PALMERSTON Emplastron
PALUDAMENT Datum-plane
PARADISAIC Paradisiac
PARADISIAC Paradisiac
PARENTALLY Paternally, Prenatally
PARTIALISM Patrialism
PARTIALITY Patriality
PARTIALIZE Patrialize
PASTICHEUR Curateship
PATERNALLY Parentally, Prenatally
PATRIALISM Partialism
PATRIALITY Partiality
PATRIALIZE Partialize
PATRIATION Tritanopia
PATRONISER Periastron
PATRONYMIC Importancy, Phyromantic
PECULATION Unpoetical
PECULATORS Speculator
PEDAL-POINT Pentaploid
PEDANTRIES Pedestrian
PEDERASTIC Predicates
PEDESTRIAN Pedantries
PENCIL-LEAD Lead-pencil
PENETRANCE Repentance
*PENNISETUM Septennium
PENNY-PINCH Pinch-penny
PENSIONERS Presension
PENTAPLOID Pedal-point
PENTATOMIC Camptonite
PENTIMENTI Impenitent
PERCEPTION Preception
PERCEPTIVE Preceptive
PERCOLATED Pre-located
PERCOLATOR Coal-porter
PERCURRENT Precurrent
PERCURSORY Precursory

PERCUSSION Croupiness,
Supersonic
PERFECTISM Imperfects
PERFORMING Preforming
PERIASTRON Patroniser
PERICENTER Pericentre
PERICENTRE Pericenter
PERISPERMS Pre-impress
PERMEATING Impregnate
PERMISSION Impression
PERMISSIVE Impressive
PERSIFLAGE Pilferages
PERSISTENT Prettiness
PERSISTING Springiest
PERTAINING Repainting
PERVERSION Pre-version
PERVIOUSLY Previously,
Viperously
PESTICIDAL Septicidal
PETITIONER Repetition
PETROLEUMS Pulsometer
PHALANGIST Asphalting
PHANEROGAM Anemograph
*PHILIPPIAN Philippina
*PHILIPPINA Philippian
PHOTONASTY Nostopathy
PHRENOLOGY Nephrology
PHYTOGENIC Pythogenic,
Typhogenic
PIANOFORTE Fortepiano
PICTORIALS Poristical, Saprolitic
PILASTERED Plaistered
PILFERAGES Persiflage
PILLOW-BEER Pillow-bere
PILLOW-BERE Pillow-beer
PILLOW-LACE Lace-pillow
PINCH-PENNY Penny-pinch
PINE-CARPET Apprentice
PISTOLLING Postilling
PITCHSTONE Open-stitch
PLAGIARIES Plagiarise
PLAGIARISE Plagiaries
PLAGUE-SORE Grape-louse
PLAISTERED Pilastered

PLANT-HOUSE Sulphonate
PLASTICISE Specialist
PLAY-ACTING Anaglyptic
PLEONASTIC Neoplastic
POLLINATOR Trolloplan
*POLYPTERUS Suppletory
PORISTICAL Pictorials, Saprolitic
PORPHYROUS Pyrophorus
PORRECTION Correption
POSITIONAL Spoliation
POSITIONED Deposition
POSTILLING Pistolling
POTTINGERS Protesting
PRAETORIAN Reparation
PRAISINGLY Aspiringly
PREADMIRER Premarried
PRE-ALTERED Pre-related
PRECEDENTS Predescent
PRECEPTIAL Tea-clipper
PRECEPTION Perception
PRECEPTIVE Perceptive
PRECESSION Encopresis
PRECLAIMED Pre-medical
PRECURRENT Percurrent
PRECURSORY Percursory
PREDEBATES Breast-deep
PREDESCENT Precedents
PREDESIGNS Depressing
PREDICANTS Discrepant
PREDICATES Pederastic
PREDICTORS Descriptor
PRE-EMINENT Repinement
PREFORMING Performing
PRE-IMPRESS Perisperms
PRE-LEASING Pre-sealing
PRELOCATED Percolated
PREMARRIED Preadmirer
PRE-MEDICAL Preclaimed
PRENATALLY Parentally
PREPOLLENT Propellent
PRE-RELATED Pre-altered
PRE-SEALING Pre-leasing
PRESENSION Pensioners
PRESENTIAL Episternal

PRESENTING Serpenting
PRESENTIVE Vespertine
PRESHARING Rangership,
Spring-hare
PRESURMISE Impressure
PRE-SYSTOLE Proselytes
PRETTINESS Persistent
PREVERSION Perversion
PREVIOUSLY Perviously,
Viperously
PRIESTLESS Stripeless
PROBATIONS Absorption
PROCLAIMER Reproclaim
PROMETHEAN Heptameron
PROPELLENT Prepollent
PROSELYTES Pre-systole
PROSTHETIC Rope-stitch
PROTESTING Pottingers
PROTOPHYTE Tropophyte
PSALMODIES Psalmodise
PSALMODISE Psalmodies
PSITTACINE Antiseptic
PULSOMETER Petroleums
PURSUINGLY Usurpingly
PYROMANTIC Importancy,
Patronymic
PYROPHORUS Porphyrous
PYTHOGENIC Phytogenic,
Typhogenic

QUESTIONER Requestion

RACEMATION Cameration,
Maceration
RACONTEUSE Nectareous
RADIOPHONY Hypodorian
RANGERSHIP Presharing,
Spring-hare
RANTIPOLES Interposal
RATIONALES Alienators,
Senatorial
RATIONALLY Notarially
REACTIONAL Creational,
Laceration

REACTIVELY Creatively
REACTIVITY Creativity
REALIGNING Engrailing
REAPPROACH Approacher
REBRIGHTEN Brightener
RECAMPAIGN Campaigner
RECENTNESS Secernents,
Sentencers
RECHRISTEN Christener
RECOMPOUND Compounder
RECONFRONT Confronter
RECOUNTING Countering
RECTIFYING Certifying,
Cretifying
REDACTIONS Draconites,
Narcotised
REDISCOVER Discoverer
REDISPATCH Dispatcher
REDOUNDING Underdoing
REDUCTIONS Discounter,
Introduces
REFORECAST Forecaster
REFORESTED Deer-forest,
Deforester
REGELATING Relegating
REGELATION Relegation
REGIONALLY Orange-lily
REGISTERER Reregister
REGULATION Urogenital
REHEARINGS Rehearsing
REHEARSING Rehearings
REIMPRISON Imprisoner
REINSERTED Residenter
REINTRENCH Intrencher
REINVENTED Intervened
RELATIVISE Revitalise
RELEASABLE Resealable
RELEGATING Regelating
RELEGATION Regelation
RELEVATION Revelation
RELOCATION Co-relation,
Iconolater
REMANIFEST Manifester
REMIGATING Emigrating

REMIGATION Emigration
REMOULDING Mouldering
REMUNERATE Renumerate
RENEGATING Generating
RENEGATION Generation
RENUMERATE Remunerate
REORNAMENT Ornamenter
REPAINTING Pertaining
REPARATION Praetorian
REPENTANCE Penetrance
REPETITION Petitioner
REPINEMENT Pre-eminent
REPROCLAIM Proclaimer

REPUTATIVE Vituperate
REQUESTION Questioner
REREGISTER Registerer
RESALUTING Granulites
RESANCTION Containers,
  Crenations, Sanctioner
RESCINDING Discerning
RESEALABLE Releasable
RESERVEDLY Reversedly
RESHOULDER Shoulderer
RESIDENTER Reinserted
RESINOUSLY Neurolysis
RESISTANTS Straitness
RESISTLESS Sisterless
RESQUANDER Squanderer
RESTOCKING Stockinger
RESULTLESS Lustreless
RESUMPTION Entropiums,
  Importunes
RESUPPRESS Suppresser
RETHREATEN Threatener
RETINALITE Trilineate
RETRACTION Triaconter
RETREADING Intergrade,
  Gradienter
REVELATION Relevation
REVERSEDLY Reservedly
REVISITANT Transitive
REVITALISE Relativise
RHAPSODIES Rhapsodise
RHAPSODISE Rhapsodies

RHEINBERRY Rhineberry
RHINEBERRY Rheinberry
RHINESTONE Enthronise
ROD-FISHING Fishing-rod
*****ROMANISTIC** Marcionist,
  Morticians
ROPE-STITCH Prosthetic
ROTULIFORM Toruliform
RUINATIONS Insinuator,
  Urinations
RUSTICNESS Crustiness
RUTHLESSLY Hurtlessly

SACCHARINE Cane-chairs
SANCTIONER Containers,
  Crenations, Resanction
SANDERLING Slandering
SAPROLITIC Pictorials, Poristical
SARMENTOSE Sea-monster
SASH-WINDOW Window-sash
SATIN-PAPER Appertains
*****SATURNALIA** Australian
SCALLOPING Collapsing
SCAPULATED Capsulated
SCARCEMENT Marcescent
SCHISMATIC Mica-schist
SCHOOL-DAME Dame-school
SCRAP-METAL Campestral
SCREICHING Scrieching
SCRIECHING Screiching
SCRUTINIES Scrutinise,
  Sinecurist
SCRUTINISE Scrutinies,
  Sinecurist
SEA-CAPTAIN Anapaestic
SEA-MONSTER Sarmentose
SECERNENTS Recentness,
  Sentencers
SELF-SLAYER Fearlessly
SEMI-LUNATE Mustelinae
SEMINARIAL Laminarise
SEMINATION Noetianism
SENATORIAL Alienators,
  Rationales

SENTENCERS Recentness, Secernents
SEPTENNIUM Pennisetum
SEPTICIDAL Pesticidal
SERIALISED Idealisers
SERIALIZED Idealizers
SERPENTING Presenting
SERVANT-MAN Man-servant
SEVENTY-SIX Sixty-seven
SEXPARTITE Extirpates
SEXPLOITER Exploiters
*SHACKLETON Chalkstone, Shecklaton
SHATTERING Straighten
SHECKLATON Chalkstone, Shackleton
SHIPMASTER Mastership
SHOPWINDOW Window-shop
SHOULDERER Reshoulder
SIGNALMENT Alignments
SILVERLIKE Sliverlike
SINECURIST Scrutinies, Scrutinise
SISTERLESS Resistless
SIXTY-SEVEN Seventy-six
SKREIGHING Skrieghing
SKRIEGHING Skreighing
SLANDERING Sanderling
SLEAZINESS Lazinesses
SLEETINESS Steeliness
SLIVERLIKE Silverlike
SOFT-BOILED Field-boots
SOMBERNESS Sombreness
SOMBRENESS Somberness
SOMNAMBULE Summonable
SORDAMENTE Emendators
SORICIDENT Directions, Discretion
SPANCELING Enclasping
SPECIALIST Plasticise
SPECULATOR Peculators
SPERMACETI Imprecates
SPIDER-CRAB Crispbread

SPINIGRADE Despairing, Diaperings
SPIROMETER Temporiser
SPOLIATION Positional
SPREAD-OVER Overdrapes, Overspread
SPRING-HARE Presharing, Rangership
SPRINGHEAD Headspring
SPRINGIEST Persisting
SQUANDERER Resquander
STABLEMATE Metastable
STAGNATION Antagonist
STANDSTILL Still-stand
STEELINESS Sleetiness
STERIGMATA Magistrate
STILL-STAND Standstill
STIMULATOR Mutilators
STINKSTONE Knottiness
STITCHWORK Throw-stick
STOCKINGER Restocking
STONE-BRASH Basset-horn
STORM-WATER Masterwort
STRAIGHTEN Shattering
STRAITNESS Resistants
STREAMIEST Tasimeters
STREAMLESS Masterless
STREPEROUS Superstore
STRETCH-OUT Outstretch
STRIKEOVER Overstrike
STRING-BAND Band-string
STRING-BEAN Banterings
STRINGENDO Grindstone
STRIPELESS Priestless
STRIPTEASE Tapestries
SULPHONATE Plant-house
SUMMONABLE Somnambule
SUPERSONIC Croupiness, Percussion
SUPERSTORE Streperous
SUPPLETORY Polypterus
SUPPRESSER Resuppress
SYMPATHIES Sympathise
SYMPATHISE Sympathies

SYMPHONIES Symphonise
SYMPHONISE Symphonies

TABLE-D'HÔTE Bottle-head
TABLEWATER Water-table
TANTARARA Tarantara
TAPE-RECORD Deprecator
TAPESTRIES Striptease
TARANTARA Tantarara
TASIMETERS Streamiest
TEA-CLIPPER Preceptial
TEA-SERVICE Eviscerate
TECHNOCRAT Trench-coat
TEMPERATED Attempered
TEMPORISER Spirometer
TENEMENTAL Lentamente
TENTER-HOOK Heterokont
TERMINABLY Liberty-man
TERMINATES Main-street,
 Martensite, Misentreats
TESTICULAR Trisulcate
THEOLOGIES Theologise
THEOLOGISE Theologies
THEOLOGIST Ethologist
THEREABOUT Outbreathe
THICKENING Kitchening
THREATENER Rethreaten
THROW-STICK Stitch-work
TIMBER-TREE Embitterer
TIME-SAVING Negativism
TONALITIVE Levitation, Velitation
TONELESSLY Notelessly
TOPOLOGIST Optologist
TORULIFORM Rotuliform
TRANCELIKE Nectarlike
TRANSIENCE Nectarines
TRANSITIVE Revisitants
TRANSONICS Constrains,
 Transonic .
TRANS-SONIC Constrains,
 Transonics
TREADBOARD Broad-tread
TRENCH-COAT Technocrat
TRIACONTER Retraction

TRIAPSIDAL Lapidarist
TRICHINOUS Unhistoric
TRIFLINGLY Flirtlingly
TRILINEATE Retinalite
TRINISCOPE Isentropic
TRISULCATE Testicular
TRITANOPIA Patriation
TRIVALENCE Cantilever
TROCHLEARS Orchestral
*TROGONIDAE Derogation,
 Gerodontia
*TROLLOPIAN Pollinator
TROPOPHYTE Protophyte
TWELVE-NOTE Twelve-tone
TWELVE-TONE Twelve-note
TYPHOGENIC Phytogenic,
 Pythogenic

*UGRO-FINNIC Finno-Ugric
ULTRAISTIC Altruistic
UNARTISTIC Naturistic
UNBUTTERED Unrebutted
UNCANNONISE Unisonance
UNCAROLLED Uncollared
UNCOLLARED Uncarolled
UNCORSETED Unescorted
UNCREDITED Undirected
UNDEIFYING Unedifying
UNDELUDING Unindulged
UNDEMANDED Unmaddened
UNDERBRUSH Undershrub
UNDERDOING Redounding
UNDERDRAWS Undersward
UNDERLYING Enduringly
UNDERNOTED Undertoned
UNDERSHRUB Underbrush
UNDERSIGNS Undressing
UNDERSWARD Underdraws
UNDERTONED Undernoted
UNDESERVER Unreserved,
 Unreversed
UNDIRECTED Uncredited
UNDREAMING Maundering
UNDRESSING Undersigns

UNEDIFYING Undeifying
UNESCORTED Uncorseted
UNFALLIBLE Unfillable
UNFILLABLE Unfallible
UNFORESTED Unfostered
UNFOSTERED Unforested
UNHALTERED Unlathered
UNHISTORIC Trichinous
UNINDULGED Undeluding
UNISONANCE Uncanonise
UNLATHERED Unhaltered
UNLICENSED Unsilenced
UNMADDENED Undemanded
UNMASTERED Unstreamed
UNPOETICAL Peculation
UNREBUTTED Unbuttered
UNRESERVED Undeserver,
  Unreversed
UNRESISTED Unsistered
UNREVERSED Undeserver,
  Unreserved
UNSEIZABLE Unsizeable
UNSILENCED Unlicensed
UNSISTERED Unresisted
UNSIZEABLE Unseizable
UNSOMBERLY Unsombrely
UNSOMBRELY Unsomberly
UNSTREAMED Unmastered
UPBRINGING Bringing-up
URINATIONS Insinuator,
  Ruinations
UROGENITAL Regulation
USURPINGLY Pursuingly

VATICINATE Inactivate
VELITATION Levitation,
  Tonalitive

VENATORIAL Voltairean
VENERATING Enervating
VENERATION Enervation
VENERATIVE Enervative
VESPERTINE Presentive
VICE-CONSUL Conclusive
VICEGERENT Viceregent
VICEREGENT Vicegerent
VIOLACEOUS Olivaceous
VIPEROUSLY Perviously,
  Previously
VISITATION Vitiations
VITIATIONS Visitation
VITUPERATE Reputative
***VOLTAIREAN** Venatorial

WARRANTISE Warranties
WARRANTIES Warrantise
WATCH-NIGHT Night-watch
WATER-BREAK Breakwater
WATER-LEMON Water-melon
WATER-MELON Water-lemon
WATER-TABLE Table-water
WATERFLOOD Floodwater
WATERINESS Ear-witness
WELL-LEASED Well-sealed
WELL-SEALED Well-leased
WHOMSOEVER Howsomever
WILDFLOWER Wildfowler
WILDFOWLER Wildflower
WINDOW-SASH Sash-window
WINDOW-SHOP Shop-window
WORK-BASKET Basketwork
WORK-MASTER Master-work

Eleven letters

ACCOUNT-BOOK Book-Account
ACTIVATIONS Vacationist
ADULTERINES Laurentides,
  Neutralised
AEROLOGICAL Areological
ALGORITHMIC Logarithmic
ALTITUDINAL Latitudinal
*AMERICANIST Creatianism
AMPHIPODOUS Hippodamous
*ANACREONTIC Canceration
ANEMOGRAPHY Phanerogamy
ANGELICALLY Englacially
ANTHOLOGIES Anthologise,
  Theologians
ANTHOLOGISE Anthologies,
  Theologians
ANTIMONIALS Laminations,
  Nationalism
ANTIPYRETIC Pertinacity
APPORTIONER Reapportion
APPREHENDER Reapprehend
AREOLOGICAL Aerological
ARMOUR-PLATE Plate-armour
ARTILLERIST Triliterals
ASTRONOMIES Astronomise
ASTRONOMISE Astronomies
ATTEMPERING Temperating
ATTENTIVELY Tentatively

BACKSCRATCH Scratch-back
BARONETICAL Carbonalite
BOOK-ACCOUNT Account-book
BOTTLE-GOURD Gutter-blood
BOTTLE-GREEN Greenbottle
BROADCASTER Rebroadcast

CABBAGE-PALM Palm-cabbage

CALLIGRAPHY Graphically
CANCERATION Anacreontic
CAPERNOITED Deprecation
CAPILLARITY Piratically
CAPTAINSHIP Ship-captain
CARBONALITE Baronetical
CATALOGUING Coagulating
CATAPULTIER Particulate
CATECHISMAL Schematical
CAVILLATION Vacillation
CEMENT-WATER Water-cement
CENTRALISED Credentials
CENTRALISES Linecasters,
  Treacliness
CERTIFIABLE Rectifiable
CHAIN-LETTER Threnetical
CHEMOTROPIC Ectomorphic
CLITORIDEAN Directional
COAGULATING Cataloguing
CO-INHERENCE Incoherence
COLONIALIST Oscillation
COMEDIETTAS Domesticate
CONDITIONER Recondition
CONSERVABLE Conversable
CONSERVANCY Conversancy
CONSIDERATE Desecration
CONSTRUCTER Reconstruct
CONSUMERIST Misconstrue
CONVERSABLE Conservable
CONVERSANCY Conservancy
CONY-CATCHER Technocracy
COPULATIONS Unapostolic
CORMOPHYTIC Mycotrophic
*CORRODENTIA Recordation
COSMETICIAN Encomiastic
CREATIANISM Americanist
CREATIONARY Reactionary

CREATIONISM Miscreation, Reactionism, Romanticise
CREATIONIST Reactionist, Recitations
CREDENTIALS Centralised
CROCIDOLITE Crocodilite
CROCODILITE Crocidolite
***CRYPTOMERIA** Imprecatory

DECURIONATE Re-education
DEGRADATION Gradationed
DEIFICATION Edification
DENUNCIATOR Underaction
DEPLORATION Periodontal
DEPRECATION Capernoited
DESCRIPTION Predictions
DESCRIPTIVE Discerptive
DESECRATION Considerate
DETERMINANT Detrainment
DETRAINMENT Determinant
DIACHRONISM Disharmonic
DIRECTIONAL Clitoridean
DISCERNABLE Rescindable
DISCERNMENT Rescindment
DISCERPTIVE Descriptive
DISHARMONIC Diachronism
DOMESTICATE Comediettas

EARTH-SHAPED Heart-shaped
ECTOMORPHIC Chemotropic
EDIFICATION Deification
ELECTORSHIP Helicopters
ELIMINATORS Misrelation, Orientalism, Relationism
EMBELLISHER Re-embellish
ENGLACIALLY Angelically
ENGRAILMENT Realignment
ENLARGEMENT Greenmantle
ENLIGHTENER Re-enlighten
ENTABLATURE Untreatable
ENTAILMENTS Sentimental
ENTERPRISES Intersperse
ENUMERATION Mountaineer
ESTABLISHER Re-establish

ETHOLOGICAL Theological
EXAMINATION Exanimation
EXANIMATION Examination

FESTINATION Infestation, Sinfonietta
FORWARDNESS Frowardness
FRACTIONALS Infracostal
FROWARDNESS Forwardness
FULL-ACORNED Uncalled-for

GALLEY-BAGGER Galley-beggar
GALLEY-BEGGAR Galley-bagger
GENEALOGIES Genealogise
GENEALOGISE Genealogies
GENERATIONS Nitrogenase
GRADATIONED Degradation
GRAMOPHONIC Monographic, Nomographic, Phonogramic
GRAPHICALLY Calligraphy
GRAPHOLOGIC Logographic
GRAPHOTYPIC Pictography, Typographic
GREEN-BOTTLE Bottle-green
***GREENMANTLE** Enlargement

HAND-PROMISE Preadmonish
HAND-RUNNING Running-land
HAPTOTROPIC Protopathic
HEART-SHAPED Earth-shaped
HELICOPTERS Electorship
HIBERNATING Inbreathing
HIPPODAMOUS Amphipodous
HISTRIONICS Trichinosis
HOMOGENESIS Homogenises
HOMOGENISES Homogenesis
HORSERIDING Riding-horse
HOUSE-LIGHTS Lighthouses
HURTFULNESS Ruthfulness

IMMORTALISE Memorialist
IMPENETRATE Intemperate
IMPERSONALS Personalism
IMPERSONATE Permeations

IMPORTUNATE Permutation
IMPRECATORY Cryptomeria
IMPRESSIBLE Permissible
IMPRESSIBLY Permissibly
INBREATHING Hibernating
INCOGNISANT Sanctioning
INCOHERENCE Co-inherence
INCORPORATE Procreation
INFESTATION Festination,
  Sinfonietta
INFRACOSTAL Fractionals
INGREDIENTS Tenderising
INOCULATORY Locutionary
INSECTOLOGY Scientology
INSEMINATOR Nitrosamine
INTEGRATION Orientating
INTEGRATIVE Vinaigrette
INTEMPERATE Impenetrate
INTERNALITY Itinerantly
INTERPRETER Reinterpret
INTERRUPTER Reinterrupt
INTERSPERSE Enterprises
INTERVIEWER Reinterview
INUSITATION Unitisation
INVOLUCRATE Countervail
ITINERANTLY Internality

KANGAROO-RAT Rat-kangaroo

LAMINATIONS Antimonials,
  Nationalism
LATITUDINAL Altitudinal
*****LAURENTIDES** Adulterines,
  Neutralised
LEVITATIONS Neovitalist
LIGHTHOUSES House-lights
LINECASTERS Centralises,
  Treacliness
LOCUTIONARY Inoculatory
LOGARITHMIC Algorithmic
LOGOGRAPHIC Graphologic
LOUVER-BOARD Louvre-bard
LOUVRE-BOARD Louver-board
LOVE-IN-A-MIST Neovitalism

MAID-SERVANT Servant-maid
MARCHIONESS Monarchises
MEMORIALIST Immortalise
MENSURATION Numerations
MESALLIANCE Miscellanea
METAPLASTIC Palmatisect
MISCELLANEA Mesalliance
MISCONSTRUE Consumerist
MISCREATION Creationism,
  Reactionism, Romanticise
MISCREDITED Misdirected
MISDIRECTED Miscredited
MISRELATION Eliminators,
  Orientalism, Relationism
MONARCHISES Marchioness
MONOGENESIS Nomogenesis
MONOGRAPHER Nomographer
MONOGRAPHIC Gramophonic,
  Nomographic, Phonogramic
MONOLOGICAL Nomological
MOUNTAINEER Enumeration
MUTILATIONS Stimulation
MYCOPHAGIST Phagocytism
MYCOTROPHIC Cormophytic
MYOGRAPHIST Pythagorism
MYTHOLOGIES Mythologise
MYTHOLOGISE Mythologies

NATIONALISM Antimonials,
  Laminations
NECESSARIAN Renaissance
NEOTERISING Nitrogenise
NEOTROPICAL Percolation
NEOVITALISM Love-in-a-mist
NEOVITALIST Levitations
NEPHOLOGIST Phenologist
NEPHROSTOME Nephrotomes
NEPHTROMES Nephrostome
NERVE-ENDING Never-ending
NEUTRALISED Adulterines,
  Laurentides
NEVER-ENDING Nerve-ending
NIGHTINGALE Tile-hanging
NINETY-SEVEN Seventy-nine

NITROGENASE Generations
NITROGENISE Neoterising
NITROSAMINE Inseminator
NOMOGENESIS Monogenesis
NOMOGRAPHER Monographer
NOMOGRAPHIC Gramophonic,
　Monographic, Phonogramic
NOMOLOGICAL Monological
NON-CREATIVE Non-reactive
NON-PARENTAL Non-paternal
NON-PATERNAL Non-parental
NON-REACTIVE Non-creative
NUMERATIONS Mensuration

OPTOMETRIST Potometrist
ORCHESTRATE Sachertorte
ORIENTALISM Eliminators,
　Misrelation, Relationism
ORIENTALIST Relationist
ORIENTATING Integration
ORTHOEPISTS Photo-resist
OSCILLATION Colonialist
OSTEOGRAPHY Ostreophagy
OSTREOPHAGY Osteography

PALMATISECT Metaplastic
PALM-CABBAGE Cabbage-palm
PARAMEDICAL Pre-adamical
PARLIAMENTS Paternalism
PARTICULATE Catapultier
PARTITIONED Trepidation
PARTITIONER Reportition
PARTNERSHIP Transhipper
PATERNALISM Parliaments
PATERNOSTER Penetrators
PATHOPHOBIA Taphophobia
PECULATIONS Speculation
PENETRATORS Paternoster
PERAMBULATE Preambulate
PERCOLATING Pre-locating
PERCOLATION Neotropical
PERIDONTAL Deploration
PERIPATETIC Precipitate
PERISTALTIC Triplicates

PERMEATIONS Impersonate
PERMISSIBLE Impressible
PERMISSIBLY Impressibly
PERMUTATION Importunate
PERPETRATOR Prêt-à-porter
PERSONALISM Impersonals
PERTINACITY Antipyretic
PESTIFEROUS Septiferous
PETROGRAPHY Pterography,
　Typographer
PHAGOCYTISM Mycophagist
PHANEROGAMY Anemography
PHENOLOGIST Nephologist
PHONEMICIST Phoneticism
PHONETICISM Phonemicist
PHONOGRAMIC Gramophonic,
　Monographic, Nomographic
PHOTO-RESIST Orthoepists
PIANO-PLAYER Player-Piano
PICTOGRAPHY Graphotypic,
　Tyrographic
PIRATICALLY Capillarity
PLANIMETERS Sempiternal
PLATE-ARMOUR Armour-plate
PLAYER-PIANO Piano-player
POENOLOGIST Stool-pigeon
POINT-SOURCE Prosecution
POLARIMETRY Temporarily
POLYPHONIST Psilophyton
POTOMETRIST Optometrist
PRE-ADAMICAL Paramedical
PREADMONISH Hand-promise
PREAMBULATE Perambulate
PRECIPITATE Peripatetic
PRECREDITOR Predirector
PREDICTIONS Description
PREDIRECTOR Precreditor
PRE-LOCATING Percolating
PRELUSIVELY Repulsively
PRERATIONAL Proletarian
PRESENTIENT Spinnerette
PRÊT-À-PORTER Perpetrator
PROBATIONER Reprobation
PROCREATION Incorporate

PROLETARIAN Prerational
PROLETARIES Proletarise
PROLETARISE Proletaries
PROSECUTION Point-source
PROTECTRESS Retrospects
PROTOPATHIC Haptotropic
PROTOPHYTIC Tropophytic
PROVISIONER Reprovision
*****PSILOPHYTON** Polyphonist
PTEROGRAPHY Petrography,
Typographer
*****PYTHAGORISM** Myographist

QUARTER-NOTE Quarter-tone
QUARTER-TONE Quarter-note

RATIONALISE Realisation
RAT-KANGAROO Kangaroo-rat
REACTIONARY Creationary
REACTIONISM Creationism,
Miscreation, Romanticise
REACTIONIST Creationist,
Recitations
REALIGNMENT Engrailment
REALISATION Rationalise
REAPPORTION Apportioner
REAPPREHEND Apprehender
REBROADCAST Broadcaster
RECITATIONS Creationist,
Reactionist
RECONDITION Conditioner
RECONNOITRE Reconnoiter
RECONNOITER Reconnoitre
RECONSTRUCT Constructer
RE-CORDATION Corrodentia
RECTIFIABLE Certifiable
RE-EDUCATION Decurionate
RE-EMBELLISH Embellisher
RE-ENLIGHTEN Enlightener
RE-ESTABLISH Establisher
REINTERPRET Interpreter
REINTERRUPT Interrupter
REINTERVIEW Interviewer

RELATIONISM Eliminators,
Misrelation, Orientalism
RELATIONIST Orientalist
REMUNERATED Renumerated
RENAISSANCE Necessarian
RENUMERATED Remunerated
REPAINTINGS Signpainter
REPARTITION Partitioner
REPROBATION Probationer
REPROVISION Provisioner
REPULSIVELY Prelusively
RESCINDABLE Discernable
RESCINDMENT Discernment
RESIDENTERS Retiredness
RESPECTLESS Sceptreless
RESPIRATION Retinispora
RETELEGRAPH Telegrapher
RETINISPORA Respiration
RETIREDNESS Residenters
RETROSPECTS Protectress
REUPHOLSTER Upholsterer
RIDING-HORSE Horseriding
ROMANTICISE Creationism,
Miscreation, Reactionism
RUNNING-HAND Hand-running
RUSTICATION Urtications
RUTHFULNESS Hurtfulness

SABURRATION Subarration
*****SACHERTORTE** Orchestrate
SANCTIONING Incognisant
SANCTUARIES Sanctuarise
SANCTUARISE Sanctuaries
SAVOURINESS Variousness
SCARLET-BEAN Tabernacles
SCEPTRELESS Respectless
SCHEMATICAL Catechismal
SCIENTOLOGY Insectology
SCORBUTICAL Subcortical
SCRATCH-BACK Backscratch
SEMPITERNAL Planimeters
SENTIMENTAL Entailments
SEPTIFEROUS Pestiferous
SERPIGINOUS Spinigerous

SERVANT-MAID Maid-servant
SEVENTY-NINE Ninety-seven
SHIP-CAPTAIN Captainship
SIGNPAINTER Repaintings
SILVESTRIAN Trivialness
SINFONIETTA Festination,
  Infestation
SPECULATION Peculations
SPINIGEROUS Serpiginous
SPINNERETTE Presentient
SPRING-HOUSE Surgeonship
SPRINGWATER Waterspring
STIMULATION Mutilations
STOOL-PIGEON Poenologist
SUBSTRACTOR Subtractors
SUBTRACTORS Substractor
SURGEONSHIP Spring-house
SWING-HANDLE Swingle-hand
SWINGLE-HAND Swing-handle

TABERNACLES Scarlet-bean
TAPHOPHOBIA Pathophobia
TAUTOLOGIES Tautologise
TAUTOLOGISE Tautologies
TECHNOCRACY Cony-catcher
TELEGRAPHER Retelegraph
TEMPERATING Attempering
TEMPORARILY Polarimetry
TENDERSING Ingredients
TENTATIVELY Attentively
TETRASPORIC Triceratops
THEATERGOER Theatregoer
THEATREGOER Theatergoer
THEOLOGIANS Anthologies,
  Anthologise
THEOLOGICAL Ethological
THEOSOPHIES Theosophise
THEOSOPHISE Theosophies
THEREWITHAL Whitleather
THRENETICAL Chain-letter
TILE-HANGING Nightingale
TILLER-CHAIN Trichinella
TRANSHIPPER Partnership

TREACLINESS Centralises,
  Linecartes
TREPIDATION Partitioned
TRICERATOPS Tetrasopric
TRICHINELLA Tiller-chain
TRICHINOSIS Histrionics
TRILITERALS Artillerist
TRIPLICATES Peristaltic
TRIVIALNESS Silvestrian
TROPOPHYTIC Protophytic
TYPOGRAPHER Petrography,
  Pterography
TYPOGRAPHIC Graphotypic,
  Pictography

UNAPOSTOLIC Copulations
UNAUCTIONED Uncautioned
UNCALLED-FOR Full-acorned
UNCAUTIONED Unauctioned
UNCERTIFIED Unrectified
UNDERACTION Denunciator
UNDERLEASED Undersealed
UNDERSEALED Underleased
UNDERSHAPEN Unsharpened
UNDISCERNED Unrescinded
UNITISATION Inusitation

UNRECTIFIED Uncertified
UNRESCINDED Undiscerned
UNRESPECTED Unsceptered
UNSCEPTERED Unrespected
UNSHARPENED Undershapen
UNTREATABLE Entablature
UPHOLSTERER Reupholster
URTICATIONS Rustication

VACATIONIST Activations
VACILLATION Cavillation
VARIOUSNESS Savouriness
VICE-GERENCY Vice-regency
VICE-REGENCY Vice-gerency
VINAIGRETTE Integrative

WATER-CEMENT Cement-water

WATERSPRING Springwater
WEATHERINGS Weather-sign
WEATHER-SIDE Wise-hearted
WEATHER-SIGN Weatherings

WELL-WISHING Wishing-well
WHITLEATHER Therewithal
WISE-HEARTED Weather-side
WISHING-WELL Well-wishing

Twelve letters

ABOLITIONISM Mobilisation
ACHERONTICAL Anchoretical
ACROSTICALLY Socratically
ALTITUDINOUS Latitudinous
AMPHITHEATER Amphitheatre
AMPHITHEATRE Amphitheater
ANCHORETICAL Acherontical
ANEMOGRAPHIC Phanerogamic
ANTI-CREATION Anti-reaction
ANTI-CREATIVE Anti-reactive
ANTI-REACTIVE Anti-creative
ANTI-REACTION Anti-creation
*ARISTOTELIAN Laterisation,
  Retaliations
ASSIMILATION Islamisation

BEHAVIOURISM Misbehaviour
BUTTER-COOLER Root-tubercle

CARTESIANISM Sectarianism
CHAPELMASTER Spermathecal
CIRRO-CUMULUS Comulo-
  cirrus
CLARE-OBSCURE Clear-obscure
CLEAR-OBSCURE Clare-obscure

COALITIONIST Solicitation
COLLIMATIONS Collision-mat
COLLISION-MAT Collimations
COMMISSIONER Recommission
COMMISSARIAT Marcatissimo
COMULO-CIRRUS Cirro-
  comulus
CONSERVATION Conversation
CONSERVATIVE Conversative
CONSOLIDATES Disconsolate
CONSTRAINERS Contrariness

CONTRARINESS Constrainers
CONVERSATION Conservation
CONVERSATIVE Conservative
CORPOREALIST Prosectorial
COUNTERCHARM
  Countermarch
COUNTERMARCH
  Countercharm
COUNTERPALED Counterplead
COUNTERPLEAD Counterpaled
COURT-MARTIAL Matriculator
CREATIVENESS Reactiveness
CREDITORSHIP Directorship
CREMATIONIST Metrications
CULVERTAILED Revictualled
CYLINDER-SEAL Seal-cylinder

DELICATENESS Delicatessen
DELICATESSEN Delicateness
DEMAGNETISER Disagreement
DEPOSITIONAL Despoliation
DESPOLIATION Depositional
DIRECTORSHIP Creditorship
DISAGREEMENT Demagnetiser
DISCONSOLATE Consolidates
DISCREETNESS Discreteness
DISCRETENESS Discreetness
DISHARMONIES Disharmonise
DISHARMONISE Disharmonies

ENERGETICIST Energetistic
ENERGETISTIC Energeticist
ENTOMOLOGIES Entomologise
ENTOMOLOGISE Entomologies
EXPERIMENTER Re-experiment

FOUNDATIONER Refoundation

GRAMOPHONIST
Monographist
GRAPHOPHONIC Phonographic

HURTLESSNESS Ruthlessness

IMPRESSIVELY Permissively
INACTIVATION Vaticination
INDISCREETLY Indiscretely,
Iridescently
INDISCRETELY Indiscreetly,
Iridescently
INOCULATIONS Inosculation
INOSCULATION Inoculations
IRIDECTOMIES Iridectomise
IRIDECTOMISE Iridectomies
IRIDESCENTLY Indiscreetly,
Indiscretely
*****ISLAMISATION** Assimilation

LATERISATION Aristotelian,
Retaliations
LATITUDINOUS Altitudinous
LOUVER-WINDOW Louvre-
window
LOUVRE-WINDOW Louver-
window

MANSLAUGHTER Slaughterman
MARCATISSIMO Commissariat
MARCH-TREASON Stream-
anchor
MATRICULATOR Court-martial
METRICATIONS Cremationist
METRONOMICAL Monometrical
MISBEHAVIOUR Behaviourism
MISCREDITING Misdirecting
MISDIRECTING Miscrediting
MOBILISATION Abolitionism
MONKEY-PUZZLE Puzzle-
monkey
MONOGRAPHIST
Gramophonist
MONOMETRICAL Metronomical

MORPHOTROPIC Protomorphic

NEBULISATION Sublineation
NEPHOLOGICAL Phenological
NEPHROLOGIST Phrenologist
NON-CERTIFIED Non-rectified
NON-RECTIFIED Non-certified
NOTELESSNESS Tonelessness

OBSCURANTIST Substraction,
Subtractions

PARADISAICAL Paradisiacal
PARADISIACAL Paradisaical
PENETRATIONS Presentation
PERCEPTIVELY Preceptively
PERFOLIATION Prefoliation
PERFORMATIVE Preformative
PERMISSIVELY Impressively
PERVIOUSNESS Previousness
PETROGRAPHER Pterographer
PETROGRAPHIC
Pterographic
PHANEROGAMIC Anemograph-
ic
PHENOLOGICAL Nephological
PHILOSOPHIES Philosophise
PHILOSOPHISE Philosophies
PHONOGRAPHIC Graphophonic
PHOTOGRAPHER Rephotograph
PHRENOLOGIST Nephrologist
PHYTOGENESIS Pythogenisis
POST-ARTERIAL Proletariats
PRECEPTIVELY Perceptively
PRE-CREDITING Pre-directing
PRE-DIRECTING Pre-crediting
PREFOLIATION Perfoliation
PREFORMATIVE Performative
PRESENTATION Penetrations
PREVIOUSNESS Perviousness
PROBATIONERS Reabsorption,
Reprobations
PROGENITRESS Resting-spore
PROLETARIATS Post-arterial

PROPORTIONER Reproportion
PROSECTORIAL Corporealist
PROTOMORPHIC
Morphotropic
PTEROGRAPHER Petrographer
PTEROGRAPHIC Petrographic
PUZZLE-MONKEY Monkey-
puzzle
PYTHOGENESIS Phytogenesis

RATEABLENESS Tearableness
REABSORPTION Probationers,
Reprobations
REACTIVENESS Creativeness
RECOMMISSION Commissioner
REDINTEGRATE Reintegrated
RE-EXPERIMENT Experimenter
REFOUNDATION Foundationer
REINTEGRATED Redintegrate
REMUNERATING Renumerating
RENUMERATING Remunerating
REPHOTOGRAPH Photographer
REPROBATIONS Probationers,
Reabsorption
REPROPORTION Proportioner
RESTING-SPORE Progenitress
RESTRAIGHTEN Straightener
RETALIATIONS Aristotelian,
Laterisation
RETRANSPLANT Transplanter
ROOT-TUBERCLE Butter-cooler
REVICTUALLED Culvertailed
RUTHLESSNESS Hurtlessness

SEAL-CYLINDER Cylinder-seal
SECTARIANISM Cartesianism
SLAUGHTERMAN Manslaughter

SOCRATICALLY Acrostically
SOLICITATION Coalitionist
SPERMATHECAL Chapelmaster
SPERMATOZOIC Zoospermatic
STRAIGHTENER Restraighten
STREAM-ANCHOR March-
treason
SUBLINEATION Nebulisation
SUBSTRACTION Obcurantist,
Subtractions
SUBTRACTIONS Obscurantist,
Substraction
SURF-BOARDING Surfing-board
SURFING-BOARD Surf-boarding

TEARABLENESS Rateableness
TILLER-CHAIN Trichinella
TONELESSNESS Notelessness
TRANSPLANTER Retransplant
TRICHINELLA Tiller-chain

UNDERLEASING Undersealing
UNDERSEALING Underleasing
UNSOMBERNESS Unsombreness
UNSOMBRENESS Unsomberness

VATICINATION Inactivation
VISITATIONAL Vitalisation
VITALISATION Visitational

WELL-CORSETED Well-escorted
WELL-CREDITED Well-directed
WELL-DIRECTED Well-credited
WELL-ESCORTED Well-corseted

ZOOSPERMATIC Spermatozoic

Thirteeen letters

ACCOUSTREMENT
Accoutrements
ACCOUTREMENTS
Accoustrement
ANTICLINORIUM
Inclinatorium
ATTENTIVENESS
Tentativeness

BALANCE-SHEETS
Teachableness

CEPHALOMETRIC
Petrochemical
CERTIFICATION
Cretification, Rectification
CHARACTERLESS
Clear-starches
CHEIROPTERANS
Terpsichorean
CLEAR-STARCHES
Characterless
COMMERCIALIST
Microclimates
CONDYLOMATOUS
Monodactylous
CONTAINERISEED
Inconsiderate
CRETIFICATION
Certification, Rectification

DESERTISATION
Disorientates
DISCRIMINATOR
Doctrinairism
DISORIENTATES
Desertisation

DOCTRINAIRISM
Discriminator

ETHOLOGICALLY
Theologically
EXPLOITATIONS
Sexploitation

GRAMOPHONICAL
Monographical, Nomographical,
Phonogramical
GRAPHOLOGICAL
Logographical

IMPRESSIONIST
Permissionist
INCLINATORIUM
Anticlinorium
INCONSIDERATE
Containerised
INTEROCEPTORS
Retrospection
INTERSPECIFIC
Prescientific

LOGOGRAPHICAL
Graphological

MICROCLIMATES
Commercialist
MONODACTYLOUS
Condylomatous
MONOGRAPHICAL
Gramophonical, Nomographical,
Phonogramical
NEPHROLOGICAL
Phrenological

13

NOMOGRAPHICAL
Gramophonical, Monographical,
Phonogramical
PERAMBULATORY
Preambulatory
PERMISSIONIST
Impressionist
PETROCHEMICAL
Cephalometric

PHONOGRAMICAL
Gramophonical, Monographical,
Nomographical
PHRENOLOGICAL
Nephrological
PREADMONITION
Predomination
PREAMBULATORY
Perambulatory
PREDOMINATION
Preadmonition
PRESCIENTIFIC
Interspecific
RECTIFICATION
Certification, Cretification
RETROSPECTION
Interoceptors
RUMEL-GUMPTION
Rumle-gumption
RUMLE-GUMPTION
Rumel-gumption

SEXPLOITATION
Exploitations
SOUNDBOARDING
Soundingboard

SOUNDINGBOARD
Soundboarding
STARTING-POINT
Train-spotting
STATELESSNESS
Tastelessness

TASTELESSNESS
Statelessness
TEACHABLENESS
Balance-sheets
TENTATIVENESS
Attentiveness
TERPSICHOREAN
Cheiropterans
THEOLOGICALLY
Ethologically
TRAIN-SPOTING
Starting-point

UNCERTIFIABLE
Unrectifiable
UNCONSERVABLE
Unconversable
UNCONVERSABLE
Unconservable
UNRECTIFIABLE
Uncertifiable

VERIFICATIONS
Versification
VERSIFICATION
Verifications

Fourteen letters

AEROHYDROPLANE
  Hydro-aeroplane
ALTITUDINARIAN
  Latitudinarian
ANTHROPOPHAGUS
  Phonautographs

CARDIOMYOPATHY
  Myocardiopathy
CONSERVATIONAL
  Conversational
CONVERSATIONAL
  Conservational
ELECTROTHERMIC
  Thermo-electric
GERMISSIVENESS
  Impressiveness
HYDRO-AEROPLANE
  Aerohydroplane
IMPRESSIBILITY
  Premissibility
IMPRESSIVENESS
  Permissiveness
INDISCREETNESS
  Indiscreteness
INDISCRETENESS
  Indiscreetness
INTEROSCULATES
  Sansculotterie

INTERROGATIVES
  Tergiversation
LATITUDINARIAN
  Altitudinarian

MYOCARDIOPATHY
  Cardiomyopathy
PERMISSIBILITY
  Impressibility
PERMISSIVENESS
  Impressiveness
PHONAUTOGRAPHS
  Anthropophagus
PREDICTIVENESS
  Vice-presidents

RUMMELGUMPTION
  Rummlegumption
RUMMLEGUMPTION
  Rummelgumption

SANSCULOTTERIE
  Interosculates

TERGIVERSATION
  Interrogatives
THERMO-ELECTRIC
  Electrothermic
VICE-PRESIDENTS
  Predictiveness

14

Fifteen letters

CONSERVATIONIST
 Conversationist
CONSTRUCTIONISM
 Misconstruction
CONVERSATIONIST
 Conservationist

ELECTROMAGNETIC
 Magneto-electric

MAGNETO-ELECTRIC
 Electromagnetic
MICROPHOTOGRAPH
 Photomicrograph

MISCONSTRUCTION
 Constructionism

PHOTOMICROGRAPH
 Microphotograph
PHOTOTELEGRAPHY
 Telephotography

TELEPHOTOGRAPHY
 Phototelegraphy